## Strategic Marketing Management: Planning, implementation and control

The Marketing Series is one of the most comprehensive collections of books in marketing and sales available from the UK today.

Published by Butterworth-Heinemann on behalf of the Chartered Institute of Marketing, the series is divided into three distinct groups: *Student* (fulfilling the needs of those taking the Institute's certificate and diploma qualifications); *Professional Development* (for those on formal or self-study vocational training programmes); and *Practitioner* (presented in a more informal, motivating and highly practical manner for the busy marketer).

Formed in 1911, the Chartered Institute of Marketing is now the largest professional marketing management body in Europe with over 22,000 members and 25,000 students located worldwide. Its primary objectives are focused on the development of awareness and understanding of marketing throughout UK industry and commerce and on the raising of standards of professionalism in the education, training and practice of this key business discipline.

**Books in the series**

*Behavioural Aspects of Marketing*
Keith C. Williams

*Business Law*
A. A. Painter and R. Lawson

*Economics: an introduction for students of business and marketing*
Frank Livesey

*Effective Sales Management*
John Strafford and Colin Grant

*Financial Aspects of Marketing*
Keith Ward

*The Fundamentals of Advertising*
John Wilmshurst

*The Fundamentals and Practice of Marketing*
John Wilmshurst

*International Marketing*
S. J. Paliwoda

*Marketing Communications*
Colin J. Coulson-Thomas

*Marketing Financial Services*
Edited by Christine Ennew, Trevor Watkins and Mike Wright

*The Marketing Primer*
Geoff Lancaster and Lester Massingham

*Mini Cases in Marketing*
Lester Massingham and Geoff Lancaster

*The Principles and Practice of Selling*
Alan Gillam

*Strategic Marketing Management: Planning, implementation and control*
Richard M. S. Wilson and Colin Gilligan with David J. Pearson

# Strategic Marketing Management
## Planning, implementation and control

Richard M. S. Wilson
University of Keele

*and*

Colin Gilligan
Sheffield Business School

*with*

David J. Pearson
Nottingham Business School

*Published in association with the Chartered Institute of Marketing*

Butterworth-Heinemann Ltd
Linacre House, Jordan Hill, Oxford OX2 8DP

 PART OF REED INTERNATIONAL BOOKS

OXFORD   LONDON   BOSTON
MUNICH   NEW DELHI   SINGAPORE   SYDNEY
TOKYO   TORONTO   WELLINGTON

First published 1992
Reprinted 1992, 1993

**British Library Cataloguing in Publication Data**
Wilson, Richard M. S.
    Strategic marketing management: Planning,
    implementation and control. – (Marketing series)
    I. Title      II. Gilligan, Colin
    III. Pearson, David J.      IV. Series
    658.8

ISBN 0 7506 0329 1


**Library of Congress Cataloguing in Publication Data**
Wilson, Richard M. S.
    Strategic marketing management: planning, implementation and
    control/Richard M. S. Wilson and Colin Gilligan with David J. Pearson
    p.   cm. – (The Marketing Series)
    'Published in association with the Chartered Institute of
    Marketing.'
    Includes bibliographical references and index.
    ISBN 0 7506 0329 1
    1. Marketing – Management.      I. Gilligan, Colin.      II. Pearson,
    David J.      III. Chartered Institute of Marketing.      IV. Title.
    V. Series: Marketing series (London, England)
    HF5415.13.W547
    658.8'02–dc20                                                     91–29728
                                                                          CIP

Composition by Genesis Typesetting, Laser Quay, Rochester, Kent
Printed and bound in Great Britain by Thomson Litho, East Kilbride, Scotland

# Contents

# Dedication

This book is dedicated to the authors' wives – Gillian, Rosie, Christine, and children – Ben Gilligan, Jane and Ruth Pearson, for their support while it was being written; and to the students whose studies will in turn be supported by the book itself.

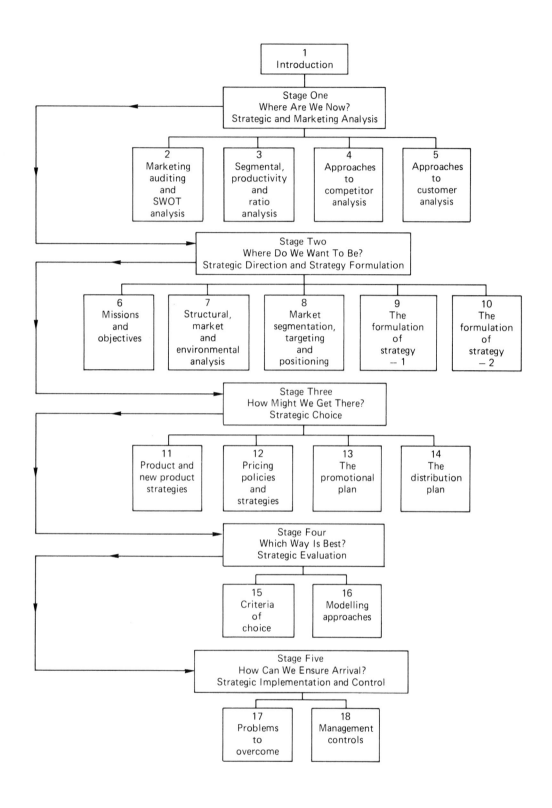

```
                        ┌──────────────────────┐
                        │          1           │
                        │    Introduction      │
                        └──────────────────────┘

        ┌──────────────────────────────────────────────────┐
        │                   Stage One                       │
        │             Where Are We Now?                     │
        │        Strategic and Marketing Analysis           │
        └──────────────────────────────────────────────────┘

   ┌──────────┐  ┌──────────┐  ┌──────────┐  ┌──────────┐
   │    2     │  │    3     │  │    4     │  │    5     │
   │Marketing │  │Segmental,│  │Approaches│  │Approaches│
   │auditing  │  │productivity│ │   to     │  │   to     │
   │  and     │  │  and     │  │competitor│  │customer  │
   │ SWOT     │  │ ratio    │  │ analysis │  │ analysis │
   │analysis  │  │analysis  │  │          │  │          │
   └──────────┘  └──────────┘  └──────────┘  └──────────┘

        ┌──────────────────────────────────────────────────┐
        │                  Stage Two                        │
        │            Where Do We Want To Be?                │
        │   Strategic Direction and Strategy Formulation    │
        └──────────────────────────────────────────────────┘

 ┌────────┐ ┌──────────┐ ┌──────────┐ ┌──────────┐ ┌──────────┐
 │   6    │ │    7     │ │    8     │ │    9     │ │   10     │
 │Missions│ │Structural,│ │Market    │ │  The     │ │  The     │
 │  and   │ │ market   │ │segmentation,│ formulation│ formulation│
 │objectives││  and     │ │targeting │ │   of     │ │   of     │
 │        │ │environmental││  and    │ │ strategy │ │ strategy │
 │        │ │ analysis │ │positioning│ │  − 1     │ │  − 2     │
 └────────┘ └──────────┘ └──────────┘ └──────────┘ └──────────┘

        ┌──────────────────────────────────────────────────┐
        │                 Stage Three                       │
        │            How Might We Get There?                │
        │                Strategic Choice                   │
        └──────────────────────────────────────────────────┘

   ┌──────────┐  ┌──────────┐  ┌──────────┐  ┌──────────┐
   │   11     │  │   12     │  │   13     │  │   14     │
   │Product and│ │Pricing   │  │  The     │  │  The     │
   │new product│ │policies  │  │promotional│ │distribution│
   │strategies│  │  and     │  │  plan    │  │  plan    │
   │          │  │strategies│  │          │  │          │
   └──────────┘  └──────────┘  └──────────┘  └──────────┘

        ┌──────────────────────────────────────────────────┐
        │                 Stage Four                        │
        │             Which Way Is Best?                    │
        │             Strategic Evaluation                  │
        └──────────────────────────────────────────────────┘

              ┌──────────┐  ┌──────────┐
              │   15     │  │   16     │
              │Criteria  │  │Modelling │
              │   of     │  │approaches│
              │ choice   │  │          │
              └──────────┘  └──────────┘

        ┌──────────────────────────────────────────────────┐
        │                 Stage Five                        │
        │          How Can We Ensure Arrival?               │
        │     Strategic Implementation and Control          │
        └──────────────────────────────────────────────────┘

              ┌──────────┐  ┌──────────┐
              │   17     │  │   18     │
              │Problems  │  │Management│
              │   to     │  │ controls │
              │overcome  │  │          │
              └──────────┘  └──────────┘
```

# Foreword

In the turbulent conditions that have already characterized the early 1990s it is more important than ever to establish and maintain high standards of marketing education and marketing practice. This book – designed by its authors to meet the requirements of the Chartered Institute of Marketing's Planning and Control syllabus – serves both ends. The message that comes through this latest addition to the successful CIM–Butterworth-Heinemann series is for marketing to spearhead the drive for corporate institutional and national wealth creation and economic progress. This well-structured and comprehensive book shows how excellence in marketing practice and performance can be encouraged by applying the lessons that Professors Wilson and Gilligan with the help of Dr Pearson put forward. It is a timely addition to the marketing literature and will appeal to students and practitioners interested in current thinking in the critical field of strategic marketing planning, implementation and control.

*Professor Donald Cowell*
*Barkers Advertising Dean,*
*Birmingham Polytechnic Business School*
*Chief Examiner, The Chartered Institute of Marketing*
*Chairman, Marketing Education Group*

# Preface

In writing this book we have been motivated by a concern to help improve the effectiveness of marketing practice – especially in Britain. In focusing on this desired end we have sought to address a number of key questions that logically follow each other in the context of strategic marketing management:

- Where are we now?
- Where do we want to be?
- How might we get there?
- Which way is best?
- How can we ensure arrival?

The themes of planning, implementing and controlling marketing activities are reflected in the answers to these questions – as offered in the eighteen chapters that follow. The structure of the book is designed to take the reader through each of the questions in turn, hence the sequencing of the chapters is significant. We have sought to build the book's argument in a cumulative way such that it will provide guidance in generating effective marketing performance within a strategic framework – once the reader has worked through each chapter in turn.

Against this background we can specify the book's aims as being:

- to make readers aware of the major aspects of the planning and controlling of marketing operations;
- to locate marketing planning and control within a strategic context;
- to demonstrate how the available range of analytical models and techniques might be applied to marketing planning and control to produce superior marketing performance;
- to give full recognition to the problems of implementation and how these problems might be overcome.

It is not intended that this should be used as an introductory text: we have deliberately assumed that readers will have had some prior exposure to marketing principles if not to marketing practice.

The intended market for the book comprises the following segments:

- students of the Chartered Institute of Marketing who are preparing for the Marketing Planning and Control paper in CIM's Diploma examinations;
- students reading for degrees involving marketing (especially MBA candidates and senior undergraduates following business studies programmes);
- marketing practitioners who will benefit from a comprehensive review of current thinking in the field of strategic marketing planning, implementation and control.

*RMSW*
*CTG*
*DJP*

# Acknowledgements

In preparing this book for publication the authors were very ably helped by Karen Hornby, Sharon Lewis, Elizabeth Singleton and Gillian Wilson to whom they would like to offer their thanks. On behalf of the publisher, Kathryn Grant took the risk of accepting a manuscript that was both late and much longer than she had anticipated, for which we are apologetic and appreciative in turn. Deena Burgess looked after the production aspects in a friendly and competent manner.

For granting copyright clearance we are grateful to the following:

- John Wiley & Sons Ltd for Figure 18.50 from R. Amit, et al. 'Thinking One Step Ahead: the Use of Conjectures in Competitor Analysis'. *Strategic Management Journal*, vol. 9, 1988 © John Wiley & Sons Ltd, 1988.
- Harvard Business School Press for Figure 18.12 from R. N. Anthony, *The Management Control Function*, © 1988 by the President and Fellows of Harvard College; and Figures 16.43–16.46 from T. V. Bonoma and B. H. Clark, *Marketing Performance Assessment*, © 1988 by the President and Fellows of Harvard College.
- MCB University Press Ltd. for the distribution productivity example (pp. 67–70) from H. M. Armitage, 'The Use of Management Accounting Techniques to Improve Productivity Analysis in Distribution Operations', *International Journal of Physical Distribution & Materials Management*, vol. 17, no. 2, 1987; and Figures 18.37 and 18.38 from T. F. Barrett, 'When the Market Says "Beware!"', *Management Decision*, vol. 24, no. 6, 1986.
- Elsevier Scientific Publishing Co. for Figure 18.46 from J. J. Brock, 'Competitor Analysis: Some Practical Approaches', *Industrial Marketing Management*, vol. 13, 1984.
- The American Marketing Association for Figure 15.14 from G. S. Day and J. R. C. Wensley, 'Assessing Advantage: A Framework for Diagnosing Competitive Superiority', *Journal of Marketing*, vol. 52, April, 1988; and Figure 18.27, adapted from J. M. Hulbert and N. E. Toy, 'Strategic Framework for Marketing Control', *Journal of Marketing*, vol. 41, April, 1977.
- The Chartered Institute of Marketing for Figure 18.32 from A. Diamanto-poulos and B. P. Mathews, 'A Model for Analysing Product Performance', *Quarterly Review of Marketing*, vol. 15, no. 3, 1990; and Figures 17.11 and 17.13, plus related discussion, from R. M. S. Wilson and N. Fook, 'Improving Marketing Orientation', *Marketing Business*, June, 1990.
- *The Times* for the pieces by M. Dynes, 'BR to Split National Network into Local Areas', 11 April, 1991; P. Strafford, 'Centuries of Discovery', 1 March,

1990; and R. Tieman, 'Taking the British out of BT', 3 January, 1991: © Times Newspaper Ltd, 1990, 1991.

- Ian Griffith (of Marketing Quality Assurance) for his piece 'Marketing Needs New Sales Pitch', which first appeared in *The Sunday Times*, 7 July, 1991.
- McGraw-Hill, Inc, for Figure 18.33 from J. P. Guiltinan and G. W. Paul, *Marketing Management: Strategies & Programs*, 3rd edition, 1988; and Figure 18.6 from G. Shillinglaw's Divisional Performance Review' in C. P. Bonini, R. K. Jaedicke, and H. M. Wagner (eds) *Management Controls: New Directions in Basic Research*, 1964.
- Macmillan Publishing Co Inc for Figures 16.21 and 16.22, plus related discussion, from J. L. Heskett, *Marketing*, 1976.
- Prentice Hall International (UK) Ltd for Figure 1.10 from G. Johnson and K. Scholes, *Exploring Corporate Strategy*, 2nd edition, 1988.
- Cassell plc for Figure 8.4 from P. Feldwick (ed), *Advertising works – 5*, 1990.
- Butterworth-Heinemann Ltd. for Figure 6 from P. McNamee, *Management Accounting: Strategic Planning & Marketing*, 1988; and Figure 14.6 from M. McDonald, *Marketing Plans: How to Prepare Them, How to Use Them*, 1984.
- L. Gilmore (of Diana Martin Ltd) for Figure 13.4.
- The Editor of *Accountancy Ireland* for Figure 1.14 from F. Milton and T. Reiss, 'Developing a Competitive Strategy', *Accountancy Ireland*, vol. 17, no. 5, 1985.
- Nissan Motor (GB) Ltd for Figure 13.15.
- Professor Nigel Piercy for Figures 17.17, 17.20, 17.23, 17.24 and 17.25 from *Marketing Organisation*, London: George Allen & Unwin Ltd, 1985.
- Frank Pyne (of Problem Resolution) for Figure 15.4 from F. Pyne, 'Better Operating Statements for the Marketing Director', *Accountancy*, vol. 95, no. 1086, February, 1984.
- The Editor of *Marketing Week* for the piece by J. Sturges, 'Mars in the Ascendent', *Marketing Week*, 22 March, 1991, reprinted in the Preamble to Stage 4.
- West Publishing Company, Inc, for Figure 10.7 from p. 120, G. S. Day, *Analysis for Strategic Marketing Decisions*, © 1986 by West Publishing Company. All rights reserved.
- The Free Press, a Division of Macmillan, Inc, for Figure 10.6 from R. D. Buzzell & B. T. Gale, *The PIMS Principles*, © 1987 by The Free Press.
- Prentice-Hall, Inc for Figure 18.17 from D. J. Luck and O. C. Ferrell, *Marketing Strategy and Plans*, 1979; and Figure 2.6 adapted from P. Kotler, *Marketing Management: Analysis, Planning, Implementation and Control*, 6th edition, 1988.
- The Editor of *Harvard Business Review* for Figure 2.2 adapted from P. Kotler, 'From Sales Obsession to Marketing Effectiveness', *Harvard Business Review*, Vol. 55, No. 6, November–December, 1977, © The President and Fellows of Harvard College.
- The Editor of *Sloan Management Review* for Figure 2.9 adapted from P. Kotler, W. Gregor and W. Rogers, 'The Marketing Audit Comes of Age', *Sloan Management Review*, Vol. 18, No. 1, Winter, 1977.

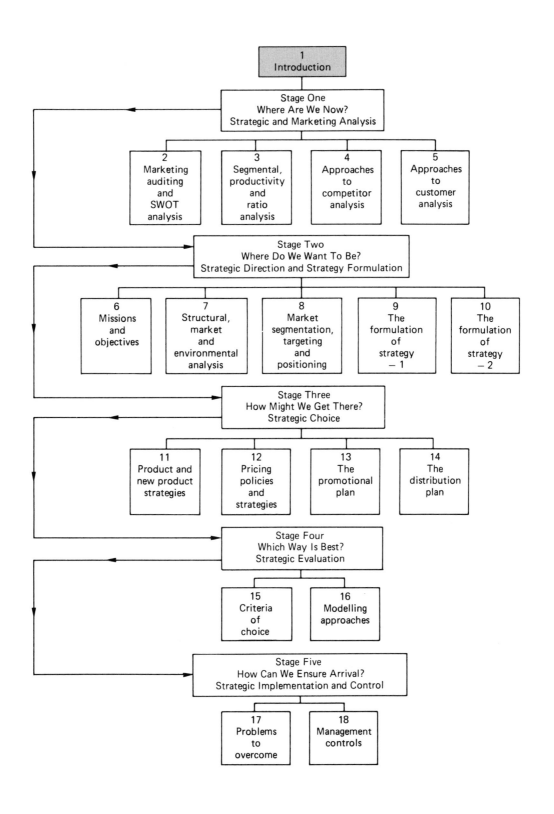

| 1 |
| :---: |
| Introduction |

**Stage One**
**Where Are We Now?**
**Strategic and Marketing Analysis**

| 2 | 3 | 4 | 5 |
| :---: | :---: | :---: | :---: |
| Marketing auditing and SWOT analysis | Segmental, productivity and ratio analysis | Approaches to competitor analysis | Approaches to customer analysis |

**Stage Two**
**Where Do We Want To Be?**
**Strategic Direction and Strategy Formulation**

| 6 | 7 | 8 | 9 | 10 |
| :---: | :---: | :---: | :---: | :---: |
| Missions and objectives | Structural, market and environmental analysis | Market segmentation, targeting and positioning | The formulation of strategy − 1 | The formulation of strategy − 2 |

**Stage Three**
**How Might We Get There?**
**Strategic Choice**

| 11 | 12 | 13 | 14 |
| :---: | :---: | :---: | :---: |
| Product and new product strategies | Pricing policies and strategies | The promotional plan | The distribution plan |

**Stage Four**
**Which Way Is Best?**
**Strategic Evaluation**

| 15 | 16 |
| :---: | :---: |
| Criteria of choice | Modelling approaches |

**Stage Five**
**How Can We Ensure Arrival?**
**Strategic Implementation and Control**

| 17 | 18 |
| :---: | :---: |
| Problems to overcome | Management controls |

## 1 | Introduction

### 1.1 LEARNING OBJECTIVES

When you have read this chapter you should be able to:

(a) define marketing in strategic terms;
(b) understand the basic structure of the book;
(c) appreciate the analytical approach to managerial planning and control that can be achieved through model building;
(d) specify the characteristics of strategy and strategic decisions.

### 1.2 THE NATURE OF MARKETING

What is marketing? Many definitions exist with differing emphases on the process of marketing, the functional activities that constitute marketing, and the orientation (or philosophy) of marketing. For example, the Chartered Institute of Marketing defines it as follows:

> Marketing is the management process for identifying, anticipating, and satisfying customer requirements profitably.

This 'process' definition can be compared with Drucker's (1973) definition of marketing orientation:

> Marketing is so basic that it cannot be considered a separate function on a par with others such as manufacturing or personnel. It is first a central dimension of the entire business. It is the whole business seen from the point of view of its final result, that is, from the customers' point of view.

A significant shift in emphasis since Drucker wrote this is to be found in the importance that is now attached to *competitive position* in a changing world. Thus the marketing concept is that managerial orientation which recognizes that success primarily depends upon identifying changing customer wants and developing products and services which match these better than those of competitors (Doyle, 1987; see also Wilson & Fook, 1990).

The contrasting emphases on customers and competitors can be highlighted as in Figure 1.1. If an enterprise is managed a little better than customers expect, and if this is done in a slightly better way than competitors can manage, then the enterprise should be successful.

Within Figure 1.1 the customer-oriented and competitor-centred categories speak for themselves. The self-centred category is characterized by an introspective orientation that focuses on year-on-year improvements in key operating ratios, or on improvements in sales volume without making direct

**FIGURE 1.1**
*Customer and
competitor
orientations*

Competitor emphasis

|  | Minor | Major |
|---|---|---|
| **Minor** | Self-centred | Competitor-centred |
| **Major** | Customer-oriented | Market-driven |

Customer
emphasis

SOURCE: Adapted from Day (1990), p. 126

comparisons with competitors. Such an orientation is potentially disastrous when viewed in strategic terms. At the opposite extreme is a market-driven approach to marketing which seeks to balance a responsiveness to customers' requirements on the one hand with direct competitor comparisons on the other.

As pointed out in Wilson (1988, p. 259), the essential requirements of marketing are:

1  the identification of consumers' needs (covering *what* goods and services are bought; *how* they are bought; by *whom* they are bought; and *why* they are bought);
2  the definition of target market segments (by which customers are grouped according to common characteristics – whether demographic, psychological, geographic, etc.);
3  the creation of a *differential advantage* within target segments by which a distinct competitive position relative to other companies can be established, and from which profit flows.

The way in which a differential advantage might be achieved – and sustained – is via the manipulation of the elements of the *marketing mix*. This comprises the 'four Ps' of marketing: product, price, promotion and place. Figure 1.2 shows these in a little more detail.

## 1.3  THE MANAGEMENT PROCESS

Management can be looked at from a variety of viewpoints. It may be seen from one perspective as being largely an *attitude* that reflects a willingness to debate issues and resolve them through the use of appropriate techniques and procedures. Alternatively, management may be viewed in terms of its *responsibility for achieving desired objectives* which requires the selection of means to accomplish prescribed ends as well as the articulation of those ends.

**FIGURE 1.2**
*The marketing mix*

This view of management can be analysed further by focusing on its *task orientation* (e.g. in the functional context of marketing) or on its *process orientation* (i.e. the way in which the responsibility is exercised). In either case it has been suggested that decision making and management are the same thing (Simon, 1960, p. 1).

The process of decision making is rendered problematic on account of the existence of risk and uncertainty. In the face of risk or uncertainty some managers postpone making a choice between alternative courses of action for fear of that choice being wrong. What they typically fail to recognize in this situation is that they are actually making another choice – they are deciding *not to decide* (Barnard, 1956, p. 193), which favours the status quo rather than change. This is not a means of eliminating risk or uncertainty since it seeks to ignore them rather than to accommodate them: the imperative to adapt is one that cannot be ignored.

If the central question in the management process concerns the need to make decisions, we need to know *what* decisions should be made and *how* they should be made. This book is intended to deal with both these issues by following a sequence of stages that reflects a problem-solving routine. Each of the five main parts of the book represents one of these stages. Figure 1.3 summarizes these stages.

*Stage 1* raises the question of where the organization is now in terms of its competitive position, product range, market share, financial position and overall effectiveness. In addressing this question we are seeking to establish a base line from which we can move forward. Chapters 2 to 5 address Stage 1.

*Stage 2* is concerned with where the organization should go in the future, which requireu the specification of ends (or objectives) to be achieved. While top management in the organization will have some discretion over the choice of ends, this is constrained by various vested interests, as we shall see later in this chapter. Chapters 6 to 10 address Stage 2.

*Stage 3* deals with the question of how desired ends might be achieved, which begs the question of how alternative means to ends might be identified. This strategy formulation stage requires creative inputs that cannot be reduced to mechanical procedures. Chapters 11 to 14 address Stage 3.

*Stage 4* focuses on the evaluation of alternative means by which the most preferred (or 'best') alternative might be selected. The need to choose may be due to alternatives being mutually exclusive (i.e. all attempting to achieve the same end) or a consequence of limited resources (which means that a rationing mechanism must be invoked). Chapters 15 and 16 address Stage 4.

**FIGURE 1.3**
*The framework*

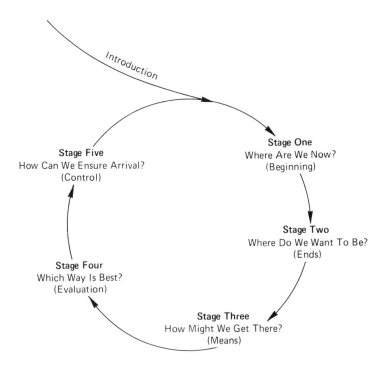

*Stage 5* covers the implementation of the chosen means, and the monitoring of its performance in order that any corrective actions might be taken to ensure that the desired results are achieved. Since circumstances both within the organization and in its environment are unlikely to stay constant while a strategy is being pursued it is necessary to adapt to accommodate such changes. Chapters 17 and 18 address Stage 5.

Within these stages are to be found the main managerial activities of:

• planning;
• decision making;
• control.

The entire sequence of Stages 1 to 5 constitutes control, within which the planning activities are to be found in Stages 1 to 4. At every stage it is necessary for decisions to be made, so you will see that these managerial activities are closely intertwined. Moreover, their links are spread across three different time dimensions which are not of equal significance: the past, the present and the future. Let us consider these in turn.

The *past* brought the organization (and its products, competitors, etc.) to their present positions. By gaining an understanding of how the organization arrived in its present position the managers of that organization might develop some insights to help them in deciding how to proceed in the future. However, there is no way in which the past can be influenced, so the best one can do is to attempt to learn from it instead of being constrained by it. If an organization simply continues on unchanging routes its viability is almost certain to be endangered as the environment changes but it does not.

Stage 1 is concerned with establishing the ways in which the past brought the organization to its present position.

The *present* is transient: it is the fleeting moment between the past and the future when one must take one's understanding of the past and link this to the development of one's aspirations for the future. Decisions are made (with both planning and control consequences) in the present, but their impact is intended to be in the future.

The time dimension that is of major relevance in any planning exercise must be the *future* rather than the present or the past. There is nothing about an organization that is more important than its future, and the spirit of this was aptly summarized by C. F. Kettering: 'I am interested in the future because that is where I intend to live.' The past may help us in deciding how to proceed in the future, but there is no way in which we can influence the past, so there is a limit to the amount of effort that should be applied to it as opposed to planning for the future. This is especially relevant when we consider what a constraint to innovation the past might be: in Goethe's terms, we see what we know, and if we are obsessed with carrying on along unchanging routes we must expect our viability to become endangered as the environment changes but we fail to adapt to those changes.

On the other hand, the anticipation of the future should not become too fanciful. In a deliberately extreme mood, de Jouvenal (1967) has stated that:

> ... world population, and also the available labour force in industrial countries, is doubling every 50 years. The GNP is doubling every 20 years, and so are the number of major scientific discoveries. The whole scientific and engineering establishment, including, for example, the numbers of graduates, membership of learned societies, and scientific publications is doubling every 15 years. The money spent on applied research is doubling every 7 years, and so also is the demand for electronics and aviation. If all these processes were to continue unchecked ... within about 100 years every one of us would be a scientist, the entire national output would be absorbed in research, and we should be spending most of our lives airborne at 40,000 feet.

This can be contrasted with a rather more serious comment made by Professor William H. Pickering of Harvard in a speech made during June of 1908 in which his lack of imagination is as extreme as de Jouvenal's excess:

> The popular mind often pictures gigantic flying machines speeding across the Atlantic carrying innumerable passengers in a way analogous to our modern steamship. It seems safe to say that such ideas are wholly visionary, and, even if the machine could get across with one or two passengers, the expense would be prohibitive to any but the capitalist who could use his own yacht.

With this uninspired perspective from a member of the establishment in the early twentieth century, it is not surprising that the vision of writers such as Jules Verne and H. G. Wells were mocked; yet their premonitions have often come to be justified, with surprising speed and accuracy in some instances. We do have Concorde, despite Professor Pickering's pessimism.

It should not be expected that any particular vision of the future will be correct in every detail, nor necessarily very detailed in its conception. Writing in 1959, Drucker made the rather careless statement that '... if anyone still suffers from the delusion that the ability to forecast beyond the shortest timespan is given to us, let him look at the headlines in yesterday's paper, and then ask himself which of them he could possibly have predicted ten years ago.' What Drucker does not take into account is the vital *level of resolution* (see p. 12): our interest over a 10-year period may be more in the continued existence of *The Times*, or even of a free press, than in specific headlines, because the level of resolution would have to be relatively low (i.e. broad horizons, broad view, little detail).

A balance must be maintained in dealing with the short-run future on the one hand and the long-run future on the other. Apart from headlines in *The Times* we can note the short-run preoccupation in the UK with financial results and contrast this with the longer-run relevance of market-building strategies; or the risk of being obsessed with tactics to the exclusion of a proper concern for strategy.

## 1.4  A MODELLING APPROACH

In dealing with managerial processes such as planning, decision making and control it would be inappropriate to presume that *objective rationality* was present. Human beings are unable to act in a wholly objective way as a result of their tendency to use *subjective judgements* in their decision making.

The type of judgement that is intended here is not that which stems purely from 'experience', but rather that which reflects value systems (see Vickers, 1968; 1972). Rationality implies objectivity and thus excludes the subjective reasoning that follows from the values that each decision maker holds. The nature of personal values (such as one's willingness to be involved in marketing cigarettes in full knowledge of the potentially detrimental effect on health by smoking, or the view one has of profit, or of capitalism, or of the use of sexual advertising themes in promoting sexless products) is not well understood, and the choice of personal values is not open to rational economic analysis. Nevertheless, the values of dominant managers will be inherent in the choice of 'organizational' objectives. (Since only individuals can have objectives while collectivities cannot, it follows that organizational objectives must reflect the aspirations of the dominant individuals in the organizational coalition. See March & Simon, 1958, and Cyert & March, 1963.)

The culture of the society in which we live determines the norms for acceptable behaviour and hence for acceptable objectives. Differences among cultures (such as British versus Japanese) will obviously lead to different value systems and different norms of behaviour. (For example, the longer-term focus of Japanese and German financial markets relative to those in the UK and the USA.) However, even within a national culture there are sub-cultures which result in different value systems developing in government, business, the armed forces, and so forth, which can be seen in the very different behaviour patterns of participants in each sub-culture (see Weinshall, 1977).

The recognition that values play such a prominent – and largely unpredictable – role in managerial behaviour may discourage some individuals and cause them to dismiss rational analysis as being inadequate in effective decision making. In the sense that decisions are not made entirely on the basis of economic rationality this may seem reasonable, but if we can apply rational economic analysis to a substantial element in each managerial decision it seems overly pessimistic to assume that this will not be helpful. If alternative courses of action can be analysed and presented in rational, neutral terms to the decision maker, it will help him to make his choice, even though this itself will be biased in accordance with his personal set of values.

The question of personal values to an individual (or perhaps of a cohesive group) can be extended to the question of ethics (or moral values) to a society (see Bartels, 1963; and Kelley in Schwartz, 1965). The consumer movement (see Aaker & Day, 1972 and 1974; Kotler, 1972b, Gaedeke & Etcheson, 1972; and McCarry, 1972) suggests that marketers are not invariably putting other people's interests in an acceptable societal perspective. It is not clear, however, to what extent management is expected to introduce and support gradual social change in so far as this reflects changing its own behaviour towards particular groups (such as consumers, employees, shareholders, and the community at large) and to what extent it should uphold the status quo (see Starr, 1971, pp. 249–58).

Business behaviour will certainly be influenced to some degree by the ethics of the prevailing social system, although defining ethical objectives becomes fraught with difficulties when society is divided in its views. (For example the divergence between the perceived importance in Britain of regenerating economic growth in the private sector, which requires innovative freedom, and the regulation of private enterprise that discourages such regeneration. Similarly, there is conflict between the 'morality' of the environmentalists and the 'morality' of economic growth.) This topic should be kept in mind through the following pages since it constitutes a constraint that may be more restrictive than statutory limitations.

We have seen that the idea of objective economic rationality is not a realistic notion in the context of managerial decision making. Equally, it is unrealistic to proceed purely on the basis of common sense (which might encourage us to think that the world is flat), or arbitrary rules (which might be termed 'conventional wisdom'). What is needed is a theoretical framework for the analysis of managerial problems, and this presupposes a *scientific* orientation.

Science can be defined as a body of knowledge about the phenomena in a particular section of the real world and of the research tools available for obtaining accurate and reliable knowledge about these phenomena. A scientific approach in any field of investigation is the direct antithesis of dogmatism (or conventional wisdom and tradition). In following such an approach the marketing decision maker should learn to rely on evidence from reality instead of hunch. However, whether marketing is, or will ever be, regarded as a science by anyone other than its own adherents is unimportant in relation to the role it has assumed in applying scientific method to the understanding of this important sphere of human activity (see Christopher, et al., 1968, pp. 231–2).

But there is some scope for 'creative intuition' (Fisk, 1967, p. 494), which requires that we view marketing as part *art* (which is usually linked to subjectivity) and part *science* (which is usually linked to a kind of objectivity). At one extreme is a totally objective, scientific approach to decision making, while at the other extreme (of a notional continuum) intuition, experience and subjective knowledge take over the decision. It should be readily appreciated that decision making at higher levels in an organization will require rather more creative intuition than will tend to be the case at lower levels where formal methods can be more widely employed.

In whatever field he is working, a scientist will proceed by attempting to develop theories concerning the behaviour of the phenomena in which he is interested. Rules of thumb and experience are not without some value, but a knowledge of the basic relationships underlying the behaviour of relevant phenomena should allow managers to make decisions even in the absence of traditional guidelines and experience (see Zaltman, et al., 1973).

A good decision maker can be said to be an individual with good theories. This may conflict with the emphasis put on 'practicality' by unenlightened, defensive individuals who are well aware of their own ignorance of the behaviour of marketing phenomena. The aim of marketing theory has been stated, in broad terms, as being '. . . to comprehend what is known and to derive a set of principles or action-guides to enable businessmen to manage their affairs better' (Rodger, 1965, p. 37). It follows therefore that if theory is concerned with knowing, those who dismiss it are recommending a policy of not knowing: the practical individual (operating without a theoretical basis) is the individual who does not really know what he is doing. This is not to say, of course, that practice is not vitally important. It is. But theory and practice are two sides of the same coin, and to emphasize one (or merely neglect the other) is potentially dangerous if one fails to appreciate that sound practice must rest on valid theories, and valid theories must facilitate sound practice.

Scientific theories in marketing enable us to:

1 Explain and understand the behaviour of marketing variables and their interrelationships. The emphais will usually be on causal relations, but one should not expect sets of precise cause-and-effect rules to emerge that are applicable under any potential sets of circumstances. 'In the management field it is never possible to say: "If I do A and B, then C will inevitably happen." The best that [the decision maker] can say is: "If I do A and B, the result is *likely* to be C. And if I neglect to do either A or B, it is *very probable* that the consequences will be unfortunate." ' (Dale & Michelon, 1969, p. 11).

2  Predict the future behaviour patterns of marketing variables and their interrelationships. The ability (from (1) above) to explain relationships is a necessary basis for prediction, and it should be apparent that a good explanatory theory can facilitate prediction across a broader range of circumstances than can the practical personal experience of any individual (whose perspective is constrained by the limits of that experience). A theorist can use his knowledge of relevant behaviour patterns in many different situations to indicate the consequences of alternative courses of action among which the decision maker must choose.
3  Produce prescriptions, by which the values of decision makers are aligned with the alternative courses of action available, thereby enabling choices to be made.
4  Achieve control over the outcomes from interactions of marketing variables.

When the marketing analyst has a validated predictive theory of cause-and-effect relationships among phenomena of interest to him, he is able to control the effects by exerting pressure on the causes. Since effects lead to the attainment of objectives this makes the achievements of purpose possible. For example, if it were known how a given amount and type of promotion (cause) affected sales (first-order effect), it would be possible to control the profitability outcome (second-order effect) since profit depends, in part, on the difference between sales revenue and promotional outlays (see Huegy, 1963; Cox, et al., 1964).

Available marketing theories are not yet comprehensive, but appreciating the role of theories and having some awareness of theory construction are essential qualities for the good decision maker. In considering the relationship between sales calls and sales, or that between speed of delivery (or level of service) and sales, a marketing manager might assume that at some stage diminishing returns set in (i.e. no matter how many sales calls are made, or how rapid delivery is, or how many orders can be filled immediately ex-stock, the level of sales will not increase to infinity). It is up to the manager to develop a theory of how, and at what rate, sales vary in response to changes in other variables (see Stasch, 1972, pp. 1–28).

An approach such as this clearly has major implications regarding the provision of data, but it also demands the formal consideration of how particular courses of action lead to particular outcomes, and thus requires an analytical framework for improving decision-making performance. By contrast, the use of practical experience as a basis for decisions is tantamount to uncontrolled experimentation with no formal explanatory foundation, thereby rendering it a faulty guide to the prediction of future events and a totally inadequate basis for control.

We can characterize the main features of theories through a simple systems model (Figure 1.4).

Controllable factors in this format are termed 'strategies' and are determined by management. A firm's pricing policy, the range of products it offers, and its forms of promotion are examples of such factors that are entirely within the control (subject to legal constraints) of the firm itself.

The uncontrollable factors are termed 'environments' or 'states of nature', and represent those variables that are independent of the firm's control (such as competitive actions, political events, movements in commodity prices, and so forth).

Together, the uncontrollable and controllable variables in a given situation constitute the inputs, or causal variables, of the theory of that situation. The inputs interact and this produces a transformation that leads to results (which may also be termed pay-offs, effects, or outputs). Since each variable on the input side could assume any one of a vast range of values (such as the controllable expenditure on advertising Product X being anything from, say, £0 to £100,000, and the uncontrollable price of copper, which might be an essential element in Product X, being anything from £750 to £1,050 per ton, and so on), the situation is one of great uncertainty and could therefore lead to any one of a large number

**FIGURE 1.4**
*Theoretical foundations*

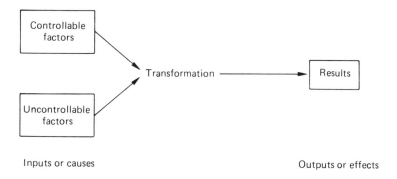

of outcomes. Under these circumstances it is necessary for us carefully to limit our concern to states of nature that are likely to occur (given our selected strategies) and that might influence the attainment of our objectives (and hence the desired outputs or effects).

It is worth pointing out that the use of the term 'control' is not unambiguous in managerial parlance. In the phrase 'controllable factors' the sense of the meaning is that the manager can influence, in any way he wishes, the behaviour of each factor. ('Behaviour' means a change in state, or value, over time, and so this covers human behaviour but is by no means restricted to this.) He can, for instance, offer Product X in 25 different colours or only in black. He cannot, however, directly influence the range of colours of competitive products, so this comes under the heading of 'uncontrollable factors' along with other states of nature or environments.

In discussing the role of theories in securing control over the behaviour of phenomena the term 'control' was used in a different sense. If we can anticipate (by predictive means) states of nature, we are in a position to respond to them when they arise, and in this way we are able to survive, adapt, and ultimately reach our objectives. This is the substantive meaning of 'control' in this book.

While the methodology of 'marketing science' is essentially the same as that of the empirical physical sciences (Montgomery & Urban, 1969a, p. 8), with the two central aspects of problem orientation and scientific approach being much in evidence, the facts which are pertinent to marketing science are more inclusive than those which are the subject of investigation in other subject areas. This is demonstrated through the eclectic nature of marketing, which is more in the form of a sub-set of a number of other disciplines rather than being a discipline in itself. As a subject of academic and professional study, marketing is composed of approaches from economics, psychology, sociology, political science, anthropology and history, with assistance from accounting, law, statistics and mathematics. The scientific method is frequently equated with rational rather than emotional deliberation; with objectivity and freedom from personal bias or prejudice; with precision in investigation and measurement; and with honesty in interpreting findings. However, the scientific method is never as easy to apply in the social sciences (which include marketing and management) as it is in the physical sciences (see Schwartz, 1973, pp. 309–10). Directly or indirectly, human behaviour is at the core of marketing problems and this is infinitely more difficult to analyse than is, say, the behaviour of either chemical compounds or white mice under controlled laboratory conditions. (The value of qualitative research, reflecting problems of quantification, is often a controversial topic in marketing; see, for example, Brighton, 1977.) One vehicle that is of great value in helping us cope with studying any form of behaviour is the model, so let us turn our attention to modelling (see Lazer, 1962a).

It is possible to state our knowledge of marketing phenomena in both verbal and quantitative ways, either of which can be equally valid. Analysis is more readily facilitated, however, when information is expressed in quantitative terms.

Not only is this likely to be more precise and concise than its verbal counterpart, but it is also amenable to statistical and mathematical manipulation in an effort to explain, predict and control the behaviour of marketing phenomena. Frequently, analysis and manipulation are made possible through the use of models.

We can define a model as a simplified representation of some part of reality. If it were not a simplification of reality it would be both too complex to use and also redundant (since there is little point in a replication of reality). Relevance will determine the features that are to be modelled in relation to a formulated problem situation.

The popularity of models in recent years is due to: an improved competence on the part of decision makers to build and use them (often in conjunction with computing facilities and the availability of spreadsheets); a greater need to incorporate the rapidly increasing uncertainty of problem situations in the decision-making process; and the utility of models in carrying out experiments (e.g. via simulation) which could not be performed in reality. If there were no evidence to suggest that 'scientific' models of marketing processes improved organizational performance the adoption of modelling would not be as popular as it has become. But there is a temptation for models to be developed for their own sake, or to satisfy the curiosity of the analyst, in relation to a matter that is of no real significance to organizational success. Many models suffer from 'rigour without relevance' (Ehrenberg, 1965) in that they are highly refined and elegant in mathematical terms but fail to reflect the key features of marketing processes and problems. It is important to see that marketing models are not ends in themselves but simply a means to an end – the making of better marketing decisions, rather than the 'unlimited postulation of irrelevant truths' (Schwartz, 1965, p. 489). (See Kotler, 1971, for a broad coverage on this theme.)

At a later stage we will look at particular types of models developed specially to tackle particular marketing problems. At this stage, however, it will be helpful to look at one very important type of model (the systems model) and one modelling approach (experimentation), both of which can supply an extremely helpful perspective in considering marketing planning and control.

The *systems model*, in its basic form, is an abstraction that can be related to *any* 'living' system. (A living system is one that is purposive or objective seeking; has interdependent and interacting parts; and exhibits changes of state over time, i.e. it behaves. Such systems are not necessarily live in a biological sense, but exhibit life – as with the economic system – through their changes of state.) (See Beer, 1967; Churchman, 1968; Emery, 1981; Ackoff, 1971; Schoderbek, et al., 1975; Beishon & Peters, 1972.) Every system has inputs, a transformation process in which the various inputs are combined, and outputs that are intended to lead to the attainment of the system's purpose. Figure 1.5 illustrates this in its simplest form.

**FIGURE 1.5**
*A simple systems model*

In order that the system might 'learn', and hence adapt its behaviour to ensure it is progressing along an acceptable path towards its objectives, it is necessary to have a link between the outputs and the inputs. This is termed a feedback loop, and it is the essential ingredient that converts a simple systems model into a control model by enabling the system's inputs to be varied in order to ensure that its behaviour (as represented by the system's outputs) is consistent with its objectives (see Figure 1.6).

The example that is usually cited is of a domestic thermostat: whenever the temperature (output) falls below the desired level (which represents the standard of performance, but which is only a surrogate for the objective which will be the

**FIGURE 1.6**
*A simple control
system*

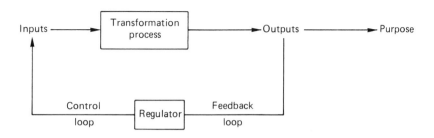

welfare of the user of the system), this message passes through the feedback loop and causes heat to be supplied (through the transformation process) in response to the provision of a signal and fuel (inputs).

To put this simple model into a managerial context we can use the example of Figure 1.7 which shows, in general terms, a range of input factors into a transformation process termed 'the firm', and some of the resulting outputs.

**FIGURE 1.7**
*A simple business
system*

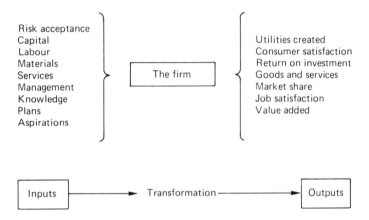

Resources, consisting of managerial skill, materials, funds, labour, etc., constitute a major class of (controllable) inputs, to which must be added such variables as risk and the aspirations or ambitions of individual employees/ managers (over which the firm has little control). In the main, however, input factors are at least identifiable even if some of these represent constraints to the most efficient attainment of objectives. Among the most obvious constraints in marketing systems are the prevailing level of technology, cultural norms, legal restrictions (such as price codes), competition, the pattern and level of demand, and nature (as seen in droughts, floods, climatic variations, etc.), all of which can limit the freedom of action of marketing decision makers.

The outputs from marketing systems indicate how the system is progressing towards its desired purpose. Marketing activities result in the creation of utilities (of time, place and ownership) and in the addition of value to goods passing through the various phases of the marketing process. Consumers derive their satisfaction from the utilities, and business firms derive their profits from the value added.

Output is relative to input, and their relationship gives a measure of efficiency or productivity (see Sevin, 1965; Narver & Savit, 1971, Ch. 15). Efficiency is concerned with the amount of output created from a given mix and amount of inputs and is often encountered in its extreme form when optimizing behaviour is being urged (by which the maximum output from given inputs, or a given output from minimum inputs, is required). Marketing is considered by such authorities as Narver & Savit, 1971, to have low efficiency in comparison with manufacturing or farming, and this gives some indication of the difficulties involved in understanding the complexities of the marketing domain.

But no matter how efficient an activity or process is, we must also have regard to its effectiveness. This refers to a system's ability to achieve its purpose, so we might have effective but inefficient systems, efficient but ineffective ones, or anything in between (see Schoderbek, 1971; Johnson, et al., 1973; Schoderbek, et al., 1975).

The boundary of any system will be drawn by the analyst in accordance with the problem at hand rather than being given in any sense. It is a system's boundary that separates the items over which we have major influence from the environmental variables over which we have little influence but which affect our ability to reach our objectives.

By thinking in terms of purposive systems one gets away from the descriptive view of marketing consisting of a number of separate departments carrying out a range of separable activities. The coherence of its elements distinguishes a system from the jumble of items that might otherwise be perceived, and this simply reflects the real world.

We can represent in systems terms any marketing activity by varying the *level of resolution*. This refers to the spatial (or space) and temporal (or time) dimensions of the problem situation we are examining. For example, if our interest is in media scheduling for a specific advertising campaign we will adopt a high level of resolution which means we will examine the limited number of items in the problem in detail over a short-time horizon. If our interest lay in, say, the adoption of solar heating systems, then we would need to consider many more variables over longer periods of time and consequently we would adopt a lower level of resolution (see Klir and Valach, 1967, Ch. 2; Lowe, 1971, pp. 96–8). The generality of the systems model is such that we can accept its fundamental relevance to the problems of adaptive systems, in general, and then use it to formulate, in precise terms, the characteristics of any particular problem we might come up against.

In summary, then, by using systems models as a means of studying marketing processes and problems we are focusing attention on certain key questions, namely:

1 What purposes are to be served by the system? (In other words, what objective is to be satisfied by the solution to the marketing problem represented by the systems model?)
2 What structure (or organization) should exist among the variables within the system in order that the desired behaviour patterns might emerge?
3 What inputs are required to achieve the system's purpose?
4 What outputs are required, and how should these be measured?
5 What constraints exist to limit the system's ability to behave in the desired manner?
6 With what degree of efficiency and effectiveness is the system operating?

As we have seen, any model is a simplified representation of a larger, more complex slice of reality. In order to make modelling useful in decision making the most general approach has been to enquire about the effects (outcomes) that result from changing the inputs (causes) to the model on a 'What if . . .?' basis. This is one feature of experimentation (in the form of a simulation) which can also be applied by restructuring the model itself.

Sensitivity analysis is one example of *experimentation*. The testing of a model for its sensitivity is aimed at discovering how the output changes in response to variations in input values, or due to variations in model parameters. This should indicate the extent to which outcomes are sensitive (i.e. are subject to change) in response to particular inputs, and which inputs can be varied and have little impact on output. A model's sensitivity should correspond with the sensitivity of the real-world situation, and in this sense there is a link between a model's sensitivity and its validity (see Montgomery & Urban, 1969b, p. 8).

Experimentation in general involves the testing of an item or idea to ascertain its suitability for a particular purpose, or its ability to bring about a desired result. Instances in which an experimental approach might be used abound, and include:

1 determining a product's design;
2 identifying the best method for training salesmen;
3 specifying a package design;
4 ascertaining the most effective advertising copy;
5 selecting a product's price;
6 estimating the demand for a product;
7 choosing the best remuneration scheme for salesmen;
8 evaluating alternative point-of-sale displays;
9 gauging the best shelf arrangements for displaying a product;
10 comparing the efficiency of alternative channels of distribution.

In essence, experiments are observations, but, unlike straightforward observation in which there is no control over either the behaviour of subjects or of the environments in which they are being observed (and hence no real awareness of causal relationships), the experimenting observer deliberately intervenes in the situation. This is done by exercising influence over the variables and conditions within the experimenter's control, and controlled experiments provide the most reliable method of demonstrating causal relationships (see Banks, 1964; Cox & Enis, 1969; Davies, 1970; Venkatesan & Holloway, 1971).

Both 'experimental' and 'control' grokps are required representing, say, two matched samples, or two test-market locations, two retail outlets, and so on. Selected stimuli (in the form of controllable inputs) will initially be identical in both the experimental situation and the control situation, but these stimuli will be selectively and systematically varied in the former while being held constant in the latter. Assuming that the uncontrolled extraneous factors (i.e. environmental inputs) vary in the same way between the experimental and control situations, the differences in observed outcomes can be wholly attributed to the changes made in the controllable variables. Let us consider the relationship between sales and advertising for a given product. We could carry out an experiment to determine the nature of this relationship by selecting two matching market situations, one of which would be the control and the other the experimental location. Initially there would be no advertising in either market-place but this would be gradually introduced into the experimental location only. Prior to the introduction of advertising, with all other controllable variables being identical in each location, there would have been sales levels that accorded with existing inputs, so the introduction of a new input should be the main factor in any subsequent variation in the ratio of sales in both locations (subject to the usual tests of statistical significance). In this way it is possible to build up an awareness of the manner in which particular variables (such as sales levels, or profit levels) depend on other variables (such as advertising, or the interaction of cost and revenue functions). Variables of the first type are termed *dependent variables* and those of the second type are termed *independent variables*: the values of independent variables can either be determined by management or emerge from an earlier interaction of variables in which we are not currently interested, and these independent variables then interact to produce the values of the dependent variables in which we are interested.

Diagrammatically, we can portray experimentation in a systems model (see Figure 1.8).

Obvious problems arise in connection with measuring the changes in marketing variables in an acceptably accurate way, especially when the variables of interest are concerned with levels of awareness or degrees of preference on the part of consumers (whether actual or potential). Difficulties also exist in matching groups of subjects prior to running an experiment. Following from the matching

**FIGURE 1.8**
*Experimentation*

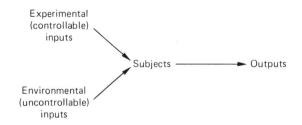

Independent variables                    Dependent variables

problem is that of ensuring comparable exposure of the subjects to the same environmental (i.e. non-controllable) stimuli during the experiment, and then ensuring that subjects behave in an authentic manner (which will tend not to be the case when human subjects know that they are participating in an experiment – see Kotler, 1972, pp. 317–18).

If the concept of experimentation brings to mind images of chemical laboratories or white mice, it is as well to remember that the precision of measurements in the physical sciences, and to a lesser extent in the life sciences, is greater than in the social sciences. The controls that are established to ensure the accuracy of experimental results in marketing cannot usually approach the reliability of those employed in scientific laboratories. This can be seen by considering the demographic variations between two towns used in a test marketing experiment, and reflecting on the variations between two samples of a chemical of known formulation. Nevertheless, experimentation is the only means available for verifying causal relationships in marketing, which suggests that it is an important aspect of marketing planning. This in turn suggests that it is essential to know the various components of an experiment. These are shown in Figure 1.9 (after Venkatesan and Holloway, 1971, p. 11), and have an applicability (in this form of abstraction) across a large number of disciplines.

The significance of carefully stating the problem to be solved has already been discussed and might be in the form of evaluating the effectiveness of a specific advertising campaign. Help may be available in the form of existing articles, research reports, etc. (collectively referred to as 'the literature'), and theories to formulate the problem precisely and maybe to provide a solution. Usually, however, it will be necessary to specify one or more hypotheses to be tested. A hypothesis is a conjectural statement about the assumed relationship between two or more variables (see Zaltman, et al., 1973). We might hypothesize, for instance, that the expenditure of £X on advertising in medium A will give more opportunities to see, and have a better effect on sales, than will the expenditure of £Y in medium B. The main relevant variables are advertising expenditure, opportunities to see on the part of members of the target group, and sales response; and their interrelationship is such that sales response depends, *inter alia*, on opportunities to see, which in turn depends on the form of advertising and the medium carrying it. It is advertising that is the independent variable in this case, and an experiment must be designed to determine which type of advertising is most effective (i.e. to test the hypothesis). This raises the problems of measurement, control groups, and so forth, to which reference has already been made. Assuming these problems can be resolved and the experiment carried out the results should then be analysed to see if the hypothesis is supported or refuted.

It will be obvious that well-designed marketing experiments provide a very sound basis for planning and control in marketing, yet they are expensive to carry out, which tends to be a discouraging factor despite the importance of having reliable information in order that the right decisions might be made on the basis

**FIGURE 1.9**
*Stages of an experiment*

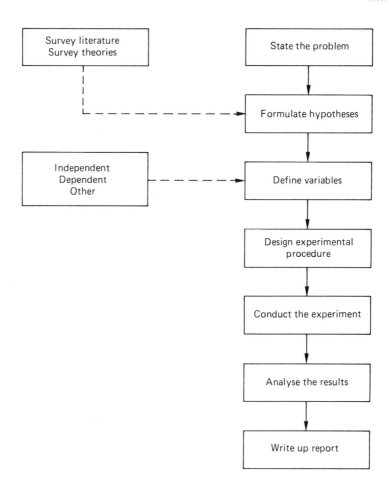

of that information. What may be useful is a phasing-in of experimental results over a period covering the preparation of several marketing plans so that the value of this information becomes apparent. Hopefully, this will lead to greater marketing effectiveness, with problems being anticipated so that experiments can be carried out to supply a basis to resolve them before crises emerge (see Adler, 1960; Boyd and Britt, 1965).

## 1.5 STRATEGIC DECISIONS AND THE NATURE OF STRATEGY

What are the characteristics of strategic decisions?

1 They are concerned with the scope of an organization's activities, and hence with the definition of an organization's boundaries.
2 They relate to the matching of the organization's activities with the opportunities of its substantive environment. Since the environment is continually changing it is necessary for this to be accommodated via adaptive decision making that anticipates outcomes – as in playing a game of chess.
3 They require the matching of an organization's activities with its resources. In order to take advantage of strategic opportunities it will be necessary to have funds, capacity, personnel, etc., available when required.
4 They have major resource implications for organizations – such as acquiring additional capacity, disposing of capacity, or reallocating resources in a fundamental way.

5 They are influenced by the values and expectations of those who determine the organization's strategy. Any repositioning of organizational boundaries will be influenced by managerial preferences and conceptions as much as by environmental possibilities.
6 They will affect the organization's long-term direction.
7 They are complex in nature since they tend to be non-routine and involve a large number of variables. As a result their implications will typically extend throughout the organization.

Decision making (whether strategic or tactical) is but a part of a broader problem-solving process. In essence this consists of three key aspects: analysis, choice and implementation.

1 *Strategic analysis* focuses on understanding the strategic position of the organization, which requires that answers be found to such questions as:

   (a) What changes are taking place in the environment?
   (b) How will these changes affect the organization and its activities?
   (c) What resources does the organization have to deal with these changes?
   (d) What do those groups associated with the organization wish to achieve?

2 *Strategic choice* has three aspects:

   (a) The generation of strategic options, which should go beyond the most obvious courses of action.
   (b) The evaluation of strategic options, which may be based on exploiting an organization's relative strengths or on overcoming its weaknesses.
   (c) The selection of a preferred strategy which will enable the organization to seize opportunities within its environment or to counter threats from competitors.

3 *Strategic implementation* is concerned with translating a decision into action, which presupposes that the decision itself (i.e. the strategic choice) was made with some thought being given to feasibility and acceptability. The allocation of resources to new courses of action will need to be undertaken, and there may be a need for adapting the organization's structure to handle new activities as well as training personnel and devising appropriate systems.

The elements of strategic problem-solving are summarized in Figure 1.10 (Johnson and Scholes (1988), p. 16).

We have given some thought to strategic decisions, but what is meant by strategy?

Hofer and Schendel (1978, p. 27) have identified three distinct levels of strategy in a commercial context. These are:

1 corporate strategy, which deals with the allocation of resources among the various businesses or divisions of an enterprise;
2 business strategy, which exists at the level of the individual business or division, dealing primarily with the question of competitive position;
3 functional level strategy, which is limited to the actions of specific functions within specific businesses.

Our main concern is in relation to business strategy (i.e. level (2) above).

Different authorities have defined strategy in lots of different ways; there is no standard definition. However, a range of elements that most writers seem to subscribe to in discussing strategy have been put forward by Simmonds (1980, pp. 7–9), as follows:

● Strategy is applicable to business within defined boundaries. While the boundaries may change, the strategy applies at any one time to actions affecting a delimited area of demand and competition.

**FIGURE 1.10**
*A summary model
of the elements of
strategic
management*

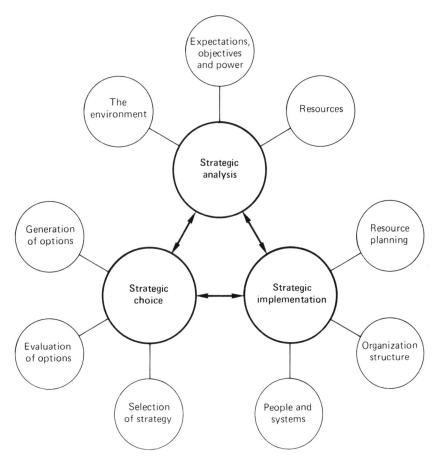

SOURCE: Johnson and Scholes (1988), p. 16

- There are specified direct competitors. These are competitors selling essentially the same products or services within the defined demand area. Indirect competitors are those operating outside the defined business and whose products are not direct substitutes. Indirect competition is usually ignored or covered by the concept of price elasticity of demand.
- There is zero-sum competition between the direct competitors for the market demand, subject to competitive action affecting the quantity demanded.
- Demand within the defined market varies over time. This variation in demand is largely independent of supplier strategies and is often referred to as the *product life cycle*. At its simplest it is depicted as a normal curve over time with regularly growing then declining demand.
- Strategy unfolds over a sequence of time periods. Competition evolves through a series of skirmishes and battles across the units of time covered by the product life cycle.
- Single period profit is a function of:
  *the price level ruling for the period;
  *the accumulated volume experience of the enterprise;
  *the enterprise's achieved volume as a proportion of capacity.
- Market share has intrinsic value. Past sales levels influence subsequent customer buying, and costs reduce with single-period volume and accumulated experience.
- Competitors differ in market share, accumulated experience, production capacity and resources. Competitors are unequal, identified and positioned.
- Objectives differ. Enterprises composed of ownership, management and employee factions and operating a range of different businesses have different

objectives. Strategic business thinking, however, will usually express these as different time and risk preferences for performance within an individual business, measured in financial terms.

- Within a given situation there will be a core of strategic actions which will be the essential cause of change in competitive position. Non-strategic, or contingent actions, will support strategic actions and should be consistent with them, but will not change competitive position significantly.
- Identification of an optimal core of strategic actions requires reasoning, or diagnosis, is not attained through application of a fixed set of procedures and is situational. In short, thinking is required.

Taken together, these elements present a view of business strategy that sees it as a chosen set of actions by means of which a market position relative to other competing enterprises is sought and maintained. This gives us the notion of competitive position.

It needs to be emphasized that 'strategy' is not synonymous with 'long-term plan' but rather consists of an enterprise's attempts to reach some preferred future state by adapting its competitive position as circumstances change. While a series of strategic moves may be planned, competitors' actions will mean that the actual moves will have to be modified to take account of those actions.

We can contrast this view of strategy with an approach to management that has been common in the UK. In organizations that lack strategic direction there has been a tendency to look inwards in times of stress, and for management to devote their attention to cost cutting and to shedding unprofitable divisions. In other words, the focus has been on *efficiency* (i.e. the relationship between inputs and outputs, usually with a short time horizon) rather than on *effectiveness* (which is concerned with the organization's attainment of goals – including that of desired competitive position). While efficiency is essentially introspective, effectiveness highlights the links between the organization and its environment. The responsibility for efficiency lies with operational managers, with top management having the primary responsibility for the strategic orientation of the organization (see pp. 11–12 above).

Figure 1.11 summarizes the principal combinations of efficiency and effectiveness (adapted from Christopher, et al., 1987, p. 80).

**FIGURE 1.11**
*Efficiency versus effectiveness*

**FIGURE 1.12**
*Interest groups*

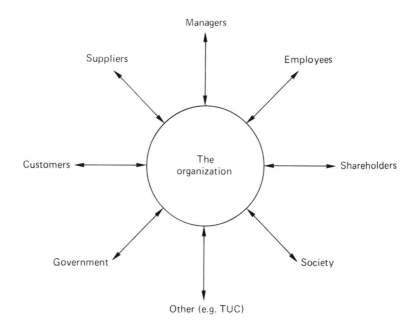

An organization that finds itself in cell 1 is well placed to thrive, since it is achieving what it aspires to achieve with an efficient output/input ratio. In contrast, an organization in cell 4 is doomed, as is an organization in cell 2 unless it can establish some strategic direction. The particular point to note is that cell 2 is a worse place to be than is cell 3 since, in the latter, the strategic direction is present to ensure effectiveness even if rather too much input is being used to generate outputs. To be effective is to survive whereas to be efficient is not in itself either necessary or sufficient for survival.

In crude terms, to be effective is to do the right thing, while to be efficient is to do the (given) thing right. An emphasis on efficiency rather than on effectiveness is clearly wrong. But who determines effectiveness? Any organization can be portrayed as a coalition of diverse interest groups each of which participates in the coalition in order to secure some advantage. This advantage (or inducement) may be in the form of dividends to shareholders, wages to employees, continued business to suppliers of goods and services, satisfaction on the part of consumers, legal compliance from the viewpoint of government, responsible behaviour towards society and the environment from the perspective of pressure groups, and so on. Figure 1.12 illustrates the way in which a range of interest groups come together to sustain (and, indeed, constitute) an organization. In so far as the inducements needed to maintain this coalition are not forthcoming the organization ceases to be effective. Thus, for example, employees may go on strike in furtherance of a pay dispute; shareholders may be unwilling to subscribe further capital if the value of their shares has fallen due to bad management; consumers may have defected in the light of superior market offerings from competitors; and each of these will remove one vital element from the coalition.

The interest groups within the coalition provide contributions (or resources) without which the organization cannot function: these are the inputs (men, machines, money, etc.) to the systems model we saw earlier in the chapter.

It should be apparent from this view of an organization that management's freedom of movement is constrained by virtue of the expectations of the interest groups within the coalition. We are unable to assume that a clean slate exists on which any strategy might be drawn, since this may be against the interests of members of the coalition. What we can say, therefore, is that any strategy is potentially available in so far as it ensures that the interests of coalition members are protected. If this is not so the organization cannot be effective, and if it is not effective it will not survive.

## 1.6  THE MARKETING/STRATEGY INTERFACE

On the basis of a literature review Greenley (1986, p. 56) has drawn some distinctions between marketing planning (seen as being an annual exercise) and strategic planning (seen as being of a long-term nature), including the following:

Table 1.1

| Strategic planning | Marketing planning |
| --- | --- |
| Concerned with overall, long-term organizational direction. | Concerned with day-to-day performance and results. |
| Provides the long-term framework for the organization. | Represents only one stage in the organization's development. |
| Overall orientation needed to match the organization to its environment. | Functional and professional orientation tends to predominate. |
| Goals and strategies are evaluated from an overall perspective. | Goals are subdivided into specific targets. |
| Relevance of goals and strategies is only evident in the long term. | Relevance of goals and strategies is immediately evident. |

These differences indicate that strategic planning logically precedes marketing planning by providing a framework within which marketing plans might be formulated. As Cravens (1986, p. 77) has stated:

> Understanding the strategic situation confronting an organization is an essential starting point in developing a marketing strategy.

This understanding can be derived from an assessment of:

- organizational capabilities;
- threats from environmental forces;
- competitors' strengths and weaknesses;
- customer needs;

and fits into an iterative setting as shown in Figure 1.13.

The strong interdependence of strategic and marketing planning is clearly seen in this diagram. We can use this interdependence to develop the marketing mix (of Figure 1.2 above) into a set of elements from which a competitive strategy might be developed (as in Figure 1.14). The aim should be to build strength in those elements that are critical to achieving superiority in areas deemed important by customers. In this way the organization should be able to challenge its competitors from a position in which it can use its relative strengths.

The potential benefits of a strategic underpinning to marketing planning are probably apparent, but what about the problem of implementation? If

**FIGURE 1.13**
*The marketing
strategy process*

**FIGURE 1.14**
*Elements of a
competitive
strategy*

**Product**
- Functional performance
- Technical developments planned
- Packaging
- Service levels
- Range extensions/deletions

**Customer**
- Customer targets
- Researching customer needs by segment
- Segmenting the market by customer needs
- Distribution channels
- Export

**Distribution**
- Identifying appropriate channels
- Accessing successful distributors
- Stock and service levels
- Operating costs

**Price**
- List prices
- Discount structure

**Advertising and promotion**
- Target audience
- Communication objective
- Media
- Advertising weight
- Promotion plans and timing
- Point of sale

**Sales force**
- Customer priorities
- Product priorities
- Incentives and rewards

**Manufacturing**
- Sustainable quality and volume levels
- Cost reduction programme:
  - raw material usage
  - yields
  - manpower
- Quality enhancement

SOURCE: Milton and Reiss, 1985, p. 23

implementation is ineffective the carefully devised strategy will be unable to help in improving the organization's performance. The question becomes, therefore: 'given a specific type of strategy, what marketing structures, policies, procedures, and programs are likely to distinguish high performing business units from those that are relatively less effective, efficient, or adaptable?' (Walker and Ruekert, 1987, p. 15). We will turn to this question in Part 5.

## 1.7 SUMMARY

This chapter seeks to offer some ideas constituting a framework for the rest of the book.

It begins by considering the nature of management and of the management process. The process is often characterized in the following stages:

- planning;
- decision making;
- control.

These are related to a series of questions, around which the book is structured:

1 Where are we now?
2 Where do we want to be?
3 How might we get there?
4 Which way is best?
5 How can we ensure arrival?

Three different time dimensions can be identified:

1 *Past*: which brought us to where we are now and from which we might learn;
2 *Present*: in which we might determine where we wish to go and how we might get there;
3 *Future*: in which our aspirations may – or may not – be realized but which represents the key time dimension.

We can inter-relate managerial processes, key questions, and time dimensions into a multi-faceted framework which can be portrayed as a 'cycle of control'. The next step is to consider the notion of strategy, and then the role of marketing in relation to strategy.

*Strategy* can be seen as a normative matter concerning what an organization would like to achieve. As such it:

- guides the organization in its relationship with its environment;
- affects the internal structure and processes of the organization;
- centrally affects the organization's performance.

*Marketing*, via its policies and programmes relating to product, price, service, distribution and communications, can provide the means to facilitate the attainment of a strategy.

The extent to which the strategy is achieved provides a measure of the organization's effectiveness. Any organization's effectiveness depends upon the balance between what is desired and what is achieved on the one hand, and on the other by paying due regard to the requirements of all stakeholders, whether internal or external. It is through the process of organizational control that managers seek to achieve organizational effectiveness, and this gives a reference point for all that follows.

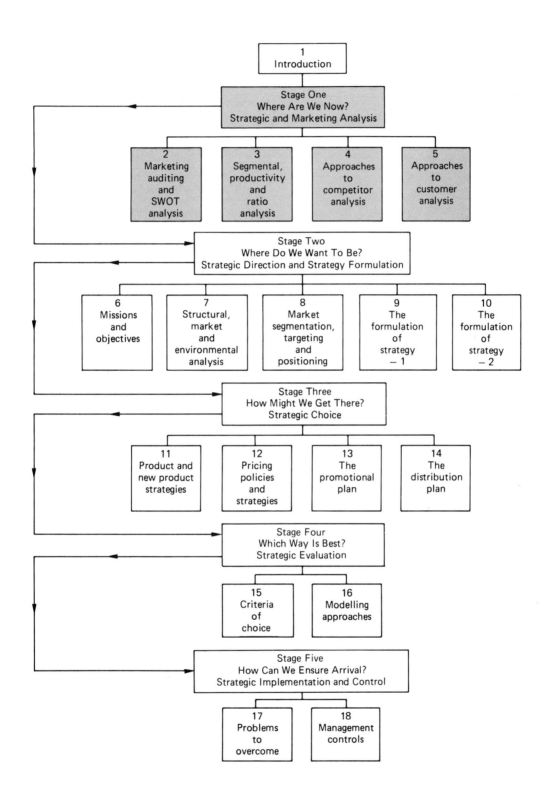

| | 1 Introduction | |
|---|---|---|

**Stage One**
**Where Are We Now?**
**Strategic and Marketing Analysis**

| 2 Marketing auditing and SWOT analysis | 3 Segmental, productivity and ratio analysis | 4 Approaches to competitor analysis | 5 Approaches to customer analysis |
|---|---|---|---|

**Stage Two**
**Where Do We Want To Be?**
**Strategic Direction and Strategy Formulation**

| 6 Missions and objectives | 7 Structural, market and environmental analysis | 8 Market segmentation, targeting and positioning | 9 The formulation of strategy – 1 | 10 The formulation of strategy – 2 |
|---|---|---|---|---|

**Stage Three**
**How Might We Get There?**
**Strategic Choice**

| 11 Product and new product strategies | 12 Pricing policies and strategies | 13 The promotional plan | 14 The distribution plan |
|---|---|---|---|

**Stage Four**
**Which Way Is Best?**
**Strategic Evaluation**

| 15 Criteria of choice | 16 Modelling approaches |
|---|---|

**Stage Five**
**How Can We Ensure Arrival?**
**Strategic Implementation and Control**

| 17 Problems to overcome | 18 Management controls |
|---|---|

# Stage One
## Where Are We Now?
## Strategic and Marketing Analysis

## Preamble

Our primary concern within this stage is with the ways in which organizations can most clearly identify their current position and the extent of their marketing capability. It is against the background of the picture that emerges from this analysis that the strategist should then be in a far better position to begin the process of deciding upon the detail of the organization's future direction and the ways in which strategy is to be formulated.

The starting point in this process of strategic and marketing analysis involves a detailed marketing audit and review of marketing effectiveness. Together, the two techniques are designed to provide the strategist with a clear understanding of:

- the organization's current market position;
- the nature of environmental opportunities and threats;
- the organization's ability to cope with the demands of this environment.

The results of this analysis are then incorporated in a statement of Strengths, Weaknesses, Opportunities and Threats (SWOT).

Although the marketing auditing process is, as we discuss in Chapter 2, a relatively under-utilized activity, a growing number of strategists and writers have over the past few years highlighted the nature of its potential contribution to effective strategy formulation.

Although there is no single format for the audit, it is generally acknowledged that if the process is to be worthwhile, account needs to be taken of six dimensions:

1 the marketing environment;
2 the current marketing strategy;
3 organizational issues;
4 the marketing systems in use;
5 levels of marketing productivity;
6 marketing functions.

Used properly, marketing auditing and a review of marketing effectiveness are recognized as potentially powerful analytical tools that are capable of providing the strategist with a detailed understanding of the organization's marketing capability and the nature of the environment that it is likely to face.

This process of analysis is taken a step further in Chapter 3 in which we discuss the ways in which the strategist can establish patterns of resource allocation and its productivity by relating inputs (resources or costs) to outputs (revenues). By doing this the process of cost-effective planning is capable of being improved significantly.

Against this background we turn in Chapters 4 and 5 to the various ways in which competitors and customers can be analysed.

It has long been recognized that marketing strategy is to a very large extent driven by the strategist's perception of competitors and customers. Because of this the failure to analyse in depth competitors' and customers' potential response profiles is likely to be reflected in strategies which lack an adequate underpinning.

In the case of competitors our understanding of how competitive relationships develop and operate has increased greatly over the past few years, largely as the result of the work of Michael Porter. Porter's work is based on the idea that the nature and intensity of competition within an industry is determined by the interaction of five key forces:

1  the threat of new entrants;
2  the power of buyers;
3  the threat of substitutes;
4  the extent of competitive rivalry;
5  the power of suppliers.

Analysis of these allows, in turn, for the identification of strategic groups and for a far clearer identification of the relative position, strengths and objectives of each competitor. In the light of this the arguments in favour of a competitive intelligence system are compelling. However, as we point out in Chapter 4, the value, and indeed the existence, of such a system is determined to a very large extent by the belief in competitive monitoring on the part of top management. Without this the evidence that emerges from the work of Davidson and others suggests that the organization will be largely introspective, with competitive analysis playing only a minor role in the planning process.

Broadly similar comments can be made about the role and value of customer analysis. As with competitive behaviour, our understanding of how buyers behave has advanced significantly in recent years, largely as the result of the work of researchers such as: Foxall; Turnbull and Cunningham; Webster; Robinson, Faris and Wind; and Hakansson. All too often, however, evidence suggests that firms devote relatively little attention to detailed customer analysis, assuming instead that because they interact with customers on a day-to-day basis they have a sufficient understanding of how and why markets behave as they do. Only rarely is this likely to be the case and, recognizing that customer knowledge is a potentially powerful source of competitive advantage, the rationale for regular and detailed analyses of customers is therefore strong.

| 2 | Marketing auditing and SWOT analysis |
|---|---|

## 2.1 LEARNING OBJECTIVES

When you have read this chapter you should be able to understand:

(a) the nature, structure and purpose of the marketing audit;
(b) the nature of the contribution made by the marketing audit to the overall management audit;
(c) the need for a regular review of marketing effectiveness and how such a review might be conducted;
(d) why a regular review of strengths, weaknesses, opportunities and threats is necessary;
(e) how the marketing effectiveness review, SWOT analysis and the marketing audit contribute to the marketing planning process.

## 2.2 INTRODUCTION

The process of marketing auditing is for many organizations still a relatively new and under-utilized activity. This is despite a substantial and growing body of evidence which suggests that an organization's performance in the market-place is influenced significantly and directly by the strategist's perception of three factors:

1 the organization's current market position;
2 the nature of environmental opportunities and threats;
3 the organization's ability to cope with environmental demands.

The marketing audit is designed to provide the strategist with a clear understanding of these three dimensions and in this way provide a firm foundation for the development of strategy. This is reflected in a comment by McDonald (1984, p. 14):

> Expressed in its simplest form, if the purpose of a corporate plan is to answer three central questions:
>
> Where is the company now?
> Where does the company want to go?
> How should the company organize its resources to get there?
>
> then the audit is the means by which the first of these questions is answered. An audit is a systematic, critical and unbiased review and appraisal of the environment and of the company's operations. A marketing audit is part of the larger management audit and is concerned (specifically) with the *marketing environment and marketing operations*. [Emphasis added.]

## What is a Marketing Audit?

The marketing audit is in a number of ways the true starting point for the strategic marketing planning process, since it is through the audit that the strategist arrives at a measure both of environmental opportunities and threats and of the organization's marketing capability. The thinking that underpins the concept of the marketing audit is straightforward: it is that corporate objectives and strategy can only be developed effectively against the background of a detailed and objective understanding both of corporate capability and environmental opportunity. The audit is, therefore, as McDonald (1984, p. 14) has suggested, 'The means by which a company can identify its own strengths and weaknesses as they relate to external opportunities and threats. It is thus a way of helping management to select a position in that environment based on known factors.'

Definitions of the audit have also been proposed by Shuchman (1950, pp. 16–17) and Kotler (1988, p. 747). Shuchman, for example, has suggested that the audit is:

> . . . a systematic, critical, and impartial review and appraisal of the total marketing operation: of the basic objectives and policies and the assumptions which underlie them as well as the methods, procedures, personnel and organization employed to implement the policies and achieve the objectives.

Kotler's view is broadly similar:

> A marketing audit is a *comprehensive, systematic, independent,* and *periodic* examination of a company's – or business unit's – marketing environment, objectives, strategies and activities with a view to determining problem areas and opportunities and recommending a plan of action to improve the company's performance.

Taken together, these definitions highlight the three major elements and potential benefits of the marketing audit:

1 the analysis of the external environment and internal situation;
2 the evaluation of past performance and present activities;
3 the identification of future opportunities and threats.

These three elements can then usefully be viewed against the background of comments made by Ansoff (1968) who has suggested that, 'irrespective of the size of the organization, corporate decisions have to be made within the constraint of a limited total resource'. Recognizing this, the strategist is then faced with the task of producing 'a resource allocation pattern which will offer the best potential for meeting the firm's objectives'. The marketing audit can therefore be seen in terms of providing a sound basis for this process of resource allocation. In this way any strategy that is then developed should be far more consistent both with the demands of the environment and the organization's true capabilities and strengths.

The rationale for the audit is straightforward and in a number of ways can be seen to derive from the more commonly known and widely accepted idea of the financial audit which, together with audits of other functional areas, is part of the overall management audit; the nature of this relationship is illustrated in Figure 2.1.

## The Structure and Focus of the Audit

In terms of its structure, the marketing audit consists of three major and detailed diagnostic steps. These involve a review of:

1 the organization's environment (opportunities and threats);
2 its marketing system (strengths and weaknesses);
3 its marketing activities.

**FIGURE 2.1**
*The place of the marketing audit in the overall management audit*

The first of these is designed to establish the various dimensions of the marketing environment, the ways in which it is likely to change and the probable impact of these changes upon the organization. The second stage is concerned with an assessment of the extent to which the organization's marketing systems are capable of dealing with the demands of the environment. The final stage involves a review of the individual components of the marketing mix.

It should be apparent from this that in conducting an audit the strategist is concerned with two types of variable. First, there are the *environmental* or *market variables* over which the strategist has little or no direct control. Second, there are the *operational variables* which can be controlled to a greater or lesser extent. This distinction can also be expressed in terms of the *macroenvironmental forces* (political/legal, economic/demographic, social/cultural, and technological) that affect the business, and *microenvironmental actors* (customers, competitors, distributors and suppliers) who subsequently influence the organization's ability to operate profitably in the market-place. Regardless of which approach to categorization is used, the process and purpose of the audit is the same. It begins with an *external audit* covering the macroenvironmental forces referred to above and the markets and competitors that are of particular interest to the company. The *internal audit* then builds upon this by assessing the extent to which the organization, its structure and resources, relate to the environment and have the capability of operating effectively within the constraints that the environment imposes.

In doing this the auditor should not view the marketing audit and its result in isolation but, as we observed earlier, should instead give full recognition to the way in which it sits within the general framework of the overall management audit and alongside the audits of the other management functions. In this way the strategist should arrive at a true measure not just of environmental opportunity but also of the ability of the organization as a whole to respond effectively.

**The Scope and Frequency of Marketing Auditing**

The frequency with which the audit should be conducted is influenced by several factors, the most important of which are the nature of the business, the rate of environmental change, and the planning cycle (annual, bi-annual). In so far as it is possible to provide a reasonably definitive guideline it is that the organization should undertake a full audit at the beginning of each major planning cycle, supplemented by less intensive but more frequent reviews of specific or key areas as conditions change. In discussing this, Baker (1985, p. 192) suggests that:

> Detailed inquiry into specific topics, e.g. pricing policy, may well be amenable to some form of rota, so that all areas will be covered within the duration of the planning cycle. For example, if the firm normally operates on an annual cycle then it may be convenient to monitor key indicators such as sales, prices, market share, etc., on a monthly basis, and the 'mix' elements on a bi-monthly rota, e.g.:
>
> | | |
> |---|---|
> | Month 2 | Pricing |
> | Month 4 | Packaging |
> | Month 6 | Promotion |
> | Month 8 | Distribution |
> | Month 10 | Sales |
> | Month 12 | Market research |

A somewhat different view of the frequency of auditing has been put forward by Bureau (1981), who has suggested that 'once every five years is psychologically about the minimum time span between audits. More frequent audits will not only demoralize marketing personnel, but would indicate that the organization's recruitment policies required serious review'.

**The Stages of the Audit**

In conducting a marketing audit both Grashof (1975) and Cannon (1968, p. 102) advocate a step-wise procedure. In this way, they argue, the approach ensures a degree of consistency that allows for a comparison from one period to another. For Grashof, these steps are:

1 *Pre-audit activities* in which the auditor decides upon the precise breadth and focus of the audit.
2 *The assembly of information* on the areas which affect the organization's marketing performance. These would typically include:

(a) the industry;
(b) the market;
(c) the firm;
(d) the product;
(e) pricing;
(f) promotion;
(g) distribution.

3 *Information analysis*.
4 The formulation of *recommendations*.
5 The development of *an implementation programme*.

Cannon's approach is broadly similar and again consists of five distinct stages as shown in Table 2.1.

Although for many organizations it is the assembly of information which proves to be the most time consuming, it is (in terms of Grashof's suggested framework) Stages 3 and 5 which often prove to be the most problematic. In analysing information the auditor needs to consider three questions:

1 What is the *absolute* value of the information?
2 What is its *comparative* value?
3 What *interpretation* is to be placed upon it?

**Table 2.1**

| | | **Key elements** |
|---|---|---|
| Step 1 | Define the market | *Develop:*<br>• Statement of purpose in terms of benefits.<br>• Product scope.<br>• Size, growth rate, maturity state, need for primary versus selective strategies.<br>• Requirements for success.<br>• Divergent definitions of the above by competitors.<br>• Definition to be used by the company. |
| Step 2 | Determine performance differentials | • Evaluate industry performance and company differences.<br>• Determine differences in products, applications, geography and distribution channels.<br>• Determine differences by customer set. |
| Step 3 | Determine differences in competitive programmes | Identify and evaluate individual companies for their:<br>• Market development strategies.<br>• Product development strategies.<br>• Financing and administrative strategies and support. |
| Step 4 | Profile the strategies of competitors | • Profile each significant competitor and/or distinct type of competitive strategy.<br>• Compare own and competitive strategies. |
| Step 5 | Determine the strategic planning structure | When size and complexity are adequate:<br>• Establish planning units or cells and designate prime and subordinate dimensions.<br>• Make organizational assignments to product managers, industry managers and others. |

It is generally acknowledged that if these questions are answered satisfactorily the recommendations will follow reasonably easily and logically. The only remaining problem is then the development of an effective implementation programme; the ways in which this might be done are discussed in detail in Stage Five of the book.

It should be apparent from the discussion so far that a marketing audit, if carried out properly, is a highly specific, detailed and potentially time-consuming activity. Because of this many organizations often do not bother with a full audit, and opt instead for a less detailed, more general and more frequent *review of marketing effectiveness*, coupled with an analysis of strengths, weaknesses, opportunities and threats.

## 2.3 REVIEWING MARKETING EFFECTIVENESS

Marketing effectiveness is to a very large extent determined by the extent to which the organization reflects the five major attributes of a marketing orientation, namely:

1  a customer-oriented philosophy;
2  an integrated marketing organization;
3  adequate marketing information;
4  a strategic orientation;
5  operational efficiency.

Each of these dimensions can be measured relatively easily, he suggests, by means of a checklist and an overall rating then arrived at for the organization; an example of this appears in Figure 2.2. It needs to be recognized, however, that an

**FIGURE 2.2**
*A marketing
effectiveness rating
instrument*

| Customer philosophy | Score |
|---|---|

1 *To what extent does management recognize the need to organize the company to satisfy specific market demands?*

| | |
|---|---|
| The managerial philosophy is to sell existing and new products to whoever will buy them. | ☐ 0 |
| Management attempts to serve a wide range of markets and needs with equal effectiveness. | ☐ 1 |
| Having identified market needs, management focuses upon specific target markets in order to maximize company growth and potential. | ☐ 2 |

2 *To what extent is the marketing programme tailored to the needs of different market segments?*

| | |
|---|---|
| Not at all. | ☐ 0 |
| To some extent. | ☐ 1 |
| To a very high degree | ☐ 2 |

3 *Does management adopt a systems approach to planning, with recognition being given to the interrelationships between the environment, suppliers, channels, customers and competitors?*

| | |
|---|---|
| Not at all; the company focuses solely upon its existing customer base. | ☐ 0 |
| To some extent, in that the *majority* of its effort goes into serving its immediate and existing customer base. | ☐ 1 |
| Yes. Management recognizes the various dimensions of the marketing environment and attempts to reflect this in its marketing programmes by taking account of the threats and opportunities created by change within the system. | ☐ 2 |

**Marketing organization**

4 *To what extent does senior management attempt to control and integrate the major marketing functions?*

| | |
|---|---|
| Not at all. No real attempt is made to integrate or control activities, and conflict between areas of marketing exists. | ☐ 0 |
| To a limited degree, although the levels of control and coordination are generally unsatisfactory. | ☐ 1 |
| To a very high degree with the result that functional areas work together well. | ☐ 2 |

5 *What sort of relationship exists between marketing management and the management of the R & D, finance, production and manufacturing functions?*

| | |
|---|---|
| Generally poor, with frequent complaints being made that marketing is unrealistic in its demands. | ☐ 0 |
| Generally satisfactory, although the feeling exists that each department is intent on serving its own needs. | ☐ 1 |
| Overall very good, with departments working together well in the interests of the company as a whole. | ☐ 2 |

6 *How well organized is the new product development process?*

| | |
|---|---|
| Not very well at all. | ☐ 0 |
| A formal new product process exists but does not work very well, | ☐ 1 |
| It is well structured, professionally managed and achieves good results. | ☐ 2 |

**Marketing information**

7 *How frequently does the company conduct market research studies of customers, channels and competitors?*

| | |
|---|---|
| Seldom, if ever. | ☐ 0 |
| Occasionally. | ☐ 1 |
| Regularly and in a highly structured way. | ☐ 2 |

**FIGURE 2.2 (contd.)**

|  | Score |
|---|---|

8 *To what extent is management aware of the sales potential and profitability of different market segments, customers, territories, products and order sizes?*

Not at all. ☐ 0

To some degree. ☐ 1

Very well. ☐ 2

9 *What effort is made to measure the cost effectiveness of different levels and types of marketing expenditure?*

None at all. ☐ 0

Some, but not in a regular or structured way. ☐ 1

A great deal. ☐ 2

**The strategic perspective**

10 *How formalized is the marketing planning process?*

The company does virtually no formal marketing planning. ☐ 0

An annual marketing plan is developed. ☐ 1

The company develops a detailed annual marketing plan and a long-range plan that is updated annually. ☐ 2

11 *What is the quality of the thinking that underlies the current marketing strategy?*

The current strategy is unclear. ☐ 0

The current strategy is clear and is largely a continuation of earlier strategies. ☐ 1

The current strategy is clear, well argued and well developed. ☐ 2

12 *To what extent does management engage in contingency thinking and planning?*

Not at all. ☐ 0

There is some contingency thinking but this is not incorporated into a formal planning process. ☐ 1

A serious attempt is made to identify the most important contingencies, and contingency plans are then developed. ☐ 2

**Operational efficiency**

13 *How well is senior management thinking on marketing communicated and implemented down the line?*

Very badly. ☐ 0

Reasonably well. ☐ 1

Extremely successfully. ☐ 2

14 *Does marketing management do an effective job with the resources available?*

No. The resource base is inadequate for the objectives that have been set. ☐ 0

To a limited extent. The resources available are adequate but are only rarely applied in an optimal manner. ☐ 1

Yes. The resources available are adequate and managed efficiently. ☐ 2

15 *Does management respond quickly and effectively to unexpected developments in the market-place?*

No. Market information is typically out of date and management responses are slow. ☐ 0

To a limited extent. Market information is reasonably up to date, although management response times vary. ☐ 1

Yes. Highly efficient information systems exist and management responds quickly and effectively. ☐ 2

**FIGURE 2.2 (contd.)**

---

**The scoring process**

Each manager works his way through the 15 questions in order to arrive at a score. The scores are then aggregated and averaged. The overall measure of marketing effectiveness can then be assessed against the following scale:

| | | |
|---|---|---|
| 0–5 | = | None |
| 6–10 | = | Poor |
| 11–15 | = | Fair |
| 16–20 | = | Good |
| 21–25 | = | Very good |
| 26–30 | = | Superior |

With a score of *10 or less* major questions can be asked about the organization's ability to survive in anything more than the short term, and any serious competitive challenge is likely to create significant problems. Fundamental changes are needed, both in the management philosophy and the organizational structure. For many organizations in this position, however, these changes are unlikely to be brought about by the existing management, since it is this group which has led to the current situation. The solution may therefore lie in major changes to the senior management.

With a score of *between 11 and 15* there is again a major opportunity to improve the management philosophy and organizational structure.

With a score of *between 16 and 25* scope for improvement exists, although this is likely to be in terms of a series of small changes and modifications rather than anything more fundamental. With a score of *between 26 and 30* care needs to be taken to ensure that the proactive stance is maintained and that complacency does not begin to emerge.

---

SOURCE: Adapted from Kotler (1977)

organization's marketing effectiveness is not always reflected in current levels of performance. It is quite possible, for example, for an organization to be performing well simply by force of circumstance rather than because of good management. In other words, good performance may be due to being in the right place at the right time as opposed to anything more fundamental. A change in strategy as the result of an effectiveness review might well have the result of improving performance from good to excellent. Equally, an organization may be performing badly despite seemingly excellent marketing planning. Again, the explanation may well be environmental rather than poor management. Recognizing this, the purpose of going through the process of a marketing effectiveness rating review is to identify those areas in which scope exists for marketing improvement. Action, in the form of revised plans, can then be taken to achieve this.

With regard to the process of arriving at a measure of marketing effectiveness, the procedure is straightforward and involves managers from a number of departments – not just marketing – completing the checklists of Figure 2.2. Scores are then summarized in order to arrive at an overall perception of marketing effectiveness. In practice, and as might be expected, few companies achieve a score in the highest range; among the few to have done this in the US, it is suggested, are McDonald's, Procter & Gamble, IBM, and General Electric. The majority of companies, however, cluster around the fair-to-good range, suggesting that scope exists for improvements in one or more of the five areas.

Having conducted a review of marketing effectiveness, the strategist may decide that the results provide sufficient insight into the organization's strengths and weaknesses. There is, however, a strong argument for viewing the marketing effectiveness rating review as the jumping-off point for the more thorough and detailed marketing audit.

## 2.4 THE ROLE OF SWOT ANALYSIS

**Identifying Opportunities and Threats**

Faced with a constantly changing environment, each business unit needs to develop a marketing information system (MIS) to track trends and developments. Each trend or development can then be categorized as an *opportunity* or a *threat*, and an assessment made of the feasibility and action needed if the organization is either to capitalize upon the opportunity or minimize the impact of the threat. However, in examining opportunities and threats the reader needs to recognize a point made by Johnson and Scholes (1988, p. 77) that

> they can never be viewed as 'absolutes'. What might appear at first sight to be an opportunity may not be so when examined against the organization's resources, its culture, the expectations of its stakeholders, the strategies available, or the feasibility of implementing the strategy. At the risk of oversimplification, however, the purpose of strategy formulation is to develop a strategy which will take advantage of the opportunities and overcome or circumvent the threats.

For our purposes an opportunity can be seen as any sector of the market in which the company would enjoy a competitive advantage. These opportunities can then be assessed according to their *attractiveness* and the organization's *probability of success* in this area: this is illustrated in Figure 2.3.

**FIGURE 2.3**
*The opportunity matrix*

Probability of success

|               |      | High | Low |
|---------------|------|------|-----|
| Attractiveness | High | 1    | 2   |
|               | Low  | 3    | 4   |

Cell 1 consists of opportunities offering the greatest scope, and management should focus upon these. Cell 4, by contrast, represents those opportunities which either are too small or which the organization is unlikely to be able to exploit effectively. Cells 2 and 3 offer certain attractions, and management should examine these closely to see whether scope exists either for improving their attractiveness or increasing the probability of success.

The probability of success is influenced by several factors, but most obviously by the extent to which the organization's strengths, and in particular its distinctive competences, match the key success requirements for operating effectively in the target market *and* exceed those of its competitors. Competence by itself is rarely sufficient in anything more than the short term since, given time, competitive forces will erode this competence. Because of this the strategist needs to concentrate upon developing *competitive advantages* which are sustainable over time. The bases of a sustainable competitive advantage are illustrated in Figure 2.4.

The significance of competitive advantage has been highlighted by a wide variety of writers and it is an issue to which we will return on a number of occasions throughout this book. At this stage, however, it is worth quoting from the Boston Consulting Group's Annual Report for 1982:

> In the real world of business competition, each survivor is uniquely superior to all others in some significant way, no matter how subtle the difference. That competitor dominates his unique niche or his life cycle is short.

The nearly infinite possible combinations of customer characteristics, costs, logistics, methodology, etc., make it possible for vast numbers of competitors to co-exist. And each competitor may simultaneously be defending its niche against multiple unique antagonists.

Market share and industry structure are ambiguous terms when such a complex spectrum of individual differences is woven into a web of relationships in which no given competitor has exactly the same competitors as any other.

Strategy development starts with the task of identifying the comparative differentials for each competitor that constitutes a constraint. The next step is to determine the

**FIGURE 2.4**
*The bases for developing a competitive advantage*

The methods for developing a sustainable competitive advantage can be divided into three main groups:

1 **Organizational advantages**
   - Economies of scope
   - Flexibility
   - Competitive stance
   - Size
   - Speed of response
   - Past performance
   - Financial strengths
   - Patterns of ownership
   - Reputation

2 **Departmental and functional advantages**
   *Marketing*
   - Customer base
   - Customer knowledge
   - New product skills
   - Pricing
   - Communication and advertising
   - Distribution
   - Sales force
   - Service support
   - Reputation

   *Research and development*
   - Product technology
   - Patents

   *Production*
   - Technology
   - Process efficiency
   - Economies of scale
   - Experience
   - Product quality
   - Manufacturing flexibility

   *Personnel*
   - Good management–worker relations
   - Workforce flexibility

3 **Advantages based on relationships with external bodies**
   - Customer loyalty
   - Channel control
   - Preferential political and legislative treatment
   - Government assistance
   - Beneficial tariff and non-tariff trade barriers
   - Cartels
   - Intra-organizational relationships
   - Access to preferential and flexible financial resources

tradeoffs and match-ups that make competitive equilibrium possible. The strategy itself must aim at enlarging either the scope or the depth of the competitive advantage.

Ability to adapt to changing competition determines each competitor's life cycle. The web of customers, suppliers and competitors and the external environment of resources and conditions are constantly shifting. When any competitor adapts to each shift, then the equilibrium between competitors is changed too. Each must adapt. Your competitor is your environment. As a consequence, the whole competitive network is constantly evolving.

Every competitor that survives must be superior to all others with respect to some unique combination of external conditions. Every company dominates its own unique competitive segment. That domination may be by a thin margin, but if a competitor fails to be superior on its own turf, it will inevitably be crowded out.

At the same time as generating opportunities the external environment also presents a series of threats (a threat being a challenge posed by an unfavourable trend or development in the environment that in the absence of a distinct organizational response will lead to the erosion of the company's market position).

Threats can be classified on the basis of their *seriousness* and the *probability of their occurrence*; an example of how this can be done is illustrated in Figure 2.5.

**FIGURE 2.5**
*The threat matrix*

Probability of occurrence

|  | High | Low |
|---|---|---|
| High | 1 | 2 |
| Low | 3 | 4 |

Seriousness

The threats in cell 1 are serious and have a high probability of occurrence. Because of this, the strategist needs to monitor developments closely and have a detailed contingency plan available to cope with any changes that take place. The threats in cells 2 and 3 need to be closely monitored in case they become critical. At this stage, contingency planning is unlikely to be necessary. Threats in cell 4 are very minor and can be largely ignored.

In putting together a picture of the major opportunities and threats facing the business the strategist is attempting to arrive at a measure of *the market's overall attractiveness*. In essence four possibilities exist:

1 an *ideal business* that is characterized by numerous opportunities but few, if any, threats;
2 a *speculative business* that is high both in opportunities and threats;
3 a *mature business* that is low both in opportunities and threats;
4 a *troubled business* that is low in opportunities but high in threats.

**Identifying Strengths and Weaknesses**

Although in many markets it is often a relatively simple process to identify a whole series of environmental opportunities, few organizations have the ability in terms of competences to capitalize upon more than a small number. Each business needs therefore to evaluate on a regular basis its *strengths* and *weaknesses*. This can be done by means of the sort of checklist illustrated in Figure 2.6.

Each factor is rated by management or an outside consultant according to whether it is a fundamental strength, a marginal strength, a neutral factor, a marginal weakness, or a fundamental weakness. By linking these ratings a general

**FIGURE 2.6**
*Strengths and
weaknesses
analysis*

| Strengths | Performance | | | | | Importance | | |
|---|---|---|---|---|---|---|---|---|
| | Fundamental strength | Marginal strength | Neutral | Marginal weakness | Fundamental weakness | High | Medium | Low |
| *Marketing factors* | | | | | | | | |
| 1 Relative market share | —— | —— | —— | —— | —— | —— —— | | —— |
| 2 Reputation | —— | —— | —— | —— | —— | —— —— | | —— |
| 3 Previous performance | —— | —— | —— | —— | —— | —— —— | | —— |
| 4 Competitive stance | —— | —— | —— | —— | —— | —— —— | | —— |
| 5 Customer base | —— | —— | —— | —— | —— | —— —— | | —— |
| 6 Customer loyalty | —— | —— | —— | —— | —— | —— —— | | —— |
| 7 Breadth of product range | —— | —— | —— | —— | —— | —— —— | | —— |
| 8 Depth of product range | —— | —— | —— | —— | —— | —— —— | | —— |
| 9 Product quality | —— | —— | —— | —— | —— | —— —— | | —— |
| 10 Programme of product modification | —— | —— | —— | —— | —— | —— —— | | —— |
| 11 New product programme | —— | —— | —— | —— | —— | —— —— | | —— |
| 12 Distribution costs | —— | —— | —— | —— | —— | —— —— | | —— |
| 13 Dealer network | —— | —— | —— | —— | —— | —— —— | | —— |
| 14 Dealer loyalty | —— | —— | —— | —— | —— | —— —— | | —— |
| 15 Geographical coverage | —— | —— | —— | —— | —— | —— —— | | —— |
| 16 Sales force | —— | —— | —— | —— | —— | —— —— | | —— |
| 17 After sales service | —— | —— | —— | —— | —— | —— —— | | —— |
| 18 Manufacturing costs | —— | —— | —— | —— | —— | —— —— | | —— |
| 19 Manufacturing flexibility | —— | —— | —— | —— | —— | —— —— | | —— |
| 20 Raw material advantage | —— | —— | —— | —— | —— | —— —— | | —— |
| 21 Pricing | —— | —— | —— | —— | —— | —— —— | | —— |
| 22 Advertising | —— | —— | —— | —— | —— | —— —— | | —— |
| 23 Unique selling propositions | —— | —— | —— | —— | —— | —— —— | | —— |
| 24 Structure of competition | —— | —— | —— | —— | —— | —— —— | | —— |
| *Financial factors* | | | | | | | | |
| 25 Cost of capital | —— | —— | —— | —— | —— | —— —— | | —— |
| 26 Availability of capital | —— | —— | —— | —— | —— | —— —— | | —— |
| 27 Profitability | —— | —— | —— | —— | —— | —— —— | | —— |
| 28 Financial stability | —— | —— | —— | —— | —— | —— —— | | —— |
| 29 Margins | —— | —— | —— | —— | —— | —— —— | | —— |
| *Manufacturing factors* | | | | | | | | |
| 30 Production facilities | —— | —— | —— | —— | —— | —— —— | | —— |
| 31 Economies of scale | —— | —— | —— | —— | —— | —— —— | | —— |
| 32 Flexibility | —— | —— | —— | —— | —— | —— —— | | —— |
| 33 Workforce | —— | —— | —— | —— | —— | —— —— | | —— |
| 34 Technical skill | —— | —— | —— | —— | —— | —— —— | | —— |
| 35 Delivery capabilities | —— | —— | —— | —— | —— | —— —— | | —— |
| 36 Supplier sourcing flexibility | —— | —— | —— | —— | —— | —— —— | | —— |
| *Organizational factors* | | | | | | | | |
| 37 Culture | —— | —— | —— | —— | —— | —— —— | | —— |
| 38 Leadership | —— | —— | —— | —— | —— | —— —— | | —— |
| 39 Managerial capabilities | —— | —— | —— | —— | —— | —— —— | | —— |
| 40 Workforce | —— | —— | —— | —— | —— | —— —— | | —— |
| 41 Flexibility | —— | —— | —— | —— | —— | —— —— | | —— |
| 42 Adaptability | —— | —— | —— | —— | —— | —— —— | | —— |

SOURCE: Adapted from Kotler (1988), p. 53

picture of the organization's principal strengths and weaknesses emerges. Of course, not all of these factors are of equal importance either in an absolute sense or when it comes to succeeding with a specific business opportunity. Because of this, each factor should also be given a rating (high, medium or low) either for the business as a whole or for a particular marketing opportunity. Combining performance and importance levels in this way leads to four possibilities emerging; these are illustrated in Figure 2.7 in the form of a performance–importance matrix.

**FIGURE 2.7**
*Performance–importance matrix*

Performance

| | Low | High |
|---|---|---|
| **High** | Concentrate efforts ¹ | Maintain efforts ² |
| **Low** | Low priority ³ | Possible over-investment ⁴ |

Importance

Cell 1 consists of those factors which are important but in which the organization is currently performing badly. Because of this the organization needs to concentrate on strengthening these factors. Cell 2 is made up of factors in which the business is already strong but in which it needs to maintain its strengths. Cell 3 consists of unimportant factors. Improvements here, while often desirable, have low priority. Cell 4 is made up of unimportant factors in which (possibly as the result of over-investment in the past) the business is unnecessarily strong.

On the basis of this analysis it should be apparent that even when a business has a major strength in a particular area this strength does not invariably translate into a competitive advantage. There are several possible explanations for this, the two most prominent of which are that it may not be a competence that is of any real importance to customers, or that it is an area in which competitors are at least equally strong. It follows from this that in order to benefit from the strength it has to be relatively greater than that of the competitor.

Having identified the organization's weaknesses the strategist needs to return to Figure 2.7 and consider again the relative importance of these weaknesses. There is often little to be gained from overcoming all of the organization's weaknesses, since some are unimportant and the amount of effort needed to convert them to a strength would quite simply not be repaid. Equally, some strengths are of little real strategic value and to use them in anything other than a peripheral way is likely to prove of little real value. Recognizing this, the strategist should focus upon those areas of opportunity in which the firm currently has major strengths or where, because of the size of the opportunity and the potential returns, it is likely to prove cost-effective in acquiring or developing new areas of strength. In commenting on this Kotler (1987, p. 54) cites the example of Texas Instruments:

> [The] managers in Texas Instruments (TI) split between those who wanted TI to stick to industrial electronics where it had clear strength and those who urged the company to go into digital watches, personal computers, and other consumer products where it did not have the required marketing strengths. As it turned out, TI did poorly in these areas, but perhaps its mistake was not in going into these areas, but rather not acquiring the required marketing strengths to do the job right.

On occasions, organizations suffer not because of a lack of individual, departmental or divisional strengths, but quite simply because the various departments or divisions do not work together sufficiently well. As part of the SWOT process the strategist therefore should also pay attention to the quality of interdepartmental and divisional relationships with a view to identifying any dysfunctional areas. One of the ways in which this can be done is by conducting a periodic survey in which each department is asked to identify the strengths and weaknesses both of itself and of each other department. Action can then be taken to overcome areas of conflict, misunderstanding and inefficiency. An example of the results of an attempt to identify interdepartmental strengths and weaknesses appears in Figure 2.8. These are based on a consultancy project conducted by one of the authors at the end of 1989. The northern-based client company operated in the engineering field and was a subsidiary of a far larger multinational organization. The company had a strong financial orientation and was rapidly being overtaken by its competitors; for obvious reasons, the client's name has been omitted.

**FIGURE 2.8**
*Identifying interdepartmental strengths and weaknesses*

| | Strengths | Weaknesses |
|---|---|---|
| **Marketing** | Market development<br>Advertising<br>Dealer development<br>Competitor analysis | Long-term planning<br>Liaising with sales<br>Liaising with production<br>Profitable new product development<br>Identifying small but potentially profitable gaps in the market<br>Expectations regarding quality and manufacturing capability<br>Pricing<br>Relations with corporate management |
| **Sales** | None identified | Expectations regarding delivery times<br>Providing market feedback<br>Often sell what can only be made with difficulty<br>Little apparent awareness of costs<br>Ignores small orders<br>Patchy productivity<br>Levels of training<br>Sales staff turnover |
| **Production** | Quality | Slow to change<br>Unwilling to cooperate with marketing and sales<br>Often late in delivering<br>Tend to want to make what they are good at<br>A lack of flexibility caused by a strong trade-union presence<br>Rising costs<br>Lack of strong management<br>Ageing plant<br>Inadequate training in CAD/CAM |
| **Personnel** | Junior management and shop-floor training | Representation at board level<br>Long-term senior management development<br>Poor negotiating skills<br>Willingness to give in to trade-union pressure<br>Lack of real personnel management skills |
| **Finance** | Tight cost control<br>Credit control<br>Relationship with corporate management<br>Access to significant financial resources | Over-emphasis on short-term returns<br>Lack of vision<br>Unwilling to cooperate with marketing and sales<br>Unwilling to provide finance for major programmes of new product development<br>Unrealistic reporting demands |

## 2.5 THE CHARACTERISTICS OF EFFECTIVE AUDITS

At an earlier stage in this chapter (see p. 26) we made reference to Kotler's definition of the marketing audit. Referring for a moment to this definition, it can be seen that he highlights four dimensions, suggesting that for an audit to be worthwhile it should be *comprehensive, systematic, independent* and *periodic*. The significance of these points is as follows:

1 *Comprehensive.* For the auditing process to be worthwhile it is essential that it covers *all* of the major elements of the organization's marketing activity, including those that seemingly are doing well, rather than just a few apparent trouble spots. In this way a distinction can be drawn between the *marketing audit* and a *functional audit* which would focus far more specifically upon a particular element of marketing activity such as sales or pricing. As an example of this, a functional audit might well suggest that a high sales-force turnover and low morale is due to a combination of inadequate sales training and a poor compensation package. A more fundamental reason, however, might be that the company has a poor or inadequate product range and an inappropriate pricing and advertising strategy. It is the comprehensiveness of the marketing audit which is designed to reveal these sorts of factors and to highlight the *fundamental* causes of the organization's problems.

2 *Systematic.* In carrying out the audit it is essential that a sequential diagnostic process is adopted covering the three areas to which reference was made earlier: the external environment, internal marketing systems, and specific marketing activities. This process of diagnosis is then followed by the development *and implementation* of both short-term and long-term plans designed to correct the weaknesses identified and, in this way, improve upon levels of marketing effectiveness.

3 *Independent.* As with a financial audit, there are several ways in which the marketing audit can be conducted. These include:

   (a) a self-audit in which managers use a checklist to assess their own results and methods of operation;
   (b) an audit by a manager of the same status but drawn from a different department or division within the organization;
   (c) an audit by a more senior manager within the same department or division;
   (d) the use of a company auditing office;
   (e) a company task force audit group;
   (f) an audit conducted by an outside specialist.

Of these it is generally recognized that an audit conducted by an outside specialist is likely to prove the most objective and to exhibit the independence which any internal process will almost inevitably lack. Adopting this approach should also ensure that the audit receives the undivided time and attention that is needed. In practice, however, many large companies make use of their own audit teams (something which 3M, for example, has pioneered).

This question of *who* should conduct the audit has been the subject of a considerable amount of research and discussion in recent years with, as indicated above, the argument revolving around the issue of objectivity (in other words, how objective can a line manager be in conducting an evaluation of activities for which he has direct responsibility?) It is largely because of this that it has been suggested that outside consultants should be used to ensure impartiality. This is likely to prove expensive if done annually, and the answer is increasingly being seen to lie in a compromise whereby an outside consultant is used every third or fourth year, with line managers from different departments or divisions being used in the intervening periods. Alternatively an organization might opt for what is in essence a composite approach, with an external auditor being used initially to validate line managers' self-audits, and subsequently to integrate them to produce an audit result for the marketing function as a whole.

To a large extent, however, it can be argued that the supposed difficulties of achieving impartiality are overstated since a sufficiently well-structured and institutionalized auditing process can overcome many of these difficulties. There is a need, therefore, for managers to be trained in how best to use auditing procedures and, very importantly, for the audit process to be endorsed by senior management; without top management commitment to the audit process and, in turn, to the need to act on the results that emerge, the entire exercise is likely to prove valueless.

4 *Periodic*. If the company is to benefit fully from the auditing process it is essential that it is carried out on a regular basis. All too often in the past companies have been spurred into conducting an audit largely as the result of poor performance. Ironically, this poor performance can often be traced to a myopia on the part of management, stemming from a failure to review activities on a sufficiently regular basis, something which has been pointed to by Shuchman (1950) who has commented that: 'No marketing operation is ever so good that it cannot be improved. Even the best *must* be better, for few if any marketing operations can remain successful over the years by maintaining the status quo.'

**Why Bother With a Marketing Audit?**

Although we have so far argued the case for marketing auditing to be carried out on a regular basis, many organizations quite simply do not bother to do this until things go wrong. Most typically this would be manifested in terms of declining sales, a loss of market share, under-utilized production capacity, a demoralized sales force, reduced margins, and so on. Faced with these sorts of problems the temptation for management is to firefight and hence fall into the trap of crisis management. In many cases this is characterized by the rapid launching and dropping of products, price cutting, and attempts at drastic cost reduction. While this sort of response will often have an immediate and apparent pay-off, it is unlikely that it will solve any underlying and fundamental problems. The audit is designed to avoid the need for crisis management both by identifying and defining these fundamental problems *before they have any opportunity to affect the organization*. In this way carrying out a regular and thorough marketing audit in a structured manner will go a long way towards giving a company a knowledge of the business, trends in the market, and where value is added by competitors as a basis for setting objectives and strategies. These points have been highlighted in a summary of the 10 most common findings of marketing audits:

1 a lack of knowledge of customers' behaviour and attitudes;
2 a failure to segment markets effectively;
3 the absence of marketing planning procedures;
4 reductions in price rather than increases in volume;
5 the absence of market-based procedures for evaluating products;
6 misunderstanding company marketing strengths;
7 short-term views of the role of promotion;
8 a perception that marketing is limited just to advertising and sales activity;
9 inappropriate organizational structures;
10 insufficient investment in the future, particularly in the area of human resources.

**The Auditing Procedure**

The auditing process should begin with agreement being reached between the organization's marketing director and the marketing auditor – someone from inside or outside the organization – regarding the specific objectives, the breadth and depth of coverage, the sources of data, the report format and the time period for the audit. Included within this should be a plan of who is to be interviewed and the questions that are to be asked.

With regard to the question of *who* is to be questioned, it needs to be emphasized that the audit should never be restricted to the company's executives; it should also include customers, the dealer network, and other outside groups. In this way, a better and more complete picture of the company's position and its effectiveness can be developed. In the case of customers and dealers, for example, the auditor should aim to develop satisfaction ratings which are capable of highlighting areas in need of attention.

Once the information has been collected, the findings and recommendations need to be presented with emphasis being given to the type of action needed to overcome any problems, the timescale over which remedial action is to be taken, and the names of those who are to be responsible for this.

**Components of the Audit**

Within the general framework of the external and internal audits, Kotler et al. (1989) suggest there are six specific dimensions that are of direct interest to the auditor. These are:

1 *The marketing environment audit*, which involves an analysis of the major macroeconomic forces and trends within the organization's task environment. This includes markets, customers, competitors, distributors, dealers, and suppliers.
2 *The marketing strategy audit*, which focuses upon a review of the organization's marketing objectives and strategy, with a view to determining how well suited they are to the current and forecasted market environment.
3 *The marketing organization audit*. This aspect of the audit follows on from 2 and is concerned specifically with an evaluation of the structural capability of the organization and its suitability for implementing the strategy needed for the developing environment.
4 *The marketing systems audit*, which covers the quality of the organization's systems for analysis, planning and control.
5 *The marketing productivity audit*, which examines the profitability of different aspects of the marketing programme and the cost effectiveness of various levels of marketing expenditure.
6 *The marketing functions audit* involving a detailed evaluation of each of the elements of the marketing mix.

The audit questions associated with each of these areas appear in Figure 2.9. In answering each of the questions it is essential that the strategist pays particular attention to the implications for the organization and its likely strategic development.

**How are the Audit Results Used?**

Having conducted the audit the question that then arises is how best to use the results. In some companies a considerable amount of time, effort and expense is given over to the auditing process, but the corrective action that is then needed simply falls by the wayside. To ensure that the results are incorporated most effectively within the strategic planning process which forms the focus of the remainder of this book, the major findings of the audit need to be incorporated within an appropriate framework. This can be done in one of several ways, although undoubtedly the most useful is the SWOT framework discussed earlier. This should focus on the *key* internal strengths and weaknesses in relation to the *principal* external opportunities and threats, and include a summary of the reasons for good or bad performance. It is then against the background of this document that the strategist should begin planning at both the functional and the corporate levels. It is this process which provides the basis for much of the rest of this book.

**FIGURE 2.9**
*The marketing*
*audit*

**The marketing environment audit**
*The macro environment*

Political/legal/fiscal
1 What legal developments are likely, nationally and internationally, that may affect marketing strategy and tactics?
2 Which governmental bodies (local, national and international) should be monitored?
3 What developments are likely to take place in areas such as product safety, product liability, labelling, packaging, advertising and pricing control, pollution control and employment legislation that might affect marketing planning?
4 What changes are likely in the levels of direct and indirect taxation?
5 Are levels of political risk likely to increase or decrease?
6 How are relations with other countries, regimes and trading blocs likely to develop, and what are their probable implications for marketing?
7 How volatile are trade-union practices likely to be in the short, medium and long term?
8 Are policies regarding nationalization or privatization likely to change?

Economic/demographic
1 What is likely to happen in the short, medium and long term to levels of inflation, unemployment, the availability of credit and savings?
2 What economic growth rates and income levels are forecast both for the organization's existing and potential markets?
3 What changes to the size, structure and regional distribution of population are likely to occur?

Social/cultural
1 What changes to consumer lifestyles and values are taking place?
2 What attitudinal changes towards business and the products/services produced by the organization are occurring?
3 What attitudinal changes are taking place towards such areas as government, the media, and pollution?

Technological
1 What changes are taking place in the areas of product and process technology?
2 What generic substitutes might replace the organization's products?
3 How well placed is the organization to cope with and/or capitalize upon such changes?

Ecological
1 What is likely to happen to the cost and availability of the natural resources and energy required by the organization?
2 What contingency plans exist to cope with shortages or sudden price rises?
3 Have any concerns been expressed about the organization's role in conservation and pollution?

*The task environment*

Markets
1 What is happening to the size, growth rate and geographical distribution of the organization's markets?
2 Which major market segments exist? How are they likely to grow and which offer the greatest opportunities?
3 Are new market segments emerging?
4 Are new or different market priorities emerging?
5 What scope exists for further market development?
6 What changes in usage patterns can be identified or are likely?
7 Are terms and conditions of sale changing?

Competitors
1 What changes are likely to take place in the structure, bases, and intensity of competition?
2 Who are the major competitors currently and in what ways might they change? Are there any likely new entrants to the market? If so, what capabilities and objectives will they have and what are the probable implications for competition?
3 What are the major strengths and weaknesses of each competitor?
4 What are the objectives, strategies and levels of profitability of each competitor?
5 What trends can be identified in the patterns of future competition and substitutes for the organization's product/service?
6 What patterns of product and market development can be identified among competitors?
7 Are any major changes likely to take place in patterns of market share? Does any competitor appear likely to pursue an aggressive share gaining strategy? If so, how well equipped to do this would they be, what are the implications for the bases of competition, and what is the probability of success?
8 What is the extent of the diversification among each competitor? What international links does each have?

**FIGURE 2.9 (contd.)**

9 What are the patterns of ownership among competitors and what level of resources can each call upon?
10 What barriers to entry and exit exist currently? In what ways might these change?

Distributors and dealers
1 What changes are taking place in the structure of the distribution network?
2 What are the efficiency levels and growth potentials of each channel?
3 Which channels are currently under-exploited?
4 What is the cost and availability outlook for warehousing and transportation facilities?

Suppliers
1 What changes are taking place in the supplier network and what affect will this have upon balances of power?
2 What new sources of supply are emerging?
3 What are the objectives and strategies of the major suppliers?
4 What changes are taking place in suppliers' patterns of selling?

Advertising and PR agencies
1 How effective are the efforts of the organization's advertising and public relations agencies?
2 What trends in agency practice are emerging?

---

*The marketing strategy audit*

The business mission
1 How clearly stated and realistic is the mission statement?
2 To what extent is it consistent and compatible with the corporate and marketing objectives?

Corporate and marketing objectives
1 Do the corporate and marketing objectives provide clear guidelines for marketing planning and control?
2 Are these objectives consistent with the organization's position, capabilities and opportunities?
3 Are the objectives for each business unit clearly stated, realistic and consistent with the overall marketing objectives?

Marketing strategy
1 How clearly stated and appropriate is the marketing strategy?
2 Is the strategy convincing? Has it been properly communicated?
3 Does the strategy take full account of the state of the economy, the stage reached on the product life cycle, and competitors' strategies?
4 Is the basis for market segmentation appropriate?
5 To what extent is there scope for developing and improving upon methods of segmentation?
6 How accurate are the profiles of each segment?
7 How well developed is the positioning strategy for each segment? Does scope exist for repositioning in order to strengthen the competitive stance?
8 Are the available resources sufficient and suitably allocated to the various elements of the marketing mix?
9 Is there scope for reallocating resources to achieve a greater degree of cost-effectiveness?
10 Are there sufficient controls built in to the strategy?

**FIGURE 2.9 (contd.)**

### The marketing organization audit

1 Is the marketing function led by a person with sufficient authority and responsibility over those areas of the organization's activities that affect customer satisfaction?
2 Are the marketing activities optimally structured along functional, product, end-user and geographical lines?
3 What need and scope exists for changing current patterns of authority and responsibility?

Functional efficiency
1 Are the lines of communication and the working relationships between marketing and other areas of the business effective?
2 What scope exists for improving and developing these relationships?
3 What needs exist for training, motivation, supervision, evaluation, and control?

### The marketing systems audit

Information systems
1 Is the MIS providing sufficiently accurate and timely information about market developments?
2 Is this information presented in the most appropriate format?
3 Is sufficient market research of the right sort being conducted and are the results being fully and properly utilized?
4 What scope exists for improving upon methods of market and sales forecasting?
5 Is the information generated by the MIS communicated to the appropriate network of staff?

Planning systems
1 How efficient and well conceived are the planning systems?
2 What scope and plans exist for its further development?

Control systems
1 Do the control procedures provide the strategist with a sufficiently clear and accurate picture of absolute and relative performance?
2 Is the performance of individual products, markets, and distribution channels monitored sufficiently regularly?
3 How frequently are marketing costs examined and validated?
4 Is behaviour modified in the light of feedback from the control systems?

New product systems
1 How well organized is the procedure for collecting, generating and evaluating new product ideas?
2 Is sufficient research and analysis conducted before proceeding with new product ideas?
3 Are the levels of product and market testing adequate?
4 Is the rate of new product development and product modification sufficient to achieve marketing objectives?
5 Is the new product success rate satisfactory? Is it better or worse than those of the major competitors?

### The marketing productivity audit

Profitability analyses
1 What is the profitability of each of the organization's products, markets, territories and distribution channels?
2 Should the company enter or withdraw from any market segment?
3 Is there a need for expansion or contraction within any market?
4 How do the organization's levels of profitability compare with those of its principal competitors?

Cost-effectiveness analysis
1 Are there any areas of marketing which appear to be incurring unrealistic costs?
2 What scope exists for cost reduction?
3 Are costs monitored sufficiently, regularly and rigorously?
4 What scope exists for modifying approaches to budgeting and control to ensure better resource allocation?
5 Does any one person have direct responsibility for measuring cost effectiveness?

**FIGURE 2.9 (contd.)**

*The marketing functions audit*

Products
1 What are the product line objectives?
2 How appropriate are these objectives?
3 How regularly are the objectives reassessed?
4 Is the current mix of products achieving the objectives?
5 Which products should be deleted?
6 What product modifications should be made?
7 What products should be added to the line?
8 How well managed is the product line?
9 What are the product lines' particular strengths and weaknesses?
10 How does the product line compare with those of the organization's competitors?
11 To what extent is the product line differentiated from those of the competitors?

Price
1 What pricing objectives, strategies and procedures exist?
2 How appropriate are the pricing objectives?
3 How consistent is pricing throughout the product range?
4 Is full advantage taken of the profit opportunities when pricing product options?
5 Is the pricing stance proactive or reactive?
6 Is sufficient attention paid to competitive criteria when setting prices?
7 What knowledge exists of competitors' objectives, costs and price levels?
8 Are competitors' prices regularly monitored and reviewed?
9 Are the organization's prices in line with customers' and distributors' perceptions of product value?
10 Is sufficient use made of price promotion?
11 At what level within the organization are pricing decisions made?
12 Are pricing decisions fully integrated with other marketing decisions?
13 How responsive to sudden market changes are prices?

Distribution
1 What distribution objectives and strategies are pursued?
2 Are the levels of market coverage appropriate?
3 What need and scope exists for improvements in service levels?
4 How effectively are distributors and dealers operating?
5 What knowledge exists of competitors' distribution structures and costs?
6 Is there scope or need for changes to be made to the distribution channels being used currently?
7 Where does the balance of power lie within the channel? In what ways is this changing and what are the implications?
8 How well motivated is the distribution channel?
9 How important to the channel are the organization's products?
10 Do distributors have adequate product knowledge? What training needs exist?
11 What scope exists for greater short- and long-term motivation of dealers?
12 What levels of dealer/distributor loyalty exist? Are these adequate? What scope exists for strengthening this loyalty?

Sales force
1 What are the sales force's short- and long-term objectives?
2 Is the sales force large enough to achieve the objectives it is set?
3 Is the organization and structure of the sales force suited to the demands of the market?
4 Does the sales force give emphasis to volume or to profitability?
5 Is the sales force made fully aware of the profit associated with different parts of the product line?
6 Is the sales force kept fully informed of marketing objectives, marketing programmes, and market developments?
7 Is there sufficient sales force training?
8 Is the sales force properly motivated? Is full use made of incentives?
9 Are the sales targets realistic?
10 Is the sales and profit performance measured and the results fed back to sales staff?
11 Is the turnover of sales staff too high? If so, what might be done to reduce it?
12 How does the sales force compare with that of competitors?
13 How is the sales force perceived by customers?
14 Is full use made of the sales force as a means of monitoring market developments?

Advertising and promotion
1 What are the promotional objectives? Are they appropriate given the overall marketing objectives?
2 How is the budget set? Is sufficient attention paid to the expenditure levels and patterns of competitors?
3 What controls over advertising expenditure exist?
4 How effective is the creative appeal?
5 What advertising research is conducted?

**FIGURE 2.9 (contd.)**

> 6  How well chosen are the media?
> 7  How regularly is the performance of the advertising agency reviewed?
> 8  How important is the account to the agency?
> 9  Are sales promotions used regularly? Are they effective?
> 10 How effective is the publicity programme?
> 11 Is effective use made of sponsorship?
> 12 Who is responsible for publicity?
> 13 What measures of effectiveness are used for advertising, sales promotion and public relations?
> 14 How do the advertising and promotional campaigns compare with those of the competitors?

SOURCE: Adapted from Kotler *et al*. (1977)

## 2.6 SUMMARY

Within this chapter we have focused upon the role and structure of marketing auditing and SWOT analysis. In doing this we have highlighted the way in which the marketing audit represents an important first step in the marketing planning process and how, as a result, the value of much of what follows within this process is determined by the thoroughness of the audit procedure. It is therefore essential that the audit exhibits a number of characteristics, the four most significant of which are that it is:

1 comprehensive in its coverage of the elements of the organization's marketing activity;
2 systematic;
3 independent;
4 conducted on a regular basis.

The purpose of the audit is to provide the strategist with a clear understanding both of environmental opportunities and threats, and of the organization's marketing capability. In doing this the strategist begins by focusing upon the principal macroenvironmental forces (pollitical/legal, economic/demographic, social/cultural and technological) that affect the business. He then moves on to consider the microenvironmental actors (customers, competitors, distributors and suppliers) who influence the organization's ability to operate effectively in the market-place. The internal audit builds upon this by providing an understanding of the extent to which the organization, its structure and resources relate to the environment and have the capability of operating effectively within the constraints that the environment imposes.

In addition to conducting the marketing audit the strategist needs also to carry out regular reviews of the organization's marketing effectiveness. This can be done most readily by means of a checklist which embraces five principal areas:

1 the nature of the customer philosophy;
2 the marketing organization;
3 marketing information;
4 the strategic perspective;
5 operational efficiency.

Against the background of the picture that emerges from the audit and the review of marketing effectiveness, the strategist should have a clear understanding both of the environment (opportunities and threats) and of the organization's marketing capability (strengths and weaknesses). It is this which then provides the basis for subsequent marketing planning.

Marketing audits are discussed further in Chapter 18, and marketing effectiveness is considered in some detail in Chapter 14.

# 3 | Segmental, productivity and ratio analysis

## 3.1 LEARNING OBJECTIVES

When you have read this chapter you should be able to:

(a) understand how cost analysis can be applied to marketing segments;
(b) appreciate the role of marketing experimentation in improving the allocation of marketing effort;
(c) recognize the value of segmental productivity analysis;
(d) perceive critically how ratio analysis can be used in order to appreciate the current position.

## 3.2 INTRODUCTION

It is helpful in relation to the question 'How have resources been allocated within this organization?' to think of the organization as a bundle of projects or activities. This is relevant whether the organization is large or small, commercial or non-commercial, engaged in manufacturing or service rendering. Typical projects might be defined as:

● reformulation and relaunch of Product X;
● continued market success with Product Y;
● the successful development and launch of Product Z.

One might go further and define projects or activities in terms of *missions*: a mission represents the provision of a product or range of products at a particular level of service to a particular customer or customer group in a particular area. Figure 3.1 illustrates this.

An organization's mix of projects – or missions – will be constantly changing, and each has resource implications. For example, the scarcity of resources

**FIGURE 3.1**
*Multi-dimensional mission characteristics*

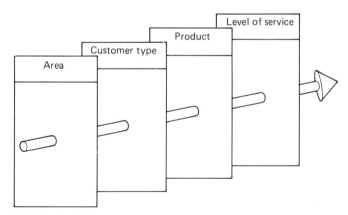

SOURCE: Barrett (1980), p. 143

inevitably means that choices must be made in rationing available resources (whether in the form of funds, management time, etc.) among competing projects. It may be that new projects can only be adopted if old ones are deleted, thereby freeing resources. But how might a manager know which projects are worth retaining, which should be added to the portfolio, and which should be deleted? One starting point is to establish the cost of each of the organization's existing projects.

We can think of cost as being equivalent in broad terms to *effort*, so what we are initially seeking to establish is how the available effort has been applied to the various activities in which the organization is engaged. Before we can really get to grips with this, however, we need to clarify our understanding of some important categories of cost.

## 3.3 THE CLARIFICATION OF COST CATEGORIES

Many of the costs of marketing are not satisfactorily identified since marketing *functions* are not always carried out by the marketing *department*. (It could be argued that any members of an organization who deal with customers, for example, are carrying out a marketing function even though they may not be recognized in any formal sense as members of the marketing staff.) This is one definitional problem, but not the only one.

In their training managers are almost indoctrinated to think, for example, of variable costs as being *manufacturing* costs that fluctuate with the level of *production* output, or to define direct costs as those that can be readily traced to units of *production* output, and so on. It is imperative that a broader view be taken in order that the analysis of marketing costs might be tackled.

In this general sense we can define costs in the following ways:

- A *fixed cost* is one that does not vary in relation to changes in the level of activity (however defined) within a given period of time.
- A *variable cost* is one that varies in proportion to changes in the level of activity (however defined).

This distinction facilitates flexible budgeting, permits cost-volume-profit analysis, and gives a basis for flexible pricing. However, the further distinction between *avoidable* and *unavoidable* costs needs to be considered since it cannot safely be assumed that a fixed cost is inevitably unavoidable. Much will depend on whether a particular fixed cost is 'committed', 'managed', or 'discretionary': the latter could almost certainly be avoided in the short term if a better use for the resources in question was available, although a committed fixed cost would not be easily avoided other than in the long run.

The base (i.e. level of activity) to be used in determining cost behaviour patterns must be carefully selected and have a clear causal relationship with the level of cost in question. In this regard it must not be assumed that sales volume *causes* order-getting costs. Let us consider some examples.

1 Advertising and sales promotion costs are not caused by sales volume since sales volume is the dependent (rather than the independent) variable. The advertising budget is likely to be a fixed sum per period of time, representing a programmed, managed or discretionary cost.
2 Personal selling costs are rather more complicated: commissions will tend to vary with sales volume (or value); salaries will be a fixed cost of a managed type that is independent of sales volume within any given financial period; and expenses will be a mixture of fixed and variable costs that are also independent of sales volume. Suitable bases for determining cost behaviour patterns may be number of calls made, number of customers, distance travelled, etc.

3  A *direct cost* is one that can be specifically traced to a cost object. In a marketing context this object may be any one of several alternatives *other than the product*. Thus, in an analysis of sales territories, the salaries, commissions and expenses of sales personnel working exclusively in one territory constitute direct costs of that territory.

4  An *indirect cost* is one that cannot be traced to a specific cost object on anything other than an arbitrary basis.

   The more specific a cost object is (e.g. a customer, or a product line), the greater will be the proportion of costs that are indirect, whereas the more broadly based a cost object (e.g. a sales territory), the greater will be the proportion of costs that can be traced directly to it. It should be borne in mind, however, that direct costs can be fixed or variable in nature (and similarly with indirect costs), so directness should not be linked in any general way with variable costs alone − whether in a marketing or any other setting.

5  A *controllable cost* is one that can be influenced by an individual whose performance is being measured by reference to such costs. Thus a sales manager will be held accountable for his sales team's expenses on the grounds that he can influence − hence control − their rate of incurrence. Controllable costs, then, usually originate in the sphere of organizational responsibility under consideration.

6  An *uncontrollable cost* is one that cannot be influenced by a particular individual (e.g. a manager cannot specify his own salary, so this is an uncontrollable cost from the viewpoint of his level of authority). It would, in general terms, be unreasonable to judge an individual's performance by reference to significant amounts of uncontrollable costs.

   Controllable costs will often, but not always, be variable in nature. However, it is unusual for any fixed costs to be controllable in the short run unless they are clearly discretionary or programmed (which will frequently include some order-getting costs, such as advertising appropriations that have not yet been irrevocably committed).

   It is not usually considered reasonable to hold an individual accountable for apportioned costs − such as may relate to head office services to divisions. Nevertheless, if one is interested in the performance of the division (rather than its manager) it may be appropriate to make cautious allocations of uncontrollable costs. (This is the basis of productivity analysis which will be discussed in the section starting on page 50).

7  A *standard cost* is one that represents the efficient performance of a repetitive task. This will include the direct labour and material inputs in a manufacturing situation, but it is by no means limited to the production arena. Distribution activities as well as certain clerical tasks are amenable to cost standards, and a range of marketing cost standards can also be developed. (This topic will be covered later − see the section starting on page 585).

Another definitional problem concerns the traditional focus that accountants have adopted which puts product costing at the centre of their costing systems. This traditional preoccupation with the manufacturing costs of products and factory processes emphasizes the attributes of whatever is currently being made. Such an orientation fails to deal with patterns of consumer preferences and competitive positioning by market segment. The attributes of market segments − from which profit is derived − are fundamentally different from those attributes that characterize production processes. Any analysis based on product costing will generate insights that are limited by their origins, thereby failing to support marketing orientation.

Whatever cost object (or activity) is selected as the focus of attention, some costs will be *direct* (in the sense of being traceable to the activity − such as direct labour, and direct material inputs into a unit of manufactured output, or a salesperson's salary and expenses in relation to the sales territory), while others will be *indirect*. By definition, indirect costs cannot be traced directly to cost objects, so any procedure whereby these costs are assigned to cost objects will mean that the resulting full (or 'absorbed') cost is inaccurate to an unknown extent. The assigning of a 'fair share' of indirect costs, along with direct costs, to cost units is at the heart of *absorption costing*.

A particular cost item can only be termed direct or indirect once the cost object has been specified. Thus a salesperson's salary will be indirect in relation to the individual product lines sold (assuming the salesperson carries a range of products), but it will be a direct cost of the territory in which that individual is operating. In the same way the costs of distributing various products to wholesalers may be indirect with regard to the goods themselves but direct if one is interested in costing the channel of distribution of which the wholesalers are part.

The same basic problems arise in attempting to determine the full cost of a cost object in every type of organization, whether a service company, a retailing enterprise, a factory or a non-commercial entity. For example, a garage (as one type of service organization) will treat the servicing of each customer's car as a separate job (or cost object) to which will be assigned the direct cost of the mechanic's time, materials, and parts, plus an allowance (usually applied as an hourly rate and associated with the utilization of mechanics' time) for the use of indirect factors (which will include power, equipment, rent, rates, insurance, salaries of reception, supervisory and stores staff, etc.). A similar approach is applied by firms of solicitors or accountants, by consulting engineers, architects and management consultants. Non-commercial organizations typically provide services (such as health care, defence, education and spiritual guidance) and use resources in carrying out their various activities in much the same way as do commercial undertakings. The logic of absorption costing is equally applicable to non-commercial as to commercial enterprises.

## 3.4 MARKETING COST ANALYSIS: AIMS AND METHODS

Establishing a base line for marketing planning can be seen to be concerned with the allocation of total marketing effort to segments, along with the profitability of these allocations. It is generally found, however, that companies do not know the profitability of segments in marketing terms. Useful computations of marketing costs and profit contributions in the multiproduct company require the adoption of analytical techniques that are not difficult in principle but which are not widely adopted in practice on account of, *inter alia*, the preoccupation with factory cost accounting that exists.

The fact that most companies do not know what proportion of their total marketing outlay is spent on each product, area, or customer group may be due to the absence of a sufficiently refined system of cost analysis, or it may be due to vagueness over the nature of certain costs. For instance, is the cost of packaging a promotional, a production, or a distribution expense? Some important marketing costs are hidden in manufacturing costs or in general and administrative costs, including finished goods inventory costs in the former and order-processing costs in the latter.

Since few companies are aware of costs and profits by segment in relation to sales levels, and since even fewer are able to predict changes in sales volume and profit contribution as a result of changes in marketing effort, the following errors arise:

1   marketing budgets for individual products are too large, with the result that diminishing returns become evident and benefits would accrue from a reduction in expenditure;

2 marketing budgets for individual products are too small and increasing returns would result from an increase in expenditure;
3 the marketing mix is inefficient, with an incorrect balance and incorrect amounts being spent on the constituent elements – such as too much on advertising and insufficient on direct selling activities;
4 marketing efforts are misallocated among products and changes in these cost allocations (even with a constant level of overall expenditure) could bring improvements.

Similar arguments apply in relation to sales territories or customer groups as well as to products. The need exists, therefore, for planning and control techniques to indicate the level of performance required and achieved as well as the outcome of shifting marketing efforts from one segment to another. As is to be expected, there exists great diversity in the methods by which managers attempt to obtain costs (and profits) for segments of their business, but much of the cost data are inaccurate for such reasons as those listed below.

- Marketing costs may be allocated to individual products, sales areas, customer groups, etc., on the basis of sales value or sales volume, but this involves circular reasoning. Costs should be allocated in relation to causal factors and *it is marketing expenditures that cause sales to be made* rather than the other way round: managerial decisions determine marketing costs. Furthermore, despite the fact that success is so often measured in terms of sales value achievements by product line, this basis fails to evaluate the efficiency of the effort needed to produce the realized sales value (or turnover). Even a seemingly high level of turnover for a specific product may really be a case of misallocated sales effort. (An example should make this clear: if a salesman concentrates on selling Product A which contributes £50 per hour of effort instead of selling Product B which would contribute £120 per hour of effort, then it 'costs' the company £70 per hour he spends on selling Product A. This is the *opportunity cost* of doing one thing rather than another and is a measure of the sacrifice involved in selecting only one of several alternative courses of action.)
- General indirect and administrative costs are arbitrarily (and erroneously) allocated to segments on the basis of sales volume.
- Many marketing costs are not allocated at all as marketing costs as they are not identified as such but are classified as manufacturing, general, or administrative costs instead.

Marketing cost analysis has been developed to help overcome these problems and aims to:

1 Analyse the costs incurred in marketing products (embracing order-getting and order-filling aspects) so that when they are combined with production cost data overall profit can be determined.
2 Analyse the costs of marketing individual products to determine profit by product line.
3 Analyse the costs involved in serving different classes of customers, different areas and other segments to determine their relative profit performance.
4 Compute such figures as cost per sales call, cost per order, cost to put a new customer on the books, cost to hold £1's worth of inventory for a year, etc.
5 Evaluate managers according to their actual controllable cost responsibilities.
6 Evaluate alternative strategies or plans with full costs.

These analyses and evaluations provide senior management with the necessary information to enable them to decide which classes of customer to cultivate, which products to delete, which products to encourage, and so forth. Such analyses also provide a basis from which estimates can be made of the likely increases in product profitability that a specified increase in marketing effort should create. In the normal course of events it is far more difficult to predict the outcome of decisions that involve changes in marketing outlays in comparison with changes in production expenditure. It is easier, for instance, to estimate the effect of a new machine in the factory than it is to predict the impact of higher advertising outlays. Similarly, the effect on productive output of dropping a production worker is easier to estimate than is the effect on the level of sales caused by a reduction in the sales force.

The methodology of marketing cost analysis is similar to the methodology of product costing. Two stages are involved:

1 Marketing costs are initially reclassified from their *natural* expense headings (e.g. salaries) into *functional* cost groups (e.g. sales expenses) in such a way that each cost group brings together all the costs associated with a particular element of the marketing mix.
2 These functional cost groups are then apportioned to control units (i.e. products, customer groups, channels of distribution, etc.) on the basis of measurable criteria that bear a causal relationship to the total amounts of the functional cost groups.

These two stages are illustrated in Figure 3.2.

**FIGURE 3.2**
*Determining segmental costs*

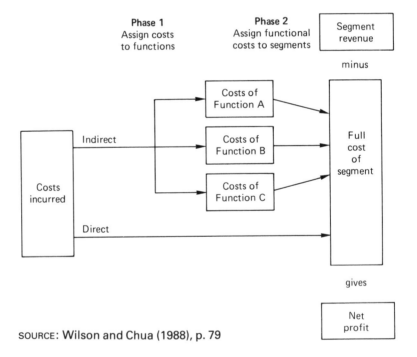

SOURCE: Wilson and Chua (1988), p. 79

Once the natural indirect expenses have been reclassified on a functional basis they are then charged to the segment in line with the usual benefit criterion (i.e. the segment is only allocated with that portion of each functional cost group that can be related to it on a cause and effect basis). The logical basis of allocation may be apparent from an analysis of the underlying data, but it is important to observe that some costs vary with the characteristics of one type of segment only. Thus inventory costs depend on the characteristics of the products rather than on those of the customers, whereas the cost of credit depends on the financial integrity and number of customers rather than on regional factors. Accordingly, all functional costs should not be allocated to products, customers and territorial segments, but only to whichever segment or segments exhibit a cause and effect relationship.

Before functional costs can be allocated to segments, certain data must be known as follows:

1 *Allocations to products*
  (a) Average inventory value of finished stock by product line.
  (b) Amount of storage space occupied by the inventory of each finished product.
  (c) The number of times each product is invoiced.
  (d) The number of 'handling units' of each product that is sold.
  (e) The weight and number of shipping units of each product sold.
  (f) The proportion of promotional effort spent on each product.
  (g) The media costs for each product.
2 *Allocations to customers*
  (a) The number of invoice lines on all orders for the period.
  (b) The weight and numbers of shipping units bought by each customer.
  (c) The number of sales calls made to each customer.
  (d) The media costs for each customer group.
  (e) The number of orders placed by each customer.
  (f) The average balance outstanding on each customer's account.
  (g) The number of invoices posted to accounts receivable (i.e. debtors ledger).
3 *Allocations to territories*
  The above information is sufficient to permit any territorial analysis.

Figure 3.3 indicates how functional marketing costs are allocated to segments once the basic data referred to above are available.

It must be remembered when using marketing cost analysis that any cost allocation involves a certain degree of arbitrariness which means that an element of error is inevitably contained within the allocation. Furthermore, it remains necessary to supplement the analysis of marketing costs with other relevant information and with managerial judgement.

Marketing cost analysis is the joint responsibility of the controller and the marketing manager, with the controller supplying most of the information and the marketing manager supplying most of the judgement. Nevertheless, the marketing manager must be fully aware of the methodology and limitations of marketing cost analysis. The high cost of establishing and maintaining a marketing costing system is justified by the benefits derived from increasing the efficiency of marketing effort. The risks involved in adopting marketing cost analysis before the benefits have been demonstrated can be reduced by initially confining the analysis to a sample of products, customers, or territories and by making periodic rather than continuous analyses.

Since a fundamental objective of marketing cost analysis lies in increasing the productivity of expenditures and not necessarily in their reduction the manager who wishes to introduce marketing cost analysis must emphasize the desire to make better use of existing funds rather than reducing future budgets. The integration of marketing costing with marketing research can assist in this matter. Confining any costing system to data provided from accounting records forces that system to be historical, but marketing research can provide estimates of future outcomes resulting from variations in marketing effort (with or without experimentation and the building of complex models) that enable the efficiency of alternate expenditure patterns to be pre-determined and evaluated in accordance with corporate aims.

While costs can be broken down in a microscopic manner, there are dangers and limitations which should not be overlooked as they can hinder the control of marketing costs. If the outcome of functionalizing all marketing costs is to compute a unit cost for every activity then this can be misleading. At the least a distinction should be made between fixed and variable costs, and the focus should be on the *purpose* for which a particular cost is to be derived and not simply on the *means* by which a figure is computed. Thus costs and units can be looked at separately, thereby avoiding myopic confusion.

An important distinction to make in marketing costs analysis – beyond the basic fixed-variable split – is that between *separable* fixed costs and *non-separable* fixed costs. A sales manager's salary is a fixed cost in conventional cost analysis but in so far as a sales manager's time can be linked to different products, sales territories, customers, etc., his or her salary (or at least portions of that salary) can be treated as being a separable fixed cost attributable to the segments in question in accordance with time devoted to each. In contrast,

**FIGURE 3.3**
*Summary chart*

| | Bases of allocation | | |
|---|---|---|---|
| | *To product groups* | *To customer groups* | *To sales territories* |
| **Direct selling expenses**<br>Personal calls by salesperson on existing accounts and prospective accounts. Sales force salaries, commissions, travelling, etc. | Selling time devoted to each product as shown by special sales call reports or other special studies | Number of calls times average call time as shown by special sales call reorts or other special studies | Direct |
| **Indirect selling expenses**<br>Field supervision. Sales administration – clerical and office costs. Sales training. Sales management expenses. Marketing research costs. Sales statistics and accounting. Communications, etc. | In proportion to direct selling time | In proportion to direct selling time | Equal charge for each salesperson |
| **Advertising**<br>Media costs. Production costs. Fees. Salaries. | Direct, or on basis of space and time by media. Other costs in proportion to media costs | Cost of space for each customer group, or equal charge to each customer | Direct, or on basis of analysis of media circulation records |
| **Sales promotion**<br>Consumer promotions (premiums, etc.) Trade promotions (exhibitions, etc.). Point of sale displays, etc. | Direct, or on basis of analysis of source records | Direct, or on basis of analysis of source records | Direct, or on basis of analysis of source records |
| **Transportation**<br>Payment to carriers. Transport department cost, etc. | Applicable rate times weight | Analysis of sample of bills of lading | Applicable rate times weight |
| **Storage and shipping**<br>Storage, packing, handling, loading, assembling shipments, preparation of documents, rent and warehouse charges. Labour costs, etc. | Space occupied times average inventory Number of shipping units The invoice line | Number of shipping units The invoice line Average order size | Number of shipping units |
| **Order processing**<br>Checking and processing orders. Coordination with production. Pricing expenses. Invoice preparation. Freight accounting. Credit management. Bad debt provision, etc. | Number of order lines Number of invoice lines | Number of order lines Number of invoice lines | Number of order lines Number of invoice lines |

corporate advertising expenditure that is concerned with the company's image is not specific to any segment, hence it is non-separable and should not be allocated. Any non-specific, non-separable cost allocations would inevitably be very arbitrary, and such costs should therefore be excluded from all detailed cost and profit computations.

If one is concerned purely with measuring profit by segment, then even separable fixed costs should be omitted from the calculations since they are not direct deductions from the sales revenue of specific segments. However, marketing cost analysis is concerned also with the most effective use of marketing effort and this form of analysis requires the inclusion of separable fixed costs. (This highlights the important difference between product costing and marketing cost analysis: the former is very much concerned with the task of simply compiling product costs whereas the latter is concerned with the cost and revenue implications of different marketing actions and activities.)

## 3.5 AN ILLUSTRATION OF SEGMENTAL ANALYSIS

A segment is any cost object that is of interest, and is synonymous with the notion of activity, project or mission as appropriate. Thus, for example, marketing segments may be one – or a combination – of the following:

- product line;
- channel of distribution;
- sales territory;
- customer group;
- size of order.

It is possible to vary the degree of aggregation of segments as shown in Figure 3.4 (adapted from Ratnatunga, 1983, p. 34).

**FIGURE 3.4**
*Segmental levels*

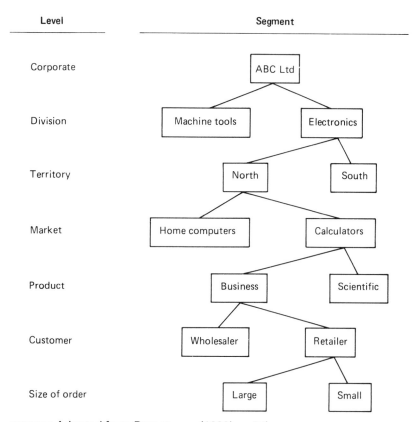

SOURCE: Adapted from Ratnatunga (1983), p. 34

Initially one must select the segment in which one is interested (e.g. territory, customer, etc.). Then one must select the approach to costing that one prefers. Essentially there are two major alternatives:

1 absorption (or full) costing;
2 variable (or direct or marginal) costing.

Our earlier discussion dealt with the first of these and we saw that this approach involves charging both direct and a portion of indirect costs to the segment in question. When set against the segment's revenue the result is a net profit figure. An example is given in Figure 3.5 of the net profit picture in an organization operating through three different channels of distribution.

**FIGURE 3.5**
*Profit analysis by channel*

| £'000s | Channel A | B | C | Total |
|---|---|---|---|---|
| Revenue | 875 | 950 | 1,225 | 3,050 |
| Cost of goods sold | 325 | 285 | 490 | 1,100 |
| Gross Profit | 550 | 665 | 735 | 1,950 |
| Direct expenses | 265 | 245 | 450 | 960 |
| Indirect expenses | 330 | 275 | 250 | 855 |
|  | 595 | 520 | 700 | 1,815 |
| Net profit | (45) | 145 | 35 | 135 |

The net profit figure reflects the result of the allocation of effort as shown by the total of:

cost of goods sold
direct expenses
indirect expenses

once this allocation has been set against the revenue figure, channel by channel. It is evident that the validity of the net profit figures that emerge depend critically upon the adequacy of the means by which indirect costs are apportioned.

An example, ABC Ltd, follows which illustrates in detail how the above approach might be implemented.

**ABC Ltd: An Exercise on Segmental Analysis**

The profit and loss acount for last month's operations of ABC Ltd is given in Figure 3.6, showing a net profit of £14,070.

Derek Needham, ABC's chief executive, is interested in knowing the profitability of the company's three customers. Since this cannot be known from Figure 3.6 as it stands, he asks his management accountant, Philip Randall, to carry out the necessary analysis.

In addition to the five *natural* accounts shown in the profit and loss account Mr Randall has identified four *functional* accounts:

● personal selling;
● packaging and despatch;
● advertising;
● invoicing and collection.

**FIGURE 3.6**
*ABC Ltd profit and loss account*

|  | £ |
|---|---|
| Sales revenue | 255,000 |
| Cost of goods sold | 178,500 |
| Gross profit | 76,500 |
| | |
| *Expenses* | |
| Salaries | 37,500 |
| Rent | 7,500 |
| Packaging materials | 15,180 |
| Postage and stationery | 750 |
| Hire of office equipment | 1,500 |
|  | 62,430 |
| Net profit | £14,070 |

His investigations have revealed that:

1 Salaries are attributable as follows:

- Sales personnel £15,000
- Packaging labour £13,500
- Office staff £ 9,000

Salesmen seldom visit the office. Office staff time is divided equally between promotional activities on the one hand and invoicing/collecting on the other.
2 The rent charge relates to the whole building, of which 20 per cent is occupied by offices and the remainder by packaging/despatch.
3 All the advertising expenditure related to Product C.
4 ABC Ltd markets three products, as shown in Figure 3.7. These products vary in their manufactured cost (worked out on absorption lines), selling price, and volume sold during the month. Moreover, their relative bulk varies: Product A is much smaller than Product B, which in turn is only half the size of Product C. Details are given in Figure 3.7.

**FIGURE 3.7**
*ABC Ltd basic product data*

| Product | Manufactured cost per unit | Selling price per unit | Number of units sold last month | Sales revenue | Relative bulk per unit |
|---|---|---|---|---|---|
| A | £105 | £150 | 1,000 | £150,000 | 1 |
| B | £525 | £750 | 100 | £75,000 | 3 |
| C | £2,100 | £3,000 | 10 | £30,000 | 6 |
|  |  |  | 1,110 | £255,000 | |

5 ABC's three customers each requires different product combinations, places a different number of orders, and requires a different amount of sales effort. As Figure 3.8 shows, James received more sales calls, Charles placed more orders, and Hugh made up most of the demand for Product C.

In the light of this information we may now seek to:

(a) Use the data that has been presented, and making any assumptions we feel to be appropriate, apply absorption costing principles in order to determine the net profit or loss attributable to each of ABC's customers.
(b) On the basis of the outcome from (a), what course of action should we propose?

**FIGURE 3.8**
*ABC Ltd basic customer data*

| Customer | Number of sales calls in period | Number of orders placed in period | Number of units of each product ordered in period | | |
|---|---|---|---|---|---|
| | | | A | B | C |
| Charles | 30 | 30 | 900 | 30 | 0 |
| James | 40 | 3 | 90 | 30 | 3 |
| Hugh | 30 | 1 | 10 | 40 | 7 |
| Totals | 100 | 34 | 1,000 | 100 | 10 |

**ABC Ltd: Segmental Analysis**

(a)  Among the given data we are told that office staff divide their time equally between two functional activities:

(i)   advertising (i.e. order-getting);
(ii)  invoicing and collections.

It seems reasonable to assume (in the absence of other guidance) that space, postage and stationery, and office equipment are used equally by these two functions. The calculations that follow are based on this assumption, but any other reasonable (and explicit) basis could be acceptable.

Rent is payable on the basis of:

- 20 per cent office space (i.e. £1,500);
- 80 per cent packaging and despatch space (i.e. £6,000).

All packaging materials are chargeable to packaging and despatch (which is a clear-cut example of a direct functional cost). Since packaging costs will vary with the bulk of the products sold rather than with, say, the number of units sold or sales revenue, we need to take note of the causal relationship between the bulk of sales and packaging costs (see Figure 3.9).

**FIGURE 3.9**
*ABC Ltd packaging units*

| Product | Number of units sold | | Relative bulk per unit | | Packaging units |
|---|---|---|---|---|---|
| A | 1,000 | × | 1 | = | 1,000 |
| B | 100 | × | 3 | = | 300 |
| C | 10 | × | 6 | = | 60 |
| | 1,110 | | | | 1,360 |

This can be done by computing (as in Figure 3.9) a measure termed 'packaging units' which incorporates both the number of units and their relative bulk. Even though only 10 units of Product C are sold during the month the bulk of that product (with a factor of 6) ensures that it uses a correspondingly high amount of packaging effort (hence cost) per unit relative to products A and B.

The bases for determining the rates to apply functional costs to segments can be built up in the following way:

(i)   *Assign natural expenses to functional activities.* This is done in Figure 3.10.
(ii)  *Select bases for assigning functional costs to segments.*
  - Sales calls can be used for personal selling expenses (although this assumes all calls took an equal amount of time).
  - The packaging costs vary in accordance with the number of packaging units handled, so a rate per product can be established by taking bulk and the number of units handled into account.

**FIGURE 3.10**
*ABC Ltd assigning natural expenses*

| Natural expense | Personal selling | Packaging and despatch | Advertising | Invoicing and collection |
|---|---|---|---|---|
| Salaries | £15,000 | £13,500 | £4,500 | £4,500 |
| Rent | – | £6,000 | £750 | £750 |
| Packaging materials | – | £15,180 | – | – |
| Postage and stationery | – | – | £375 | £375 |
| Hire of equipment | – | – | £750 | £750 |
| Total | £15,000 | £34,680 | £6,375 | £6,375 |

- Advertising can be related to the number of units of Product C sold during the period (which assumes that advertising was equally effective for all sales, and that all its benefits were obtained during the period in question).
- The costs of invoicing can be assumed to vary in accordance with the number of orders (hence invoices) processed during the period.

Relevant calculations are given below:

$$\text{Cost per sales call} = \frac{\text{functional costs}}{\text{no. of sales calls}} = \frac{£15,000}{100} = £150.00$$

$$\text{Packaging costs} = \frac{\text{functional costs}}{\text{no. of packaging units}} = \frac{£34,680}{1,360} = £25.50$$

$$\text{Product A} = £25.50 \times 1 = £25.50$$

$$\text{Product B} = £25.50 \times 3 = £76.50$$

$$\text{Product C} = £25.50 \times 6 = £153.00$$

$$\text{Advertising cost} = \frac{\text{functional costs}}{\text{units of C sold}} = \frac{£6,375}{10} = £637.50$$

$$\text{Invoicing cost per order} = \frac{\text{functional costs}}{\text{no. of orders}} = \frac{£6,375}{34} = £187.50$$

(iii) *Assign functional costs to segments.* Before this step can be executed fully it is necessary to calculate the cost of goods sold on a customer-by-customer basis. Data in Figure 3.7 of the question includes the manufactured cost per unit of each product, and from Figure 3.8 in the question we can see how many units of each product are bought by each customer. From this we can calculate the data in Figure 3.11 below:

**FIGURE 3.11**
*ABC Ltd assigning functional expenses*

| Product | Unit COGS | Charles Units | Charles COGS | James Units | James COGS | Hugh Units | Hugh COGS |
|---|---|---|---|---|---|---|---|
| A | £105 | 900 | 94,500 | 90 | 9,450 | 10 | 1,050 |
| B | £525 | 30 | 15,750 | 30 | 15,750 | 40 | 21,000 |
| C | £2,100 | 0 | 0 | 3 | 6,300 | 7 | 14,700 |
| | | | £110,250 | | £31,500 | | £36,750 |

We can now turn to the assigning of functional costs to segments. If we take the case of Charles we know that he can be attributed with (see Figure 3.12):

**FIGURE 3.12**
*ABC Ltd Charles'
costs*

| | | |
|---|---|---|
| 30 sales calls @ £150.00 | | £4,500 |
| 30 orders      @ £187.50 | | £5,625 |
| Packaging costs for: | | |
| Product A 900 × £25.50 | £22,950.00 | |
| Product B  30 × £76.50 | £2,295.00 | |
| Product C | 0 | |
| | | £25,245 |
| Advertising | | 0 |
| Segmental marketing cost | | £35,370 |

A similar computation needs to be carried out for James and Hugh, which gives us the data in Figure 3.13:

**FIGURE 3.13**
*ABC Ltd costs of
James and Hugh*

| James | | | Hugh | | |
|---|---|---|---|---|---|
| 40 sales calls @ £150.00 | £6,000.00 | | 30 sales calls @ £150.00 | £4,500.00 | |
| 3 orders      @ £187.50 | £562.50 | | 1 order      @ £187.50 | £187.50 | |
| Packaging | | | Packaging | | |
| A 90 × £25.50 | £2,295 | | A 10 × £25.50 | £255 | |
| B 30 × £76.50 | £2,295 | | B 40 × £76.50 | £3,060 | |
| C  3 × £153.00 | £459 | | C  7 × £153.00 | £1,071 | |
| | £5,049.00 | | | £4,386.00 | |
| Advertising 3 × £637.50 | £1,912.50 | | Advertising 7 × £637.00 | £4,462.50 | |
| Segmental marketing cost | £13,524.00 | | Segmental marketing cost | £13,536.00 | |

Finally, the revenue generated from each customer must be calculated as in Figure 3.14:

**FIGURE 3.14**
*ABC Ltd revenue by
customer*

| | | Customer | | | | | |
|---|---|---|---|---|---|---|---|
| | | Charles | | James | | Hugh | |
| Product | Unit selling price | Units | Revenue | Units | Revenue | Units | Revenue |
| A | £150 | 900 | 135,000 | 90 | 13,400 | 10 | 1,500 |
| B | £740 | 30 | 22,500 | 30 | 22,500 | 40 | 30,000 |
| C | £3,000 | 0 | 0 | 3 | 9,000 | 7 | 21,000 |
| | | | £157,500 | | £45,000 | | £52,500 |

(iv) *Compile a net profit statement*. All the pieces can now be put together to show the profit or loss of each customer account with ABC Ltd. The resulting figures (Figure 3.15) show that Charles and Hugh are profitable accounts while James is marginally unprofitable.

**FIGURE 3.15**
*ABC Ltd net profit by customer*

|  | Customer | | | |
|---|---|---|---|---|
|  | Charles | James | Hugh | *ABC Ltd* |
| Sales revenue | £157,500 | £45,000 | £52,500 | £255,000 |
| COGS | 110,250 | 31,500 | 36,750 | 178,500 |
| Gross profit | 47,250 | 13,500 | 15,750 | 76,500 |
| Marketing expenses | 35,370 | 13,524 | 13,536 | 62,430 |
| Net profit | £11,880 | £(24) | £2,214 | £14,070 |

In productivity terms we have:

$$\text{Charles:} \quad \frac{\text{Outputs}}{\text{Inputs}} = \frac{£157,000}{£(110,250 + 35,370)} = 1.08$$

$$\text{James:} \quad \frac{\text{Outputs}}{\text{Inputs}} = \frac{£45,000}{£(31,500 + 13,524)} = 0.99$$

$$\text{Hugh:} \quad \frac{\text{Outputs}}{\text{Inputs}} = \frac{£52,000}{£(36,750 + 13,536)} = 1.04$$

$$\text{ABC Ltd:} \quad \frac{\text{Outputs}}{\text{Inputs}} = \frac{£255,000}{£(178,500 + 62,430)} = 1.06$$

(b) *Interpretation of data*

A danger in using an absorption-based approach in segmental analysis is that the 'bottom line' might be taken as a criterion for *action*. It should not be; the aim is to determine the net profit as a criterion for *investigation*. (In a sense, of course, this is one type of action, but the type of action that should be avoided is the eliminating of James's account due to the marginal loss revealed in Figure 3.15.)

Charles's account contributed almost 85 per cent of the total net profit, and he bought three times as much from ABC Ltd as did Hugh, and more than three times the purchases of James. However, the number of sales calls to Charles was fewer than to James, although Charles placed a much larger number of orders than both James and Hugh together.

The mix of products purchased clearly affects the profit performance of different customer accounts. While the COGS does not vary from one product to another (being 70 per cent of sales revenue for each product line), the variation in relative bulk of the product lines caused differences in packaging costs. Thus Charles (whose orders were for 900 units of A, 30 of B, and none of C) was charged with relatively less packaging cost than either James or Hugh due to the smaller packaging bulk of Product A. On a similar basis, since Charles bought no units of C his account was not charged with any advertising costs, so the profit performance of Charles's account would clearly be better than either of the others.

One possible way forward could be to consider calling less often on James; encourage Charles to place fewer (but larger) orders; and to rethink the wisdom of the advertising campaign for Product C.

It is vital to recognize that this net profit approach to segmental analysis can only raise questions: it cannot provide answers. (The reason for this, of course, is that the apportionment of indirect costs clouds the distinction between avoidable and unavoidable costs, and even direct costs may not all be avoidable in the short run.)

The application of the above steps to a company's product range may produce the picture portrayed in Figure 3.16.

**FIGURE 3.16**
*Segmental profit
statement*

| Product | % contribution to total profits |
|---|---|
| Total for all products | 100.0 |
| *Profitable products:* | |
| A | 43.7 |
| B | 35.5 |
| C | 16.4 |
| D | 9.6 |
| E | 6.8 |
| F | 4.2 |
| Sub-total | 116.2 |
| G | −7.5 |
| H | −8.7 |
| Sub-total | −16.2 |

The segment could equally be sales territory, customer group, etc., and after the basic profit computation has been carried out it can be supplemented (as in Figure 3.17) by linking it to an analysis of the effort required to produce the profit result. (Clearly this is a multi-variate situation in which profit depends upon a variety of input factors, but developing valid and reliable multi-variant models is both complex and expensive.) As a step in the direction of more rigorous analysis one can derive benefits from linking profit outcome to individual inputs – such as selling time in the case of Figure 3.17.

From Figure 3.17 one can see that Product A generates 43.7 per cent of total profits, requiring only 16.9 per cent of available selling time. This is highly productive. By contrast, Product E produces only 6.8 per cent of total profits but required 10.2 per cent of selling effort. Even worse, however, is the 24.8 per cent of selling effort devoted to Products G and H, which are unprofitable.

**FIGURE 3.17**
*Segmental
productivity
statement*

| Product | % contribution to total profits | % total selling time |
|---|---|---|
| Total for all products | 100 | 100 |
| *Profitable products* | | |
| A | 43.7 | 16.9 |
| B | 35.5 | 18.3 |
| C | 16.4 | 17.4 |
| D | 9.6 | 5.3 |
| E | 6.8 | 10.2 |
| F | 4.2 | 7.1 |
| Sub-total | 116.2 | 75.2 |
| *Unprofitable products:* | | |
| G | −7.5 | 9.5 |
| H | −8.7 | 15.3 |
| Sub-total | −16.2 | 24.8 |

A number of obvious questions arise from this type of analysis. Can the productivity of marketing activities be increased by:

- increasing net profits proportionately more than the corresponding increase in marketing outlays?
- increasing net profits with no change in marketing outlays?
- increasing net profits with a decrease in marketing costs?
- maintaining net profits at a given level but decreasing marketing costs?
- decreasing net profits but with a proportionately greater decrease in marketing costs?

If these analyses are based purely on historical information they will provide less help than if they relate to plans for the future. One way of overcoming the limitations of historical information is to plan and control the conditions under which information is gathered. This can be achieved through *marketing experimentation.*

## 3.6 MARKETING EXPERIMENTATION

As we saw in Chapter 1 (see pp. 12–15 above, and see also Chapter 16, pp. 487–489 below), attempts are made in a marketing experiment to identify all the controllable factors that effect a particular dependent variable, and some of these factors are then manipulated systematically in order to isolate and measure their effects on the performance of the dependent variable.

It is not possible, of course, to plan or control all the conditions in which an experiment is conducted; for example, the timing, location, and duration of an experiment can be predetermined, but it is necessary to measure such uncontrollable conditions as those caused by the weather and eliminate their effects from the results. Irrespective of these uncontrollable influences, the fact that experiments are concerned with the deliberate manipulation of controllable variables (i.e. such variables as price and advertising effort) means that a good deal more confidence can be placed in conclusions about the effects of such manipulation than if the effects of these changes had been based purely on historical associations.

Studies of marketing costs can provide the ideas for experiments. Questions such as the following can be answered as a result of marketing experimentation.

1 By how much (if any) would the net profit contribution of the most profitable products be increased if there were an increase in specific marketing outlays, and how would such a change affect the strategy of competitors in terms of the stability of, say, market shares?
2 By how much (if any) would the net losses of unprofitable products be reduced if there were some decrease in specific marketing outlays?
3 By how much (if any) would the profit contribution of profitable products be affected by a change in the marketing effort applied to the unprofitable products, and vice versa, and what would be the effect on the total marketing system?
4 By how much (if any) would the total profit contribution be improved if some marketing effort were diverted to profitable territories or customer groups from unprofitable territorial and customer segments?
5 By how much (if any) would the net profit contribution be increased if there were a change in the method of distribution to small unprofitable accounts, or if these accounts were eliminated?

Only by actually carrying out properly designed marketing experiments can management realistically predict with an acceptable degree of certainty the effects of changes in marketing expenditure on the level of sales and profit of each differentiated product, territory, or customer segment in the multiproduct company.

## 3.7 An Alternative Approach to Segmental Analysis

The alternative approach to segmental analysis is the variable costing approach in which only direct costs are allocated to arrive at a measure of profit. Using the data from Figure 3.5 above, this has been reworked in Figure 3.18 to illustrate the variable costing approach.

**FIGURE 3.18**
*A direct costing profit statement*

| £'000s | Channel | | | Total |
|---|---|---|---|---|
| | A | B | C | |
| Revenue | 875 | 950 | 1,225 | 3,050 |
| Variable COGS | 225 | 175 | 300 | 700 |
| Manufacturing contribution | 650 | 775 | 925 | 2,350 |
| Variable direct marketing expenses | 115 | 105 | 190 | 410 |
| Variable contribution | 535 | 670 | 735 | 1,940 |
| Fixed direct marketing expenses | 150 | 140 | 260 | 550 |
| Marketing contribution | 385 | 530 | 475 | 1,390 |
| Indirect expenses | | | | 855 |
| Fixed manufacturing expenses | | | | 400 |
| | | | | 135 |

It has been assumed that the cost of goods sold figures in Figure 3.5 included £700,000 of variable manufacturing costs and £400,000 of fixed manufacturing costs; that the direct expenses are all of a marketing nature and can be split into fixed and variable components as shown in Figure 3.18; and that the indirect expenses are all non-allocable to channels. The result is a clear statement that sufficient revenue is being generated via each channel to cover the variable expenses and the directly allocable fixed expenses. Moreover, there is sufficient total contribution to cover the indirect expenses and the fixed manufacturing costs while still making a net profit of £135,000.

## 3.8 Customer Profitability Analysis

An approach to segmental analysis that is of increasing interest is customer profitability analysis (CPA). If marketing effort is to be directed at customers or market segments with the greatest profit potential it is essential that marketing managers have information showing both the existing picture with regard to customer profitability and prospects for the future.

Customer profitability analysis has been defined (Anandarajan & Christopher, 1986, p. 86) as:

... the evaluation, analysis and isolation of:

- all the significant costs associated with servicing a specific customer/group of customers from the point an order is received through manufacture to ultimate delivery;
- the revenues associated with doing business with those specific customers/ customer groups.

The implementation of CPA can be achieved by a series of steps which parallel the steps suggested earlier for other types of segmental analysis. In outline these steps are:

## Step 1
Clearly define customer groups and market segments in a way that distinguishes the needs of customers in one group from those of customers in another group.

## Step 2
For the customer groups or market segments of interest identify those factors that cause variations in the costs of servicing those customers. This can be done by identifying the key elements of the marketing mix used for each customer group or segment from which some indication of the costs of servicing each group should be drawn.

## Step 3
Analyse the ways in which service offerings are differentiated between customer groups. For example, terms of trade may vary between home-based and overseas customers, or between large and small customers, as might the level of service (i.e. speed of delivery) to key accounts.

## Step 4
Clearly identify the resources that have been used to support each customer group or segment – including personnel, warehouse facilities, administrative back-up, etc.

## Step 5
Determine ways in which the costs of resources (step 4) can be attributed to customer groups.

## Step 6
Relate revenues and costs to each customer group, with profit emerging as the difference.

The total of the costs for a given customer group is a measure of the effort that has been allocated to that group, and the profit is a measure of the return from that effort. Until the existing pattern of allocation is known, along with its profitability, it is not possible to devise ways of improving that allocation.

## 3.9  THE NATURE OF PRODUCTIVITY

Productivity can be considered at either a macro level (i.e. in relation to entire industries or whole economies) or at a micro level (i.e. in relation to particular organizations, or in relation to particular activities within organizations). Our interest is in the latter – productivity at a micro level – although we must avoid being too introspective by focusing exclusively on one organization or function as if it were independent of its context.

At its simplest, productivity can be conceived of as the relationship between outputs and inputs. Thus marketing productivity can be expressed as:

$$\frac{\text{marketing outputs}}{\text{marketing inputs}}$$

Sevin (1965, p. 9) has defined marketing productivity in more specific terms as:

> . . . the ratio of sales or net profits (effect produced) to marketing costs (energy expended) for a specific segment of the business.

This equates productivity and profitability, which seems acceptable to some writers (e.g. Thomas, 1984; 1986) but not to others (e.g. Bucklin, 1979). The major objection to Sevin's definition is due to the effects of inflation since sales, net profit, and costs are all financial flows subject to changes in relative prices. For example, any increase in the value of sales from one period to another during inflationary times will be made up of two elements:

1 an increase due to a higher physical volume of sales;
2 an increase due to higher prices.

If the value of the pound sterling were constant this would remove the problem, but since this is not the case it means that any financial data is necessarily suspect. The answer is to make some adjustments to ensure that measurement is made in *real* terms rather than simply in *monetary* terms – and to make these adjustments to both numerator and denominator in a way that allows for differential rates of inflation. Once measurement is made in real terms it is possible to use the ratio that emerges as an index of efficiency. This can be used in relation to two types of question:

1 How much output was achieved for a given input?
2 How much input was required to achieve a given output?

These questions can be asked retrospectively (as above) or prospectively (for example, how much output should be achieved from a given mix and quantity of inputs?). The first relates to the notion of *technical efficiency*, whereby one seeks to maximize the output from a given input, whereas the second relates to the notion of *economic efficiency*, whereby one seeks to minimize the input costs for a given output.

Having specified in operational terms the numerator (output) and the denominator (input), and having eliminated the impacts of inflation, the result represents a measure of resource allocation (i.e. the pattern of inputs) and resource utilization (i.e. the generation of outputs), and these can be depicted via *ratio pyramids* which we will look at later in this chapter (see p. 71 *et seq.*). What we need to recognize at this point is that the array of ratios within a ratio pyramid can give us a vivid picture of the manner in which the organization has allocated its resources, and the efficiency with which those resources have been utilized. The next step, of course, is to consider how the allocation and its efficiency might be improved, which will mean changes in inputs and outputs. In turn this requires an understanding of the causal relationships between inputs and outputs.

Let us be a little more specific and consider a particular productivity index from the distribution domain. The relevant output may be expressed in terms of the number of orders shipped during a given period, and the associated input may be the number of labour hours worked in the period. Thus:

$$\text{productivity index} = \frac{\text{number of orders shipped}}{\text{number of labour hours worked}}$$

It will be apparent that this index relates one physical measure to another, hence there is no need to worry about inflationary distortions. However, had the numerator been expressed in terms of the *sales value* of orders shipped, and/or the denominator in terms of the *cost* of labour hours worked, it would have been necessary to adjust the figures to eliminate the effects of inflation – even though the index that results is a true ratio (i.e. it is not stated in terms of specific units).

It should also be apparent that any productivity index that is calculated is meaningless in isolation from some comparative figure. With what should an index be compared? There are a number of alternatives that will be examined later in more detail, but for the present we should be aware of the following:

- *internal comparisons* can be made with either
  1 figures from previous periods, which give a basis for trend analysis;
  2 figures representing efficient or desired performance, which give a basis for budgetary control.
- *external comparisons* can be made with other organizations operating within the same markets.

The importance of external reference points cannot be overemphasized. As Christopher (1977) has stated:

> Business success is achieved where the client is, more than in our plants. External returns from the market are more appropriate measures than internal returns on investment. Success is more in manufacturing satisfied, repeat customers than in manufacturing products.

Within the distribution domain it has been estimated that order-filling activities (i.e. transportation, stockholding and associated administration) account for between 18 per cent and 45 per cent of total company costs. Outlays of this magnitude clearly warrant attention, and the example following is focused on measuring productivity in the distribution function. It is drawn from Armitage (1987, pp. 42–5).

## A Distribution Productivity Example

In virtually any warehousing situation, certain tasks are routinely performed. Evaluating the performance of the individuals working on these tasks dictates that work areas or responsibility centres be established, and that data about individuals be collected by such work areas or responsibility centres. How the areas are defined will vary with the nature and size of each organization's warehousing facilities. A large multiproduct distribution centre contains many employees performing homogeneous sets of tasks resulting in numerous specific work areas. On the other hand, the management of a smaller warehouse may require their employees to perform more heterogeneous tasks resulting in a broader definition of work areas. Despite these variations, however, there will be certain logical groupings of activities which may be accounted for as a separate work unit.

As an example, Figure 3.19 illustrates a set of activities occurring at a corporation's manufacturing warehouse (MW), its regional distribution centres (RDC) and its local distribution centres (LDC). These activities begin with the receipt of goods from either production facilities (PF) or vendors, and continue until the goods are shipped between distribution centres or to customers. The figure also illustrates that those activities which require close coordination can be clustered and treated as work areas. This exists, for example, in the case of receiving and storing, and in the case of packing and shipment. The picking or selection activity, while not independent of other activities, is usually important enough to warrant a separate accounting.

### Definition of Output in Each Work Area

Although the basic nature of the activities taking place at each MW, RDC and LDC are the same, Figure 3.19 indicates some important differences in the manner in which they are carried out. At the MW cost centres, for example, inventory is received in single cases via a conveyor belt system linking the production areas and MWs. The cases are then palletized and moved by mechanized vehicle to predetermined storage slots. At RDC and LDC cost centres, on the other hand, inventory arrives by truck and consists predominantly of full pallet loads with smaller amounts arriving on partial pallets or as single

**FIGURE 3.19**
*Diagram illustrating sequence of procedures at inventory locations*

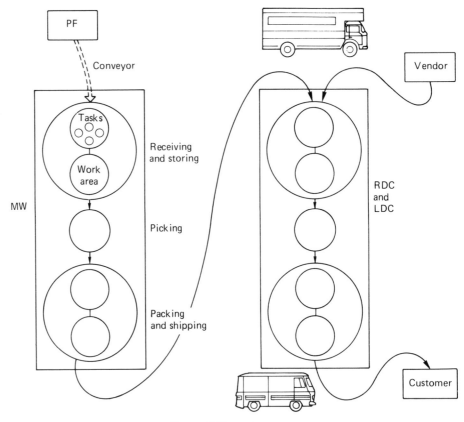

*Responsibility centres*

*Cost centres*
MW  — Manufacturing
      warehouse
RDC — Regional distribution
      centre
LDC — Local distribution
      centre
PF   — Production facilities

*Work areas*
Receiving and storing
Picking
Packing and shipping

*Tasks*
Full pallet task
Partial pallet task
Loose case task
Damaged case task

cases. On arrival the goods are either stored directly into predetermined locations or are reassembled before they are stored. Similarly, the packing and shipping operations of the RDCs and LDCs differ from those of the MWs. At MW locations, a high proportion of shipments are palletized full truck loads requiring less labour effort per unit shipped than is the case at RDC and LDC locations. At these locations, shipments regularly consist of partial pallets or single cases, and require different handling techniques.

The determination of an acceptable level of performance in such diverse conditions is a difficult task. Not only do the work practices at various cost centres differ, but the mix of work practices may vary within a single cost centre. In addition, changes in work methods are made occasionally in the hope of improving labour productivity. Consequently, any measure of output adopted must take these variations and changes into account.

### Productivity Effectiveness and Productivity Efficiency
This requires a distinction between productivity gains and losses due to effectiveness* and productivity gains and losses due to efficiency. In locations

_____
*Effectiveness is defined as the ability to reach a desired objective. Efficiency is defined as the optimum relationship between inputs and outputs given a specific set of work methods.

where work methods are reasonably stable, the overriding purpose of the accounting system is to monitor the efficiency with which individual tasks are carried out. On the other hand, if structural changes are considered or adopted, the accounting system should reflect the productivity effectiveness associated with the change. At issue are the following two questions.

1 Given the accepted set of work methods, what should the productivity level be? (Efficiency)
2 Given a change in work methods, what differences should occur in productivity? (Effectiveness)

The first question deals with control and seeks to measure the efficiency with which individual activities are conducted. In a warehousing environment where the same outputs require different labour inputs (picking 1000 palletized cases by forklift requires less labour input than picking 1000 loose cases by hand), the efficiency measure must recognize the existence of these diversities. In other words, individual managers must not be penalized for the work methods currently used, provided their efforts are efficiently carried out.

The second question recognizes that there may be a greater (i.e. more productive) way to produce the output, even though the current operation is performing as efficiently as possible. For example, the ability periodically to ship full pallets of inventory to customers (rather than shipping a case or two at irregular intervals) would lead to higher productivity effectiveness even though the current procedure is being carried out efficiently.

## Measuring Productivity Efficiency

Developing a useful measure for the efficiency question is the more troublesome of the two issues but can be accomplished by drawing from the literature on process costing. Process costing is a type of cost system found in a homogeneous manufacturing situation. A key feature of this system is the measurement of the outputs of a particular process or work area in terms of the number of equivalent units of production completed.

To illustrate the notion of an equivalent unit and how it is used, assume that the following activity took place in a recent month.

| | | |
|---|---|---|
| Units started | 1000 | |
| Units completed | 700 | |
| Units remaining in process | 300 | to which all necessary materials but only ¼ of the required labour and overhead components have been added. |

For purposes of conducting cost analysis, a material equivalent unit of 1000 (700 + 1.00(300)) and a labour and overhead equivalent unit of 775 (700 + 0.25(300)) would be used.

Adopting a variation of this feature in the warehousing environment can lead to a more consistent measure of output which in turn leads to a more useful productivity measure for control purposes. The productivity efficiency ratio can be expressed by equation (1).

$$\text{Productivity efficiency} = \frac{\text{equivalent cases of output}}{\text{allowed man hours worked}} \qquad (1)$$

## Measuring Productivity Effectiveness

Improving effectiveness, on the other hand, is a managerial prerogative. Despite the fact that the various tasks may be operating with equal efficiency, it is clear, for example, that handling cases on full pallets is more effective in raising labour productivity than is the handling of loose cases. Thus, a measure which portrays this difference is also necessary. Such a measure can be called the productivity effectiveness ratio and is calculated by equation (2).

$$\text{Productivity effectiveness} = \frac{\text{actual cases of output}}{\text{allowed man hours worked}} \qquad (2)$$

## 3.10  THE USE OF RATIOS

Whether one's primary interest is in the productivity of an organization as a whole, or in the productivity of a highly specific activity within an organization, ratios can be computed at a suitable level of aggregation. Their value lies in the relative measures (as opposed to absolute measures) on which they are based.

It is possible to calculate a great range of ratios, but a word of warning is needed to ensure that only useful ratios are calculated. Thus, for example, the ratio of

$$\frac{\text{advertising expenditure}}{\text{miles travelled by salesmen}}$$

within a given period is not likely to be very useful for at least two reasons:

1  it seeks to relate two input factors (rather than one input and one output);
2  the resulting ratio (of advertising expenditure per mile travelled by salesmen) is not meaningful.

On the other hand, the ratio of

$$\frac{\text{incremental sales}}{\text{incremental promotion}}$$

relates one input to a relevant output and is potentially useful as a measure of promotional effectiveness. Discretion, therefore, is most important in choosing which ratios to calculate as a means towards assessing productivity within marketing.

Another warning needs to be given over the way in which ratios tend to average out any patterns in the underlying data. Consider the case of a seasonal business making 90 per cent of its sales in the first six months of every year and the remaining 10 per cent during the other six months. Average monthly sales over the whole year will differ significantly from the average monthly sales in each half year, so one must choose carefully the period over which one gathers data, and the frequency with which one calculates ratios.

At an organizational level the ultimate measure of short-term efficiency is the relationship between net profit and capital employed, typically expressed in percentage terms as the rate of return on capital employed or the rate of return on investment (ROI).

$$\frac{\text{Net profit}}{\text{Capital employed}} \times 100 = \text{ROI}$$

This ratio shows the return (i.e. net output) that has been generated by the capital employed (i.e. input) during a given period of time. Problems exist in connection with the definitions, hence measurement, of both numerator and denominator, which highlights another note of caution in using ratios: always be sure to establish the definition of numerators and denominators. For example, is the net profit pre-tax or post-tax? Is the capital employed based on historic cost or replacement cost figures?

Given that profit is the residual once costs have been deducted from revenues, it is clear that ROI can be improved by either increasing revenues, decreasing costs, or reducing capital employed – or by any combination of these. This gives us the basic idea underlying the ratio pyramid. At the apex is ROI, but this can be decomposed into two secondary ratios:

Primary ratio $\dfrac{\text{net profit}}{\text{capital employed}}$

Secondary ratios $\dfrac{\text{net profit}}{\text{sales}}$ $\dfrac{\text{sales}}{\text{capital employed}}$

Each of the secondary ratios can help explain the ROI. The first is the profit rate on sales and the second is the capital turnover. Their interrelationship is such that:

$$\text{Profit rate} \ \times \ \text{capital turnover} \ = \ \text{ROI}$$

Even the secondary ratios are highly aggregated, so it is necessary to proceed to measure tertiary ratios as one moves down the ratio pyramid using its structure as a diagnostic guide.

The general cause of any deviation in ROI from standard may be found by computing the profit ratio and the capital turnover ratio, but this is only a starting point. Before corrective action can be taken a study of specific causes must be made, hence *tertiary ratios* need to be worked out.

Tertiary ratios are those that constitute the secondary ratios. The profit ratio reflects the relationship between the gross profit rate, the level of sales, and operating costs (i.e. net profit + operating costs = gross profit), while the rate of capital turnover is affected by the level of sales and the capital structure mix (of fixed and working capital, etc.). From these details it is a simple step to compute four tertiary ratios as follows:

1 $\dfrac{\text{Gross profit}}{\text{Sales}}$

2 $\dfrac{\text{Sales}}{\text{Operating costs}}$

3 $\dfrac{\text{Sales}}{\text{Fixed assets}}$

4 $\dfrac{\text{Sales}}{\text{Working capital}}$

Many other levels of the ratio pyramid can be identified, and the process of decomposing broad ratios into their component parts can be continued further and further until the reasons for outcomes are known. If, for example, the tertiary ratio of sales to working capital ((4), above) was broken down further, it will be seen to be made up of two ratios, which themselves are made up of many more subordinate ratios. See Figure 3.20.

**FIGURE 3.20**
*Sales to working capital ratio*

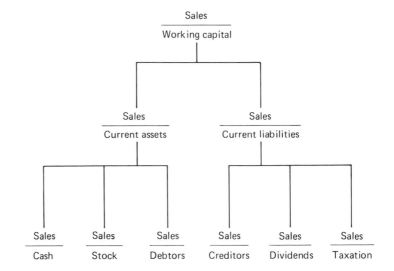

**FIGURE 3.21**
*Sales to stock ratio*

**FIGURE 3.22**
*Ratio pyramid*

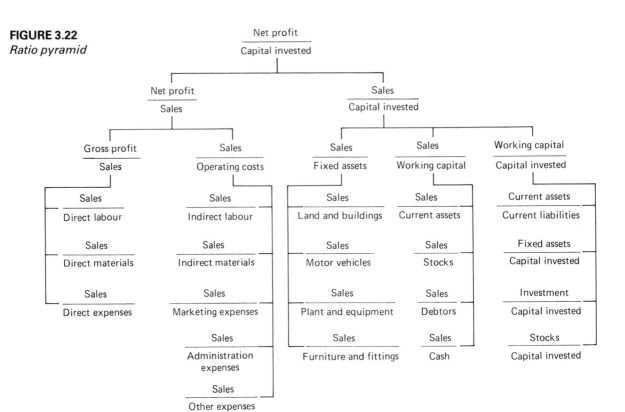

The decomposition can still go on because, for instance, the ratio of sales to stock is made up as shown in Figure 3.21.

An overall ratio pyramid is given in Figure 3.22 and part of this (relating to marketing) is developed and examined in greater detail in Figure 3.23.

Figure 3.24 shows the constituents of ROI.

**FIGURE 3.23**
*Marketing ratio pyramid*

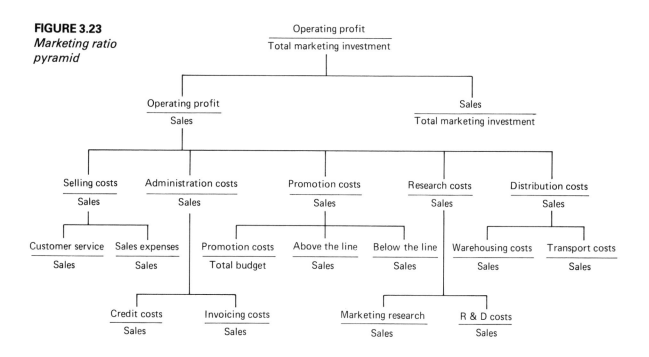

**FIGURE 3.24**
*Constituents of return on investment*

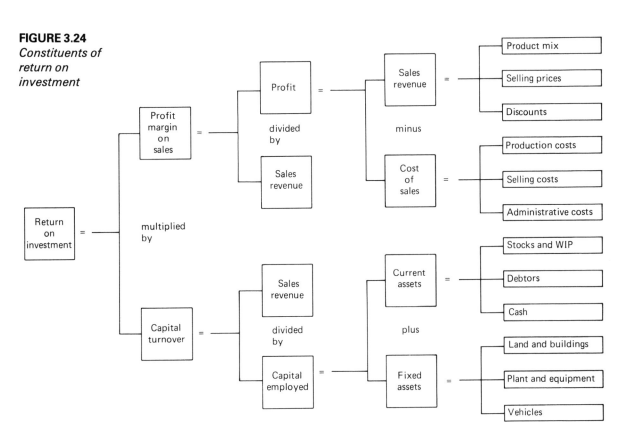

## 3.11 ANALYSING RATIOS AND TRENDS

It is possible to indicate trends in a company's performance over time by plotting successive ratios on a graph and thereby showing trends. Some important trends may only become apparent over a number of months (or even years), and ratio analysis can ensure that such trends do not develop unnoticed. Figure 3.25, for example, shows a continuing decline in a company's profitability. The causes for this trend may be found by breaking it down into its secondary components and so on through the ratio pyramid. These secondary trends – profit rate and capital turnover – are shown in Figure 3.26 and can be seen to be falling and rising respectively. Figure 3.27 then takes the former of these trends (falling profit rate) and decomposes it into a falling gross profit trend and a rising indirect cost to sales trend.

It could prove necessary in a specific instance to work right through the ratio pyramid in plotting trends in order to isolate the causes of variations from the desired trend line in high levels of the ratio hierarchy, and it may also be necessary to apply some imagination and common sense. This last mentioned requirement can be illustrated in two ways. First, the declining ROI noted in Figure 3.25 may be thought, prima facie, to be due to the falling net profit to sales trend shown in

**FIGURE 3.25**
*Primary trend*

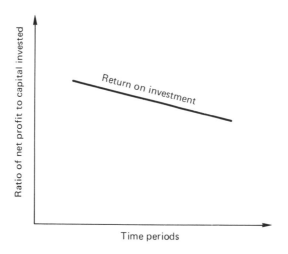

Figure 3.26, and so the rising capital turnover trend as in Figure 3.26 may be ignored. But ROI is clearly the combined outcome of a particular level of profit and a particular quantity of capital investment, so any variation in either will inevitably affect the ROI. Furthermore, a rising aggregate trend of capital turnover will almost certainly conceal many more compensating highs and lows in tertiary and subsequent levels of the ratio hierarchy. It follows that attention in the light of a falling ROI should not necessarily be focused exclusively on the net profit trend, but some consideration should be given to the rate and trend of capital turnover.

The second common-sense point to note is that a rising indirect cost to sales trend, as in Figure 3.27, cannot be controlled until the specific items that cause the trend have been identified and appropriate steps taken to bring them under control. Of course, the extent to which the decline of the profit rate (a secondary trend) is caused by either of its constituent tertiary trends should be carefully established.

**FIGURE 3.26**
*Secondary trends*

**FIGURE 3.27**
*Tertiary trends*

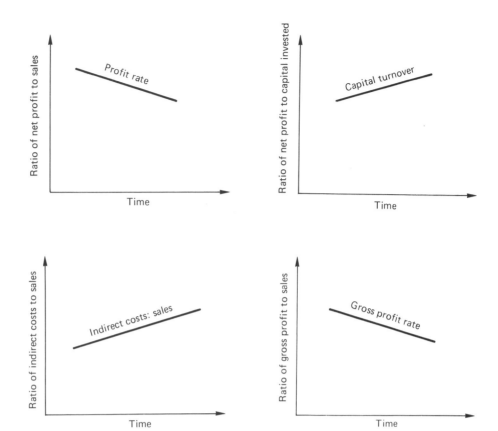

## 3.12 RATIOS AND INTERFIRM COMPARISON

In many industries – and especially in those in which production methods, technology, product characteristics, and general operating conditions are very similar – it is helpful to have comparative figures for one's own company and for other companies within the industry. From published accounts it is possible to see the primary, secondary, and tertiary ratios (hence trends) of competing companies, but no reasons for divergences between one's own company's results and other companies' results can be discerned from such accounts due to a lack of detail relating to the lower part of the ratio pyramid (i.e. below the tertiary level) and so there is no guidance for future actions.

One major cause of divergence between the results of any two companies can be found in their use of differing accounting techniques and definitions. This will be seen, for example, if two companies purchase a similar asset each at the same point and one company chooses to depreciate the asset over four years while the other company chooses to take a 100 per cent depreciation allowance in the first year. It follows, therefore, that a meaningful comparison must be based on common definitions and usage. This can best be achieved (for comparative purposes) by a central organization and for this reason the Centre for Interfirm Comparison was set up.

**Examples of the Use of Interfirm Comparison**

While interfirm comparison figures are expressed in relation to quartiles and the median (i.e. if all results are ranked in descending order of size, the median is represented by the figure that comes half-way down, and the third quartile is three-quarters of the way down), the following example (OPQ Ltd) simplifies this by just giving the general approach to interfirm comparisons. The necessary steps in such an exercise are:

1 ensure that the reports, etc., that are to be compared incorporate figures that have been prepared on a comparable basis;
2 compute the required ratios, percentages, and key totals from submitted reports;
3 compare the results of each company with the aggregate results;
4 introduce intangible or qualitative factors that may aid in interpreting the results of each individual company in the light of the whole picture;
5 examine the numerator, denominator, and lower ratios in instances where a ratio differs significantly from the external standard (or average, median, or whatever);
6 determine the adjustment (if any) that is required to bring a given company's divergent ratio into line with the aggregate norm.

## OPQ Ltd – Ratio Analysis

The following is a simple example of interfirm comparison. Figure 3.28 shows the ratios of OPQ Ltd, a firm in a light engineering industry, for the two years 1990 and 1991.

This looks like a success story. Profit on assets employed has gone up from 8.25 per cent to 10 per cent due to an increase in the firm's profit on sales (Ratio 2) and

**FIGURE 3.28**
*OPQ's own figures*

| | Ratio | Unit | 1990 | 1991 |
|---|---|---|---|---|
| 1 | Operating profit / Assets employed | % | 8.25 | 10.0 |
| 2 | Operating profit / Sales | % | 5.5 | 6.1 |
| 3 | Sales / Assets employed | times | 1.5 | 1.65 |
| 3(a) | Assets employed / Average daily sales | days* | 249 | 222 |
| 4 | Production cost of sales / Sales | % | 71.0 | 70.4 |
| 5 | Distribution and marketing expenses / Sales | % | 17.7 | 17.7 |
| 6 | General and administrative expenses / Sales | % | 5.8 | 5.8 |
| 7 | Current assets / Average daily sales | days* | 215 | 188 |
| 8 | Fixed assets / Average daily sales | days* | 34 | 34 |
| 9 | Material stocks / Average daily sales | days* | 49 | 45 |
| 10 | Work-in-progress / Average daily sales | days* | 53 | 46 |
| 11 | Finished stocks / Average daily sales | days* | 52 | 39 |
| 12 | Debtors / Average daily sales | days* | 61 | 54 |

\* Days required to turn the asset item over once.

the better use it seems to have made of its assets (Ratios 3 and 3a). The higher profit on sales seems to have been achieved through operational improvements which results in a lower ratio of cost of production (Ratio 4). The firm's faster turnover of assets (Ratio 3) is due mainly to a faster turnover of current assets (Ratio 7), and this in turn is due to accelerated turnovers of material stocks (Ratio 9), work in progress (Ratio 10), finished stock (Ratio 11) and debtors (Ratio 12).

The firm's illusion of success was shattered when it compared its ratios with those of other light engineering firms of its type. Figure 3.29 is an extract from the results – it gives the figures of only five of the 22 participating firms. OPQ Ltd's figures are shown under letter C.

In this year the firm's operating profit on assets employed is well below that of two other firms, and this appears to be due to its profit on sales (Ratio 2) being relatively low. This in turn is mainly due to the firm's high distribution and marketing expenses (Ratio 5). In the actual comparison further ratios were given helping Firm C to establish to what extent its higher Ratio 5 was due to higher costs of distribution and warehousing; higher costs of advertising and sales promotion; or higher costs of other selling activities (e.g. cost of sales personnel).

**FIGURE 3.29**
*The interfirm comparison*

| | Ratio | | A | B | C | D | E |
|---|---|---|---|---|---|---|---|
| 1 | Operating profit / Assets employed | (%) | 18.0 | 14.3 | 10.0 | 7.9 | 4.0 |
| 2 | Operating profit / Sales | (%) | 15.0 | 13.1 | 6.1 | 8.1 | 2.0 |
| 3 | Sales / Assets employed | | 1.20 | 1.09 | 1.65 | 0.98 | 2.0 |
| 3(a) | Assets employed / Average daily sales | * | 304 | 335 | 222 | 372 | 182 |
| 4 | Production cost of sales / Sales | (%) | 73.0 | 69.4 | 70.4 | 72.5 | 79.0 |
| 5 | Distribution and marketing expenses / Sales | (%) | 8.0 | 13.1 | 17.7 | 13.7 | 15.0 |
| 6 | General and administrative expenses / Sales | (%) | 4.0 | 4.4 | 5.8 | 5.7 | 4.0 |
| 7 | Current assets / Average daily sales | * | 213 | 219 | 188 | 288 | 129 |
| 8 | Fixed assets / Average daily sales | * | 91 | 116 | 34 | 84 | 53 |
| 9 | Material stocks / Average daily sales | * | 45 | 43 | 45 | 47 | 29 |
| 10 | Work-in-progress / Average daily sales | * | 51 | 47 | 46 | 60 | 52 |
| 11 | Finished stocks / Average daily sales | * | 71 | 63 | 39 | 94 | 22 |
| 12 | Debtors / Average daily sales | * | 36 | 84 | 54 | 18 | 26 |

* Days required to turn the asset item over once.

## 3.13 SUMMARY

This chapter is concerned primarily with the existing allocation of resources within the enterprise. Both ratio analysis and productivity analysis can help in establishing the pattern of resource allocation and its productivity by relating inputs (resources or costs) to outputs (revenue). From this base, marketing managers will be able to derive greater insights into relationships between inputs and outputs to help them in planning (and controlling) future activities.

If the allocation of 'effort' (i.e. resources) across an organization's various activities can be measured and related to the revenues generated by those activities it is possible to determine their productivity. In essence this is the ratio of outputs/inputs. While the outputs are fairly easy to establish the same is not true of the inputs, so most of the discussion focused on the measurement of inputs.

The starting point is the specification of the objects of interest, for example productivity of operating via different channels, or serving different customer groups. Costs will be *direct* or *indirect*, depending upon the objects of interest. Full cost needs to be determined for each object (i.e. segment), and the ways in which this can be done were discussed and demonstrated. Once this has been done the productivity of each segment can be measured and from these measurements questions can be raised about the adequacy of each segment's productivity. For example, can effort be reallocated from Segment A to Segment B to improve these segments' productivity?

The key role of ratio analysis and productivity analysis lies in the basis they give for raising questions in the light of the existing state of play. Such techniques cannot generate answers.

A pyramid of marketing ratios was constructed to show the pattern of ratios (reflecting resource allocation and productivity) across relevant activities in a way that highlights interdependencies in an overall context.

# 4 | Approaches to competitor analysis

## 4.1 LEARNING OBJECTIVES

When you have read this chapter you should be able to understand:

(a) the importance of competitor analysis;
(b) how firms can best identify against whom they are competing;
(c) how to evaluate competitive relationships;
(d) how to identify competitors' likely response profiles;
(e) the components of the competitive information system and how the information generated feeds into the process of formulating strategy.

## 4.2 INTRODUCTION

Although the vast majority of marketing strategists acknowledge the importance of competitive analysis, it has long been recognized that less effort is typically put into detailed and formal analysis of competitors than, for example, of customers and their buying patterns. In many cases this is seemingly because marketing managers feel that they know enough about their competitors simply as the result of competing against them on a day-by-day basis. In other cases there is almost a sense of resignation, with managers believing that it is rarely possible to understand competitors in detail, and that as long as the company's performance is acceptable there is little reason to spend time collecting information. In yet others, there is only a general understanding of who it is that the company is competing against. The reality, however, is that competitors represent a major determinant of corporate success and any failure to take detailed account of their strengths, weaknesses, strategies and areas of vulnerability is likely to lead not just to a less than optimal performance, but also to an unnecessarily greater exposure to aggressive and unexpected competitive moves. Other probable consequences of failing to monitor competition include an increased likelihood of the company being taken by surprise, its relegation to being a follower rather than a leader, and to a focus on the short term rather than on more fundamental long-term issues.

It follows from this that competitive analysis should be a central element of the marketing planning process, with detailed attention being paid to each competitor's apparent objectives, resources and competitive stance as well as to the individual elements of the marketing mix. In this way, areas of competitive strength and weakness can more readily be identified, and the results fed into the process of developing an effective marketing strategy. Better and more precise attacks can then be aimed at competitors and more effective defences erected to fight off competitors' moves. An additional benefit of competitor analysis, in certain circumstances at least, is that it can help in the process of understanding buying behaviour by identifying the particular groups or classes of customer to whom each competitor's strategy is designed to appeal. This can then in turn be used as the basis for determining the most effective probable positioning strategy for the organization.

Recognition of these points faces the strategist with the need to answer five questions:

1 Who is it that we are competing against?
2 What are their objectives?
3 What strategies are they pursuing and how successful are they?
4 What strengths and weaknesses do they possess?
5 How are they likely to behave and, in particular, how are they likely to react to offensive moves?

Taken together, the answers to these five questions should provide the marketing strategist with a clear understanding of the competitive environment and, in particular, *who* the company is competing against, and *how* they compete; an example of this appears in Figure 4.1.

It is then against the background of the picture that emerges from this analysis that the marketing strategist can begin to formulate strategy. In the example cited in Figure 4.1, for example, the central issue for Kodak revolved around the costs, risks, and possible long-term returns from penetrating new markets in instant cameras and office copiers, as opposed to sustaining and defending the company's position as the market leader in the photographic paper market. The principal environmental inputs to the company's strategic planning process at this time were therefore competitive forces and new technology.

Having developed a picture of the market in this way, the analysis can then be taken a step further by a compilation of each competitor's likely response profile; the various inputs needed for this are illustrated in Figure 4.2.

In using this model, the strategist begins by focusing upon the competitor's current strategy and then moves successively through an examination of competitive strengths and weaknesses; the assumptions that the competitor appears to hold about the industry and itself; and then, finally, the competitor's probable future goals and the factors which drive it. It is an understanding of

**FIGURE 4.1**
*The competitive environment for selected Eastman Kodak products in the late 1970s*

| Kodak's products | Principal competitor(s) | Kodak's market position | Intensity and bases of competition | Likelihood of new entrants | Kodak's core strategy |
|---|---|---|---|---|---|
| Instant cameras and instant film | Polaroid | Challenger to a well-established leader | High and increasing with greater emphasis being placed on innovation | High | Penetration pricing to sell cameras as fast as possible to build a base for the sales of film |
| Photographic paper | Fuji Photo Film Co | Leader but being threatened by Fuji and other Japanese companies | High – the attack is based on lower prices and statements of quality | Medium | Share maintenance by emphasizing the quality of Kodak paper and making consumers aware that some processors do not use Kodak paper |
| Office copiers | Xerox, IBM, 3M | Late entrant to a highly competitive market in which Xerox held a 75 per cent share | Very high with ever greater emphasis being given to innovation, cost and service | Very high (particularly from Japanese firms) | The establishment of a separate sales and service network utilizing the firm's image and marketing capabilities in the microfilm equipment area |

Source: Adapted from 'The Market Mishandles a Blue Chip', *Business Week*, 20 June 1977.

**FIGURE 4.2**
*Identifying a
competitor's
response profile*

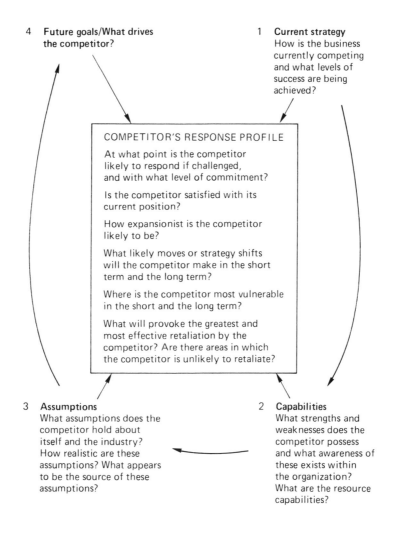

these four dimensions that then allows the marketing strategist to begin compiling the detail of the response profile and to answer four principal questions:

1 Is the competitor satisfied with its current position?
2 What moves is the competitor likely to make?
3 In which segments or areas of technology is the competitor most vulnerable?
4 What move on our part is likely to provoke the most effective retaliation by the competitor?

Against the background of the answers to those questions, the marketing strategist needs then to consider one further issue: where are we most vulnerable to any move on the part of each competitor and what can we realistically do in order to reduce this vulnerability?

**Porter's
Approach to
Competitive
Structure
Analysis**

Undoubtedly one of the major contributions in recent years to our understanding of the ways in which the competitive environment influences strategy has been provided by Michael Porter (1980, Ch. 1). Porter's work, which is discussed in detail in Chapter 10, is based on the idea that 'competition in an industry is rooted in its underlying economics, and competitive forces that go well beyond the established combatants in a particular industry' (1979, p. 138). He has also emphasized that the first determinant of a firm's profitability is the attractiveness of the industry in which it operates. The second determinant is competition:

> The second central question in competitive strategy is a firm's relative position within its industry. Positioning determines whether a firm's profitability is above or

below the industry average.... The fundamental basis of above average performance in the long run is sustainable competitive advantage.

This leads Porter to suggest that the nature and intensity of competition within any industry is determined by the interaction of five key forces:

1 the threat of new entrants;
2 the power of buyers;
3 the threat of substitutes;
4 the extent of competitive rivalry;
5 the power of suppliers.

This work is, as we commented above, examined in Chapter 10 and the reader may therefore find it of value to turn to that chapter before going any further and attempting to answer the five questions referred to earlier.

## 4.3 AGAINST WHOM ARE WE COMPETING?

**Identifying Present Competitors and New Entrants**

Although the answer to the question of who it is that a company is competing against might appear straightforward, the range of actual and potential competitors faced by a company is often far broader than appears to be the case at first sight. The strategist should therefore avoid competitive myopia both by adopting a broad perspective and recognizing that, in general, companies tend to overestimate the capabilities of large competitors and either underestimate or ignore those of smaller ones. In the 1970s, for example, the large manufacturers of computers were preoccupied with competing against one another and failed for some time to recognize the emergence and growing threat in the PC market posed by what were at the time small companies such as Apple.

In a more general sense, business history is full of examples of companies that have seemingly been taken by surprise by organizations they had failed to identify as competitors, or whose competitive capability they drastically underestimated. In Chapter 9, for example, we discuss the experiences of the Swiss watch industry which was brought to its knees in the late 1960s and early 1970s by new manufacturers of inexpensive watches that incorporated digital technology, a technology that, ironically, the Swiss themselves had developed. Equally, in the reprographic market, companies such as Gestetner suddenly and unexpectedly found themselves in the 1970s having to fight aggressive new entrants to the market such as Xerox. Xerox entered this market with a new, faster, cleaner, and infinitely more convenient product to which Gestetner, together with a number of other companies in the market at the time, experienced difficulties in responding. Similarly, the British and US television and motorcycle manufacturers either failed to recognize the Japanese threat or underestimated their expansionist objectives. The result today is that neither country has a domestic manufacturing industry of any size in either of these sectors. Less drastic but in many ways equally fundamental problems have been experienced in the car industry.

It is because of examples such as these that astute strategists have long acknowledged the difficulties of defining the boundaries of an industry and have recognized that companies are more likely to be taken by surprise and hit hard by *latent* competitors than by *current* competitors whose patterns of marketing behaviour are largely predictable. It is therefore possible to see competition operating at four levels:

1 *Competition consists only of those companies that offer a similar product or service to the target market, utilize a similar technology, and exhibit similar degrees of vertical integration.* Thus, Nestlé sees General Foods with its Maxwell House brand as a similar competitor in the instant coffee market, while Penguin sees its direct competitors in the chocolate snack bar market to be Kit-Kat's six pack, Twix and Club.

2 *Competition consists of all companies operating in the same product or service category.* Penguin's indirect competitors, for example, consist of crisps and ice-creams.
3 *Competition consists of all companies manufacturing or supplying products that deliver the same service.* Thus, long-distance coach operators compete not just against each other, but also against railways, cars, planes and motorcycles.
4 *Competition consists of all companies competing for the same spending power.* An example of this is the American motorcycle manufacturer, Harley Davidson, which does not necessarily see itself as competing directly with other motorcycle manufacturers. Instead, for many buyers it is a choice between a Harley Davidson motorcycle and a major consumer durable such as a conservatory or a boat; this is discussed in greater detail in Illustration 4.1.

---

## Illustration 4.1: Harley Davidson and Its Perception of Competition

Harley Davidson, the last remaining American motorcycle, is seen by many as one of the icons of the design world. As a symbol of freedom and adventure, the socio-economic profile of Harley Davidson owners differs significantly from that of virtually all other motorcycle riders. The late Malcolm Forbes, the owner of *Forbes* magazine, for example, rode Harleys with his 'gang' called the Capitalist Tools and did much to promote the bike among clean-cut executives known as Rich Urban Bikers – RUBs. This image has been reinforced by the bike's appearance in numerous commercials, including a Levis' advertisement in which a monstrous Harley is ridden on to a Wall Street dealing-room floor.

Although it is acknowledged that the bikes are technically antiquated, few current or aspiring owners see this as a drawback. Most Harley owners do not actually ride them a great deal. They are, as one commentator has observed, social statements rather than forms of transport. One consequence of this is that Harley Davidson, at least in the UK, competes only very indirectly with other motorcycle manufacturers. Instead, as Steve Dennis of Harley Street, a dealership specializing in used and customized bikes, puts it: 'We're competing against conservatories and swimming pools, not other bikes.'

*Source:* Sunday Times, *23 September 1990*

---

It should be apparent from this that the marketing strategist needs not only to identify those competitors who reflect the same general approach to the market, but also to consider those who 'intersect' the company in each market, who possibly approach it from a different perspective, and who ultimately might pose either a direct or an indirect threat. As part of this, he needs also to identify potential new entrants to the market and, where it appears necessary, develop contingency plans to neutralize their competitive effect. Newcomers to a market can, as Abell and Hammond (1979, p. 52) have pointed out, enter from any one of several starting points:

- They already sell to your customers, but expand their participation to include new customer functions which you currently satisfy (e.g. they initially sell a component of a computer system and expand into other system components which you supply).
- They already satisfy customer functions which you satisfy but expand their participation into your customer market from activities in other customer

84 *Strategic Marketing Management*

markets (e.g. they initially sell pumps for oil exploration only and then expand into the marine pump business where you are active).
- They already operate in an 'upstream' or 'downstream' business (e.g. Texas Instruments entered calculators from its position as a semi-conductor manufacturer, while some calculator manufacturers have integrated backwards into the manufacture of semi-conductors).
- They enter as a result of 'unrelated' diversification.

Taken together, these comments lead to two distinct viewpoints of competition: the industry point of view and the market point of view.

## The Industry Perspective of Competition

The industry perception of competition is implicit in the majority of discussions of marketing strategy. Here, an industry is seen to consist of firms offering a product or class of products or services that are close substitutes for one another; a close substitute in these circumstances is seen to be a product for which there is a high cross-elasticity of demand. An example of this would be a dairy product such as butter, where if the price rises a proportion of consumers will switch to margarine. A logical starting point for competitor analysis therefore involves understanding the industry's competitive patterns, since it is this which determines the underlying competitive dynamics. A model of this process appears in Figure 4.3.

**FIGURE 4.3**
*The competitive dynamics of an industry*

SOURCE: Adapted from Scherer (1980), p. 4

From this it can be seen that competitive dynamics are influenced initially by conditions of supply and demand. These in turn determine the *industry structure* which then influences *industry conduct* and, subsequently, *industry performance*.

Arguably the most significant single element in this model is the structure of the industry itself, and in particular the number of sellers, their relative market shares, and the degree of differentiation that exists between the competing companies and products; this is illustrated in Figure 4.4.

**FIGURE 4.4**
*Five industry structure types*

|  |  | Undifferentiated product | Differentiated product |
|---|---|---|---|
| Number of sellers | One | 1 Pure monopoly | |
| | Few | 2 Pure oligopoly | 3 Differentiated oligopoly |
| | Many | 4 Monopolistic competition | 5 Pure competition |

*Characteristics and marketing implications*

1 *Pure monopoly*: prices tend to be high, there is little advertising, service levels tend to be low, and barriers to entry often exist.
2 *Pure oligopoly*: differentiation is difficult to achieve and prices are set at the going rate. The only way in which to achieve a sustainable competitive advantage is by means of cost reductions.
3 *Differentiated oligopoly*: differentiation is achieved by pursuing a strategy of quality, adding features or styling. The extent to which leadership or premium pricing can be achieved is a measure of the success of the strategy.
4 *Monopolistic competition*: companies typically focus on particular market segments where scope exists either for minimizing the degree of direct competition or in which scope for premium pricing exists.
5 *Pure competition*: at its most extreme, there is no scope for differentiation and prices are at the same level. Advertising is only worthwhile if it can create a degree of psychological differentiation (where this is feasible, the market should be more correctly labelled as monopolistically competitive). Relative profit levels are directly determined by each company's ability to manage costs.

The interrelated issue of the number of sellers and their relative market shares has long been the focus of analysis by economists who have typically categorized an industry in terms of five types:

1 an absolute monopoly in which because of patents, licences, scale economics, or some other factor, only one firm provides the product or service;
2 a pure oligopoly in which a few firms produce broadly the same commodity;
3 a differentiated oligopoly where a few firms produce products that are partially differentiated;
4 monopolistic competition in which the industry has many firms offering a differentiated product or service;
5 pure competition in which numerous firms offer broadly the same product or service.

Although industries can at any given time be categorized in these terms, competitive structures do of course change. British Rail, for example, faced significant competition from National Express coaches after deregulation within the industry in 1980 and was forced into making a series of changes to its marketing strategy. Equally, patterns of competition in many other industries such as cars, consumer electronics, and white goods, have changed dramatically in a relatively short period as the result of the growth of import penetration. In the case of white goods such as refrigerators, washing machines, tumble driers and freezers, for example, the domestically-based manufacturers such as Hoover and Hotpoint found themselves in the 1970s facing new, aggressive and often price-based competition from, among others, Zanussi, Indesit, Electrolux and Candy. The issue that then needs to be faced is how best the company can respond.

Although a substantial increase in levels of import penetration are in many ways the most conspicuous causes of a change in competitive structures, a series of other factors exist which can have equally dramatic implications for the nature and bases of competition. These include:

- changes within the distribution channels – the emergence of large national DIY retailers such as B & Q and Do-It-All, for example, has led to a shift in the balance of power between manufacturers and retailers, with the retailers adopting an ever more proactive stance regarding product acceptance, new product development, price points, and advertising support;
- changes in the supplier base;
- legislation;
- the emergence of new technology.

## The Market Perspective of Competition

As an alternative to the industry perspective of competition, which takes as its starting point companies making the same product or offering the same service, we can focus on companies that try to satisfy the same customer needs or which serve the same customer groups. Theodore Levitt has long been a strong advocate of this perspective and it was this which was at the heart of his classic article 'Marketing Myopia'. In this article, Levitt (1960, pp. 45–56), pointed to a series of examples of organizations that had failed to recognize how actual and potential customers viewed the product or service being offered. Thus in the case of railways, the railway companies concentrated on competing with one another and in doing this failed to recognize that because customers were looking for transport, they compared the railways with planes, buses and cars. The essence of the market perspective of competition therefore involves giving full recognition to the broader range of products or services that are capable of satisfying customer needs. This should, in turn, lead to the marketing strategist identifying a broader set of actual and potential competitors and adopting a more effective approach to long-run market planning.

## 4.4 EVALUATING COMPETITIVE RELATIONSHIPS AND ANALYSING HOW THEY COMPETE

Any analysis of *how* firms compete falls into four parts:

1  What is each competitor's current strategy?
2  How are they performing?
3  What are their strengths and weaknesses?
4  What can we expect from each competitor in the future?

However, before moving on to the detail of these four areas, the strategist should spend time identifying what is already known about each competitor. There are numerous examples of companies which have collected information on competitors only to find out at a later stage that this knowledge existed already within the organization, but that for one reason or another it had not been analysed or disseminated. In commenting on this, Davidson (1987, p. 133) has suggested that:

> Recorded data tends not to be analysed over time, and often fails to cross functional barriers. Observable data is typically recorded on a haphazard basis, with little evaluation. Opportunistic data is not always actively sought or disseminated.

This failure to collect, disseminate or make full use of competitive information is for the majority of organizations a perennial problem and often leads to the same information being collected more than once. It is, however, an issue that we discuss in greater detail at a later stage, and at this point we will therefore do no more than draw attention to it.

In attempting to arrive at a detailed understanding of competitive relationships, it is essential that each competitor is analysed separately, since any general analysis provides the strategist with only a partial understanding of competitors, and tells little either about potential threats that might emerge, or opportunities that can be exploited. It is worth remembering, however, that what competitors have done in the past can often provide a strong indication of what they will do in the future. This is particularly the case when previous strategies have been conspicuously successful. Companies such as Mars, for example, have traditionally pursued an objective of market leadership, while the Japanese are often willing to accept long pay-back periods. Recognition of points such as these should then be used to guide the ways in which strategy is developed.

Other factors that need to be borne in mind include:

- patterns of investment in plant;
- links with other competitors;
- patterns of advertising expenditure;
- relative cost positions;
- major changes in the senior management structure and in particular the appointment of a new chief executive who might act as an agent for change.

## Identifying Strategic Groups

In the majority of industries competitors can be categorized, at least initially, on the basis of the similarities and differences that exist in the strategies being pursued. The strategist can then begin to construct a picture of the market showing the strategic groups that exist; for our purposes here, a strategic group can be seen to consist of those firms within the market that are following a broadly similar strategy. An example of how strategic groupings can be identified is illustrated in Figure 4.5.

Having identified strategic groups in this way, the strategist then needs to identify the relative position and strength of each competitor. This can be done in one of several ways, including the categorizing of firms on the basis of whether

**FIGURE 4.5**
*Strategic groups in the construction industry*

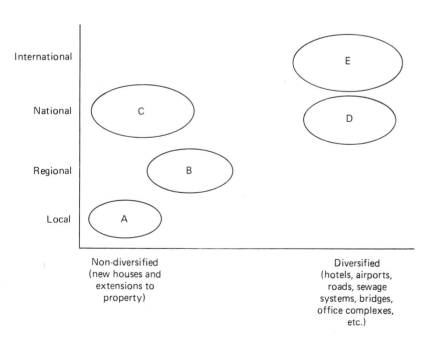

their position within the market overall and within the strategic group is dominant, strong, favourable, tenable, weak or non-viable. Having done this, the strategist needs to consider the bases of any competitive advantages that exist; this is illustrated in Figure 4.6.

**FIGURE 4.6**
*The five types of competitive status and the implications for competitive advantage*

| Level | Competitive status | Examples |
|-------|--------------------|----------|
| 1 | One or more sizeable advantages | Honda, Sony, Seiko & Coca Cola |
| 2 | A series of small advantages which combine to form one large advantage | McDonald's |
| 3 | Advantages exist but these are either not recognized or not exploited fully | |
| 4 | No obvious or sustainable competitive advantages | Petrol retailers, estate agents and high street banks |
| 5 | Competitive disadvantages because of the organization's limited size, inflexibility, inefficient manufacturing practices, distribution networks, cost structures, culture, lack of skills, or poor image | Eastern European car manufacturers |

SOURCE: Adapted from Davidson (1987), p. 160

The experiences of many companies suggest that the easiest starting point from which to improve an organization's competitive position is Level 3, since this can often be achieved by good management. One example of a company that did this with considerable success was Beecham with its Lucozade brand.

There are several points that emerge from identifying strategic groups in this way. The first is that the height of the barriers to entry and exit can vary significantly from one group to another. The second is that the choice of a strategic group determines which companies are to be the firm's principal competitors. Recognizing this, a new entrant would then have to develop a series of competitive advantages to overcome, or at least to neutralize, the competitive advantages of others in the group.

There is, of course, competition not just *within* strategic groups but also *between* them, since not only will target markets develop or contract over time and hence prove to be either more or less attractive to other firms, but customers might not fully recognize major differences in the offers of each group. One consequence of this is that there is likely to be a degree of comparison buying across groups, something which again argues the case for the marketing strategist to adopt a market, rather than an industry, perspective of competition.

Although in Figure 4.6 we have made use of just two dimensions in plotting strategic groupings, a variety of other factors can typically be expected to be used to differentiate between companies and to help in the process of identifying group membership. A summary of these characteristics appears in Figure 4.7.

The particular relevance to any given industry of these characteristics is in practice influenced by several factors, the most significant of which are the history and development of the industry, the types of environmental forces at work, the nature of the competitive activities of the various firms, and so on. It should be evident from this that each company does therefore have a different strategic make-up which needs to be profiled separately. Often, however, a strategy proves difficult to describe since it encompasses so many different dimensions, but Abell and Hammond (1979, p. 53) have outlined a useful framework for thinking about the strategic decision process:

- How is the competitor defining the business in terms of customer groups, customer functions, and technologies, and how vertically integrated is he? And at a lower level of aggregation, how is he segmenting the market and which segments are being pursued?
- What mission does this business have in his overall portfolio of businesses? Is it being managed for sales growth? market share? net income? ROI? cash? What goals does he appear to have for each major segment of the business?
- What is his marketing mix, manufacturing policy, R & D policy, purchasing policy, physical distribution policy, etc.?
- What size are his budgets and how are they allocated?

In so far as it is possible to generalize, it is the third of these areas in which marketing managers find it most easy to collect information. This should not, however, be seen as a reason for ignoring the other three areas, since it is here that insights to what really drives the competition can best be gained.

This leads us to a position in which we are able to begin to construct a detailed list of the areas in which we need to collect competitive information. In the case of each competitor's current performance, this list includes sales, growth rates and patterns, market share, profit, profitability (return on investment), margins, net income, investment patterns and cash flow. Other areas to which attention needs to be paid include the identification of the importance of each market sector in which the competitor is operating, since this allows the marketing strategist to probe the areas of weakness or least concern at the minimum of risk.

**FIGURE 4.7**
*Some characteristics for identifying strategic groups*

- *Size* and relative share
- The extent of *product* or *service diversity*
- The degree of *geographic coverage*
- The number and type of *market segments served*
- The type of *distribution channels* used
- The *branding* philosophy
- Product or service *quality*
- *Market position* (leader or follower)
- *Technological position* (leader or follower)
- *R & D capability*
- *Performance*
- *Cost structure* and behaviour
- Patterns of *ownership*
- Organizational *culture*
- The degree of *vertical integration*
- *Reputation*

SOURCE: Adapted from Johnson and Scholes (1988), p. 75

**The Character of Competition**

The final area that we need to consider when examining how firms compete is what can loosely be termed 'the character of competition'. Because competition within a market is influenced to a very high degree by the nature of customer behaviour, the character of competition can not only take many forms, but is also likely to change over time. One fairly common way of examining the character of competition is therefore by means of an analysis of the changes taking place in the composition of *value added* by different firms. (The term 'value added' is used to describe the amount by which selling prices are greater than the cost of the bought out goods or services embodied in market offerings.) An analysis of changes in the value added component can therefore give the strategist an understanding of the relative importance of such factors as product and process development, selling, after-sales service, price, and so on, as the product moves through the life cycle. See Figure 4.8 for an example of this for a hypothetical product.

**FIGURE 4.8**
*A comparison of
the value added
components across
the product life
cycle*

SOURCE: Adapted from Abell and Hammond (1979), p. 59

The marketing strategist can also arrive at a measure of the character of competition by considering the extent to which each competitor develops new total industry demand (primary demand) or quite simply competes with others for a share of existing demand (selective demand). When a competitor's objective is the stimulation of primary demand, it is likely that efforts will focus upon identifying and developing new market segments. When, however, a competitor concentrates upon stimulating selective demand, the focus shifts to an attempt to satisfy existing customers more effectively than other companies. The obvious consequence of this is that the intensity of competition on a day-to-day basis is likely to increase significantly.

## 4.5 IDENTIFYING COMPETITORS' OBJECTIVES

Having identified the organization's principal competitors and their strategies, we need then to focus upon each competitor's objectives. In other words, what drives each competitor's behaviour? A starting point in arriving at an answer to this is to assume that each competitor will aim for profit maximization either in the short term or the long term. In practice, of course, maximization is an unrealistic objective that for a wide variety of reasons many companies are willing to sacrifice. A further assumption can be made – that each competitor has a variety of objectives, each of which has a different weight. These objectives might typically include cash flow, technological leadership, market share growth, service leadership, or overall market leadership. Gaining an insight into this mix of objectives allows the strategist to arrive at tentative conclusions regarding how a competitor will respond to a competitive thrust. A firm pursuing market share growth is likely to react far more quickly and aggressively to a price cut or to a substantial increase in advertising than a firm that is aiming for, say, technological leadership.

The differences that exist between the objectives of companies has been referred to by a variety of writers, including Doyle, Saunders and Wong (1986) who have contrasted the objectives typically pursued by Japanese and British firms. See Illustration 4.2 for a discussion of their work.

In a general sense, however, company objectives are, as is pointed out in Chapter 6, influenced by a wide variety of factors, but particularly the organization's size, history, culture, and the breadth of the operating base.

# Illustration 4.2: The Difference Between Japanese and British Company Objectives

In 1986, Doyle, Saunders and Wong published the results of a study in which they compared the objectives and strategies of 15 leading Japanese companies operating within the United Kingdom with those of their British counterparts. Their findings proved to be illuminating, and highlighted some of the principal causes of Japanese success. In commenting subsequently on their research, Saunders (1987, pp. 24–26) has given emphasis to several points:

> There was a striking contrast between these two national groups in the clarity of their strategic thinking, and in their determination to achieve the objectives that they set themselves. Indeed, only one-third of the British (compared with two-thirds of the Japanese) even believed themselves to be good at sales and marketing. When entering a new market, the British usually arrived late, and few had a strong commitment to it. Two-thirds of UK companies gave defensive reasons for entry: 'We had to in order to survive'. Several admitted that they 'had never really thought it out'. In contrast, the Japanese were much more professional: over 70 per cent said that their moves were 'part of a planned global expansion', or related to the 'potential of the UK market'. Once in the market, the British lack of commitment to beating the competition was again striking. Some 87 per cent of the Japanese gave 'aggressive growth' or 'market domination' as their goal, but only 20 per cent of the British thought these targets applied to them. Maintenance of the status quo or the prevention of decline were the most typical British objectives. Short term profit was also much more important to the UK companies (93 per cent) than to the Japanese (40 per cent). The British were willing to allow their market position to be eroded in order to bolster short term profitability.

He went on to emphasize the difference that exists between the strategic focus, customer targets, competitor targets, differential advantages, management of the marketing mix, and approaches to organization and implementation.

In the case of strategic focus, for example, the Japanese concentrated on stimulating primary demand, entering newly emerging market segments and building market share by weaning customers away from their competitors. By contrast, the British tended to focus on cost cutting, range reduction and rationalization as ways of preventing margin erosion.

In the area of customer targets, equally significant differences emerged with the Japanese concentrating on high-potential segments while the British either made little attempt to focus their efforts or positioned themselves at the lower and cheaper end of the market.

It was perhaps because of this that only 20 per cent of Japanese companies in the study saw European firms as their major rivals; the remainder saw their main competition in the UK coming from other Japanese groups. This was in turn reflected in the recognition by many British companies of their lack of skill at differentiating themselves from the competition. By contrast, 87 per cent of the Japanese pointed to superior quality, reliability and customer service as their bases of differentiation and competitive advantage.

*Source: Saunders, J., 'Marketing and Competitive Success' in* The Marketing Book, *edited by Baker, M. (1987), Heinemann. See also: Doyle, P., Saunders, J. and Wong, V. (1986), 'A Comparative Study of Japanese Marketing Strategies in the British Market',* Journal of International Business Studies, *17(1), Spring.*

Where, for example, a company is part of a larger organization, a competitive thrust always runs the risk of leading to retaliation by the parent company on what might appear to be a disproportionate scale. Conversely, the parent company may see an attack on one of its divisions as being a nuisance, but little more, and not bother to respond in anything other than a cursory fashion. This has been discussed in some detail by Rothschild (1989, Ch. 5) who argues that the potentially most dangerous competitive move involves attacking a global company for which this is the only business.

It follows that the marketing strategist should give explicit consideration to the relative importance of each market to a competitor in order to understand the probable level of commitment that exists. By doing this, it is possible to estimate the level of effort that each competitor would then logically make in order to defend its position. Several factors are likely to influence this level of commitment, the five most important of which are likely to be:

1 the proportion of company profits that this market sector generates;
2 the managerial perceptions of the market's growth opportunities;
3 the levels of profitability that exist currently and that are expected to exist in the future;
4 any interrelationships between this and any other product or market sector in which the organization operates;
5 managerial cultures – in some companies, for example, any threat will be responded to aggressively almost irrespective of whether it is cost effective.

As a general rule of thumb, therefore, competitive retaliation will be strong whenever the company feels its core business is being attacked. Recognizing this, the marketing strategist should concentrate on avoiding areas which are likely to lead to this sort of response, unless of course the target has a strong strategic rationale. This sort of issue is discussed in detail in Chapter 10.

## 4.6  IDENTIFYING AND EVALUATING COMPETITORS' STRENGTHS AND WEAKNESSES

By this stage it should be apparent that the identification and evaluation of competitors' strengths and weaknesses is at the very heart of a well-developed competitive strategy. The marketing strategist should as a first step therefore concentrate upon collecting information under a number of headings as a prelude to a full comparative assessment. These include:

- sales;
- market share;
- cost and profit levels and how they appear to be changing over time (discussed in some detail in Chapter 12);
- cash flows;
- return on investment;
- investment patterns;
- production processes;
- levels of capacity utilization;
- organizational culture;
- products and the product portfolio;
- product quality;
- the size and pattern of the customer base;
- the levels of brand loyalty;
- dealers and distribution channels;
- marketing and selling capabilities;

- operations and physical distribution;
- financial capabilities;
- management capabilities and attitudes to risk;
- human resources, their capability and flexibility;
- previous patterns of response;
- ownership patterns and, in the case of divisionalized organizations, the expectations of corporate management.

Obtaining this sort of information typically proves to be more difficult in some instances than in others. Industrial markets, for example, rarely have the same wealth of published data that is commonly available in consumer markets. This should not, however, be used as an excuse for not collecting the information, but rather emphasizes the need for a clearly developed competitive information system which channels information under a wide variety of headings to a central point. This information needs to be analysed and disseminated as a prelude to being fed into the strategy process.

The sources of this information will obviously vary from industry to industry, but will include most frequently the sales force, trade shows, industry experts, the trade press, distributors, suppliers and, perhaps most importantly, customers. Customer information can be gained in several ways, although periodically a firm may find it of value to conduct primary research among customers, suppliers and distributors to arrive at a profile of competitors within the market. An example of this appears in Figure 4.9 where current and potential buyers have been asked to rate the organization and its four major competitors on a series of attributes. A similar exercise can then be conducted among suppliers and distributors in order to build up a more detailed picture.

**FIGURE 4.9**

*The comparative assessment of competitors*

| Significant buying factors | Our company | Competitors | | |
|---|---|---|---|---|
| | | *1* | *2* | *3* |
| *Products* | | | | |
| Product design | Good | Exc | Fair | Good |
| Product quality | Good | Exc | Fair | Exc |
| Product performance | Good | Good | Fair | Good |
| Breadth of product line | Fair | Fair | Poor | Good |
| Depth of product line | Fair | Fair | Poor | Good |
| Reliability | Good | Exc | Fair | Exc |
| Running costs | Fair | Good | Equal | Good |
| *Promotion and pricing* | | | | |
| Advertising/sales promotion | Fair | Exc | Fair | Good |
| Image and reputation | Fair | Exc | Fr/Pr | Exc |
| Product literature | Poor | Exc | Poor | Good |
| Price | Equal | Fair | Good | Equal |
| *Selling and distribution* | | | | |
| Sales force calibre | Fair | Good | Poor | Good |
| Sales force experience/knowledge | Fair | Good | Fair | Exc |
| Geographical coverage | Good | Good | Poor | Good |
| Sales force/customer relations | Fair | Exc | Poor | Exc |
| *Service* | | | | |
| Customer service levels | Fair | Exc | Poor | Exc |
| Performance against promise | Fair | Exc | Poor | Exc |

The classification of factors from excellent (Exc) to poor should be determined by marketing intelligence, including studies of the perceptions of current and potential buyers, as well as those of suppliers and distributors.

**Competitive Product Portfolios**

In many cases, one of the most useful methods of gaining an insight into a competitor's strengths, weaknesses and general level of capability is by means of portfolio analysis. The techniques of portfolios analysis, which include the Boston Consulting Group matrix, are by now well developed and are discussed in detail in Chapter 9. The reader might therefore find it of value at this stage to turn to page 223 in order to understand more fully the comments below.

Having plotted each major competitor's portfolio, the marketing strategist needs to consider a series of questions:

1  What degree of internal balance exists within each portfolio? Which competitors, for example, appear to have few, if any, 'cash cows' but a surfeit of 'question marks' or 'dogs'? Which of the competitors appears to have one or more promising 'stars' that might in the future pose a threat?
2  What are the likely cash flow implications for each competitor of his portfolio? Does it appear likely, for example, that he will be vulnerable in the near future because of the cash demands of a disproportionate number of 'question marks' and 'stars'?
3  What trends are apparent in each portfolio? A tentative answer to this question can be arrived at by plotting the equivalent growth-share display for a period three to five years earlier, and superimposing on this the current chart. A third display that reflects the likely development of the portfolio over the next few years, assuming present policies are maintained, can in turn then be superimposed on this to show the direction and rate of travel of each product or strategic business unit (SBU).
4  Which competitors' products look suited for growth and which for harvesting? What are the implications for us and in what ways might we possibly pre-empt any competitive actions?
5  Which competitor appears to be the most vulnerable to an attack? Which competitor looks likely to pose the greatest threat in the future?

In plotting a competitor's portfolio, the marketing strategist is quite obviously searching for areas of weaknesses which subsequently can be exploited. In commenting on this, Davidson (1987, pp. 139–40) identifies 17 major sources of vulnerability. A summary of his ideas appears in Illustration 4.3.

At this point it is perhaps worth uttering a word of caution. The marketing strategist should not of course limit competitive analysis just to a series of marketing factors, but should also focus upon other areas, including financial and production measures. In this way it is possible to identify far more clearly who, within the industry, is relatively weak and who might therefore be vulnerable to a price attack or a takeover. Equally, it can identify who within the industry should, by virtue of their financial strength or production flexibility, be avoided.

## 4.7 IDENTIFYING COMPETITORS' LIKELY RESPONSE PROFILES

Although a knowledge of a competitor's size, objectives and capability (strengths and weaknesses) can provide the strategist with a reasonable understanding of possible responses to company moves such as price cuts, new products, and so on, other factors need to be examined. One of the most important of these is the organization's culture, since it is this which ultimately determines how the firm will do business and hence how it will act in the future.

The issue of how a competitor is likely to behave in the future has two components. First, how is a competitor likely to respond to the general changes taking place in the external environment and, in particular, in the market-place?

# Illustration 4.3:  What Makes a Competitor Vulnerable?

A knowledge of a competitor's weaknesses can often be used to great effect by an astute marketing strategist. According to Davidson (1987, pp. 139–40), the sorts of factor that make a competitor vulnerable include:

- a lack of cash;
- low margins;
- poor growth;
- high cost operations or distribution;
- overdependence on one market;
- overdependence on one account;
- strength in falling sectors;
- short-term orientation;
- people problems;
- taking their eyes off the ball;
- predictability;
- product or service obsolescence/weakness;
- high market share;
- low market share;
- premium price positioning;
- slow moving/bureaucratic structures;
- fiscal year fixation.

*Source: J. H. Davidson, 1987,* Offensive Marketing, *Penguin*

Second, how is he likely to respond to specific competitive moves that we, or indeed any other company, might make? For some companies at least there is also a third question that needs to be considered: how likely is it that the competitor will initiate an aggressive move, and what form might this move be most likely to take? In posing questions such as these we are trying to determine where each competitive company is the most vulnerable, where it is the strongest, where the most appropriate battleground is likely to be, and how, if at all, it will respond.

Kotler (1988, p. 247) identifies four common reaction profiles among competitors:

1 *The laid-back competitor.* Some competitors do not react quickly or strongly to a given competitor move. They may feel that their customers are loyal; they may be harvesting the business; they may be slow in noticing the initiative; they may lack the funds to react. The firm must try to assess the reasons for the competitor's laid-back behavior.

2 *The selective competitor.* A competitor might react to certain types of assault and not to others. It might, for example, always respond to price cuts in order to signal that these are futile. But it might not respond to advertising expenditure increases, believing these to be less threatening. Knowing what a key competitor reacts to gives a clue as to the most feasible types of attack.

3 *The tiger competitor.* This company reacts swiftly and strongly to any assault on its terrain. Thus P & G does not let a new detergent come easily into the market. A tiger competitor is signalling that another firm had better avoid any attack because the defender is going to fight to the finish if attacked. It is always better to attack a sheep than a tiger.

4 *The stochastic competitor.* Some competitors do not exhibit a predictable reaction pattern. Such a competitor might or might not retaliate on any particular occasion, and there is no way to foresee what it will do based on its economics, history, or anything else.

This general theme has, in turn, been developed by Bruce Henderson (1982) of the Boston Consulting Group who, in discussing competition, argues that much depends on the competitive equilibrium. Henderson's comments on this have been summarized by Kotler (1988, p. 247) in the following way:

1 *If competitors are nearly identical and make their living in the same way, then their competitive equilibrium is unstable.*
   There is likely to be perpetual conflict in industries where competitive ability is at parity. This would describe 'commodity industries' where sellers have not found any major way to differentiate their costs or their offers. In such cases, the competitive equilibrium would be upset if any firm lowers its price. This is a strong temptation, especially for a competitor with overcapacity. This explains why price wars frequently break out in these industries.
2 *If a single major factor is the critical factor, then competitive equilibrium is unstable.*
   This would describe industries where cost differentiation opportunities exist through economies of scale, advanced technology, experiences curve learning, etc. In such industries, any company that achieves a cost breakthrough can cut its price and win market share at the expense of other firms who could only defend their market shares at great cost. Price wars frequently break out in these industries as a function of cost breakthroughs.
3 *If multiple factors may be critical factors, then it is possible for each competitor to have some advantage and be differentially attractive to some customers. The more the multiple factors that may provide an advantage, the more the number of competitors who can coexist. Each competitor has his competitive segment defined by the preference for the factor trade-offs that he offers.*
   This would describe industries where many opportunities exist for differentiating quality, service, convenience, and so on. If customers also place different values on these factors, then many firms can coexist through niching.
4 *The fewer the number of competitive variables that are critical, the fewer the number of competitors.*
   If only one factor is critical, then no more than two or three competitors are likely to coexist. Conversely, the larger the number of competitive variables, the larger the number of competitors, but each is likely to be smaller in its absolute size.
5 *A ratio of 2 to 1 in market share between any two competitors seems to be the equilibrium point at which it is neither practical nor advantageous for either competitor to increase or decrease share.*

**The Significance of Costs**

In attempting to come to terms with the structure of competition, the marketing strategist should also take account of *cost structures* and *cost behaviour*. Cost structure is usually defined as the ratio of variable to fixed costs and is typically capable of exerting a significant influence upon competitive behaviour. In businesses where, for example, the fixed costs are high, profits are sensitive to volume. Companies are therefore forced to behave in such a way that plants operate as near to full capacity as possible. Where demand is price sensitive, the industry is likely to be characterized by periodic bouts of aggressive price wars. Where, however, it is the case that variable costs are high, profits are influenced far more directly by changes in margins. Recognizing this, the marketing strategist needs to focus upon differentiating the product in such a way that prices and hence margins can be increased.

The second cost dimension is that of its behaviour over time and in particular how the organization can make use of learning and experience effects, as well as scale effects; these are discussed in detail in Chapters 12 and 16.

**The Influence of the Product Life Cycle**

Competitive behaviour is typically affected in several ways by the stage reached on the product life cycle (PLC). Although the product life cycle (see Chapter 9) is seen principally as a model of product and market evolution, it can also be used as a framework for examining probable competitive behaviour. Used in this way, it can help the strategist to anticipate changes in the character of competition. In the early stages of the life cycle, for example, advertising and promotion is generally high, and prices and margins are able to support this. The natural growth of the market allows firms to avoid competing in an overtly direct way. As maturity approaches and the rate of growth slows, firms are forced into more direct forms of competition, a situation which is in turn exacerbated by the often generally greater number of companies operating within the market. This greater intensity of competition manifests itself in several ways, but most commonly in a series of price reductions. The role of advertising changes as greater emphasis is placed upon the search for differentiation. In the final stages, some firms opt to leave the market, while others engage in perhaps even greater price competition as they fight for a share of a declining sales curve. It follows from this that the PLC is yet one more of the myriad of factors that the marketing strategist needs to consider in coming to terms with competitors.

# 4.8 THE COMPETITIVE INFORMATION SYSTEM (CIS)

It should be apparent from the discussion so far that the need for an effective competitive intelligence system (CIS) is paramount. In establishing such a system, there are five principal steps:

1 setting up the system and deciding what information is needed;
2 collecting the data;
3 analysing and evaluating the data;
4 disseminating the conclusions;
5 incorporating these conclusions into the subsequent strategy and feeding back the results so that the information system can be developed further.

The mechanics of an effective CIS are straightforward, as Davidson (1987, p. 134) has pointed out:

- Select key competitors to evaluate. Focus on three or four per market at most.
- Select and brief data collectors in each department. This should include people in sales, purchasing, engineering, marketing, R & D and finance.
- Apply the right resource levels to the task. It is usually worthwhile having at least a part-time competitive analyst, to chase, coordinate and evaluate competitive data.
- Insist on regular returns from data collectors.
- Publish regular tactical and strategic reports on competition. The tactical ones could be fortnightly and widely circulated. The strategic ones would be less frequent, perhaps quarterly, and go to senior management only.

The sources of data are, as we observed at an earlier stage, likely to vary significantly from one industry to another. However, a useful framework for data collection involves categorizing information on the basis of whether it is recorded, observed or opportunistic. The major sources of data under each of these headings is shown in Figure 4.10.

With regard to the question of precisely what information is needed, this will of course vary from one industry to another and from one company to another. It is, however, possible to identify with relative ease the sorts of headings under which information should be gathered; these are identified in Figure 4.11.

Given this information, the strategist should be able to determine far more precisely who is operating in the same strategic group. From here, he can then go on to decide far more readily who and when to attack and the basis on which this should be done. Equally, he is also able to decide who is to be avoided. Although these issues are discussed in some detail in Chapter 10, there are several points that can usefully be made at this stage.

**FIGURE 4.10**

*The major sources of competitive data*

| Recorded data | Observable data | Opportunistic data |
|---|---|---|
| Market research | Competitors' pricing | Raw material suppliers |
| Secondary data | Promotions | Equipment suppliers |
|   sources, e.g. Mintel | Patent applications | Trade shows |
| Business press | Competitive advertising | Customers |
| Trade press | Planning applications | Packaging suppliers |
| Technical journals | Sales force feedback | Distributors |
| BRAD (British Rate & | Buying competitors' | Sub-contractors |
|   Data) |   products and taking | Internal newsletters |
| Government sector |   them apart to | Disgruntled employees |
|   reports, e.g. |   determine costs of | Poaching competitors' |
|   Monopolies |   production and |   employees |
|   Commission |   manufacturing | Conferences |
| Stockbrokers' reports |   methods | Placing advertisements and |
| Credit reports | |   holding interviews for jobs |
| Annual reports | |   that do not exist in order |
| Public documents | |   to entice competitors' |
| | |   employees to spill the |
| | |   beans |
| | | Private investigators |

SOURCE: Adapted from Davidson (1987), p. 134

Assuming that the company is to go on the offensive, the strategist needs to begin by deciding *who* to attack. In essence, this represents a choice between strong and weak competitors, close and distant competitors, and good and bad competitors.

Although *weak competitors* are by their very nature the most vulnerable, the potential pay-off needs to be examined carefully. It may be the case, for example, that the share gained, while useful, is of little long-term strategic value since it takes the company into segments of the market offering little scope for growth. Equally, they may require substantial long term investment. By contrast, competing against *strong competitors* requires the firm to be far leaner, fitter and more aggressive, a point that has been argued in some considerable detail for almost two decades by Michael Porter, and which was developed further in his book *The Competitive Advantage of Nations* (1990).

The second decision involves deciding between *close* and *distant competitors*. We have already commented that the majority of companies compete against those within the strategic group they resemble the most. Thus, as we observed earlier, Nestlé's Nescafé is in direct competition with General Foods' Maxwell House. The strategist needs, however, in certain circumstances at least, to beware of destroying these close competitors, since the whole competitive base may then change. In commenting on this, Porter (1985, pp. 226–7) cites several examples:

> Bausch & Lomb in the late 1970s moved aggressively against other soft lens manufacturers with great success. However, this led one after another competitor to sell out to larger firms such as Revlon, Johnson & Johnson, and Schering-Plough, with the result that Bausch & Lomb now faced much larger competitors . . .

> A speciality rubber manufacturer attacked another speciality rubber manufacturer as its mortal enemy and took away market share. The damage to the other company allowed the speciality divisions of the large tyre companies to move quickly into speciality rubber markets, using them as a dumping ground for excess capacity.

Porter expands upon this line of argument by distinguishing between 'good' and 'bad' competitors. A good competitor, he suggests, is one who adheres to the rules, avoids aggressive price moves, favours a healthy industry, makes realistic assumptions about the industry growth prospects, and accepts the general status quo. Bad competitors, by contrast, violate the unspoken and unwritten rules.

**FIGURE 4.11**
*What companies
need to know about
their competitors*

Although it is not possible to develop an exhaustive list of headings under which competitive information should be collected, these are nine principal areas to which the strategist should pay attention on a regular basis:

1 **Sales**
Number of units sold
Sales by product line
Sales trends
Market shares
Share trends

2 **Customers**
Customer profiles
Buying motives
Patterns of usage
New accounts/buyers
Lost accounts/buyers
Proportion of repeat business/degree of brand loyalty
Depth of brand loyalty
Identity and image among buyers
Satisfaction levels with the product's design, performance, quality and reliability
The existence of special relationships

3 **Products**
Breadth and depth of the product range
Comparative product performance levels
New product policies
Investment in R & D
New product introduction and modifications
Size assortments
New packaging

4 **Advertising and promotion**
Expenditure levels and patterns
Effectiveness
Product literature
Sales promotions
Customers' brand preferences
Image and levels of recognition

5 **Distribution and sales force**
Types of distribution network used
Relationships and the balance of power
Cost structures
Flexibility
Special terms and the existence of agreements
Dealer objectives
Distributors' performance levels

Size, calibre and experience of the sales force
Sales force customer coverage
Levels of technical assistance available
Dealer support levels and capabilities
Stock levels
Shelf facings
After-sales service capabilities
Customer service philosophy
Location of warehouses
Degree of customer satisfaction

6 **Price**
Cost levels
Cost structure
List prices and discounts by product and customer type
Special terms

7 **Finance**
Performance levels
Margins
Depth of financial resources
Patterns of ownership and financial flexibility

8 **Management**
Objectives (short and long term)
Philosophy and culture
Expectations
Attitudes to risk
Identity of key executives
Skills and special expertise
Competitive strategies
'Ownership' of strategies and the commitment to them
Organizational structures
Investment plans
Key success factors

9 **Other**
Sales per employee
Plant capacity utilization
Type of equipment used
Labour rates and relationships
Raw material purchasing methods
Principal suppliers
Degree of vertical and horizontal integration
Commitment to market sectors.

They engage in unnecessarily aggressive and often foolhardy moves, expand capacity in large steps, slash margins and take significant risks.

The implications of this is that good competitors should work hard to develop an industry that consists only of good companies. They can do this, Kotler (1988, p. 252) suggests, by coalitions, selective retaliation and careful licensing. The pay-off will then be that:

1 competitors will not seek to destroy each other by behaving irrationally;
2 they will follow the rules of the industry;
3 each player will be differentiated in some way;
4 companies will try to earn share increases rather than buying them.

He goes on from this to develop the larger point:

> that a company really needs and benefits from competitors. The existence of competitors confers such strategic benefits as the following: (1) They lower the antitrust (monopolies) risk, (2) they may increase total demand, (3) they lead to more differentiation, (4) they provide a cost umbrella for the less efficient producers, (5) they share the cost of market development and legitimise a new technology, (6) they improve bargaining power versus labour or regulators, and (7) they may serve less-attractive segments.

## 4.9 SUMMARY

Within this chapter we have emphasized the need for constant competitor analysis and for the information generated to be fed into the strategic marketing planning process.

Although the need for competitor analysis has long been acknowledged, a substantial number of organizations still seemingly fail to allocate to the process the resources that are needed, relying instead upon a far less detailed understanding of competitive capabilities and priorities. It does therefore need to be recognized that if an effective system of competitive monitoring is to be developed, and the results used in the way intended, it is essential that top management commitment to the process exists.

In developing a structured approach to competitive analysis the strategist needs to give explicit consideration to five questions:

1 Who is it that we are competing against?
2 What are their objectives?
3 What strategies are they pursuing and how successful are they?
4 What strengths and weaknesses do they possess?
5 How are they likely to behave and, in particular, how are they likely to react to offensive moves?

Taken together, the answers to these five questions can be used to develop a detailed response profile for each competitive organization, and the probable implications for competitive behaviour fed into the planning process.

Several methods of categorizing competitors were discussed, including Porter's notion of strategic groups. We then examined the ways in which these ideas can be taken a step further by focusing upon the character of competition and how this is likely to change over the course of the product life cycle.

Particular emphasis was given to the need for the strategist to take account of each competitor's probable objectives, its competitive stance, and the relative importance of each market sector. Again, a variety of frameworks that can help in this process of understanding were discussed, including portfolio analysis.

Against this background we discussed the ways in which an effective competitive intelligence system (CIS) might be developed and the nature of the inputs that are required. Much of the information needed for such a system is often readily available, and emphasis needs therefore to be placed upon developing a framework that will ensure that this information is channelled, analysed and disseminated in the strategically most useful way. This theme is further developed in Chapter 18.

# 5 | Approaches to customer analysis

## 5.1 LEARNING OBJECTIVES

When you have read this chapter you should be able to understand:

(a) the factors that influence consumer behaviour;
(b) the structure of the consumer buying decision process;
(c) the nature of organizational buying;
(d) how an understanding of buying processes can be used in the development of marketing strategy.

## 5.2 INTRODUCTION

It has long been recognized that marketing planning is ultimately driven by the marketing strategist's perception of how and why customers behave as they do, and how they are likely to respond to the various elements of the marketing mix. See Illustration 5.1.

In the majority of markets, however, buyers differ enormously in terms of their buying dynamics. The task faced by the marketing strategist in coming to terms with these differences is consequently complex. In consumer markets, for example, not only do buyers typically differ in terms of their age, income, educational levels and geographical location, but more fundamentally in terms of their personality, their lifestyles and their expectations. In the case of organizational and industrial markets, differences are often exhibited in the goals being pursued, the criteria employed by those involved in the buying process, the formality of purchasing policies, and the constraints that exist in the form of delivery dates and expected performance levels.

Despite these complexities, it is imperative that the marketing strategist understands in detail the dynamics of the buying process, since the costs and competitive implications of failing to do so are likely to be significant. In the case of new product development, for example, it is generally recognized that some 80 per cent of all new products launched fail, a statistic that owes much to a lack of understanding of customers' expectations. It is for these sorts of reasons that a considerable amount of research has been conducted in the post-war period in order to provide us with a greater understanding of buying patterns, and to enable us to predict more readily *how* buyers will behave in any given situation. Within this chapter we therefore focus upon some of the factors which influence behaviour and how subsequently they influence marketing strategy. It does need to be emphasized, however, that a series of interrelationships exist between this material and the areas covered in Chapter 8 in which we examine approaches to segmentation, targeting and positioning. The reader might therefore find it useful at this stage to turn briefly to Chapter 8 to identify the nature of these interrelationships before reading the present chapter in detail.

## Illustration 5.1: The Advantages of Understanding Customer Needs

Although the arguments for constant and detailed customer analysis have been well rehearsed, numerous organizations fall into the trap of believing that because they deal with their customers on a day-to-day basis, they have a clear understanding of their needs and motivations. The reality is, however, often very different, as is shown for example by the ways in which companies are seemingly taken by surprise by the decline of major market sectors, the loss of long-standing accounts, and by the way in which some 80 per cent of all new products launched fail. There is therefore an overwhelming argument for regular assessments (and reassessments) of what customers really want, their current levels of satisfaction, and the scope that exists for developing new products and services that existing customers might buy. Among those to have done this are:

- Accounting firms which having been heavily committed to a mature product – the annual company audit – used this as the entry point for developing a wide range of consultancy services. They are now firmly positioned in the rapidly-expanding management consultancy market, having retained their stable core auditing business.
- One of the great success stories of the 1980s was the Sony Walkman. Its development was brought about as the result of Sony's Chairman, Akio Morita, observing that the quality of stereo on planes was poor. The Sony Walkman technology was therefore developed initially for global travellers. Once the technology was available, Sony recognized the product's potential for a younger and far larger market.
- Dulux Solid Emulsion Paint which overcame the perennial problem faced by the DIY decorator, that of paint spattering over the floor. The advantages of/ the product were capitalized upon in an intensive advertising campaign and confirmed Dulux's position as the market leader.

*Source: Davidson, J. H. (1987)* Offensive Marketing, *Penguin p. 60*

## 5.3 A SIMPLE MODEL OF BUYER BEHAVIOUR

Irrespective of whether the marketing strategist is operating in a consumer, industrial or organizational market, there are seven questions which underpin any understanding of buyer behaviour:

1 Who is in the market and what is the extent of their power with regard to the organization?
2 What do they buy?
3 Why do they buy?
4 Who is involved in the buying?
5 How do they buy?
6 When do they buy?
7 Where do they buy?

It is the answers to these questions which should provide the marketing strategist with an understanding of the ways in which buyers are most likely to

**FIGURE 5.1**
*A stimulus-
response model of
buyer behaviour*

respond to marketing stimuli. It then follows from this that the organization which makes the best use of the information should be in a position to gain a competitive advantage. For this reason, a considerable amount of time, effort and money has been spent over the past few decades in attempting to provide the marketing strategist with a series of answers.

The starting point for much of this work has been a straightforward stimulus-response model of the sort illustrated in Figure 5.1.

Here, stimuli in the form both of the external environment and the elements of the marketing mix enter the buyer's 'black box' and interact with the buyer's characteristics and decision processes to produce a series of outputs in the form of purchase decisions. Included within these is the question of whether to buy and, if so, which product and brand, which dealer, when, and in what quantities. The task faced by the marketing strategist therefore involves understanding how the black box operates. To do this, we need to consider the two principal components of the box: firstly, the factors which the individual brings to the buying situation, and secondly, the decision processes that are used. We will therefore begin by focusing upon these background factors – cultural, social, personal and psychological – as a prelude to examining the detail of the decision process itself. However, as a general background to this discussion, the reader should first read Michael Porter's analysis of competitive structures which we examine in detail on page 242. In essence, Porter argues that five forces of competition can be at work in any market. It is then that interplay between these elements that determines the attractiveness and intensity of competition within any given market sector. Included within these five forces are the issues of buyer and supplier power. *Buyer power*, he suggests, is likely to be at its highest when:

- there is a concentration of buyers;
- there are alternative sources of supply;
- buyers have access to useful information and tend to shop around;
- there is a threat of backward integration if the buyer does not obtain satisfactory supplies and prices.

By contrast, *supplier power* is likely to be high if:

- there is a concentration of suppliers;
- the costs of switching from one supplier to another are high;
- suppliers are likely to integrate forward if they do not obtain the price/profits they seek;
- the organization has little countervailing power.

The nature of buyer-seller relationships is therefore of potentially considerable significance and needs to be taken into account when examining any market sector. In the majority of consumer markets, for example, buyer power is typically low, while supplier power is high. In many industrial markets, however, the situation is reversed and it is the buyer who is often in the position of greatest power. The implications of these different relationships are reflected most obviously in terms of how marketing strategy is developed and the relative degree of freedom that the market structure gives to the strategist. An important element therefore of any customer analysis is the insight that it provides to our understanding of buyer–supplier relationships, and hence to the market's competitive structure.

## 5.4 FACTORS INFLUENCING CONSUMER BEHAVIOUR

From the viewpoint of the marketing strategist, the mix of cultural, social, personal and psychological factors which influence behaviour and which are illustrated in Figure 5.2 are largely non-controllable. Because of the influence they exert upon patterns of buying, it is essential that as much effort as possible is put into understanding *how they interact* and, ultimately, *how they influence* purchase behaviour. In doing this, the reader should not lose sight of the differences that exist between customers and consumers, and the implications of these differences for strategy. The term 'consumer' is typically taken to mean the final user, who is not necessarily the customer. In the case of foodstuffs such as breakfast cereals, for example, the buyer (generally still the housewife) acts on behalf of her family. For the marketing mix to be effective, it is quite obviously essential that the strategist therefore understands not just what the *customer* wants (e.g. value for money) but also what the *consumer* wants (e.g. taste, free gifts, image).

**FIGURE 5.2**
*Factors influencing consumer behaviour*

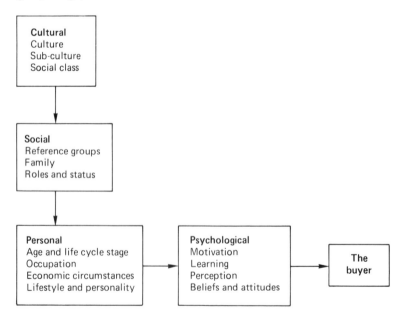

**The Significance of Culture**

The most fundamental of the four influencing forces, and hence the logical starting point for any analysis of behaviour, is the buyer's set of *cultural* factors. These include culture, subculture and social class. Of these, it is the culture of the society itself which typically proves to be the most fundamental and enduring influence on behaviour. Human behaviour is, as Kotler (1988, p. 175) has observed, 'largely the result of a learning process and as such individuals grow up learning a set of values, perceptions, preferences and behavior patterns as the result of socialization both within the family and a series of other key institutions'. From this we develop a set of values which, in the western world at least, Schiffman and Kanuk (1983, pp. 404–20) suggest include achievement, success, efficiency, progress, material comfort, practicality, individualism, freedom, humanitarianism, youthfulness and practicality. It is these which to a very large extent determine and drive our patterns of behaviour.

This broad set of values is then influenced in turn by the subcultures in which we develop. These include nationality groups, religious groups, racial groups and geographical areas, all of which exhibit degrees of difference in ethnic taste, cultural preferences, taboos, attitudes and lifestyle.

The influence of subcultures is subsequently affected by a third set of variables, that of *social stratification* and, in particular, *social class*. The significance of social class as a determinant of behaviour is discussed in some detail in Chapter 8. At this stage we will simply highlight its key characteristics which, traditionally at least, it has been suggested are as follows:

1 people within a particular social class are more similar than those from different social classes;
2 social class is determined by a *series* of variables such as occupation, income, education and values rather than by a single variable;
3 individuals can move from one social class to another.

Although research in recent years has led to a modification of these ideas, the most important single implication of social class is the still valid assumption that it exerts a significant degree of influence in areas such as clothing, cars, leisure pursuits and media preferences.

## Social Factors

Against this background of cultural forces, the strategist needs then to turn to an examination of the influence exerted by a series of social factors, including reference groups, family, social role and status.

Although influence groups have been defined in a variety of ways, one of the most useful definitions is that of 'all the groups that have a direct (face-to-face) or indirect influence on the person's attitudes or behavior' (Kotler, 1988, p. 177).

Reference groups can be divided into four types.

1 *Primary membership groups*, which are generally informal and to which individuals belong and within which they interact. These include family, neighbours, colleagues and friends.
2 *Secondary membership groups*, which tend to be more formal than primary groups and within which less interaction typically takes place. Included within these are trade unions, religious groups and professional societies.
3 *Aspirational groups* to which an individual would like to belong.
4 *Dissociative groups* whose values and behaviour the individual rejects.

The influence exerted by reference groups tends to vary considerably from one product and brand to another, as well as at different stages of the product life cycle. Among the products and brands that Hendon (1979, pp. 752–61) found were influenced most directly by reference group behaviour were cars, beer, clothing, restaurants and cigarettes. He went on to highlight the ways in which this behaviour changes over the course of the product life cycle. In the introductory stage, for example, the question of *whether* to buy is heavily influenced by others, although the influence upon the choice of brand is not particularly significant. In the growth stage, the group influences both product and brand choice, while in maturity it is the brand but not the product which is subject to this influence. The influence of reference groups in the decline stage is almost invariably weak in terms of both the product and brand choice.

The implications of these findings are significant and provide the marketing strategist with a series of guidelines, the most important of which centres around the need to identify the *opinion leaders* for each reference group. Our understanding of opinion leadership has developed considerably over the past few years, and whereas at one time it was believed that opinion leadership was limited primarily to prominent figures within society this is now no longer seen to be the case. Rather, it is recognized that an individual may well be an opinion leader in certain circumstances, but an opinion follower in others. Quite obviously, this makes the task of identifying opinion leaders more difficult and gives emphasis to the need to understand not just the demographic, but particularly the psychographic characteristics of the group which the strategist is attempting to influence.

For many products, however, it is the family which exerts the greatest single influence on behaviour. This includes both the *family of orientation* (parents, brothers and sisters) and the *family of procreation* (spouse and children). The significance of the family as a determinant of buying behaviour has long been recognized and for this reason it has been the subject of a considerable amount of research in order to identify the roles and relative influence exerted by different family members. Although it is not our intention to examine this area in detail, there are several general conclusions that have emerged from this research and that at this stage merit emphasis:

1   Husband and wife involvement in purchase decisions varies greatly from one product category to another, with women still playing the principal role in the purchasing of food and clothing. Although this has changed somewhat over the past few years as the proportion of working women has increased and divorce rates have escalated, the Institute of Grocery Distribution has estimated that women still account for some 78 per cent of food purchases.
2   Joint husband and wife decision making tends to be a characteristic of more expensive product choices where the opportunity cost of a 'wrong' decision is greater.

At a more general level, however, research in the United States (see, for example, Davis, 1970) has identified three patterns of decision making within the family and the sorts of product category with which each is typically associated. These are:

*   husband dominant: life insurance, cars, and televisions.
*   wife-dominant: washing machines, carpets, kitchenware and non-living-room furniture.
*   equal: living-room furniture, holidays, housing, furnishings and entertainment.

Although this research is useful in that it distinguishes between the different decision-making patterns, the results need to be treated with a degree of caution, if only because of the ways in which roles within the family have, and indeed still are, changing significantly.

The final social factor that typically influences purchase behaviour consists of the individual's actual and perceived *roles* and *statuses* both within society in general and within groups in particular. The significance of status symbols and the messages they communicate has long been recognized and is discussed in some detail in Chapter 13. The obvious implication, however, for the marketing strategist is to position products and brands in such a way that they reinforce the messages suited to particular individuals and groups.

**Personal Influences on Behaviour**

The third major category of influences upon behaviour is made up of the buyer's set of *personal characteristics*, including age and life-cycle stage, occupation, economic circumstances, lifestyle, and personality (see Illustration 5.2). The majority of these factors have been used extensively by marketing strategists in segmenting markets, and the reader should therefore turn to pages 200–217 in which we discuss this.

---

## Illustration 5.2: The Influences of Personality on Product Choice

A large number of writers and researchers over the past 30 years have argued that an individual's personality influences his or her choice of product and brand. Assuming that this is indeed the case, the scope that should then exist for using personality to guide marketing strategy by, for example, segmenting markets, repositioning brands, developing new products, and modifying advertising messages, would be considerable. In practice, however, consumer researchers have, as Foxall (1987, p. 132) has pointed out,

> ... failed to find more than a handful of significant relationships between measures of personality and aspects of consumer choice despite a great many empirical investigations. Particularly disappointing was the fact that personality measures often turned out to be less accurate predictors of consumer behaviour than more traditional segmentation variables such as social class, age and previous patterns of choice.

Foxall's comment is based very largely on the inconclusive results which have emerged from a series of studies, the best known of which was conducted by Evans (1959). This study was stimulated by the way in which in the United States Fords and Chevrolets were promoted as having different personalities. Ford buyers, for example, were identified as 'independent, impulsive, masculine, alert to change and self-confident', while Chevrolet owners were 'conservative, thrifty, prestige conscious, less masculine, and seeking to avoid extremes'. Evans investigated the validity of these descriptions by applying the Edwards Personal Preference Test which measures needs for achievement, dominance, change, aggression, and so on, to Ford and Chevrolet owners. The scores achieved by the two groups of owners proved not to be significantly different and Evans concluded that 'the distribution of scores for all needs overlap to such an extent that (personality) discrimination is virtually impossible'.

---

**Psychological Influences**

The fourth and final set of influences upon behaviour consists of the four principal *psychological factors* – motivation, perception, learning, and beliefs and attitudes. The first of these, motivation, is in many ways both the most important to understand and the most complex to analyse. The starting point involves recognizing the differences between *biogenic* needs which are physiological (hunger, thirst and discomfort) and *psychogenic* needs which are essentially psychological states of tension (these include the need for esteem and the desire for recognition or belonging). It is these needs which, when they become sufficiently intense, create a motivation to act in such a way that the tension of the need is reduced. The search to understand the detail of this process has led to a considerable amount of research over the past 100 years and, in turn, to a variety of theories of human motivation. The best known of these are the theories of Marshall, Freud, Veblen, Herzberg and Maslow.

The first of these, the Marshallian model, is in many ways the most straightforward and is based on the idea that a person's behaviour is inherently rational and motivated by economic factors. The economic individual therefore attempts to maximize total satisfaction by buying goods and services from which the marginal utility is, in theory at least, equivalent to the marginal utility of the alternatives. Although such an overtly rational view of behaviour has long been criticized as being too partial and inadequate an explanation, Kotler (1972) has highlighted several ways in which the Marshallian model contributes to our understanding of buyer behaviour:

1 It is axiomatic that every buyer acts in the light of his own best interest. The question is whether an economist would describe these actions as 'rational' or not.
2 The model is normative in the sense that it provides a logical basis for purchase decisions, i.e. how one should decide rather than being descriptive, i.e. how one actually decides.
3 The model suggests a number of useful behavioral hypotheses, e.g. the lower the price, the greater the sales; the lower the price of substitute products, the lower the sales of this product; the lower the price of complementary products, the higher the sales of this product; the higher the real income, the higher the sales of this product, provided that it is not an 'inferior' good; the higher the promotional expenditure, the higher the sales.

Freud's work, by contrast, suggests that the psychological factors which influence behaviour are for the most part unconscious, and that as a consequence we can only rarely understand our true motivations. Equally, in the process of growing up and conforming to the rules of society, we repress a series of urges. The obvious implication of this for marketing is that a consumer's *stated* motive for buying a particular brand or product may well be very different from the more fundamental *underlying* motive. Thus, in the case of a fast car, the stated motive might be the ability to get from A to B quickly. The underlying motive, however, might well be the desire for status and to be noticed. Similarly, with an expensive watch the stated motive might be the product's reliability, while the real – and unconscious – motive might again be status and the desire to impress others.

The best known exponent of Freudian theory in marketing is Ernest Dichter who in the 1950s developed a series of techniques, under the general heading of *motivational research*, designed to uncover consumers' deepest motives. Motivation research was subjected to a considerable amount of criticism on the grounds that buyers were subsequently being manipulated and persuaded to act against their own interests. Two of the most vociferous opponents of motivation research proved to be Galbraith and Packard. Galbraith (1958), for example, levelled a series of criticisms against the development of the consumer society, arguing that consumers were being persuaded to act against their true interests. Packard's criticisms, in his book *The Hidden Persuaders* (1957), were aimed even more specifically at techniques of motivation research and raised the spectre of the wholesale manipulation of society by marketing people for their own ends. Largely because of the subsequent publicity, motivation research became a less acceptable research technique and this, coupled with a whole series of problems experienced in its use, led to its gradual decline.

The Freudian view that a consumer's stated motives may well be very different from the true motives is echoed in Veblen's social-psychological interpretations of behaviour (1899). Many purchases, he argued, are motivated not by need but by a desire for prestige and social standing. Although Veblen's views, and in particular his emphasis upon conspicuous consumption, have subsequently been modified by research findings, his contribution to our understanding of buyer behaviour is significant, not least because it stresses the importance of social relationships as an influence upon choice.

The fourth major theory of motivation and one which has received considerable attention from marketing analysts over the past 15 years, was developed by Herzberg. Labelled the 'Two Factor Theory' of motivation, it distinguishes between *satisfiers* (factors that create satisfaction) and *dissatisfiers* (factors that create dissatisfaction). In the case of a car, for example, the absence of a warranty would be a dissatisfier. The existence of a warranty, however, is not a satisfier since it is not one of the principal reasons for buying the product. These are more likely to be the car's looks, its performance and the status that the buyer feels the product confers upon the driver.

There are several implications of this theory for marketing, the two most significant of which are, first, that the seller needs to be fully aware of the dissatisfiers which, while they will not by themselves sell the product, can easily 'unsell' it. The second implication, which follows logically from this, is that the strategist needs to understand in detail the various satisfiers and then concentrate not just upon supplying them, but also giving them full emphasis in the marketing programme.

The fifth and final principal theory of motivation was put forward by Maslow who suggested that behaviour can be explained in terms of a hierarchy of needs; this is illustrated in Figure 5.3.

**FIGURE 5.3**
*Maslow's hierarchy of needs*

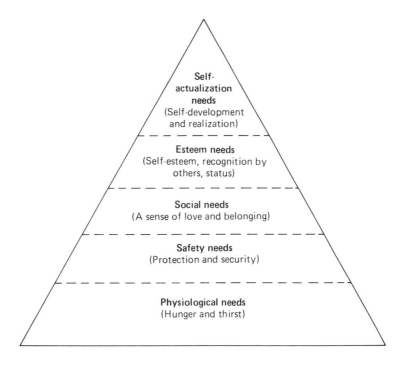

The model suggests that a person begins by concentrating upon satisfying the most important and most basic physiological needs before moving on to the higher levels of need. Thus, as each level is satisfied, the next level is likely to become the focus of attention.

Although from the viewpoint of the marketing strategist Maslow's theory is arguably of less direct value than that of, say, Herzberg, it is of value in that it provides yet another insight into the ways in which products fit into the goals and lives of consumers.

**Issues of Perception**

Against the background of an understanding of the factors influencing motivation, the marketing strategist needs then to consider the influence of *perception*, since it is the way in which motivated individuals perceive a given situation that determines precisely how they will behave. It has long been understood that because of the three elements of the perceptual process – selective attention, selective distortion and selective retention – individuals can perceive the same object in very different ways. It is the failure to recognize and take account of this that often leads to a confusion of, for example, advertising messages. Research in this area has provided a series of insights into the perceptual process, and subsequently to a series of guidelines for marketers. In the case of *selection attention*, for example, simply because of the enormous number of stimuli that we are exposed to each day (more than 1000 advertisements alone), a substantial number are either ignored or given only cursory attention. If a marketing message is to succeed it therefore has to fight against this screening process. This can be done in one of several ways, including:

1 the use of black and white advertisements when others are in colour, or vice versa;
2 the use of shock messages – in 1990, for example, the RSPCA drew attention to the number of stray dogs being destroyed each year by showing a mountain of bodies;
3 the sheer size of the advertisement;
4 substantial money-off offers;
5 the unexpected – a glue manufacturer used his product to stick a car to a hoarding in London some 15 feet above the pavement.

Even when a message does reach the consumer, there is no guarantee that it will be interpreted in the way that was intended. Each person modifies information in such a way that it fits neatly into the existing mind set. This process of *selective distortion* means that messages that confirm preconceived notions are far more likely to be accepted than those that challenge these notions. Although a mind set can be changed, this is typically both costly and time consuming. However, one example of where this has been done with considerable success is with Japanese products. The image reputation of the majority of Japanese products in the 1960s was undoubtedly poor, and a factor which had implications for, among other areas, distribution and pricing. Throughout the 1970s and 1980s, however, the Japanese concentrated on quality and product innovation to the point at which even the most die-hard and conservative European or American has been forced to admit that in many markets it is now the Japanese who set the lead.

A similar example is likely to be provided in the 1990s by the Czechoslovakian car manufacturer, Skoda. Long seen as rugged, cheap and utilitarian, their take-over by Volkswagen in the early part of the decade and the strategic changes which will inevitably be made will force changes in the ways in which the product is perceived.

The third element of perception is that of *selective retention*. Quite simply, individuals forget much of what they learn. To ensure therefore that a message is retained, it needs to be relevant, generally straightforward, one which reinforces existing positive attitudes, and in the case of certain products, catchy. Many people for example still remember simple advertising slogans such as 'Beanz Meanz Heinz', 'Drinka Pinta Milk A Day', 'Go to work on an egg', and 'Guinness is good for you', even though in some cases the message has not been used for well over a decade.

Once individuals have responded to an advertisement, they go through a process of learning. If the experience with the product is generally positive, the likelihood of repeat purchase is obviously increased. If, however, the experience is largely negative, not only is the likelihood of repeat purchase reduced, but the negative attitude that develops is likely to be extended to other products from the same manufacturer and possibly the country of origin. It is the set of *beliefs* and *attitudes* that emerge both from our own experiences and from those of individuals in our reference groups that build up a set of product and brand images. These, in turn, lead us to behave in relatively consistent ways. An obvious problem that can therefore be faced by a manufacturer stems from the difficulties of changing attitudes and images once they have been established.

## 5.5 THE BUYING DECISION PROCESS

Having identified the various factors which influence behaviour, the marketing strategist is then in a position to examine the buying process itself. This involves focusing on three distinct elements:

1 the buying roles within the decision-making unit;
2 the type of buying behaviour;
3 the decision process.

**The Five Buying Roles**

In the majority of cases and for the majority of products, identifying the buyer is a relatively straightforward exercise. In some instances, however, the decision of what to buy involves several people, and here we can identify five distinct roles:

1 the *initiator* who first suggests buying the product or service;
2 the *influencer* whose comments affect the decision made;
3 the *decider* who ultimately makes all or part of the buying decision;
4 the *buyer* who physically makes the purchase;
5 the *user(s)* who consumes the product or service.

Identifying who plays each of these roles, and indeed *how* they play them, is important since it is this information which should be used to determine a wide variety of marketing decisions. In the case of advertising, for example, the question of who plays each of the buying roles should be used to decide on who the advertising is to be aimed at, the sort of appeal, the timing of the message, and the placing of the message.

**The Types of Buying Behaviour**

So far in our discussion, we have referred simply to 'buying behaviour'. In practice, of course, it is possible to identify several types of buying decision and hence several types of buying behaviour. The most obvious distinction to make is based on the expense, complexity, risk and opportunity cost of the purchase decision – the process a consumer goes through in deciding on a new car or major holiday, for example, will be radically different from the process in deciding whether to buy a chocolate bar. Recognition of this has led Assael (1987, Chapter 4) to distinguish between four types of buying behaviour, depending on the degree of buyer involvement in the purchase and the extent to which brands differ. This is illustrated in Figure 5.4.

**FIGURE 5.4**
*The four types of buying behaviour*

|  |  | Degree of involvement | |
|---|---|---|---|
|  |  | Low | High |
| Significant differences between brands | Few | 1 Habitual buying behaviour (e.g. baked beans) | 3 Dissonance reducing behaviour (e.g. furniture) |
|  | Many | 2 Variety seeking behaviour (e.g. chocolate bars and breakfast cereals) | 4 Complex buying behaviour (e.g. computers) |

SOURCE: Adapted from Assael (1987), p. 87

**Understanding the Buying Decision Process**

The third and final stage that we are concerned with here is the structure of the buying decision process that consumers go through. In other words, precisely how do consumers buy particular products? Do they, for example, search for information and make detailed comparisons, or do they rely largely upon the advice of a store assistant? Are they influenced significantly by price or by advertising? Questions such as these have led to a considerable amount of research into the buying process (see Illustration 5.3) and subsequently to consumers being categorized either as deliberate buyers or compulsive buyers.

---

# Illustration 5.3: Using Research to Get into the Consumer's Mind

Customer analysis is designed to provide the strategist with a clear understanding of *how* and *why* people behave as they do. To help with this, two sets of techniques have been developed.

1 *Consumer research* which deals with attitudes and opinions towards existing products and possible new ones. The techniques used include simple structured interviews of large samples of consumers and lengthy discussions with small groups.
2 *Market research* which observes what happens in the market-place. The findings are then projected into estimates of total market size, trends, brand shares, and so on.

Although both sets of research techniques have developed significantly over the past 20 years, Davidson (1987, pp. 48–9) has argued that:

> Despite much clever talk in the marketing world about complicated and novel research techniques, it is apparent that most of the really successful new consumer products introduced in the past decade have fulfilled relatively obvious needs which the simplest form of investigation would have revealed. The critical reason for their success was not shrewd investigation, but skilful design and selling. Most of the outstanding new products of the 1980s succeeded for these reasons.

*Source: Davidson, J. H. (1987),* Offensive Marketing, *Penguin*

---

To help in coming to terms with this, a series of models have been proposed which focus not simply upon the purchase *decision*, but upon the *process* leading up to this decision, the decision itself, and then subsequently post-purchase behaviour. An example of this sort of model is illustrated in Figure 5.5.

This process begins with the consumer's *recognition of a problem*, or perhaps more commonly, a want. This may emerge as the result of an internal stimulus (hunger or thirst) or an external stimulus in the form of an advertisement or a colleague's comment. This leads to the *search for information*, which might be at the level simply of a heightened awareness or attention to advertising, or at the deeper level of extensive information searching. In either case, the search process is likely to involve one or more of four distinct sources:

1 *personal sources* such as family, friends, colleagues and neighbours;
2 *public sources* such as the mass media and consumer organizations – a typical example would be the Consumers' Association *Which?* magazine;
3 *commercial sources* such as advertising, sales staff and brochures;
4 *experimental sources* such as handling or trying the product.

**FIGURE 5.5**
*A sequential model
of the buying
process*

The relative importance of each of these varies greatly from person to person and product to product, a point that has been emphasized by Kotler (1988, p. 196):

> Generally speaking, the consumer receives the most information exposure about a product from commercial sources, that is, marketer-dominated sources. On the other hand, the most effective exposure come from personal sources. Each type of source may perform a somewhat different function in influencing the buying decision. Commercial information normally performs an informing function and personal sources perform a legitimizing and/or evaluation function.

To illustrate this, Kotler goes on to cite an example of doctors learning about the existence of new pharmaceuticals from commercial sources, but who then typically rely upon other doctors for evaluative information.

By gathering information in this way consumers develop an awareness, knowledge and understanding of the various brands in the market. An obvious task then faced by marketing strategists is how best to ensure that their brand stands out from the others available and is subsequently purchased. In essence this involves moving the product or brand from the *total set* available, through to the consumer's *awareness set* and *consideration set* to the *choice set* from which the consumer ultimately makes the buying decision; this is illustrated diagrammatically in Figure 5.6.

**FIGURE 5.6**
*The move from the
consumer's total
set to the choice
set*

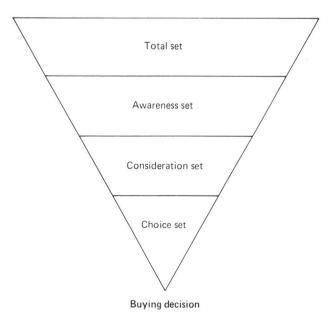

# Illustration 5.4: Customers Buy Benefits, Not Products

Recognition of the idea that customers do not buy products but are instead interested in the benefits gained from using the product has long been at the heart of successful marketing. This has been commented on by, among others, Malcolm McDonald (1984, p. 56):

> The difference between benefits and products is not just a question of semantics. It is crucial to the company seeking success. Every product has its features: size, shape, performance, weight, the material from which it is made, and so on. Many companies fall into the trap of talking to customers about these features rather than what those features mean to the customer. This is not surprising. For example, if, when asked a question about the product, the salesman could not provide an accurate answer, the customer might lose confidence and, doubting the salesman, wiill soon doubt his product. Most salesmen are therefore very knowledgeable about the technical features of the products they sell. They have to have these details at their fingertips when they talk to buyers, designers and technical experts.
>
> However, being expert in technical detail is not enough. The customer may not be able to work out the benefits which particular features bring and it is therefore up to the salesman to explain the benefits which accrue from every feature he mentions.
>
> A simple formula to ensure that this customer-oriented approach is adopted is always to use the phrase 'which means that' to link a feature to the benefit ir brings:
>
> 'Maintenance time has been reduced from 4 to 3 hours which means that most costs are reduced by . . .'
>
> 'The engine casing is made of aluminium which means that six more units can be carried on a standard truck load, which means that transport costs are reduced by . . .'

McDonald goes on to argue that companies should undertake detailed analyses to identify the full range of benefits *they are able to offer* the customer as a prelude to identifying the range of benefits that *customers actually want* or will respond to. Benefits typically fall into four categories:

1  *standard benefits* which arise from the company and its products;
2  *double benefits* which bring a benefit to the customer and subsequently, through an improvement in the customer's product, to the end user;
3  *company benefits* which emerge as the result of a relationship that develops by virtue of having bought a particular product – a typical example would be worldwide service back-up;
4  *differential benefits* which distinguish the product from those offered by competitors.

Among others to have discussed the significance of benefits is Theodore Levitt who takes as an example drill bits. The customer, he suggests, does not buy a quarter-inch drill for its own sake, but for the quarter-inch holes it gives. The implication for the manufacturer is that he needs to define his business in terms of the means of making holes in materials. By limiting the definition to the manufacture of drills he is likely to fail to recognize the opportunity offered by, for example, industrial lasers which are capable of making holes more rapidly and accurately.

However, for this to be done effectively, the strategist needs to have a clear understanding of the evaluative criteria used by consumers in comparing products. Much of the research in this area has focused primarily upon the cognitive element, suggesting that consumers make product judgements on a rational basis (see Illustration 5.4). Whether this is the case in practice is debatable.

Nevertheless, there are several influencing factors which have emerged from this research which merit consideration. These include:

1 the *product's attributes* such as its price, performance, quality and styling;
2 their *relative importance* to the consumer;
3 the consumer's perception of each *brand's image*;
4 the consumer's *utility function* for each of the attributes.

By understanding consumers' perceptions in this way, the strategist can then begin modifying the product offer. This can be done in one of six ways:

1 changing the physical product by, for example, adding features (real repositioning);
2 changing beliefs about the product by giving greater emphasis to particular attributes (psychological repositioning);
3 changing beliefs about competitors' products by comparative advertising and 'knocking copy' (competitive depositioning);
4 changing the relative importance of particular attributes – as a product moves through the product life cycle, for example, and consumers become more familiar with the concept and the technology, the emphasis in the advertising can be shifted from, say, reassuring consumers about reliability and service back-up, to a range of additional uses;
5 emphasizing particular product features which previously have been largely ignored;
6 changing buyers' expectations.

Against the background of these comments, the strategist should then be in a position to consider the act of purchase itself, and in particular *where* the purchase will be made, the *quantities* in which it will be made, the *timing*, and the *method* of payment.

## An Overview of Models of Consumer Behaviour

Throughout the 1960s attempts were made to integrate a variety of theories, research findings and concepts from the behavioural sciences into a general framework which could be used to explain and predict consumer behaviour. In doing this, the principal writers, such as Nicosia (1966), Engel, Kollat and Blackwell (1968), and Sheth (1969), moved away from the general perspective that had previously been adopted by economists and which in a number of ways is typified by Marshall's work and the Marshallian model of 'economic man'. Instead of viewing consumer behaviour simply as a single act made up of the purchase itself and the post-purchase reaction, a far greater recognition was given to the consumer's psychological state before, during and after the purchase. This process has been summarized by Howard (1983) who suggested that buyer behaviour is 'largely determined by how the customer thinks and processes information'.

This idea of an information–attitude–intention–purchase sequence has also been commented on by Foxall (1987, p. 126):

All of the models . . . are founded upon such a rational decision sequence. They credit consumers with considerable capacities for receiving and handling quantities of information and undertaking extensive prepurchase searches and evaluations. They rely heavily upon the idea of cognitive decision making in which information is received and classified by the individual and, via mental processing, transformed into the attitudes and intentions which determine brand choice and related aspects of purchase and consumption. Consumer information processing has sometimes been described as analogous with that of computers; the consumer has been depicted in terms of a 'central control unit' and the cognate elements of information technology. Whatever the details of explanation, however, hypothesized decision makers use evaluation criteria to predict the outcomes of each available option in terms of their objectives; employ decision rules or other methods of comparative evaluation in order to decide upon a course of action; receive and process information, storing it in and retrieving it from memory – all in the course of making a decision or solving a problem before purchasing a brand.

The three best known of these so-called comprehensive models were developed in the United States by Nicosia, Engel et al., and Sheth. A brief summary of their structure and key features appears in Illustration 5.5.

Although these models have been of value in extending our understanding of the decision process, their value has been questioned in recent years. The principal criticisms that have been made by Foxall (1987, p. 128) are as follows:

1  the models assume an unrealistic degree of consumer rationality;
2  observed behaviour often differs significantly from what is described;
3  the implied decision process is too simplistic and sequential;
4  insufficient recognition is given to the relative importance of different types of decisions – each decision is treated by comprehensive models as significant and of high involvement, but the reality is very different and by far the vast majority of decisions made by consumers are relatively insignificant and of low involvement;
5  the models assume consumers have a seemingly infinite capacity for receiving and ordering information – in practice, consumers ignore, forget, distort, misunderstand or make far less use than this of the information with which they are presented;
6  attitudes towards low involvement products are often very weak and only emerge after the purchase and not before as comprehensive models suggest;
7  many purchases seem not to be preceded by a decision process;
8  strong brand attitudes often fail to emerge even when products have been bought on a number of occasions;
9  consumers often drastically limit their search for information, even for consumer durables;
10 when brands are similar in terms of their basic attributes, consumers seemingly do not discriminate between them but instead select from a repertoire of brands.

In the light of these criticisms, it is perhaps not surprising that the results that have emerged from attempts to test the models have proved disappointing.

## 5.6  ORGANIZATIONAL BUYING BEHAVIOUR

Although there are certain factors common to both consumer and organizational buying behaviour, there are also numerous points of difference. Perhaps the most obvious feature of commonality in approaching the two areas is the fundamental need to understand how and why buyers behave as they do. There are, however, certain features of organizational buying which are not found in consumer markets. Kotler (1988, p. 208) identified these as being:

- Organizations buy goods and services to satisfy a variety of goals: making profits, reducing costs, meeting employee needs, and meeting social and legal obligations.
- More persons typically participate in organizational buying decisions than in consumer buying decisions, especially in procuring major items. The decision

# Illustration 5.5: Comprehensive Models of Consumer Behaviour

### The Nicosia Model
The Nicosia model consists of a flow diagram designed to illustrate how a potential consumer responds to news of a new brand. The model's three-stage sequence begins with the consumer being made aware of the brand's existence and then traces the decision process through from purchase to post-purchase evaluation and feedback. This sequence is assumed to begin with advertising which makes the consumer aware of the brand's existence and an unfilled want. Perception of the message is influenced by attributes of both the company and the consumer, and may lead to the development of an attitude towards the brand. The consumer is then assumed to search for alternative brands which are evaluated by means of other consumers, advertising messages, previous experiences with each company, and so on. This search process leads the consumer either to dismiss or to purchase the product. The experience of purchase and consumption then has the effect of modifying the consumer's psychological state and acts as a feedback loop leading either to a decision to repeat the purchase or not to buy it again.

### The Engel, Kollat and Blackwell Model
The starting point for the EKB model is the consumer's perception of a want which must be satisfied. This stimulates a search for information internally (memory), externally (neighbours, colleagues, and friends), and from market sources (advertisements, trade literature, magazine reports). This search process identifies the various ways in which the want can be satisfied and leads to the consumer setting the criteria by which the alternatives can be compared and evaluated. This leads in turn to the emergence of a set of attitudes and beliefs which ultimately determine choice. The outcome of this choice then feeds back to influence future behaviour.

### The Howard and Sheth Model
Howard and Sheth's approach is broadly similar to those of Nicosia and Engel, et al., in that it again attempts to pull together a disparate set of variables. These are grouped under four main headings:

1 *inputs* which stimulate the buying process. These include product related factors (price, quality and distinctiveness), symbolic factors (images that stem from the mass media and sales people), and social factors (family, reference groups and social class influences);
2 *perceptual constructs* which explain the consumer's cognitive activity in terms of information processing;
3 *learning constructs* which represent the results of information processing;
4 *outputs* which include not just the purchase itself but also the implications for perception and learning.

As with the two previous models, the output acts as a feedback loop to influence attitudes and future behaviour.

participants usually have different organizational responsibilities and apply different criteria to the purchase decision.
- The buyers must heed formal purchasing policies, constraints, and requirements established by their organizations.
- The buying instruments, such as requests for quotations, proposals, and purchase contracts, add another dimension not typically found in consumer buying.

These points are in turn reflected in Webster and Wind's (1972, p. 2) definition of organizational buying as 'the decision making process by which formal organizations establish the need for purchased products and services, and identify, evaluate, and choose among alternative brands and suppliers'.

The significance of organizational buying practices has been pointed to by a variety of writers, including Turnbull (1987, p. 147) who has highlighted the impact of professional procurement on profitability in the telecommunications equipment market:

> Some telecommunications equipment manufacturers now buy in items accounting for up to 80 per cent of total cost. Thus even a 2 per cent procurement saving can have a marked effect on profitability or give the company a significant price advantage in the marketplace. Additionally, professional purchasing also helps secure long term and improved sources of supply.

The strategic significance of consistently good buying has long been recognized within the Dixons retail chain and has been a major contributor to their performance in recent years. Their experiences are discussed in Illustration 5.6.

Although quite obviously, as with consumers in consumer markets, no two companies behave in the same way, both research and experience have demonstrated that patterns of similarity do exist in the ways in which organizational buyers approach the task of buying, and that they are sufficiently uniform to simplify the task of strategic marketing planning.

In analysing patterns of organizational buying, the starting point is in many ways similar to that for consumer markets, with the strategist posing a series of questions:

- *Who* makes up the market?
- What *buying decisions* do they make?
- Who are the *key participants* in the buying process?
- What are the *principal influences* upon the buyer and what organizational rules and policies are important?
- What *procedures* are followed in selecting and evaluating competitive offerings and how do buyers arrive at their decisions?

## Who Makes Up the Industrial Market?

The term 'industrial market' is used to refer to individuals who and organizations which buy goods and services that are then used in the production of other goods and services subsequently supplied to others. As a group, it therefore includes agriculture, manufacturing, construction, transportation, communications, banking, financial services, insurance, mining, and so on. These markets typically possess a set of characteristics which are not shared with consumer markets and which have a series of implications for the way in which the marketing strategist needs to approach the marketing task. The most significant of these characteristics are:

1 the existence of a smaller number of buyers each of whom typically buys in larger quantities than is the case in consumer markets;
2 a (high) degree of buyer concentration, with a limited number of buyers often accounting for the bulk of purchasing within the industry;
3 geographical concentration;
4 close relationships between suppliers and customers, with products often being modified to fit the specific needs of the customer;
5 inelastic demand, particularly in the short term;

---

# Illustration 5.6:  The Dixon's Success Story: a Lesson in Buying

'Retailing is about buying rather than selling,' according to Stanley Kalms, the founder of Dixons. 'It is based on products and is about "competitive edge" and unique propositions.' Certainly the success of Dixon's, the high street electrical and camera retailer, owes much to its professional purchasing operations.

Buyers at Dixon's are seasoned veterans who know their industry inside out. Buying activities break down into three categories. Firstly there are the deals with leading manufacturers of brown goods (e.g. TVs; videos; computers) and white goods (e.g. washers; cookers, fridges and freezers). Dixon's has a successful record of working with leading manufacturers to develop new products, too. Secondly, and of growing importance are Dixon's own label products (labelled with Japanese type names such as Saisho). These are made for Dixon's by foreign manufacturers and provide the organisation with the opportunity to beat famous brand prices and still make bigger margins. Finally, and most excitingly (according to some Dixon's buyers), are the 'one off' bargain deals Dixon's are able to strike with manufacturers. Such deals are forged with manufacturers who need to move stocks. Often the success of such transactions is down to Dixon's better understanding of what will sell and how to sell in the market place. The financial capability of Dixon's enables it to take massive stocks (the entrepreneurial spirit within the organisation makes acceptable the risk involved). This capability often means very low purchasing prices per unit. In the summer of 1985, for example, Dixon's doubled its order of computer stock from the troubled Sinclair organisation. Ten thousand units represented an order of such magnitude that it might well have been beyond the scope of Dixon's prior to their takeover of the family firm, Curry's the year earlier. As it turned out an aggressively marketed package of a Spectrum computer together with software, disc drive and joystick, all at a lower price, made reordering possible.

The marketing operation is the mirror image of purchasing. Purchasing managers work closely with their marketing counterparts – even share the same office. They are jointly responsible for the selection of product ranges and for their margins. While according to the firm, 'good purchasing personnel ripen with age', marketing people are constantly moved to new product areas to maintain a continuous injection of new ideas.

The constant search is to find ways of making customers feel 'it is worth their while coming into Dixon's, always worthwhile passing by someone else'. Exclusive merchandise, own label products, 'how to' books, better credit, better ranges, longer guarantees and an exciting, 'sexy' shop atmosphere have been hallmarks of the Dixon marketing approach.

*Source: Richardson and Richardson (1989),* Business Planning: an approach to strategic management, *Pitman.*

---

6 demand is generally derived, with the result that the strategist needs to examine the secondary markets which influence the demand for the primary product;

7 professional purchasing which is performed by buyers who often work as part of a buying team and who in attempting to satisfy particular performance or quality criteria employ a greater degree of overtly rational thinking than is generally the case in consumer markets;

8 reciprocal trading patterns often exist, making it difficult for new suppliers to break into the market.

**The Three Types of Buying Decision**

Much of the research conducted over the past 25 years into the nature of the industrial buying process has made either explicit or implicit use of a categorization first proposed in 1967 by Robinson, Faris and Wind. There are, they suggested, three distinct buying situations or buy classes, each of which requires a different pattern of behaviour from the supplier. They are the *straight rebuy*, the *modified rebuy*, and the *new task*.

Of these, the straight rebuy is the most straightforward and describes a buying situation where products are reordered on a largely routine basis, often by someone at a fairly junior level in the organization. Among the products ordered in this way is office stationery. Here, the person responsible for the ordering simply reorders when stocks fall below a pre-determined level and will typically use the same supplier from one year to another until either something goes wrong or a potential new supplier offers a sufficiently attractive incentive for the initial decision to be reconsidered. The implications of this sort of buying situation are for the most part straightforward and require the supplier to maintain both product and service quality. Perhaps the biggest single problem in these circumstances stems from the need on the part of the supplier to avoid complacency setting in and allowing others to make an approach which causes the customer to reassess the supplier base.

The second type of buying situation – the modified rebuy – often represents an extension of the straight rebuy and occurs when the buyer wants to modify the specification, price or delivery terms. Although the current supplier is often in a relatively strong position to protect the account, the buyer will frequently give at least cursory consideration to other possible sources of supply.

The third type of buying situation – the new task – is the most radical of the three and provides the marketing strategist with a series of opportunities and challenges. The buyer typically approaches the new task with a set of criteria which have to be satisfied, and in order to do this will frequently consider a number of possible suppliers each of whom is then faced with the task of convincing the buyer that his product or service will outperform or be more cost-effective than the others. The buyer's search for information is often considerable and designed to reduce risk. Where the costs are high there will typically be several people involved in the decision, and the strategist's task is therefore complicated by the need not just to identify the buying participants, but also their particular concerns and spheres of influence. In doing this, the strategist should never lose sight of the significance of attitudes to risk and the ways in which individuals may work to reduce their exposure to it. Chisnall (1989, p. 72), for example, has commented that: 'A buyer's professional activities may be tempered by the fundamental instinct he has for survival and for enhancing his career.' This point has also been made by McClelland (1961): 'A great part of the efforts of business executives is directed towards minimising uncertainties.'

This general theme has been examined in detail by Cyert and March (1963) who in their behavioural theory of the firm identify four types of buying determinants: individual, social, organizational, and environmental. Within this framework they then distinguish between 'task' and 'non-task' factors. Task factors are for the most part rational and include price, delivery, quality, performance levels, and so on. The non-task factors include personal values, and political, cultural and social elements, as well as the personality traits of the decision maker. Although identifying and analysing the impact and relative importance of these 'soft' elements is difficult, their effects should be neither underestimated nor ignored.

**Who is Involved in the Buying Process?**

A major characteristic of organizational buying is that it is a group activity, and only rarely does a single individual within the organization have sole responsibility for making all the decisions involved in the purchasing process. Instead, a number of people from different areas and often with different statuses are involved either directly or indirectly. Webster and Wind (1972, p. 6) have referred to this group both as the decision-making unit (DMU) of an organization and as the buying centre, and define it as 'all those individuals and groups who participate in the purchasing decision-making process, who share some common goals and the risks arising from the decisions'. There are, they suggest, six roles involved in this process, although on occasions all six may be performed by the same person:

1 *users* of the product or service who in many cases initiate the buying process and help in defining the purchase specifications;
2 *influencers* who again help to define the specification, but who also provide an input to the process of evaluating the alternatives available;
3 *deciders* who have the responsibility for deciding on product requirements and suppliers;
4 *approvers* who give the authorization for the proposals of deciders and buyers;
5 *buyers* who have the formal authority for selecting suppliers and negotiating purchase terms (a summary of the different types of buyer that have been identified appears in Illustration 5.7).
6 *gatekeepers* who are able to stop sellers from reaching individuals in the buying centre. These can range from purchasing agents through to receptionists and telephone switchboard operators.

---

# Illustration 5.7: The Seven Different Types of Buyer

The issue of the buyer's style and its implications for marketing strategy has been the subject of research in the United States by Dickinson (1967, pp. 14–17) who identified seven types of buyer:

1 *loyal* buyers who remain loyal to a source for considerable periods;
2 *opportunistic* buyers who choose between sellers on the basis of who will best further his long-term interests;
3 *best deal* buyers who concentrate on the best deal available at the time;
4 *creative* buyers who tell the seller precisely what they want in terms of the product, service and price;
5 *advertising* buyers who demand advertising support as part of the deal;
6 *chisellers* who constantly demand extra discounts;
7 *nuts and bolts* buyers who select products on the basis of the quality of their construction.

---

Although Webster and Wind's categorization of buying centre roles is the best known and the most widely used, a variety of other analytical approaches have been developed. Hill (1972), for example, has argued the case for analysing the buying centre not on the basis of the participants' roles, but on the basis of functional units. There are, he suggests, five such units:

1 *control units* which are responsible for the policy making which influences buying and which imposes certain constraints – these might include buying where possible only from British suppliers or from local small firms;
2 *information units* which provide information relating to the purchase;
3 *the buying unit* which consists of those with formal responsibility for negotiating the terms of the contract;
4 *user units* consisting of anyone in the organization who will be involved in using the product or service;
5 *the decision-making unit* which consists of those in the DMU who will make the decision.

Of these, it is only the control, information and decision-making units that he believes are of any real importance in influencing buying decisions. Regardless of which of these two frameworks the strategist uses in trying to understand the organizational buying process, a considerable amount of research has been conducted that provides a series of interesting insights to each of these elements; a brief summary of a selection of these findings appears in Illustration 5.8.

Although the size, structure and formality of the buying centre will quite obviously vary depending both upon the size of the organization and the product decision involved, the strategist needs always to consider five questions:

1  Who are the principal participants in the buying process?
2  In what areas do they exercise the greatest influence?
3  What is their level of influence?
4  What evaluative criteria do each of the participants make use of and how professional is the buying process?
5  To what extent in large organizations is buying centralized?

In considering these questions, there are several pieces of research which are worth examining because of the insights they provide to the ways in which buying centres behave. The findings of two of the most useful studies are illustrated in Figures 5.7 and 5.8.

**FIGURE 5.7**
*Buying influences and company size*

| | Average number of: | |
|---|---|---|
| Number of employees | (I) Buying influences | (II) Contacts by members of the sales force |
| 0–200 | 3.42 | 1.72 |
| 201–400 | 4.85 | 1.75 |
| 401–1000 | 5.81 | 1.90 |
| More than 1000 | 6.50 | 1.65 |

SOURCE: Adapted from McGraw-Hill (1963)

**FIGURE 5.8**
*Sources of information*

| | Small firms (%) | Large firms (%) |
|---|---|---|
| Trade and technical press | 27 | 60 |
| Calls by the sales force | 46 | 19 |
| Direct mail | 19 | 9 |
| Exhibitions | 8 | 12 |

SOURCE: McLean Hunter

## The Principal Influences on Industrial Buyers

Much of the early research into industrial buying processes was based on the assumption that industrial buyers, unlike consumers, are wholly rational. More recently it has been recognized that while economic factors play a significant role, a variety of other elements also needs to be taken into account. Chisnall (1989, p. 71), for example, in recognizing this, says that:

> Organisational buyers do not live like hermits; they are influenced by the personal behaviour of their colleagues, by the trading practices of other enterprises, and by the standards of the society to which they belong.

# Illustration 5.8:   Research Findings on Roles
# within the Buying Centre

Each of the roles in the organizational decision-making unit has been subjected to a substantial amount of research. Among the findings to have emerged from this, Turnbull (1987, p. 149) has highlighted 12 of the most significant:

- The buyer or purchasing agent in many circumstances is little more than a clerical officer whose input to the buying decision is limited to filling out the order forms (Weigand, 1968).
- The buyer's role and influence is determined to a very large extent by senior management's purchasing philosophy. Where this is seen to be significant, the role and influence of the buyer will be far greater than is otherwise the case (Feldman and Cardozo, 1968).
- Buyers' perceptions of their role and status can be major determinants of the influence they exert. Where the buyer is ambitious, they work to enhance their role by feeding information on new technical developments to management and by trying to become involved in as many aspects of the buying process as possible (James, 1966).
- Where buyers have little authority, they often attempt to simplify the purchasing process (Kettlewood, 1973).
- Users with specialist knowledge may exert sufficient influence to override traditional commercial considerations such as delivery times and price (Weigand, 1966).
- Purchasing staff and technologies in certain European countries such as Germany and Sweden have been shown to be more highly qualified and demanding than their British counterparts. This apparent lack of technical competence on the part of British companies has led in turn to exporters facing unexpected barriers to entry (Turnbull and Cunningham, 1981).
- The composition of the buying centre is heavily dependent upon the company's orientation. Where, for example, it is technology orientated, engineers dominate the buying process and decisions (Sheth, 1973).
- The larger the company, the greater the number of buying influences (Sheth, 1973).
- Large organizations typically exhibit a far greater degree of purchasing expertise and formality than smaller firms (Various).
- The composition of the buying centre tends to vary depending upon the characteristics of the product being purchased and, in particular, the degree of perceived risk (Cyert and March, 1963).
- The composition of the buying centre is influenced by the organization's previous experience with the seller (Robinson, Faris and Wind, 1967).
- Buyers often only examine a limited range of suppliers, largely because of the costs of collecting information (Buckner, 1967). This finding has subsequently been taken a step further by White (1969) whose research suggested that a major reason for limiting the search process is in fact to avoid or simplify work.

It is unrealistic, therefore, to approach the study of buying behaviour – personal or organisational – without an appreciation of the multiplexity of buying motivations. A balanced view is necessary; explanations of buying behaviour should not go from the one extreme of regarding 'rational' economic factors as solely responsible to the equally extreme view that emotional or 'irrational' influences entirely account for the purchase of products and services.

A similar view has been expressed by Harding (1966, p. 76) who has suggested that:

> Corporate decision-makers remain human after they enter the office. They respond to 'image'; they buy from companies to which they feel 'close'; they favour suppliers who show them respect and personal consideration, and who do extra things 'for them'; they 'over-react' to real or imagined slights, tending to reject companies which fail to respond or delay in submitting requested bids.

This point has in turn been developed by Kotler (1988, p. 214) and reflected subsequently in a model of the influences on industrial buying behaviour proposed by Webster and Wind (1972, pp. 32–7). Kotler, for example, has said:

> Industrial buyers actually respond to both economic and personal factors. Where there is substantial similarity in supplier offers, industrial buyers have little basis for rational choice. Since they can satisfy the purchasing requirements with any supplier, these buyers can place more weight on the personal treatment they receive. On the other hand, where competing products differ substantially, industrial buyers are more accountable for their choice and pay more attention to economic factors.

Webster and Wind's model classifies the influences on industrial buyers under four headings: environmental, organizational, interpersonal, and individual influences. These are illustrated in Figure 5.9.

**FIGURE 5.9**
*Factors influencing industrial buying behaviour*

SOURCE: Adapted from Webster and Wind (1972), pp. 33–7

The question of what influences buyers and how various sources of information are perceived has also been examined by Webster (1970). He was particularly interested in the relative importance of formal and informal information sources and how they differ from consumer markets. His findings suggest that informal sources tend to be used far less frequently in industrial markets than in consumer markets and that sales people are often regarded as highly reliable and useful sources of information. By contrast, opinion leadership, which often plays a significant role in consumer markets, was found to be largely ineffective; a possible explanation of this is the perception that no two companies experience the same problem and that there is therefore little to be gained. Perhaps the most significant single finding to emerge from Webster's research was the significance of the role that the industrial sales person is capable of playing *throughout* the buying process; this is illustrated by the summary of Webster's work which appears in Figure 5.10.

**FIGURE 5.10**
*Percentage of respondents considering information sources to be important at each stage of the buying process*

| | Awareness | Interest | Evaluation | Trial | Adoption |
|---|---|---|---|---|---|
| Manufacturers's sales staff | 84 | 90 | 64 | 70 | 56 |
| Trade journals and the technical press | 90 | 38 | 22 | 16 | 8 |
| Buying staff in other companies | 18 | 22 | 28 | 16 | 8 |
| Engineering staff in other companies | 26 | 34 | 44 | 20 | 18 |
| Trade associations | 42 | 24 | 14 | 4 | 8 |
| Trade shows and exhibitions | 76 | 38 | 16 | 12 | 4 |

SOURCE: Adapted from Webster (1970)

The relative importance of sources of information has also been examined by Martilla (1971) and Abratt (1986). Martilla's work led to a series of conclusions that are broadly similar to those of Webster, although in addition he highlighted the importance of word of mouth communication within firms, particularly in the later stages of the adoption process. Abratt's research, which focused on high technology laboratory instrumentation, adds a further dimension to our understanding of the buying process, suggesting that in markets such as these buying personnel often have 'only a token administrative function'. Instead, the question of what to buy is the responsibility of groups of two to three people, with the most significant purchasing criteria proving to be product reliability and technical and sales service back-up, while price was relatively unimportant.

Perhaps the most underestimated and, in research terms, ignored elements of the buying process is that of the *gatekeeper*. Although the identity of the gatekeeper is often difficult to determine, it is the gatekeeper who in many organizations either blocks or facilitates access and who can therefore play a pivotal role in determining which products are considered. This has been recognized by Pettigrew (1975) who, in a study of the way in which a computer system was purchased, demonstrated how the gatekeeper is capable of filtering the information flow to suit his own objectives.

Although as Chisnall (1989, p. 78) has observed, 'Generalisations about buying behaviour – industrial or consumer – appear to be unwise,' it is generally acknowledged that the role and status of buyers is typically lower in high technology organizations than elsewhere. There are several explanations for this, the most obvious being the need for specialist inputs from technical staff. The ways in which this erodes the authority of the professional buyer and how they typically respond has been examined by Strauss (1962). He identified a series of techniques ranging from the rigid enforcement of highly routinized techniques through to extremes of persuasion and cooperation. This led him in turn to propose a five-part framework:

1 rule-orientated tactics;
2 rule-evading tactics;
3 personal–political tactics;
4 persuasion–educational tactics;
5 organizational–interactional tactics.

The success of the buyer's behaviour was, he suggested, ultimately due to whether the strategy pursued was broadly expansionist or contractionist. Those who tried to expand their role and sphere of influence and who subsequently succeeded did so, he concluded, where: managerial relationships were still developing (perhaps because of new management); the technology of the industry was complex; and there was a need for learning.

## How do Buyers Arrive at Their Decisions?

One of the major differences between consumer and industrial buying decisions is the buying motive. Whereas the majority of consumer purchases are made for the individual's personal consumption or utility, industrial purchases are typically designed to reduce operating costs, satisfy legal obligations, provide an input to the manufacturing process, and ultimately to make money. In order to provide a greater understanding of this process, Robinson, Faris and Wind (1967) of the Marketing Science Institute have identified eight stages or buy-phases of the industrial buying process. They then related these to the three types of buying situation that we discussed earlier to form what they referred to as the *buy-grid framework*. This is illustrated in Figure 5.11.

**FIGURE 5.11**
*The Buygrid model*

| | | | Buy classes | | |
|---|---|---|---|---|---|
| | | | Straight rebuy | Modified rebuy | New task |
| **Buy phases** | 1 | Problem recognition | No | Possibly | Yes |
| | 2 | Determination of the general need | No | Possibly | Yes |
| | 3 | Specific description of the required product | Yes | Yes | Yes |
| | 4 | Search for potential suppliers | No | Possibly | Yes |
| | 5 | Evaluation of suppliers | No | Possibly | Yes |
| | 6 | Selection of a supplier | No | Possibly | Yes |
| | 7 | Order-routine established | No | Possibly | Yes |
| | 8 | Review of performance and feedback | Yes | Yes | Yes |

SOURCE: Adapted from Robinson, et al. (1967)

This buying process, which begins with the recognition of a problem, can be sparked off by either internal or external stimuli. Internal stimuli typically include: the decision to develop a new product, and the recognition that this will require new equipment or materials; machine breakdowns; the belief on the part of the purchasing manager that better prices or quality can be obtained from an alternative supplier; curiosity; and organizational policy decisions. External stimuli include: the launch of a new product by a competitor; advertisements; sales representatives; and ideas that emerge as the result of trade shows.

This recognition of a problem is then followed by a *general need description* in which the buyer identifies the characteristics and quantity of the products required to overcome the problem. This leads to the development of *product specifications* and subsequently to a *search for suppliers*.

The question of precisely *how* buyers select suppliers has been the subject of a considerable amount of research with some of the most significant findings emerging from the work of Dempsey (1978), Cunningham and Roberts (1974), Lehmann and O'Shaughnessy (1974), and Green, Faris and Wind (1968). Dempsey, for example, in a survey of purchasing managers found the 20 most important selection criteria to be:

1 delivery capability;
2 quality;
3 price;
4 repair and after sales services;
5 technical capability;
6 performance history;
7 production facilities;
8 help and advice;
9 control systems;
10 reputation;
11 financial position;
12 attitude towards the buyer;
13 compliance with bidding procedures;
14 training support;
15 communications on the progress of the order;
16 management and organization;
17 packaging;
18 moral/legal issues;
19 location;
20 labour relations.

Cunningham and Roberts' research, which covered the British valve and pump industry, highlighted a series of similar factors: delivery reliability; technical advice; test facilities; replacement guarantee; speed of quotations; ease of contact; and a willingness/ability to supply a wide range.

Lehmann and O'Shaughnessy's findings were again broadly similar, although they introduced an additional element in the form of the *type of buying situation*. This led them to suggest that:

1 for routine order products delivery, reliability, price and reputation are extremely important;
2 in the case of procedural-problem products (e.g. computers and other types of office machinery) the important criteria are technical service, supplier flexibility, and product reliability;
3 for political-problem products which are capable of creating organizational rivalries, the most important attributes are price, the reputation of the supplier, product reliability, service reliability, and supplier flexibility.

These general patterns were in turn reflected in the research findings of Green, Faris and Wind (1968), which are illustrated in Figure 5.12.

**FIGURE 5.12**
*The relative importance of product selection criteria in industrial markets*

| Performance characteristics | Scaling value |
|---|---|
| Price/quality ratio | 3.61 |
| Reliability of delivery | 2.94 |
| Technical knowledge and abilities | 1.95 |
| Information services | 1.86 |
| Reputation and image | 1.65 |
| Location geographically | 1.63 |
| Technical and related issues | 1.61 |
| Degree of previous contact | 1.44 |
| Significance of client-supplier reciprocal relations | 0.61 |

SOURCE: Adapted from Green, et al. (1968)

In so far as it is possible to identify a common theme in this process of deciding between suppliers, it is the reduction, containment and management of risk. In commenting on this, Chisnall (1989, p. 83) has suggested that:

> The element of risk in buying decisions could be considered along a continuum ranging from routine (low risk purchases) at one extreme to novel (high risk) purchases at the other end of the scale. In the centre would fall many industrial transactions where the hazards could reasonably be calculated sufficiently to allow decisions of tolerable risk to be made.

This is illustrated in Figure 5.13.

**FIGURE 5.13**
*The buying risk continuum*

SOURCE: Adapted from Chisnall, P. M. (1989), *Strategic Industrial Marketing* (second edition), Prentice Hall, p. 83

Buyers typically cope with these risks in several ways, including:

1 exchanging technical and other information with their customers and prospects;
2 dealing only with those suppliers with which the company has previously had favourable experiences;
3 applying strict (risk reducing) decision rules;
4 dealing only with suppliers who have a long-established and favourable reputation;
5 the introduction of penalty clauses for, for example, late delivery;
6 multiple sourcing to reduce the degree of dependence upon a single supplier.

Although for many buyers the pursuit of a risk-reducing strategy has a series of attractions, it needs to be recognized that such a strategy can also possess drawbacks. The most obvious of these stems from the way in which it is likely to lead to the company becoming and remaining a follower rather than becoming a leader. Developments both in product and process technology on the part of a supplier often provide significant opportunities for the development of a competitive edge, and unless this is recognized by the company it runs the risk of adopting new ideas only when they have been well tried by others. In commenting on this, Chisnall (1989, p. 84) has said:

> The industrial buyer is, to some extent, in a dilemma regarding innovating products. He will not wish to retard the development of his own organisation but, at the same time, he will be reluctant to accept unduly heavy risk. Yet he will be conscious of his status within the management hierarchy and of the opportunities which he should use to enhance his career. It has been seen that progressive buyers . . . deliberately involved technical managers in discussions and decisions regarding supplies, and were skilled in using formal and informal approaches. In this way the corporate or organisation man aims to steer a careful course between satisfying his personal need for status and security and the development of his company as a progressive organisation . . . Suppliers should obviously (therefore) try to reduce the element of risk as perceived by buyers, through imaginative marketing strategies, particularly where new products are being introduced.

Perhaps the final aspect of risk that needs to be considered here stems from the significance of post-purchase dissonance. Undoubtedly the best known writer on dissonance is Festinger (1957), who has referred to it as a state of psychological discomfort. This discomfort is, in essence, the result of the individual questioning whether the decision made is correct. According to Festinger, a buyer will try to reduce this discomfort by seeking reassurance for the decision. This can be done by, for example, seeking the support of others, avoiding conflicting messages such as competitive advertising, and searching for editorials and advertisements which state how good the product just purchased is. The more expensive and significant the purchase, the greater the dissonance is likely to be. The implications for a supplier in these circumstnaces should be obvious: buyers need reassurance and this can best be provided by continuing to 'sell' the product and providing supporting evidence of the wisdom of the decision even after the sale itself has been made. Other ways in which dissonance can be reduced include giving emphasis to the quality of the after-sales service, maintaining regular contact with customers, and giving prominence in advertising to the market leaders who have also bought the product. One example of an organization that recognizes the need for managing dissonance is IBM, whose experiences are discussed in Illustration 5.9.

---

## Illustration 5.9:  IBM and its Development of the Total Sales Programme

IBM says that it sells solutions, not products. In doing this, the company concentrates upon gaining – and retaining – the customer's confidence from the moment of contact through until well after the sale has been made. One result of this is that long-term relationships are established, repeat purchases are guaranteed, and the likelihood of post-purchase dissonance reduced so that it is to all intents meaningless. Some of the ways in which this is done are listed below:

- Inviting the customer contact and other members of the company to conferences and seminars that may be useful to them. Often these seminars feature major international figures.
- Inviting the contact to visit prestigious customers who have successful IBM installations.
- Inviting the contact and others in the company to visit IBM's factories to look at projects that may be of interest.
- Sending out articles, newsletters and house magazines.
- Ensuring that IBM's service engineers and systems specialists channel back information gained when working at the customer's plant so that as full a picture as possible is built up of the client's needs.
- The development of 'account planning sessions' in which IBM, together with the customer, draws up an action plan for the next few years covering the systems and products that the customer may need.
- Ensuring a regular and worry-free relationship is developed and maintained.

*Adapted from Duro, R. (1989)* Winning the Marketing War, *John Wiley & Son*

---

Having decided upon the choice of supplier, the buyer moves on to the *order-routine specification* by identifying such features as the technical specification, the order quantities, delivery schedules, maintenance requirements and payment terms.

The final stage involves a *review of suppliers' performance* and is designed, in one sense at least, to close the loop by feeding back information that will be used when purchasing in the future.

**An Assessment of the Buygrid Framework**

Although the buygrid framework is undoubtedly useful and provides a series of insights into the various phases of buying, the reader should recognize that it fails to give full recognition of the complexity of the behavioural factors which are likely to influence those involved in making specific purchase decisions. Because of this, other models of organizational buying have been proposed, four of which are discussed in Illustration 5.10.

# Illustration 5.10: An Overview of Models of Organizational Buying Behaviour

During the past 25 years a wide variety of models of industrial buying behaviour have been developed. These fall into four main categories:

1 task related models;
2 non-task related models;
3 complex and multidisciplinary models;
4 interactive models.

The first of these – *task related models* – is by far the most straightforward and is the organizational equivalent of the Marshallian model of economic man that we discussed at an earlier stage. These models, which have to a large extent been invalidated by subsequent research, emphasize rationality and constrained choice:

By contrast, *non-task models* recognize the personal interests of the decision maker. In discussing this, Turnbull (1987, pp. 155–6) identifies the key concepts as being:

- Individual desire for ego enhancement or personal gain.
- Desire to avoid risk in decision making.
- Gratification of buyer and seller through a dyadic relationship.
- Lateral relationships between buyer and colleagues.
- Relationships with significant other persons from within the company and their effect on transmission and interpretation of information.

The third category consists of *complex* and multidisciplinary models which incorporate a larger number of variables. Included within this are Robinson, Faris and Wind's buygrid model, and Sheth's multidisciplinary model, both of which are discussed in the text. A key feature of complex models is that explicit recognition is given to social, cultural, psychological and economic variables.

The final category – the *interaction approach* – places far greater emphasis upon the nature of the process and relationships which develop both within and between buying and selling organizations. Thus:

- buyers and sellers are both active participants and buyers often attempt to influence what they are offered;
- relationships are often long term and based on mutual trust rather than any formal commitment;
- patterns of interaction are frequently complex and extend within the organizations as well as between them;
- emphasis is given to supporting these relationships as well as to the process of buying and selling;
- links between buyers and sellers often become institutionalized.

The best known of the multidisciplinary models was developed by Sheth (1973). Within this model he attempts both to identify and show the interrelationship of the multiplicity of factors involved in industrial buying. These factors, he suggests, can be examined under three headings:

1 the psychological world of the individuals involved in organizational buying;
2 the conditions which precipitate joint decisions among these individuals;
3 the process of joint decision making with the inevitable conflict among the decision makers and its resolution by resorting to a variety of tactics.

In putting forward this model, Sheth does not argue that it is definitive. Rather it is a framework which illustrates the complexity of the process and attempts to present the various inputs to this process systematically.

This approach to modelling industrial buying has in turn provided one of the foundations for the work of Hakansson and the IMP (International Marketing and Purchasing of Industrial Goods) group. Their research focused upon industrial buying and selling behaviour in five European countries – West Germany, the United Kingdom, France, Italy and Sweden – and led to the development of a model which views this behaviour as a process in which both sides play active roles within a given environment. They suggest that four elements influence the patterns of buyer–seller interaction. These elements, which are illustrated in Figure 5.14, are:

1 the interaction process;
2 the participants in this process;
3 the interaction environment;
4 the atmosphere created by this interaction.

**FIGURE 5.14**
*The interaction model of industrial marketing and purchasing*

SOURCE: Adapted from Hakansson (1983)

The real value of this model, which makes use both of inter-organizational theory and new institutional economic thinking, is that it gives far greater emphasis than earlier work to the idea that industrial buying and selling is concerned with the management of relationships. In commenting on this, Chisnall (1989, p. 93) has said:

That business negotiation is essentially a dynamic process will hardly surprise experienced executives who, although they may not be able to articulate the theory, know full well the complexities involved in successful business deals. The interdependence of buyers and sellers in industrial product and service markets is well recognised in practice, although even long-established relationships and loyalties may be vulnerable to new levels of competition from, for instance, the newly industrialised countries.

Hakansson's theory is helpful in drawing attention to the need for executives – in both purchasing and marketing – to develop negotiating skills appropriate to specific products and market conditions. Both formal and informal contacts contribute to the establishment of relationships that can result in mutually satisfactory business transactions. Since the research enquiries covered several countries, it is perhaps not surprising that attitudes towards participation and authority were found to be 'quite different' in France and Germany compared with Sweden, although it was considered that more extensive research would be needed before this cultural phenomenon could definitely be established.

## 5.7 THE INFLUENCE OF THE PRODUCT ON MARKETING STRATEGY

Although a variety of frameworks for classifying products have at one time or another been proposed, one of the most useful was put forward by Aspinall (1962). There are, he suggests, five product characteristics that should provide the basis for identifying the product's potentially most effective marketing strategy. These are:

1 the rate at which the product is purchased, consumed and replaced (*the replacement rate*);
2 the *gross margin*;
3 the *amount of adjustment* that needs to be made to the product so that it matches the precise needs of the customer;
4 the *time of consumption* over which the product delivers the utilities demanded by the consumer;
5 the amount of *searching time* that the consumer is willing to give to the product. This is typically a measure of the average time and distance from the retail outlet.

Aspinall argues that this framework can then be used as the basis for a scoring system and the subsequent classification of products into broad categories. He then goes on to identify three categories of products, each of which is assigned a colour. Thus:

- *Red goods* which have a high replacement rate, a low gross margin, require little adjustment, and have a limited consumption and searching time;
- *orange goods* which have a medium score across all five dimensions;
- *yellow goods* which have a low rate of replacement, a high gross margin, require substantial adjustment, and have a significant consumption and searching time.

## 5.8 SUMMARY

Within this chapter we have focused on the detail of consumer and industrial buying structures and processes and on the ways in which an understanding of these contributes to effective marketing planning.

A variety of factors influence consumer behaviour, the most significant of which are a network of cultural, social, personal, and psychological forces. Each of these was discussed in some detail and the nature of their interrelationships explored. Against this background we then considered the structure of buying decision processes, and in particular:

- the buying roles within the decision-making unit;
- the different types of buying behaviour;
- the process through which a consumer goes in making a decision.

A variety of attempts have been made over the past 25 years to model the complexities of the buying process, the best known of which are those proposed by Nicosia; Engel, Kollat and Blackwell; and Sheth. These models have been the subject of a certain amount of criticism, one consequence of which has been that the strategist's ability to predict with any real degree of accuracy the probable response of consumers to marketing behaviour is still relatively limited.

Research into organizational buying behaviour has pursued broadly similar objectives to that in the consumer field, with attention being paid to the questions of:

- Who makes up the market?
- What buying decisions do they make?
- Who are the key participants in the buying process?
- What influences the buyer?
- How do buyers arrive at their decisions?

Each of these areas was examined in some detail and the best known of the models of organizational buying behaviour were reviewed. As with models of consumer behaviour, the majority of these have been heavily criticized, largely because of their poor analytical or predictive ability. There are, however, exceptions to this, as we discussed, including Robinson, Faris and Wind's buygrid model, and Hakansson's interaction approach in which use is made of inter-organizational theory and new institutional economic thinking. It is in these areas that future developments in our understanding of organizational buying processes are most likely to be made.

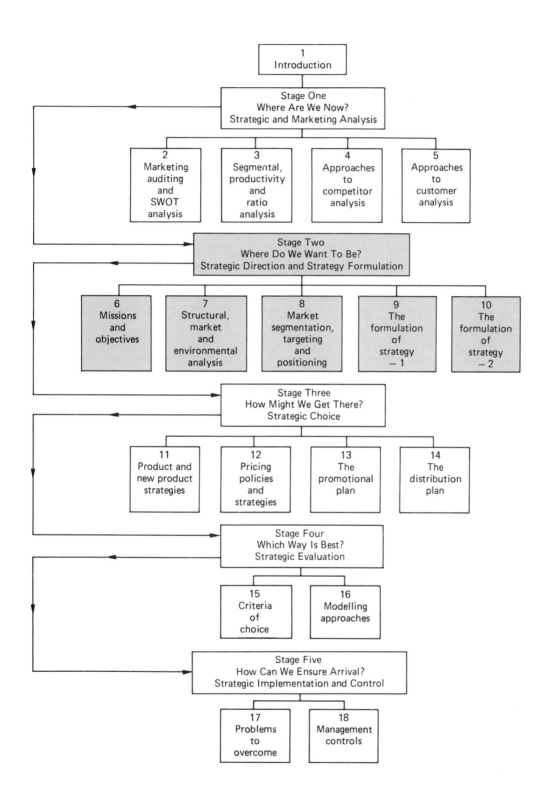

# Stage Two
## Where Do We Want To Be?
### Strategic Direction and Strategy Formulation

## PREAMBLE

Within this stage we focus on where the organization wants to go. In doing this we take as our foundation the material of Stage One in which we examined where the organization is currently, and the nature of its marketing capability.

We begin by considering the organizational mission and the nature of marketing objectives (Chapter 6). We then turn to an examination of the changing structure of the marketing environment (Chapter 7) and to the ways in which this structure needs to be reflected in the approach adopted when segmenting the market (Chapter 8). In the following chapter we examine a number of the models that have been developed to help in the process of strategy formulation, as a prelude – in Chapter 10 – to a discussion of the factors that influence the nature of the strategy pursued.

Mission statements have been the subject of considerable discussion in recent years, with the majority of commentators pointing to their potential for providing employees with a clear understanding of core corporate values. Although many organizations still lack a mission statement, while others have statements which reflect a degree of wishful thinking rather than reality, the guidelines for developing a meaningful corporate mission are now well developed. The significance of the mission statement can be further highlighted by recognizing that it is against the background of the mission statement that the strategist should set objectives at both the corporate and the functional level (in the case of marketing, these objectives revolve around two major dimensions: products and markets). It follows from this that a poorly developed mission statement is likely to have consequences for the nature and appropriateness of any subsequent objectives.

As well as being influenced by the corporate mission, organizational objectives are typically influenced by a wide variety of other factors, including the nature and demands of the environment. The marketing strategist typically analyses the environment within the PEST (Political, Economic, Social and Technological) framework, the individual elements of which are in the majority of markets undergoing a series of significant and often unprecedented changes, each of which needs to be taken into account both when setting objectives and formulating strategies.

The changing environment also has consequences for methods of segmentation. Effective segmentation is at the heart of a well-developed marketing strategy, and has implications for virtually everything else that follows in the strategy process. It is therefore a source of concern that work by Saunders has highlighted the fact that senior managers in many British organizations seemingly fail to recognize this, and pay little or no attention either to the need for segmentation or to the ways in which it can be carried out most effectively.

The strategic significance of segmentation is reinforced by the way in which decisions on how the organization's markets are to be segmented subsequently has implications for targeting and market positioning. The failure to segment effectively is therefore likely to weaken much of the marketing process.

In Chapters 9 and 10 we focus upon approaches to the formulation of marketing strategy. In the first of these chapters we consider some of the developments that have taken place over the past 20 years in techniques of portfolio analysis. The portfolio approach to management emerged largely as a result of the turbulence of the early 1970s and is based on the idea that an organization's businesses should be viewed and managed in a similar way to an investment portfolio, with a strategic perspective being adopted in the management of each major element.

Although a wide variety of portfolio techniques have been developed and have contributed to a greater understanding on the part of management of what is meant by strategy, research findings are beginning to emerge which suggest that usage levels of even the best-known methods are low. Several explanations for this have been proposed, including unrealistic expectations on the part of managers, difficulties with the data inputs, and an over-zealous adherence to the strategic guidelines that typically accompany the models. Nevertheless, models of portfolio analysis need to be seen as one of the major developments in strategic thinking over the past 20 years and, if used wisely, are capable of contributing greatly to a structured approach to marketing management. (See Morrison and Wensley (1991).)

The type of marketing strategy pursued by an organization is often the result of the interaction of a series of factors, including past performance, managerial expectations and culture, competitive behaviour, the stage reached on the product life cycle, and the firm's relative market position. Porter has attempted to provide a structure for examining the strategic alternatives open to an organization and suggests that in order to compete successfully the strategist needs to select a generic strategy and pursue it consistently. The three generic strategies that he identifies are:

- cost leadership;
- differentiation;
- focus.

Dangers arise, Porter suggests, when the firm fails to pursue one of these and instead is forced or drifts into a 'middle-of-the-road' position where the message to the market is confused and the likelihood of a successful competitive attack is increased.

A considerable amount of work has been done in recent years in drawing parallels between military warfare and marketing strategy with a view to identifying any lessons that the marketing strategist might learn. A number of general lessons have emerged from this, and guidelines on how best either to defend a market position or attack other organizations are now well developed. Within this chapter we have attempted to draw upon the experiences of successful organizations and to highlight particular dangers. Included within these is the danger of adhering to a particular strategy for too long a period, labelled 'strategic wear out'. There is an obvious attraction in sticking to a well-proven strategy, although evidence exists to suggest that even the best formulated strategy has a limited life. The marketing strategist should therefore closely monitor the effectiveness of any given strategy and be willing to change it in order to reflect the environment, different managerial expectations, and the progression through the product and market life cycles.

# 6 | Missions and objectives

## 6.1 LEARNING OBJECTIVES

When you have read this chapter you should be able to understand:

(a) the purpose of planning;
(b) the nature of the corporate mission and how a mission statement can best be developed;
(c) the factors influencing objectives and strategy;
(d) the nature of corporate objectives;
(e) the nature of marketing objectives.

## 6.2 INTRODUCTION

To be effective, a strategic planning system must be goal driven. The setting of objectives is therefore a key step in the marketing planning process, since unless it is carried out effectively, everything that follows will lack focus and cohesion. In terms of its position within the overall planning process that forms the basis of this book, objectives setting can be seen to follow on from the initial stage of analysis and, in particular, the marketing audit which provided the focus of Chapter 2 (see Figure 6.1).

**FIGURE 6.1**
*The strategic planning process*

Initial environmental and business analysis

Develop the mission statement

Detailed marketing audit

Corporate objectives and strategy formulation

Marketing objectives and strategy formulation

Estimate expected results

Identify alternative plans and mixes

Implementation

Review

By setting objectives, the planner is attempting to provide the organization with a sense of direction. In addition, however, objectives provide a basis for motivation as well as a bench-mark against which performance and effectiveness can subsequently be measured. The setting of objectives is thus at the very heart of the planning process and is the prelude to the development of strategies and detailed plans. (For a discussion of the interrelationships between objectives, strategies and plans, refer to Illustration 6.1). Perhaps surprisingly therefore in view of its fundamental importance, the literature on *how* to set marketing objectives is surprisingly thin, something that is reflected in a comment by McDonald (1984, p. 82):

> The literature on [marketing planning] is not very explicit, which is surprising when it is considered how vital the setting of marketing objectives is. An objective will ensure that a company knows what its strategies are expected to accomplish and when a particular strategy has accomplished its purpose. In other words, without objectives, strategy decisions and all that follow will take place in a vacuum.

A possible explanation of this is that, in principle at least, the process of setting objectives is relatively straightforward and as such merits little discussion. In practice, however, the process is infinitely more difficult, particularly in divisionalized organizations, or where the company has an extensive product range being sold across a variety of markets. Regardless of whether we are talking about principles or practice, the sequence should be the same, beginning with an identification of the organization's current position and capabilities, a statement of assumptions about environmental factors affecting the business, and then agreement among stakeholders as to the objectives themselves.

In moving through this process, the majority of commentators recommend that the planner moves from the general to the specific and from the long term to the short term. This frequently translates into statements on three aspects of the business:

1 the nature of the current business (what business *are* we in?);
2 where it should go (what business *should* we be in?);
3 how it should get there.

Identifying where the company is currently is often far more difficult than it might appear, something which is reflected in a comment by the ex-Chairman of ICI, Sir John Harvey-Jones (1988):

> There is no point in deciding where your business is going until you have actually decided with great clarity where you are now. Like practically everything in business this is easier said than done.

Recognizing the validity of this point should encourage the strategist to focus not just upon the business's current position, but also *how* and *why* it has achieved its current levels of success or failure. Having done this, he is then in a far better position to begin specifying the *primary* or *most important* corporate objectives, as well as a series of statements regarding the key results areas such as sales growth, market penetration, and new product development in which success is essential to the organization. Following on from this, the strategist should then begin developing the *secondary* or *sub-objectives* such as geographical expansion and line extension which will need to be achieved if the primary objectives are to be attained.

This process of moving from the general to the specific should lead to a set of objectives which are not just attainable within any budgetary constraints that exist, but which are also compatible with environmental conditions as well as organizational strengths and weaknesses. It follows from this that the process of setting objectives should form what is often referred to as an internally consistent and mutually reinforcing hierarchy. As an illustration of this, if we assume that corporate management is concerned first and foremost with, say, long-term profits and growth, it is these objectives which provide the framework within which the more detailed subset of operational objectives, including market expansion and product specific increases in sales and share, are developed. Taken together, these then contribute to the achievement of the overall corporate objectives.

It is these operational objectives which are the principal concern of those in the level below corporate management. Below this, managers are concerned with objectives that are defined even more specifically such as creating awareness of a new product, increasing levels of distribution, and so on. This hierarchy points in turn to the interrelationship, and in some cases the confusion, that exists between corporate objectives and marketing objectives. The distinction between the two is an important one and is discussed at a later stage in this chapter. However, as a prelude to this, and indeed to the process of objectives setting, there is a need for the strategist to decide upon the business mission. We therefore begin this chapter with a discussion of the role and purpose of planning as the background against which we can more realistically examine approaches to the development of the mission statement and, subsequently, corporate and marketing objectives. See Illustration 6.1.

---

## Illustration 6.1: Objectives, Strategies and Plans

The interrelationships between objectives, strategies and plans have been spelled out by Davidson (1987, p. 122) who, in discussing BMW's recovery efforts in Germany in the 1960s, comments:

> In 1960 BMW was on the verge of bankruptcy. It was producing motor cycles for a dwindling market, and making a poor return on its bubble cars and six-cylinder saloons. A takeover bid by Daimler-Benz, the makers of Mercedes, was narrowly avoided, and the group was rescued by a Bavarian investment group.
>
> Paul G. Hahnemann, Opel's top wholesale distributor, was appointed Chief Executive. His first objective was obviously to get BMW back on an even keel, where it was sufficiently profitable to survive in the long-term. Having got there, he would then move to a more ambitious objective of challenging Mercedes for leadership of the market for high-quality executive cars.
>
> He was convinced that there was an unexploited market for a sporty saloon car, which Mercedes was not tapping. As he pointed out, 'If you were a sporty driver and German, there was no car for you. The Mercedes is big, black and ponderous. It's for parking, not driving.'
>
> Consequently, he evolved a strategy for producing a range of high-quality cars with better performance and a more sporty image than any other saloon. This strategy has remained broadly unchanged since. But the plans for executing it have evolved and been refined.

*Source: Davidson, H. (1987),* Offensive Marketing, *Penguin*

---

## 6.3 THE PURPOSE OF PLANNING

In discussing the nature and role of the planning process, Jackson (1975) comments that:

> Planning attempts to control the factors which affect the outcome of decisions; actions are guided so that success is more likely to be achieved. To plan is to decide

what to do before doing it. Like methods, plans can be specially made to fit circumstances or they can be ready made for regular use in recurrent and familiar situations. In other words, a methodical approach can be custom built or ready made according to the nature of the problems involved.

The purpose of planning can therefore be seen as an attempt to impose a degree of structure upon behaviour by allocating resources in order to achieve organizational objectives. This is in turn reflected in a somewhat cumbersome but nevertheless useful comment by Drucker (1959) who suggests that:

> business planning is a continuous process of making present entrepreneurial decisions systematically and with best possible knowledge of their futurity, organizing systematically the effort needed to carry out these decisions against expectations through organized feedback.

While not particularly succinct, this definition has a certain value in that it highlights the three major elements of planning:

1 the need for systematic decision making;
2 the development of programmes for their implementation;
3 the measurement of performance against objectives, as a prelude to modifications to the strategy itself.

It follows from this that if the planning process is to be effective, then the planner needs to give full recognition to the changing nature and demands of the environment, and to incorporate a degree of flexibility into both the objectives and the plan itself. Any failure to do this is likely to lead to a plan that quickly becomes out of date. Simmons (1972) has pointed to the dangers of this both in the planning carried out by the Eastern bloc countries and by American business. In the case of the Eastern bloc countries in the 1940s, 50s and 60s, for example, he suggests that:

> They tried to impose a fixed five year plan on changing conditions. Unfortunately, some American businesses are still making this mistake ... frequently a well constructed plan only six months old will be found to be very much out-of-date.

If planning is to prove effective, there is an obvious need for a regular review process, something which is particularly important when the environment in which the organization is operating is changing rapidly. As an example of this, Chisnall (1989, pp. 133–34) has pointed to the Post Office and the increasingly competitive environment it faced following the Post Office Act of 1969, which:

> ... transformed the Post Office from a Department of State into a State Corporation that had to achieve a predetermined level of profits. The establishment of a marketing department in 1972 added to the keen commercial awareness and new professional skills which were needed to tackle, for instance, the fast-growing and aggressive competition in parcels traffic from several new market suppliers.

The principal purpose and indeed benefit of planning can therefore be seen in terms of the way in which it imposes a degree of order upon potential chaos and allocates the organization's resources in the most effective way. Among the other benefits are the ways in which the planning process brings people together and, potentially at least, leads to 'a shared sense of opportunity, direction, significance and achievement'. The planning process can therefore be seen to consist of four distinct stages:

1 evaluation (where are we now, where do we want to go, and what level of resource capability do we have?);

2 strategy formulation (how are we going to get there?);
3 detailed planning;
4 implementation and review.

For many organizations, it is the implementation stage which proves to be the most difficult but which paradoxically receives the least attention. There are several possible explanations for this. Peters & Waterman (1982, pp. 9–12), for example, suggest that all too often emphasis is placed upon what they refer to the 'hard-ball' elements of strategy, structure and systems, with too little recognition being given to the significance of the 'soft-ball' elements of style, skills, staff and subordinate systems. (This is discussed in greater detail on pages 528–529.)

## 6.4 ESTABLISHING THE CORPORATE MISSION

Referring back to Figure 6.1 (see page 137), it can be seen that following an initial environmental and business analysis, the development of a mission statement is the starting point both for corporate and marketing planning since it represents a vision of what the organization is or should attempt to become. This is typically expressed in terms of the two questions to which we have already referred: 'What business are we in?' and 'What business should we be in?' It is the answer to this second question in particular which sets the parameters within which objectives are subsequently established, strategies developed, and action programmes implemented. The mission statement should therefore be capable of performing a powerful integrating function, since it is in many ways a statement of core corporate values and is the framework within which individual business units prepare their business plans, something which has led to the corporate mission being referred to as an 'invisible hand' which guides geographically scattered employees to work independently and yet collectively towards the organization's goal. A similar sentiment has been expressed by Ouchi (1983, p. 74) who suggests that the deliberate generality of the mission statement performs an integrating function of various stakeholders over a long period of time. This is illustrated in the case of the earth-moving equipment manufacturer J. C. Bamford which has a clearly stated policy of quality and product improvement, something of which everyone in the organization is fully aware and which acts as a consistent guideline in determining behaviour at all levels, but particularly within the planning process.

For a mission statement to be worthwhile, it should be capable of providing personnel throughout the company with a shared sense of opportunity, direction, significance and achievement, factors which are particularly important for large organizations with divisions which are geographically scattered.

The potential benefits of a strong binding statement of fundamental corporate values and good communication have been highlighted by a variety of writers, including Pilditch (1987, p. 34) who has pointed to research in the United States which 'found that companies that do better had excellent communications. Everyone knew the corporate goals and was encouraged to help to achieve them'. Equally a study of European managers by Management Centre Europe found that what gave highly successful companies an edge over their competitors was the importance they attached to basic corporate values. In commenting on these findings, Chisnall (1989, pp. 138–39) has said:

> As with comparable studies in the United States, there often seemed to be a rather curious inverse relationship between those companies which emphasised profitability as a primary corporate value and the actual profitability achieved. On the other hand, companies generally ranking customer satisfaction as the most important corporate value were highly profitable. It is important to note, however, that professed commitment to high corporate values needs to be translated into practice:

strong declarations themselves may sound impressive, but implementation has to be effected by management at every level of organisation and expressed in many ways, such as high standards of customer service, good teamwork between executives in different departments as well as in the same section, keeping promised delivery dates, etc. Clearly, these duties should always be undertaken by those responsible for them but, too often, such everyday tasks are just not well done.

In many ways, therefore, the mission statement represents a visionary view of the overall strategic posture of an organization and, as Johnson & Scholes (1988, p. 8) comment 'is likely to be a persistent and resistant influence on strategic decisions'. Richards (1983, p. 104) has referred to the mission in much the same way, calling it 'the master strategy' and suggesting that it is a visionary projection of the central and overriding concepts on which the organization is based. He goes on to suggest that 'it should not focus on what the firm is doing in terms of products and markets currently served, but rather upon the services and utility within the firm'.

It follows from this that any failure to agree the mission statement is likely to lead to fundamental problems in determining the strategic direction of the firm. Recognizing this, Debenhams, Sainsbury, and Marks & Spencer have all concentrated upon developing *and communicating to their staff* their mission statements. The rationale in each case is straightforward and is a reflection of the fact that a mission statement is of little value unless it is understood by everyone in the organization and *acted upon*.

In the case of Debenhams, for example, the mission statement is printed on a card which employees are expected to carry with them:

We will be the leading countrywide speciality store, the first choice for fashion and home furnishings for middle and upper income customers, characterised by our:

- Visual excitement and easy to shop environment
- Fashion authority
- Dominance in the most wanted merchandise categories
- Above average quality and value for money
- Merchandise organised by end use, activity or emerging trend
- Customer dedication

We will produce above average profits for Department Stores to meet Group financial objectives.

We will develop an organisational environment which will attract, retain, develop and motivate high calibre staff, dedicated to the implementing of our mission.

Similarly, Sainsbury has stated its mission as being:

To discharge the responsibility as leaders in our trade by acting with complete integrity, by carrying out our work to the highest standards, and by contributing to the public good and to the quality of life in the community.

To provide unrivalled value to our customers in the quality of the goods we sell, in the competitiveness of our prices and in the range of choice we offer.

In our stores, to achieve the highest standards of cleanliness and hygiene, efficiency of operation, convenience and customer service, and thereby create as attractive and friendly a shopping environment as possible.

To offer our staff outstanding opportunities in terms of personal career development and in remuneration relative to other companies in the same market, practising always a concern for the welfare of every individual.

To generate sufficient profit to finance continual improvement and growth of the business whilst providing our shareholders with an excellent return on their investment.

Marks & Spencer's mission is broadly similar:

To offer our customers a selective range of high quality well-designed and attractive merchandise at reasonable prices.

To encourage our suppliers to use the most modern and efficient techniques of production and quality control dictated by the latest discoveries in science and technology.

With the co-operation of our suppliers, to ensure the highest standards of quality control.

To plan the expansion of our stores for the better display of a widening range of goods (and) for the convenience of our customers.

To simplify operating procedures so that our business is carried on in the most efficient manner.

To foster good human relations with customers, suppliers and staff.

In all three cases the mission statement represents a reflection of basic corporate values and in doing this provides an overall purpose and sense of direction.

**The Characteristics of Good Mission Statements**

Good mission statements can be seen to exhibit certain characteristics, the most notable being that they are, as Wensley has commented, 'short on numbers and long on rhetoric while (still) remaining succinct' (1987, p. 31). Having said this, Toyota's mission statement, expressed in 1985, did contain a useful and significant number. Sometimes called the Global 10 mission, it expressed Toyota's intention to have 10 per cent of the world car market by the 1990s. In many cases, however, the mission statement emerges as little more than a public relations exercise. In making this comment we have in mind the temptation that exists for over-ambition which is typically reflected in the too frequent use of phrases such as 'first in the field', 'excellent', and so on. For a mission statement to be worthwhile, it is essential that it is realistic and specifies the business domain in which the company will operate. According to Abell (1980, Ch. 3) this domain is best defined in terms of three dimensions;

1 the *customer groups* that will be served;
2 the *customer needs* that will be met;
3 the *technology* that will satisfy these needs.

**Modifying the Mission Statement Over Time**

Having developed a mission statement, it should not be seen as a once-and-for-all expression of the organization's purpose, but rather as something which changes over time in response to changing internal conditions and external environmental opportunities, and threats. A mission statement developed in the 1970s, for example, is unlikely to be appropriate in the 1990s when issues such as environmentalism and the green consumer are of considerably greater importance. Equally, the mission statement needs to reflect changing emphases as the organization grows, adds new products and moves into new markets. Over the past decade, for example, Uniroyal has gradually moved out of the tyre business and in doing this has redefined its mission statement on several occasions.

**Influences on the Mission Statement**

In developing the mission statement for a company there are likely to be five major factors which need to be taken into account:

1 *The company's history and in particular its performance and patterns of ownership.* In commenting on this, Kotler (1988, p. 37) has pointed out that 'every organization has a history of aims, policies and accomplishments. In

reaching for a new purpose, the organization must honour the salient characteristics of its past history.'

2 *The preferences, values and expectations of managers, owners and those who have power within the organization.* In commenting on this in the context of the nature of strategic decisions, Johnson & Scholes (1988, p. 7) suggest that 'strategy can be thought of as a reflection of the attitudes and beliefs of those who have the most influence in the organization. Whether an organization is expansionist or more concerned with consolidation, or where the boundaries are drawn for a company's activities, may say much about the values and attitudes of those who most strongly influence strategy'.

3 *Environmental factors*, and in particular the major opportunities and threats that exist and are likely to emerge in the future.

4 *The resources available*, since these make certain missions possible and others not.

5 *Distinctive competences.* While opportunities may exist in a particular market, it would not necessarily make sense for an organization to enter the market if it would not be making the fullest use of its areas of distinctive competence.

For the majority of organizations, the development of a mission statement often proves to be a difficult process, involving a series of decisions on strategic trade-offs between different groups of stakeholders both inside and outside the organization. These stakeholders can conveniently be grouped under three main headings (see Figure 1.12, p. 19):

1 *internal stakeholders* including owners, decision makers, unions and employees;
2 *external stakeholders* such as the government, the financial community, trade associations, pressure groups and society;
3 *market-place stakeholders* including customers, competitors, suppliers and creditors.

Of these three groups it is the *internal stakeholders* who undoubtedly exert the greatest and most immediate effect upon the mission and subsequently the objectives pursued, since it is their expectations and patterns of behaviour which influence the organization most directly on a day-to-day basis.

The impact of *external stakeholders* is by contrast less direct although still felt in a variety of ways. The implications of legislation, for example, in the form of, say, compulsory seat belts in the rear of cars has an effect both upon the manufacturers of cars and seat belts. Equally, the financial community represents a significant influence in that the availability and cost of finance, as well as financial expectations in terms of returns, will all force the planner to behave in particular ways. In the case of pressure groups, the most obvious factor in recent years has been the emergence of environmental issues with the 'greening' of business policies having subsequently been felt across a wide spectrum of products, including petrol, foodstuffs, and white goods such as refrigerators.

The third category of stakeholders is made up of those in the *market-place*. Of the four major types of market-place stakeholders, it is customers and competitors who have the most obvious and direct impact upon planning, since in order to succeed the company needs to understand in some detail their expectations and likely patterns of behaviour. It follows from this that both the organizational mission and the objectives pursued must of necessity be a direct reflection of both elements. By contrast, the influence of suppliers is generally seen to be less direct. There is, however, an obvious need for planning to take account of issues of supply availability, consistency and quality, since without this problems of shortfall or irregular supply are likely to be experienced.

Before attempting to write a mission statement the strategist needs to spend time preparing a meaningful statement about the purpose of the firm. In doing this he needs to recognize the organization's capabilities, the constraints upon it both internally and externally, and the opportunities that exist currently and that might feasibly develop.

For a mission statement to be useful therefore it needs to exhibit certain characteristics. It should, for example, focus upon *distinctive values* rather than upon every opportunity that is likely to exist. A statement that includes comments on producing the highest-quality product, offering the most service, achieving the widest distribution network, and selling at the lowest price is both unrealistic and too ambitious. More importantly, it fails to provide the sorts of guidelines needed when trade-offs are necessary. Equally, the mission statement must define what we can refer to as the *competitive domain* within which the organization will operate. This competitive domain can be classified by a series of statements on scope:

1 *Industry scope*: this is the range of industries that are of interest to the organization. Some organizations, for example, will operate in just one industry sector, while others are willing to operate in a series. Equally some organizations will only operate in an industrial or consumer goods market while others are willing to operate in both.
2 *Geographical scope*: the geographical breadth of operations in terms of regions, countries or county groupings is again part of the mission statement, and varies from a single city right through to multinationals which operate in virtually every country of the world.
3 *Market segment scope*: which covers the type of market or customer that the company is willing to serve. For a long time, for example, Johnson & Johnson sold its range of products only to the baby market. Largely because of demographic shifts, the company redefined its market segments and, with considerable success, moved into the young adult market.
4 *Vertical scope*: which refers to the degree of integration within the company. Thus Ford, as part of its car manufacturing operations, also owns rubber plantations, glass manufacturing plants and several steel foundries. Others, by contrast, buy in everything and simply act as middlemen.

It should be apparent therefore that in developing the mission statement a variety of considerations need to be borne in mind. The end purpose, however, should be that of *motivation* by ensuring that stakeholders recognize the significance of their work in a far broader sense than simply that of making profits.

The third aspect of the mission statement is that it should only give emphasis to the *major policies* that the organization wishes to pursue. These policies are designed to narrow the range of individual discretion, with the result that the organization should operate in a more consistent manner.

**The Need for Communication**

Once a mission has been developed it is of course imperative that it is communicated to employees so that everyone in the organization is aware of it, since as we suggested earlier, the statement is designed to provide a sense of vision and direction for the organization over the next 10 to 20 years. A mission statement is of little value therefore if employees are either not made aware of it or misunderstand it, or if it is revised every few years in response to minor environmental changes. There is, however, a need for it to be redefined either when it has lost its appropriateness or when it no longer defines the optimal course for the organization.

## 6.5 INFLUENCES ON OBJECTIVES AND STRATEGY

Having developed the mission statement, the strategist is then in a position to turn to the objectives and strategy. It has long been recognized that any organization represents a complex mix of cultural and political influences, all of which come to bear in some way on the objectives that are pursued. It follows from this that objectives and strategy are not simply set in a vacuum or just by reference to environmental factors, but rather that they emerge as the product of a complex interaction at various levels of the organization. This is reflected in Figure 6.2 which illustrates the various layers of cultural and political influences on objectives (and subsequently strategy), ranging from the values of society to the far more specific influences such as organizational objectives, individuals' expectations, and indeed the power structures that exist within and around the organization.

**FIGURE 6.2**
*Influences on organizational objectives (and strategy)*

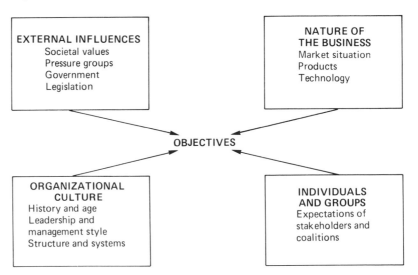

SOURCE: Adapted from Johnson and Scholes (1988), p. 114

It follows from this that if we are to understand fully the process of setting objectives, we need to recognize the complexities of these interrelationships. These have been commented on by Johnson & Scholes (1988, pp. 113–15), and it is worth quoting them at some length:

- There are a number of cultural factors in an organization's *environment* which will influence the internal situation. In particular the values of society at large and the influence of organized groups need to be understood.
- The *nature of the business*, such as the market situation and the types of product and technology are important influences not only in a direct sense but in the way they affect the expectations of individuals and groups.
- Most pervasive of all these general influences is the organizational *culture* itself.
- At a more specific level, individuals will normally have shared expectations with one or more groups of people within the organization. These shared expectations may be concerned with undertaking the company's tasks and reflect the formal structure of the organization, e.g. departmental expectations. However, *coalitions* also arise as a result of specific events, and can transcend the formal structure.
- Internal groups and individuals are also influenced by their contacts with *external stakeholders* – groups who have an interest in the operation of the company such as customers, shareholders, suppliers or unions. For example, sales staff may be pressurized by customers to represent their interests within the company.
- Individuals or groups, whether internal or external, cannot influence an organization's strategies unless they have an influencing mechanism. This mechanism is called *power*, which can be derived in a variety of ways.
- Organizational *objectives* traditionally have been afforded a central/dominant role in influencing strategy, i.e. strategy is seen as the means of achieving preordained and unchangeable objectives. That is not our view. Whereas organizations do have objectives, which are often valuable in strategy formulation, they should not be regarded as an unchangeable set of expectations.

They should be viewed as an important part of the strategic equation, and open to amendment and change as strategies develop.

- Objectives tend to emerge as the wishes of the most dominant coalition, usually the management of the organization although there are notable exceptions. However, in pursuing these objectives the dominant group is very strongly influenced by their reading of the political situation, i.e. their perception of the power struggle. For example, they are likely to set aside some of their expectations in order to improve the chance of achieving others.

## External Influences on Objectives

By referring back to Figure 6.2 (see pp. 146) it can be seen that the most general of the influences upon individuals and groups, and hence on organizational objectives and strategy, are external factors, the nature of the business, and the organizational culture. Taking the first of these, arguably the two most important external factors are the *values of the society* in which the organization is operating and the *behaviour of organized groups* both inside and outside the organization. The influence of social values is likely to be felt in a variety of ways, but most significantly in terms of what society will and will not tolerate in terms of business behaviour. As an example of this, it is worth considering how attitudes to environmental pollution have changed dramatically over the past 20 years. An obvious consequence of this has been to force changes on business behaviour and to increase the pressures for safer and more environmentally friendly products. In the case of petrol, for example, a growing awareness of the dangers of airborne lead pollution and an increasing unwillingness on the part of society to accept this prompted the oil companies to develop unleaded petrols. Equally, it was an awareness of a growing opposition to the testing of products on animals that led Anita Roddick's Body Shop to offer a range of cosmetics that has been developed without the need for testing on animals.

Objectives and strategy are also affected by the behaviour of organized groups within the organization. The most obvious of these are trade unions and trade associations which attempt to influence members both formally and informally through codes of conduct and norms of behaviour. In the case of the travel industry, for example, ABTA (the Association of British Travel Agents) has over the past few years worked hard to monitor and improve the standards within the industry so that clients receive better and more professional standards of service.

## The Nature of the Business

The second general influence on objectives and strategy is the *nature of the business itself*, and in particular the market situation faced by the organization, the life-cycle stages of its products, and the types of technology being used. The influence of market situation can perhaps best be understood by referring back to the mid-1980s when much of British industry was undergoing fundamental restructuring in order to survive. The markets in which the industries were operating had changed dramatically over a 20-year period with an upsurge in the market of often low priced foreign competition which made operating profitably difficult. Faced with this, organizations such as British Steel and the National Coal Board (subsequently renamed British Coal) were forced into the position of massive restructuring, changed working practices and radically different product/market strategies in order to survive. This, in turn, was reflected in the type of technology that could be used, attitudes within the industry, and subsequently in the ways in which employees viewed policy.

## Organizational Culture

The third general influence on objectives and strategy is *organizational culture*. Culture has been defined in a variety of ways over the past few years but for our purposes here it can be seen as the commonly held core beliefs of the organization. As such, it determines how people within the organization behave and respond. In examining and trying to understand organizational culture, Johnson & Scholes (1988, pp. 39–43) argue the case for what is referred to as the 'cultural web'. This web, they suggest, is made up of four major dimensions:

1 stories and myths;
2 rituals and symbols;
3 leadership and management style;
4 structure and systems.

Together, these four factors determine the type and profile of the organization and hence how it is likely to behave in the market-place. Factors such as these led Miles and Snow to identify three types of organization: defenders, prospectors and analysers. The implications of each type for objectives, strategies, and planning and control systems appear in Figure 6.3.

**FIGURE 6.3**
*Different types of organizational culture and their influences on policy making*

| Organization type and dominant objectives | Characteristics of policy making (preferred strategy) | Nature of the planning and control systems |
|---|---|---|
| 1 *Defenders* Desire for stability | Specialization with cost efficient production; a marketing emphasis on price and service to defend current business A tendency for vertical integration | Generally, centralized with detailed control and an emphasis on cost-efficiency Extensive use of formal planning procedures |
| 2 *Prospectors* Search for and exploitation of new product and market opportunities | Growth through product and market development Constant monitoring of environmental change Multiple technologies | Emphasis on flexibility and decentralization with use of ad-hoc measurements |
| 3 *Analysers* Desire to match new ventures to present shape of business | Steady growth through market penetration Exploitation of applied research Followers in the market | Often extremely complicated Coordinating roles between functions Intensive planning |

SOURCE: Adapted from Miles and Snow (1978)

**Individual and Group Expectations**

The fourth and final influence on objectives and strategy is that of the *expectations of individuals, stakeholders and coalitions*. In most cases it is the expectations of coalitions that exert the greatest influence on the organization, in that while individuals may well have a variety of personal aspirations, they often share expectations with a number of others. This, together with the relative inability of any single individual to exert a major influence upon the organization, leads to the emergence of groups within departments, regions and levels of the hierarchy, all of which attempt in one way or another to influence the direction of the organization. In practice, however, and particularly in the case of a multinational or large divisionalized organization, the ability of any one group to exert any significant degree of influence may well be limited. Almost inevitably, of course, conflicts between the expectations of different groups are likely to exist and this, in turn, leads to a series of trade-offs. This was referred to in a slightly different context at an earlier stage in this chapter when talking specifically about marketing objectives. More generally, the sorts of conflicts that are likely to emerge are between growth and profitability; growth and control/independence; cost efficiency and jobs; and volume/mass provision versus quality/specialization.

## 6.6 GUIDELINES FOR ESTABLISHING OBJECTIVES AND SETTING GOALS AND TARGETS

Few businesses pursue a single objective; instead they have a mixture, which typically includes profitability, sales growth, market share improvement, risk containment, innovativeness, usage, and so on. Each business unit should therefore set objectives under a variety of headings and then *manage by objectives*. In other words, it is the pursuit of these objectives which should provide the framework both for the planning and control processes. However, for this to work, several guidelines must be adhered to, with objectives being:

1 *hierarchical*: going from the most important to the least important;
2 *quantitative*: in order to avoid ambiguity – the objective 'to increase market share' is not as satisfactory a guideline as 'to increase market share by 5 per cent' or indeed 'to increase market share by 5 per cent within 18 months';
3 *realistic*: it is only too easy for objectives to reflect a degree of wishful thinking – instead they should be developed as the result of a detailed analysis of opportunities, corporate capability, competitive strengths and competitive strategy;
4 *consistent*: it is quite obviously unrealistic to pursue incompatible objectives. As an example of this, to aim for substantial gains in both sales and profits simultaneously is rarely possible.

## Primary and Secondary Objectives

Although for a long time economists argued that firms aimed to maximize profits, it is now generally recognized that the modern large corporation, managed by professionals, pursues a far broader and infinitely more diverse set of objectives. As a consequence, traditional views of profit maximization as the principal objective have been challenged by the reality of the behaviour of corporate management. With this in mind, two types of objective can be identified: *primary* and *secondary*.

Traditionally the primary objective was, as we observed above, profit maximization. Other objectives are, however, often seen by managers to be of more immediate relevance and, as Chisnall (1989, p. 137) points out, may affect the organization's profit-earning ability:

These secondary objectives which are not in any way inferior to the primary objective, are necessary if a company is to plan effectively for its future progress. In the short term, for instance, a profit maximisation policy may be affected by changes in economic conditions which demand some restructuring of corporate resources to meet new levels of competition. Survival or market share defences may, in fact, become primary objectives.

This issue of the multiplicity of objectives has also been discussed by Drucker (1955) who isolated eight areas in which organizational objectives might be developed and maintained:

1 market standing;
2 innovation;
3 productivity;
4 financial and physical resources;
5 manager performance and development;
6 worker performance and attitude;
7 profitability;
8 public responsibility.

See also the discussion in Chapter 15 on the GE approach to multiple objectives.

## Objectives and Time Horizons

It should be apparent by this stage that in setting objectives the marketing planner needs to take account of a wide variety of factors. Perhaps the final influence that we need to examine here before focusing upon the detail of corporate and marketing objectives is that of the time horizons involved. In the case of those industries which are highly capital intensive, for example, the planning horizons tend to be considerably longer than is the case in faster-moving consumer goods markets. We can therefore usefully distinguish between the short, medium and long term.

From the planner's point of view, the short term is concerned essentially with issues of tactics, while the long term is concerned with the major issues of strategy and the allocation and reallocation of resources. The medium term then sits neatly between these in that it provides the focus for determining how effectively resources are being used. Although there is a perhaps understandable temptation to tie each of these phases to specific periods of time (e.g. up to one year in the case of the short term, one to five years for the medium term and over five years for the long term), such an exercise is generally only useful when carried out in relation to a specific industry or company.

At a more general level, the significance of planning time horizons relates rather more to the degree of environmental change being experienced and the ability of the organization to respond by reallocating resources. The significance of this from the point of view of establishing objectives can therefore be seen in terms of the need to identify objectives both for the short term and the long term. The long-term objectives will then be concerned with the direction in which the organization is heading, while the short-term objectives will be allied far more closely with the stages through which the organization will have to move in order to achieve this position.

## The Nature of Corporate Objectives

In the light of our discussion here and in Chapter 1 (see pages 18–19) it should be apparent that corporate management, having established the corporate mission, then has to take the mission a stage further by developing a series of specific objectives for each level of management. Most typically these objectives are expressed in terms of sales growth, profitability, market share growth and risk diversification. Because the majority of organizations generally pursue a number of objectives, it is, as we have seen, important that they are stated in a hierarchical manner going from the most important to the least important, with this hierarchy being both internally consistent and mutually reinforcing. By doing this, the strategist is clarifying priorities so that if at a later stage a conflict of objectives emerges, a decision can then be made on which particular objective is to dominate. At the same time it is essential that the objectives established are realistic both in terms of their magnitude and the time scale over which they are to be achieved. Almost invariably, however, organizations experience difficulties and conflicts in establishing objectives, problems which are in turn compounded by the need to establish multiple objectives. It is seldom, if ever, possible for example for an organization to satisfy concurrently objectives of rapid growth *and* risk aversion, or to maximize both sales *and* profits. Recognizing this, Weinberg (1969) has identified eight basic strategic trade-offs facing firms. These are, he suggests:

1 short-term profits versus long-term growth;
2 profit margins versus competitive position;
3 direct sales effort versus market development effort;
4 penetration of existing markets versus the development of new markets;
5 related versus non-related new opportunities as a source of long-term growth;
6 profit versus non-profit goals;
7 growth versus stability;
8 a 'riskless' environment versus a high-risk environment.

It follows from this that the strategist has to decide upon the relative emphasis that is to be given to each of these dimensions. Any failure to do this is ultimately likely to lead to conflict and reduce the extent to which the objectives provide useful strategic guidelines.

However, while the need for clear objectives may well be self-evident, it is rare, as Baker (1985, p. 41) has pointed out, 'to find any explicit reference as to just *how* one should set about formulating these objectives in the first place'. One of the few who has attempted to provide guidelines for formulating objectives is McKay (1972), who suggests that it is possible to identify two categories of issues that should be considered: the general issues which apply to all organizations, and the more specific which force a more detailed examination. These general issues are:

(i)   *business scope*: what business should we be in?
(ii)  *business orientation*: what approach is most appropriate for our business scope and to our purposes of survival, growth and profit?
(iii) *business organization*: to what extent is our organizational style, structure and staff policy suited to the orientation chosen?
(iv)  *public responsibility*: is there a match between our selection of opportunities and the existing and future social and economic needs of the public?
(v)   *performance evaluation*: is there a match between our appraisal and planning systems?

The *specific* areas that then follow from this he suggests relate to each strategic business unit (SBU) and include:

- customer classes;
- competitors;
- markets and distribution;
- technology and products;
- production capability;
- finance;
- environment.

**Taking Account of Competitors' Objectives**

Objectives should never be set in a vacuum. Instead they should be set against the background of a detailed understanding of environmental demands and opportunities. In doing this particular attention needs to be paid to the objectives that are likely to be pursued by competitors, since these will often have a direct impact upon subsequent levels of performance.

A competitor's objectives are likely to be influenced by many factors, but particularly by its size, history, managerial culture, and performance. They are also affected by whether the company is part of a larger organization. If this is the case, the strategist needs to know whether it is being pressured to achieved growth or whether it is viewed by the parent as a 'cash cow' and is being milked. Equally, we need to know just how important it is to the parent; if it is central to the parent company's long-term plans, this will have a direct influence upon how much money will be spent in fighting off an attack. Rothschild (1984, Ch. 5), for example, argues that the worst competitor to attack is the competitor for whom this is the sole or principal business, and who has a global operation.

There is therefore, as we discussed in Chapter 4, a strong argument for the strategist to develop a detailed competitive map in which issues of competitive capability and priority figure prominently. In doing this, a useful assumption, at least initially, is that competitors will aim for profit targets and choose their strategies accordingly. Even here, however, organizations differ in the emphasis they put on short-term as opposed to long-term profits. In reality, of course, few organizations aim for profit maximization, be it in the short or long term, but instead opt for a degree of satisficing. They have target profit figures and are satisfied to achieve them, even if greater profits could have been achieved by other strategies with perhaps a greater degree of risk. In discussing this, Kotler (1988, p. 242) suggests that:

> An alternative assumption is that each competitor has a mix of objectives with different weights. We want to know the relative weights that a competitor places on

current profitability, market share growth, cash flow, technological leadership, service leadership, and so on. Knowing a competitor's weighted mix of objectives allows us to know whether the competitor is satisfied with its current financial results, how it might react to different types of competitive attack, and so on. For example, a competitor that pursues low cost leadership will react much more strongly to a manufacturing process breakthrough by another competitor than to an advertising step-up by the same competitor.

The argument for looking in detail at your competitors as a prelude to developing your own objectives has also been pursued by Davidson (1987, p. 136):

> You know what your competitors have done in the past, and buried in there are many clues as to what they are likely to do in the future ... The attitudes and philosophies of your competitors (therefore) deserve close study. With successful competitors, their attitudes tend to be deeply ingrained and change little, if at all. Any competitor of General Electric or Mars will know that their objective in any market is likely to be brand leadership, with little interest in being number two or number three for long. Many Japanese competitors are prepared to wait five or ten years before receiving a return on their investments when entering new markets.

Competitive attitudes, objectives and strategies do, of course, change over time, even when a particular strategy is proving to be successful. History has shown that the probability of change is far greater when a particular strategy is not working, or when there is a change in management at the top of the organization. There are therefore several specific factors that should be taken into account as well as the rather more general issue of competitive posture referred to above. These include:

1 *Each competitor's previous successes and failures.* It is quite normal to continue with a successful formula and to change one that is not working.
2 *The volume and direction of investment in advertising and plant.* A rational competitor will concentrate his advertising effort on the products and markets which appear to offer the greatest scope. Monitoring patterns of competitive advertising spend can therefore provide the strategist with a good indication of the directions in which to concentrate. Equally, a knowledge of competitors' investment in plant, which can often be picked up from equipment suppliers, planning applications and the trade press, provides an invaluable guide to profitable future plans.
3 *Each competitor's relative cost position.* The starting point for this is to arrive at an assessment of each competitor's relative cost position in each major market sector. Working on the assumption that each competitor will have conducted a similar exercise, it is reasonable to suppose that they will give priority to cost-reduction strategies in those markets in which they are currently high-cost operators.

By focusing upon areas such as these, the strategist should be in a far better position to answer four fundamental questions:

1 What is each competitor seeking?
2 What is it that drives each competitor?
3 What is each competitor's true competitive capability?
4 In what ways might this capability be translated into objectives and strategy?

It is against this background that the strategist can then define and perhaps redefine his own organization's objectives.

**Developing Offensive Corporate Objectives**

Firms can be broadly classified as *proactive* or *reactive*. The former are characterized by an entrepreneurial and highly positive attitude to their markets, with a constant searching and pursuit of new business opportunities; in essence they try to shape the environment to fit the organization's resources and objectives. By contrast, reactive firms adopt a far more passive and less entrepreneurial posture, responding to rather than initiating environmental change. These contrasting styles have an obvious effect upon the sorts of objectives pursued and indeed, in most cases, upon subsequent levels of trading performance.

The implications of this for marketing have been spelled out by Davidson (1987, p. 149) who suggests that:

> Objective setting is a good measure of a company's success in offensive marketing. Unless ambitious objectives are established, there is little incentive for executives to apply the offensive marketing approach.

With regard to the specific objectives that an offensive or proactive organization might pursue, these will depend to a large degree upon the organization's market position. If, for example, it is intent on increasing its market share, the starting point involves deciding upon which competitor(s) to attack. The options open to it are essentially:

1 *to attack the market leader*: this is typically a high risk but potentially high return strategy and one which makes sense if the leader is generally complacent or not serving the market as well as he might – Xerox, for example, chose to attack 3M by developing a cleaner, faster and more convenient copying process (dry copying rather than wet);
2 *it can attack firms of its own size*: firms that are either underfinanced or undermanaged;
3 *it can attack local and regional firms*: again, firms that again are underfinanced or undermanaged – this strategy was pursued with considerable success in the 1960s and 70s by a small number of large brewers who gobbled up the small, regional brewers.

This question of *who* to attack is at the very heart of an effective offensive strategy, since to make the wrong choice is likely to prove immensely costly. Thus while in the razor market BIC might well try to increase its market share, it carefully avoids attempting to topple Gillette.

The differences between reactive and proactive organizations have also been the subject of a considerable amount of analysis at the national level over the past few years. In part this has been due to the relatively poor economic performance of British companies in world markets. Japanese organizations, by contrast, have achieved far greater levels of success; it is the reasons for this and the apparent differences between British and Japanese marketing approaches that has provided the focus for a considerable body of research. In essence, the results of this research have highlighted a largely proactive approach on the part of Japanese firms, but an essentially reactive approach on the part of British firms. One example of this research is summarized in Illustration 6.2.

**Establishing the Marketing Objectives**

Against the background of the comments made so far, we can identify a firm's competitive situation and hence its marketing decisions as being concerned with just two major elements: products and markets. This has been discussed by a variety of writers but most obviously by McKay (1972), Guiltinan and Paul (1988) and Ansoff (1968). McKay, for example, identifies just three fundamental marketing objectives:

1 to enlarge the market;
2 to increase market share;
3 to improve profitability.

# Illustration 6.2: The Differences Between Japanese and Western Business Objectives

That major differences exist betwen the objectives of Japanese companies and their European and North American counterparts has long been recognized. Kotler (1988, p. 242), for example, has stated that:

> US firms operate largely on a short-run profit maximization model, largely because their current performance is judged by stockholders who might lose confidence, sell their stock, and cause the company's cost of capital to rise. Japanese firms operate largely on a market share maximization model. They need to provide employment for more than 100 million people in a resource-poor country. Japanese firms have lower profit requirements because most of the capital comes from banks that seeks regular interest payments rather than high returns at somewhat higher risks. As a result, Japanese firms can charge lower prices and show more patience in building and penetrating markets. Thus competitors who are satisfied with lower profits have an advantage over their opponents.

A similar line of argument has been pursued by Doyle, et al., (1986) who, in a comparative investigation of Japanese marketing strategies in the British market, highlighted a variety of differences between Japanese and British companies. Prominent among these were:

1 market share versus short-term profitability – the marketing of western companies, they suggest, is oriented to profitability, that of the Japanese to market share;
2 an emphasis upon fast market adaption rather than innovation;
3 more aggressive marketing tactics on the part of the Japanese;
4 a greater orientation by Japanese firms towards environmental opportunities.

Underpinning these four points were fundamental differences in the strategic objectives being pursued:

> The marketing objectives of a company express its ambition and commitment. There was a striking contrast between the two groups in these strategic objectives. In entering a new market the British usually arrived late and few had a strong commitment to it. Two-thirds of British companies gave defensive reasons for entry: 'we had to in order to survive' and several admitted they 'had never really thought it out'. In contrast, the Japanese were much clearer and professional: over 70% noted the motives were 'part of a planned global expansion' or 'potential of the UK market'. Once in the market, the British lack of commitment to beating competition was again striking. Whereas 87% of the Japanese gave 'aggressive growth' or 'market domination' as the goal, only 1 in 5 British companies thought these statements applied to them. 'Maintenance' or the 'prevention of decline' were the most the typical British competitor sought. As hypothesized, short-term profit was much more important to the British than the Japanese (93% vs 40%), and they were willing to cut costs and allow their market position to erode if necessary to bolster short-term profitability. If these attitudes are typical, the poor record of much of British manufacturing industry in defending its home market becomes more comprehensible.

The authors went on to suggest that a company can improve profitability by a strategic focus based either upon raising volume or improving productivity. Organizations with ambitious strategic objectives would be expected to focus on the former, a defensive one on the latter. The Japanese firms in their sample almost invariably chose volume. By contrast, the British, rather than pushing aggressively into new, high-growth markets or competing for market share, tended to focus on cost cutting, range reduction and rationalization as the basis for preventing margins being eroded. The differences between these British and Japanese firms can perhaps best be illustrated by the two tables below:

**What was your market share/sales strategy?**

|  | British (%) | Japanese (%) |
| --- | --- | --- |
| Prevent decline | 20 | 0 |
| Defensive | 20 | 0 |
| Maintain position | 40 | 0 |
| Steady growth | 0 | 13 |
| Aggressive growth | 13 | 60 |
| Dominate market | 7 | 27 |

**How well does 'good short-term profits are the objective' describe your company?**

| British (%) | Japanese (%) |
| --- | --- |
| 93 | 40 |

McKay's ideas of three principal marketing objectives have been taken several steps further by Guiltinan and Paul, who argue that there are six objectives which should be given explicit consideration:

1  market share growth;
2  market share maintenance;
3  cash flow maximization;
4  sustaining profitability;
5  harvesting;
6  establishing an initial market position.

In many ways, however, the thinking underpinning both approaches can be seen to come together in Ansoff's ideas of a product/market matrix. This is illustrated in Figure 6.4.

This matrix, which focuses upon the product (what is sold) and to whom it is sold (the market), highlights four distinct strategic alternatives open to the strategist:

1  selling existing products to existing markets;
2  extending existing products to new markets;
3  developing new products for existing markets;
4  developing new products for new markets.

**FIGURE 6.4**
*Ansoff's growth
vector matrix*

|  |  | Product | |
|  |  | Current | New |
| **Market** | Current | Market penetration    1 | Product development    3 |
|  | New | Market extension    2 | Diversification    4 |

SOURCE: Ansoff (1957)

Although in practice of course there are *relative* degrees of newness both in terms of products and markets, and hence the number of strategies open to the organization is infinite, Ansoff's matrix is useful in that it provides a convenient and easily understood framework within which marketing objectives and strategies can be readily developed.

It follows from this that setting objectives and strategies *in relation to products and markets* is a fundamental element of the marketing planning process. These marketing objectives then represent performance commitments for the future and are typically stated in terms of market share, sales volume, levels of sterling distribution, and profitability. For these to be worthwhile, however, they need to be stated both quantitatively and unambiguously. In this way they are capable of measurement, something which is not possible if they are stated only in broad directional terms. In commenting on this McDonald (1984, p. 88) suggests that:

> Vague objectives, however emotionally appealing, are counter-productive to sensible planning, and are usually the result of the human propensity for wishful thinking which often smacks more of cheerleading than serious marketing leadership. What this really means is that while it is arguable whether directional terms such as 'decrease', 'optimize', 'minimize' should be used as objectives, it seems logical that unless there is some measure, or yardstick, against which to measure a sense of locomotion towards achieving them, then they do not serve any useful purpose.

The argument for explicit and quantitatively expressed objectives is therefore overpowering, since any failure to do this simply offers scope for confusion and ambiguity at a later stage, not just in terms of the sort of action required but also in terms of the performance measurement standards that are to be used. In stating objectives they also need to be related to the fundamental philosophies and policies of a particular organization, something which again argues the case for a clear and well-communicated mission statement. The *process* of setting objectives is therefore central to its effectiveness, a comment reflected by McDonald (1984, p. 30) who, in discussing the findings of a research programme carried out at the Cranfield School of Management, has suggested that:

> . . . it is inadequacies in the objective-setting process which lie at the heart of many of the problems of British companies. Since companies are based on the existence of markets, and since a company's sole means of making profit is to find and maintain profitable markets, then clearly setting objectives in respect of these markets is a key business function. If the process by which this key function is performed is inadequate in relation to the differing organizational settings in which it takes place, it follows that operational efficiency will be adversely affected.
>
> Some kind of appropriate system has to be used to enable meaningful and realistic marketing objectives to be set. A frequent complaint is the pre-occupation with short-term thinking and an almost total lack of what has been referred to as 'strategic thinking'. Another complaint is that plans consist largely of numbers, which are difficult to evaluate in any meaningful way, since they do not highlight and quantify opportunities, emphasize key issues, show the company's position

clearly in its markets, or delineate the means of achieving the sales forecasts. Indeed, very often the actual numbers that are written down bear little relationship to any of these things. Sales targets for the sales force are often inflated in order to motivate them to higher achievement, while the actual budgets themselves are deflated in order to provide a safety net against shortfall. Both act as demotivators and both lead to the frequent use of expressions such as 'ritual', 'the numbers game', 'meaningless horsetrading', and so on.

**Ansoff's Matrix Revisited**

Against the background of the comments so far it should be apparent that marketing objectives relate to the four categories of Ansoff's product/market matrix, with decisions being needed on:

1 existing products in existing markets;
2 new products in existing markets;
3 existing products in new markets;
4 new products in new markets.

The general nature and direction of these decisions is influenced both by the product life cycle and the current shape of the company's product portfolio. This in turn leads to a series of choices for each product/market condition, choices which can be expressed in terms of five types of strategy:

1 *Maintenance* of the current competitive position.
2 *Improvement* of the current competitive position.
3 *Harvesting* which involves reducing or relinquishing the current competitive position in order to capitalize upon short-term profit and improve cash flow.
4 *Exiting*. This typically occurs when the company is suffering from a weak competitive position or recognizes that the cost of staying in the market and/or improving upon the position is too high. As an example of this, ICI sold its loss-making European fertilizer business to Europe's second largest fertilizer producer, the Finnish company Kemira Oy. The decision to withdraw from this market sector was made after ICI had experienced losses for four years, despite having made major attempts to improve the business including vigorous cost reductions and investment in new technology.
5 *Entry* to a new sector.

However, while considering either the need or the feasibility of each of these strategies, the marketing manager needs to recognize the danger of adhering slavishly to any particular set of rules relating to the five categories and to be fully aware of the major constraints within which he is operating. Among the most commonly used and useful frameworks for identifying these is the concept of the limiting factor (see Illustration 6.3) and techniques of gap analysis which are designed to highlight any gaps that exist between long-term forecasts of performance and the sales or financial objectives that have been set (see Figure 6.5).

In the case of Figure 6.5(a), the lowest curve represents a projection of expected sales from the organization's current portfolio of businesses. The highest curve traces the sales targets for the next 10 years which, as can be seen, are more ambitious than the current portfolio will permit. The question that then quite obviously follows is how best to fill this strategic planning gap. The courses of action open to the strategist can then be examined in several ways. The first involves subdividing the gap into the *operations gap* and the *new strategies gap*. In the case of the *operations gap*, the approaches to reducing or eliminating it totally include:

1 greater productivity by means of reduced costs;
2 improvements to the sales mix or higher prices;
3 higher levels of market penetration.

---

# Illustration 6.3:  BOC and the Limiting Factor

A few years ago, the British Oxygen Company recognized that its limiting factor was the nature of demand for its products: this was essentially reactive and dependent on industrial activity. In addition, BOC products could not economically be transported more than 150–200 miles from the point of production.

The invasion of the British market by Air Products faced BOC with an entirely new competitive situation; for years they had enjoyed a virtual monopoly situation in the British gas market. BOC, in the words of the chairman of their industrial and medical cases group, were forced to start marketing gases: a task for which they were ill prepared. The defensive posture adopted against Air Products' aggressive marketing in the late 1960s was abandoned and BOC sought to regain ground by positive marketing not only of gases but of the technological expertise and advice which they could offer to customers.

Another outcome of the changed market environment was that BOC vigorously pursued a policy of diversification, so that its activities now range across welding products, vacuum engineering, medical equipment, refrigeration equipment, frozen food retailing and specialized food distribution.

*Source: Chisnall, P. M. (1989),* Strategic Industrial Marketing, *Prentice Hall International, p. 143.*

---

**FIGURE 6.5**

*The strategic planning gap*

(a)

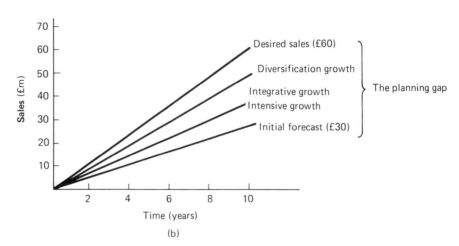

(b)

In the case of the *new strategies gap*, the courses of action include:

1 a reduction in objectives;
2 market extension in the form of new market segments, new user groups or expansion geographically;
3 product development;
4 diversification by selling new products to new markets.

An alternative way of looking at the strategic planning gap is illustrated in Figure 6.5(b). Here, the solutions to the shortfall have been categorized as:

1 identifying further opportunities to achieve growth within the company's current business (intensive growth);
2 identifying opportunities to build or acquire businesses related to the current sphere of operations (integrative growth);
3 adding businesses that are unrelated to current operations (diversification).

In weighing up which of these alternatives to pursue, the planner needs to give consideration to a variety of issues. For many companies the most attractive option proves to be greater market penetration since this is concerned with existing products and markets and typically therefore involves less cost and risk than would be incurred by moving outside existing areas of knowledge. Equally, it generally pays an organization to search for growth within existing and related markets rather than moving into new markets, since by doing this it is more readily able to build upon its reputation. If, however, the company decides to move into new and possibly unrelated areas, there is then a need not only to establish itself against a new set of competitors but also to build new distribution networks and come to terms with a different technology. This should not in itself be seen as an argument against moving into new markets with new products, but rather an argument for the planner to develop objectives and strategies against the background of a firm understanding of the organization's strengths and weaknesses and overall corporate capability, all of which should emerge clearly from the marketing audit.

The levels of risk associated with each of the strategic alternatives identified in the Ansoff matrix can perhaps be better understood by considering an extension to the basic model. While undoubtedly useful as a framework, Ansoff's four-cell matrix is not able to reflect different *degrees* of technological or market newness, or indeed of the risk associated with the four alternatives. By returning for a moment to Figure 6.4, it should be apparent that, all other things being equal, the lowest level of risk is associated with the market penetration strategy of Cell 1. This then increases through Cells 2 and 3, peaking in Cell 4 with a strategy of diversification. The diagrams that appear in Figures 6.6 and 6.7 are both designed to add a further dimension to Ansoff's original model.

Figure 6.6, for example, gives recognition to the fact that strategies involving new products (hence technology) generally entail a greater degree of risk than those limited just to new markets.

**FIGURE 6.6**
*Levels of risk associated with various product/ market combinations – 1*

**FIGURE 6.7**
*Levels of risk
associated with
various product/
market
combinations – 2*

| | | Newness of product | | | |
|---|---|---|---|---|---|
| | | Same product | Extended model | Modified or improved design | New product |
| **Newness of market** | Same market | 1 | 2 | 4 | 8 |
| | Better market coverage | 2 | 4 | 8 | 16 |
| | New coverage but in related areas | 4 | 8 | 16 | 32 |
| | Totally new market | 8 | 16 | 32 | 64 |

SOURCE: Adapted from Ward (1968)

Figure 6.7 takes this model somewhat further by distinguishing between the different types and degrees of market and product development, and in doing this illustrates the relative degrees of risk more precisely. It can be seen from this how risk levels escalate as the organization moves away from its existing product and market base. It then follows that the issue of corporate capability, and in particular the ability of the organization to cope with risk, needs to be understood in some detail by the marketing planner. Without this understanding there is a very real danger that the organization will move too far and too fast into areas in which it will find difficulties in operating effectively. Again, however, this should not be seen simply as an argument for the company to stay where it is currently, since the product life cycle alone necessitates changes both to products and markets if sales and profits are to be maintained or increased. Rather it is an argument for strategic development to reflect objectives, opportunities and capabilities, together with an understanding of the entry and exit barriers to possible market areas. The implications of entry and exit barriers for a market's attractiveness are illustrated in Figure 6.8.

**FIGURE 6.8**
*Barriers and
profitability*

| | | Exit barriers | |
|---|---|---|---|
| | | Low | High |
| **Entry barriers** | Low | Low, stable returns | Low, risky returns |
| | High | High, stable returns | High, risky returns |

The most attractive segment from the viewpoint of profit is one in which entry barriers are high and exit barriers are low. Few new firms are able to enter, and the poor performers can exit easily. When both entry and exit barriers are high the profit potential is high, although this is generally accompanied by greater levels of risk as the poorer performers, finding it difficult to leave, are forced to fight for share. When both entry and exit barriers are low, firms find it easy both to enter and leave, and returns tend to be stable and low. The worst case scenario is when barriers to entry are low but exit barriers are high: here firms enter when the market is buoyant, but then find it difficult to leave when there is a downturn. The result is overcapacity which affects all the players.

## 6.7  THE DEVELOPMENT OF STRATEGIES

In the light of what has been discussed so far it should be apparent that a marketing objective is what the organization wants to achieve in terms of sales volume, market share, and so on. How the organization then sets out to achieve these objectives is the *strategy*. An effective strategy statement should therefore make reference not just to the allocation of resources but also to timescales; inevitably it is broad in scope. Following on from this, the planner then moves to develop the *tactics* and *programme for implementation*. From the viewpoint of the marketing planner, the major aspects of strategy with which he is involved are the individual elements of the marketing mix, each of which is covered in greater detail at a later stage in the book. Before moving on, however, it is worth focusing on one of the other major influences upon strategic success. Although decisions are typically taken against a background of resource constraint, their effects can often be minimized by the strategist giving full recognition to the importance of the *leverage* that can be gained by the development of one or more *distinctive competences* to gain a comparative marketing advantage. Although the importance of distinctive competences has long been recognized, their strategic significance was highlighted by the results of a study carried out by the American management consultants, McKinsey & Co. Prominent among their findings was that:

> the distinguishing characteristic shared by (successful companies) was that they did one particular thing well. They had developed significant strength in one feature of their business which gave them a comparative advantage over their competitors.

This theme has, in turn, been developed by Chisnall (1989, p. 143) who has made the observation that while the concept of a distinctive competence is well known and understood, one of the main problems of applying it is that of changing the basis of competitive advantage in line with changes in the environment. Among the companies which have failed to come to terms with this are Bowman in the hand-held calculator market, Sinclair in home computers, and Texas Instruments in digital watches.

It follows from this that in developing strategies the planner needs to identify these distinctive competences, and to build on them. As an example of how this can be done, the Dominos Pizza chain in the United States developed as its USP (unique selling proposition) rapid delivery times with a refund to the customer if delivery of the pizza took longer than it should.

## 6.8  SUMMARY

In this chapter we have focused on three main areas:

- the nature and purpose of planning;
- the significance of the corporate mission;
- the nature and purpose of corporate and marketing objectives.

The starting point in the planning process involves the strategist in identifying where the organization is currently (where are we now?) and the short- and long-term direction for the organization (where should we go?). In addressing this second question a variety of issues need to be considered, including:

- environmental opportunities and threats (see Chapter 2);
- the organization's strategic capability (again, see Chapter 2); and
- stakeholders' expectations.

Having done this it then becomes possible to give far more explicit and realistic consideration to the question of how the organization should go about achieving its objectives.

As a background to the planning process there needs to be agreement on the corporate mission, the mission statement being a vision of what the organization is or should attempt to become. The significance of the mission statement has been highlighted by a wide variety of writers, most of whom have given emphasis to its integrating role and to the way in which it provides a strong binding statement of fundamental corporate values.

In developing a mission statement the strategist needs to take account of a variety of factors, including:

- the organization's history, performance and patterns of ownership;
- managerial values and expectations;
- the environment;
- resource availability;
- the existence of any distinctive competences.

Having developed a mission statement the strategist is in a far stronger position to begin the process of establishing corporate and marketing objectives. Objectives are typically influenced by several issues, including:

- the nature of the business (products, markets and technology);
- external factors (societal values, pressure groups, government and legislation);
- organizational culture;
- individuals and groups within the organization.

Having identified the organization's corporate and marketing objectives the strategist needs to ensure that they satisfy certain criteria, the four most significant of which are that they are arranged hierarchically, that they are expressed quantitatively, that they are realistic and that there is internal consistency. It is at this stage also that the strategist is in a position to identify the nature and size of any gaps that are likely to emerge between where the organization wants to go and where in practice it is capable of going. Once this has been done it then becomes possible to begin the process of developing the strategies that are to be used to achieve the agreed objectives.

# 7 | Structural, market and environmental analysis

## 7.1 LEARNING OBJECTIVES

When you have read this chapter you should be able to understand:

(a) why a regular and detailed analysis of the organization's environment is important;
(b) the key elements of the environment;
(c) how firms go about analysing the environment;
(d) how environmental factors are changing;
(e) the dimensions of environmental scanning systems.

## 7.2 INTRODUCTION

Strategic marketing is, as we discussed in the introduction to this book, an essentially iterative process. It is iterative for a number of reasons, the most significant of which is that as the company's external environment changes, so opportunities and threats emerge and disappear only to re-emerge perhaps in a modified form at a later stage. Because of this, the marketing strategist needs to recognize the fundamental necessity both for an environmental monitoring process that is capable of identifying in advance any possible opportunities and threats, and for a planning system and organizational structure that is capable of quite possibly radical change to reflect the environment so that the effects of threats are minimized and that opportunities are seized.

In essence, therefore, the formulation of marketing strategy is concerned with matching the *capabilities of the organization* with the *demands of the environment*. In doing this, the strategist is faced with a difficult problem, since what we typically refer to as the environment encapsulates a wide variety of influences. The difficulty lies therefore in coming to terms with this diversity in such a way that it contributes to effective decision making, since it is this that has a direct influence upon performance. This difficulty in coping with the environment can be viewed under two headings:

1 understanding the *extent* to which the environment affects strategy;
2 understanding the ways in which environmental pressures can be *related* to the capabilities of the organization.

A possible danger that has been highlighted by several commentators is that of adopting a 'balance sheet' approach to environmental analysis and simply listing all possible environmental influences and then categorizing each as either an opportunity or a threat. If environmental analysis is limited to this alone, the strategist is left with far too broad and unsophisticated a picture of what really affects the organization. In addition, such an approach is likely to lead to the organization responding in a fragmented way rather than in a more integrated and strategic fashion.

Within this chapter we therefore focus on the various elements of the marketing environment with a view to illustrating the nature of their interaction and, subsequently, their effect on the organization. Against this background, we then move on to consider the ways in which an effective environmental monitoring process can best be developed and then, subsequently, how environmental forces are capable of determining the nature of the strategy pursued. We begin, however, by examining an approach to analysing the environment.

## 7.3  ANALYSING THE ENVIRONMENT

In analysing the environment, Johnson and Scholes (1988, p. 54) argue for a step-wise approach. This involves an initial audit of general environmental influences, followed by a series of increasingly tightly focused stages that are designed to provide the strategist with an understanding of the *key opportunities and threats* as a prelude to identifying the organization's *strategic position*. This process, which is illustrated in Figure 7.1, consists of five stages:

1  The starting point in this process is the *general audit of environmental influences*. The purpose of this is to identify the types of environmental factors that have influenced the organization's development and previous perform-ance, and to arrive at an initial conclusion of the likely important influences in the future.

2  From here the strategist moves to an *assessment of the nature of the environment* and the degree of uncertainty and change that is likely to exist. If from this the strategist concludes that the environment is relatively static then historical analysis is likely to prove useful. If, by contrast, the environment shows signs of instability, then a stronger emphasis upon the future is needed.

3  The third phase then involves focusing upon *specific environmental factors* such as the nature and structure of the market.

4  This in turn leads to an analysis of the firm's *competitive position*. A detailed discussion of how this can be done appears in Chapter 4. In essence, however, this involves a combination of *strategic group analysis* in which competitors are mapped in terms of their similarities, dissimilarities, their capabilities and the strategies they follow, and *market share analysis* to highlight their relative degrees of market power.

**FIGURE 7.1**
*The five stages of environmental analysis*

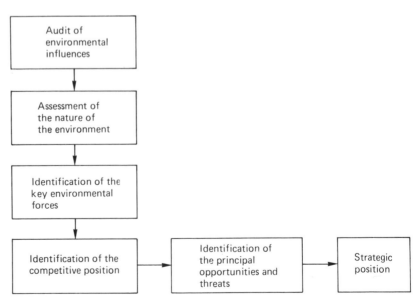

SOURCE: Adapted from Johnson and Scholes (1988), p. 54

5 This information is then used as the basis for identifying *in detail* how environmental forces are likely to affect the organization and, in particular, the *opportunities and threats* that are likely to exist. This in turn provides the basis for a detailed understanding of the organization's strategic position and the degree to which there is match between strategy, structure and environment.

At this point we will examine the first three stages of this step-wise approach; the fourth stage is discussed at the end of this chapter, while the fifth stage was covered in some detail in Chapter 2.

Referring back to Figure 7.1, it can be seen that the first step in the process involves the *general audit of environmental influences*. The starting point for this involves the strategist in developing a list of those factors which are likely to have an impact on the organization and which will therefore need further analysis. In doing this, the purpose is to develop a detailed understanding of what environmental factors have influenced the organization in the past, and the degree to which any changes that are taking place are likely to increase or reduce in impact. Although quite obviously such a list has to be company specific, it is possible to identify a broad framework to help with this audit. This framework, which is typically referred to as PEST (Political, Economic, Social and Technological) analysis, is illustrated in Figure 7.2.

**FIGURE 7.2**
*The PEST framework for environmental auditing*

| | |
|---|---|
| **POLITICAL/LEGAL FACTORS**<br>Legislative structures<br>Monopoly restrictions<br>Political and government stability<br>Political orientations<br>Taxation policies<br>Employment legislation<br>Foreign trade regulations<br>Environmental protection legislation<br>Pressure groups<br>Trades union power | **SOCIO-CULTURAL FACTORS**<br>Demographics<br>Lifestyles<br>Social mobility<br>Educational levels<br>Attitudes<br>Consumerism |
| | **TECHNOLOGICAL FACTORS**<br>Levels and focuses of government and industrial R & D expenditure<br>Speed of technology transfer<br>Product life cycles<br>Joint ventures |
| **ECONOMIC FACTORS**<br>Business cycles<br>Money supply<br>Inflation rates<br>Investment levels<br>Unemployment<br>Energy costs<br>GNP trends<br>Patterns of ownership | |

Against this background, the strategist can then move to an assessment of the *nature of the environment*. In essence, this is concerned with answering three questions:

1 How uncertain is the environment?
2 What are the sources of this uncertainty?
3 How should this uncertainty be dealt with?

Levels of uncertainty are directly attributable to the extent to which environmental conditions are dynamic or complex. *Dynamism* is due largely to the rates and frequency of change, while *complexity* is the result either of the diversity of environmental influences, the amount of knowledge required to cope with them, or the extent to which environmental factors are interconnected. The implications for environmental analysis of these different types of environmental condition are illustrated in Figure 7.3.

**FIGURE 7.3**
*Handling different environmental conditions*

| | | Conditions | |
|---|---|---|---|
| | Simple/static | Dynamic | Complex |
| **Aims** | To achieve thorough (historical) understanding of the environment | To understand the future rather than simply relying on past experiences | The reduction of complexity Greater structural understanding |
| **Methods** | Analysis of past influences and their effect on organizational performance Identification of key forces Analysis of existing relationships | Managers' sensitivity to change Scenario planning Contingency planning Sensitivity planning | Specialist attention to elements of complexity Model building |
| **Dangers** | The sudden emergence of unpredicted change Mechanistic organizational structures Lack of skills Focus on existing relationships Lack of willingness to accept that conditions are changing Stereotyped responses | Management myopia Mechanistic organizational structures Lack of skills Inappropriate forecasting Failure to recognize significant new players | Unsuitable organizational structure or control systems Inappropriate reactions Inappropriate focuses Over-reaction |

SOURCE: Adapted from Johnson and Scholes (1988)

## Environment Types

The question of *how* to categorize environments has been discussed in some detail by Miles (1980, Ch. 8) who developed a framework for a comprehensive and systematic analysis of environment types. The model calls for a 'measurement' response by those performing the analysis and is based upon the answers to six questions:

1 How complex is the environment? (Complexity is a measurement of the number of different environmental forces which have an impact, or potential impact, upon the organization.)
2 How routine and standardized are organizational interactions with elements of the environment?
3 How interconnected and how remote, initially, are the significant environmental variables?
4 How dynamic and how unpredictable are the changes taking place around the organization?
5 How receptive is management to the ways in which environmental pressures adversely affect the input and output processes of the organization?
6 How high is flexibility of choice and to what extent is the organization constrained from moving into new areas?

Using this checklist of questions, the strategist should then be able to establish the organization's environmental position on a number of continuums:

Simple ↔ Complex
Routine ↔ Non-routine
Unconnected ↔ Interconnected
Proximate ↔ Remote
Static ↔ Dynamic

Predictable  ↔  Unpredictable
High input receptivity  ↔  Low input receptivity
High output receptivity  ↔  Low output receptivity
High domain choice flexibility  ↔  Low domain choice flexibility

**The Implications of Environmental Change**

Undoubtedly one of the major problems faced by managers comes when the organization, having operated for some time in a largely predictable environment, is faced with having to come to terms with a far more complex, uncertain and possibly malevolent environment. Among those who have had to do this in recent years are solicitors, estate agents and opticians, all of whom have been affected by the Conservative government's moves to reduce barriers to competition. Solicitors, for example, have had to come to terms with a new form of competition in the form of licensed conveyancers. Similarly, the structure of estate agency changed dramatically in the mid to late 1980s as a series of financial institutions moved into the business by buying individual agencies and regional chains, and then offered clients packages of financial services in addition to the normal estate agency service. Prominent among those doing this were Lloyds Bank, Prudential Insurance, and the large building societies such as the Halifax and Abbey National. Those estate agents which were still independent found themselves having to cope with a radically different and generally more sophisticated form of competition than that to which most were accustomed.

The significance of changes such as these needs to be seen in terms of *how* the organization monitors the environment and, subsequently, *how* it *responds*. Quite obviously, what is appropriate to a static environment is not suited to either a dynamic or a complex environment.

**Static, Dynamic and Complex Environments**

With regard to the question of how the organization monitors the environment, evidence suggests that in *broadly static conditions* straightforward environmental scanning is likely to be a useful and generally adequate process. In a *dynamic environment*, however, the organization is typically faced with major change in the areas of technology and markets with the result that decisions can no longer be based upon the assumption that what broadly has happened in the past will continue in the future. As a consequence of this, the focus needs to be upon the future with a far greater degree of inspirational interpretation. Among the techniques that have been used to do this is Delphic forecasting. The results are then used as the basis for building alternative scenarios.

This idea of alternative futures can then be used to identify the likely impact upon consumers, suppliers, competitors, government, the financial institutions, their probable responses, and subsequently their impact upon the organization.

For organizations faced with a *complex* environment, many of the issues and problems to which reference has been made are exacerbated. In discussing how to cope with this, Johnson and Scholes (1988, p. 61) suggest that there are organizational and information processing approaches:

> Complexity as a result of diversity might be dealt with by ensuring that different parts of the organisation responsible for different aspects of diversity are separate and given the resources and authority to handle their own part of the environment. Where high knowledge requirements are important it may also be that those with specialist knowledge in the organisation become very powerful because they are relied upon, not only to make operational decisions, but are trusted to present information in such a way that a sensible strategic decision can be made: or indeed they themselves become responsible for the strategic decisions. As an information processing approach there may be an attempt to model the complexity. This may be done through a financial model, for example, which seeks to simulate the effects on an organisation of different environmental conditions. In its extreme form there may be an attempt to model the environment itself. The Treasury Office draws on a model of the UK economy for example. However, for most organisations facing complexity, organisational responses are probably more common than extensive model building.

Regardless, however, of the degree of complexity in the environment, there appear to be certain common strands in the ways in which managers cope with their environments. The most significant of these is that managers develop over time what can loosely be referred to as the accepted wisdom of the industry and the workable solutions to the various situations that are likely to emerge. One consequence of this is that the major competitive threats to organizations often come from companies *outside* the industry which, on entering the market, adopt a strategy which falls outside this area of standardized expectation which allows for the conventional wisdom of response to change to be adopted.

## 7.4  THE NATURE OF THE MARKETING ENVIRONMENT

The marketing environment has been defined in a variety of ways. Churchman (1968), for example, has referred to it in terms of factors which are outside the system's control but which determine, in part at least, how the system performs.

For our purposes, however, the most useful working definition is that proposed by Kotler (1988, p. 135):

> The company's marketing environment is made up of the sectors and forces outside the firm's marketing function which infringe upon the ability of marketing management to develop and maintain a successful relationship with the firm's target group.

Within the environment there are two distinct components: the *microenvironment* and the *macroenvironment*. These are illustrated in Figure 7.4.

**FIGURE 7.4**
*The organization's marketing environment*

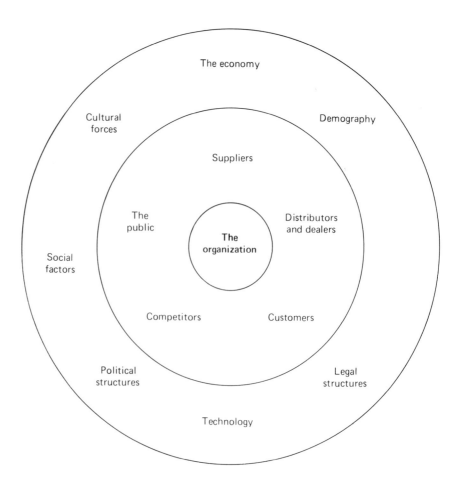

The *microenvironment* is made up of those elements which are closest to the company and which exert the greatest and most direct influence over its ability to deal with its markets. This includes the organization itself, its suppliers, its distribution network, customers, competitors, and the public at large. The *macroenvironment* consists of the rather broader set of forces that have a bearing upon the company, including economic, demographic, technological, political, legal, social and cultural factors. Together, these elements of the environment combine to form what we can loosely refer to as the non-controllable elements of marketing which, in many ways, act as a series of constraints on the parameters within which the marketing planner is required to operate.

In labelling these elements as non-controllable, the reader should recognize that, in some cases at least, the marketing planner may well adopt a highly proactive stance in an attempt to alter the nature and impact of the environment upon the organization. He might, for example, attempt a merger or take-over in order to minimize a competitive threat. Equally, a large organization may well lobby the government in order to have legislation developed or changed so that the company benefits in some way. The car, foodstuffs, cigarettes, and brewing industries, for example, all have powerful lobby groups that attempt to exert a degree of influence over government to ensure that any legislation is beneficial or at least not harmful to their interests. In other cases, however, the organization may adopt a rather more reactive stance and simply view the environment as something that has to be lived with and responded to.

Regardless of which approach an organization adopts, it needs to be recognized that the environment is a significant determinant both of strategy and organizational performance, something which has been reflected in the work of a considerable number of writers including Baker (1985, p. 85) who has described it as 'the ultimate constraint upon the firm's strategy', Drucker (1969) who referred to the environment of the 60s and 70s as the 'age of discontinuity', and Toffler (1970, p. 28) who, in looking ahead, referred to it as a time of 'future shock'. In making these comments, each author was giving recognition to the volatility, and indeed the potential malevolence, of environmental factors. As an example of this, the early 1970s witnessed the oil crisis, which in turn precipitated an economic upheaval throughout the world which was reflected for some considerable time in higher levels of unemployment, interest rates, the development of new economic thinking, and perhaps most importantly, levels of business confidence. However, although the oil crisis was without doubt a significant environmental upset, its impact was obviously felt far more directly by some organizations than others. It needs therefore to be remembered that what is a key environmental issue for one organization is not necessarily a key environmental issue for another. For a multinational corporation, for example, the major areas of concern are likely to be government relations, spheres of influence and the various political complexions throughout the world. For a retailer, the more *directly* important environmental influences are likely to be customer tastes and behaviour, and interest rates, while for a manufacturer in the high technology fields it is issues of technical development and speeds of obsolescence that are important.

The question of the extent to which environmental change, particularly of something as significant as the oil crisis, can be anticipated by business organizations has been the subject of considerable discussion, and in the case of the oil crisis, has led to both a 'yes' and a 'no' answer. 'Yes' in the sense that the techniques of environmental analysis undoubtedly existed at the time, but 'no' in that few people were willing, or indeed able, to recognize that one economic era was in the process of coming to an end, that another was about to start and that balances of power throughout the world were beginning to change in a number of significant ways.

Although a number of commentators have suggested that environmental change of this magnitude is so rare as to be seen almost as a one-off, other writers' views differ and suggest that it is simply the *scale* of the oil crisis that separates it from the more commonly experienced and less dramatic forms of environmental change. The lesson to be learned in either case is straightforward, in that it points to the need for companies to engage in careful, continuous and fundamental monitoring of the environment with a view to identifying *potential* threats before they become *actual* threats, and opportunities before they are missed. This has in turn led to the idea of 'strategic windows', a concept which has been discussed by Abell and Hammond (1979, p. 63):

> The term strategic window is used to describe the fact that there are often only limited periods when the 'fit' between the 'key requirements' of a market and the particular competences of a firm competing in that market are at an optimum. Investment in a product line or market area has to be timed to coincide with periods in which a strategic window is open, i.e. where a close fit exists. Disinvestment should be considered if, during the course of the market's evolution, changes in market requirements outstrip the firm's capability to adapt itself to the new circumstances.
>
> The strategic window concept can be useful to incumbent competitors as well as to would-be entrants into a market. For the former it provides a way of relating future strategic moves to market evolution and of assessing how resources should be allocated to existing activities. For the latter it provides a framework for diversification and new entry.

The consequences of failing to identify strategic windows can, of course, be significant and is typically manifested in terms of a loss of opportunity, market share or competitive advantage. This was illustrated by the Swiss watch industry in the 1970s and 1980s when it failed to recognize the significance of new, low price market segments, new quartz technology, and a new, low cost and aggressive form of competition from Japan and, subsequently, Hong Kong. The net effect of this was that the Swiss saw their share of the world watch industry drop from 80 per cent in 1948 to just 13 per cent in 1985; this is discussed in detail in Illustration 7.1.

That they have subsequently fought back with the Swatch watch is, in one sense at least, incidental. Perhaps the more important lesson to be learned from their experience is that a different approach to environmental monitoring might well have led to the industry avoiding the traumas that it undoubtedly faced.

## 7.5 THE EVOLUTION OF ENVIRONMENTAL ANALYSIS

Recognition of the potential significance of environmental change highlights the need for a certain type of organizational structure and culture which is then reflected both in a balanced portfolio of products and in an adaptive management style supported by a well-developed intelligence and information monitoring system. Without this, the likelihood of the firm being taken unawares by environmental changes of one sort or another increases dramatically. Against the background of these comments, the need for environmental analysis would appear self-evident. All too often, however, firms appear to pay only lip service to such a need. In commenting on this, Diffenbach (1983, pp. 107–16) has identified three distinct stages in the evolution of corporate environmental analysis. These are, he suggests:

1 An *appreciation stage* typically resulting from the emergence of books and articles which argue the case for looking beyond the short term and for considering the wider implications of the economic, technological, social and political factors which make up the business environment.
2 An *analysis stage* which involves 'finding reliable sources of environmental data, compiling and examining the data to discuss trends, developments and

# Illustration 7.1: The Swiss Watch Industry and the Consequences of New (and Unexpected) Competition

In 1948 the Swiss watch industry accounted for 80 per cent of all watches sold in the world. By 1985 its share of the market had dropped to just 13 per cent with the Japanese, a relatively new entrant to the market, having taken over as market leader (see Figure 7.5).

**FIGURE 7.5** *Estimated brakdown of world watch production*

|      | World production* | Switzerland | Japan | Hong Kong | USA | Rest of world |
|------|-------------------|-------------|-------|-----------|-----|---------------|
| 1948 | 31                | 80          | –     | –         | –   | 20            |
| 1970 | 174               | 43          | 14    | –         | 11  | 32            |
| 1975 | 218               | 34          | 14    | 2         | 12  | 38            |
| 1980 | 300               | 29          | 22    | 20        | 4   | 25            |
| 1985 | 440               | 13          | 39    | 22        | 0.4 | 25            |

\* million watches and movements

SOURCE: Federation of the Swiss Watch Industry

This surprising and remarkably rapid change in the market's structure was attributable to several factors, the most important of which can be identifed as:

1 A failure on the part of the Swiss to come to terms with the explosive growth in the less expensive sector of the market.
2 The speed of the switch away from mechanical (i.e. spring-powered) watches to the far more accurate quartz-powered watches. Whereas 98 per cent of all watches and movements produced in 1974 were mechanical and only 2 per cent were quartz, in 1984 the breakdown was 24 per cent mechanical and 76 per cent quartz. Ironically, in the light of the source and the technological base of the attack upon the Swiss watch industry, the quartz electronic watch was invented in Switzerland in 1968, but first marketed in the United States.
3 A failure to come to terms with the increasing Asian penetration of the large and lucrative American market. While Switzerland's estimated contribution to American import volume decreased from 99 per cent in 1950 to 4 per cent in 1984, the percentage of import volume from Asia increased from 10 per cent in 1970 to 92 per cent in 1984.

The Japanese, and subsequently the Hong Kong manufacturers, owed their success to a combination of aggressive marketing, a high degree of production concentration, and perhaps most importantly, a relatively complacent competitor who was taken by surprise by the sudden inroads made by the Japanese and who subsequently found it difficult to retaliate. With regard to the first two points, the nature of the challenge has been summed up in the following way.

The Japanese industry was highly concentrated with the two major firms, Hattori Seiko and Citizen, stressing the development of automated production lines and maximum vertical integration of operations. Compared with the multitude of Swiss watch brands, the combined product lines of these two plus Casio, the third major Japanese watchmaker, did not exceed a dozen brands. In contrast, the industry in Hong Kong was highly fragmented, with several manufacturers producing 10–20 million watches per year, and hundreds of small firms producing less than 1 million annually. These firms could not afford to invest in quartz analog technology but with virtually no barriers to entry for watch assembly, they produced complete analog watches from imported movements and modules, often Swiss or Japanese. Design costs were also minimized by copying Swiss or Japanese products. The competitive advantages of the Hong Kong firms were low-cost labour, tiny margins and the flexibility to adapt to changes in the market.

The spectacular rise of Japan and Hong Kong, particularly in the middle and low-price categories, was primarily due to their rapid adoption of quartz technology, a drive to achieve a competitive cost position through accumulation of experience, and economies of scale. Whereas in 1972 the digital watch module cost around $200, the same module cost only $50 in 1984. The Asian watchmaking industry had been ensuring a chronic state of world oversupply, mainly in the inexpensive quartz digital range. This had been the cause of a number of bankruptcies and had incited watch manufacturers to turn to the quartz analog market where added value was higher. Since in contrast to quartz digital technology, quartz analog technology was available only within the watch industry, the hundreds of watch assemblers scattered throughout the world were increasingly dependent on the three major movement manufacturers, Seiko, ETA and Citizen.

The fightback by the Swiss began at the beginning of the 1980s and was spearheaded by Dr Ernest Thomke. Thomke concluded that '. . . the future was in innovative finished products, aggressive marketing, volume sales and vertical integration of the industry'. Quartz analog technology was more complex than digital, but as ETA was known for the technology it possessed for the production of high-priced, ultra-thin 'Delirium' movement, Thomke decided to develop a 'low-price prestige' quartz analog wristwatch that could be mass produced in Switzerland at greatly reduced cost. Two ETA micromechanical engineers specializing in plastic injection moulding technology, Jacques Muller and Elmar Mock, were given the challenge of designing a product based on Thomke's concept. This required inventing entirely new production technology using robots and computers for manufacture and assembly. By 1981 a semi-automated process had been designed to meet Thomke's goal of a 15 SF ex-factory price, and seven patents were registered. The watch's movement, consisting of only 51 instead of the 90–150 parts in other watches, was injected directly into the one-piece plastic case. The casing was sealed by ultrasonic welding instead of screws, precluding servicing. The watch would be simply replaced and not repaired if it stopped. The finished product, guaranteed for one year, was shock resistant, water resistant to 100 feet (30 metres) and contained a three-year replaceable battery.

Launched as the Swatch, the success of the marketing campaign is now legendary. However, the question that must be faced is to what extent might the problems faced by the Swiss watch industry have been avoided by a far more careful monitoring of the environment and the identification of a major competitive and technological threat?

*Source:* I've Got a Swatch *case study, INSEAD, 1987*

key relationships. It also includes monitoring developments and anticipating the future'. It was the emergence of this thinking which led to the appearance in the 1960s and 1970s of numerous books on environmental scanning, Delphic analysis and environmental forecasting.

3 The *application stage* in which very real attempts are made to monitor the environment, assess the implications for change and incorporate staff evaluations into strategy and plans.

Assuming therefore that a firm intends to develop an effective system for environmental analysis, there is a need first to identify those dimensions which are likely to have the greatest impact upon the organization, and second to establish a mechanism whereby each of these elements is monitored on a regular basis. For most companies these elements are contained within the PEST analytical framework referred to earlier. Although in practice other factors can be added to this list, we will for convenience use this framework as a prelude to illustrating how environmental factors influence, and occasionally dictate, strategy. However, before examining these various dimensions, it is worth making reference to the way in which environmental analysis has developed, and to the areas upon which managers typically focus. In doing this, the most obvious starting point is Aguilar's (1967) work.

In what is now seen as a classic study, Aguilar interviewed 137 managers drawn from 41 chemical firms in Europe and the United States. His work highlighted the lack of a systematic approach to environmental monitoring, something which has been reinforced more recently by the work of, among others, Thomas (1980, pp. 20–8) and Fahey, et al. (1981, pp. 32–9).

In carrying out his research, Aguilar identified that managers typically collected 16 types of environmental information. These he subsequently classified under five headings:

1 market tidings;
2 acquisition leads;
3 technical tidings;
4 broad issues (e.g. general conditions and government actions);
5 other tidings (e.g. suppliers and resources).

These information needs are developed in Figure 7.6.

**FIGURE 7.6**
*The types of environmental information required by managers*

**Market tidings**

Market potential
Structural change
Competitors and industry
Pricing
Sales negotiations
Customers

**Acquisition leads**

Leads for mergers, joint ventures or acquisitions

**Technical tidings**

New products, processes and technology
Product problems
Costs
Licensing and patents

**Broad issues**

General conditions
Government actions and policies

**Other tidings**

Suppliers and raw materials
Resources available
Miscellaneous

SOURCE: Adapted from Aguilar (1967)

Of these, market tidings proved to be the most commonly collected pieces of environmental information, with 52 per cent of participants placing emphasis upon them. This was followed by technical tidings (17 per cent) and broad issues (12 per cent). The research also revealed four approaches to market monitoring:

1 undirected viewing;
2 conditioned viewing;
3 informal search;
4 formal search.

Aguilar concluded from this work that for a process of environmental monitoring to work effectively and make a worthwhile contribution to a company's operations, it must be carried out systematically and not in the fragmented and frequently purposeless fashion (i.e. largely undirected viewing) revealed by his study. In suggesting how best to overcome these problems, Aguilar gave prominence both to the necessity for *top management commitment* to environmental monitoring and to the *incorporation* within the decision-making process of the information generated. This should, he argued, lead to a far greater degree of top management involvement in the specification of the information to be collected, and hence to a sense of 'ownership'. Without this, the benefits of the system are likely to be limited.

Subsequent work in this area has continued to reveal a general picture of the partial and largely unstructured development of environmental monitoring processes, although Fahey, et al. (1981, pp. 32–9) identified a more positive picture in a sample of 12 large American firms. This work led them to suggest a typology of models of scanning characterized by an increasing degree of structure, systemization, sophistication and resource intensity. These are:

1 *Irregular systems* which predominate in companies with a poorly developed planning culture and in which the focus is upon *responding* to environmentally generated crises. The net effect of this is that emphasis is simply placed upon finding solutions to short-term problems with little real attention being paid to identifying and assessing the likely impact of future environmental changes.
2 *Periodic models* which represent a general development of the irregular system and which are more systematic, resource intensive and sophisticated. The environment is reviewed regularly and a longer-term perspective is developed.
3 The *continuous model* which is yet a further development and involves focusing upon the business environment generally and upon the long term as opposed to short term and specific issues.

Fahey, et al., went on to suggest that although there is a general shift within American companies towards more sophisticated systems, this movement is slow and compared with its apparent impact, has still to justify the level of resources required.

Nevertheless, the argument for continuous environmental monitoring in order to identify strategic issues and market signals in advance of their impact upon the company is a strong one and has led Brownlie (1987, pp. 100–5) to identify the three basic premises upon which continuous environmental analysis is based. These are, he suggests, that:

1 the determinants of success are dictated by the business environment;
2 the firm's response to environmental change therefore represents a fundamental strategic choice;
3 a knowledge of the business environment must precede the acquisition of any degree of control over it.

Acknowledging the validity of these three assumptions leads to a recognition that effective management cannot take place in an information vacuum, or indeed in circumstances in which information is at best partial and poorly structured. There is, therefore, an obvious need for the organization to develop an effective information system which *collects*, *analyses* and then *disseminates* information both from within and outside the company.

There are, however, problems that are commonly associated with the first of these, that of information collection and the development of a worthwhile database. Brownlie identifies these as being that all too often the information is:

- poorly structured;
- available only on an irregular basis;
- often provided by unofficial sources;
- qualitative in nature;
- ambiguous in its definitions;
- opinion based;
- poorly quantified;
- based on an insecure methodology;
- likely to change.

Because of problems such as these, the need to collect and analyse environmental information in a well-structured and useable fashion is essential, and it is this that frameworks such as PEST are designed to achieve. It must be emphasized, however, that the organization should avoid focusing just upon the immediate task environment, since all too frequently history has demonstrated that the most significant threats faced by companies often come from firms outside the task environment. We have already pointed to the example of the Swiss watch industry which was significantly damaged by the introduction of microchips and digital technology on the part of firms that the Swiss did not see as competitors. Equally, companies in markets as prosaic as carbon paper were decimated by photocopying technology, while in the same period the British motorcycle manufacturers of the 1960s, seeing their competitors as being one another, were taken by surprise by the Japanese. In making these comments we are therefore arguing for a *breadth* of perspective within the general structure of PEST analysis.

However, although the environment exerts a significant and obvious influence upon the organization, it should not necessarily be seen as the most direct determinant of strategy. Porter (1980, Ch. 1), for example, has argued that industry structure is a more important factor than environmental conditions:

> Industry structure has a strong influence in determining the competitive rules of the game as well as the strategies potentially available to the firm. Forces outside the industry are significant primarily in a relative sense; since outside forces usually affect all firms in the industry, the key is found in the differing ability of the firms to deal with them.

Before going on to consider some of the ways in which industry structure influences strategy, we need to examine the various dimensions of the political, economic, social and technological environments. It is this that provides the basis of the next section.

## 7.6 THE POLITICAL, ECONOMIC, SOCIAL AND TECHNOLOGICAL ENVIRONMENTS

At the beginning of this chapter we suggested that effective marketing planning is based on two important analytical ingredients. First, market opportunity must be analysed, and second, the company's ability to take advantage of these opportunities and cope with threats must be assessed.

Under the first heading, there are four basic building blocks:

1 customers must be analysed to determine how the market can be segmented and what the requirements of each segment are;
2 competitors must be identified and their individual strategies understood;
3 environmental trends (social, economic, political, technological) affecting the market must be isolated and forecasted;
4 market characteristics in terms of the evolution of supply and demand and their interaction must be understood.

It is point 3 to which we now turn our attention.

**The Political (and Legal) Environment**

Marketing decisions are typically affected in a variety of ways by developments in the political and legal environments. This part of the environment is composed of laws, pressure groups and government agencies, all of which exert some sort of influence and constraint on organizations and individuals in society.

With regard to the legislative framework, the starting point involves recognizing that the amount of legislation affecting business has increased steadily over the past two decades. This legislation has been designed to achieve a number of purposes, including:

1 protecting companies from each other by means of laws such as the Restrictive Trade Practices Acts (1956 and 1976) and the Fair Trading Act (1973), all of which are designed to prevent unfair competition;
2 Protecting consumers from unfair business practice – legislation such as this, which includes the Trade Descriptions Act (1968), the Consumer Credit Act (1974), the Sale of Goods Act (1979), and the Unfair Contract Terms Act (1977), is intended to ensure that certain safety standards are met, that advertising is honest, and that generally companies are not able to take advantage of the possible ignorance, naivety and gullibility of consumers;
3 protecting society at large from irresponsible business behaviour.

It is important therefore that the marketing planner is aware not only of the current legislative framework, but also of the ways in which it is likely to develop and how, by means of industry pressure groups and lobbying of parliament, the direction of legislation might possibly be influenced so that it benefits the company. At a broader level the strategist should also be familiar with the way in which legislation in other countries differs, and how this too might provide opportunities and constraints. The Scandinavian countries, for example, have developed a legislative framework to protect consumers that is far more restrictive than is generally the case elsewhere in Europe. Norway, for example, has banned many forms of sales promotion such as trading stamps, contests and premiums as being inappropriate and unfair methods for sellers to use in the promotion of their products. Elsewhere, food companies in India require government approval to launch a new brand if it will simply duplicate what is already on offer in the market, while in the Philippines food manufacturers are obliged to offer low price variations of their brands so that low income groups are not disadvantaged.

Although legislation such as this tends to be country-specific, examples such as these are potentially useful in that they highlight the need for marketing managers to be aware not just of the situation in their immediate markets, but also of how legislation might develop in order to restrict marketing practice. In a broader sense, marketing planners also need to monitor how public interest groups are likely to develop and, subsequently, influence marketing practice. In commenting on this in the context of American pressure groups, Salancik and Upah (1978) have said:

There is some evidence that the consumer may not be King, nor even Queen. The consumer is but a voice, one among many. Consider how General Motors makes its cars today. Vital features of the motor are designed by the United States government; the exhaust system is redesigned by certain state governments; the production materials used are dictated by suppliers who control scarce material resources. For other products, other groups and organizations may get involved. Thus, insurance companies directly or indirectly affect the design of smoke detectors; scientific groups affect the design of spray products by condemning aerosols; minority activist groups affect the design of dolls by requesting representative figures. Legal departments also can be expected to increase their importance in firms, affecting not only product design and promotion but also marketing strategies. At a minimum, marketing managers will spend less time with their research departments asking 'What does the consumer want?' and more and more time with their production and legal people asking 'What can the consumer have?'

In the light of comments such as these, the need for careful and continual monitoring of the political and legal environment should be obvious, since at the heart of all such analysis is the simple recognition of the idea of political risk.

**The Economic and Physical Environments**

Within the majority of small and medium sized firms, the economic environment is typically seen as a constraint, since the ability of a company to exert any sort of influence on this element of the environment is to all intents and purposes negligible. As a consequence, it is argued, firms are typically put into the position of responding to the state of the economy. Having said this, larger companies, and particularly the multinationals (MNCs), are perhaps able to view the economic environment in a rather different way, since they are often able to shift investment and marketing patterns from one market to another and from one part of the world to another in order to capitalize most fully on the opportunities that exist. For a purely domestic operator, however, the ability to do this is generally non-existent. For both types of company there is still a need to understand *how* the economic environment is likely to affect performance, a need which received a significant boost in the 1970s in the wake of the oil crisis when parallels were being drawn between that period and the Great Depression of the 1930s. More specifically, however, the sorts of change that are currently taking place in the economic environment can be identified as:

1  a slowdown in real income growth;
2  continuing inflationary pressures;
3  changings in the savings/debt ratio;
4  concern over levels of Third World debt;
5  different consumer expenditure patterns.

The significance of changes such as these should not be looked at in isolation, but should be viewed instead against the background of changes in the *political/economic balances of power* (e.g. the rise of Japan over the past 20 years, the opportunities today in Central and Eastern Europe, and the possible economic development of China), and major changes in the *physical environment*.

Concern with the physical environment has increased dramatically over the past few years, with the origins being traceable to the publication in the 1960s of Rachael Carson's book *Silent Spring* (1963). In this Carson drew attention to the possibly irrevocable damage being done to the planet and the possibility that we would exhaust the world's resources. This concern was echoed in the coining of the phrase 'eco-catastrophe' and reflected subsequently in the formation of powerful lobby groups such as Friends of the Earth who have had an impact upon business practice. The four major areas of concern expressed by pressure groups such as these are:

1  an impending shortage of raw materials;
2  the increasing costs of energy;

3  increasing levels and consequences of pollution;
4  an increasing need for governments to become involved in the *management* of natural resources.

It should be apparent from this that a broad perspective needs to be adopted in looking at the economic environment. From the viewpoint of the marketing planner, analysis of short-term and long-term economic *patterns* is of vital importance. Although it is not possible to develop an all-embracing list of economic issues to which attention needs to be paid, the strategist almost invariably needs to take account of the following areas:

1  patterns of real income distribution;
2  patterns of saving and debt;
3  expenditure patterns;
4  inflationary and deflationary pressures.

## The Social, Cultural and Demographic Environments

In analysing this aspect of the environment, arguably the most useful and indeed logical starting point is that of demography, since not only is demographic change readily identifiable, but it is the size, structure and trends of a population that ultimately exert the greatest influence on demand. There are several reasons for this, the two most significant of which are, first, that there is a strong relationship between population and economic growth, and second, that it is the absolute size of the population that acts as the boundary condition determining potential or primary demand. A detailed understanding of the size, structure, composition and trends of the population is therefore of fundamental importance to the marketing planner. It is consequently fortunate that in the majority of developed countries information of this sort is generally readily available and provides a firm foundation for forecasting.

In the case of the UK, for example, the population is expected to have grown by 1.2 per cent from 56.4 million in 1980 to 57.5 million in 1998. Although this is a relatively slow rate of growth, particularly when compared with some other countries (the USA for example is expected to have grown by 11 per cent in the same period), a variety of other and in many ways more significant structural changes in the population will have taken place during the same period. In commenting on these, the market research firm Mintel has identified the most significant as being:

- 9 per cent more children up to the age of 14;
- 18 per cent fewer teenagers and young adults aged 15–29;
- 13 per cent more 30–54-year-olds;
- 7 per cent fewer 55–69-year-olds;
- 5 per cent more 70-year-olds and over.

The key marketing factor to emerge from this, it is argued, is the swing from teenagers and young adults to middle-aged marrieds.

At the same time, a variety of other equally important and far reaching changes are currently taking place including the following.

1  *A growth in the number of one-person households.* The size of this SSWD group (single, separated, widowed, divorced) has grown dramatically over the past few years, partly as the result of more young adults leaving home early and partly by a rise in the divorce rate. The significance of this has been highlighted by a government forecast that the number of one-person households will have increased by more than 30 per cent in the period 1976–94. At the same time, the number of pensioner one-person households is expected to have increased

from 2.9 million in 1979 to almost 4 million by the mid 1990s. The net effect of changes such as these, together with a rather more general move towards smaller families, will lead to a drop in the average household size from 2.7 in 1979 to 2.4 in 1995.

The implications for marketing of changes such as these have already proved significant in a variety of ways and have been reflected in an increase in demand for more starter homes, smaller appliances, food that can be purchased in smaller portions, and a greater emphasis on convenience products.

2 *A rise in the number of two-person cohabitant households.* It has been suggested by several sociologists that cohabitation is becoming increasingly like the first stage of marriage, with more people of the opposite sex sharing a house. At the same time, the number of households with two or more people of the same sex sharing has also increased.

3 An increase in *group households* with three or more people of the same or opposite sex sharing expenses by living together, particularly in the larger cities. This figure looks set to increase yet further.

The needs of these non-family households differ in a variety of ways from those of the more conventional family household which in the past has typically provided the focus for marketing attention. By virtue of their increasing importance, non-family households are likely to require ever more different strategies over the next few years if full advantage of the opportunities they offer is to be realized.

At the same time a variety of other significant demographic shifts are taking place throughout the world, all of which need to be reflected in the planning process.

1 *An explosion in the world's population.* With an annual and exponential growth rate of 1.8 per cent, the world population will have grown from 4.4 billion in 1980 to 6.2 billion by the year 2000. Much of this growth will be concentrated in those nations which, by virtue of currently low standards of living and economic development, can least afford it. Nevertheless, significant opportunities will be generated as a result of this growth both domestically and internationally.

2 *A slowdown in birth rates* in many of the developed nations. Many families today, for example, are opting for just one child and this has had significant implications for a variety of companies. Johnson & Johnson, for example, responded to the declining birth rate by very successfully repositioning its baby oil, baby powder and baby shampoo in such a way that the products also appealed to young female adults. Similarly, cosmetics companies have placed a far greater emphasis on products for the over-fifties.

3 *An ageing population* as advances in medical care allow people to live longer. One result of this trend, which has in turn been exacerbated by the slowdown in birth rate, has been an increase in the number of empty nesters (see the section on the family life cycle on page 205) who have substantial sums of discretionary income and high expectations.

4 *Changing family structures* as a result of:
   - later marriage
   - fewer children
   - increased divorce rates
   - more working wives
   - an increase in the number of career women.

5 *Higher levels of education* and an increasing number of families in what has traditionally been seen as the middle class.

6 *Geographical shifts* in population and, in Britain at least, the emergence of a north-south divide characterized by radically different levels of economic activity and employment.
7 *A growth in the number of people willing to commute long distances to work,* and an upsurge in the opportunities for telecommuting whereby people work from home and interact with colleagues via computer terminals.

The net effect of changes such as these has been significant, and is continuing to prove so, with the marketing strategies of nearly all companies being affected in one way or another. At their most fundamental, these changes have led to a shift from a small number of mass markets to an infinitely larger number of micromarkets differentiated by age, sex, lifestyle, education and so on. Each of these groups differs in terms of its preferences and characteristics, and as a consequence requires different, more flexible and more precise approaches to marketing which no longer take for granted the long established assumptions and conventions of marketing practice. The implications of these trends are therefore of considerable significance and from the viewpoint of the strategist have the advantage of being both reliable and largely predictable, at least in the short and medium term. There is thus no excuse either for being taken unawares by them or for ignoring them.

Against the background of fundamental demographic and social shifts such as these a wide variety of other changes can be seen to be taking place, particularly in the area of social and cultural factors. Albrecht (1979), for example, has identified five major lifestyle changes that are currently taking place. There are, he suggests, shifts:

- from rural living to urban living;
- from stationary to mobile;
- from self-sufficient to interconnected;
- from isolated to interconnected;
- from physically active to sedentary.

The full impact of these changes is in many cases still to be felt, although Albrecht highlights their physiological and psychological effects, which have increased levels of stress and in turn influenced lifestyle. At the same time, however, the social and cultural environment is being influenced by a seemingly ever greater concern with the environment. At one level this has seen the development of consumerism and concern for equal opportunities while at another level, however, it is reflected in a far deeper and more fundamental concern for the physical environment and the way in which certain products such as the fluorocarbons contained in some aerosols have harmed the ozone layer. Equally, attitudes with regard to such things as acid rain, pollution of the seas, and the danger of nuclear power have all changed over the past decade and, directly or indirectly, seem likely to influence marketing behaviour, with an ever greater emphasis being given to environmentally friendly products. In part this can be seen as a result of: the possible shift in emphasis from a 'me society' to a 'we society' that is characterized by less self-interest and a greater concern with longer lasting relationships; an increase in the number of people concerned with a healthy lifestyle; a decline in the work ethic and institutional loyalty; and a greater concern with the physical environment. Others have argued that the shift in social and cultural values is in fact the other way.

Regardless of the direction in which attitudes are shifting, the relationship between people and society can be expressed in terms of the Stanford Research Institute's *life ways concept* which suggests that people fall into one of six groups. The key elements of each of these groups have been summarized by Kotler (1988, p. 162) as being:

- *Makers*. Makers are those who make the system work. They are the leaders and the up-and-comers. They are involved in worldly affairs, generally prosperous and ambitious. They are found in the professions and include the managers and proprietors of business.
- *Preservers*. Preservers are people who are at ease with the familiar and are proud of tradition. They are a powerful force in promoting stability in a changing world.
- *Takers*. Takers take what they can from the system. They live only marginally in the work world, finding their pleasures outside. They are attracted to bureaucracies and tenured posts.
- *Changers*. Changers tend to be answer-havers; they commonly wish to change things to conform with their views. They are the critics, protestors, radicals, advocates, and complainers – and a significant segment of the doers. Their focus is chiefly outward.
- *Seekers*. Seekers are the ones who search for a better grasp, a deeper understanding, a richer experience, a universal view. The pathways of their seeking and the rewards sought tend to be internal. They often originate and promulgate new ideas.
- *Escapers*. Escapers have a drive to escape, to get away from it all. Escape takes many forms from dropping out, to addiction, to mental illness, to mysticism.

These life groups differ in a variety of significant ways and need to be seen as market segments with specific material and symbolic needs. The makers, for example, are high achievers for whom success symbols such as cars, houses and brand names are important forms of expression, while changers, represent a far more austere lifestyle, characterized by smaller cars and less emphasis in their clothing on fashion. This shift in cultural values has also led to the following trends:

Other centredness → self-fulfilment
Postponed gratification → immediate gratification
Hard work → the easy life
Formal relationships → informal open relationships
Religious orientation → secular orientation

Taken together, the changes that we have pointed to in this section can be seen as fundamental, and have been described by Albrecht (1979) in the following ways:

> The period from 1900 until the present stands apart from every other period in human history as a time of incredible change. Mankind, at least in the so-called 'developed' countries, has lost its innocence entirely. The great defining characteristics of this period – the first three-quarters of the twentieth century – have been change, impermanence, disruption, newness and obsolescence, and a sense of acceleration in almost every perceptible aspect of American society.
>
> Philosophers, historians, scientists, and economists have given various names to this period. Management consultant Peter F. Drucker (1968) has called it the Age of Discontinuity. Economist John Kenneth Galbraith (1977) has called it the Age of Uncertainty. Media theorist Marshall MacLuhan (1964, 1968) called it the Age of the Global Village. Writer and philosopher Alvin Toffler (1970, 1975) called it the Age of Future Shock. Virtually all thoughtful observers of America, Americans, and American society have remarked with some alarm about the accelerating pace with which our life processes and our surrounds are changing within the span of a single generation. And this phenomenon is spreading all over the industrialized world. I call this the Age of Anxiety.

A number of these themes have been picked up and developed by social forecasters. Among them is an ad-hoc group established by the management consultants, the Hay Group; their views of the future are discussed in Illustration 7.2.

# Illustration 7.2:  Headlines 2000

In 1988, Hay Management Consultants took 14 people – seven from their own organization and seven from a variety of other organizations* – who are likely to be in a senior position in the year 2000, and asked them to think about the world as it might be in AD 2000. In doing this, they were looking for the *inevitable*, the *unexpected*, the *possibilities*, and the *problems*. Among their conclusions were:

 1 Throughout Europe we are running short of young people. The number of 16 to 19-year-olds will have fallen by up to 25 per cent by 1995 alone. Although this has been an established fact for at least 10 years, it will still prove to be unexpected to a surprising number of employers. The result will be a shortage of qualified people, which will have to be overcome by a combination of fewer early retirements, more married women being wooed back into the workforce, the replacement of people with technology, an ever greater investment in education, and possibly a drawing in of skilled labour from the old European empires, Africa, Asia and China.
 2 The 50–54 age group will increase by a third, and the over-75 group by a quarter. Markets and tastes will be dominated by the middle-aged. The competition for the fewer affluent young will be more intense with the growth market being in health and personal services for the 'greying battalions'. A major problem, however, will be the cost to society of an ageing population; the cost per head of health services is six times higher for the over 75s, and the cost of social services 26 times higher.
 3 The further development of office technology, and in particular business communications, will make the truly personal mobile office feasible.
 4 The next scientific revolution will be biotechnology which will allow a far greater range of diseases to be cured, including cancer and AIDS. Transplants will be more common, with pigs as the likely new donors.
 5 In agriculture, biotechnology will be able to solve many of the world's food problems.
 6 The family car will still exist but new materials and new manufacturing techniques will mean that every car can be different, with the driver effectively able to design a customized car. Components will be cheaper to replace than to repair.
 7 In monetary terms the global village will have arrived, with notes and coins virtually obsolete.
 8 A new mood of détente will result in a fall in defence spending, enabling the United States' double-deficit problem to be a single-deficit one.
 9 The highly educated baby-boomers are increasingly likely to adopt a portfolio lifestyle in their later years doing a variety of different jobs at the same time.
10 More and more information about our public and private lives will be stored on computer, with an increased ability to corrupt or misuse the information.
11 An ever greater number of employees will be on short-term specific contracts with organizations, and pay will be more directly geared to outputs.

*British Aerospace, The Civil Service, Eurotunnel, ICI, Prudential Corporation, Saatchi & Saatchi, Tesco.

*Source*: Headlines 2000: the world as we see it, *Hay Management Consultants, 1989*

# The Technological Environment

The fourth and final strand of the environment is that of technology. Seen by many people as the single most dramatic force shaping our lives, technological advance needs to be seen as a force for 'creative destruction' in that the development of new products or concepts has an often fatal knock-out effect on an existing product. The creation of the Xerography photocopying process, for example, destroyed the market for carbon paper, while the development of cars damaged the demand for railways. The implications for the existing industry are often straightforward: change or die. The significance of technological change does, however, need to be seen not just at the corporate or industry level but also at the national level, since an economy's growth rate is directly influenced by the level of technological advance (see Wills, et al., 1972).

Technology does, therefore, provide both opportunities and threats, some of which are direct while others are far less direct in their impact. As an example of this, the development of the contraceptive pill led to smaller families, an increase in the number of working wives, higher levels of discretionary income and then subsequently to a greater emphasis on holidays, consumer durables, and so on. Recognizing then that the impact of technology is to all interests inevitable, the areas to which Kotler (1988, pp. 154–6) suggests the marketing planner should pay attention include:

1 *The accelerating pace of technological change.* In his book *Future Shock*, Toffler (1970) makes reference to the accelerative thrust in the invention, exploitation, diffusion and acceptance of new technologies. An ever greater number of ideas are being developed, and the time period between their development and implementation is shortening. This theme was developed further by Toffler in *The Third Wave* (1980) in which he forecast the rapid emergence and acceptance of telecommuting (the electronic cottage) with direct implications for such things as family relationships, home entertainment and, less directly, levels of car exhaust pollution.
2 *Unlimited innovational opportunities* with major advances being made in the areas of solid state electronics, robotics, material sciences and biotechnology.
3 *Higher research and development budgets*, particularly in countries such as Japan. One implication of this is that organizations are likely to be forced into the position of spending ever greater amounts on R & D simply to stay still.
4 *A concentration of effort in some industries on minor product improvements* that are essentially defensive, rather than on the riskier and more offensive major product advances.
5 *A greater emphasis upon the regulation of technological change* in order to minimize the undesirable effects of some new products upon society. Safety and health regulations are most evident in their application in the pharmaceutical, foodstuffs and car industries, although across the entire spectrum of industry far more emphasis today is being given to the idea of technological assessment as a prelude to products being launched commercially.

From the viewpoint of marketing, the implications of each of these areas is of potential significance, and argues the case for careful technological monitoring in order to ensure that emerging opportunities are not ignored or missed. This, in turn, should lead to more market-oriented, rather than product-oriented, research and to a generally greater awareness of the negative aspects of any innovation.

Underlying all of these points is, of course, a recognition of the product life cycle (PLC) concept. The pros and cons of the PLC are detailed elsewhere in this book, and at this stage we are therefore concerned with the way in which simple recognition of the concept argues the case for the development of a formal technological forecasting system which then acts as an input to the process of developing marketing strategy.

# Illustration 7.3: Megatrends 2000

In 1982, two of the world's leading social forecasters, John Naisbitt and Patricia Aburdene, published their book *Megatrends* in which they identified a series of factors likely to influence patterns of world development. The book, with sales of eight million copies, proved to be immensely successful and was followed at the beginning of 1990 by *Megatrends 2000* which identified the major social, economic, political and technological changes likely to shape the 1990s. They introduced the book with the following passage.

> Before us is the most important decade in the history of civilization, a period of technological innovation, unprecedented economic opportunity, surprising political reform and great cultural rebirth. It is a decade like none that has come before because it culminates in the millennium, AD 2000. Already we have fallen under its dominion. The year 2000 is like a powerful magnet on humanity, intensifying the Nineties. It is amplifying emotions, accelerating change, heightening awareness and compelling us to re-examine our values and institutions.
>
> In the Nineties apocalyptic themes will emerge with stunning regularity. Disaster, it seems, will always be just around the corner; the superpowers having just signed a nuclear arms agreement, we have the 'greenhouse' effect.
>
> The Nineties present a new world view. The cold war ended in the Eighties, and the arms race has slowed, perhaps halted. The postwar nationalism is over and a new era of globalism has begun. The arts flourish. There is an international call to environmentalism. Communist countries experiment with democracy and market mechanisms. Among nations, the urge for economic co-operation is stronger than for military adventure. In an increasingly interconnected world there is a new respect for the human spirit.

Within the body of the book they discuss a wide series of factors likely to influence our development up the year 2000, some of the most prominent of which are:

1 a global economic boom;
2 a decade of women in leadership;
3 a religious revival;
4 a renaissance in the arts;
5 the privatization of the welfare state;
6 free-market socialism;
7 the rise of the Pacific Rim;
8 an age of biology;
9 the growth of global lifestyles and nationalism;
10 the triumph of the individual.

## 7.7 APPROACHES TO ENVIRONMENTAL ANALYSIS AND SCANNING

Against the background of our discussion so far it should be clear that environmental analysis and forecasting are capable of making a major contribution to the formulation of strategy. Indeed it has been argued by a number of strategists that environmental analysis and forecasting is the true starting point of any effective planning system, since strategy is based not only on a detailed understanding of the firm's capacity but also on a full knowledge and appreciation of environmental forces and changes that are likely to have an impact on the firm. At its most extreme, the failure to do this is highlighted by Theodore Levitt's ideas of 'Marketing Myopia' which he discussed in his now classic *Harvard Business Review* article (1960, pp. 45–56).

In this article Levitt argued that declining or defunct industries generally reached this position because of a product rather than a marketing orientation. In other words, they focused too firmly on products rather than the environment in which they operated. As a consequence, these companies were often taken by surprise by environmental change, found it difficult to respond, and in many cases, either lost significant market shares or were forced into liquidation.

A system of environmental analysis and forecasting consists of two elements: the first of these is concerned with the *generation* of an up-to-date data base of information, while the second involves the *dissemination* of this information to decision makers and influencers. The effectiveness of such a system, and in particular of this second part, is in practice likely to be influenced by a variety of factors, including:

1 the technical skills of those involved in the process of analysis and forecasting;
2 the nature of the managerial environment that exists within the company.

The significance of this second point is in many companies all too often ignored, but highlights the importance of a planning culture which is both endorsed and promoted by top management. In addition, the managerial environment affects the process in the sense that in large companies at least, those who are involved in the mechanics of analysis and forecasting are rarely the decision makers themselves. Instead, they are generally in an advisory role. This role can lead to the emergence of an important political process within the system whereby the analyst presents information in such a way that the decision maker's perception of the environment and, in turn the options open to the company, is distorted in a particular way. By the same token, the decision maker will often place a particular interpretation on the information presented by the analyst, depending on his perception of the analyst's track record. In commenting on this political process, Brownlie (1987, p. 99) suggests that:

> students of history will recognise that many a bloody political intrigue was spawned by the jealously guarded, and often misused privilege of proximity to the seat of power which was conferred on privy counsellors and advisors. Thus in addition to the technical skills demanded of environmental analysts and forecasters, astute political skills could be said to be the hallmark of an effective operator.

It should therefore be recognized that the effectiveness of a planning system is not determined solely by its methodology, but that it is also affected by several other factors, including the willingness and ability of a management to recognize and subsequently respond to the indicators of coming environmental change.

Taken together, these comments argue the case for what we can refer to as *formal environmental scanning*, a process which covers the full spectrum of activities firms use in order to understand environmental changes and their implications. The essential element of formal environmental scanning is that it should be seen as an activity that becomes an *integral* part of the ongoing process by which companies develop, implement, control and review strategies and plans at both the corporate and the business unit level.

## The Benefits of Environmental Scanning

In practice, the precise role of an environmental scanning process is influenced by a variety of factors, the most significant of which is typically that of management expectations. This, in turn, is often a function of the size of the organization and managerial perceptions of the complexity of its environment. Thus in the case of many small firms the focus is likely to be on the general trends that are likely to influence short- and medium-term levels of performance. In large firms, however, and in particular the multinationals, the focus tends to be far broader with a greater emphasis being placed upon longer-term and more fundamental issues, including possible changes in the political, economic, social and technological variables which provided the focus for the first part of this chapter.

With regard to the specific benefits of environmental scanning Diffenbach (1983, pp. 107–16), in a study of 90 American corporations, has suggested that there are seven principal pay-offs:

1 an increased general awareness by management of environmental changes;
2 better planning and strategic decision making;
3 greater effectiveness in government matters;
4 better industry and market analysis;
5 better results in foreign business;
6 improvements in diversification and resource allocations;
7 better energy planning.

It should be noted that from this study Diffenbach found that although environmental scanning is widely practised and generally considered to be important by the majority of those firms that do it (73 per cent), a sizeable number of companies (27 per cent) simply did not bother with scanning, or did it but found it to be of only limited value (28 per cent).

These benefits of environmental scanning have also been expanded upon by Jain (1985, p. 250) who has listed the major attractions to be that the process:

1 helps firms to identify and capitalize upon opportunities rather than losing out to competitors;
2 provides a base of objective qualitative information;
3 makes the firm more sensitive to the changing needs and wishes of customers;
4 provides a base of 'objective qualitative information' about the business environment that can subsequently be of value to the strategist;
5 provides a level of intellectual stimulation for strategists;
6 improves the image of the firm with the public by illustrating that it is sensitive to its environment;
7 provides a continuing broad based education for executives in general, and the strategist in particular.

Having said this, the complexity of the scanning process varies greatly from one company to another. In commenting on this, Ansoff (1984) has suggested that it is determined by two factors:

1 perceptions within the company of the degree of environmental uncertainty (most typically this is a function of the rate of environmental change);
2 perceptions of the degree of environmental complexity (this is generally influenced by the range of activities and markets in which the firm is currently and prospectively involved).

The significance of this second factor needs to be seen in terms of the implications for the structure of the scanning process which the firm then develops. Recognizing the dangers of overload within a system, there is a need for those involved in scanning to organize the process in such a way that the environment can be reduced to something manageable, while at the same time ensuring that extraneous factors are not ignored. What this means in practice is that a process of filtration generally operates in which the full breadth of environmental stimuli is reduced to something more manageable.

The question of who should decide on these elements has been referred to by Ansoff (1984) who has argued that it is the *user* of the information who should exert the major influence; in practice, however, it is often the scanner who determines the choice of approach.

Returning for a moment to the filtration process through which a structure is imposed upon the full breadth and complexity of the environment, Brownlie (1987, pp. 110–12) identifies three levels:

1 *The surveillance filter* which provides a broad and generally unstructured picture of the business environment. However, although this picture is broad it will, by virtue of the perceptions of those involved, 'be selective and partial' (Brownlie, 1987, p. 110).
2 *The mentality filter* which emerges as the result of past successes and failures and which in turn leads to the idea of bounded rationality allowing those involved to cope with the volume and complexity of the information being generated. However, while this mentality filter is undoubtedly useful in helping to provide a structure, bounded rationality can create problems in that environmental signals which are extreme in nature and outside the manager's historical experience are likely to be perceived to be of little significance and subsequently screened out. There is a need therefore to balance the benefits of the mentality filter with a willingness to assess and possibly incorporate novel and perhaps extreme signals.
3 *The power filter* which is in essence an attitude of mind on the part of top management and which reflects a willingness to incorporate material in the strategic decision-making process that falls outside the bounds of previous practice and preconceived notions. Recognition by the scanner of the existence of an attitude such as this is then likely to be reflected in the scanner's own willingness to build into the process a breadth of perspective rather than a straightforward identification and assessment of largely predictable environmental changes.

Against the background of comments such as these, it is possible to identify the features which are most likely to lead to an effective environmental scanning system. These include:

1 top management involvement and commitment;
2 a detailed understanding of the dimensions and parameters of the scanning model that it is intended should operate;
3 an established strategic planning culture.

In addition, attention needs to be paid to the *boundaries of the firm's environment* and hence to those areas which are deemed to be either relevant or irrelevant, and to the *time horizon* which is felt to be meaningful. In the case of the chemicals and pharmaceuticals industries, for example, the planning time horizon – and hence the scanning period – may easily be in excess of 30 years, while in the clothing industry it may be a year or less.

**The Responsibility for Scanning**

Brownlie's work (1983, 1987) suggests that environmental scanning is typically the responsibility of one of three levels of management.

1 *Line management* with one or more line managers being given the task of scanning in addition to their normal responsibilities. In practice, however, such an approach typically suffers from limitations, the most obvious of which is that it is an additional responsibility and may not therefore get the attention it deserves. On top of this, the perspective is likely to be at best medium term, since the manager is unlikely to have the full range of specialist skills needed for the task to be performed effectively.
2 *Strategic planning* in which environmental scanning is made part of the overall process of strategic analysis. While this is arguably more likely to succeed than is the case if responsibility is passed to line management, other problems are

likely to emerge largely because corporate staff may not necessarily understand the detail of the firm's business on a day-to-day basis. Because of this, it is argued, they are unlikely to be able to define and interpret the relevant parameters of the environment any more effectively than a line manager.

3 *A specialist organizational unit* with specific responsibilities for environmental monitoring.

Of these, the third approach may be seen as an ideal that few firms have yet to embrace. As a result, it is a mixture of the first two that predominates in business today. Most typically the mixture operates on a largely unstructured basis, with corporate planners focusing upon the general environment, while line managers focus upon the product market. The two perspectives, together with the general forecasts that can be bought from consultants and organizations such as the Henley Centre, are then assessed before the overall picture is developed.

Recognizing these sorts of organizational problems has led Diffenbach (1983) to identify the specific difficulties of environmental analysis that act as deterrents to the development and implementation of an effective scanning system:

1 the interpretation of results and the assessment of their specific impact upon the organization is rarely clear-cut;
2 the output of environmental analysis may be too inaccurate, general or uncertain to be taken seriously;
3 a preoccupation with the short term pre-empts attention being paid to longer-term environmental issues;
4 long-term environmental analyses are often treated sceptically;
5 in diversified businesses the amount of analysis needed is likely to be both considerable and complex, particularly when interrelationships are considered;
6 perceptions and interpretations of scenarios identified may differ significantly between one manager and another.

## 7.8 SUMMARY

Marketing strategy is concerned with matching the capabilities of the organization with the demands of the environment. There is therefore a need for the strategist to monitor the environment on an ongoing basis so that opportunities and threats facing the organization are identified and subsequently reflected in strategy.

In analysing the environment a step-wise approach is needed. This begins with an initial audit of general environmental influences followed by a series of increasingly tightly focused stages designed to provide the strategist with a clear understanding of the organization's strategic position.

Although a variety of approaches can be used for analysing the environment, arguably the most useful is the PEST framework. This involves the strategist focusing in turn upon the Political/legal, Economic, Social/cultural, and Technological elements of the environment. Each of these elements was discussed in detail.

The environmental conditions faced by an organization are capable of varying greatly in their complexity and need to be reflected both in the ways in which environmental analysis is conducted and in the ways in which strategy is subsequently developed. The consequences of failing to take account of a changing environment have, as we discussed, been illustrated by a wide variety of organizational experiences, including those of the Swiss watch industry in the 1970s.

It is widely recognized that the pace of environmental change is increasing and that the need for organizations to develop a structured approach to environmental analysis with the results then being fed into the strategic marketing planning process is greater than ever. Despite this the evidence suggests that in many organizations environmental scanning systems are only poorly developed. If this is to change, top management commitment both to the development of a scanning system and to the incorporation of the results into the planning process is essential.

# 8 | Market segmentation, targeting and positioning

## 8.1 LEARNING OBJECTIVES

When you have read this chapter you should be able to understand:

(a) the nature and purpose of market segmentation;
(b) the contribution of segmentation to effective marketing planning;
(c) how markets can be segmented, and the criteria that need to be applied if segmentation is to prove cost effective;
(d) how product positioning follows from the segmentation process and the bases by which products and brands can be positioned effectively.

## 8.2 INTRODUCTION

In the previous chapter we focused on approaches to environmental analysis and the frameworks within which strategic marketing planning can best take place. Against this background we now turn to the question of market segmentation and to the ways in which companies need to position themselves in order to maximize their competitive advantage and serve their target markets in the most effective manner. It does need to be recognized, however, that for many organizations the strategic issues of segmentation and positioning often take on only a minimal role. Saunders (1987, p. 25), for example, points to research which suggested that a substantial proportion of British companies still fail to segment their market. He quotes the marketing director of one consumer durables company as saying:

> We have not broken the customers down. We have always held the opinion that the market is wide . . . and the product has wide appeal, therefore why break the market down at all?

A similar comment emerged from a sales director who stated:

> We do not see the market as being made up of specific segments. Our market is made up of the whole industry.

There are several possible reasons for views such as these, although in the case of companies with a broadly reactive culture, it is often due largely to a degree of organizational inertia, which leads to the firm being content to stay in the same sector of the market for some considerable time. It is only when the effects of a changing environment become overwhelmingly evident that serious consideration is given to the need for repositioning in order to appeal to new sectors of the market. For other organizations, however, a well thought out policy of segmentation plays a pivotal role in the determination of success. It is the recognition of this that has led to the suggestion in recent years that the essence of strategic marketing can be summed up by the initials STP – segmentation, targeting and positioning. This is illustrated in Figure 8.1.

**FIGURE 8.1**

*The eight stages of the segmentation, targeting and positioning process*

Not all writers are in favour of segmentation and before we examine the methods used to segment markets, it is worth looking briefly at their views. Bliss (1980), for example, has suggested that while many marketing managers acknowledge the rationale of segmentation, many are dissatisfied with it as a concept, partly because it is inapplicable or difficult to apply in many markets, but also because emphasis is too often given to the techniques of segmentation at the expense of the market itself and the competitive situation that exists. Equally, Resnik, Turney and Mason (1979, pp. 100–6) have suggested that changing values, new lifestyles and the rising costs of products and services argue the case for what they call 'countersegmentation'; in other words, an aggregation of various parts of the market rather than their subdivision. The majority of writers, however, acknowledge the very real strategic importance of segmentation and, in particular, the ways in which it enables the organization to use its resources more effectively and with less wastage.

## 8.3 THE NATURE AND PURPOSE OF SEGMENTATION

During the past 20 years market segmentation has developed and been defined in a variety of ways. In essence it is the process of dividing a varied and differing group of buyers or potential buyers into smaller groups within which broadly similar patterns of buyers' needs exist. By doing this, the marketing planner is attempting to break the market into more strategically manageable parts which can then be targeted and satisfied far more precisely by making a series of perhaps small changes to the marketing mix. The rationale is straightforward and can be expressed most readily in terms of the fact that only rarely does a single product or marketing approach appeal to the needs and wants of all buyers. Because of this, the marketing strategist needs to categorize buyers on the basis both of their characteristics and their specific product needs with a view then to adapting either the product or the marketing programme or both to satisfy these different tastes and demands.

The potential benefits of a well-developed segmentation strategy can therefore be considerable since an organization should be able to establish and strengthen its position in the market and in this way operate more effectively. Not only does it then become far more difficult for a competitor to attack, but it also allows the organization to build a greater degree of market sector knowledge and customer loyalty.

Although the arguments for segmentation appear strong, it is only one of three quite distinct approaches to marketing strategy which exist. These are:

1 undifferentiated or mass marketing;
2 product-variety or differentiated marketing;
3 target or concentrated marketing.

These are illustrated in Figure 8.2.

**FIGURE 8.2**
*Undifferentiated,
differentiated and
concentrated
marketing*

**Undifferen-
tiated,
Differentiated
and
Concentrated
Marketing**

A policy of *undifferentiated or mass marketing* emerges when the firm deliberately ignores any differences that exist within its markets and decides instead to focus upon a feature that appears to be common or acceptable to a wide variety of buyers. Perhaps the best known and most frequently quoted example of this is Henry Ford's strategy with the Model T that buyers could have 'in any colour as long as it is black'. A more recent example of undifferentiated marketing is provided by Black & Decker which in the late 1970s was faced with a drop in its worldwide market share of the power tool market from 20 per cent to 15 per cent as Japanese firms began marketing their brands in a far more aggressive manner. In an attempt to counter this, Black & Decker moved away from a policy of customizing products for each market and concentrated instead on making a smaller number of products that could be sold everywhere with the same basic marketing approach. The success of this undifferentiated global marketing strategy was subsequently reflected in the fact that by the mid 1980s Black & Decker had more than regained its 20 per cent share of the market.

The obvious advantage of an undifferentiated strategy such as this is that it offers scope for enormous cost economies in production, promotion and distribution, since the organization is dealing with a standardized product. At the same time it needs to be recognized that undifferentiated marketing is becoming increasingly rare, largely because of ever greater degrees of competition and the increasingly sophisticated and fragmented nature of the majority of developed markets. In these circumstances, the scope that exists for marketing a product aimed at a broad sector of the market is reduced significantly.

This de-massification of markets has led many organizations towards strategies of *product-variety marketing* and, ultimately, target marketing. As an example of this, Coca-Cola for many years produced only one type of drink for the entire market in the expectation that it would have a mass market appeal. The success of the strategy is now part of marketing folklore. The company's strategy was changed, however, partly to cope with an increasingly aggressive competitive environment and partly to develop and capitalize on different patterns of consumer demand. As a result, the company's marketing effort today now reflects buyers' needs for a far wider variety of tastes and demands which are packaged in a number of different sizes and types of container. It should be emphasized that the move on the part of many organizations in recent years towards product differentiated or product-variety marketing has often had as its primary purpose the need to offer existing buyers greater variety, rather than to new and different market segments. In many ways, therefore, product variety marketing can be seen as an interim step in the move towards *target marketing* in which the strategist identifies the major market segments, targets one or more of these segments, and then develops marketing programmes tailored to the specific demands of each segment.

For some organizations target marketing leads to a concentration of effort on a single target market with a single marketing mix. Referred to as *concentrated segmentation*, it is a strategy that has been pursued with great success by the piano makers Steinway. The company defines its market as the concert and professional pianist and while, quite obviously, others may buy the product, they are not part of the strategic target market. The obvious advantage of an approach such as this is that having identified a particular market, the firm can then control costs by advertising and distributing *only* to the market it views as its primary target.

In so far as disadvantages exist with a strategy of concentration, they stem from the possibility of missed opportunities; it may be the case, for example, that significant opportunities exist elsewhere but that the firm's single-minded approach to just one part of the market fails to recognize this. Equally, the organization can prove vulnerable either to a direct and sustained attack by a competitor or to a downturn in demand within the target market. Because of this, many marketing strategists pursue a policy of *multiple segmentation* in which the firm focuses upon a variety of different segments and then develops a different marketing mix for each. This is often described as a 'rifle' rather than a 'shotgun' approach in that the company can focus on buyers they have the greatest chance of satisfying rather than scattering the marketing effort. An example of its use is that of the Burton Group which during the 1980s has developed and refined a highly segmented strategy. In doing this specific attention was paid to a variety of distinct customer groups by means of different types of retail outlet, each with its own distinct target market, image and customer appeal.

The ways in which a segment's characteristics influence the allocation of marketing effort has been illustrated in the case of the retail banking sector by Channon (1987) who identified four distinct customer groups:

1 *the very rich*: a small but strategically significant group with substantial assets in excess of £1 million – customers within this category are typically over 50 years of age and expect a high level of personal service;
2 *the rich*: a far larger group with assets of around £100,000;
3 *high net worth individuals (HNWIs)*: a semi-mass market with assets available for investment of £15,000 to £100,000.
4 *medium net worth individuals (MNWIs)*: the bulk of the market both for the high street banks and building societies.

Each of these groups has very different sets of expectations which need to be reflected in the organization's marketing strategy.

The rationale for target marketing and multiple segmentation can be seen to be straightforward and stems from an expectation on the part of the organization that it will be able to generate a higher total level of sales by making specific appeals to a variety of different target groups. At the same time, however, a strategy of multiple segmentation almost invariably leads to cost increases in several areas, including production, promotion, distribution, inventory and administration. The choice between undifferentiated marketing, product-variety marketing, and target marketing does therefore involve a series of trade-offs, the most obvious of which is an increase in cost against an expectation of higher total returns. As a prelude to deciding which of these three approaches to adopt, the strategist needs to identify clearly the organization's capability, the opportunities that exist and the level of market coverage that is possible or realistic.

Perhaps the most extreme example of a trade-off is to be seen in *customized marketing* where the product or service is modified to match the specific demands of each buyer. This is discussed in Illustration 8.1.

Where there are no apparent natural segments, a more formal procedure needs to be adopted. Several approaches exist, the most popular of which consists of three steps and has been spelled out by Kotler (1988, p. 284):

1 *Survey stage*. The researcher conducts informal interviews and focus groups with consumers to gain insight into their motivations, attitudes and behaviour. Based on these findings, the researcher prepares a formal questionnaire that is administered to a sample of consumers to collect data on:

- Attributes and their importance ratings.
- Brand awareness and brand ratings.
- Product usage patterns.
- Attitudes toward the product category.
- Demographics, psychographics, and mediagraphics of the respondents.

The sample should be large in order to gather enough data to profile each segment accurately. If the researcher guesses that there are, say, four segments, and generally two hundred interviews are desired per segment, then the questionnaire might be administered to eight hundred consumers.
2 *Analysis stage*. The researcher applies factor analysis to the data to remove highly correlated variables. Then the researcher applies cluster analysis to create a specified number of maximally different segments. Each cluster is internally homogenous and externally very different from every other cluster.
3 *Profiling stage*. Each cluster is now profiled in terms of its distinguishing attitudes, behaviour, demographics, psychographics, and media consumption habits. Each segment can be given a name based on a dominant distinguishing characteristic. Thus in study of the leisure market, Andreasen and Belk (1980, pp. 112–20) found six market segments:

---

# Illustration 8.1: The (Re)Emergence of Customized Marketing

The ultimate expression of market segmentation is customized marketing with the product or service being tailored to the specific demands of each buyer. Although, because of the cost implications, few industries have in the past been able to do this, a number of commentators have argued that policies of customization which were relatively common at the turn of the century are returning, albeit in a modified form. Among these is Kotler who suggests that:

> Today customized marketing is coming back, in a form that Stanley Davis calls mass customization. This is a strange oxymoron, like 'jumbo shrimp', 'permanent change', and so on, but it well describes new marketing possibilities opened up by advances in manufacturing technology. Mass customization is the ability to prepare on a mass basis individually designed products to meet each customer's requirements. Here are some examples.
>
> As a result of General Motors' Saturn project, American car buyers will be able to walk into a GM dealership, sit down at a computer terminal, and select the car's color, engine, seat material, radio, and so on. Their order will be transmitted to the auto plant, which will then produce the desired car.
>
> In Japan, home buyers can sit down with a sales representative at a computer terminal and design their home. They can choose from twenty thousand different standardized parts, make the rooms as large or small as they want, and design the overall layout. The information is sent electronically to the factory where the parts are put together on an assembly line stretching one-third of a mile long. The prefabricated modules are delivered to the site within thirty days, and the room and walls are assembled in one day. The finishing touches take another thirty days, and the family can then move into its customized home.
>
> There are some men's clothing stores in Japan that can custom-tailor suits without any tailors! The customer is measured electronically, and the information travels to a cutting shop where laser equipment directs the cutting and sewing of the cloth. The customer comes back the next day to pick up his custom-tailored suit. Another development is an electronic mirror that superimposes images of various suits on the customer's body in different colours, styles, and materials. After the customer finds a pleasing combination, the information is sent electronically to the factory to cut that suit.
>
> In general, as the cost of customization falls and approaches the cost of segmentation, more companies will turn to customized marketing.

*Source: Kotler, P. (1988),* Marketing Management: analysis, planning, control and implementation, *Prentice Hall, p. 282*

---

- The passive homebody.
- The active sports enthusiast.
- The inner-directed self-sufficient.
- The culture patron.
- The active homebody.
- The socially active.

They found, for example, that the culture patron is the best target for both theatre and symphony subscriptions. The socially active can also be drawn to symphonies (though not theatres) in order to satisfy social needs.

**The
Development
of Segments
Over Time**

Having identified segments within a market, the strategist needs to recognize that this is not a once-and-for-all exercise, but rather that it is one which needs monitoring and updating if it is to maintain its usefulness. This is illustrated by the ways in which attitudes to a given product's country of origin can change, possibly dramatically, over time. Twenty years ago, for example, attitudes in Britain to Japanese products were generally negative, largely because of perceptions of poor quality and inadequate levels of after-sales support. These attitudes began changing in the 1970s and today Japanese products are generally perceived very differently. The implications of this for preference patterns is significant and does, of course, need to be reflected in methods of segmentation.

## 8.4 APPROACHES TO SEGMENTING MARKETS

The majority of markets can be segmented in a variety of ways. For the marketing strategist, the process of identifying the potentially most effective way begins with an initial examination of the market with a view to identifying whether 'natural segments' already exist.

In the United States in the 1960s, for example, both Volkswagen and Toyota identified the growth potential of a market sector that was concerned with car size and fuel economy, a segment that the three major domestic manufacturers had either failed to identify or had chosen to ignore. Following the Arab–Israeli conflict of the early 1970s and the subsequent oil crisis, consumers became far more energy conscious and this part of the market grew dramatically. It was several years before domestic manufacturers were able to capitalize on these opportunities.

There are several lessons to be learned from this sort of example, including the ways in which new segments can be identified by examining the sequence of variables that consumers consider when choosing a product. One way of doing this involves categorizing current consumer segments on the basis of a hierarchy of attributes. There are those, for example, whose major preoccupation is price (price-dominant), while others are more concerned with the brand (brand-dominant), quality (quality-dominant), or country of origin (nation-dominant).

In the case of hi-fi and audio equipment, for example, a buyer might only be willing to consider products from a Japanese manufacturer; this would be the first-level preference. The second-level preference may then be for, say, Sony. After this, issues of the price range and choice of outlet begin to emerge.

Recognition of hierarchies of attitudes such as these has led to the emergence of market-partitioning theory, with segments being determined on the basis of particular combinations such as quality/service/brand, price/type/brand, and so on. Underlying this is the belief that each combination will then reflect distinct demographic and psychographic differences.

The question of *how* to segment the market provides the basis for much of the remainder of this chapter. In essence, however, this involves deciding between *a priori* and *post hoc* methods. An *a priori* approach is based on the notion that the planner decides in advance of any research which basis for segmentation he intends using. Thus typically he will categorize buyers on the basis of their usage patterns (heavy, medium, light, and non-users); demographic characteristics (age, sex, and income); or psychographic profiles (lifestyle and personality). Having decided this, he then goes on to conduct a programme of research in order to identify the size, location and potential of each segment as a prelude to deciding on which of the segments the marketing effort is to be concentrated.

*Post hoc* segmentation, by contrast, involves segmenting the market on the basis of research findings. Thus, research might highlight particular attitudes, attributes or benefits with which particular groups of customers are concerned. This information can then be used as the basis for deciding how best to divide the market. As an example of this, Haley's research into the toothpaste market in the early 1960s highlighted levels of concern among mothers about tooth decay in their children (1963, pp. 30–5). Although a number of brands claiming decay prevention existed at the time, the size and potential for the growth of this segment had not previously been recognized. One result of Haley's work was to increase the number of companies that recognized the value of targeting this segment.

In making these comments, it must be emphasized that both approaches to segmentation have their place and that their real value to the strategist depends largely on how much knowledge of the market the strategist has. If, for example, previous research or experience has enabled the planner to identify key segmentation dimensions within the market, then an *a priori* approach is likely to be adequate. When, however, the market is new, changing or unrelated to the planner's experience, a *post hoc* approach to determine the key segmentation variables is likely to prove more valuable.

## 8.5 FACTORS AFFECTING THE FEASIBILITY OF SEGMENTATION

For a market segment to justify attention, six conditions typically need to be satisfied. The segment must be:

1 *Measurable*. Although in many consumer markets measurement is generally a relatively straightforward exercise, it is often a more difficult process with industrial or technical goods. This is due largely to the relative lack of specific published data.
2 *Accessible*. In some cases it may be possible to identify a sizeable and potentially profitable segment, but then either because of a lack of finance or in-house expertise this potential may be difficult to exploit.
3 *Substantial*. If the strategist is to justify the development of a segment the exercise must be cost effective. The size and value of the segment is therefore an important determinant of this decision. Size should, of course, be seen in relative rather than absolute terms, since what may be too small to be considered by one organization may be appropriate to another, smaller, company. Morgan, for example, has concentrated on a very small and specialized part of the car market which is of no interest to the larger firms such as Ford, Toyota and Volkswagen.
4 *Unique* in its response, so that it can be distinguished from other market segments.
5 *Appropriate* to the organization's objectives and resources.
6 *Stable*, so that its behaviour in the future can be predicted with a sufficient degree of confidence.

## 8.6 APPROACHES TO SEGMENTATION

Although a wide variety of methods of segmentation have been developed over the past 30 years, their real value to the strategist in any given situation depends to a very large extent on the nature and characteristics of the product and the market in which the company is operating. The task that the strategist is faced with involves deciding upon the most appropriate single method or combination of methods for dividing up the market. In the case of consumer goods, for example, the most commonly used methods have typically been geographic, demographic and benefit measures, while in the industrial sector they have typically been usage rate, source loyalty and location. Most of these measures, however, are at best partial, and the past few years have witnessed a growing willingness on the part of many companies, particularly in the consumer sector, to make greater use of more complex methods of segmentation in order to build up more detailed and useful pictures of their target markets. One result of this has been an upsurge of the interest expressed in behavioural and psychographic techniques as a means of gaining a greater insight into the question of *why* people behave in particular ways.

The thread that runs through all of these approaches is the need to understand in detail the structure of the market. This is most typically done by focusing on three areas:

1 developing a spatial map of consumers' perceptions of brands within a given market sector;
2 identifying consumers' ideal points on this map so that demand for a particular product might then be estimated by examining its position in relation to the ideal;
3 developing a model which will provide a basis for predicting consumers' responses to new and modified products.

An example of a perceptual map that was developed for the launch of Paul Masson California Carafes at the beginning of the 1980s appears in Figure 8.3.

Here, the wine market is mapped on two key dimensions: heavy versus light drinkers, and above and below average usage according to the most often usage occasion.

**FIGURE 8.3**
*A perceptual map of the wine market*

SOURCE: TGI (1982)

By mapping the market in this way, the company's advertising agency, Abbott Mead Vickers, was able to examine the duplication or repertoires of brand usage among wine drinkers and establish the degrees of overlap between the different brands. By doing this, clusters of brands emerged according to usage and provided the agency/strategist with an understanding of the market's structure, the existence of any gaps, the nature and intensity of competition, and the type of marketing mix needed to establish or support a brand.

This sort of picture of the market can then be taken a step further by superimposing a second map illustrating in greater detail consumer profiles. This might typically include sex (male versus female), age (young, middle-aged, old), income group (high earners versus low earners), and marital status (married versus single).

The importance and role of brand mapping is also illustrated by the way in which Brooke Bond's Red Mountain brand of coffee was positioned and then subsequently repositioned in the instant coffee market. This is discussed in Illustration 8.2.

# Illustration 8.2: Brand Mapping of the Coffee Market

The British Coffee market has long been dominated by two major companies, Nestlé (Nescafé) and General Foods (Maxwell House). The decision by Brooke Bond to enter the market with its Red Mountain brand was therefore one which had significant competitive and financial implications. The brand, a quality freeze-dried instant coffee, was launched on a platform of 'Move Up to the Bigger Taste' with advertising that attempted to capture the spirit of adventurous outdoor people who liked their coffee strong. This imagery with its use of, among others, cowboys backfired with consumers perceiving it as a cheap coffee but finding at the point of purchase that it was more expensive than the market leader, Nescafé. In an attempt to overcome this, the company tried to build on the launch strategy by appealing to those with a sense of adventure. This was then followed by a relaunch to highlight a new, improved blend, together with a reduction in price to below Nescafé levels.

Dissatisfaction by Brooke Bond with the drift in positioning of the brand led to the appointment of a new advertising agency, Still Price Court Twivy D'Souza. The brief given to the agency centred around the need for repositioning and in particular to provide reassurance about the taste and to associate the brand with quality and aspirational images.

The respositioning exercise began with a market research programme which concentrated initially on developing a brand map. The results are illustrated in Figure 8.4.

**FIGURE 8.4** *Initial perceptions of instant coffee brands*

| Expensive ← | | → Cheap | |
|---|---|---|---|
| Gold Blend<br>Blend 37 | Nescafé<br>Maxwell House | Red Mountain | Own label |
| • The best instants<br>• Special<br>• Expensive<br>• When one has<br>  people round<br>• Christmas | • Popular<br>• Everyday<br>• Reliable<br>• 'The Standard'<br>• Frequent use<br>• Old favourites<br>• Ordinary | • Cheaper<br>• Not as classy<br>• Middle of the<br>  road<br>• Cheap and<br>  cheerful | • Cheap and nasty<br>• Weak<br>• Bitter<br>• Lack flavour |

SOURCE: Feldwick (1990) p. 210

These perceptions of Red Mountain were in turn confirmed by qualitative research which had elicited the image and personality as being:

Outdoor, rugged, American, working class, eccentric, ordinary, scruffy, lumberjack, macho, farmer, normal, dull, boring, rough and ready, strange, untidy, basic.

Against the background of these findings, the decision was made not to compete directly with Gold Blend but at the half of the market accounted for by Nescafé and Maxwell House. The brand proposition eventually decided on was 'Ground coffee taste without the grind'.

The first commercial was the highly successful 'Dinner party' in which the hostess goes in the kitchen, pushes the filter coffee maker to one side, turns on the kettle, spoons Red Mountain into the jug of the coffee maker and then mimics the clacking noise that coffee makers make as they finish brewing.

This was followed over the next few months by several other commercials such as 'Apartment' and 'Restaurant' in which one of those involved goes through the same routine.

The campaign proved to be a significant success with levels of spontaneous awareness, attitude ratings, sales and brand share all increasing dramatically. Equally significantly, rival brands were forced to retaliate with higher levels of advertising spend and/or new advertising. Gold Blend, for example, started a 'soap opera' campaign.

*Source:* Advertising Works 5, *Holt, Rinehart Winston, 1990*

## 8.7 BASES FOR SEGMENTATION

In 1978, Wind (1978, p. 317) commented that 'over the years almost all variables have been used as bases for market segmentation'. There are several possible explanations for this, the most significant of which is the difficulty that is typically encountered in putting into practice the normative theory of segmentation. In other words, while the marketing planner might well recognize that customer characteristics should determine strategy, all too often this is reversed with managers focusing on the probable response of different segments to a previously determined strategy. Although quite obviously in the majority of circumstances feedback will ensure that changes are subsequently made to the strategy to take account of the response received, it is often the case, as Baker (1985, p. 142) has pointed out, that 'the managerial approach is more closely akin to product differentiation than a normative approach to market segmentation'.

Although, as we observed earlier, a wide variety of variables have been used to segment markets, the majority of these can be grouped into four categories:

1 geographic and geo-demographic;
2 demographic;
3 behavioural;
4 psychographic.

Only rarely, however, can just one of these dimensions be used to segment a market effectively, something which is reflected both in Illustration 8.3 and in a comment by Wind (1978, p. 318).

> In contrast to the theory of segmentation that implies that there is a single best way of segmenting a market, the range and variety of marketing decisions suggest that any attempt to use a single basis for segmentation (such as psychographic, brand preference, or product usage) for all marketing decisions may result in incorrect marketing decisions as well as a waste of resources.

**FIGURE 8.5**
*The major bases for segmenting consumer markets*

---

**Geographic and geodemographic**

Geographic: region, climate, population density.
Geodemographic: ACORN, MOSAIC, PiNPOINT, SUPERPROFILES, DEFINE, PiN, FiNPiN

**Demographic**

Age, sex, education, occupation, religion, race, nationality, family size, family life cycle, SAGACITY

**Behavioural**

Attitudes, knowledge, benefits, user status, usage rate, loyalty status, readiness to buy, occasions

**Psychographic**

Personality, lifestyle, VALS, AIO, 4Cs, Monitor

# Illustration 8.3:  Recommendations for the Bases of Segmentation

Some of the most interesting work on market segmentation has been carried out in the United States by Yoram Wind (1978). One of the undoubted attractions of his work is its strong element of pragmatism and the recognition that he gives to the problems typically experienced by marketing managers in trying to develop and implement an effective segmentation strategy. This has led him to a series of recommendations for the bases of segmentation which Baker (1985, pp. 142–3) has neatly summarized:

*For general understanding of a market*:
- benefits sought (in industrial markets, the criterion used is purchase decision);
- product purchase and usage patterns;
- needs;
- brand loyalty and switching pattern;
- a hybrid of the variables above.

*For positioning studies*:
- product usage;
- product preference;
- benefits sought;
- a hybrid of the variables above.

*For new product concepts* (and new product introduction):
- reaction to new concepts (intention to buy, preference over current brand, etc.);
- benefits sought.

*For pricing decisions*:
- price sensitivity;
- deal proneness;
- price sensitivity by purchase/usage patterns.

*For advertising decisions*:
- benefits sought;
- media usage;
- psychographic/lifestyle;
- a hybrid of the variables above and/or purchase/usage patterns.

*For distribution decisions*:
- store loyalty and patronage;
- benefits sought in store selection.

## 8.8 GEOGRAPHIC AND GEODEMOGRAPHIC TECHNIQUES

**Geographic Techniques**

Geographic segmentation – one of the earliest and still most commonly used methods of segmentation both within the consumer and the industrial sectors – involves dividing markets into different geographical units such as countries, regions, counties and cities. The strategist then chooses to operate either in just a few or in all of these. Typically, however, if a company pursues this second approach, minor modifications are often made to the marketing mix used for different geographical areas in order to take account of different regional tastes and preferences. In the case of the car industry, for example, manufacturers such as Ford and General Motors, while selling a particular model throughout Europe, will typically make a series of minor changes to the design and to the way in which the product is promoted and sold in order to reflect local differences, preferences and legislative demands. Similarly, the manufacturers of potato crisps modify the taste of the product to cater for regional taste differences, with a greater emphasis being placed upon strong flavours in the north of England and Scotland. In the United States, General Foods with its Maxwell House brand of coffee varies the flavour regionally to reflect preferences for stronger or weaker coffees. With other products such as consumer electronics, geographical differences also need to be reflected in strategy. Makers of stereophonic equipment, for example, offer products that vary by region. Europeans tend to want small, unobtrusive, high-performance equipment, while many Americans prefer large speakers that, as one anonymous commentator said, 'rise from the floor of living rooms like the columns of an ancient temple'.

Among the undoubted attractions of geographic segmentation to the strategist is its flexibility and its apparent simplicity. It is the combination of these, together with its broad applicability, that has led to its widespread use. At the same time, however, it is a relatively unsophisticated approach to categorization and one that at best gives only a partial view of buying motives.

**Geodemographic Techniques**

Largely because of the limitations of geography, a considerable amount of work has been done in Britain over the past few years in an attempt to improve on the traditional methods of geographic segmentation. One outcome of this has been the development of a variety of geodemographic systems such as ACORN (A Classification Of Residential Neighbourhoods) which classify people by where they live. Based on the idea that 'birds of a feather flock together', it gives recognition to the fact that people with broadly similar economic, social and lifestyle characteristics tend to congregate in particular neighbourhoods and exhibit similar patterns of purchasing behaviour and outlook, something which is reflected in a comment by Rothman (1989, p. 1) who in discussing the central theme of geodemographics suggests that:

> . . . two people who live in the same neighbourhood, such as a Census Enumeration District, are more likely to have similar characteristics than are two people chosen at random. . . . neighbourhoods can be categorized in terms of the characteristics of the population which they contain, and . . . two neighbourhoods can be placed in the same category, i.e. can contain similar types of people, even though they are widely separated.

The essential purpose of geodemographics is therefore to provide the base for targeting customers in particular areas who exhibit similar behaviour patterns.

The first attempt to formalize this and demonstrate its potential to the strategist was carried out in Liverpool in 1973 by Richard Webber. Working subsequently with the Census Office at a national level, Webber applied techniques of cluster analysis to identify 38 separate neighbourhood types, each of which was different in terms of its population, housing and socio-economic characteristics. The

**FIGURE 8.6**
*The 1981 ACORN profile of Great Britain*

| ACORN groups | | 1981 | |
| --- | --- | --- | --- |
| | | **Population** | **%** |
| A | Agricultural areas | 1811485 | 3.4 |
| B | Modern family housing, higher incomes | 8667137 | 16.2 |
| C | Older housing of intermediate status | 9420477 | 17.6 |
| D | Poor quality older terraced housing | 2320846 | 4.3 |
| E | Better-off council estates | 6976570 | 13.0 |
| F | Less well-off council estates | 5032657 | 9.4 |
| G | Poorest council estates | 4048658 | 7.6 |
| H | Multi-racial areas | 2086026 | 3.9 |
| I | High status non-family areas | 2248207 | 4.2 |
| J | Affluent surburban housing | 8514878 | 15.9 |
| K | Better-off retirement areas | 2041338 | 3.8 |
| U | Unclassified | 388632 | 0.7 |

potential value of this to the market research industry was subsequently recognized by Kenneth Baker (1982) of the British Market Research Bureau, who identified the scope that the system offered for controlling the fieldwork of the bureau's Target Group Index (TGI). The 2400 respondents in the TGI survey were categorized on the basis of Webber's neighbourhood groups, and illustrated graphically 'that respondents in different neighbourhood groups displayed significantly different propensities to buy specific products and services'.

Following this, Webber subsequently joined Consolidated Analysis Centres Inc. (CACI) and concentrated on developing the technique further in order to achieve higher levels of discrimination. The result was the 11-group classification (see Figure 8.6) which today is used as a major method of market location. Specific applications of the technique include:

1 the identification of new retail sites;
2 the selection of sales territories;
3 the allocation of marketing resources;
4 media selection;
5 leaflet distribution;
6 decisions on which products and services to promote in particular retail outlets.

Using this profile, specific areas of high and low consumption can be identified from the ACORN 'buying power' indices. As an example of this, ACORN type J35, which consists of 'villages with wealthy older commuters, have 2.4 times the national average proportion of households with two cars, and 2.7 times the proportion of those living in seven or more rooms'. Using information such as this, market targeting becomes both easier and far more accurate.

This work on the ACORN system of classification has led subsequently to a major reassessment of the ways in which geographic techniques might be used in the most effective way. One result of this has been the development of a variety of other geodemographic forms of classification, including CCNs MOSAIC, CDMSs SUPERPROFILES, Infolink's DEFINE, and PiNPOINT Analysis's PiN and FiNPIN.

The common element in all geodemographic systems is their use of census enumeration district (ED) data. ACORN, for example, uses 40 regularly updated census variables which take account of the demographic, housing, and social aspects of EDs. Their clustering techniques then enable customers to be matched to an ACORN type and, by the postcode, to the relevant ED.

Other geodemographic systems are broadly similar to this, although each uses a variety of other variables. MOSAIC, for example, includes financial data at postcode level and then relies on aggregated individual addresses within a postcode to reduce the errors encountered in matching postcodes to EDs. Other systems such as PiNPOINT base their clustering techniques on a larger sample and improvements to the grid referencing of EDs so that they more accurately match postcodes. Such developments represent a very real attempt to overcome some of the inevitable problems and inaccuracies of geodemographic analysis. In commenting on this, Joseph and Yorke (1989, p. 12) have said:

> It must be recognized that despite claims from commercial companies, there are inaccuracies within all the geodemographic systems. Many of the errors are bound up firstly with the difficulty of matching EDs to postcodes and secondly trying to reflect as far as possible the changes in housing since the last census.

These sorts of problem have also been referred to by Openshaw (1989, p. 121) who, in discussing how geodemographics should develop, has said that:

> ... users with a large customer data base spending big sums of money on segmentation based direct mail ... banks, building societies, insurance companies, home shopping organisations, telemarketers, etc., should be seriously considering using a system which has been explicitly tailored to meet their own unique purposes in preference to any of the standard geo-demographic products.

Although on the face of it, comments such as these might appear to suggest that geodemographic techniques are, at least in part, questionable, the reality is that they represent an enormous step forward in accurate targeting. Recognizing this, a considerable amount of work in recent years has been devoted to developing industry and market specific systems. One example is PiNPOINT's FiNPIN, a 40-variable classification system that uses data from Financial Research Services to define geographical areas in terms of financially active/inactive customers.

## 8.9 DEMOGRAPHIC SEGMENTATION

The second major method of segmentation, and probably the one most frequently used, rests on the assumption that markets can be subdivided into groups on the basis of one or more demographic variables such as age, sex, income, education, occupation, religion, race, nationality, family size and stage reached in the family life cycle. Here, we will concentrate on just three of these variables: age and the family life cycle, income and occupation, and sex.

An undoubted attraction of demographic segmentation is the wide availability and easy interpretation of the data, and it is this, together with the fact that not only can most consumer markets generally be divided relatively easily along these lines but also that purchase behaviour often correlates highly with demographic segmentation, that have combined to make it such a convenient, easily understood and frequently used approach. In recent years, considerable attention has been paid to the ways in which specific demographic variables can be used more effectively, with the result that variables such as age and life cycle, income, and sex have all been greatly refined. As an example of this, firms such as Fisher Price give full recognition to the differences that exist between children of various ages, with the result that toys are now designed to fall into highly specific age categories. In this way not only is the development potential of the child maximized, but the task of choosing toys by parents, friends and relatives is made infinitely easier. A similar if perhaps rather more esoteric recognition of the importance of age and life cycle is reflected in the marketing strategies of various petfood manufacturers who over the past few years have developed different dog foods for puppies and adult dogs. In the United States, this has been taken several steps further by General Foods which has also targeted owners of older dogs and overweight dogs. More frequently, however, the significance of life cycle is reflected in the notion of a *family life cycle* (FLC), the details of which are illustrated in Figure 8.7.

**FIGURE 8.7**
*The family life cycle
and its implications
for buying
behaviour*

| Stages in the family life cycle | Buying patterns |
|---|---|
| 1 Bachelor stage: young, single people living at home | Few financial commitments. Recreation and fashion orientated.<br>Buy: cars, entertainment items, holidays |
| 2 Newly married couples: young, no children | Better off financially than they are likely to be in the near future. High purchase rate of consumer desirables.<br>Buy: cars, white goods, furniture |
| 3 Full nest 1: youngest child under six | House buying is at a peak. Liquid assets are low. Dissatisfied with level of savings and financial position generally.<br>Buy: medicines, toys, baby food, white goods |
| 4 Full nest 2: youngest child six or over | Financial position is improving. A higher proportion of wives are working.<br>Buy: wider variety of foods, bicycles, pianos |
| 5 Full nest 3: older married couples with dependent children | Financial position is improving yet further. A greater proportion of wives work and some children get jobs. Increasing purchase of desirables.<br>Buy: better furniture, unnecessary appliances and more luxury goods |
| 6 Empty nest 1: older married couples, no children at home, head of household still in the workforce | Home ownership is at a peak. The financial situation has improved and savings have increased. Interested in travel, recreation and self-education. Not interested in new products.<br>Buy: holidays, luxuries and home improvements |
| 7 Empty nest 2: Older married, no children living at home, head of household retired | Substantial reduction in income.<br>Buy: medical products and appliances that aid health, sleep and digestion |
| 8 Solitary survivor in the workforce | Income still high but may sell home |
| 9 Solitary survivor, retired | Same medical and product needs as group 7. Substantial cut in income. Need for attention and security. |

SOURCE: Adapted from Wells and Gubar (1966)

**The Family Life Cycle**

The idea of a family life cycle can be traced back to Rowntree's work at the beginning of the century and while changes have occurred since then to the pattern through which the family passes, the concept is still the same. Today, the nine-stage FLC proposed by Wells and Gubar (1966, pp. 355–63) is the one to which reference is made most frequently. The potential strategic value of the FLC stems from the way in which it highlights the different and changing financial situation and priorities of the family as it moves through the nine stages. By recognizing and taking account of these differences, the strategist should be more easily able to develop a marketing programme that satisfies the *specific* rather than the general demands of target groups.

Despite its apparent attractions, the FLC has been subjected to a series of criticisms in recent years. For the most part, these stem from the significance and implications of changes taking place within society which are at best reflected only marginally in the basic FLC model. Implicit in FLC thinking, for example, is a particular view of the role of women which is some way removed from today's reality where the proportion of women working even during the early stages of their children's lives is high. Equally, the model fails to reflect high divorce rates and the large numbers of single-parent families. Because of criticisms such as these, fundamental questions have been raised about the model's validity and usefulness. Defenders of the model, however, have argued that it is a summary demographic variable that combines the effects of age, marital status, career status (income), and the presence or absence of children. This can then be used *together* with other variables to reflect reality. This view is supported by a number of writers, including Dominguez and Page (1984) whose research in the United States for a mid-Western bank found that the FLC is a major determinant of consumer banking interest and behaviour. Similarly, Reading (1988, p. 9) has pointed out that:

> There is a distinctive life time pattern to saving and spending when we are in our twenties and thirties – getting married, buying houses, having children – we borrow and spend. When we are old and retired, we 'dissave' and spend. In middle age, therefore, we have to save like blazes to repay debts and build up capital for our old age.

A slightly different version of the family life cycle has in recent years been proposed by Research Services in the form of SAGACITY. The basic thesis of the SAGACITY grouping is that people have different aspirations and behaviour patterns as they go through their life cycle. Four main stages of the life cycle are defined which are subdivided by income and occupation groups. This is illustrated in Figure 8.8.

**FIGURE 8.8**
*The SAGACITY life-cycle model*

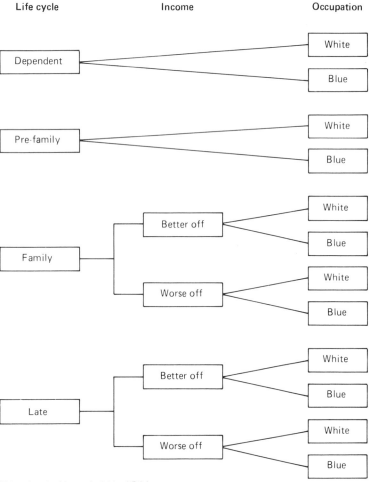

White: head of household in ABC1 groups
Blue: head of household in C2DE groups

**The Psychological Life Cycle**

As an extension both to the traditional thinking and the family life cycle and to the more current ideas of SAGACITY, work recently has focused upon the idea of a *psychological life cycle* in which chronological age by itself is not necessarily the factor of greatest significance in determining consumption patterns. Rather it is the transformation of attitudes and expectations that becomes a more important factor; something which is reflected in the Neugartens' research in the United States:

> Age has become a poor predictor of the timing of life events, as well as a poor predictor of a person's health, work status, family status, and therefore, also of a person's interests, pre-occupations, and needs. We have multiple images of persons of the same age: there is the 70-year-old in a wheelchair and the 70-year-old on the tennis court. Likewise, there are 35-year-olds sending children off to college and 35-year-olds furnishing the nursery for newborns, producing in turn, first-time grandparenthood for persons who range in age from 35 to 75.

**Income and Occupation**

The second major category of demographic variable focuses upon *income* and *occupation*, the combination of which is reflected in the JICNARS approach to social classification; this is illustrated in Figure 8.9.

Developed in the immediate post-war period, the JICNARS classification of social class has proved to be a popular, enduring and easily understood method of classification. It is, however, an imprecise method of segmenting a market since social class today is a far less accurate predictor of income and spending patterns than was once the case. It has also been argued that social class is unable to give any real insight into a household's level of disposable income, particularly where there are several wage earners. Largely because of this, a considerable amount of work has been done in recent years in an attempt to develop it further and to identify better alternative methods of discrimination.

The problems of social class as a basis for segmentation have been highlighted by O'Brien and Ford (1988, pp. 289–331) who have commented,

> The trends today are towards a more disparate family group, less inclined to share their meals and leisure time as a household unit, but following their own interests and tastes with like minded peers. Whether peer groups share the same 'social' background is less important than their shared pursuit. Equally, Social Class does not act as an accurate guage of disposable income. A C2 or D may not intellectually be performing the same role in the job market as a B or C1, but may well have more cash with which to acquire the trappings of our society. The financial chains of private education are likely to constrain the AB as much as the black economy and overtime can enhance the apparently lower wage of the C2 and D. From a different standpoint, social class categories are difficult to apply consistently. The variety and complexity of people's jobs make many social classifications inherently subjective rather than objective.

**FIGURE 8.9**
*The JICNARS social classification*

| Grade | |
|---|---|
| A | Upper middle class: higher managerial administrative or professional |
| B | Middle class: middle to senior management, up and coming professionals |
| C1 | Lower middle class: Junior management, supervisory, secretarial, and clerical grades |
| C2 | Skilled working class: manual trades |
| D | Working class: semi and unskilled workers |
| E | Pensioners and widows and those on the breadline, using social security and state benefits |

It is because of problems such as these that Coleman (1961, pp. 171–84) has drawn a distinction between the 'underprivileged' and the 'overprivileged' segments of each social class. 'The most economical cars are not bought by the really poor', he argues, but rather 'by those who think of themselves as poor relative to their status aspirations and to their needs for a certain level of clothing, furniture, and housing which they could not afford if they bought a more expensive car'. He goes on to point out that medium-priced and expensive cars tend to be purchased by the overprivileged segments of each social class.

Recognition of the problems of defining social class and of the limitations of traditional methods of social classification led the Market Research Society in 1990 to publish an up-to-date guide to socio-economic status. The guide, which defines the pecking order of 1500 jobs, is based not on earnings, but on qualifications and responsibility. A summary of this appears in Figure 8.10.

**FIGURE 8.10**
*The Market Research Society's occupation groupings*

> A: admiral, advocate, air marshal, ambassador, archbishop, attorney, bank manager, bishop, brigadier, chemist shop manager (more than 25 staff); chief constable, chief engineer, chief fire officer, chief rabbi, chiropodist (more than five staff); national orchestra conductor, coroner, university dean, dental surgeon with own practice, chartered estate agent, self-employed farmer (more than 10 staff), financier, general practitioner (own practice/partner), school head-teacher (more than 750 pupils), homoeopath, insurance underwriter, magistrate, hospital matron, judge, MP, professor and town clerk.
>
> B: advertising account director, archdeacon, area sales manager, ballistics expert, qualified brewer, bursar, church canon, chef (more than 25 staff), police chief inspector, computer programmer, stock exchange dealer, deputy power station manager, drawing office manager, fund manager, master mariner, orchestra leader, parish priest, parson, prison governor, probation officer, rabbi, senior buyer, senior engineer, qualified social worker, secondary-school teacher, television newscaster, lecturer and nursing sister.
>
> C1: advertising account executive, accounts clerk, announcer (television, radio or station platform), art buyer, articled clerk, athlete, band master, bank cashier, boxer, bus inspector, calligrapher, campanologist, telephone canvasser, cardiographer, cartographer, chef (five to 24 staff), chemist dispenser, chorister, chorus girl, clown, sports coach, coastguard, computer operator, skilled cook, police constable, advertising copywriter, travel courier, curate, cricketer, dancer, dental hygienist, private detective, dietician, driving examiner/instructor, estate agent (not chartered), fashion model, film projectionist, golfer, hospital houseman, book illustrator, disc jockey, juggler, domestic loss adjuster, magician, maitre d'hotel, masseur/masseuse, midwife, monk, nun, staff nurse, non-manual office worker, pawn-broker, plant breeder, RSPCA inspector, receptionist, secretary, telephone operator, sports umpire, youth worker.
>
> C2: AA patrolman, self-employed antique dealer, boat builder, bus driver, shoe-maker, bricklayer, carpenter, chimney sweep, bespoke tailoring cutter, deep-sea diver, dog handler, hair-dresser, skilled electrician, fireman, thatcher, train driver, Rolls-Royce trained chauffeur, skilled miner.
>
> D: au pair, bingo caller, dustman, bodyguard, bus conductor, chauffeur, croupier, dog breeder, lumberjack, unskilled miner, nursemaid and ratcatcher.
>
> E: anyone brave enough to admit it.

SOURCE: MRS (1990)

**Sex**

The third demographic category is that of sex. While this variable has obvious applications to such products as clothes, cosmetics, magazines and so on, ever greater attention has been paid in recent years to the ways in which it can be used as a key element in the strategies to market a far wider range of products. In part, this has been brought about by a series of fundamental changes that are taking place within society, including a greater number of working women and the generally higher levels of female independence. One result of this has been an increase in the number of marketing campaigns targeted specifically at women; examples include cigarettes, cars and hotels.

## 8.10 BEHAVIOURAL SEGMENTATION

The third major approach to segmentation is based on a series of behavioural measures including attitudes, knowledge, benefits sought by the buyer, a willingness to innovate, loyalty status, usage rates, and response to a product. Of these, *benefit segmentation* is probably the best known and most widely used and is based on the assumption that it is the benefits people are seeking from a product that provide the most appropriate bases for dividing up a market.

In applying this approach the marketing planner begins by attempting to measure consumers' value systems and their perceptions of various brands within a given product class. The information generated is then used as the basis for the marketing strategy. One example of this is the work conducted on the watch market by Yankelovich (1964, pp. 83–90). His findings that 'approximately 23 per cent of the buyers bought for lowest price, another 46 per cent bought for durability and general product quality, and 31 per cent bought watches as symbols of some important occasion' were subsequently used by the US Time Company which created its Timex brand to capitalize on the first two of these segments. The majority of other companies at this stage focused either largely or exclusively on the third segment and Timex therefore faced little direct competition in the early years.

Benefit segmentation begins therefore by determining the principal benefits customers are seeking in the product class, the kinds of people who look for each benefit, and the benefits delivered by each brand. Amstrad, for example, a late entrant into the microcomputer market, gained market share largely as the result of concentrating on two distinct benefit segments: initially, those who were non-computer literate and who wanted a basic machine they could simply plug in and use, and then, subsequently, those who wanted a cheap and easy-to-use word processor.

One of the first pieces of benefit research, and probably the best known, was conducted by Russell Haley (1963, pp. 30–5). On the basis of his work in the toothpaste market, Haley identified four distinct segments which, he argued, were sufficiently different to provide a platform for selecting advertising copy, media, commercial length, packaging and new product design; the four segments he identified were: seeking economy, decay prevention, cosmetic, and taste benefits respectively.

Haley demonstrated that each group exhibited specific demographic, behavioural and psychographic characteristics. Those concerned primarily with decay prevention, for example, typically had large families, were heavy toothpaste users and were generally conservative in their outlook. By contrast, the group which was more concerned with bright teeth (the cosmetic segment) tended to be younger, were more active socially and, in many cases, were smokers. Each of these groups, he then demonstrated, exhibited preferences for particular brands: Crest in the case of those concerned with decay prevention, and Macleans and Ultra-Brite for those preoccupied with bright teeth.

In a similar type of study, Doyle and Newbould (1974) examined the building society market and identified three distinct categories of customer and the benefits each is seeking:

1 a building society's investors currently;
2 investors who also have accounts in other building societies;
3 those without any building society investments.

Having identified these three primary segments, they went on to identify a secondary stage:

- bankers: those who use the society in a similar way to a bank – they typically have an account with few funds and have a high withdrawals to deposit rate;
- savers: who use their account primarily as a means of saving for special purchases – balances tend to be high and withdrawals infrequent;

- investors: who have relatively large accounts, and who switch funds to maximize interest payments.

The information generated by studies such as these can, as we observed earlier, be used in a variety of ways. Most obviously they prove useful in classifying the specific benefits being sought by particular customer groups, the segment's behavioural, demographic and psychographic characteristics, and the major competitive brands. An additional by-product of this sort of research can also be that it highlights a benefit that customers are seeking, but which currently is not being satisfied. As an example of this, General Foods identified a sizeable and predominantly female segment which found the majority of instant coffees to be too strong and bitter. Using this as the starting point, the company went on to develop and launch Mellow Birds instant coffee which took as its major appeal a far less bitter taste. More recently, benefit segmentation research has also highlighted the size of the potential market for caffeine-free coffees. The result has been a substantial upsurge in the number of coffees targeted at this segment which was served previously only by Café Hag.

In many markets benefit segmentation results in the company focusing upon satisfying just one benefit group, with the benefit offered being the unique selling proposition (USP). This is, however, just one of four choices that exist:

1 single benefit positioning;
2 primary and secondary benefit positioning;
3 double benefit positioning;
4 triple benefit positioning.

These will be discussed in greater detail at a later stage in the chapter (see pp. 219–221).

**User Status**

As an alternative to benefit segmentation, markets can be subdivided on the basis of what is referred to as *user status*. Thus a number of segments can typically be identified including non-users, ex-users, potential users, first-time users and regular users. These final two categories can then be subdivided further on the basis of *usage rate* (this is sometimes referred to as *volume segmentation*).

For many firms the marketing task is seen in terms of moving buyers and potential buyers along the buying continuum; thus non-users and potential users all need to be persuaded to try the product, while first-time users need to be persuaded to become medium users, and medium users to become heavy users. The essence of this approach is reflected in the strategies of a variety of organizations, including those of a number of cigarette companies which, having been affected by changing smoking habits over the past two decades, have targeted particular user status groups. In the United States, for example, young females in particular have been identified as a potentially valuable segment and a variety of brands developed to appeal specifically to this part of the market.

The attraction of different user status groups tends to vary from one type of organization to another. High market share companies, for example, typically focus on converting potential users into actual users, while smaller and lower share firms will often concentrate upon users of competitive brands with a view to persuading them to switch brands.

**Loyalty Status and Brand Enthusiasm**

The third technique encompassed by behavioural segmentation is that of *loyalty status* in which buyers are categorized on the basis of the extent and depth of their loyalty to particular brands or stores. Most typically this leads to the emergence of four categories: hard core loyals, soft core loyals, shifting loyals, and switchers.

- *Hard core loyals* consist of consumers who consistently buy the same brand or use the same store. Their buying pattern over time can therefore be represented as XXXXXX.

- *Soft core loyals* are those willing to choose from a limited brand set. Their buying pattern of XXYXYY reflects their divided loyalty between brands X and Y.
- *Shifting loyals* who shift their loyalty from one brand to another. Their buying pattern is therefore likely to be XXXYYYZZZ.
- *Switchers* who show no loyalty to any single brand. Their buying pattern is typically determined either by the special offers available ('offer prone'), or by their search for variety (variety prone). This is then reflected in a buying pattern of XYXZYX.

The implications of loyalty are of course significant, since in the case of those markets in which high patterns of loyalty exist, the ability to persuade buyers to shift from one brand to another is likely to be limited, even in the face of high levels of marketing expenditure. Thus, in these circumstances, a share gaining or market entry strategy may well prove to be at best only marginally cost effective. However, the process of categorization referred to above is not by itself sufficient for the strategist. Rather it is the starting point from which the specific characteristics of each category then need to be examined. It may be the case, for example, that those buyers with the highest degrees of loyalty exhibit certain common characteristics in terms of age, socio-economic profile, and so on, while those with lower degrees of loyalty exhibit a very different but common set of characteristics. Research designed to identify these differences may well then provide the planner with a far greater understanding and insight to the ways in which patterns of loyalty may prove vulnerable to attack. Equally, analysis of this sort can provide an insight into the ways in which a competitor's products are vulnerable to attack. In the case of soft core loyals, for example, the strategist needs to identify the brands which compete either directly or indirectly with its own. By doing this, it can then strengthen its position, possibly by means of knocking copy or direct comparison advertising.

Analysis of the final group – the switchers – is also of potential strategic value since this can provide the basis for understanding in greater detail the brand's weaknesses and the basis for attack.

As an alternative or addition to loyalty status, consumers can often be categorized on the basis of their *enthusiasm* for the product, the five categories that are used most frequently being *enthusiastic, positive, indifferent, negative* and *hostile*. Its major value as a technique is principally as a screening step, in that having identified the category within which the consumer falls the organization can then focus its energies on the most likely prospects. This process can then be taken a step further by focusing on the *occasions* on which consumers develop a need, purchase or use a product.

Greeting cards companies, for example, have concentrated on increasing the number of occasions on which cards are given in relation to what was the case, say, 20 years ago. A glance at the shelves of any newsagent will reveal the enormous variety of cards that now exist, ranging from Father's Day and Mother's Day through to Get Well and Congratulations on Your Examination Success/New Baby/Moving House/New Job/Passing Your Driving Test, and so on. Ice-cream manufacturers have pursued a broadly similar strategy in order to move away from a pattern of sales that was overly dependent on hot, sunny weather. The result in this case has been the development of a whole series of ice-cream based desserts such as Vienetta, and ice-cream cakes that can be used throughout the year.

**Critical Events**

As a further development of occasion-related segmentation, the past few years have seen the emergence of what is usually referred to as *critical event segmentation* (CES). This is based on the idea that major or critical events in an individual's life generate needs that can then be satisfied by the provision of a collection of products and/or services. Typical examples of these critical events are marriage, the death of someone in the family, unemployment, illness, retirement and moving house. Among those who have recognized the potential of CES are estate agents, who during the past decade have moved away from simply selling houses to providing the whole range of legal and financial services surrounding house sale and purchase.

## 8.11 PSYCHOGRAPHIC AND LIFESTYLE SEGMENTATION

The fourth and increasingly popular basis of consumer segmentation stems from work in the early 1950s by Riesman, et al. (1950) which led to the identification of three distinct types of social characterization and behaviour:

1 *tradition directed behaviour* which changes little over time and which as a result is easy to predict and use as a basis for segmentation;
2 *other directedness* in which the individual attempts to fit in and adapt to the behaviour of the peer group;
3 *inner directedness* where the individual is seemingly indifferent to the behaviour of others.

Although this relatively simplistic approach to categorization has subsequently been subjected to a degree of criticism, it has provided the basis for a considerable amount of further work, all of which has been designed to provide the strategist with a far more detailed understanding of personality and lifestyle.

The attempts to use personality to segment markets began in earnest in the United States in the late 1950s when both Ford and Chevrolet gave emphasis to the brand personalities of their products in order to appeal to distinct consumer personalities (see Illustration 5.2, p. 107). Buyers of Fords, for example, were identified as 'independent, impulsive, masculine, alert to change, and self confident, while Chevrolet owers were conservative, thrifty, prestige-conscious, less masculine, and seeking to avoid extremes'. The validity of these descriptions was subsequently questioned by Evans (1959, pp. 340–69) who, by using a series of psychometric tests, argued that Ford and Chevrolet owners did not in fact differ to nearly the extent that had been suggested. More recent research has with just one or two possible exceptions been equally inconclusive. Among these exceptions is the work of Westfall (1962, pp. 34–40) and Young (1972, pp. 61–82). Westfall, for example, has reported finding evidence of personality differences between the buyers of convertible and non-convertible cars, with the former seemingly being 'more active, impulsive and sociable', while Young has pointed to the successful development of personality trait based segmentation strategies in the cosmetics, drinks and cigarettes markets.

Largely because of the difficulties encountered in using personality as an easy, consistent and reliable basis for segmentation, attention in recent years has switched to *lifestyle* and to the ways in which it influences patterns of consumer demand. Lifestyle has been defined in a variety of ways, but is in essence, as Kotler (1988) states:

> the person's pattern of living in the world as expressed in (their) activities, interests and opinions ... [it] portrays the 'whole person' interacting with his or her environment. Lifestyle reflects something beyond the person's social class, on the one hand, or personality, on the other ... [it] attempts to profile a person's way of being and acting in the world.

Because of the apparent insights offered by lifestyle analysis, a variety of models for categorizing consumers have emerged over the past few years, prominent among these being the VALS and AIO frameworks, Young and Rubicam's 4Cs, and Taylor Nelson's Monitor.

**The VALS Framework**

Developed in the United States by Arnold Mitchell of the Stanford Research Institute, the VALS framework used the answers of 2713 respondents to 800 questions to classify the American public into nine value lifestyle groups. These nine groups, together with estimates of the percentages of the US population within each group, are:

1  *survivors* who are generally disadvantaged and who tend to be depressed, withdrawn, and despairing (4%);
2  *sustainers* who are again disadvantaged but who are fighting hard to escape poverty (7%);
3  *belongers* who tend to be conventional, nostalgic, conservative and generally reluctant to experiment with new products or ideas (33%);
4  *emulators* who are status conscious, ambitious and upwardly mobile (10%);
5  *achievers* who make things happen, and enjoy life (23%);
6  *'I-am-me'* who are self-engrossed, respond to whims and generally young (5%);
7  *experientials* who want to experience a wide variety of what life can offer (7%);
8  *societally conscious* people with a marked sense of social responsibility and who want to improve the conditions of society (9%);
9  *integrateds* who are psychologically fully mature and who combine the best elements of inner and outer directedness (2%).

The thinking that underpins the VALS framework is that individuals pass through a series of developmental stages, each of which influences attitudes, behaviour and psychological needs. Thus people typically move from a stage which is largely need driven (survivors and sustainers) towards either an outer-directed hierarchy of stages (belongers, emulators and achievers) or an inner-directed hierarchy (I-am-me, experientials, societally conscious); relatively few reach the nirvana of the integrated stage.

From the marketing point of view, the need-driven segments have little apparent appeal since it is this part of society which lacks any real purchasing power. Outer-directed consumers, by contrast, represent a far more attractive part of the market and in general buy products with what has been described as 'an awareness of what other people will attribute to their consumption of that product'. Typically, therefore, brand names such as Rolex, Gucci, Benetton, Chanel and Cartier will prove to be important. Inner directed consumers by contrast are those people who in their lives place far greater emphasis on their individual needs as opposed to external values. Although in terms of overall numbers this group represents only a small part of the total market, it is often seen to be an important sector in terms of its ability to set trends. It is this group also which currently is showing the fastest growth rate within society, while the number of need-driven consumers declines and outer-directed remains about the same.

**The AIO Framework**

The AIO framework is broadly similar in concept to VALS in that again it attempts to classify distinctive lifestyle groups. This is done by means of a questionnaire designed to measure Activities, Interests and Opinions (AIO). Using this, the advertising agency Needham, Harper and Steers has identified the five major male and five major female lifestyle types:

Male Lifestyle Types
1  the self-made businessman (17 per cent);
2  the devoted family man (17 per cent);
3  the frustrated factory worker (19 per cent);
4  the successful professional (21 per cent);
5  the retiring homebody (26 per cent).

Female Lifestyle Types
1 the socialite (17 per cent);
2 the contented housewife (18 per cent);
3 the militant mother (20 per cent);
4 the suburbanite (20 per cent);
5 the traditionalist (25 per cent).

Against the background of this sort of classification, the strategist needs then to decide the group(s) at which the product is targeted, and an advertising message that should appeal specifically to the AIO characteristics of that lifestyle group.

This sort of thinking was used by Levi Strauss at the beginning of the 1980s in their development of a new range of clothes as the company diversified away from their core business of denim jeans. Although the new line eventually proved disappointing, their research identified five basic lifestyle segments, each of which exhibited specific characteristics. These are:

● Q1: *mainstream traditionalist* – over 45, he is a department-store shopper, conservative, and the main target for Levi action slacks and action suits (semi-smart casual wear). He shops with wife and values her opinion.

Proportion of population 19 per cent

● Q2: *classic independent* – aged between 20 and 60, a specialist store shopper, he dresses traditionally, but not unfashionably. Looking right is important. Shops alone and spends more on clothes than any other group.

Proportion of population 20 per cent

● Q3: *utilitarian jeans buyer* – all ages, a department store shopper who doesn't care much about clothes, he wears jeans for work and play; a Levi loyalist.

Proportion of population 26 per cent

● Q4: *trendy casual* – aged 16–45, he shops in department and specialist stores, likes to be noticed, may wear jeans for work, certainly wears them for play sometimes.

Proportion of population 19 per cent

● Q5: *price shopper* – all ages, department and discount store shopper who looks for bargains. Appearance is only important within certain parameters.

Proportion of population 15 per cent

**Young and Rubicam's 4Cs and Taylor Nelson's Monitor**

Developed by the advertising agency, Young & Rubicam, 4Cs (A Cross-Cultural Consumer Characterization) divides people into three main groups, each of which is further subdivided along the following lines:

(a) *the constrained*
   (i)   the resigned poor;
   (ii)  the struggling poor.
(b) *the middle majority*
   (i)   mainstreamers;
   (ii)  aspirers;
   (iii) succeeders.
(c) *the innovators*
   (i)   transitionals;
   (ii)  reformers.

The largest single sub-group in the United Kingdom is the mainstreamers, said to account for between 30 and 35 per cent of the population.

The principal benefit of 4Cs is that it defines in a fairly precise manner individual or group motivational needs. It does this by acknowledging the multidimensional nature of people and groups by taking the key motivational factors (e.g. success in the case of a succeeder) and overlaying this with other important motivational values to develop a motivational matrix. The technique has been used by Young and Rubicam over a number of years to develop strategic frameworks for marketing and advertising campaigns both domestically and internationally. In the case of the domestic market, for example, both the British Gas 'Tell Sid' shares campaign and Legal and General's 'Umbrella Campaign' were based on 4Cs analysis.

In the case of Legal and General, the objectives of the campaign were to make L & G sound new, interesting and at the forefront of innovating policies (without weakening its solid, safe, secure, mainstream image), as they wished to introduce new and larger investors without alienating their mainstream investors. Here, the 4Cs was used to identify the main motivational factors that would influence succeeders and aspirers to invest with them, while at the same time not alienating mainstreamers.

A similar framework, labelled Monitor, has been developed by the market research agency, Taylor Nelson. The Monitor typology again divides people into three main groups which are then subdivided:

1 *Sustenance-driven.* Motivated by material security, they are sub-divided into:
   (a) aimless, who include young unemployed and elderly drifters and comprise 5 per cent of the UK population;
   (b) survivors, traditionally-minded working class people (16% of the population);
   (c) belongers. These conservative family-oriented people form 18 per cent of the population, but only half of them are sustenance driven.
2 *Outer-directed.* Those who are mainly motivated by the desire for status. They are subdivided into:
   (a) belongers;
   (b) conspicuous consumers (19 per cent).
3 *Inner-directed.* Subdivided into:
   (a) social resisters, who are caring and often doctrinaire (11 per cent);
   (b) experimentalists, who are hedonistic and individualistic (14 per cent);
   (c) self explorers, who are less doctrinaire than social resisters and less materialistic than experimentalists.

The development of approaches such as these has also led to the emergence of a wide variety of acronyms and labels. Prominent among these are Yuppies (Young Upwardly Mobile Professional), Bumps (Borrowed-to-the-hilt, Upwardly Mobile Professional Show-offs), Jollies (Jet-setting Oldies with Lots of Loot), Woopies (Well Off Older Persons), and Glams (Greying Leisured Affluent Middle Aged). Although a number of these labels are now rather passé – Yuppies, for example, proved to be a phenomenon of the 1980s and the Big Bang – they have proved to be useful in that they characterize in an easily understood fashion a particular style of life.

## 8.12 APPROACHES TO SEGMENTING INDUSTRIAL MARKETS

Although much of the work that has been done on segmentation analysis over the past 20 years has focused on consumer markets, many of the variables such as benefits sought, geography, and usage rates can be applied with equal validity to industrial markets. Recognizing this, a number of writers, including Cardozo (1983, pp. 264–76), and Bonoma and Shapiro (1983) have concentrated on demonstrating, developing and refining their applicability. Cardozo, for example, has identified four dimensions which can be used either separately or collectively to classify organizational buying situations.

1 familiarity with the buying task and in particular whether it is a new task, modified rebuy or straight rebuy;
2 the type of product and the degree of standardization;
3 the significance of the purchase to the buying organization;
4 the level of uncertainty in the purchase situation.

Baker (1985, p. 159) has argued that these last two factors are of particular significance in that they reflect the fact that buyers too try to segment potential suppliers by developing assessment criteria and establishing formal vendor rating systems. This general line of thinking has been developed by Johnson and Flodhammer (1980, pp. 201–5) who, in arguing that the need to understand buyers' needs is as important in industrial markets as in consumer markets, have suggested that 'Unless there is knowledge of the industrial users' needs the manufactured product usually has the lowest common denominator – price. Quality and service are unknown qualities.'

A slightly different line of argument has been pursued by Bonoma and Shapiro (1983) who have concentrated on developing a classification of industrial segmentation variables and listing the questions that industrial marketers should pose in deciding which customers they want to serve. A summary of these questions in declining order of importance appears in Figure 8.11.

From this it can be seen that the starting point is the question of which industry to serve, followed by a series of decisions on customer size and purchase criteria.

**FIGURE 8.11**
*The major industrial market segmentation variables*

**Demographic**

*Industry*: on which industries that use this product should we concentrate?

*Company*: on what size of company should we concentrate?

*Location*: in which geographical areas should we concentrate our efforts?

**Operating variables**

*Technology*: which customers technologies are of the greatest interest to us?

*User status*: on which types of user (heavy, medium, light, non-user) should we concentrate?

*Customer capabilities*: should we concentrate on customers with a broad or a narrow range of needs?

**Purchasing approaches**

*Buying criteria*: should we concentrate on customers seeking quality, service, or price?

*Buying policies*: should we concentrate on companies that prefer leasing, systems purchases, or sealed bids?

*Current relationships*: should we concentrate on existing or new customers?

**Situational factors**

*Urgency*: should we concentrate on customers with sudden delivery needs?

*Size of order*: should we concentrate on large or small orders?

*Applications*: should we concentrate on general or specific applications of our product?

**Personal characteristics**

*Loyalty*: should we concentrate on customers who exhibit high or low levels of loyalty?

*Attitudes to risk*: should we concentrate on risk taking or risk avoiding customers?

SOURCE: Adapted from Bonoma and Shapiro (1983)

This methodology has been employed to great effect by, among others, IBM. IBM's starting point for segmentation has always been the idea that the company sells solutions rather than products. They therefore segment the market by commercial type: banking, transportation, insurance, processing industry, and so on, so as to be able to tailor solutions to specific problem areas. Each segment is then divided in a series of subsegments. Transportation, for example, can be divided into road, air, sea and rail.

## 8.13 MARKET TARGETING

Having decided how best to segment the market, the strategist is then faced with a series of decisions on how many and which segments to approach. Three factors need to be considered.

1 the size and growth potential of each segment;
2 their structural attractiveness;
3 the organization's objectives and resources.

The starting point for this involves examining each segment's size and potential for growth. Obviously, the question of what is the 'right size' of a segment will vary greatly from one organization to another. Morgan, for example, as mentioned earlier, has chosen to concentrate on a very small and specialized segment of the car market. Its customers are seeking the nostalgia of a pre-war sports car and the company has tailored its marketing mix accordingly. In commenting on this and giving the product a four-star rating, *What Car?* (1985) said:

> The ride's as hard as a rock, comfort and space minimal, noise levels deafeningly high, and overall the sports car has about as much refinement as a tractor. Wonderful!

This is neither a specification nor a segment that has any appeal for, say, General Motors or Ford, but Morgan operates within it with a degree of success.

In so far as it is possible to develop broad guidelines, we can say that large companies concentrate on segments with large existing or potential sales volumes and quite deliberately overlook or ignore small segments simply because they are rarely worth bothering with. Small firms, by contrast, often avoid large segments partly because of the level of resource needed to operate effectively, and partly because of the problems of having to cope with a far larger competitor.

With regard to the question of each segment's *structural attractiveness*, the strategist's primary concern is profitability. It may be the case that a segment is both large and growing but that, because of the intensity of competition, the scope for profit is low. Several models for measuring segment attractiveness exist, although arguably the most useful is Michael Porter's five-force model. This model, which is discussed at the beginning of Chapter 10, suggests that segment profitability is affected by five principal factors:

1 *industry competitors* and the threat of segment rivalry;
2 *potential entrants* to the market, and the threat of mobility;
3 the threat of *substitute products*;
4 *buyers* and their relative power;
5 *suppliers* and their relative power.

Having measured the size, growth rate and structural attractiveness of each segment, the strategist needs then to examine each one in turn against the background of the organization's objectives and resources. In doing this, the strategist is looking for the degree of compatibility between the segment and the organization's long-term goals. It is often the case, for example, that a seemingly attractive segment can be dismissed either because it would not move the organization significantly forward towards its goals, or because it would divert organizational energy. Even where there does appear to be a match, consideration needs to be given to whether the organization has the necessary skills competences, resources and commitment needed to operate effectively. Without these, entry is likely to be of little strategic value.

## 8.14  DECIDING ON THE BREADTH OF MARKET COVERAGE

The final segmentation decision faced by the strategist, is concerned with which and how many segments to enter. In essence, five patterns of market coverage exist:

1 *Single segment concentration* in which the organization focuses on just one segment. Although a potentially high risk strategy in that the firm is vulnerable to sudden changes in taste or the entry of a larger competitor, concentrated marketing along these lines has often proved to be attractive to small companies with limited funds. Left to itself, an organization which opts to concentrate upon a single segment can develop a strong market position, a specialist reputation, and above average returns for the industry as a whole.
2 *Selective specialization.* As an alternative to concentrating upon just one segment, the strategist may decide to spread the risk by covering several. These segments need not necessarily be related, although each should be compatible with the organization's objectives and resources. One organization to have done this with a high degree of success is Land Rover. Launched at the end of the 1940s as a rugged, utilitarian and easily maintained off-road vehicle, the Land Rover was targeted at a wide variety of geographically dispersed agricultural and military markets. Having dominated these markets for a considerable time the company subsequently developed the far more luxurious (and expensive) Range Rover which proved to have an immediate appeal to a very different type of market altogether. Their strategy was then developed further in 1990 by the launch of the Land Rover Discovery (see Gabb, 1991).
3 *Product specialization* in which the organization concentrates on marketing a particular product type to a variety of target markets. As an example of this, the Burton Group has concentrated upon selling fashion clothing to a predominantly young market.
4 *Market specialization.* Here the organization concentrates on satisfying the range of needs of a particular target group. An example of this would be an agro-chemicals manufacturer whose principal target market is farmers.
5 *Full market coverage.* By far the most costly of the five patterns of market coverage, a strategy of full market coverage involves serving all customer groups with the full range of products needed.

**Market Niching and Focusing**

For small companies in particular, market niching offers a degree of security that is often denied to them if they try to compete in segments which, by virtue of their size, appeal to larger and better funded organizations.

An undoubted attraction of many niche markets is the scope they offer for premium pricing and above-average profit margins. In addition, an effective niche strategy has for many firms provided a convenient jumping off point for entry into a larger market. Both Volkswagen and Toyota, for example, niched when they first entered the North American car market. Their strategies, together with the subsequent growth of the small car market, combined to change what had previously been a niche into a sizeable segment which the American big three

(Ford, General Motors, and Chrysler) found difficult to attack because of the entrenched positions of VW and Toyota. Elsewhere, the Japanese have often used a niche as the entry point to a larger market. In the case of motorcycles, for example, 50cc 'toys' proved to be the niche which gave Honda in particular the basis for expansion. Similarly, Volvo developed what was previously a niche that wanted a safe, functional and long-lasting car into a mass market.

There is, however, a hidden danger in looking at what appear to be niche markets. Many strategists with small brands often deceive themselves by believing they have a niche product. The reality may in fact be very different with the product being a vulnerable number four or number five brand in a mass market. To clarify whether a brand is a true market nicher, Davidson (1987, p. 168) therefore suggests posing three questions:

1 Is the niche or segment recognized by consumers and distributors, or is it just a figment of marketing imagination?
2 Is your niche product distinctive, and does it appeal strongly to a particular group of consumers?
3 Is your product premium-priced, with above average profit margin?

Unless the answer to all three of the questions is 'yes', he argues, it is unlikely that the brand is a true nicher, but is instead a poor performer in a far larger market segment. He goes on to say:

> Anyone can find a niche . . . The secret is to ensure that it is the right size – large enough to be profitable, but not sufficiently large to attract the supertankers, at least not in the early days when you are establishing a position. Some niche marketers are small companies. Others are large but have developed the knack of operating with small-volume products. Two of the most skilful exponents of niche marketing – American Home Products and Reckitt & Colman – are major companies.

In the light of comments such as these, the characteristics of the ideal niche are:

1 it is of sufficient size to be potentially profitable;
2 it offers scope for an organization to exercise its distinctive competences;
3 it has the potential for growth.

Other characteristics that favour niching would be patents, a degree of channel control, and the existence of customer goodwill.

Niching should not, however, be seen as a strategy limited just to small organizations. Among the large firms to have recognized the benefits of niching is 3M, which has long pursued a highly effective niching strategy by finding sectors of the market that have either been missed or ignored by others.

## 8.15 PRODUCT POSITIONING

The third strand of what we referred to at the beginning of this chapter as STP marketing involves deciding on the position within the market that the product is to occupy. In doing this, the strategist is stating to customers what the product means and how it differs from current and potential competing products. Porsche, for example, is positioned in the prestige segment of the car market with a differential advantage based on performance, while Mothercare is positioned to appeal to mothers of young children. Its differential advantage is based on the breadth of merchandise for that target group.

Positioning is therefore the process of designing an image and value so that customers within the target segment understand what the company or brand stands for in relation to its competitors. This can perhaps best be understood by considering an example such as grocery retailing where the major UK retailers have set out to establish distinct market positions. Marks & Spencer, for example, occupies a service and quality position. Kwik Save, Aldi and Netto, by contrast, have pursued the low price/no frills position, while Sainsbury and Tesco occupy the quality, breadth of range, and convenience position. In doing this, the organization is sending a message to consumers and trying to establish a competitive advantage that it hopes will appeal to customers within a subsegment of the target segment. In the case of M & S, therefore, the company hopes that its quality/service position will appeal to the customer to whom these two dimensions are far more important than low prices.

It should be apparent from this that positioning is a fundamental element of the marketing planning process, since any decision on positioning has direct and immediate implications for the whole of the marketing mix. In essence, therefore, the marketing mix can be seen as the tactical details of the organization's positioning strategy. Where, for example, the organization is pursuing a high quality position, this needs to be reflected not just in the quality of the product that is to be sold, but in every element of the mix including price, the pattern of distribution, the style of advertising, and the after-sales service. Without this consistency, the believability of the positioning strategy reduces dramatically.

For some organizations the choice of a positioning strategy proves to be straightforward. Where, for example, a particular positioning strategy and image has already been established in a related market, there are likely to be synergistic benefits by adopting the same approach in a new market or with a new product. For other organizations, however, the choice of position proves to be more difficult or less clear and the firm ends up by pursuing the same position as several others in the market. Where this happens the degree and costs of competition increase dramatically. There is a strong case therefore for the strategist to decide in detail on the basis of differentiation; in other words, the organization must identify and build a collection of competitive advantages that will appeal to the target market and then communicate these effectively.

In the light of these comments, it should be apparent that the process of positioning involves three steps:

1 identifying the organization's or brand's possible competitive advantages;
2 deciding on those that are to be emphasized;
3 implementing the positioning concept.

Points 1 and 2 are discussed in detail in Chapter 10 and here we will therefore consider only point 3.

## Capitalizing on the Competitive Advantage

Having identified the competitive advantage (see Chapter 10) that appears to offer the greatest potential for development, the final step in the process involves communicating this to the market. Ries and Trout (1982), who in the eyes of many are the founding fathers of positioning theory, argue that positioning is first and foremost a communication strategy and that any failure to recognize this will undermine the whole of the marketing mix. All too often, however, and despite having identified potentially valuable competitive advantages, organizations fail to signal these advantages sufficiently strongly. This then leads to one of three errors:

1 confused positioning where buyers are unsure of what the organization stands for;
2 over-positioning where consumers perceive the organization's products as being expensive and fail to recognize the full breadth of the range;
3 under-positioning where the message is simply too vague and consumers have little real idea of what the organization stands for.

Recognition of these dangers has led to the development of six major positioning strategies:

1 positioning by attribute;
2 positioning by price/quality;
3 positioning by competitor;
4 positioning by application;
5 positioning by product user;
6 positioning by product class.

In order to select the most effective market position, the strategist needs to begin by identifying the structure of the market and the positions currently held by competitors. This can be done in a variety of ways, including by means of the sort of brand map to which we referred to earlier in Figure 8.4. With maps such as these the planner sets out firstly to plot where the product lies in relation to competitive products, and secondly, to identify those areas in which marketing opportunities might exist either for a new brand or for the existing brand if it was to be repositioned. In taking this second step the strategist is setting out to position the product in such a way that its marketing potential is fully realized. As an example of this, the West German car manufacturer Audi set out in the 1980s to reposition its range of products in order to move further up-market. In doing this, the company recognized that the organizations against which it would be competing would change and that in this particular case it would bring itself into more direct competition with both BMW and Mercedes-Benz. In electing for a repositioning strategy, the strategist therefore needs to feel confident that, first, he will be able to reach the new market position he is aiming for, and second, that he will be able to operate and compete effectively and profitably in this new position. For many organizations, however, repositioning proves to be a less than successful exercise. Among those that have succeeded are Lucozade and Babycham.

Against the background of these comments, it should be recognized that very different positioning strategies need to be followed depending upon whether the firm is a market leader, follower or challenger, and that as a general rule market followers should try to avoid positioning themselves too closely or directly against the market leader. The reasoning behind this is straightforward, since a smaller firm is most likely to succeed if it can establish its own position within the market and develop its own customer base. To compete head-on against the market leader is to invite retaliation and a costly marketing war.

## 8.16 SUMMARY

Within this chapter we have focused upon the ways in which a well-developed strategy of market segmentation, targeting and positioning contributes to effective marketing planning.

The rationale for segmentation is straightforward and based on the idea that only rarely can a single product or marketing approach appeal to the needs and wants of a disparate group of potential customers. Because of this there is a need for the marketing strategist to categorize buyers on the basis both of their characteristics and their specific product needs with a view then to adapting either or both of the product and the marketing programme to satisfy more specifically these different tastes and demands. An effective policy of segmentation is therefore a key contributory factor to the development of a competitive advantage.

A wide variety of approaches to segmentation have been developed and these were discussed in some detail in the text. Many of the early approaches to segmentation are uni-dimensional and are incapable of providing the marketing planner with a sufficiently detailed picture of buyers' motives to be of real value. A considerable amount of work has therefore been conducted over the past decade to improve segmentation techniques, with the greatest emphasis being placed upon geodemographics and psychographics.

Work within the industrial products sector has for the most part tended to lag behind that in the consumer goods field, although the work of Cardozo, and Bonoma and Shapiro has gone some way towards rectifying this.

Having segmented the market the strategist should then be in a position to identify those segments which, from the organization's point of view, represent the most attractive targets. In deciding where to focus the marketing effort the strategist needs to give consideration to three elements:

1  the size and growth potential of each segment;
2  the structural attractiveness of different segments;
3  the organization's objectives and resources.

Once a decision has been made on the breadth of market coverage the strategist needs then to consider how best to position the organization, the product range, and brand within each target segment. A number of guidelines for market positioning were discussed and emphasis was placed upon the need to avoid making any one of the three most common positioning errors:

1  confused positioning;
2  over-positioning;
3  under-positioning.

We concluded by returning to the significance of competitive advantage and to the ways in which a well-conceived and properly implemented strategy of segmentation, targeting and positioning can contribute to a truly effective marketing programme.

# 9 | The formulation of strategy 1: analysing the product portfolio

## 9.1 LEARNING OBJECTIVES

When you have read this chapter you should be able to understand:

(a) how strategic perspectives have developed over the past 20 years;
(b) how the responsibilities for planning vary throughout the organization;
(c) how portfolio analysis has developed and how it can be used in the development of strategy;
(d) the limitations and current status of portfolio analysis.

## 9.2 INTRODUCTION

Against the background of the material covered so far we are now in a position to turn our attention to the ways in which organizations approach the development of a marketing strategy. In this, the first of two chapters on strategy, we begin by examining how strategic perspectives have developed over the past 20 years. We then turn our attention to a variety of models of portfolio analysis. In Chapter 10 we concentrate upon the issues surrounding growth, the approaches that are most typically used to achieve it, methods of developing a sustainable competitive advantage, and the ways in which market position influences strategy.

## 9.3 THE DEVELOPMENT OF STRATEGIC PERSPECTIVES

Although a considerable amount has been written on strategic planning, it should be recognized that as a discipline strategic planning and the associated concepts and techniques did not emerge fully until the early 1970s. There are several reasons for this, perhaps the most significant of which is that, as Kotler (1988, pp. 33–4) has pointed out, largely because of the growing and continuously buoyant markets of the 1950s and 1960s, many companies prospered on the back of largely short-term operational planning. The turbulence of the early 1970s that followed a series of crises, including oil supply restrictions, energy and material shortages, high inflation, economic stagnation, labour unrest, increased unemployment and then recession, caused many managers to search for a radically different approach to the running of their businesses. At the same time an influx of low-price but relatively high-quality products from countries such as Japan began to flood Western markets, changing drastically the economics of manufacturing. The revised approach to management planning that emerged was designed to provide organizations with a far stronger and more resilient framework that would enable managers both to recognize opportunities more readily and overcome threats more easily. This new planning process was based on three central premises:

1 The company's business should be viewed and managed in a similar way to an investment portfolio with each aspect of the business being closely monitored and decisions subsequently made on which products or specific parts of the business should be developed, maintained, phased out, or deleted.

2 Emphasis should be placed upon identifying in detail the future profit potential of each aspect of the business.

3 A strategic perspective to the management of each major element of the business should be adopted. This notion of what has sometimes been referred to as a 'game plan' for achieving long-term objectives, required the strategist to plan on the basis of industry position, objectives, opportunities and resources.

It needs to be recognized, however, that for the strategist to be able to adopt this approach to management, there is a need to understand in detail the complexities of the interrelationships that exist between different parts of the organizational structure. In the majority of businesses, three different organizational levels can be identified: the corporate level, the business unit level, and the product level.

At the corporate level, the decisions made are concerned principally with the corporate strategic plan and how best to develop the long-term profile of the business. This, in turn, involves a series of decisions on the levels of resource allocation to individual business units, be it a division or subsidiary, and on which new potential business should be supported. Following on from this, each business unit should, within the resources allocated by corporate headquarters, then develop its own strategic plan. Finally, marketing plans need to be developed at the product level. Plans at all three levels need then to be implemented, the results monitored and evaluated and, where necessary, corrective action taken; this cycle of planning, implementation and control, which underpins the structure of this book, is illustrated in Figure 9.1.

**FIGURE 9.1**
*The strategic planning, implementation and control cycle*

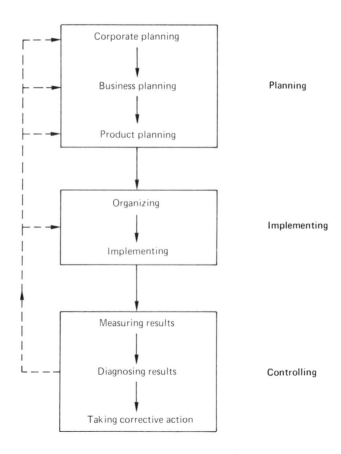

**Strategic Planning and Issues of Responsibility**

It should be apparent from what has been said so far that the ultimate responsibility for the planning process rests firmly with corporate management. This process, which involves statements of mission, policy and strategy, establishes the broad framework within which plans at the business unit level are then developed. In practice, of course, organizations differ greatly both in how they go about this and in the degree of freedom given to the managers of individual business units. Some organizations, for example, allow business units considerable scope in developing their own objectives and strategies, requiring only that the promised levels of performance are then obtained; this is typically referred to as *bottom-up planning*. Others, by contrast, adopt an approach which is diametrically opposed to this in that they not only establish the objectives, but also subsequently insist on being involved in the development and implementation of strategy (*top-down planning*). Still others are content to establish the goals and then leave the business unit to develop the strategies for their achievement (*goals down/plans up*). Irrespective of which approach is adopted, however, corporate management has the ultimate responsibility for the four major dimensions of planning:

1 the definition of the business mission;
2 establishing the company's strategic business units (SBUs);
3 evaluating the existing business portfolio;
4 identifying new areas for the business to enter.

The first of these – the definition of the business mission – provided the focus for Chapter 6 and, as we emphasized at that stage, is designed to provide the organization with an overall sense of purpose. Once this has been done, the strategist is then in a position to move on and identify the organization's *strategic business units* (SBUs).

The idea of SBUs as the basis for planning first emerged in the 1960s and gave recognition to the fact that the majority of companies operate a number of businesses, not all of which will necessarily be immediately apparent or identifiable. It does not follow, for example, that a company with four operating divisions will have four businesses and hence four SBUs, since one division may in practice contain several quite separate businesses. This typically comes about when the division produces different products for very different customer groups. Equally, two or three divisions may overlap or be interrelated in such a way that in effect they form a single business. It is therefore important that the planner understands in detail the nature and extent of these interrelationships so that the organization's strategy can be developed in the most logical way.

In commenting on this, Levitt (1960, pp. 45–56), along with a number of other writers, has warned against the dangers of simply defining businesses in terms of the products being made. Doing this, he argues, is myopic since the demand for a particular product is likely to be transient. By contrast, basic needs and customer groups are far more likely to endure. In arguing this, Levitt is reminding us that businesses need to be seen as a *customer satisfying process* rather than as a *goods-producing process*. Numerous examples exist of industries that have failed to recognize this, including the American railway companies in the 1950s, the British motorcycle industry in the 1960s, and the Swiss watch industry in the 1970s. (For a more detailed discussion of the problems experienced by the Swiss watch industry, refer to Illustration 7.1). The net effect of this has been either that opportunities have been missed, or the business – and on some occasions the entire industry – has gone into decline. It was in an attempt to force managers to recognize the transient nature of demand that Drucker (1973, Ch. 7) recommended that periodically they should pose the questions 'What business are we in?' and 'What business should we be in?'

This general theme has also been pursued by Abell (1980, Ch. 3) who suggests that businesses should be defined in terms of three elements:

1 the customer groups that will be served;
2 the customer needs that will be satisfied;
3 the technology that will be used to meet these needs.

Having done this, the planner can then move on to consider how best to manage each business strategically. A variety of frameworks to help with this have emerged over the past 20 years, although at the heart of virtually all of them is the concept of the *strategic business unit* or *strategy centre*. The term 'strategy centre' was first used by the American management consultants Arthur D. Little (1974) who defined it as:

> A business area with an external market place for goods or services, for which management can determine objectives and execute strategies independently of other business areas. It is a business that could probably stand alone if divested. Strategic Business Units are the 'natural' or homogeneous business of a corporation.

It follows from this definition that SBUs exhibit a number of characteristics, the three most important of which are that an SBU:

1 is a single business or a collection of related businesses which offer scope for independent planning and which might feasibly stand alone from the rest of the organization;
2 has its own set of competitors;
3 has a manager who has responsibility for strategic planning and profit performance, and who has control of profit-influencing factors.

**Planning with SBUs**

The ideal of planning based on SBUs developed throughout the 1970s and has proved to be useful, not least because for many managers it has to a very large extent clarified what is meant by strategic marketing planning. The identification of SBUs is therefore a convenient starting point for planning since once the company's strategic business units have been identified, the *responsibilities* for strategic planning can be more clearly assigned. In practice, the majority of companies work on the basis that strategic planning at SBU level has to be agreed by corporate management. Thus plans are typically submitted on an annual basis with corporate management then either agreeing them or sending them back for revision.

In going through this process of review, corporate management attempts to identify future potential and hence where investment can most profitably be made. This has in turn led to the development of a variety of frameworks in which products are categorized on the basis of their potential. One of the best known of these was put forward by Drucker (1963) who labelled products as:

1 tomorrow's breadwinners;
2 today's breadwinners;
3 products that are capable of making a contribution assuming drastic remedial action is taken;
4 yesterday's breadwinners;
5 the also-rans;
6 the failures.

By categorizing products or SBUs in this way, corporate management is moving towards a position where decisions regarding patterns of investment in the overall portfolio can be made with a far higher degree of objectivity than is typically the case when each SBU is viewed in partial or total isolation. To help with this and in order to ensure that the process is analytical rather than impressionistic, a number of models of portfolio evaluation have been developed. Among the best known of these are the Boston Consulting Group's Growth-Share and Growth-Gain matrices.

# 9.4 MODELS OF PORTFOLIO ANALYSIS

**The Boston Consulting Group's Growth-Share and Growth-Gain Matrices**

Undoubtedly the best-known approach to portfolio analysis, the Boston Consulting Group's (BCG) growth-share model, involves SBUs being plotted on a matrix according to the *rate of market growth* and their *market share relative to that of the largest competitor*. This is illustrated in Figure 9.2.

In using these dimensions as the basis for evaluating the product portfolio, the Boston Consulting Group forces management to give explicit consideration both to the *future potential of the market* (i.e. the annual growth rate) and to the *SBU's competitive position*. (At this stage it might be worth referring back to Chapter 4 and our discussion of Michael Porter's work concerned with the forces governing competition in an industry.) Within the model, competitive position is measured on a logarithmic scale against the share of the firm's largest competitor; thus a relative market share of 0.3 in Figure 9.2 signifies that the SBU's sales volume is 30 per cent of the leader's sales volume, while 4.0 would mean that the company's SBU is the market leader and has four times the market share of the next largest company in the market. A ratio of 1.0 signifies joint leadership. The vertical axis is then used to illustrate the largely uncontrollable annual rate of market growth in which the business operates. In Figure 9.2 this ranges from 0 to 20 per cent, with a growth rate in excess of 10 per cent being seen as high.

**FIGURE 9.2**
*The Boston Consulting Group's growth-share matrix*

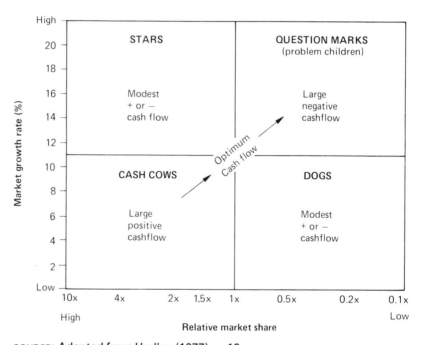

SOURCE: Adapted from Hedley (1977), p. 12

The 2 × 2 matrix that emerges from this is based on four assumptions:

1 margins and the funds generated increase with market share largely as the result of experience and scale effects;
2 sales growth demands cash to finance working capital and increases in capacity;
3 increases in market share generally need cash to support share gaining tactics;
4 growth slows as the product reaches life-cycle maturity and at this stage a surplus of cash can often be generated without the organization experiencing any loss of market share; this can then be used to support products still in the growth stages of their life cycles.

The matrix itself is divided into four cells, each of which indicates a different type of business with different cash using and cash generating characteristics; the characteristics of each of these cells are discussed in Figure 9.3.

**FIGURE 9.3**
*The Boston Consulting Group's SBU classification*

**Dogs (low share, low growth)**
Dogs are those businesses that have a weak market share in a low-growth market. Typically they generate either a low profit or return a loss. The decision faced by the company is whether to hold on to the dog for strategic reasons (e.g. in the expectation that the market will grow, or because the product provides an obstacle, albeit a minor one, to a competitor). Dog businesses frequently take up more management time than they justify and there is often a case for phasing out (shooting) the product.

**Question marks (low share, high growth)**
Questions marks are businesses operating in high-growth markets but with a low relative market share. They generally require considerable sums of cash since the firm needs to invest in plant, equipment and manpower to keep up with market developments. These cash requirements are, in turn, increased significantly if the company wants to improve its competitive position. The title of *question mark* comes about because management has to decide whether to continue investing in the SBU or withdrawing from the market.

**Stars (high share, high growth)**
Stars are those products which have moved to the position of leadership in a high growth market. Their cash needs are often high with the cash being spent in order to maintain market growth and keep competitors at bay. As stars also generate large amounts of cash, on balance there is unlikely to be any positive or negative cash flow until such time as the state of market growth declines. At this stage, provided the share has been maintained, the product should become a cash cow.

**Cash cows (high share, low growth)**
When the rate of market growth begins to fall, stars typically become the company's cash cows. The term *cash cow* is derived from the fact that it is these products which generate considerable sums of cash for the organization but which, because of the lower rate of growth, use relatively little. Because of the SBU's position in the market, economies of scale are often considerable and profit margins high.

Two further groups of SBU's have been identified by Barksdale and Harris (1982). These are *war horses* (high market share and negative growth) and *dodos* (low share, negative growth).

Having plotted the position of the organization's SBUs, the balance and health of the portfolio can be seen fairly readily. A balanced portfolio typically exhibits certain characteristics, including a mixture of cash cows and stars. By contrast, an unbalanced and potentially dangerous portfolio would have too many dogs or question marks and too few stars and cash cows; the likely consequence of this is that insufficient cash will be generated on a day-to-day basis to fund or support the development of other SBUs.

Having identified the shape of the portfolio, the planner needs then to consider the objectives, strategy and budget for each SBU. In essence, four major strategies can be pursued:

1 *Build*. In following a building strategy, the primary objective is to increase the SBU's market share in order to strengthen its position. In doing this, short-term earnings and profits are quite deliberately forsaken in the expectation that long-term returns will be far greater. It is a strategy which is best suited to question marks so that they become stars.
2 *Hold*. The primary objective in this case is to maintain the current share. It is the strategy which typically is used for cash cows to ensure they continue to generate the maximum amounts of cash.
3 *Harvest*. By following a harvesting strategy management tries to increase short-term cashflows as far as possible, even at the expense of the SBUs's longer term future. It is a strategy best suited to cash cows that are weak or which are in a market with seemingly only a limited future life. It is also used

on occasions when the organization is in need of cash and is willing to mortgage the future of the product in the interests of short-term needs. Harvesting is also used for question marks when there appear to be few real opportunities to turn them into stars, and for dogs.

4 *Divest.* The essential objective here is to rid the organization of SBUs that act as a drain on profits or to realize resources that can be used to greater effect elsewhere in the business. It is a strategy which, again, is often used for question marks and dogs.

Having decided which of these four broad approaches to follow, the strategist needs then to give consideration to the way in which each SBU is likely to change its position within the matrix over time. SBUs typically have a life cycle which begins with their appearance as question marks and their progression through the stages of star, cash cow and, finally dog. It is essential therefore that the BCG matrix is used not simply to obtain a snapshot of the portfolio as it stands currently, but rather that it is used to see how SBUs have developed so far and how they are likely to develop in the future. In doing this, it is possible to gain an impression of the probable shape and health of the portfolio in several years' time, any gaps that are likely to exist, and hence the sort of strategic action that is needed in the form of decisions on new products, marketing support, and indeed product deletion. This process can then be taken a step further if similar charts are developed for each major competitor, since by doing this the strategist gains an insight to each competitor's portfolio strengths, weaknesses, and potential gaps. The implications can then be fed back into the organization's own strategy.

## The Pitfalls of Portfolio Analysis

Although portfolio analysis is capable of providing a picture of the organization's current position, the strategists need to adopt a degree of care in their interpretation and when developing a future policy. A common mistake in portfolio analysis is to require each SBU to achieve an unrealistic growth rate or level of return; the essence of portfolio analysis involves recognizing that each SBU offers a different potential and as such requires individual management. Other typical mistakes include:

1 Investing too heavily in dogs hoping that their position will improve, but failing.
2 Maintaining too many question marks and investing too little in each one with the result that their position either fails to change or deteriorates. Question marks should either be dropped or receive the level of support needed to improve their segment position dramatically.
3 Draining the cash cows of funds and weakening them prematurely and unnecessarily. Alternatively, investing too much in cash cows with the result that the money available for question marks, stars and dogs is insufficient.

It should be apparent from the discussion so far that cash cows are essential to the health and long-term profitability of the organization since they provide the funds needed if it is to develop and realize its full potential. The reality in many companies, however, is that cash cows are often in short supply and may already have been too vigorously milked. Booz, Allen & Hamilton (1988), for example, have estimated that, in traditional portfolio analysis terms, 72 per cent of business units in the United States are dogs, 15 per cent are cash cows, 10 per cent question marks, and only 3 per cent stars. There is little evidence to suggest that the proportions in the UK are radically different. Recognizing this, the strategist needs to focus upon the long term and consider how best to manage the portfolio and ensure that the organization benefits from a succession of cash cows. Any failure to do this is likely to lead to suboptimal management and the sorts of disaster sequences that are illustrated in Figure 9.4.

**FIGURE 9.4**
*Success and disaster sequences in the product portfolio*

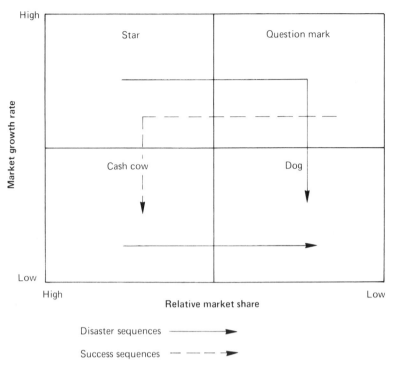

Disaster sequences ──────▶

Success sequences ── ── ── ▶

SOURCE: The Boston Consulting Group (1970)

A second model developed by the Boston Consulting Group – the growth-gain matrix – can go some way towards helping the strategist avoid problems such as those shown in Figure 9.4. The alternative matrix, which is often used in conjunction with growth-share analysis, illustrates the extent to which the growth of each product or SBU is keeping pace with market growth. The matrix, which is illustrated in Figure 9.5(a), features the growth rate of the product (or of its capacity) on the horizontal axis, and the growth rate of the market on the vertical axis. Products with a growth rate just equal to the market growth rate are located on the diagonal. Share losers therefore appear above the diagonal, while share gainers are below.

Figure 9.5(b) shows the ideal location of products within a portfolio. Here, the dogs are clustered along or near the market growth axis, a position which reflects zero capacity growth. Cash cows are concentrated along the diagonal showing that market share is being maintained. Stars should appear in the high-growth sector since they should be gaining, or at the very least holding, market share. Question marks then appear in two clusters with one group receiving little support, while the other is receiving the considerable support needed to maximize its chances of producing stars.

In discussing how best to use and interpret the growth-gain matrix, Alan Zakon (1971) of the Boston Consulting Group highlights the significance of the firm's *maximum sustainable growth*; this is plotted as a solid vertical line on the matrix. 'The weighted average growth rate of the products within the portfolio cannot', he emphasizes, 'exceed this maximum sustainable rate.' Where, however, the 'centre of gravity' (i.e. the weighted average growth rate) is to the left of this line, scope exists for further growth. This would typically be achieved by a series of strategy changes to reposition products. As an example of this, extra funds might be shifted to one of the stars in order to achieve even higher rates of growth.

**FIGURE 9.5**
*The product
portfolio and
maximum
sustainable growth*

(a) Positive diversified portfolio

(b) Idealized distribution of the portfolio

SOURCE: The Boston Consulting Group (1971)

Used in this way, the growth-gain matrix provides a basis for moving the portfolio closer to the 'ideal' position of maximum sustainable growth. Equally, by plotting growth-gain matrices for each major competitor, the strategist can, as with growth-share analysis, gain an insight into the areas of competitive emphasis and react accordingly.

**Portfolio
Analysis: An
Initial
Assessment**

Although the BCG matrices have a number of obvious attractions, a word of caution needs to be uttered, since they do not represent the ultimate management panacea that many of their advocates in the early days argued. It should be recognized that the practical value of portfolio analysis is influenced significantly both by the quality of the basic data inputs, many of which are difficult to define and measure, and the broader political and social environments within which decisions are made. It was therefore in an attempt to give greater specific recognition to a broader spectrum of factors that other approaches to portfolio analysis, including the General Electric multifactor matrix, the Shell directional policy matrix, the Arthur D. Little strategic condition matrix, and Abell and Hammond's 3 × 3 relative investment opportunity chart have been developed. It is to these models, which are concerned with market attractiveness and business position, that we now turn our attention.

## 9.5 MARKET ATTRACTIVENESS AND BUSINESS POSITION ASSESSMENT

The two BCG matrices we have discussed so far are capable of providing the strategist with an understanding of several important strategic relationships, including internal cashflows, and market share and growth trajectories. It is generally acknowledged, however, that while the insights provided by these models is undoubtedly of significant value, they are in the majority of cases insufficient if truly worthwhile investment decisions affecting the future of the business are to be made. More specifically, critics such as Abell and Hammond (1979, pp. 211–12) have highlighted the three major shortcomings of relying simply on growth-share analysis:

1 Often, factors other than relative market share and industry growth play a significant role in influencing cashflow.
2 Cashflow may well be viewed as being of less significance than ROI as a means of comparing the attractiveness of investing in one business rather than another.
3 Portfolio charts provide little real insight into how one business unit compares with another in terms of investment opportunity. Is it the case, for example, that a star is always a better target for investment than a cash cow? Equally, problems are often encountered in comparing question marks when trying to decide which should receive funds to make it a star, and which should be allowed to decline.

Recognition of these sorts of problems has led to the development of an approach which is labelled '*market attractiveness – business position assessment*', the best known of which is the General Electric model.

**The General Electric Multifactor Portfolio Model**

The thinking behind General Electric's multifactor model is straightforward and based on the argument that it is not always possible or appropriate to develop objectives or to make investment decisions for an SBU solely on the basis of its position in the growth-share matrix. The General Electric model therefore takes the general approach a step further by introducing a greater number of variables against which the position of SBUs might be plotted. This model, which appears in Figure 9.6, involves SBUs being rated against two principal dimensions: *industry attractiveness* and *competitive position*.

**FIGURE 9.6**
*The General Electric multifactor portfolio model*

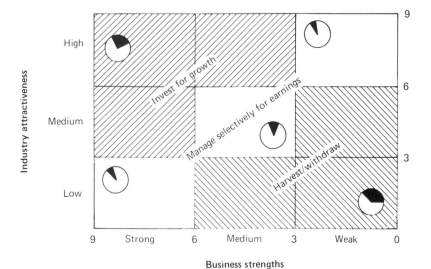

The circles then represent not the size of the SBU, but rather the size of the market in question, with the shaded part of the circle representing the SBU's market share.

The thinking behind the choice of the two axes is based on the notion that the success of a company is determined, first, by the extent to which it operates in attractive markets, and second by the extent to which it possesses the sorts of competitive business strengths needed to succeed in each of these markets. The failure on the part of the company to recognize this is likely to lead to long-term problems, since, as Kotler (1988, p. 43) suggests, 'neither a strong company operating in an unattractive market nor a weak company operating in an attractive market will do very well'.

Recognizing this requires the planner to measure each of the two dimensions. In order to do this, the factors underlying each dimension must be identified, measured and then combined to form an index. Although within each dimension the list of factors that combine to form a measure of attractiveness will be specific to each company, it is possible to identify the sorts of factor that will in nearly every instance be of relevance. Industry attractiveness, for example, is determined to a very large extent by the market's size, its rate of growth, the degree of competition, the pace of technological change, the extent to which it is constrained by government or legislative regulations, the sorts of profit margins that historically have been achieved, and so on. Equally, business strength is influenced by such factors as market share, product quality, the brand's reputation, the distribution network, production capacity and production effectiveness. (See Chapter 16 for a fuller discussion.)

It can be seen from Figure 9.6 that the nine cells of the General Electric matrix fall into three distinct areas, each of which requires a different approach to management and investment. The three cells at the top left of the matrix are the most attractive in which to operate and require a policy of investment for growth. The three cells that run diagonally from the top right to the bottom left have a medium attractiveness rating; the management of the SBUs within this category should therefore be rather more cautious with a greater emphasis being placed upon selective investment and earnings retention. The three cells at the bottom right of the matrix are the least attractive in which to operate and management should therefore pursue a policy of harvesting and/or divestment.

As with the BCG matrix, it needs to be recognized that the General Electric approach to portfolio analysis also needs to take account of the probable future of each SBU. The planner should therefore attempt to look ahead by considering life cycles, new forms of technology and their probable impact, likely competitive strategies, and so on. This can then be reflected in the matrix by adding a series of arrows showing how each SBU is likely to move over the next few years.

**Other Portfolio Models**

Although the BCG and GE models are undoubtedly the best-known approaches to portfolio analysis, a variety of other models have appeared over the years, including the Shell directional policy matrix (DPM) (1975), Abell and Hammond's 3 × 3 matrix (1979), and the Arthur D. Little strategic condition model (1974).

Shell's directional policy matrix which is illustrated in Figure 9.7 again has two key dimensions, the company's *competitive capabilities* and the *prospects for sector profitability*. As with the General Electric matrix, each dimension is then subdivided into three categories. SBUs are located within the matrix and the strategic options open to the company then identified. The directional policy matrix has, in turn, provided the basis for Abell and Hammond's 3 × 3 chart (see Figure 9.8), which is designed to depict relative investment opportunities.

Although the terminology used by Abell and Hammond differs slightly from that of Shell's DPM – company competitive capability, for example, is referred to as business position, while prospects for sector profitability is termed market

**FIGURE 9.7**
*The Shell
directional policy
matrix*

Prospects for sector profitability

|  | | Unattractive | Average | Attractive |
|---|---|---|---|---|
| **Enterprise's competitive capabilities** | Weak | Disinvest | Phased withdrawal | Double or quit |
| | Average | Phased withdrawal | Custodial  Growth | Try harder |
| | Strong | Cash generation | Growth  Leader | Leader |

SOURCE: Shell Chemical Co. (1975)

**FIGURE 9.8**
*Abell and
Hammond's 3 × 3
investment
opportunity matrix*

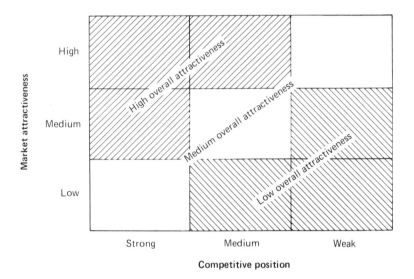

SOURCE: Adapted from Abell and Hammond (1979), p. 213

attractiveness – the thinking behind the model is similar and indeed can be seen to link back to the General Electric approach.

The Arthur D. Little model (ADL) (Wright, 1974) which is illustrated in Figure 9.9 is again similar in concept, although here the two dimensions used are the firm's *competitive position* and the *stage of industry maturity*. Competitive position, they suggest, is influenced by the geographical scope of the industry and the specific product – market sectors in which the SBU operates. It is not therefore simply market share that influences competitive position but also competitive economics and a series of other factors, including technology. This led ADL to the recognition of five main categories of competitive position:

1 *Dominant*. This is a comparatively rare position and in many cases is attributable either to a monopoly or a strong and protected technological leadership. The implications are that the firm is able to exert considerable influence over the behaviour of others in the industry and has a wide variety of strategic options open to it.

**FIGURE 9.9**

*The Arthur D. Little strategic condition matrix*

Stage of industry maturity

| Competitive position | Embryonic | Growth | Mature | Ageing |
|---|---|---|---|---|
| Dominant | Grow fast. Build barriers. Act offensively. | Grow fast. Aim for cost leadership. Defend position. Act offensively. | Defend position. Increase the importance of cost. Act offensively. | Defend position. Focus. Consider withdrawal. |
| Strong | Grow fast. Differentiate. | Lower cost. Differentiate. Attack small firms. | Lower costs. Differentiate. Focus. | Harvest. |
| Favourable | Grow fast. Differentiate. | Focus. Differentiate. Defend. | Focus. Differentiate. Hit smaller firms. | Harvest. |
| Tenable | Grow with the industry. Focus. | Hold-on or withdraw. Niche. Aim for growth. | Hold-on or withdraw. Niche. | Withdraw. |
| Weak | Search for a niche. Attempt to catch others. | Niche or withdraw. | Withdraw. | Withdraw. |

SOURCE: Adapted from ADL

2 *Strong.* By virtue of this position, the firm has a considerable degree of freedom over its choice of strategy and is often able to act without its market position being unduly threatened by competitors.

3 *Favourable.* This position, which generally comes about when the industry is fragmented and no one competitor stands out clearly, results in the market leaders having a reasonable degree of freedom. Companies with a favourable market position often have strengths that can be exploited by particular strategies and hence a greater than average opportunity to increase market share.

4 *Tenable.* Although firms within this category are able to perform satisfactorily and can justify staying in the industry, they are generally vulnerable in the face of increased competition from stronger and more proactive companies in the market. The opportunities for an organization to strengthen its position tend to be lower than average. The profitability of the tenable firm is best achieved and sustained through a degree of specialization.

5 *Weak.* The performance of firms in this category is generally unsatisfactory although opportunities for improvement do exist. Often, however, the firm is either too big and inefficient to compete with any real degree of effectiveness, or it is too small to cope with competitive pressures. Unless the firm changes, it is ultimately likely to be forced out of the market or exit of its own accord.

A sixth position, that of *non-viability*, can be added to this list and applies when the firm's performance is unsatisfactory and there are few, if any, opportunities for improvement. In these circumstances it is essentially a case of the strategist recognizing the reality of the situation and withdrawing from the market in the least costly way.

The second dimension of the model – the *stage of industry maturity* ranging from embryonic to ageing – has, ADL argue, significant implications for the strategies open to the organization. Thus once a basic strategy has been identified, there are certain things the strategist must do, might do, and should not do if consistency is to be maintained.

This combination of competitive position and industry maturity provides the basis for determining the SBU's strategic condition and subsequently the identification and evaluation of the strategic options open to the company; this typically is a choice between investing in order to strengthen or maintain position, spending in order to maintain the status quo, harvesting, or exiting from the industry. In commenting on this, ADL state that 'there is a finite set of available strategies for each Business Unit' and that these can be seen in terms of six generic strategic groups:

- market strategies (domestic and international);
- product strategies;
- technology strategies;
- operations strategies;
- management and systems strategies;
- retrenchment strategies.

In choosing among these, ADL identify several guiding principles, the most important of which is that 'strategy selection (should) be driven by the condition of the business, not the condition of its managers'. In making this comment, ADL are arguing for realism in strategic planning and that it is this that should prevail if the organization is not to overreach itself.

## 9.6 CRITICISMS OF PORTFOLIO ANALYSIS

Despite the rapid growth, adoption and indeed the apparent attractions of the underlying logic of portfolio analysis, it has been subject to a considerable and growing volume of criticism over the past 10 years. Although it is acknowledged by its critics that the sort of models referred to here have encouraged managers to think strategically, consider the economics of their businesses in greater detail, examine the nature of interrelationships, and adopt a more proactive approach to management, many writers have argued that the models are generally too simplistic in their structure. In commenting on this, Kotler (1988, p. 46) suggests that:

> Portfolio analysis models must be used cautiously. They may lead the company to place too much emphasis on market-share growth and entry into high growth businesses, to the neglect of managing the current businesses well. The results are sensitive to the ratings and weights and can be manipulated to produce a desired location in the matrix. Furthermore, since an averaging process is occurring, two or more businesses may end up in the same cell position but differ greatly in the underlying ratings and weights. A lot of businesses will end up in the middle of the matrix due to compromises in ratings, and this makes it hard to know what the appropriate strategy should be. Finally, the models fail to accommodate the synergies between two or more businesses, and this means that making decisions for one business at a time may be risky.

These sorts of criticisms have been echoed by others, including Baker (1985, p. 75) who has pointed to the way in which many firms managed to cope with the recession of the 1970s and early 1980s not because of a portfolio of products or even a high market share, but rather as the result of a strategy of concentrating upon a single product and market. Equally, many other firms, and especially those in mature markets, he suggests, have not only survived but have also prospered despite having products which in portfolio analysis terms would be universally classified as dogs. Brownlie (1983) also discusses these criticisms in some detail, and is worth quoting at length. He suggests that:

> Additional criticism of the BP [business portfolio] approach tends to focus on its over-simplified, and somewhat misleading, representation of possible strategy positions; and its use of the dimensions growth rate and market share, which are themselves considered to be inadequate measures of, respectively, industry attractiveness, and competitive position. As Wensley concludes, this approach to strategy development 'encourages the use of general rather than specific criteria as well as implying assumptions about mechanisms of corporate financing and market behaviour which are rather unnecessary or false'. Indeed, it has been observed that market leadership does not always offer the benefits of lower costs, more positive cash flow and higher profits. On the contrary: the number of highly viable companies occupying market 'niches' is legion, and growing by the day. Recent trends that have favoured the development of greater specialisation in some markets include the growth of private label consumer products and the emergence of differential preferences in some industrial markets, for example computers, as customers become familiar with product, or develop relevant in-house expertise.
>
> The BP also tends to overlook other important and strategic factors which are more a function of the external competitive environment, for example, technological change; barriers to entry; social, legal, political and environmental pressures; union and related human factors; elasticity of demand; and cyclicality of sales. The application of the BP to strategic decision-taking is in the manner of a diagnostic rather than a prescriptive aid in instances where observed cash flow patterns do not conform with those on which the four product-market categories are based. This commonly occurs where changes in product-market strategies have short-term transient effects on cash flow.

The limitations and problems of portfolio analysis have also been highlighted by McDonald (1990, p. 2), albeit from a rather different viewpoint from that of most writers. McDonald suggests that the gap between theory and practice is greater in the case of marketing than any other discipline. One consequence of this according to McDonald is that little evidence exists to show that some of the more substantive techniques such as the Ansoff Matrix, the Boston Matrix, and the Directional Policy Matrix are used in practice. This is supported by research findings not just in the UK but also in Australia and Hong Kong. Reid and Hinckley (1989, p. 9), for example, concluded:

> Respondents were asked which techniques they were familiar with. The results were skewed towards ignorance of all the techniques to which they were exposed. The majority were not familiar with any by name.

Similarly, from a study of Australian management practice, McColl-Kennedy, et al. (1989, p. 28) stated that 'The awareness and usage of planning tools is low.'
McDonald suggests that there are three possible explanations for this:

1 companies have never heard of them;
2 companies have heard of them, but do not understand them;
3 companies have heard of them, have tried them and found that they are largely irrelevant.

More fundamentally, however, he argues that the gap between theory and practice is due to the failure of most writers' attempts to explain the strategic methodologies underpinning such techniques. He illustrates this by discussing the directional policy matrix which, he suggests, is a well-known but under-utilized and misunderstood planning tool. This misunderstanding is in one form or another common to virtually all approaches to portfolio analysis. However, in the case of the DPM, the problems stem from the complexity of the analytical process that is needed if the model is to be used effectively. Thus:

> The criteria for the vertical axis (market attractiveness) can only be determined once the population of 'markets' has been specified. Once determined, those criteria cannot be changed during the exercise. Another common mistake is to misunderstand that unless the exercise is carried out twice – once for t0 and once for t+3 – the circles cannot move vertically. Also, the criteria have to change for *every* 'market' assessed on the horizontal axis each time a company's strength in that market is assessed. Some way has also to be found of quantifying the horizontal axis to prevent every market appearing in the left hand box of the matrix. If we add to this just some of the further complexities involved, such as the need to take the square root of the volume or value to determine circle diameter, the need to understand that the term 'attractiveness' has more to do with future *potential* than with any externally derived criteria, and so on, we begin to understand why practising managers rarely use the device.

Despite criticisms such as these, portfolio analysis has many defenders, including Day (1983) who suggests that

> current criticisms (of portfolio analysis) are unwarranted because they reflect a serious misunderstanding of the proper role of these analytical methods . . . what must be realised is that these methods can facilitate the strategic planning process and serve as a rich source of ideas about possible strategic options. But on their own, these methods cannot present the appropriate strategy or predict the consequences of a specific change in strategy.

In many ways, Day's comments help to put the true role and value of portfolio analysis into perspective. It is not as some managers appeared to believe in the early days a set of techniques that guarantees greater success. Rather it is an approach to the formulation of strategy which, if used in the way intended, should force a deeper analysis and give far greater recognition to the interrelationships and implications of these interrelationships to the portfolio of brands or businesses being managed by the company. This, in turn, should lead to a far firmer base for effective decision making.

This final point in particular was highlighted in 1979 by the results of a *Harvard Business Review* sponsored study of strategic portfolio planning practices in *Fortune*'s 1000 companies. The study by Haspeslagh (1982) found that portfolio planning helped managers to strengthen their planning processes, particularly in divisionalized and diversified organizations. The secret to success, however, was found to lie not just in the techniques themselves, but also in the challenge of incorporating the theory of the techniques into managerial practice. The findings of the study did highlight several problems of portfolio planning including:

1 if done properly, the process is time consuming and firms often experience difficulties of implementation;
2 if the techniques are seen simply as analytical tools, the company sees only limited benefits;
3 all too often, the strategist focuses upon factors that are in a sense inappropriate e.g. levels of cost efficiency rather than organizational responsiveness;
4 the techniques are of only limited value in addressing the issue of new business generation.

Despite problems such as these, the techniques were found to be popular for a number of reasons:

1 they were felt to lead to improvements in strategies;

2  the allocation of resources was improved;
3  they provided an improved base for adapting planning to the needs of individual businesses;
4  levels of control improved.

## 9.7  SUMMARY

In this, the first of two chapters on strategy, we took as our primary focus the nature and development of portfolio analysis. As a prelude to this we examined the development of strategic perspectives over the past 20 years, highlighting the way in which the environmental turbulence that characterized the early 1970s led to many managers rethinking their approaches to running their businesses. The new planning perspective that emerged was, we suggested, based on three central premises:

1  a need to view and manage the company's businesses in a similar way to an investment portfolio;
2  an emphasis upon each business's future profit potential;
3  the adoption of a *strategic* perspective to the management of each business.

The starting point for portfolio analysis involves identifying the organization's *strategic business units*, an SBU being an element of the business as a whole which:

- offers scope for independent planning;
- has its own set of competitors;
- has a manager with direct profit responsibility who also has control over the profit-influencing factors.

A variety of approaches to portfolio analysis and planning have been developed, the best known of which are:

- the Boston Consulting Group's growth-share matrix;
- the General Electric multifactor matrix;
- the Shell directional policy matrix;
- the Arthur D. Little strategic condition matrix;
- Abell and Hammond's 3 × 3 investment opportunity chart.

The conceptual underpinnings in each case are broadly similar, with consideration being given in one form or another to the SBU's *competitive position* and *market attractiveness/potential*. Each of the portfolio models also encompasses a series of strategic guidelines and these were examined.

Against this background we focused upon the limitations of portfolio analysis. Although it is acknowledged that these models have encouraged managers to think strategically, to consider the economics of their businesses in greater detail, and to adopt a generally more proactive approach to management, critics have argued that the models are overly simplistic in their structure, and often require data inputs which are complex and difficult to obtain. Because of this, it is suggested, usage levels are generally low.

| 10 | The formulation of strategy 2: generic strategies for leaders, followers, challengers and nichers |
|----|---|

## 10.1 LEARNING OBJECTIVES

When you have read this chapter you should be able to understand:

(a) the need for a clear statement of marketing strategy;
(b) the types of marketing strategy open to an organization;
(c) the forces which govern competition within an industry and how they interact;
(d) the sources of competitive advantage;
(e) the influence of market position on strategy;
(f) how organizations might attack others and defend themselves;
(g) how the product life cycle influences strategy.

## 10.2 INTRODUCTION

Having used the techniques discussed in the previous chapter to identify the strengths and weaknesses of the product portfolio, the strategist should be in a far stronger position to focus upon the ways in which the organization is best capable of developing. Against this background, we now turn our attention to an examination of some of the principal factors that influence marketing strategy. We begin by examining Michael Porter's work in which emphasis is given to the need for a clear statement of a generic strategy and for this to be based upon a detailed understanding of corporate capability and competitive advantage. This is then used as the basis for a discussion of the ways in which the organization's position in the market, ranging from market leader through to market nicher, influences strategy. Finally, we turn our attention to the ways in which market and product life cycles need to be taken into account.

## 10.3 TYPES OF STRATEGY

Throughout this book we have tried to give full emphasis to the need for objectives and strategy to be realistic, obtainable, and based firmly on corporate capability. In practice, of course, this translates into an almost infinite number of strategies that are open to an organization. Porter (1980) has, however, pulled them together and identified three generic types of strategy – *overall cost leadership*, *differentiation*, and *focus* – that provide a meaningful basis for strategic thinking (see Figure 10.1). In doing this, he gives emphasis to the need for the strategist to identify a clear and meaningful selling proposition for the organization. In other words, what is our competitive stance, and what do we stand for in the eyes of our customers? Any failure on the part of the strategist to identify and communicate the selling proposition and strategy is, he suggests, likely to lead to a dilution of the offer and to the company ending up as stuck in the middle or, as it appears in Figure 10.1, a middle-of-the-roader.

**FIGURE 10.1**
*Porter's three generic strategies*

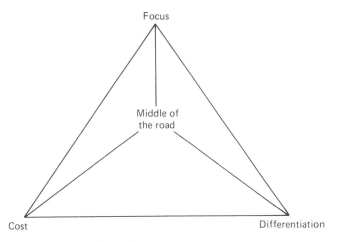

SOURCE: Adapted from Porter (1980)

Porter's thesis is therefore straightforward: to compete successfully the strategist needs to select a generic strategy and pursue it consistently. Quite obviously, there is no single 'best' strategy even within a given industry, and the task faced by the strategist involves selecting the strategic approach which will best allow it to maximize its strengths vis-à-vis its competitors. This needs to be done, Porter (1979, pp. 137–45) suggests, by taking into account a variety of factors, the five most significant of which are:

1  the bargaining power of suppliers;
2  the bargaining power of customers;
3  the threat of new entrants to the industry;
4  the threat of substitute products or services;
5  the rivalry among current competitors.

Taken together, these factors represent the forces governing the nature and intensity of competition within an industry, and they are the background against which the choice of a generic strategy should be made. The key features of these five forces are shown in Figure 10.2.

In identifying these three generic strategies, Porter suggests that the firms that pursue a particular strategy aimed at the same market or market segment make up a *strategic group*. It is the firm that then manages to pursue the strategy most effectively that will generate the greatest profits. Thus in the case of firms pursuing a low-cost strategy, it is the firm that ultimately achieves the lowest cost that will do best.

## 10.4  PORTER'S THREE GENERIC COMPETITIVE STRATEGIES

**Overall Cost Leadership**

By pursuing a strategy of cost leadership, the organization concentrates upon achieving the lowest costs of production and distribution so that it has the *capability* of setting its prices at a lower level than its competitors. Whether it then chooses to do this depends on its objectives and its perception of the market. Saunders (1987, p. 12) for example, points to IBM and Boeing, both of which are cost leaders who have chosen to use their lower costs not to reduce prices but rather to generate higher returns which have subsequently been invested in marketing, R & D and manufacturing as a means of maintaining or strengthening their position. More commonly, however, firms that set out to be cost leaders

**FIGURE 10.2**

*Porter's approach
to competitive
structure analysis*

Understanding the forces at work in any market segment is a necessary prerequisite to deducing whether – and if appropriate, how – the firm should use that segment as a strategic business area. The five forces are:

1  new entrants, potential entrants and the threat of entry;
2  substitute products/services;
3  buyers and buyer power;
4  suppliers and supplier power;
5  competitors and the nature of inter-firm rivalry.

The greater the intensity of any of these sources of competition, the harder it will be for an organization to earn profits and the greater will be the need for strategic sophistication. In the UK the intensity of competition in markets is growing. A checklist of questions can assist strategists in thinking through the strategic implications of the competitive structures of an industry:

1  What is the threat of entry into the industry and from where does it arise?
2  Where are present and potential substitute products/services located and what is their impact or likely impact on the organization and the industry?
3  Who are the buyers and what is the extent of their power with regard to the organization?
4  Who are our suppliers and what is their power with regard to the organization?
5  Who are our present and potential competitors and how intense is (or will be) present and potential competitive rivalry?

Each of these key areas can in turn be analysed to determine the intensity of competition:
1  *Potential entrants.* Threat of entry depends on the extent of barriers to entry, so:
   ● Is the potential customer base sufficient to support new operations?
   ● How heavy is the capital investment requirement in the industry? Is finance available?
   ● Is there a strong brand image to overcome?
   ● How costly will be access to distribution channels?
   ● What operating cost advantages might existing competitors hold (e.g. experienced staff, patent protection, etc.)?
   ● Is there governmental/legislative protection afforded to existing organizations?
   ● How vigorously will existing operators react against new entry attempts?
2  *Substitute products/services* will be more prevalent if:
   ● customers perceive other offers to perform the same function as ours;
   ● substitute products offer higher value for money;
   ● substitute products earn higher profits.
3  *Buyer power* is likely to be high if:
   ● there is a concentration of buyers;
   ● there are alternative sources of supply;
   ● buyers have access to useful information and tend to shop around;
   ● there is a threat of backward integration if the buyer does not obtain satisfactory supplies and prices.
4  *Supplier power* is likely to be high if:
   ● there is a concentration of suppliers;
   ● the costs of switching from one supplier to another are high;
   ● suppliers are likely to integrate forward if they do not obtain the price/profits they seek;
   ● the organization has little countervailing power.
5  *Intensity of rivalry* will be greater if:
   ● competitors are of equal size and are seeking dominance;
   ● the market is mature and subject to 'shake out' activities;
   ● high fixed costs provoke price wars to maintain capacity;
   ● product homogeneity necessitates activity to maintain share;
   ● new influxes of capacity have created excess capacity;
   ● high 'exit' barriers (legal constraints; high cost non-transferable plant and equipment; emotional commitment) exist.

SOURCE: Richardson and Richardson (1989), pp. 52–3

then use this lower cost base to reduce prices and in this way build market share – Amstrad in the 1980s was a case in point.

Although cost reduction has always been an important element of competitive strategy, Porter has commented that it became increasingly popular in the 1970s, largely because of a greater awareness of the experience curve concept. For it to succeed, he suggests that:

Cost leadership requires aggressive construction of efficient-scale facilities, vigorous pursuit of cost reductions from experience, tight cost and overhead control, avoidance of marginal customer accounts, and cost minimisation in areas like R & D, service, sales force, advertising, and so on (1980, p. 35).

In tackling costs the strategist therefore needs to recognize in advance the potential complexity of the task, since the evidence suggests that true cost leaders generally achieve this by very tight and consistent control across *all* areas of the business, including engineering, purchasing, manufacturing, distribution and marketing. An important additional element of course is the scale of operations and the scope that exists for economies of scale. However, scale alone does not necessarily lead to lower costs; rather it provides management with an *opportunity* to learn how the triad of technology, management and labour can be used more effectively (see Chapter 12). Whether these opportunities are then seized depends on the management stance and determination to take advantage of the *potential* that exists for cost cutting. Research has shown, for example, that the Japanese are most adept at gaining experience, doing so at a faster rate than the Americans, who in turn are faster than the Europeans.

While the experience curve (see pages 339–41) can provide the basis for cost reductions, manufacturers can also turn to a variety of other areas including:

1 *the globalization of operations*, including brands, in order to benefit from the economies that are not possible by operating purely on a regional basis;
2 *concentrating the manufacturing effort* in one or two very large plants in countries such as South Korea, Taiwan, and the Philippines which, currently at least, offer a low-cost base;
3 *modifying designs* to simplify the manufacturing process and make use of new materials;
4 *achieving greater labour effectiveness* by investing in new plant and processes.

The potential benefits of being a low-cost producer are quite obviously significant, since the organization is then in a far stronger position to resist all five competitive forces, out-perform its rivals, and erect barriers to entry that will help protect the organization's long-term position. In practice, however, many organizations find the long-term pursuit and maintenance of a cost-leadership strategy to be difficult. The Japanese, for example, based much of their success in the 1960s on aggressive cost management but then found that because of a combination of rising domestic costs and the emergence of new and even lower-cost competitors such as Taiwan, the position was not necessarily tenable in the long term. Although this realization coincided in many cases with a desire on the part of firms to move further up market where the scope for premium pricing is greater, the Japanese experience helps to illustrate the potential danger of an overreliance upon cost leadership. It is largely because of this that many organizations opt sooner or later for an alternative policy such as that of differentiation.

The difficulties of maintaining a cost-leadership position were also illustrated in the late 1980s and early 1990s in the UK grocery retailing sector where the low cost position had been occupied with some considerable success for a number of years by Kwik Save. The organization came under attack from an aggressive new German entrant to the market, Aldi, and faced with this, Kwik Save was forced into deciding whether to place greater emphasis on differentiation.

The effect of Aldi's entrance was not felt just by Kwik Save. Others, such as Sainsbury and Tesco, both of which had for a number of years pursued with considerable success a strategy of differentiation, were also forced to respond, albeit in a less direct way. In part, this need to respond can be seen as virtually inevitable in any mature market where the opportunities for substantial growth are limited and a new entrant is therefore able to gain sales only at the expense of firms already in the market. (This is sometimes referred to as a zero-sum game in that one organization's gain is necessarily another organization's loss.)

It is largely because of the difficulties of maintaining the lowest cost position over time and the vulnerability to a price-led attack that many organizations view cost leadership with a degree of caution and opt instead for one or other of Porter's generic strategies. Most frequently this proves to be differentiation.

**Differentiation**

By pursuing a strategy of differentiation, the organization gives emphasis to a particular element of the marketing mix that is seen by customers to be important and that as a result provides a meaningful basis for competitive advantage. The firm might therefore attempt to be the quality leader (Mercedes Benz with cars, Bang and Olufsen with hi-fi, and Marks and Spencer with food), service leader (McDonald's), marketing leader (the Japanese with cars), or the technological leader (Makita with rechargeable power tools in the early 1980s, and Dolby with noise suppression circuits for tape decks).

Differentiation can also be achieved by means of the brand image and packaging, a ploy that is particularly suited to mature markets in which the products are for the most part physically indistinguishable. This might arguably include cigarettes and beer where blind tests have shown that even highly brand loyal customers experience difficulties in identifying their favourite brand. The significance of labels and brand images, and hence their potential for differentiation, is also shown in the fashion clothing industry where brand names and logos such as Benetton, Nike and Lacoste are often prominently displayed and, by virtue of the images associated with them, used as the basis for premium pricing.

In discussing how a strategy of differentiation can be developed most effectively, Saunders (1987, p. 13) discusses the airlines industry:

> Perhaps one of the most difficult differentiation tasks is faced by the airlines who, because of bilateral agreements, are all forced to fly the same aeroplanes, to the same destinations, and charge the same prices. But as any international traveller will know, there is wide divergence in the services offered by the airlines. Singapore Airlines, Thai Airlines and Japanese Airlines have all gained their high reputation on the basis of the inflight services they provide. Some of these are on the basis of better food with more choice, free movies, many accessories freely available to passengers, and slightly more modern aircraft, but it all depends upon the attentiveness and professionalism of their cabin crews.

Differentiation can, however, prove costly if the basis for differentiation that is chosen subsequently proves to be inappropriate. Sony, for example, developed the Betamax format for its video recorders, but ultimately found that the market preferred JVC's VHS system. Despite this, differentiation is potentially a very powerful basis for strategic development, as companies such as Marks and Spencer and Sainsbury have demonstrated. Its potential is also illustrated by a McGraw-Hill study of industrial buying which estimated that most buyers would require incentives that equated to a price reduction of between 8 and 10 per cent before considering a switch to a new supplier. In commenting on this, Baker (1985, p. 110) suggests that:

> Assuming this applies to the average product with a minimum of objective differentiation, it is clear that sellers of highly differentiated products can require an even larger premium. Given higher margins the firm following a differentiated strategy is able to plough back more into maintaining the perception of differentiation through a policy of new product development, promotional activity, customer service, etc., and thereby strengthen the barriers to entry for would be competitors.

It should be apparent from this that if a strategy of differentiation is to succeed there is a need for a very different set of skills and attitudes than is suited to cost leadership. Instead of a highly developed set of cost control skills, the strategist needs to be far more innovative and flexible so that me-too companies are kept at a distance.

**Focus**
The third of the generic strategies identified by Porter involves the organization in concentrating its efforts upon one or more narrow market segments, rather than pursuing a broader based strategy. By doing this the firm is able to build a greater in-depth knowledge of each of the segments, as well as creating barriers to entry by virtue of its specialist reputation. Having established itself, the firm will typically then, depending upon the specific demands of the market, develop either a cost-based or differentiated strategy. Among those that have used this approach successfully, at least in the short term, are both Laura Ashley and Land Rover. Other firms that have used a focused strategy are Morgan with cars, Steinway with pianos, and in its early days, Amstrad with microcomputers which were designed for those with a low level of computer literacy and those who wanted low-price, easy-to-use word processing equipment.

One of the biggest problems faced by companies adopting this approach stems paradoxically from its potential for success, since as the organization increases in size, there is a tendency both to outgrow the market and to lose the immediacy of contact that is often needed. As a general rule, therefore, a focused strategy is often best suited to smaller firms since it is typically these which have the flexibility to respond quickly to the specialized needs of small segments.

Specializing in this way also enables the organization to achieve at least some of the benefits of the other two strategies since, although in absolute terms the scale of operations may be limited, the organization may well have the largest economies of scale *within* the chosen segment. Equally, the greater the degree of concentration upon a target market, the more specialized is the firm's reputation and hence the greater the degree of perceived product differentiation.

Although Porter presents competitive strategies in this way, many companies succeed not by a blind adherence to any one approach, but rather by a combination of ideas. In commenting on this, Saunders (1987, p. 14) has suggested that:

> It is apparent ... that some leading companies have not succeeded by being exclusively cost leaders, differentiators or focused. Many top companies are both cost leaders and differentiators. The buying power and expertise of Marks and Spencer make it a low cost company but it trades on quality, service and its brand name; IBM is a cost leader which also trades on customer service and Boeing has lower costs than any other aeroplane manufacturer but the 747, its most profitable product, is unique. Many of the successful low volume manufacturers complement differentiation with a clear focus. For example, Jaguar, Land Rover and Morgan in the automobile industry, and J. C. Bamford in earthmoving. Lastly, Amstrad's success needs explaining in terms of both cost leadership and focus. Its success in the hi-fi market has been based on integrated systems at the bottom of the market which the major Japanese manufacturers were neglecting. Equally, although Amstrad were cost leaders, it was its identification of segment needs which enabled it to become a major supplier with the audacity to challenge IBM.

It follows from this that the identification, development and maintenance of a competitive advantage, and hence a strong selling proposition, is at the very heart of an effective marketing strategy. In practice though, many organizations find this to be a difficult exercise. Without an advantage, however, the stark reality is that the organization runs the risk of drifting into the strategic twilight zone of being a middle of the roader or, in Porter's terms, 'stuck in the middle'.

## 10.5 IDENTIFYING POTENTIAL COMPETITIVE ADVANTAGES

**Making Use of the Value Chain**

In discussing competitive advantage, Porter (1985, Ch. 2) suggests that it:

> grows out of the value a firm is able to create for its buyers that exceeds the firm's cost of creating it. Value is what the buyer is willing to pay, and superior value stems from offering lower prices than competitors for equivalent benefits or providing unique benefits that more than offset a higher price. There are two basic types of competitive advantage: cost leadership and differentiation.

He goes on to suggest that a convenient tool for identifying and understanding the potential competitive advantages possessed by a firm is by means of value chain analysis. In making this comment, Porter gives recognition to the way in which a firm is a collection of activities that are performed to design, produce, market, deliver and support its product.

The value chain disaggregates a firm into nine strategically significant activities so that the strategist is more easily able to understand the source and behaviour of costs in the specific business and industry, and the existing and potential sources of differentiation; these nine value activities consist of five primary activities and four support activities.

The five *primary* activities that Porter refers to are concerned with the process of bringing raw materials into the organization and then modifying them in some way as a prelude to distribution, marketing and servicing them. The *support* activities, which take place at the same time, are then concerned with procurement, technology development, human resource management, and the firm's infrastructure (i.e. its management, planning, finance, accounting, and legal affairs). The strategist's job therefore involves focusing upon the levels of cost and performance in each of the nine value areas in order to identify any opportunities for improvement. The extent to which this is achieved is a measure of competitive advantage.

In searching for competitive advantage through the value chain, Porter also gives emphasis to the need to look outside the organization and to consider the value chains of supplier, distributors and customers, since improvements to each of these will also help in the search for an advantage. As an example of this, a supplier or distributor might be helped to reduce costs, with all or part of the savings then being passed to the company and used as another means of gaining cost leadership. Equally, an organization might work closely with its suppliers to ensure that particular levels of quality or service are achieved. Marks and Spencer, for example, has traditionally worked very closely with its suppliers to ensure that quality levels are maintained. Similarly, the major food retailers work with their suppliers in areas such as product development and cost control. In each case, the rationale is the same – that of achieving a competitive advantage.

Although the value chain is generally recognized to be a useful framework for searching systematically for greater competitive advantage, its usefulness in practice has been shown to vary from one industry to another. Recognition of this has led the Boston Consulting Group to develop a matrix in which they distinguish between four types of industry (see Figure 10.3).

**FIGURE 10.3**
*The Boston Consulting Group's strategic environment matrix*

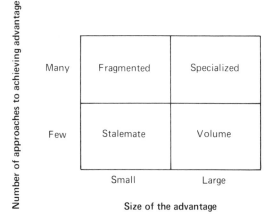

It can be seen from this that the scope for benefiting from cost or performance opportunities can vary considerably from one type of industry to another. In some industries, for example, it will be the case that the only opportunities for advantage are small and easily copied. Faced with this, an organization needs to institutionalize the process for searching for new ideas so that although it is unlikely ever to gain a significant or long-term advantage, it benefits from a whole series of small and constantly updated advantages.

The two dimensions they identify in doing this are concerned with the *size of the competitive advantage* and the *number of approaches to gaining advantage*. The characteristics of the four types of industry are outlined in Figure 10.4.

**FIGURE 10.4**
*Industry type and the scope for competitive advantage*

*Volume industry.* A volume industry is one in which organizations can typically gain only a few, but generally large, advantages. In the construction equipment industry, for example, firms can pursue either the low-cost position or the highly differentiated position, and succeed in either case. Profitability is therefore a function both of size and market share.

*Stalemated industry.* Here there are few potential competitive advantages and those that do exist are generally small. An example of this is the steel industry where scope for differentiation is limited, as indeed are the opportunities for significant cost reduction. In these circumstances, size is unrelated to profitability.

*Fragmented industry.* A fragmented industry is one in which companies have numerous opportunities for differentiation, although each is of limited value. The hairdressing industry typically exhibits this characteristic where hairdressers can be differentiated in a wide variety of ways but increases in market share tend to be small. Profitability is rarely related to size and both small and large operations can be equally profitable or unprofitable.

*Specialized industry.* In a specialized industry the opportunities for differentiation are numerous and the payoffs from each can be significant. An example would be the specialist machine tool industry where machinery is made for specific customers and market segments. Here profitability and size are rarely related.

**Developing a Sustainable Advantage**

This need to understand the bases of competition and the way in which competitive advantage is achieved has also been referred to by Bruce Henderson (1981, p. 8), the founder of the Boston Consulting Group:

> A market can be viewed in many different ways and a product can be used in many different ways. Each time the product-market pairing is varied, the relative competitive strength is varied too. Many businessmen do not recognise that a key element in strategy is choosing the competitor whom you wish to challenge, as well as choosing the market segment and product characteristics with which you will compete.

The problem faced by many companies, therefore, is not how to *gain* a competitive advantage, but how to *sustain* it for any length of time. Most marketers are, for example, fully aware of the profit potential associated with a strategy based on, say, premium quality or technological leadership. The difficulty that is all too often faced in practice, however, is how to guard against predators and capitalize on these benefits *over the long term*. Business history is full of examples of companies that having invested in a particular strategy, then fall victim to a larger organization. The question faced by many marketing strategists at one time or another is therefore how best to sustain a competitive advantage. In discussing this, Wensley (1987, p. 34) has suggested that there are three possible approaches:

1 advantages residing in the organization;
2 advantages stemming from specific functional areas;
3 advantages based on relationships with external entities.

These points were discussed in some detail in Figure 2.4.

The issue of how to develop and sustain a competitive advantage has also been discussed in detail by Davidson (1987, p. 153) 'Competitive advantage', he suggests,

> is achieved whenever you do something better than competitors. If that something is important to consumers, or if a number of small advantages can be combined, you have an *exploitable* competitive advantage. One or more competitive advantages are usually necessary in order to develop a winning strategy, and this in turn should enable a company to achieve above-average growth and profits.

For Davidson, the eight most significant potential competitive advantages are:

1 *a superior product benefit* such as the application by the Japanese of solid state technology in televisions in the 1970s,
2 *a perceived advantage*: Marlboro, with its aggressively masculine image featuring cowboys, holds a 22 per cent share of the US cigarette market; the brand is well marketed but there is no reason to believe the cigarettes are objectively superior in consumer acceptance;
3 *low-cost operations* as the result of a combination of high productivity, low overheads, low labour costs, better purchasing skills, a limited product range, or low cost distribution;
4 *legal advantage* in the form of patents, copyright, sole distributorships, or a protected position;
5 *superior contacts*;
6 *superior knowledge* as the result of more effective market research, a better understanding of costs, or superior information systems;
7 *scale advantages*;
8 *offensive attitudes* or, as Procter & Gamble label it, an attitude of competitive toughness and a determination to win.

A fundamental understanding of the significance of competitive advantage has long been at the heart of Marks and Spencer's strategies. Their performance has consistently outstripped the vast majority of retailers and has led not just to the company maintaining its position as the market leader in the clothing market, but also to its enormously successful development of food retailing. The company has concentrated on developing a series of competitive advantages which, taken together, represent a strong selling proposition, provide consumers with a powerful reason to buy, and put competitors at a disadvantage. These advantages are summarized in Illustration 10.1.

# Illustration 10.1: Marks and Spencer and its Use of Competitive Advantage to Create Distinctive Competences

Marks and Spencer have consistently been one of the most successful organizations in the UK retail sector. This success has been due to a combination of factors, but in particular to a well-developed marketing strategy that builds on a series of competitive advantages that have been used to create several distinctive competences.

| Sources of competitive advantage | Competition most affected | Distinctive competence |
|---|---|---|
| Multiple operation | Independents | |
| Systems retailer | Independents | |
| Simplified business | Department stores | |
| Emphasis on quality 100 per cent own label } | Most other retailers | Control |
| Involvement in product technology | Multiples | |
| Emphasis on economic rather than market planning | Many multiples and coops | Management of change |
| Family influence | Some 'corporate' multiples | |
| Increase in income and mobility of customers | Independents | |
| Theory Z company | Most employers | |
| Attitude to staff | Many other retailers | Human relations |
| Community involvement | Some retailers | |
| Returns policy | Many other retailers | |
| Public image | Most retailers | |

*Source: Davies, G. (1988) Marks & Spencer UK Case Study, Manchester Polytechnic*

## 10.6 THE INFLUENCE OF MARKET POSITION ON STRATEGY

In discussing how best to formulate marketing strategy, we have focused so far on the sorts of model and approach to planning that can help to formalize the analytical process. In making use of models such as these the strategist needs to pay explicit attention to a series of factors, including the organization's objectives and resources, managerial attitudes to risk, the structure of the market, competitors' strategies and, very importantly, the organization's position within the market. The significance of market position and its often very direct influence upon strategy has been discussed in detail by a wide variety of writers, most of whom suggest classifying competitive position along a spectrum from market leader to market nichers:

- *Market leader*. In the majority of industries there is one firm which is generally recognized to be the leader. It typically has the largest market share, and by virtue of its pricing, advertising intensity, distribution coverage, technological advance, and rate of new product introductions, it determines the nature, pace and bases of competition. It is this dominance which typically provides the benchmark for other companies in the industry.
- *Market challengers and followers*. Firms with a slightly smaller market share can adopt one of two stances. They may choose to adopt an aggressive stance and attack other firms, including the market leader, in an attempt to gain share and perhaps dominance (*market challengers*), or they may adopt a less aggressive stance in order to maintain the status quo (*market followers*).
- *Market nichers*. Virtually every industry has a series of small firms which survive, and indeed often prosper, by choosing to specialize in parts of the market which are too limited in size and potential to be of real interest to larger firms; a case in point would be Morgan specializing in traditional sports cars. By concentrating their efforts in this way, market nichers are able to build up specialist market knowledge and avoid expensive head-on fights with larger companies.

This approach to classification has in turn led to a considerable discussion of the strategic alternatives for leaders, challengers and nichers, with numerous analogies being drawn between business strategy and military strategy. The idea has been to show how the ideas of military strategists, and in particular Von Clausewitz, Sun-Tzu and Liddell-Hart, might be applied to the alternatives open to a company intent on gaining or retaining a competitive advantage. Within this section we will therefore examine some of these ideas and show how market leaders might defend their current position, how challengers might attempt to seize share, and how followers and nichers are affected by this.

## 10.7 STRATEGIES FOR MARKET LEADERS

Although a position of market leadership has undoubted attractions both in terms of the scope that often exists to influence others and a possibly higher return on investment, leaders have all too often in the past proved to be vulnerable in the face of an attack from a challenger or when faced with the need for a major technological change. If therefore a market leader is to remain as the dominant company, it needs to defend its position constantly. In doing this, there are three major areas to which the marketing strategist needs to pay attention:

1  how best to expand the total market;
2  how to protect the organization's current share of the market;
3  how to increase market share.

Of these, it is an *expansion of the overall market* from which the market leader typically stands to gain the most. It follows from this that the strategist needs to search for new users, new uses and greater usage levels of his or her firm's products. This can be done in a variety of ways. In the 1960s and 1970s, for example, Honda increased its sales by targeting groups that traditionally had not bought motorcycles. These groups, which included commuters and women, were seen to offer enormous untapped potential. The company unlocked this by developing a range of small, economic and lightweight machines which they then backed with a series of advertising campaigns giving emphasis to their convenience and style. Moving into the 1980s, the strategy began to change yet again as the company recognized the potential for selling motorcycles almost as an adjunct to fashion. Styling therefore became far more important. This repositioning was then taken several steps further in the late 1980s as Honda, along with other manufacturers, began targeting the middle-aged executive market with a series of larger motorcycles that were supported by advertising campaigns giving emphasis to the re-creation of youthful values.

As a second stage the strategist might search for *new uses* for the product. Perhaps the most successful example of this is Du Pont's Nylon which was first used as a synthetic fibre for parachutes and then subsequently for stockings, shirts, tyres, upholstery and carpets. This is illustrated in Figure 10.5.

**FIGURE 10.5**
*Nylon's product life cycle*

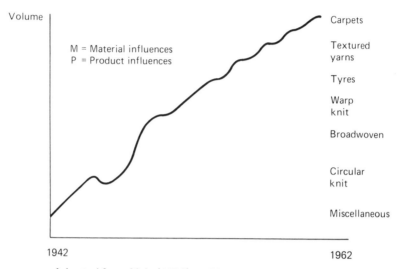

SOURCE: Adapted from Yale (1964), p. 33

The third approach to market expansion involves encouraging *existing users* of the product to *increase their usage rates*, a strategy pursued with considerable success by Procter & Gamble with its Head & Shoulders brand of shampoo which was promoted on the basis that two applications were more effective than one.

At the same time as trying to expand the total market, the market leader should not lose sight of the need to *defend its market share*. It has long been recognized that leaders represent a convenient target since, because of their size, they are often vulnerable to attack. Whether the attack is successful is often determined largely by the leader's ability to recognize its vulnerability and position itself in such a way that the challenger's chances of success are minimized. The need for this is illustrated by examples from many industries including photography (Kodak having been attacked in the film market by Fuji and in the camera market by Polaroid, Minolta, Nikon and Pentax); soft drinks (Pepsi Cola attacking Coca Cola); care hire (Avis against Hertz), potato crisps (Golden Wonder attacking Smiths, and then subsequently both companies being attacked by Walker's), razors (Bic and Wilkinson Sword attacking Gillette), and computers (IBM being attacked by, among others, Apple and Amstrad).

Although there are obvious dangers in generalizing, the most successful strategy for a leader intent on fighting off attacks such as these lies in the area of continuous innovation. This, Kotler (1988, p. 321) argues, involves the leader refusing

to be content with the way things are and leading the industry in new-product ideas, customer services, distribution effectiveness, and cost cutting. It keeps increasing its competitive effectiveness and value to customer. The leader applies the 'military principle of the offensive': the commander exercises initiative, sets the pace, and exploits enemy weaknesses. The best defence is a good offence. The dominant firm, even when it does not launch offensives, must at least guard all of its fronts and not leave any exposed flanks. It must keep its costs down, and its prices must be consonant with the value customers see in the brand. The leader must 'plug holes' so that attackers do not jump in.

Among the ways in which this can be done in the consumer goods sector at least is by producing a product in several forms (e.g. liquid soap as well as bars of soap) and in various sizes (small, medium, large and economy) to tie up as much shelf space as possible.

Although the cost of 'plugging holes' in this way is often high, the cost of failing to do so and being forced out of a product or market segment can often be infinitely higher. As an example of this, Kotler cites the camera market and the way in which Kodak withdrew from the 35 mm sector because its product was losing money. The Japanese subsequently found a way of making 35 mm cameras profitably at a low price and took share away from Kodak's cheaper cameras.

Similarly, in the United States, the major car manufacturers paid too little attention in the 1960s and early 1970s to the small car sector because of the difficulties of making them at a profit. Both the Japanese (Toyota, Mazda and Honda) and the Germans (Volkswagen) took advantage of this lack of domestic competition and developed the small car sector very profitably. The long-term consequence of this has been that the domestic manufacturers, having initially conceded this market sector, have subsequently entered into a series of joint ventures with the Japanese (e.g. Ford with Mazda, General Motors with Toyota, Isuzo, and Suzuki, and Chrysler with Mitsubishi).

The third course of action open to market leaders intent on remaining leaders involves *expanding market share*. This can typically be done in a variety of ways including by means of heavier advertising, improved distribution, price incentives, new products and, as the brewers demonstrated in the 1970s, by mergers and take-overs.

## The PIMS Study and the Pursuit of Market Share

The significance of market share, and in particular its influence upon return on investment, has long been recognized, and has been pointed to by a variety of studies over the past 20 years, the best known of which is the PIMS (Profit Impact of Market Strategy) research.

The aim of the PIMS programme, which now has a database of more than 2800 businesses, has been to identify the most significant determinants of profitability. The factors that have shown themselves to be persistently the most influential are:

1  *competitive position* (including market share and relative product quality);
2  *production structure* (including investment intensity and the productivity of operations;
3  the *attractiveness of the served market* (as shown by its growth rate and customers' characteristics.

Taken together, these factors explain 65–70 per cent of the variability in profitability among the firms in the PIMS data base. By examining the determinants of profitability it is possible to address a series of strategic questions such as:

● What rate of profit and cash flow is normal for this type of business?
● What profit and cashflow outcomes can be expected if the business continues with its present strategy?
● How will future performance be affected by a change in strategy?

One of the key notions underlying strategic marketing management is, as we have already emphasized, that of the relative position of a firm among its competitors, particularly with regard to unit costs, profitability and market share. This is reflected in the PIMS approach which is illustrated in Figure 10.6.

**FIGURE 10.6**
*Some PIMS linkages*

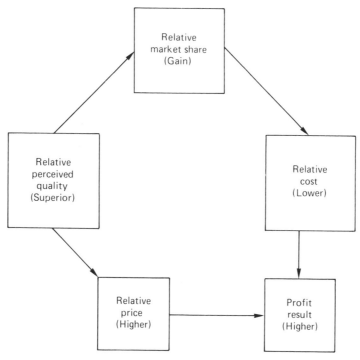

SOURCE: Buzzell and Gale (1987), p. 81

The respective contribution of each of the variables in Figure 10.6 to overall profitability is estimated by means of a multiple regression model. This allows the impact of weak variables to be offset by strong variables; a low market share might, for example, be offset by high product quality. Once the model has been applied to a given company, it can then be used to assess the relative strengths and weaknesses of competitors in order to identify the best source of competitive advantage. From the viewpoint of the marketing strategist, this has most typically been seen in terms of the organization's relative market share, a factor which has been given considerable emphasis by successive PIMS reports: 'The average ROI for businesses with under 10 per cent market share was about 9 per cent ... On the average, a difference of 10 percentage points in market share is accompanied by a difference of about 5 points in pretax ROI.' The study has also shown that businesses with a market share of more than 40 per cent achieve ROIs of 30 per cent, or three times that of firms with shares under 10 per cent.

In the light of these findings, it is not at all surprising that many organizations have pursued a goal of share increases, since it should lead not just to greater profits but also to greater profitability (that is, return on investment). Williams Holdings, for example, has consistently – and successfully – pursued an acquisition and marketing strategy that reflects this by focusing upon current or potential market leaders (see Illustration 10.2).

Although the findings and conclusions of the PIMS study have an initial and pragmatic appeal, the general approach has been subjected to an increasing amount of critical comment in recent years. In particular, critics have highlighted:

- measurement errors;
- apparent deficiencies in the model;
- the interpretations of the findings.

---

# Illustration 10.2: Williams Holdings and Its Pursuit of Market Leadership

In just eight years, Williams Holdings PLC, under the chairmanship of Nigel Rudd, grew from an annual turnover of £6 million to more than £1000 million. This was achieved by aggressive management of the firm's portfolio and a series of carefully targeted acquisitions.

The company, which now operates throughout Europe and the United States, has relentlessly pursued an objective of growth by focusing much of its efforts on 'businesses which are pre-eminent in their sphere of operations' (Annual Report for 1989, p. 13). The company's publicly stated policies include:

- owning businesses which have significant shares in their relevant markets;
- generating above average margins and cashflow to enable the companies to market their products and services aggressively;
- to invest capital consistently to create the position of lowest cost producer.

*Source: Williams Holdings PLC Annual Report, 1989, pp. 13–14*

---

Perhaps the main concern, however, is over the practice of deriving prescriptions about strategy from unsupported causal inferences. It is therefore important in using PIMS data to understand the limitations of the approach. When used in this way the PIMS programme can, its defenders argue, provide valuable insights to effective marketing and corporate strategy. In particular, they point to some of the broad conclusions from the programme which can be summarized as:

1 In the long-run, the single most important factor affecting performance is the quality of an enterprise's products/services relative to those of its competitors.
2 Market share and profitability are strongly related:
   - ROI increases steadily as market share increases;
   - enterprises having relatively large market shares tend to have above-average rates of investment turnover;
   - the ratio of marketing expenses to sales revenue tends to be lower for enterprises having high market shares.
   The PIMS programme has demonstrated the linkages among superior relative quality, higher relative prices, gains in market share, lower relative costs and higher profitability. These linkages are portrayed in Figures 10.6 and 10.7 which indicate the causal role that relative quality plays in influencing business performance.
3 High investment intensity acts as a powerful drag on profitability:
   - the higher the ratio of investment to sales, the lower the ROI;
   - enterprises having high investment intensity tend to be unable to achieve profit margins sufficient to sustain growth.
4 Many dog and wildcat activities generate cash, while many cash cows do not.
5 Vertical integration is a profitable strategy for some kinds of enterprise but not for others.
6 Most of the strategic factors that boost ROI also contribute to long-term value.

**FIGURE 10.7**
*The determinants of profitability*

SOURCE: Day (1986), p. 120

Despite these comments, however, the reader should bear in mind the very real reservations that have been expressed about the study. Baker (1985, p. 110), for example, has said that 'one should be cautious about accepting too readily the relationship between profit and market share claimed as the result of the PIMS study which is more the result of flexible definitions than reality'. Similarly, Porter (1980, p. 44) suggests:

> There is *no single relationship* between profitability and market share, unless one conveniently defines the market so that focused or differentiated firms are assigned high market shares in some narrowly defined industries and the industry definitions of cost leadership firms are allowed to stay broad (they must because cost leaders often do not have the largest share in every sub-market). Even shifting industry cannot explain the high returns of firms who have achieved differentiation industry wide and held market shares below that of the industry leader.

A number of other writers have also argued that the study's findings are generally spurious. Hamermesh, et al. (1987) for example, have pointed to numerous successful low-share businesses. Similarly Woo and Cooper (1982) identified 40 low-share businesses with pretax ROIs of 20 per cent or more.

Findings such as these suggest the existence not of a linear relationship between market share and profitability but, in some industries at least, of a V-shaped relationship. This is illustrated in Figure 10.8.

In such an industry there will be one or two highly profitable market leaders, several profitable low-share firms, and a number of medium-share, poorly focused and far less profitable organizations. This has been commented on by Roach (1981, p. 21):

The large firms on the V-curve tend to address the entire market, achieving cost advantages and high market share by realising economies of scale. The small competitors reap high profits by focusing on some narrower segments of the business and by developing specialised approaches to production, marketing, and distribution for that segment. Ironically the medium sized competitors at the trough of the V-curve are unable to realise any competitive advantage and often show the poorest profit performance. Trapped in a strategic 'No-Man's Land', they are too large to reap the benefits of more focused competition, yet too small to benefit from the economies of scale that their larger competitors enjoy.

**FIGURE 10.8**
*The relationship between market share and profitability*

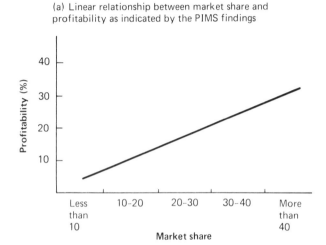
(a) Linear relationship between market share and profitability as indicated by the PIMS findings

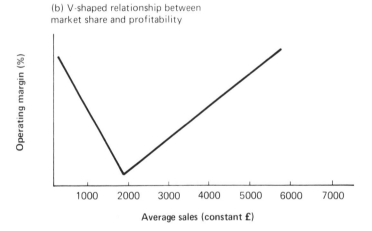
(b) V-shaped relationship between market share and profitability

Perhaps the most important point to come from this sort of observation is that the marketing strategist should not blindly pursue market share in the expectation that it will automatically improve profitability. Rather it is the case that the return will depend upon the *type* of strategy pursued. In some cases, for example, the cost of achieving a share gain may far exceed the returns that are possible. There are therefore four factors which need to be taken into account in pursuing share gains:

1 the possibility of running foul of anti-monopolies legislation;
2 the economic cost of the gain – there is considerable evidence in many markets of what might be seen as the optimal market share for any company. To go beyond this is unlikely to prove cost effective since it will involve moving into ever smaller and less appealing market segments;

3 the likelihood of competitive warfare which increases dramatically as other organizations feel threatened and begin fighting to retain share;
4 radical and possibly costly changes to the marketing mix strategy are likely to be needed if share gains are to be retained for any length of time.

These sorts of points have also been referred to by Jacobson and Aaker (1985) who in an article entitled 'Is Market Share All That It's Cracked Up To Be?' raised a series of fundamental questions about the value of chasing share gains. It is, however, possible to identify the two conditions under which higher share generally does lead to higher profits. These are, first, when the company offers a superior quality product which is then sold at a premium price which more than offsets the extra costs of achieving higher quality, and second, when unit costs fall significantly as sales and share increase.

These two points have been developed by Buzzell and Wiersema (1981) who, by using PIMS data, concluded that companies which successfully achieved gains in market share generally out-performed their competitors in three areas: *new product activity*, *relative product quality*, and *levels of marketing expenditure*. Thus:

1 the successful share gainers developed and added a greater number of new products to their range than their competitors;
2 companies that increased their relative product quality achieved greater share gains than those whose quality stayed constant or declined;
3 those companies which increased their marketing expenditures more rapidly than the rate of market growth gained share;
4 companies that cut their prices more rapidly than competitors rarely – and perhaps surprisingly – did not achieve significant share gains.

## 10.8 MARKETING STRATEGY AND MILITARY ANALOGIES: LESSONS FOR MARKET LEADERS

The greater intensity of competition that has taken place throughout the world in recent years has led to many managers developing an interest in models of military warfare with a view to identifying any lessons that might be learned and applied to business. From the viewpoint of a market leader intent on defending his position, there are six military defence strategies that can be used: position defence, mobile defence, flanking defence, contraction defence, pre-emptive defence, and counter-offensive defence. However, if military history is to teach the marketing or business strategist anything at all, it has to be that some of these strategies are likely to be far less successful than others.

**Position Defence**

Arguably one of the consistently least successful methods of defence, the position defence or fortress, relies on the apparent impregnability of a fixed position. Militarily, parallels are often drawn between this and the wartime French Maginot and German Siegfried lines, neither of which achieved their purpose. To overcome a position defence an attacker therefore typically adopts an indirect approach rather than the head-on attack that the defender expects. Among the companies that have adopted a position defence only to see it fail is Land Rover which was attacked by Toyota, Suzuki and Subaru. The company, which had developed a strong international reputation for well-made and very rugged four-wheel drive vehicles, did relatively little in the 1960s and 1970s either in terms of product or market development, and subsequently fell victim to an attack based on a lower price and 'fun' appeal. Rather than responding in an aggressive way to this, Land Rover continued with only small modifications to its strategy of selling primarily to farmers and the military, and was then faced with a second wave attack from Mitsubishi.

There are therefore several lessons to be learned from examples such as this, as Saunders (1987, p. 15) has highlighted:

> A company attempting a fortress defence will find itself retreating from line after line of fortification into shrinking product markets. The stationary company will end up with outdated products and lost markets, undermined by competitors who find superiority in new products in the market place. Even a dominant leader cannot afford to maintain a static defence. It must continually engage in product improvement, line extensions and product proliferations. For instance, giants like Unilever spread their front into related household products; and Coca-Cola, despite having over 50 per cent of the world soft drinks market, has moved aggressively into marketing wines and has diversified into desalination equipment and plastics. These companies defend their territory by breaking it down into units and entrenching in each.

## Mobile Defence

The second approach, a mobile defence, is based in part on the ideas discussed by Theodore Levitt in 'Marketing Myopia' (1960), in that rather than becoming preoccupied with the defence of current products and markets through the proliferation of brands, the strategist concentrates upon market broadening and diversification. The rationale for this is to cover new territories that might in the future serve as focal points both for offence and defence. In doing this the intention is to achieve a degree of strategic depth which will enable the firm not just to fight off an attacker, but to retaliate effectively. At the heart of a mobile defence therefore is the need for management to define carefully, and perhaps redefine, the business it is in. Several years ago, for example, the bicycle manufacturer Raleigh redefined its business by recognizing that its future was that of leisure and health rather than that of cheap and generally functional transport. Similarly, Coloroll in the mid 1980s recognized that its future was the home fashion market, including textiles and ceramics, rather than simply the wallpapers that it was making at the time.

However, in pursuing a strategy of market broadening, the marketing stategist should never lose sight of two major principles – the *principle of the objective* (pursue a clearly defined and realistic objective) and the *principle of mass* (focus your efforts upon the enemy's point of weakness). The implications of these are perhaps best understood by considering for a moment the oil industry. Faced with the likelihood of oil reserves being exhausted in the twenty-first century, the oil companies have been encouraged to redefine their business from that of petrol and oil to that of 'energy'. This has led several companies to experiment with, and in some cases invest in, nuclear energy, coal, hydroelectric power, solar energy and wind power. In the majority of cases, however, success has at best been limited and in some instances has diluted the company's mass in the markets it is operating in currently. A strategy of market broadening should therefore be realistic and reflect not just the two principles referred to above but also, and very importantly, company capability.

The second dimension of a mobile defence involves *diversification* into unrelated industries. Among those who have done this, in some cases with considerable success, are the tobacco manufacturers who, faced with a declining market, have moved into industries such as food and financial services, both of which offer greater long-term stability and profits. The net effect of this has been that their vulnerability to predators has been reduced significantly.

## Flanking Defence

It has long been recognized that the flank of an organization, be it an army or a company, is often less well protected than other parts. This vulnerability has several implications for the marketing strategist, the most significant of which is that secondary markets should not be ignored. This lesson was learned the hard way in the 1960s by Smith's Crisps, which at the time dominated the potato crisp market. This market consisted primarily of adults, with distribution being achieved mainly through pubs. The children's market was seen by the company to be of secondary importance and it was therefore this flank that Imperial Tobacco's Golden Wonder attacked with a strategy aimed at children. Distribution to this market then took place through newsagents, sweet shops and the grocery trade. The net effect of this was that within just a few years Golden Wonder had taken over as market leader.

This need to monitor closely the organization's flanks is shown also by Birds Eye's experiences in the frozen foods market. Although the company was subjected initially to a head-on attack from Findus, this achieved little. By contrast, a series of flanking moves at a later stage had the effect of changing the market structure in a variety of dramatic ways. These are discussed in Illustration 10.3.

---

# Illustration 10.3: The Frozen Foods Battleground

One of the consistently most aggressive business battlegrounds of the past 30 years has been the market for frozen foods. Pioneered in the UK by Birds Eye, the company in the 1960s held a 60 per cent market share. The remaining 40 per cent was split between Findus with 20 per cent, a number of smaller brands and a few private labels.

The first move in the market was a series of generally half-hearted head-on attacks by Findus which copied Birds Eye's strategy of superior quality – premium price. This was fought off with relative ease. A few years later in the 1970s, however, two rather more successful flanking moves took place, the first by Ross Foods and the second by stores seeking to build their private label portfolios. The private label move concentrated initially upon sectors of the market which were of little real interest to Birds Eye – the low price, moderate quality almost commodity sectors such as peas, fish fingers and burgers. Although these moves were successful, Birds Eye continued to dominate the high-quality end of the market.

Having established themselves in the commodity sector, the private label operators such as Tesco and Sainsbury shifted from a flanking strategy to a head-on attack as they concentrated on moving up-market, strengthening their reputation for frozen foods, and developing new products. At the same time, Ross Foods, which previously had been a very small player with just 2–3 per cent share of the market made use of flanking to displace Findus as the number two brand. It achieved this initially by developing a wide range of reasonable quality products in large economy packs, and then aggressively concentrating upon the private label market. Neither of these sectors was of interest either to Birds Eye or Findus. By the mid 1980s, however, the success of this strategy encouraged Ross to shift from flanking to a series of head-on attacks against Birds Eye. At the same time as this was taking place, a number of other companies were, in Michael Porter's words, jockeying for position. One of the most successful was McCain. Its strategy in the 1970s was straightforward and designed to create a niche. By the early 1980s this had changed to a flanking attack on Birds Eye, Findus and Ross. Towards the end of the 1980s this had changed yet again and began exhibiting all the characteristics of an emerging head-on attack.

The effects of these moves upon market share were significant. Although in 1985 Birds Eye was still the market leader, this was with a reduced share. Ross held 9 per cent of the market, while Findus was firmly in third place. Most dramatically, store private labels held 34 per cent.

*Source: Davidson, J. H. (1987)* Offensive Marketing, *Penguin, pp. 163–4*

## Contraction Defence

There are occasions when, faced with an actual or potential attack, a company will recognize that it has little hope of defending itself fully. It therefore opts for a withdrawal from those segments and geographical areas in which it is most vulnerable or in which it feels there is the least potential. It then concentrates its resources in those areas in which, perhaps by virtue of its mass, it considers itself to be less vulnerable. Militarily, it is a strategy which was used by Russia to great effect in defending itself against Napoleon and, subsequently, Hitler. It was, however, a strategy that was used far less effectively by the British motorcycle industry in the 1960s and 1970s, as Saunders (1987, p. 17) illustrates:

> The British motorcycle industry provides an example of a contracting defence that failed. When the Japanese attacked the moped market, and particularly the markets in South-East Asia, the British retreated and convinced themselves that the Japanese development of the sector would, in the long term, stimulate demand for larger British bikes. The retreat continued through 125 cc bikes, to 250 cc and 350 cc bikes, until eventually the only British manufacturers remaining were the super-bike manufacturers – Norton and Triumph. By the time Honda launched its own super-bikes these two, now small, British manufacturers were in no position to defend against the now much larger Honda.

## Pre-emptive Defence

Recognizing the possible limitations both of a position defence and a contraction defence, many strategists, particularly in recent years, have begun to recognize the potential value of pre-emptive strikes. This involves gathering information on potential attacks and then, capitalizing upon competitive advantages, striking first. This strike can take one of two broad forms: either the company behaves aggressively by, for example, hitting one competitor after another, or it uses psychological warfare by letting it be known how it will behave if a competitor acts in a particular way, a strategy which has been labelled FUD marketing – that is spreading 'fear uncertainty and despair'.

Among the companies that have successfully used pre-emptive defences are Procter & Gamble, and Seiko. In the case of P & G, pre-emptive behaviour has been a fundamental element of their strategy for the past few decades and takes the form of consistent and broad ranging product development, heavy advertising, aggressive pricing and a general philosophy of what is sometimes referred to as 'competitive toughness'. A similar philosophy has been pursued by Seiko which, with more than 2000 different models of watch worldwide, has made it difficult for competitors to get a foothold. The general lesson to be learned from these two companies, and indeed other market leaders, is that the company should never rest even after it has achieved domination, but should instead offer a broad range of products which are replaced frequently and supported aggressively. Any competitor is then faced with a target that is infinitely more difficult to penetrate.

## Counter-Offensive Defence

The final form of defence tends to come into play once an attack has taken place. Faced with a competitor's significant price cut, major new product, or increase in advertising, a market leader needs to respond in order to minimize the threat. This response can take one of three forms:

1 meet the attack head-on;
2 attack the attacker's flank;
3 develop a pincer movement in an attempt to cut off the attacker's operational base.

Of these, it is the first which arguably is the most straightforward and was seen in the way in which airlines responded in the 1970s to Freddie Laker's attack on prices on the North Atlantic routes. Faced with Laker's price cutting, other airlines flying these routes also cut their prices. Laker's company was eventually forced into liquidation though an inability to service its debts.

As an alternative to this sort of response, market leaders can try searching for a gap in the attacker's armour, a strategy that was used in the United States by Cadillac when faced with a stronger marketing push by Mercedes. Cadillac responded by designing a new model, the Seville, which, it claimed, had a smoother ride and more features than the Mercedes.

The final counter-offensive move involves fighting back by hitting at the attacker's base. In the United States, for example, Northwest Airlines was faced with a price cutting attack on one of its biggest and most profitable routes by a far smaller airline. Northwest responded by cutting its fares on the attacker's most important route. Faced with a significant drop in revenue, the attacker withdrew and prices were restored to their original levels.

## 10.9 STRATEGIES FOR MARKET CHALLENGERS

Companies that are not market leaders are faced with a straightforward strategic choice: either they attack other firms – including perhaps the market leader – in an attempt to build market share and achieve leadership themselves (*market challengers*), or they pursue a far less aggressive strategy and in doing so accept the status quo (*market followers*). In deciding between the two, several factors need to be taken into account, the most significant of which are the costs of attacking other firms, the likelihood of success, the eventual probable returns, and the willingness of management to engage in what in most cases will prove to be a costly fight. In commenting on the issue of returns, Fruhan (1972, p. 100) has highlighted the dangers of spending unwisely, arguing that, particularly in mature markets, management can all too easily fall into the trap of chasing market share which proves not to be cost effective.

This theme has, in turn, been picked up by Dolan (1981) who has suggested that competitive rivalry is typically most intense in industries faced with stagnant demand, high fixed costs and high inventory costs. The implications for a firm in this situation are potentially significant, since, while there may well be a need to gain share in order to benefit from greater economies of scale, not only are the costs of doing this high, but the likelihood of the sort of pyrrhic victory referred to above also increases dramatically. Recognition of this should then lead the strategist to a clearer perception of the course of action that is likely to be the most cost effective. In practice, this means choosing between:

1 attacking the market leader;
2 attacking firms of similar size to itself but which are either under-financed or re-active;
3 attacking smaller regional firms.

In making this choice a variety of factors need to be considered, but particularly the competitive consequences. Picking off a series of small regional players is, for example, often far more profitable than attacking the market leader. This point has been highlighted by Porter (1985, p. 91) who suggests that:

> trying to take business away from the competitor that holds the largest share of a market, or makes the most money from that market, may be the most dangerous move a company can make ... the leader, by virtue of its preeminent position, can afford to cut prices, rain down new products on rivals, or bury their offerings under an advertising blitz – in short the big guy can make the business miserable for everyone else.

If, however, a company does take on the market leader and succeeds, the rewards both in terms of the power and financial returns that are possible can be considerable. It is largely because of this that many challengers opt for the high risk–high return route. For those who do pursue this route there are several guidelines that emerge from the experience of others. These involve the challenger meeting three basic conditions:

1 He must have a *sustainable* competitive advantage either in terms of cost or differentiation.
2 He must be able to partly or wholly neutralize the leader's advantages, typically by doing almost as well as the leader that which the leader does best.
3 There must be some impediment to the leader retaliating. Most commonly this might be because the leader will run foul of anti-monopolies legislation or has an enormous and inflexible commitment to a particular technology that the challenger can side-step. (For a discussion of how this was used by Michelin, see Illustration 10.4.)

---

# Illustration 10.4:  Michelin and Its Use of Technological Flanking

Michelin, the French tyre manufacturer, used a strategy of technological flanking to enormous effect in the United States when it moved from an exporting base to local manufacture in 1975. The market at the time was dominated by four US manufacturers – Goodyear, Firestone, Uniroyal and Goodrich – who had for years concentrated on supplying the original equipment market (OEM) with cross-ply tyres. Although the profit margins were very low (according to one analyst, they were only pennies per tyre), the strategy guaranteed long production runs, kept brand names in front of consumers, ensured a lucrative replacement market 12–15000 miles later and, because the technology was well established, meant only a minimal sum needed to be spent on research and development. Michelin, by contrast concentrated its efforts on supplying the specialist replacement market with high quality radial tyres.

In the mid to late 1970s, the market for tyres began to change in a number of fundamental ways. The catalyst for this was the Arab–Israeli war at the beginning of the 1970s and the consequent rise in fuel prices. Motorists responded by driving fewer miles, with the result that the lucrative replacement market slowed down. The major car manufacturers responded to the call for greater fuel efficiency by switching to radial tyres as original equipment; radial tyres can reduce fuel consumption by 5–7 per cent. Michelin capitalized on this by aggressively forcing its way into the OEM market and by careful use of its reputation for quality and innovation, captured 25 per cent of the $4 billion market.

Faced with this, the US manufacturers' response was disorganized. More significantly, they were hampered by a lack of manufacturing know-how. Firestone's response, for example, involved counter-attacking with its '500' series, but this failed because of problems of quality. Other, and broader, problems also began to emerge as the industry slowly came to terms with the consequences for the replacement market of the new technology. Radial tyres typically last twice as long as cross-plys and, given the average car, reduced the replacement market opportunities substantially. Faced with a rapidly shrinking market, fixed capacity and substantial inventories, the US manufacturers were forced into an agressive and unprofitable cut-throat price war.

*Source: James, B. G. (1985)* Business Wargames, *Penguin, p. 54*

Although ideally the challenger will meet all three of these conditions, fulfilling just one or two can often offset a degree of weakness in meeting the others. In the United States, for example, the no-frills airline People Express began with the benefits of a lower cost base than its competitors – pilots' salaries were lower than the norm, staffing levels were low, and there was little job demarcation – which were passed on to customers in the form of lower prices. Their product, a cramped seat, was sufficiently similar to the cramped seats of other operations for the market leaders to be unable to persuade customers there was a difference. The condition that People Express was unable to meet was the lasting impediment to retaliation, and eventually others in the industry fought back by matching the People Express prices. Having exhausted the growth potential offered on routes that the majors had largely neglected, People Express was forced to look to the more competitive routes if it was to continue growing, and this sparked off a further round of price cutting and retaliation (see Richardson (1988) pages 17–19, 38).

A successful attack by a challenger is therefore typically based on a degree of reconfiguration of the activities that make up the business, be it in the form of design, manufacture or delivery. If the challenger is unable to do this, the safest option is often to ignore the leader and to pursue instead others in the industry who are of equal size or who are smaller and potentially more vulnerable. In this way, any competitive response is likely to be more manageable.

The choice of *who* to challenge is thus fundamental and is a major determinant not just of the likelihood of success, but also of the costs and risks involved. However, once this has been done, the strategist is then in a position to consider the detail of the strategy that is to be pursued. Returning to the sorts of military analogies discussed earlier, this translates into a choice between five strategies: a frontal attack, a flanking attack, an encirclement attack, a bypass attack, and a guerilla attack. But before choosing among these we need to return for a moment to the more fundamental issue referred to above of *who* to attack and *when*. In deciding this, the options, as we have suggested, can be seen in terms of an assault on the market leader (a high-risk but potentially high-return strategy); an attack upon companies of similar size; or an attack upon the generally larger number of smaller and possibly more vulnerable firms in the industry. In choosing among these various targets, the strategist is likely to be influenced by a variety of factors, including perception of the leader's likely response, the availability of the resources needed to launch an effective attack, and the possible pay-offs. In addition, however, the strategist should also perhaps be influenced by the findings of the military historian, Liddell-Hart. In an analysis of the 30 most important conflicts of the world from the Greek wars up to World War One (this included 280 campaigns), Liddell-Hart concluded that a direct head-on assault succeeded on only six occasions. By contrast, indirect approaches proved not only to be far more successful, but also more economic. This thinking, when applied to business, has led to a series of guidelines for challengers which are summarized in Figure 10.9.

**Frontal Attacks**

The conventional military wisdom is that for a frontal or head-on attack to succeed against a well-entrenched opponent, the attacker must have at least a 3:1 advantage in firepower; history suggests that broadly similar lessons apply to business.

In launching a frontal attack, a market challenger can opt for either the *pure frontal atack* by matching the leader product for product, price for price, and so on, or a rather more *limited frontal attack* by attracting away selected customers. Although the record of success with a pure frontal attack is, as we commented above, generally limited, examples of companies that have adopted this approach and succeeded do exist. Included among these is Xerox who in the copying market attacked companies such as Gestetner and 3M and who by virtue of a better product captured the market. (Subsequently, Xerox has itself been attacked

**FIGURE 10.9**

*Attack strategies for market challengers*

It has long been recognized that market challengers only rarely succeed by relying on just one element of strategy. Instead, success depends on designing a strategy made up of several strands which, by virtue of their cumulative effect, give the challenger a competitive advantage. The 10 most commonly used and successful strategic strands used by challengers are:

1 *Price discounting*. Fuji attacked Kodak by offering photographic film and paper which they claimed was of the same quality as the market leader, but 10 per cent cheaper. A similar strategy was pursued by Amstrad in the personal computer market.

2 *Cheaper goods*. Aldi's attack in the grocery retailing market was based on providing a different quality – price combination than that of the other players in the market. Similarly, the coach travel company National Express has based its attack upon British Rail on a strategy of lower prices.

3 *Product innovation*. By offering a constant stream of new and updated products, a challenger gives buyers a powerful reason for changing their purchasing patterns. Among those to have done this successfully are Polaroid with cameras and, in the 1970s, Apple with microcomputers.

4 *Improved services*. Avis challenged Hertz, the market leader in the car hire market, with a strategy that promised a faster and higher level of service. Its advertising slogan, 'Avis, we're number two, we try harder', is now part of advertising mythology.

5 *Distribution innovation*. Timex watches achieved considerable sales success as the result of a strategy which pioneered a new approach to watch distribution. Rather than selling the product through specialist jewellery stores, the company opted for a far broader approach by distributing through chain stores and supermarkets.

6 *Intensive advertising*.

7 *Market development*. Walker's Crisps achieved considerable success in the 1960s by focusing on the previously ignored market sector of children. The market leader, Smiths, had traditionally concentrated on adults and had distributed through pubs. The attack on such a different front took Smiths by surprise.

8 *Prestige image*. Much of the success achieved in the car market by Mercedes and BMW has been based on the development of an image of quality, reliability and consumer aspiration.

9 *Product proliferation*. The success of Seiko's attack on other watch manufacturers owes much to its strategy of developing some 2400 models designed to satisfy fashion, features, user preferences and virtually anything else that might motivate consumers.

10 *Cost reduction*. Many Japanese companies entered the European and North American markets in the 1960s and 1970s on the back of a cost-reduction, price-led strategy designed to put pressure on domestic manufacturers. Subsequently, a large number of these Japanese companies have modified their approach and repositioned by, for example, emphasizing quality, reliability and prestige. Their place has now been taken by a second wave of companies, this time from Korea, Taiwan and the Philippines which are emphasizing cost reduction and lower prices.

by a large number of companies including Sharp, Canon, Panasonic, Toshiba and Mita.)

A similar frontal attack was used to great effect by the Japanese producers of magnetic recording tape. Having pioneered the market in the 1960s, 3M fell victim to a series of aggressive pricing moves in the 1970s led by TDK. The effect on 3M was significant and by 1982 it had been forced into the position of a minor player.

More frequently, however, it is the case that, as Saunders (1987, p. 18) has pointed out, a pure frontal attack proves to be an expensive failure as was shown by Laker's attack on larger airlines such as British Airways, Pan Am and TWA, and in the main frame computer market in the early 1970s by the attacks by RCA, Xerox and General Electric upon IBM.

Returning for a moment to 3M, the company seemingly learned a great deal from its experience with magnetic tape and acted to ensure that the same thing did not happen with videotapes. As the market leader and with a strong reputation for quality, 3M launched a second brand, EXG, to ensure dominance in the premium-quality, premium-priced sector. It then capitalized on its distribution strengths by opting for intensive distribution covering office suppliers to chain stores. With regard to price, it matched the Japanese blow for blow to ensure that it maintained its leadership position.

**Flank Attack**

As an alternative to a costly and generally risky frontal attack many strategists have learned the lesson from military history that an indirect approach is both more economical and more effective. In business terms, a flanking attack translates into an attack on those areas where the leader is geographically weak and in market segments or areas of technology which have been neglected. It was the geographical approach that was used in the late 1960s and early 1970s by Honeywell in competing in the United States against IBM. Quite deliberately, the company concentrated its efforts on the small- and medium-sized cities in which IBM's representation, while still high, was not as intense as in the major cities. A similar geographical approach was adopted by the Japanese motorcycle industry which concentrated its efforts progressively on Asia, the United States and then Europe.

As an alternative, many companies have opted for *technological flanking* or leap-frogging. Among those to have done this with considerable success are the Japanese in the car industry who rewrote the rules of how to mass produce cars to such an extent that not only did they manage to undercut the traditional market leaders, but also reversed the flow of technology transfer in the industry.

Others to have used technological flanking include Michelin, whose experiences were discussed in Illustration 10.4, and the state-owned French helicopter manufacturer, Aerospatiale. Aerospatiale's competitors – Bell Helicopter, Sikorsky and Boeing – worked to full capacity for several years to satisfy the enormous military demand for helicopters in the Vietnam war and had little time for major technological developments. Aerospatiale took advantage of this and in 1980 simultaneously introduced three new generation fast twin-turbine models designed to cover all conceivable military and civilian needs. These models all featured Aerospatiale developed fail-safe rotor blades manufactured not from conventional metal but from composite materials.

Segmental flanking has been used to equal effect by numerous companies, including Hewlett-Packard with mini computers, Apple with micros, and Toyota and Volkswagen in the United States with small, economical cars. The lesson in each case is straightforward: identify the areas of market need not being covered by the market leader and then concentrate resources on building both size and share. In doing this, it is, however, essential that the attacker moves quickly, since the challenge becomes clearer over time and can lead to a sudden competitive response in which the company being attacked regains the initiative. In the majority of cases, however, the company being attacked either fails to recognize the significance of the challenge or is unsure of how best to retaliate and as a result responds only slowly. Bic, for example, flanked Gillette in razors by developing the low-priced sector, while Knorr and Batchelor flanked Heinz with the introduction of low-priced soups shortly after Heinz had fought off a head-on attack by Campbells. In both cases, the defender was slow to respond, possibly because of a fear that a stronger reaction would speed up the growth of the low-price sector.

**Encirclement Attack**

Whereas flanking in its purest form involves an attack on just one front, encirclement has parallels with a blitzkrieg in that it involves launching an attack on as many fronts as possible in order to overwhelm the competitor's defences. In this way, the defender's ability to retaliate effectively is reduced dramatically. Although quite obviously an expensive strategy to pursue and one which is almost guaranteed to lead to significant short-term losses, its record of success in the hands of certain types of company is impressive. Seiko, for example, has made use of a strategy of encirclement not just with the sheer number of models which are changed constantly, but also by acquiring distribution in every watch outlet possible and by heavy advertising which gives emphasis to fashion, features, user preferences, and everything else that might motivate the consumer. Equally, the Japanese motorcycle, audio and hi-fi manufacturers, having started with flanking strategies, quickly developed these into encirclement strategies with an emphasis on rapid product life cycles, frequent and radical new product launches, wide product ranges, aggressive pricing, strong dealer support and, in the case of the motorcycle companies, a successful racing programme. Other companies that have made use of encirclement, admittedly with varying degrees of success, include Yamaha against Honda (see Illustration 10.5), and the Japanese construction machinery manufacturer Komatsu in its attack on the market leader, Caterpillar.

---

## Illustration 10.5:  Yamaha and Its Attack Upon Honda

By the early 1960s, Honda had established itself in the United States as the undisputed marker leader in the motorcycle market. Its aggressive sales, distribution, and product development strategy had had a significant effect on the size and profitability of the market, and led Yamaha to enter the market against Honda. It began by identifying Honda's weaknesses and areas of potential vulnerability. These included a number of successful but complacent dealers, a series of management changes, and the discouragement of some new and more aggressive franchise seeking dealers.

Yamaha offered its own franchises to the best of these dealers and recruited an ambitious sales force to train and motivate them. It then invested heavily in the design of its motorcycles so that it could justifiably claim and demonstrate their mechanical superiority. The company capitalized on this with an extensive and costly advertising programme designed to increase buyer awareness and dealer motivation. When motorcycle safety became a significant issue, Yamaha invested in safety features and promoted them extensively.

The combined effect of these strategies led to Yamaha achieving the clear number two position in the market. Yamaha's president, Hisao Koike, then launched a major attack on Honda in order to achieve leadership. With an advertising slogan 'Yamaha take the lead', new models were launched in an attempt to encircle Honda. The plan failed and Yamaha found itself with high inventory levels. This forced the company to reduce its workforce by 2000 employees. Koike resigned, and what was subsequently labelled 'Yamaha's Kamikaze attack' was withdrawn.

---

In the case of Komatsu and Caterpillar, Komatsu's attack on the market leader was based on the slogan used internally, 'Encircle Caterpillar'. This translated into a series of attacks on market niches, improvements in product quality, extensions to its product range, and pricing at levels 10–15 per cent lower than those of Caterpillar.

**Bypass Attack**    The fourth approach, a bypass attack, is in the short term at least the most indirect of assaults, in that it avoids any aggressive move against the defender's existing products or markets. Instead, the strategist typically concentrates on developing the organization by focusing on *unrelated products* (the Japanese consumer electronics firms developing video recorders and compact discs rather than traditional audio-visual products); *new geographical markets* for existing products and, in the case of the hi-tech industries, by *technological leap-frogging*. Among those to have used a bypass attack successfully are Sturm Ruger and YKK.

Sturm Ruger, a small US gun manufactuerr, recognized in the early 1950s that it did not have the resources to develop a product range that would enable it to compete effectively against Colt, Remington and Browning. It therefore concentrated on a bypass strategy by producing a limited range of high quality and competitively produced guns that earned a reputation for being the best in their class. In this way, Sturm Ruger managed over a 30-year period to capture almost 20 per cent of the US domestic sporting guns market.

A broadly similar strategy was pursued in the zip fasteners market by YKK. The North American market had long been dominated by Talon. YKK therefore concentrated on avoiding a head-on confrontation with the market leader and, by selling direct to fashion houses, managed both to bypass Talon and turn their zip fasteners into a high-fashion item which commanded a premium price. By doing this, YKK captured 30 per cent of the US market. The same strategy was subsequently used in Europe to achieve broadly similar results.

**Guerilla Attack**

The fifth option open to a challenger is in many ways best suited to smaller companies with a relatively limited resource base. Whereas frontal attacks, flanking, encirclement and even bypass attacks are generally broad based and costly to pursue, a guerilla attack is made up of a series of hit-and-run moves designed to demoralize the opponent as a prelude to destabilizing and keeping the competitor off-balance. In practice, this typically involves drastic short-term price cuts (see Illustration 10.6), sudden and intensive bursts of advertising, product comparisons, damaging public relations activity, poaching a competitor's key staff, legislative moves, and geographically concentrated campaigns. The success of such a strategy has been shown to depend in part upon the competitor's response. In some cases, for example, the competitor chooses to ignore the attack, as has been seen with the way in which the major airlines have deliberately not responded to Virgin's lower prices on the North Atlantic routes. In others, however, the competitor fights back quickly and aggressively in order to minimize any long-term threat. All too often, dealing with guerilla attacks proves to be difficult. In the cream-cracker biscuits market, for example, Nabisco's Jacob's brand has long been the market leader. United Biscuits, which has only a small share of the market with its Crawford's brand, has made use of the brand to harass Jacob's with a series of guerilla attacks, normally in the form of low-priced activity.

## Illustration 10.6: Boots and Its Guerilla Pricing Strategy in the United States

The success of an unconventional and aggressive approach to competition was graphically illustrated by Boots' launch of its Rufen brand of ibuprofen, an anti-arthritic drug, into the US in the late 1980s. The company had previously licensed ibuprofen to Upjohn who had marketed the drug as Motrin.

On entering the market with Rufen, Boots pursued an unexpectedly radical penetration pricing strategy to gain market share. The drug was sold at a 20 per cent discount under Motrin's price, plus a $1.50 rebate to patients every time they bought a 100-tablet bottle, an approach which had never previously been used in the industry.

Because the government's Medicare and Medicaid programmes reimbursed pharmacists only for the lowest cost drug suited to the treatment, Boots rapidly gained a substantial part of the 20 per cent of Motrin's sales to the two programmes. In addition, because a substantial proportion of arthritis sufferers are elderly, Boots' strategy proved to be particularly appealing to a large number of price-sensitive consumers who paid for treatment themselves.

*Source: James, B. G. (1985)* Business Wargames, *Penguin, p. 64*

The value of guerilla attacks is also shown by the way in which Lever Bros responded to a new formulation of Daz by Procter & Gamble. The new formulation, which involved adding more bleach and a fluorescer to the product, gave P & G the opportunity to claim a superior whiteness, something which is, of course, a major selling proposition in the washing powder market. The product's selling price was not increased, even though the costs of development and advertising were high; P & G's assumption seemingly was that the major competitor, Omo, would be deterred from following because of this cost. In the event, Lever Bros responded not with Omo, but instead with its smaller fighting brand, Surf. In this way, Lever managed to invalidate the Daz claim at a relatively low cost.

## 10.10  STRATEGIES FOR MARKET FOLLOWERS

As an alternative to challenging for leadership, many companies are content to adopt a far less proactive posture simply by following what others do. The attractions of this have been pointed to by a variety of writers, including Levitt (1966, p. 63) and Kotler (1988, p. 339). Levitt, for example, suggested that a strategy of product imitation can often be as profitable as a strategy of innovation. Similarly, Kotler has pointed to the way in which

> the innovator bears the huge expense of developing the new product, getting it into distribution, and informing and educating the market. The reward for all this work and risk is normally market leadership. However, another firm can come along, copy or improve the new product, and launch it. Although this firm probably will not overtake the leader, the follower can achieve high profits, simply because it did not bear any of the innovation expense.

For many firms, therefore, the attractions of being and indeed remaining a market follower can be considerable. This is particularly so when the true costs and risks of challenging an entrenched leader are recognized. If a company is to challenge a market leader successfully, it is essential that the basis for challenging is truly worthwhile and meaningful; in practice, this would generally mean a major breakthrough in terms of innovation, price or distribution, something which in relatively long-established and stable industries is often difficult to achieve. Without a major breakthrough such as this, any attack is almost certain to fail since most market leaders will not only have the benefit of better financing, but will also be more firmly entrenched.

Recognizing this leads the majority of market followers to accept the status quo, and to pursue a course of action that avoids the risk of confrontation and retaliation. In strategic terms this often translates into copying the market leaders by offering broadly similar products, prices and levels of service; this is sometimes referred to as a *me-too strategy*. The net effect is that direct competition is avoided and market shares tend to remain relatively stable over a considerable period.

These comments should not, however, be taken to mean that market followers do not have their own distinct strategies. Indeed, as Saunders (1987, p. 21) has pointed out, the strategies of successful low-share followers tend to exhibit a number of common characteristics, including:

1 Careful market segmentation, competing only in areas where their particular strengths were highly valued.
2 Efficient use of limited R & D budgets – they seldom won R & D battles but channelled their R & D spending into areas that were most likely to generate the greatest financial payoff, in terms of return on R & D expenditure. Where R & D capabilities were available, they concentrated on truly innovative products.

3 They thought small and stayed small. They tended to emphasise profitability rather than sales growth and market share, concentrating on specialisation rather than diversification, high value added rather than mass products, quality rather than quantity.

4 The companies were willing to challenge conventional wisdom – their leaders were often strong willed, committed and involved in almost all aspects of their companies' operations.

It follows from this that the need for a follower to develop a clear and well-formulated strategy is just as great as it is for an infinitely more proactive market leader or challenger. In practice, however, many market followers fail to recognize this and pursue a 'strategy' that is largely implicit and derivative. At the very least a follower needs to recognize the importance of positioning itself so that its customer base is not eroded, that sales increase in line with rates of market growth, and that it is not overly vulnerable to more aggressive and predatory market challengers. This is particularly important when it is remembered that challengers can gain share in three ways, including by taking sales from smaller or equal sized competitors (see page 261). A market follower in these circumstances can often prove to be an attractive and vulnerable target.

Followers do therefore need to decide how they intend operating and, in particular, how closely they intend following the market leader. In doing this it is essential that the firm reduces its vulnerability as much as possible by a combination of tight cost control, an early recognition of developing opportunities, and a clear product and service strategy. This final point is particularly significant since there is a danger of seeing market followers quite simply as imitators of the market leader. Where this does happen the dangers of confusion among customers increases and the reasons for buying from the follower decrease markedly.

It is possible to identify three quite distinct postures for market followers, depending on just how closely they emulate the leader:

1 *following closely* with as similar a marketing mix and market segmentation combination as possible;
2 *following at a distance* so that although there are obvious similarities, there are also areas of differentiation between the two;
3 *following selectively* both in product and market terms so that the likelihood of direct competition is minimized.

## 10.11 STRATEGIES FOR MARKET NICHERS

The fourth and final strategic position for a firm is that of a market nicher. Although niching is typically associated with small companies, it is in practice a strategy that is also adopted by divisions of larger companies in industries in which competition is intense and the costs of achieving a prominent position are disproportionately high. The advantages of niching can therefore be considerable, since if properly done it is not only profitable, but also avoids confrontation and competition.

The attractiveness of a market niche is typically influenced by several factors, the most significant of which Kotler (1988, p. 342) identifies as follows:

1 [It] is of sufficient size and purchasing power to be profitable;
2 the niche has growth potential;
3 the niche is of negligible interest to major competitors;
4 the firm has the required skills and resources to serve the niche effectively;
5 the firm can defend itself against an attacking major competitor through the customer goodwill it has built up.

It is specialization that is at the heart of effective niching, something which was recognized by retailers such as Sock Shop, Tie Rack and Knickerbox in the 1980s, and, as discussed ind Illustration 10.7, by Avon in the tyre market.

---

# Illustration 10.7: Avon and the Development of a Niche Market

As one of the world's smallest tyre producers, Avon is dwarfed by multinationals like Goodyear, Michelin, Pirelli and Continental. Despite this, the organization proved to be remarkably successful during a period in which the industry was plagued with problems of chronic overcapacity, inefficient production processes, and a series of changes in buying patterns as radial tyres took over from cross-plys and the sales of remoulds and secondhand tyres increased.

Faced with changes such as these, Avon's initial response in the early 1980s was to cut its manufacturing capacity by a third and make 800 people redundant. Recognition, however, that this was at best a short-term solution led to a slow but fundamental change in the entire business and in particular to the search for market niches. The two that were identified as offering the greatest scope were high-performance motorcycle tyres and high-performance car tyres.

Although the motorcycle market is small in comparison with the car market – 50 000 tyres against some 20 million – it has the advantage not just of being far easier to target, but more discerning, selective and potentially far more brand loyal.

Although the company also still makes conventional car tyres, the strategy has concentrated upon developing an image of high quality to avoid being sucked into the bottom end of the market. In doing this, Avon invested in developing a car racing division and, by avoiding Formula One racing where tyres are supplied free of charge to the racing teams, makes a profit.

The third part of the organization's strategy involved developing tyres for the high-performance sector of the car market. This sector accounts for around 25 per cent of the UK car market and within this Avon has built its reputation on its involvement with racing and on the fact that it has long been an original equipment supplier to Rolls Royce, Bentley and Aston Martin.

*Source: Crainer, S. (1990) A Niche for High Performance, Marketing Business, 13 October, pp. 14–15*

---

Specialization can, however, prove dangerous if the market changes in a fundamental way either as the result of greater competition or an economic down turn and the nicher is left exposed. For this reason, there is often a strong argument for multiple niching rather than single-sector niching.

The potential profitability of niching has been pointed to by a variety of consultants and authors over the past few years, including McKinsey, and Biggadike. Two of McKinsey's consultants, Clifford and Cavanagh (1985) for example, found from a study of successful mid-size companies that their success was directly attributable to the way in which they niched within a large market rather than trying to go after the whole market. Equally, Biggadike (1977) in a study of 40 firms that entered established markets found that the majority chose to concentrate upon narrower product lines and narrower market segments than the rather better established incumbents.

In terms of how market nichers operate, there are several guidelines that can be identified. These include:

1 specializing geographically;
2 specializing by the type of end user;
3 specializing by product or product line;
4 specializing on a quality/price spectrum;
5 specializing by service;
6 specializing by size of customer;
7 specializing by product feature.

## 10.12 THE DANGERS OF STRATEGIC WEAR-OUT

Regardless of whether the company is a leader, follower, challenger or nicher, the marketing strategist needs to recognize that even the most successful of strategies will, sooner or later, begin to wear out and lose its impact. It is therefore essential that strategies are modified both to anticipate and meet changing competitive challenges and consumer needs. Among the companies that have failed to do this are Polaroid and the large mail order companies. In the case of Polaroid, its winning strategies of the 1960s and 1970s failed to change sufficiently to come to terms with the radically different markets of the 1980s as non-instant competitors improved product performance and the high street witnessed an explosion in the number and reliability of shops offering one-hour and 24-hour photographic development services.

Similarly, the mass market mail-order companies failed in the 1970s to come to terms with the changing role of women, their greater spending power, the smaller numbers staying at home during the day, the greater attractions of the high street, and the greater availability of instant credit. The result was a rapid decline in their share of consumer spending, an increasingly tired looking sales formula, and perhaps more fundamentally, an apparent absence of any real understanding of how to fight back.

Quite obviously, the vulnerability of a company to a predator in these circumstances increases enormously and highlights the need for regular reviews of strategy. In many cases, however, and particularly when a company has been successful, management often proves reluctant to change what is seen to be a winning strategy. The need for change often becomes apparent only at a later stage when the gap between what the company is doing and what it should be doing increases to a point at which performance and prospects begin to suffer in an obvious way. It is by this stage that an observant and astute competitor will have taken advantage of the company's increased vulnerability. The argument in favour of regular environmental and strategic reviews is therefore unassailable and reinforces the discussion of Chapter 2. Specifically, the sorts of factor which contribute to strategic wear-out include:

- changes in market structure as competitors enter or exit;
- changes in competitors' stances;
- competitive innovations;
- changes in consumers' expectations;
- economic changes;
- legislative changes;
- technological changes; these include in some instances the emergence of a new technology which at first sight is unrelated or only indirectly related to the company's existing sphere of operations;
- distribution changes;
- supplier changes;
- a lack of internal investment;
- poor control of company costs;
- a tired and uncertain managerial philosophy.

We commented at an earlier stage in this book that for many companies strategic development often proves to be a painful and unnatural process. Recognizing this, it is perhaps understandable that having developed a seemingly successful strategy, many management teams are content either to stick with the strategy or change it only marginally over time.

## 10.13  THE ATTRACTIONS OF BEING A MARKET PIONEER

A variety of studies over the past decade covering a broad range of mature consumer and individual goods businesses have shown that market pioneers – the companies that did most to develop particular market sectors in their early days – typically have a substantially higher market share than late entrants to the market. The attractions of market leadership have already been highlighted within this chapter and it follows from this that a pioneering approach can have considerable benefits. Among those who have pointed to this are the PIMS researchers, and Robinson and Fornell.

Within the PIMS research a business is classified as:

1  one of the *pioneers* responsible for developing products or services within the market;
2  an *early follower* of the pioneer in a still growing and dynamic market;
3  a *later entrant* to a longer established market sector.

Using this framework, Robinson and Fornell (1985 and 1986) examined average market shares for each of these categories. The results are shown in Table 10.1.

Table 10.1  **Average market share**

|  | Consumer goods | Industrial goods |
|---|---|---|
| Pioneer | 29% | 29% |
| Early follower | 17% | 21% |
| Late entrant | 13% | 15% |

Recognizing the potential attractions in this way should lead a market pioneer to consider carefully the strategic options open to the firm. In doing this, the strategist needs to take account of a variety of factors, but especially the anticipated life of the market. If, for example, it seems likely that the market will have only a short life, the strategy should be designed to maximize short-term returns. If, however the market offers longer-term scope, the pioneer should identify first which particular product markets it should focus on, and then second how best to sustain its competitive advantage. Returning for a moment to the work of Robinson and Fornell, there appear to be several guidelines for success which can be summarized as 'pioneers tend to have higher product quality and broader product lines than late entrants . . . [and] they gain a brand name advantage because being first is an effective way to secure a position in the consumer's mind. This is especially important in markets where consumers buy out of habit'. Perhaps surprisingly they did not find that pioneers benefited from significant direct cost savings:

> while cost savings are roughly 1 to 2 per cent, the associated market share impact is less than one share point. In these mature markets, patents and trade secrets do not benefit pioneers . . . sustainable competitive advantages are typically developed in the market place and not in the patent office.

For a firm to remain as a market pioneer requires therefore a degree of forethought, with attention being paid both to the short- and long-term profit opportunities of each segment and to the likely entry points and strategies of competitors. In commenting on this, Frey (1982) discusses the shape and implications of the competitive life cycle that pioneers are likely to encounter. This begins with the pioneers being in the position of the sole supplier with 100 per cent of the market's production capacity and sales. There follows a stage of competitive penetration in which the pioneer's share of production capacity and sales begins to fall. As others enter the market the degree of price competition tends to increase, with the result that the scope for premium pricing on the part of the pioneer declines. As the market develops yet further and more firms enter the market the perceived value of the product tends to decline, with the result that there is a gradual shift towards what Frey describes as 'commodity competition'. At this stage profit margins throughout the industry tend to be low and one or more firms may decide to withdraw. The pioneer, who is likely still to dominate the market, may take this opportunity either to increase his share further or instead withdraw from the market altogether. This cycle is illustrated in Figure 10.10.

**FIGURE 10.10**
*The competitive life cycle*

SOURCE: Frey (1982)

## 10.14 THE INFLUENCE OF PRODUCT EVOLUTION AND THE PRODUCT LIFE CYCLE ON STRATEGY

The product life cycle is arguably one of the best-known but least understood concepts in marketing. In making this comment, we have in mind the idea that although the concept has an inherent appeal and logic, there is little hard evidence that marketing managers use it in a particularly effective manner when developing strategy. There are several reasons for this, the most obvious being the difficulty in identifying the precise shape of the life-cycle curve and the position of the company on the curve at any particular time. Nevertheless, the idea of the product life cycle has undoubtedly influenced the thinking of many marketing strategists, albeit at a general rather than a specific level.

The rationale of the life cycle is straightforward and reflects the way in which, as Kotler (1988, p. 347) points out,

> not only are economic conditions changing and competitors launching new assaults, but in addition, the product is passing through new stages in the role that it plays in

its market. Consequently, the company needs to plan for a succession of strategies appropriate to each stage in the product's life cycle. The company must think about how to extend the product's life and profitability in the face of knowing that it will not last forever.

The strategic implications of the life cycle are thus potentially significant and can be summarized as follows:

1 products have a finite life;
2 during this life, they pass through a series of different stages, each of which poses different challenges to the seller;
3 virtually all elements of the organization's strategy need to change as the product moves from one stage to another;
4 the profit potential of products varies considerably from one stage to another;
5 the demands upon management and the appropriateness of managerial styles also varies from stage to stage.

In terms of operating practice, the most obvious and immediate implication of a model of product and market evolution such as this can be seen as the need for strategy to change over time and to reflect the particular demands of the different stages. These stages, which are illustrated in Figure 10.11, are typically designated as introduction, growth, maturity and decline, and follow an S-shaped curve.

**FIGURE 10.11**
*Sales and product life cycles*

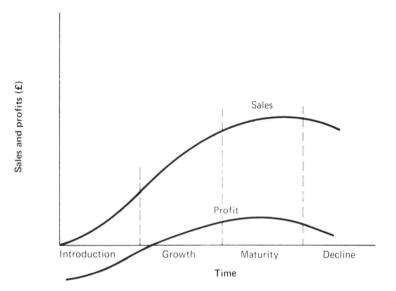

However, despite the simplicity and apparent logic of the life cycle concept, a series of problems are typically experienced in its use. The most common of these stems from the difficulty of identifying where on the life cycle a product is and where each stage begins and ends. In most cases, the decision is arbitrary, although several commentators have proposed rather more objective criteria. Probably the best known of these is an approach devised by Polli and Cook (1969) which is based on a normal distribution of percentage changes in real sales from year to year. Others such as Cox (1967) advocate an historically based approach whereby the strategist examines the sales histories of similar products in his industry. If this reveals that in the past the average length of the introductory, growth and maturity periods has been five, 14 and 48 months respectively, these time-scales are, all other factors being equal, are assumed to apply to the product in question. The problem of course is that other factors almost invariably do intrude with the result that historical analysis is at best only a vague guide to strategy and at worst misleading. This is particularly so when levels of competitive intensity increase. Equally, the strategist should not lose sight of the way in which life cycles generally are shortening. Other problems with historical analysis stem from the very different life-cycle curves that products exhibit; one particular piece of research, for example, has identified 17 different life-cycle patterns (see Swan and Rink, 1982), the three most common of which are illustrated in Figure 10.12. The combined effect of these few points raises a significant question mark over historical analysis and argues the case for a rather more cautious and individual approach than is normally suggested.

**FIGURE 10.12**
*Three common product life-cycle curves*

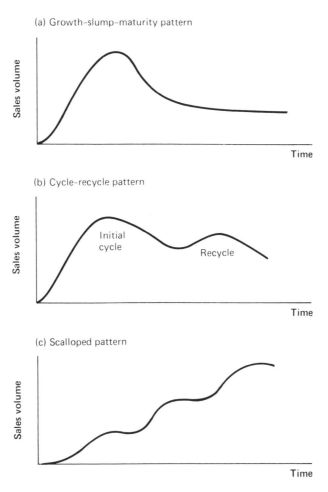

(a) Growth-slump-maturity pattern

(b) Cycle-recycle pattern

Initial cycle

Recycle

(c) Scalloped pattern

Nevertheless, despite these criticisms, the PLC does offer some scope as a broad planning, control and forecasting tool. As a planning tool its value should be seen in terms of the way in which it highlights the need for marketing strategy to change over time and indeed identifies the types of strategy that are best suited to each of the four stages. As a control tool it can be used as a basis for a comparison of a product's performance against broadly similar products in the past, while as a means of forecasting it provides a broad indication of how a product might develop. These are brought together in Figure 10.13 which summarizes the characteristics of the life cycle, and the objectives and strategies best suited to each of the four major stages.

**The Influence of Market Evolution on Strategy**

The product life cycle is, as we commented earlier, a model of both product and market evolution. In practice, emphasis tends to be placed on the *product's* life cycle rather than that of the *market*, with the result that many strategists work to a product-oriented picture rather than to a market-oriented picture. There is, however, a strong argument for the strategist to take a step sideways and to focus periodically upon the market overall in an attempt to identify how it is likely to evolve and how it will be affected by changing needs, new technology, developments in the channels of distribution, and so on. This, in turn, points to the need for the strategist to recognize the nature of the interrelationships between the demand life-cycle curve and the technology life-cycle curve, and how in turn these should be reflected in the management of particular brands.

**FIGURE 10.13**
*The characteristics of the PLC and the implications for strategy*

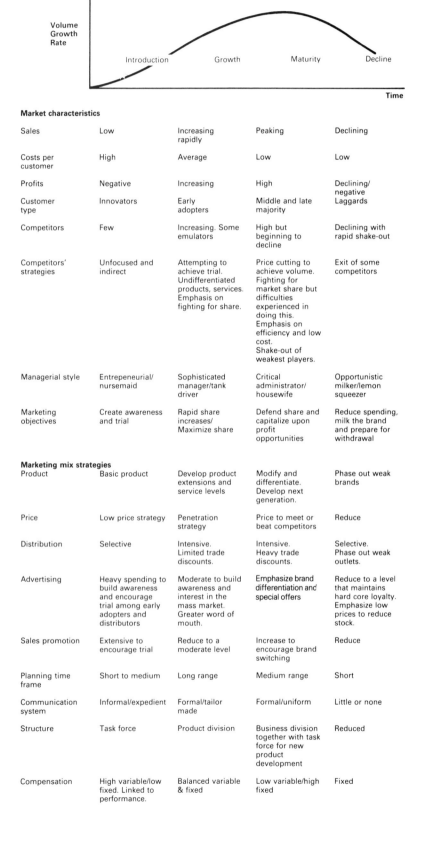

| Market characteristics | Introduction | Growth | Maturity | Decline |
|---|---|---|---|---|
| Sales | Low | Increasing rapidly | Peaking | Declining |
| Costs per customer | High | Average | Low | Low |
| Profits | Negative | Increasing | High | Declining/ negative |
| Customer type | Innovators | Early adopters | Middle and late majority | Laggards |
| Competitors | Few | Increasing. Some emulators | High but beginning to decline | Declining with rapid shake-out |
| Competitors' strategies | Unfocused and indirect | Attempting to achieve trial. Undifferentiated products, services. Emphasis on fighting for share. | Price cutting to achieve volume. Fighting for market share but difficulties experienced in doing this. Emphasis on efficiency and low cost. Shake-out of weakest players. | Exit of some competitors |
| Managerial style | Entrepeneurial/ nursemaid | Sophisticated manager/tank driver | Critical administrator/ housewife | Opportunistic milker/lemon squeezer |
| Marketing objectives | Create awareness and trial | Rapid share increases/ Maximize share | Defend share and capitalize upon profit opportunities | Reduce spending, milk the brand and prepare for withdrawal |

| Marketing mix strategies | | | | |
|---|---|---|---|---|
| Product | Basic product | Develop product extensions and service levels | Modify and differentiate. Develop next generation. | Phase out weak brands |
| Price | Low price strategy | Penetration strategy | Price to meet or beat competitors | Reduce |
| Distribution | Selective | Intensive. Limited trade discounts. | Intensive. Heavy trade discounts. | Selective. Phase out weak outlets. |
| Advertising | Heavy spending to build awareness and encourage trial among early adopters and distributors | Moderate to build awareness and interest in the mass market. Greater word of mouth. | Emphasize brand differentiation and special offers | Reduce to a level that maintains hard core loyalty. Emphasize low prices to reduce stock. |
| Sales promotion | Extensive to encourage trial | Reduce to a moderate level | Increase to encourage brand switching | Reduce |
| Planning time frame | Short to medium | Long range | Medium range | Short |
| Communication system | Informal/expedient | Formal/tailor made | Formal/uniform | Little or none |
| Structure | Task force | Product division | Business division together with task force for new product development | Reduced |
| Compensation | High variable/low fixed. Linked to performance. | Balanced variable & fixed | Low variable/high fixed | Fixed |

In doing this, the starting point involves focusing upon the demand life cycle, since it is the demand life cycle which is concerned with the underlying need. The technology life cycle, by contrast, is concerned with the particular ways in which this need is satisfied. One of the most commonly used examples to illustrate this point is that of the need for calculating power. The demand life cycle for this is still growing rapidly and looks as if it will continue to do so for the foreseeable future. The technology life cycle is concerned with the detail of how this need is met. This was done initially with fingers and then subsequently with abacuses, slide rules, adding machines, handheld calculators and then, most recently, with computers. Each of these has a technology life cycle which exists within the overall framework of the demand life cycle. The strategic implications of this need to be seen in terms of what and who the firm is competing against, something which takes us back to Peter Drucker's questions of 'what business *are* we in?' and 'what business *should* we be in?' In practical terms, this can be seen by a manufacturer of slide rules in the 1960s continuing to see its competitors as other manufacturers of slide rules rather than the new and emerging forms of technology such as adding machines and low-priced calculators which subsequently forced slide rules into decline. For a computer manufacturer today the issues are broadly similar.

The need for a company to identify clearly what type of demand technology to invest in and when to shift emphasis to a new technology has been discussed in some detail by Ansoff (1984) who refers to a demand technology as a *strategic business area* (SBA), 'a distinctive segment of the environment in which the firm does or may want to do business'. The problem faced by many firms, however, is that, confronted by a variety of different markets and technologies, all of which are changing, there is little scope for mastering them all. The strategist is faced with the need to decide where the firm's emphasis is to be placed. In essence this involves a choice between investing heavily in one area of technology or less heavily in several. This latter strategy, while offering less risk, has the disadvantage of making it less likely that the firm will either become or retain market leadership. Rather it is the pioneering firm that invests heavily in the new technology that is likely to emerge and remain as the leader.

This line of thought can be taken a step further by relating the development stage of an industry – growth, maturity, or decline – to the organization's strategic position – leader, challenger, or follower. The strategic implications of the interplay between these two dimensions is illustrated in Figure 10.14.

## Life Cycles and Managerial Style

Although a considerable amount has been written on product and market life cycles and how strategies need to reflect life cycle stages, relatively little has been said about the appropriateness of managerial style. There is, however, a strong argument for the style of management to be tailored to the particular demands of different stages. In the introductory stage, for example, there is a need for an *entrepreneurial* style of management in which emphasis is placed upon the rapid identification and seizing of opportunities, flexible structures and a risk-taking culture. In the growth stage this needs to be modified slightly with greater attention being paid to long-term planning and control. In maturity this needs to change again in order to capitalize on the profit opportunities that exist, something which argues the case for what Arthur D. Little refers to as a *critical administrator* and which is particularly important bearing in mind that the majority of products spend most of their lives in the mature stage. In the final stage of the life cycle the managerial needs change yet again with the focus tending to shorten, costs being reduced and the need for an increased emphasis upon *opportunities milking* styles. These ideas have been expressed in a slightly different, albeit more colourful, way by Clarke and Pratt (1985) who argue for four styles of management: nursemaid, tank driver, housewife and lemon squeezer.

**FIGURE 10.14**
*Competitive strategies for leaders, followers and challengers*

| | Stage of industry development | | |
| --- | --- | --- | --- |
| | **Growth** | **Maturity** | **Decline** |
| **Strategic position of the firm**<br><br>Leader | Keep ahead of the field<br>Discourage other possible entrants<br>Raise entry barriers<br>Develop a strong selling proposition and competitive advantage<br>'Lock in' distributors<br>Build loyalty<br>Advertise extensively | Hit back at challengers<br>Manage costs aggressively<br>Raise entry barriers further<br>Increase differentiation<br>Encourage greater usage<br>Search for new uses<br>Harass competitors<br>Develop new markets<br>Develop new products and product variations<br>Tighten control over distributors | Redefine scope<br>Divest peripherals<br>Encourage departures<br>Squeeze distributors<br>Manage costs aggressively<br>Increase profit margins |
| Challenger | Enter early<br>Price aggressively<br>Develop a strong alternative selling proposition<br>Search for the leader's weaknesses<br>Constantly challenge the leader<br>Identify possible new segments<br>Advertise aggressively<br>Harass the leader and followers | Exploit the weaknesses of leaders and followers<br>Challenge the leader<br>Leapfrog technologically<br>Maintain high levels of advertising<br>Price aggressively<br>Use short-term promotions<br>Develop alternative distributors<br>Take over smaller companies | If the challenging strategy has not been successful, manage the withdrawal in the least costly way to you but in the most costly way to others |
| Follower | Imitate at lower cost if possible<br>Search for joint ventures<br>Maintain vigilance and guard against competitive attacks<br>Look for unexploited opportunities | Search for possible competitive advantages in the form of focus or differentiation<br>Manage costs aggressively<br>Look for unexploited opportunities<br>Monitor product and market developments | Search for opportunities created by the withdrawal of others<br>Manage costs aggressively<br>Prepare to withdraw |

## 10.15 ACHIEVING ABOVE AVERAGE PERFORMANCE AND EXCELLENCE

Throughout this book we have tried to emphasize the importance of internal and external analysis, and for strategy to be based not just on corporate objectives, but also on a fundamental understanding of corporate capability. This theme is a reflection of the paradigm which can be traced back to the work of Mason in the late 1950s and Chandler (1962) in the early 1960s which 'relates the constructs of strategy, structure, environment and performance in a formulation which verbally states that a firm's performance is a function of its environment, its strategy and its structure'. These ideas have been reflected in a series of empirical studies in recent years by, among others, Peters and Waterman (1982), Goldsmith and Clutterbuck (1985), and Hooley et al. (1983). Of these, it is undoubtedly the work of Peters and Waterman that has had the greatest impact. Their research, which has subsequently provided the basis for a variety of other studies, was designed to identify the organizing characteristics of successful American companies. The characteristics which they suggested led to above average performance and excellence in ambiguous environments were:

1 *A bias for action.* Successful organizations showed an ability and desire to try things – to respond to situations rather than to sit back and hope for environments to change in favour of the organization.
2 *Closeness to the customer.* Success for these firms was founded on understanding customers and in serving them well.
3 *Autonomy and entrepreneurship.* In order to avoid some of the problems of 'bigness', many successful firms pushed responsibility and authority (autonomy) 'down the line' to product managers and venture teams. In addition they encouraged staff to be entrepreneurial.
4 *Productivity through people.* The 'excellent' companies treated their workers as mature people who would respond better to high expectations and peer-group assessment rather than to heavy handed 'boss' control.
5 *Hands-on value-driven.* This characteristic refers to the way that leaders, through personal example and involvement, have indoctrinated their organizations to accept and adhere to those core values that are essential to the organization's identity and success.
6 *Sticking to the knitting.* According to Peters and Waterman, organizations that do branch out into new operating areas which are related enough to benefit from existing 'excellent' skills perform more successfully than the 'out and out' conglomerates.
7 *Simple form, lean staff.* The successful companies had avoided two dangers that expansion creates – complex organization structures and large numbers of staff personnel. Excellent companies seem to have few people working at corporate level – most are out 'in the field' getting things done. Despite the hugeness of many of these winning organizations, staff knew their job and their place in the structure – even though jobs and structures might be in a constant state of flux.
8 *Simultaneous loose–tight properties.* While the excellent firms encouraged autonomy and entrepreneurship, employees knew that discretionary decision making operated within the constraints of adherence to the organization's core values. Excellence in these areas was often achieved through attention to, and control of, the finest detail.

Although Peters and Waterman's work has had a significant influence on management thinking, a number of critics have pointed out that by the time their book was published in 1982 several of its 'excellent' firms, including Hewlett Packard and Caterpillar, had begun to experience difficulties. In the case of Caterpillar, for example, it was, as we observed earlier (see page 266), coming under increasing attack from the Japanese firm Komatsu, and finding it difficult to respond effectively. Their response to this was that this did not in any way invalidate their research, but rather it was an illustration of the difficulties of adhering to the characteristics of excellence. This has in turn been reflected in a comment by Brownlie (1987, p. 101) who has suggested that, 'Despite the lessons of Peters and Waterman, the history of many firms reveals that success and excellence remain temporary and elusive phenomena.' Recognition of this highlights the need for constant monitoring of the businesses environment and for the results to be reflected in an updating of the assumptions underpinning the firm's strategic thinking.

This theme has in turn been discussed in detail by Hugh Davidson in his book *Offensive Marketing* (1987). Davidson argues that offensive marketing is a practice which combines the age-old virtues of risk taking with a modern approach to marketing. It is practised, he suggests, by only a handful of successful companies and differs enormously from the sluggish and specialized concept that passes for marketing in most companies. For Davidson (1987(b), pp. 24–9), offensive marketing is summed up by the acronym POISE – Profitable, Offensive, Integrated, Strategic, and Effectively Executed. These elements work as follows:

> *Profitable*: marketing is not just to increase market share or provide good value for consumers, but to increase profit. Offensive marketers will encounter conflicts between giving the consumer what he or she wants, and running the firm efficiently. One of their skills is to reach the right balance between these sometimes opposing elements.
> *Offensive*: an offensive approach calls for an attitude which decides independently what is best for a company, rather than waiting for competition to make the first move.
> *Integrated*: where marketing is integrated it permeates the whole company. It challenges all employees to relate their work to the needs of the marketplace and to balance it against the firm's profit needs.
> *Strategic*: winning strategies are rarely developed without intensive analysis and careful consideration of alternatives. A business operated on a day-to-day basis, with no long-term marketing purpose, is more likely to be a follower than a leader.
> *Effectively executed*: an intelligent approach is no use without effective execution, which is vitally dependent on the relationship between marketing and other departments, and on the existence of common strategies.

Among the companies to which Davidson points as exhibiting all the characteristics of offensive marketing is Sainsbury which over the past 15 years has performed well above the industry norms on virtually every conceivable dimension. At the same time, it has reduced its dependence upon food by a series of joint ventures with, among others, BHS and the Belgian retailer BG-Inno.

Offensive marketing is, Davidson suggests, 'less a matter of intelligence and ability – since most companies have plenty of both – than of attitudes, structure and strategy. It is also a set of attitudes and approaches leading to winning strategies executed with flair, and a serious approach to providing excellent value to the consumer and strong profit growth' (1987(b), p. 29).

## 10.16  SUMMARY

Within this chapter we have focused on the need for a clear statement of marketing strategy and for this strategy to be based on a detailed understanding of corporate capability and competitive advantage. In doing this we took as our initial framework the work of Michael Porter. Porter's thesis is straightforward and suggests that in order to compete successfully the strategist needs to select a generic strategy and pursue it consistently. In deciding on this strategy consideration needs to be given to a variety of factors, the most significant of which Porter suggests are:

- the bargaining power of suppliers;
- the bargaining power of customers;
- the threat of new entrants to the industry;
- the threat of substitute products or services;
- the intensity of competitive rivalry.

The generic strategies that he identifies as being open to an organization are:

- cost leadership;
- differentiation;
- focus.

The failure to pursue one of these positions is likely to lead to a confused strategic message both internally and externally and to the organization being 'stuck in the middle'.

Any strategy needs to be based on a firm understanding of corporate capability and, in particular, any competitive advantages possessed by the organization. Several approaches to identifying and developing competitive advantage exist, including Porter's approach to value-chain analysis which is designed to help the strategist understand more readily the source and behaviour of costs within the industry, and the existing and potential sources of differentiation.

Against the background of an understanding of the organization's competitive advantages the strategist needs then to begin developing the detail of the strategy. In doing this explicit consideration needs to be given both to the organization's objectives and to its position within the marketplace. In part this position is determined by the competitive stance that has been adopted in the past. Thus organizations have a choice between a *market leader* strategy, a *market challenger* strategy, a *market follower* strategy, and a *market nicher* strategy. Each of these requires distinct courses of action and these were explored in some detail with parallels being drawn between marketing strategy and military strategy.

An important marketing objective for many private sector organizations is the pursuit of market share. The attractions of market share were explored and the findings of the PIMS research examined. Included within these is that:

- market share and profitability are strongly related;
- in the long run the single factor most affecting performance is the organization's relative product/service quality;
- most of the strategic factors which boost ROI also contribute to long-term value.

Marketing strategy needs also to take account of the stage of market evolution and the position reached on the *product life cycle* (PLC) by the product or brand. Although the PLC has been the subject of considerable criticism over the years, work recently has improved our understanding of the ways in which the concept can be used and these were incorporated into a model highlighting the implications of the PLC for strategy.

We concluded by making reference to the work done over the past decade in identifying the characteristics of high performing organizations. In doing this we made particular reference to the work of Peters and Waterman, who suggested that excellence comes from:

- a bias for action;
- autonomy and entrepreneurship;
- a closeness to the customer;
- productivity through people;
- 'sticking to the knitting';
- hands-on, value-driven;
- simple form, lean staff;
- simultaneous loose–tight properties.

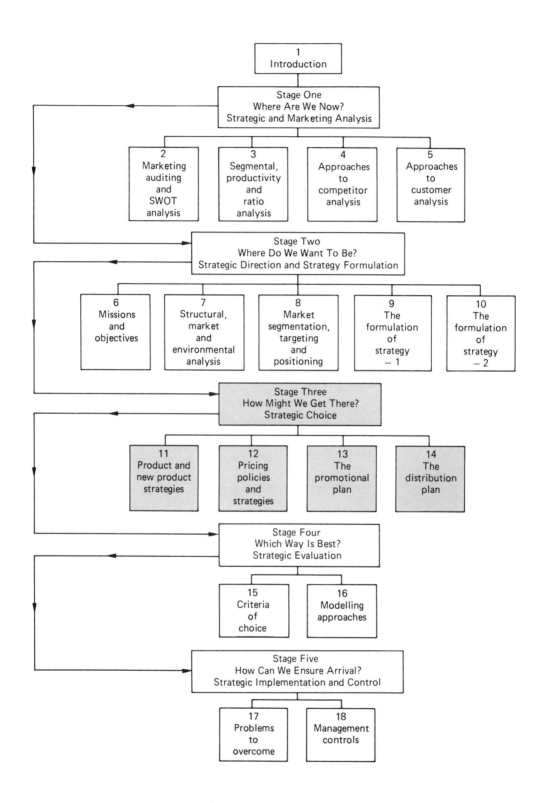

```
                        ┌──────────────────┐
                        │        1         │
                        │   Introduction   │
                        └──────────────────┘

              ┌────────────────────────────────────────┐
              │              Stage One                  │
              │          Where Are We Now?              │
              │   Strategic and Marketing Analysis      │
              └────────────────────────────────────────┘

  ┌──────────┐   ┌──────────┐   ┌──────────┐   ┌──────────┐
  │    2     │   │    3     │   │    4     │   │    5     │
  │Marketing │   │Segmental,│   │Approaches│   │Approaches│
  │ auditing │   │productivity│ │   to     │   │   to     │
  │   and    │   │   and    │   │competitor│   │ customer │
  │  SWOT    │   │  ratio   │   │ analysis │   │ analysis │
  │ analysis │   │ analysis │   │          │   │          │
  └──────────┘   └──────────┘   └──────────┘   └──────────┘

         ┌────────────────────────────────────────────────┐
         │                 Stage Two                      │
         │           Where Do We Want To Be?              │
         │ Strategic Direction and Strategy Formulation   │
         └────────────────────────────────────────────────┘

 ┌────────┐ ┌──────────┐ ┌──────────┐ ┌──────────┐ ┌──────────┐
 │   6    │ │    7     │ │    8     │ │    9     │ │   10     │
 │Missions│ │Structural,│ │ Market  │ │  The     │ │  The     │
 │  and   │ │ market   │ │segmentation,│ │formulation│ │formulation│
 │objectives│ │  and    │ │targeting │ │   of     │ │   of     │
 │        │ │environmental│ │  and   │ │ strategy │ │ strategy │
 │        │ │ analysis │ │positioning│ │  − 1     │ │  − 2     │
 └────────┘ └──────────┘ └──────────┘ └──────────┘ └──────────┘

          ┌────────────────────────────────────────┐
          │             Stage Three                │
          │         How Might We Get There?         │
          │           Strategic Choice              │
          └────────────────────────────────────────┘

  ┌──────────┐   ┌──────────┐   ┌──────────┐   ┌──────────┐
  │   11     │   │   12     │   │   13     │   │   14     │
  │Product and│  │ Pricing  │   │  The     │   │  The     │
  │new product│  │ policies │   │promotional│  │distribution│
  │strategies │  │  and     │   │  plan    │   │  plan    │
  │          │   │strategies│   │          │   │          │
  └──────────┘   └──────────┘   └──────────┘   └──────────┘

          ┌────────────────────────────────────────┐
          │             Stage Four                 │
          │          Which Way Is Best?            │
          │          Strategic Evaluation          │
          └────────────────────────────────────────┘

              ┌──────────┐   ┌──────────┐
              │   15     │   │   16     │
              │ Criteria │   │Modelling │
              │   of     │   │approaches│
              │ choice   │   │          │
              └──────────┘   └──────────┘

          ┌────────────────────────────────────────┐
          │             Stage Five                 │
          │        How Can We Ensure Arrival?       │
          │ Strategic Implementation and Control    │
          └────────────────────────────────────────┘

              ┌──────────┐   ┌──────────┐
              │   17     │   │   18     │
              │ Problems │   │Management│
              │   to     │   │ controls │
              │ overcome │   │          │
              └──────────┘   └──────────┘
```

# Stage Three
## How Might We Get There?
### Strategic Choice

## PREAMBLE

The principal contribution made by marketing to the achievement of objectives is via the marketing mix. This essentially entails developing products and services to meet target segments' needs (established by marketing research), communicating their benefits to target audiences and ensuring they are available in the right place, at the right price and at the right time.

In writing here on the marketing mix, it has been recognized that most readers will already be familiar with the basics. Also that several books are available which are devoted to individual elements of the marketing mix such as selling, advertising and distribution, for those readers wishing to access a more detailed treatment.

As we said in Chapter 1, at its simplest, the marketing mix can be seen to consist of four major elements; these were referred to by McCarthy (1974) as the four Ps, namely:

P1: Product (or service)
P2: Price
P3: Promotion (communications)
P4: Place (distribution)

Each of these four elements does, however, subsume a series of other elements or submixes. The exact nature or make-up of these submixes is determined partially by the type of product or service and partially by the marketer. For example, branding may not be a major consideration for industrial raw materials. For a consumer goods marketer, however, branding is likely to play a pivotal role in achieving a degree of differentiation. Equally, the roles and relative importance of advertising and packaging are likely to differ greatly between one sector and another.

The approach to marketing planning advocated in this book is consistent with that used by many other authors but it encompasses the standard components of a typical plan within a series of logically sequenced questions, including the vital one of 'which way is best?' The relationship of our approach to the more generally used framework can be stated as:

Where are we now?            = Audits (and analyses and research)
Where do we want to be?   = Objectives (and mission, analysis and research)
How might we get there?   = Strategy and tactics
Which way is best?            = Evaluation
How do we ensure arrival? = Controls (including budgets and organization)

The major emphases in the following chapters in Part Three – How Might We Get There? – are therefore on the strategy and tactics of the marketing mix. Other aspects of the planning structure are only lightly touched on in an illustrative way since these are covered in more detail by the other parts of this book.

We would also emphasize the importance of feed-forward as well as feed-back in our planning approach. For example, the auditing process would advise all stages of the plan and not just the marketing objectives. In evaluating which way is best we would consider not only the objectives but also the environmental and competitor audits. We would additionally take into account the budgetary considerations and how effectively we could control the chosen strategy.

One way of getting to grips with the complexities of marketing mix planning is to understand that all plans exhibit similar features and that they occupy a position in the hierarchy of the total planning process. Thus in Figure 1 the overall marketing plan can be seen as a subplan of the corporate plan and in Figure 2 each element of the marketing mix plan can be seen as part of the total marketing plan.

**FIGURE 1**
*Marketing planning
and corporate
planning*

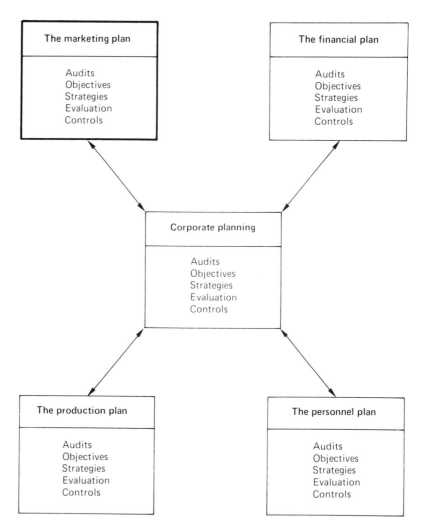

Readers are reminded that Chapter 1 comments in some detail on the interrelationships between marketing planning and corporate planning. Also that the distinction between strategy and tactics lies in the degree of detail. Thus at a broad level the chosen marketing mix can be viewed as resulting from a series of strategic decisions, whilst detail would normally be regarded as tactics. (For example, deciding to compete in the market for bicycles is strategy whilst the colour schemes to be offered is tactics.)

Each element of the marketing mix can be regarded as a subplan for which a similar framework to that of the total marketing plan can be applied.

## THE INTERDEPENDENCY OF ELEMENTS OF THE MARKETING MIX

One of the major problems involved in gaining a proper understanding of the nature of the marketing mix lies in its treatment in the literature, since authors typically tend to devote discrete chapters or sections to each of the individual elements of the marketing mix, focusing initially on the product and then moving successively through price, promotion and place.

**FIGURE 2**
*Marketing mix
planning and the
total marketing plan*

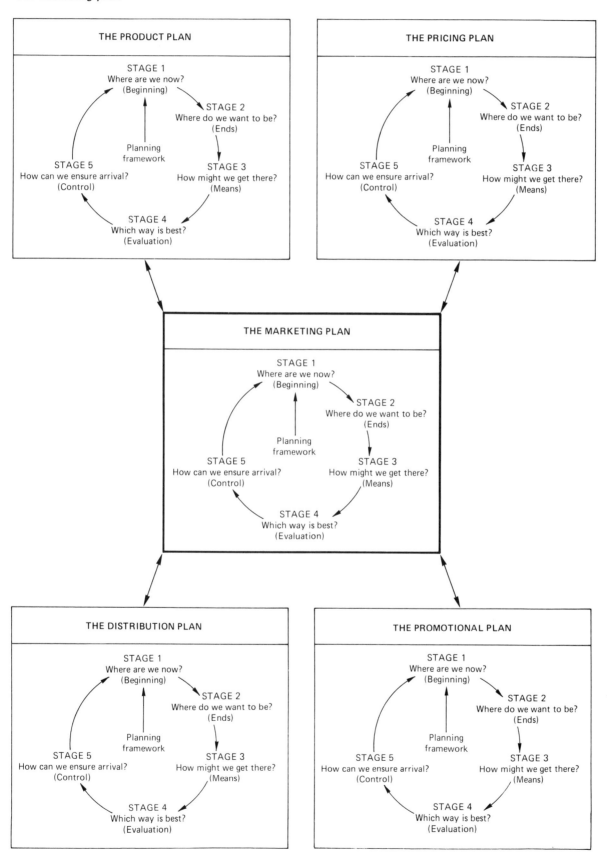

The sequential treatment can be justified by the decision-taking process adopted in many organizations in that the product is often the starting point in a series of decisions that embrace price, promotion and distribution.

The reader should recognize, however, that decisions made with regard to one element of the marketing mix inevitably affect other elements of the mix. For example, product, promotion and place all have cost implications which can affect price. Furthermore, where goods are placed (i.e. distribution) will affect both promotion (in the media used, need for branding, etc.) and product (in its packaging).

The true nature of the marketing mix is therefore that of a set of interdependent variables as indicates in Figure 3 below.

**FIGURE 3**
*Interdependency of elements in the marketing mix*

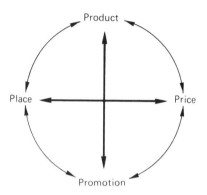

## INTEGRATING THE ELEMENTS OF THE MARKETING MIX

Recognition of the interdependency that exists among the elements of the mix highlights the need for these elements to be integrated in a harmonious way so that the greatest possible attractiveness of the total mix to its target market segment can be achieved.

It would, for example, be fatuous to advertise Rolls Royce cars in a children's comic or to endeavour to sell such cars door-to-door with an incentive of free balloons. A high-priced, high-status product such as a Rolls Royce car is aimed to meet the needs of particular types of adults – usually in particular occupations. Its promotion would be made in quality media and its distribution would be effected via exclusive dealers to the highest service standards.

By integrating the elements of the mix, dissonance and confusion in the messages being sent to the target audiences can be avoided.

The need for harmonious integration of the elements of the marketing mix applies equally to the marketing of services, as shown in Illustration 1.

---

### Illustration 1:  An Unnamed Local Authority's Bus Service in a Major City

The situation is one where the buses are clean and modern. Fare prices are among the lowest in the country and the frequency of service is excellent. Information on all the bus services is available in easy-to-read pamphlets placed in dispensers on each bus.

It would seem that all the ingredients in the mix are harmoniously integrated.

However, there is one problem in this otherwise happy situation and that is the drivers. Some of the drivers are sullen. They stop short or pass the bus stop to the irritation and inconvenience of the passengers. They also drive the buses in a series of jerks which makes the ride extremely uncomfortable as well as dangerous when passengers are leaving/occupying their seats.

As a consequence of this treatment an increasing number of previous passengers are using other forms of transport.

## EXPANDING THE FOUR PS AND MAINTAINING INTEGRATION

In practice the framework of the four Ps is, as we we suggested earlier, an over-simplification of a more complex reality. For instance, we can expand the element of product to include services, as shown in Illustration 1. Similarly we can expand the elements of promotion into at least four constituents, namely, personal selling, advertising, sales promotion and PR. Further breakdowns of these sub-elements can be made, e.g. sales promotion into sales incentives, literature, point-of-sale display materials, etc.

Each of these sub-elements also needs to be harmoniously integrated for maximum marketing effectiveness, as shown in Illustration 2.

---

## Illustration 2: Harmonizing of Sales Promotion with the Other Elements of the Promotional Mix

One of the most successful sales promotions in the baking division of Spillers was one which fully integrated all aspects of the promotional mix. This promotion increased sales of bread by over 1 million loaves.

The campaign was one of the first to use television advertising to make households aware of a sales promotion rather than the product itself. The television advertisements featured 10 saloon cars going round a circus ring and then each was seen bursting through a giant paper hoop. One of these cars was to be won each week under a free entry competition with an unlimited number of tries. All that was needed was a particular cutting from the loaf wrapper for each entry submitted. The contestants were asked to put in rank order seven interior car colour choices in terms of their preference against whatever exterior car colour was featured that week. Whichever rank order list matched that of an independent panel set up by Spillers would win the car on offer for that week. Due to the possibilities of more than one winning entry being received, competitors were asked to complete the statement 'I buy Wonderloaf because . . .' in not more than 12 words. The best answer in the opinion of the panel would receive the prize. Such a device is known as a 'tie-breaker'.

To ensure the campaign's success a team of female merchandisers was hired from a London agency whose job it was to tour round major outlets, to promote the competition in-store. They were to check the availability of competition entry forms from dispensers placed on the bread fixtures and to hand these out to customers as an encouragement to buy Wonderloaf that day instead of a competitive brand. These merchandisers were provided with cars of the marque featured in the television advertisements, decorated with details of the competition. The several thousand delivery vehicles operated by the baking division also carried a special livery promoting the competition.

Special point-of-sale (POS) display material had been commissioned at high cost and it was seen as essential not only that competition entry leaflets but aisle banners, shelf talkers and window bills all featured prominently in outlets. To this end permission to place these POS materials was negotiated with store managers prior to the campaign breaking and strict penalties were enforced by Spillers management on members of the salesforce who failed to achieve the level of placements. As a result, an extremely high penetration of POS display material was achieved in well over 80 per cent of the outlets.

Managers of the stores which sold the winners their bread received a substantial prize, as indeed did the van salesmen who delivered the bread to that store. In addition to the prize incentive, van salesmen and their supervisors received extra commission on sales increases achieved. Special incentives for the Account Executives who handled the major multiples and other members of the salesforce were introduced for obtaining window displays, extra shelf space, the placing of dump-bins and so on. Tie-up promotions and exhibitions were arranged with car distributors in order to gain additional coverage.

A separate budget was established for the purposes of gaining maximum publicity from the presentation of the prize cars to winners by 'personalities' well known locally or nationally. In the East Midlands, for example, a winning car was presented by the comedian Ken Dodd at Trentham Gardens in front of an audience of thousands. After making the presentation, Ken Dodd took part in a news programme featuring the event on local radio. Local newspapers also ran articles and photographs concerning the winning of the car by the local resident. A major objective of the campaign was not only to gain increased sales in existing outlets but to use the campaign to gain entry into new outlets. Again special incentives were used to support salesforce initiatives towards this objective.

In summary the campaign successfully and harmoniously engaged all elements of the promotional mix – advertising, selling, PR and sales promotion (including packaging, salesforce/dealer/consumer incentives, POS material and special displays). It was considered by all concerned that the degree of integration achieved was one of the major reasons for the campaign's success. Greatly improved relations were achieved not only with customers but internally throughout the baking division as a result of all employees uniting in this highly successful initiative.

The marketing mix can also usefully be seen as a set of variable inputs (means) to a process which generates desirable outputs (ends), as indicated in Figure 4.

**FIGURE 4**
*The marketing mix as a systems model*

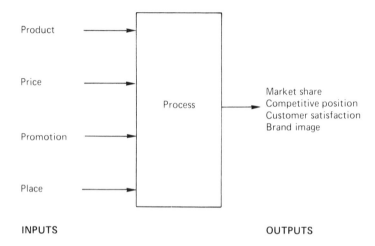

## MARKETING RESEARCH AND THE MARKETING MIX

In a marketing-led organization we would expect decisions on the elements of the marketing mix (and their sub-elements) to be influenced by information inputs drawn from marketing research. That is to say product/service features would reflect identified customer needs and wants; advertising might be pre-tested to ensure impact and retention of desire-arousing messages; products would be placed in prime, attention-getting instore positions and perhaps accompanied by point-of-sale display materials again researched for cost effectiveness.

## ELEMENTS OF THE MARKETING MIX AND THEIR SUBMIXES

Given this broad understanding of the nature of marketing mix planning we can now move on to a more detailed examination of each element of the marketing mix. In doing so it should be appreciated that just as the corporate plan breaks down into the functional plans and just as the functional marketing plan breaks down into the marketing mix plans – so each marketing mix element plan breaks down into submixes, as indicated above.

An attempt to portray these submixes is illustrated in more detail in Figure 5. These submixes represent the different types of decisions and considerations which might need to be addressed at the strategic or tactical planning level depending upon the nature of the product or service and its target market.

Any writer on marketing planning faces the problem of just what to include in these submixes so as to best represent the interests of the readers. Different product-markets

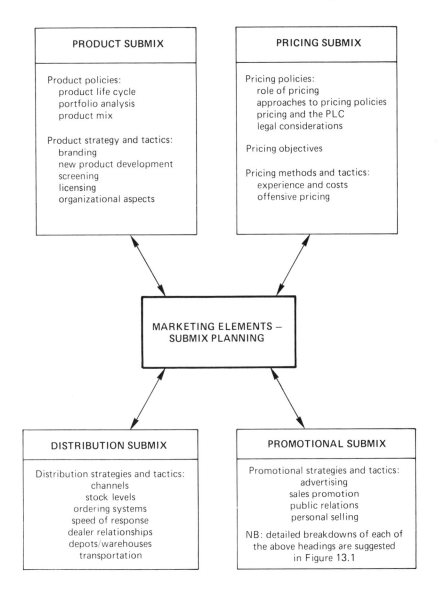

**FIGURE 5**
*Marketing elements
and their submixes*

involve different issues and emphases. Hence patenting could be a key issue to decision taking for a technological breakthrough in the engineering industry but of relatively little importance for a distributor of grain in bulk. For this reason the submixes which are given need to be seen as illustrative rather than exhaustive.

Another factor in detailing submixes is the dynamism of markets. New products and services and new market segments are being continuously developed as new needs/wants are identified. Examples include the combination of mail-order catalogue services with standard retailing by such companies as Argos and the rise of franchising illustrated by the provision of printing services in the high street (e.g. Prontaprint).

The problem of exactly how to treat marketing research is more debatable. A case could be made for treating marketing research as part of marketing operations and therefore part of the marketing mix, i.e. a fifth 'P' which we could label 'Probe'. Certainly a growing number of organizations have a marketing research department with a planning process entailing audits, objectives, strategies, tactics, budgets and controls, in its own right.

Other organizations prefer to conduct research within each element of the marketing mix, e.g. product research, advertising research, etc. In this instance research could be treated as part of the auditing process and/or (since it involves people, costs and time) as one of the submix decision areas.

# 11 | Product and new product strategies

## 11.1 LEARNING OBJECTIVES

When you have read this chapter you should be able to understand:

(a) the nature and importance of product strategy;
(b) the role of the product within the overall marketing mix;
(c) the dimensions of brand strategy;
(d) the strategic importance of new product development;
(e) how the new product development process should operate.

These objectives are contained within Figure 11.1.

**FIGURE 11.1**
*The product plan and its likely submix*

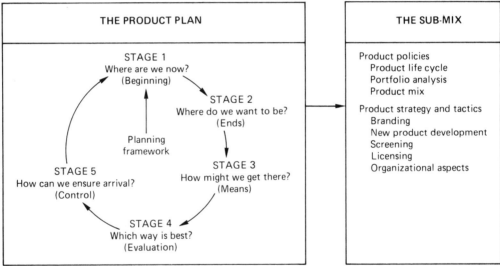

## 11.2 INTRODUCTION

In this chapter, the first of four dealing with the elements of the marketing mix, we focus on what is commonly acknowledged to be the most important single element of the marketing mix, the product. Product policy is or should be the principal preoccupation of marketing managers since it is as Thomas (1987, p. 238) has pointed out 'the product or service offering of a company or organisation [which] ultimately determines the nature of the business and the marketplace perception of the business. In this sense it is the core of the marketing management function'. In making this comment Thomas gives implicit recognition to the idea that, although in an ideal world marketing management starts with the identification and selection of opportunities, in practice resources have generally already been committed. The principal concern of most organizations is therefore *product* policy and management rather than *market* policy and management. Given this, the task faced by the strategist in developing an effective product policy can be seen to consist of two distinct but interrelated elements: first, the management of the organization's existing range of products or services, and second, the development of new or modified products or services. It is to these two areas that we now turn our attention.

## 11.3  WHAT IS A PRODUCT?

The term 'product' is used throughout this chapter to refer both to physical goods and to intangibles: Hoover, for example, sells vacuum cleaners which are *goods*; Prudential sells insurance and pension schemes which are *services*; and Weight Watchers sells an *idea* – that of losing weight through changed eating habits and greater self-control. An organization's 'product' may therefore fall into any one of these three categories.

In discussing the nature of the product, Kotler (1988, p. 446) suggests that three distinct elements need to be considered: the product's attributes, its benefits, and the nature of the support services. These are illustrated in Figure 11.2.

- *Product attributes* are associated with the core product and include such elements as features, styling, quality, brand name, packaging, and size and colour variants.
- *Product benefits* are the elements that consumers perceive as meeting their needs – this is sometimes referred to as the 'bundle of potential satisfactions' that the product represents. Included within this bundle is the product's performance and its image.
- *The marketing support services* consist of all the elements that the organization provides in addition to the core product. These typically include delivery, installation, guarantees, after-sales service, and reputation.

**FIGURE 11.2**
*The three basic elements of the product*

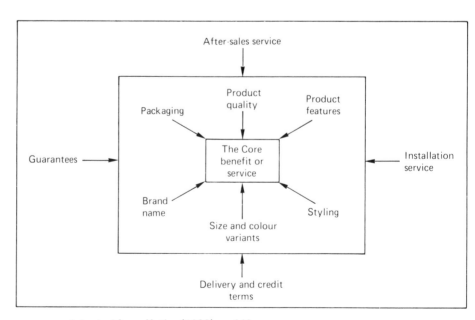

SOURCE: Adapted from Kotler (1988), p. 446

The relative importance of each of these three elements can of course vary significantly from one product category and brand to another. A consumer buying a car such as a Porsche, for example, is likely to be more concerned with the intangible attributes such as image, brand and quality than with the economic benefits of the car. The significance of this from the viewpoint of the manufacturer and the dealer needs to be seen in terms of how the product is presented through advertising and supported by the dealer network.

Recognition of this leads in turn to two distinct views of the product:

1 that the product is simply a physical entity which has a precise specification;
2 that it is a far broader concept which consists of anything, be it favourable or unfavourable, that a buyer receives in the exchange process.

From the viewpoint of the marketing strategist, it is the second of these two views which is the most meaningful and which is encapsulated in the idea of the product as a 'bundle of potential satisfactions'. This has been elaborated upon by Abbott (1955, p. 9) who has emphasized that 'What people really desire are not the products but satisfying experiences.' This view has in turn been expanded upon by Levitt (1976) who argues that products need to be seen in terms of the benefits they provide rather than the functions they perform. Thus, he suggests, 'One million quarter-inch drills were sold not because people wanted quarter-inch drills, but because they wanted quarter-inch holes.'

Views such as this provide strong support for the suggestion that in developing product policy the strategist needs to give explicit recognition both to the objective and the subjective elements of the product. The objective elements in the form of, for example, the physical specification and price are often easily copied by a competitor. The subjective element, however, which consists of among other things the image and reputation is generally more difficult to copy and in many markets provides the most effective basis for differentiation. In practice, of course, the objective and subjective dimensions are interrelated: a strong image and positive reputation, for example, develop largely as the result of high quality and reliability. It is therefore the recognition of this sort of interrelationship that is at the heart of effective product policy, since it is the combination of the two which delivers 'value' to the customer. This point has been elaborated on in the context of the American car industry by Bennett and Cooper (1982, pp. 52–69). The success of the Japanese and the Europeans in the 1970s in taking share away from domestic manufacturers was due, they suggest, not simply to lower prices and better fuel economy. Rather, it was the case that 'The European and Japanese car makers have simply been better competitors; they anticipated market needs; they built a better product – one that is more reliable, has better workmanship, and is better engineered; and they did it effectively. In short, these manufacturers delivered better value to the American consumer.'

## 11.4 THE DIMENSIONS OF PRODUCT POLICY

Effective product management is to a very large extent based on an understanding and application of two major concepts, the product life cycle and portfolio analysis, both of which were discussed in some detail in Chapters 9 and 10. The reader should therefore return briefly to the discussion on pp. 227–39 and 273–8 for a detailed discussion of these two concepts, since here we will concentrate simply on some of the key points.

**The Product Life Cycle: Its Contribution to Product Policy**

In our earlier discussion we referred to the product life cycle (PLC) as one of the best-known but least understood concepts in marketing. The ideas that underpin the concept are, as we pointed out, straightforward, suggesting that sales following a product's launch are initially slow but then increase as awareness grows. Maturity is reached when the rate of sales growth levels off and repeat purchasers account for the majority of sales. Ultimately, sales begin to decline as new products and new technologies enter the market, leading eventually to the product being withdrawn.

Although a considerable amount has been written about the product life cycle and how it might or should be used, surprisingly few empirical studies of the concept's real scope for application within an organization's product policy have been conducted. It is perhaps because of this that the literature on the life cycle still tends to lean towards one extreme or the other, with some arguing that life-cycle analysis offers a strong foundation for effective product management, while others dismiss the idea as being conceptually attractive but pragmatically worthless. Prominent among those within this second category are Dhalla and Yuspeh (1976, pp. 102–112) who, in an article entitled 'Forget the Product Life Cycle', argued that the PLC is conceptually and operationally flawed. The bases of their argument were that:

- The biological metaphors used to suggest that products are living entities is misleading.
- Attempts to match empirical sales data to life-cycle curves have proved difficult and the results are largely meaningless.
- The life cycle of a product and hence the shape of the curve is determined by how the product is managed over time. It is not an independent variable as is suggested by traditional PLC theory.
- The PLC is not equally valid for product class, product form and for brands as is often argued.
- The stages of the life cycle are difficult to define.
- Identifying where on the life cycle a product is at any particular time is difficult to determine.
- The scope for using the concept as a planning tool is limited.
- Evidence exists to suggest that where organizations have tried to use the PLC as a planning tool, opportunities have been missed and costly mistakes made.

In the light of these comments, what then is the status of the PLC and what contribution might it be expected to make to product policy? Quite obviously, it is not a model with universal applicability, but rather an ideal type from which insights into the general behaviour of most product forms can be deduced, but which in its application requires a possibly high degree of caution. This is reflected in a comment by Thomas (1987, p. 242) who suggests that:

> as a means to an end – that end being more sensitive management of the product over time, no sensible product manager should ignore the intellectual inheritance represented by the product life cycle literature. Using the product cycle concept is a means to creating an optimal life cycle, rather than being controlled by it. Sales history is a fundamental tool of the product manager, but sales history is not the only variable controlling the future of the product.

This general line of argument has also been pursued by Michael Porter (1980) who has highlighted the significance of the context in which the PLC is applied. Porter argues that the nature of the industry and its evolution from embryonic to declining is at least of equal importance as the stage of the product's life cycle. (For a more detailed discussion of this, refer to pp. 273–8.)

**The Role of Portfolio Analysis in Product Policy**

The second key contributor to effective product policy is portfolio analysis and management. The techniques of portfolio analysis are discussed in detail in Chapter 9 and so here we will limit ourselves to identifying some of the principal elements of its contribution to product policy. The starting point involves recognizing that portfolio analysis provides a firm foundation both for developing and evaluating marketing plans. The data required, for example, for the growth-share and market-attractiveness/business-position type matrices help not only in the process of allocating resources, but also in deciding upon the current and future mix and balance of the organization's portfolio. This in turn provides the basis for identifying the contribution that each strategic business unit (SBU) is capable of making to short-term and long-term strategy and, where this contribution is perceived to be inadequate, for adjustments to be made.

For Haspeslagh (1982), the principal role of portfolio analysis within product policy is that of resource allocation and, subsequently, a series of decisions regarding each product or SBU. These decisions revolve around the issue of how to manage each product and, in particular, whether to adopt a custodial, harvesting, penetration, phased withdrawal, divestment, acquisition, or new product development stance.

In many ways, this view of portfolio analysis represents a neat summary of its potential role and contribution. Portfolio displays are not intended as strategic answers to the resource allocation problem, but are instead designed to help in the process of communication and decision making at brand management and strategic management levels.

**The Product Mix and the Product Line: the Issue of Definition**

The group of products sold by a company is referred to as the firm's *product mix*. Thus all of the products sold by Heinz, including soups, baby foods, and baked beans, make up its product mix. Although the number of products within a firm's mix can vary enormously, the majority of firms begin with a single product. Ford, for example, began in this way and satisfied consumers' needs for a low-cost car. Over time, however, companies typically recognize that their single product does not satisfy the needs of all consumers and that other opportunities exist. At this stage it begins to develop a *product line*. Thus, in the case of Ford, it began developing other types of car. A product line can therefore be seen as a group of broadly similar products targeted at a broadly similar group of consumers who will use them in a broadly similar fashion. In many cases, of course, companies develop multiple product lines either to capitalize on other opportunities or to reduce a potential competitive threat. Volvo, for example, has developed a series of product lines including cars, trucks, buses and marine engines. Equally, Procter & Gamble which began life as a soap manufacturer has developed or acquired product lines in, among other areas, foods, coffee, paper products and baby products.

The advantages of multiple product lines can be considerable and not only help a company to grow more rapidly than would be the case with a single product line, but also help to reduce the risk associated with being overly dependent on one product and market sector.

**The Product as a Strategic Variable**

Because the product is at the very heart of marketing strategy, the need to manage it strategically is of paramount importance, since how well this is done is the key both to the organization's overall financial performance and to the gaining and retaining of market share. The question of *how* to manage the product strategically is not necessarily answered easily, however, and for many firms involves a careful balancing of costs, risks and returns. In doing this, explicit consideration needs to be given to competitors and in particular to the probable implications of any moves that they are likely to make.

In many cases, time is a critical dimension of product strategy and exerts a significant influence on any marketing manager's freedom of movement. In the long term, say five to 10 years, products can be changed radically in almost all industries and can therefore make a major contribution to corporate objectives. In the short term, however, the product is often much more inflexible. In the car industry, for example, a period of four years or so is often needed to develop and introduce a totally new model. In the shorter term, the strategist's flexibility is consequently more limited and restricted to a series of minor and often cosmetic changes. For this reason, innovation tends not to be a major element of short-term marketing strategy. Instead, the strategist is limited to a series of package and label changes, new varieties, accessories, options, and combinations of products that inject a degree of newness into the market.

In developing an effective product strategy, a variety of factors need to be considered. The first, and in many ways the most important, is the question of the *type* of product strategy that is to be pursued. Is it, for example, to be broadly offensive or broadly defensive? If it is to be offensive the strategist needs to consider not just how this is to be translated into action, but also its feasibility and the costs and risks that are associated with it. We can identify four types of product strategy:

1 a market leader product strategy;
2 a leadership challenging product strategy, which might translate, initially at least, into 'the strategy of the fast second' whereby the firm allows the existing leader to incur the costs and risks of developing a new product and then moves in rapidly after the launch with a copy or an improved version of the product;
3 a product following strategy;
4 a me-too product strategy.

The issue of how firms pursue a strategy of leading, challenging or following was examined in detail in Chapter 10 and the reader may find it useful to turn back to pp. 257–69 for a discussion of the key points. Where, however, an organization is intent either on leading or challenging, the implications for product strategy are considerable and are likely to make heavy demands upon resources. The majority of leaders retain their leadership position by means of a series of small and large innovations, supported by a heavy investment in advertising and distribution. For a challenger to succeed, the implications are straightforward and in many industries require an even greater level of investment.

The question of which strategy to pursue cannot be made in isolation, but requires a detailed understanding both of the organization's current position and capabilities, and of each competitor's stance and likely response pattern when challenged. The starting point should therefore be an assessment of the organization's current portfolio. Such an assessment can be carried out in one of several ways, including using the product life cycle and techniques of portfolio analysis, both of which were reviewed briefly at an earlier stage in this chapter. Based on this sort of analysis, Drucker (1963) recommends classifying products in one of six ways:

1 tomorrow's breadwinners;
2 today's breadwinners;
3 products that are capable of making a contribution assuming that drastic action is taken;
4 yesterday's breadwinners;
5 the also-rans;
6 the failures.

This approach to classification then provides the basis for posing three questions:

- Should we continue to market the product?
- If so, should the strategy and level of resource allocation be changed in a minor way?

● Should there be a major rethink of the product's strategy (e.g. a relaunch, a repositioning, or a major styling change)?

In answering these questions, the strategist needs to consider a variety of factors, but most importantly how the product is perceived by consumers and distributors; its probable future sales pattern; the scope that exists for repositioning or extending the life of the product; the availability of resources; the returns that are being generated currently; the ways in which returns are likely to increase or decrease in the future; possible competitive moves that will affect consumers' perceptions of the product; and the nature of any competing demands for the resources currently being absorbed by the product. In addition, consideration needs to be given to the relative rates of product and market growth, and whether the product is growing at a faster or slower rate than the overall market. Regardless of whether the growth rate is faster or slower, the strategist needs to consider first why this is the case and second the strategic implications (see Figure 11.3).

**FIGURE 11.3**
*Product and market growth rates*

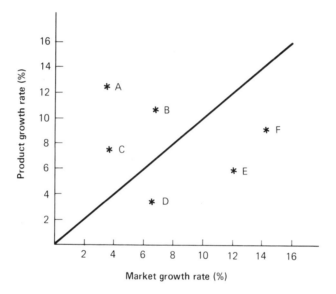

Products A, B and C are all growing at a faster rate than the rate of market growth. Products D, E and F are growing more slowly than the market. In both cases, the strategist needs to consider why this is so.

Much of the information needed for this should be generated on a regular basis by the organization's marketing information system, although in some instances specific studies of buyers, distributors, and competitors will be needed. By studying the product on a regular basis and, in particular, by focusing upon changing consumer needs and competitors' moves, the strategist should be able to identify more readily any inadequacies that exist and the scope or need for product development. As an example of this, the chewing gum manufacturers Wrigley identified that denture wearers would not buy gum because its stickiness loosened their dentures. The solution the company came up with was Freedent gum.

## 11.5 BRAND STRATEGIES

An important element of any product strategy is the role played by brand names. Brands are designed to enable customers to identify products or services which promise specific benefits. As such, they are a form of shorthand in that they create a set of expectations in the minds of customers about purpose, performance, quality and price. This, in turn, allows the strategist to build added-value into products and to differentiate them from competitors. Because of this, well-known brand names such as Rolex, Cartier, Chanel and Lacoste are of enormous strategic and financial value and are in many cases the result of years of investment in advertising. The significance of this in the case of IBM has been highlighted by the suggestion that the company's brand name is worth more than the gross national product of many nations. It also helps to explain why pirating of brand names has developed with enormous rapidity over the past decade.

In developing a brand strategy, an organization can pursue one of four approaches:

1 corporate umbrella branding;
2 family umbrella branding;
3 range branding;
4 individual branding.

The first of these – *corporate umbrella branding* – can be used in one of two ways: either as a lead name such as Heinz, Kellogg's or Cadbury's, or as a supporting brand name such as Allied-Lyons. In the case of Cadbury's, for example, the umbrella is used to cover a wide variety of chocolates and sweets including Cream Eggs, Flake, Dairy Milk, Milk Tray, Bournville, Roses, Fry's Chocolate Cream, and Turkish Delight.

*Family umbrella names*, by contrast, are used to cover a range of products in a variety of markets. A case in point is Marks and Spencer with its St Michael brand which is used for food, clothing and household textiles. The common link exists in terms of the quality, style and packaging. A broadly similar approach is used by C & A with its Canda label.

*Range brand names* are used for a range of products which have clearly identifiable links in a particular market. An example of this is the Lean Cuisine ranges of low calorie foodstuffs.

The fourth approach – *individual brand names* – is typically used to cover one type of product in one type of market, possibly with different combinations of size, flavour and service options or packaging formats. Examples of this include Lucozade, Marmite and Penguin.

## Approaches to Brand Development

To be truly effective, a brand strategy has to develop over time and reflect environmental conditions. There is therefore a need for brand development, the seven principles of which have been identified by Davidson (1987, pp. 299–303):

1 understand your brands;
2 determine how all your brand names fit;
3 decide which brand names can be stretched and how far;
4 know when to develop new brand names;
5 consider licensing your brand name;
6 cover your tracks;
7 have a five-year brand development plan.

The starting point for this involves analysing the brand in order to understand in detail what it means to customers. In doing this, the strategist needs to identify the core values, the scope that exists for extending the brand name into other product or market sectors, and the areas which must at all costs be avoided. The core values relate to the essential meaning of the brand and can be subdivided into the *inner core values* or intrinsic qualities which if altered would seriously damage the brand's integrity, and the *outer core values* which have a greater degree of flexibility.

From here, the strategist needs to move on to consider the interrelationships between the brand names used. In the case of the Volkswagen Golf GTi, for example, Volkswagen is the umbrella name, Golf the model, and GTi the designation for performance. The issue here therefore is the extent to which names can be used, how they might be extended and how they might be used in combination with other models in the range.

The third stage involves deciding how far brand names can be stretched and still be meaningful. A company that has done this with considerable success in the 1990s is Mars which, having developed a very strong brand name and image with Mars Bars, then stretched the name into a Mars drink and Mars ice cream. Similarly, Johnson & Johnson, best known for its babycare products, stretched its brand name to cover a range of toiletry products for men, while Marks & Spencer stretched its name for clothes into foods and home furnishings.

In attempting to stretch a brand, the strategist needs to tread carefully. The obvious danger, of course, is that of moving into an area in which the brand name has little relevance or which detracts from the value of the brand in its core market. The aim should therefore be to operate only in the three cells in the bottom right-hand corner of Figure 11.4.

**FIGURE 11.4**
*Brand stretching and market attractiveness*

SOURCE: Adapted from Davidson (1987)

As an alternative to brand stretching, or indeed in addition to brand stretching, the strategist can opt for the development of new brand names. There are, of course, significant costs associated with this, particularly when put against the background of the traditionally high failure rate of new products. Estimates of the costs of successfully developing a new brand name vary considerably, but as a broad rule of thumb in the food or confectionery market it is unlikely to be much less than £3 million. Again, therefore, the strategist needs to tread carefully and consider developing a new brand name only when certain criteria can be satisfied. These include:

1 the product has a series of distinctive values;
2 the consumer benefits are both strong and obvious;
3 acceptance of the new product is highly likely;
4 when using an existing brand name would be inappropriate because there is little apparent linkage between the existing and new products;
5 when using an existing name would weaken the novelty impact of the new product.

For those organizations with very strong brand names there is often scope for generating additional profits by means of licensing. Among those to have done this with considerable success are Disney and Christian Dior.

The sixth stage of offensive brand development involves 'covering your tracks', a step which is designed to safeguard the brand name from the often illegal moves of others, particularly in the form of pirating.

The final stage of offensive brand development stems from the need for an explicit brand development plan. There is little real evidence to suggest, despite the growing recognition of the need for planning, that this extends into the area of brand name development. Because of this, and because of the significance of the brand name, the strategist should concentrate upon developing a brand development plan showing how each brand name is to be used over the next five years. In doing this, Davidson (1987, p. 303) suggests that five areas be considered:

1 What is the meaning of the brand today and what do we want it to mean in five years' time?
2 What line extensions and new products do we wish to develop under this brand name?
3 What changes in market needs and consumer demographics do we forsee that will require us to modify or change the brand meaning?
4 What are the detailed plans by year for achieving these changes in the next five years? What are the sales, spending and profit implications?
5 Bearing in mind the new markets we wish to enter, which ones can be covered with existing brand names and which need new brand names?

A final issue that needs to be considered at this stage stems partly from the developments taking place in the media with the emergence of larger media footprints, and partly from the growing internationalism of companies. The combination of these factors has led several manufacturers to reconsider their branding policies. Whereas previously different brand names have been used for the same product in different countries, there is now a move towards a greater commonality. Among those to have done this is Mars which changed its M&Ms to Snickers.

## How Much is a Brand Worth?

Towards the end of the 1980s a number of companies, some threatened by take-overs, argued that a substantial part of their net worth was the ownership of well-known and strategically valuable brand names. As such, they should be treated as assets and should appear in the balance sheet. Among those to have done this were Guinness who in their 1988 accounts recognized acquired brands to a value of £1695 millions, and Ranks-Hovis-McDougall (RHM) whose inclusion of more than 50 brands added £678 millions to their 1988 balance sheet.

Although the inclusion on the balance sheet of an intangible fixed asset is allowed under the 1985 Companies Act, valuing brands was seen to be potentially problematic. The starting point for valuation that has subsequently emerged attempts to simplify this by distinguishing between brands that have been acquired, perhaps as the result of a take-over, and brands which have been created and developed internally. In the case of Guinness, the figure of £1695 millions referred to above was arrived at by considering a series of criteria including:

1 title to the brand had to be clear and separately disposable from the rest of the business;
2 its value had to be substantial and long term, based on separately identifiable earnings that had to be in excess of those achieved by unbranded products.

RHM's approach was somewhat more elaborate and was developed by the Interbrand Group. Here the method was based on an elaborate scoring system against seven criteria:

1 The brand's market position. A market leader clearly counts for more than those in lower positions.
2 The age of the brand and its stability.
3 The nature of the market. Food and drink brands score more highly than those in, say, fashion or computers where names are less well known and often have a shorter life cycle.
4 Geographic spread. Is the brand known overseas and how much has been spent overseas on its promotion?
5 The market trend. Is it growing or declining?

6 The existence of trade marks or any other form of protection.
7 The levels and consistency of advertising and promotion.

Once a score had been arrived at against these criteria, account was taken of the brand's earning power. This was done by taking a weighted average of the profits over the preceding three years, minus any depreciation, tax and costs. The two factors were then put together to produce an earnings multiple.

The strategic value of a brand name was dramatically highlighted in 1990 when it was announced that minute traces of benzene, a carcinogenic substance, had been found in bottles of Perrier water in the United States. The company's subsequent action to reassure the public and minimize the damage to the brand are now seen to be a model for others as the company fought desperately not to retain short-term sales, but rather to safeguard the meaning and value of the brand. The company's experiences are discussed in Illustration 11.1.

## Illustration 11.1: And If One Green Bottle Should Accidentally Fall

Although the strategic importance and commercial value of strong brand names has long been recognized, their potential vulnerability was dramatically illustrated on a number of occasions in the 1980s and early 1990s. In the United States, for example, Procter & Gamble had to contend with rumours, based on the company's corporate logo, of satanic influences within the company. Equally, Heinz and Johnson & Johnson were both hit by cases of product tampering and contamination. In each case it was shown that the company's ability to defend the brand depended on the nature and speed of the response.

The need for a fast and decisive response was also illustrated in 1990 when minute traces of benzene, a carcinogenic substance, were found in bottles of Perrier water in the United States. The company responded immediately and very publicly by withdrawing 160 million bottles of Perrier from shelves throughout the world. The cause of the problem, a faulty filter at the company's Vergeze plant in south-west France, was replaced, the public was given unequivocal reassurances of the product's safety, and quality control measures were stepped up.

This need for a fast response can be seen both in terms of a company's social responsibility and because of the necessity of defending the market value of the brand. In the case of Perrier, the company's success owes much to the public's perceptions of the product's purity, and any erosion of this has dramatic and obvious implications for the brand itself, particularly when the brand has a high profile.

The growth of the bottled water market throughout the 1980s had been dramatic, with total annual sales for 1989 of £1.2 billion in the United States, £851 million in France, £1.4 billion in West Germany, £791 million in Italy, and £150 million in the UK. As the market leader in many of these markets (60 per cent in the UK, for example), the stakes were therefore high. Having withdrawn its bottles from the shelves and having seen many of its competitors gaining sales and share, Perrier then went on the offensive. This began with a series of advertising campaigns, and continued with an aggressive policy of selling into the distribution network new stock with a green flash on the pack saying 'New Production'. In doing this, Perrier was acutely aware of the costs of failure. Having spent enormous sums of money achieving market leadership and with more than half its FFr 1 billion profits derived from mineral water, the value of the brand was immeasurable.

## 11.6 THE DEVELOPMENT OF NEW PRODUCTS

The development and introduction of new products has traditionally been seen to be a costly and risky activity. For an organization intent on either maintaining or improving its position in the market-place there are, however, few alternatives to new product activity of one sort or another. The issues faced by many marketing strategists thus revolve around the issue of the type of new product activity that is to be pursued and how best to manage and, hopefully, reduce risk levels.

In the majority of industries, there are two principal ways in which new products can be added to the product range: first, acquisition and second, internal new product development. Of the two, acquisition is often the faster and involves one of three approaches:

1 the organization can buy other firms;
2 the organization can buy a licence or franchise;
3 the organization can buy patents.

New product development (NPD) can in turn involve two approaches with products either being developed internally by an in-house R & D team, or by means of outside agencies used to develop products that satisfy internally generated criteria.

In the majority of firms, of course, both routes are pursued with a greater or lesser emphasis being placed on one or other activity as environmental conditions and pressures change.

**What is a New Product?**

Definitions of what constitutes a new product have over the years varied greatly. For our purposes, however, the term is used to refer to products that are *totally new to the world, product improvements, product modifications* and *new brands*. This issue of definition has been discussed in detail by the American management consultants Booz, Allen and Hamilton (BAH) (1982). There are, they suggest, two principal dimensions that need to be considered: how new is the product to the company, and how new is it to the market-place? This led them to propose a six-stage classification, as shown below. The figures in brackets represent the percentage of products appearing in each of these categories in the United States at the beginning of the 1980s and which are felt by BAH still to be broadly valid:

1 New to the world products that create an entirely new market. An example would be the launch of the Sony Walkman (10 per cent).
2 New product lines that are designed to enable a company to enter for the first time an existing product sector (20 per cent).
3 Additions to existing product lines (26 per cent).
4 Improvements and revisions to existing products (26 per cent).
5 Repositionings where existing products are retargeted in order to appeal to new market segments (7 per cent).
6 Cost reductions where products are modified to provide similar performance but at a lower cost (11 per cent).

An alternative approach to classification has been proposed by Robertson (1967) who placed innovations in three groups:

1 Continuous innovations which simply involve the modification of existing products and lead to few if any changes in consumer behaviour.
2 Dynamically continuous innovations which, while more disruptive than the previous category, do not change behaviour patterns in any fundamental way.
3 Discontinuous innovations which are dramatically new and which lead to significant changes in patterns of behaviour and usage. Included within this are the jet engine, television, stainless steel, antibiotics, and so on.

## The Increasing Risks of New Product Development

We commented earlier that new product development has traditionally been seen as a high-risk activity. There are several sources of this risk, the most significant of which represent a mixture of financial, social, psychological and physical elements. For a variety of reasons these risks have increased over the 1980s and seem likely to continue increasing throughout the 1990s. There are several explanations for this, the most obvious of which are that buyers are becoming increasingly demanding and discriminating; markets are becoming more fragmented; product life cycles are shortening, with the result that pay-back periods are reducing; the expectations of distributors and dealers are increasing; the pace of technology is becoming ever faster; and competition generally is increasing. Recognition of this has led to what can be referred to as 'the new product development dilemma' in which, while there is widespread agreement that new products are needed if the firm is to grow, the likelihood of success appears to be getting ever smaller.

The causes of the high failure rate of new products have been examined within a variety of organizations and have led to a series of conclusions, the most prominent of which are:

- the size of the market is frequently overestimated;
- the product fails to perform at the levels demanded or expected by users;
- competitors prove to be too firmly entrenched;
- the product is poorly positioned, inadequately advertised, or priced at too high a level;
- distributors lack commitment to the launch and fail to provide the support needed;
- the new product is pushed through the development by a senior executive, despite market research findings which point to the product's likely failure.

These points are elaborated on at a later stage in this chapter (see pp. 316–19).

If anything, however, failure rates seem likely to increase over the next decade as the new product development process becomes more complex. For Kotler (1988, p. 407) this greater complexity is due to seven pressures:

1 the growing shortage of new product ideas in certain areas;
2 increasingly fragmented markets which means smaller market segments, more precise needs and reduced sales and profit potentials;
3 increased societal and governmental constraints;
4 the costliness of the NPD process;
5 shortages of capital;
6 shorter time spans between the emergence of the idea and the physical launch of the product;
7 shorter life spans as competitors either copy the product idea or develop improved technologies.

In the light of these factors, it seems likely that the pressures on the marketing strategist will increase, possibly dramatically, over the next decade. Insofar as it is possible to identify how this might be dealt with most effectively, it is clear that attention needs to be paid first to the new product development process, and second to the organizational arrangements for dealing with new products.

## The Role of New Product Development

Although organizations have in the past demonstrated that they develop new and modified products for a wide variety of reasons, the underlying strategic purpose should always be either to help create and maintain a competitive advantage or to reduce the advantages of a competitor. Recognizing this, the specific role of new product development can be stated in terms of:

1 ensuring that the product mix matches changing environmental conditions and that product obsolescence is avoided;

2 enabling the organization to compete in new and developing segments of the market;
3 reducing the organization's dependence upon particular elements of the product range or vulnerable market segments;
4 matching competitive moves – where, for example, a competitor moves into a new and potentially valuable segment there is often a strong argument for following so that the competitor's advantage is kept to a minimum;
5 filling excess capacity;
6 achieving greater long-term growth and profit.

The relative importance of these factors is influenced both by the nature and culture of the organization and by the nature of the market. Where, for example, the organization is either poorly resourced or has a risk averse culture, the perceived role and importance of new products is likely to be fairly minimal. Where, however, there is a greater availability of resources and the competitive stance is more proactive, new product development is likely to take on a far more important role. At the same time, the nature of the market often exerts a series of pressures which are capable of dictating levels of new product activity. Where, for example, competition is intense, the need both for differentiation and a regular flow of new and modified products increases dramatically. The strategist should nevertheless avoid falling into the trap of seeing the solution purely in terms of new products.

Recognizing that products consist of two interrelated dimensions, an *objective* or *physical* element and a *subjective* or *perceived* element, changes in the product's advertising and packaging can often be achieved with *relatively* low levels of investment in cost and time, but lead to strategically significant different sets of perceptions. These then provide the strategist with a foundation for moving into new sectors of the market both at a lower cost and with a smaller degree of risk.

It should be apparent from this that the parameters for new product development must be set by corporate management. These parameters need to cover the product categories and market sectors in which the organization intends operating in the future, and should be set against the background of the general stance of leader or follower that the organization intends adopting. What the strategist should never lose sight of is that NPD is often a slow process and one which cannot simply be turned on or off as economic conditions dictate. The most successful companies in the field of NPD have tended to be those that recognize its *strategic* role and that allocate resources consistently. Recognizing this, Drucker (1955) has emphasized that not only is innovation a slow process, but that many market leaders owe their position to the NPD activity of earlier generations. The real consequences of cutting back on innovation and new product development are therefore likely to be felt by the next generation of management who will be faced with a significant reduction in competitive capability.

This question of the strategic role of new product development has been examined in detail by Booz, Allen and Hamilton. Their research highlighted six principal roles. The figures in percentages below show the proportion of new products in each category:

1 maintain the organization's position as a product innovator (46 per cent);
2 defend a market share position (44 per cent);
3 establish a foothold in a new market sector (37 per cent);
4 preempt a market segment (33 per cent);
5 exploit technology in a new way (27 per cent);
6 capitalize on distribution strengths (24 per cent).

Perceptions of the role of NPD have also been examined by Ansoff (1968) who subsequently classified firms as reactors, planners or entrepreneurs. 'Reactors', he suggested, wait for problems to occur (e.g. the decline of an existing product) before trying to solve them; 'planners' try to anticipate problems; while 'entrepreneurs' deliberately focus upon and attempt to anticipate both problems and opportunities. The implications for the ways in which new product development is then handled are significant, with reactors typically assigning it a low status. In entrepreneurial firms, by contrast, NPD is seen to be of central strategic importance and allocated resources accordingly.

This general theme has in turn been reflected in Myers and Marquis's (1969) idea that NPD is broadly either *offensive* or *defensive*. Offensive NPD is designed to open up new markets or enlarge existing ones by a conscious effort to introduce new products. Defensive NPD is, by contrast, often stimulated by competitive forces or other changes in the market-place and is typically designed to maintain market share or current rates of growth.

These ideas can be taken a step further by categorizing firms as *pioneers* or *imitators*. Firms that are broadly imitative can then be further subdivided into those content to follow at a distance, and those that adopt a deliberate policy of monitoring the leaders (the pioneers) and move in as soon as the market begins to grow or a new product shows signs of success (a wait and see approach). By behaving in this way it is often possible to capitalize at a relatively low cost on the mistakes made by the pioneer. The attractions of this approach were highlighted by Freeman (1965) in a study of the electronic capital goods market.

> The performance of the first laboratory prototypes and early commercial deliveries almost always leaves a great deal to be desired, so that the scope for improvement is very great. For this reason, some entrepreneurs have followed a deliberate policy of being *second* with a new product development rather than first. Success in such a policy often requires a greater capacity for moving fast with new developments once the time is considered ripe.

The attractions of imitation have also been pointed to by Majaro (1972), who suggested that 'imitation is not only more abundant than innovation, but actually a much more prevalent road to business growth and profits. IBM got into computers as an imitator. Texas Instruments into transistors . . . Holiday Inns into motels'.

## Proactive and Reactive New Product Strategies

Although for many organizations the idea of a proactive new product strategy has a certain appeal, the reality is that proactive strategies are typically associated with a significant degree of risk and a need for heavy and sustained investment in money, skill and time, not only in the development and launch stages, but also throughout the product's life. If, therefore, an organization is intent on adopting a proactive stance, certain criteria need to be met. Included within these are:

- a fundamental and sustained commitment to new product development and a willingness to accept the associated costs and risks;
- an ability to protect the new product, possibly by patents, but certainly by a sustained and aggressive investment in marketing;
- an ability to target high-volume or high-margin markets, and subsequently to capitalize on them;
- the availability of the financial, staff, and time resources needed, as well as a willingness to commit them;
- a degree of flexibility so that the strategy can be modified to reflect changing environmental conditions;
- top management commitment;
- a previously successful NPD track record (the new product chicken and egg syndrome).

Where these criteria cannot be met, the organization is likely to do far better by opting for a less proactive stance. This typically translates into one of four postures:

1 rapidly responsive;
2 second but better;
3 imitative (me-too);
4 defensive.

Overall, therefore, reactive strategies are best suited to an organization when:

- its strengths lie in managing existing products;
- it is faced with a competitor who has an aggressive and successful new product strategy and who has the capability and willingness to increase the pace of innovation within the industry;
- there is a lack of specialist NPD skills within the organization;
- organizational resources are relatively limited;
- only limited protection of an innovation exists;
- markets are too small to guarantee the recovery of development costs.

In making these comments, a point that needs emphasizing is that neither a proactive nor a reactive stance is inherently better than the other. Rather it is the case that their suitability is a function of the organization's capability and as such needs to be reflected in the NPD strategy pursued.

## The Different Types of Innovation

The question of what drives new product development has been the subject of considerable research. There are, in essence, two extremes: technology push and demand pull. Technology push is based on the idea that a discovery is made for which an application then needs to be found. Demand pull, by contrast, represents a customer need that must be satisfied. In discussing this, Langrish, et al. (1972) have identified two subdivisions within each approach:

1 *Discovery push*
   - science discovers, technology applies;
   - technological discovery, e.g. Pilkington's float glass process.

2 *Need pull*
   - customer needs which emerge as the result of customer requests or from marketing research;
   - management by objectives where, for example, by recognizing the need to lower costs, research into new processes achieves positive results.

The relative importance of technology push or demand pull varies greatly from one industry to another. In the packaged goods industry, for example, the majority of new products are driven by demand pull. This typically begins with a programme of market research designed to identify unsatisfied needs, segments or niches. The attributes of the ideal product can be determined by means of techniques such as attribute listing. The R & D team is then asked to develop a product that matches this specification. Following this, preference and taste testing can be used to refine the product, which is then launched with a specific positioning strategy.

By contrast, in the consumer durables and industrial sectors there is typically a far greater emphasis on technological push. There is a danger, however, that technologial push can lead to innovations emerging with no obvious or sizeable market. There is thus a strong need for R & D and marketing to work closely together, something to which both Canon and Honda have paid considerable attention. Their experiences are discussed in Illustration 11.2.

## Illustration 11.2: Canon and Honda and their Approaches to Technology Push

Canon, the Japanese camera and office equipment manufacturer, has a straightforward approach to new product development: 'You create good technology and then you try to make a business out of it. Some products succeed and some don't; the process is painful.' In making this comment, Canon's senior managing director and head of research, Dr Hajime Mitarai, summarized an approach used by many large Japanese corporations with a reputation for innovation.

Canon's view of the process begins with a belief in the need to master the key areas of technology. Useful products, it is believed, will then to a large degree flow automatically. Despite the demonstrable success of this approach, the majority of Western companies have been reluctant to pursue such an explicitly technologically-driven philosophy, the normal argument being that R & D staff would tend to lose sight of the market. The Japanese technology-driven businesses overcome this problem with a highly systemized communication process designed to keep their researchers in constant touch with sales and production staff. In this way, it is argued, the R & D teams become more aware of market trends and manufacturing techniques with the result that the number of blind alleys pursued is reduced dramatically. Nevertheless, Canon acknowledges that a significant proportion of the projects started each year by the company's 4000 R & D staff fail to move into the production cycle.

A similar philosophy is pursued at Honda, a company which, despite its marketing successes, does not have a marketing department. Instead, the majority of the marketing functions, such as identifying customers' future needs, are carried out by the company's research staff who work in a separate company, Honda R & D. This company operates with a budget fixed at 6 per cent of the total sales of the group, and a general absence of parent company formal guidelines.

Again, as with Canon, Honda recognizes that a substantial proportion of the research conducted does not lead anywhere, at least in the short term, and accepts this as one of the by-products of such a heavy focus upon innovation.

The emphasis that both Honda and Canon place on formal liaison betwen research staff and commercial people is a characteristic of many Japanese firms which, critics argue, inhibits scientists from moving into radically new areas of research and taking risks. Others argue that the approach leads to a far greater degree of continuity and that the discontinuity that characterizes many Western companies is avoided. One result is that over the medium and long term, researchers in Japan are likely to come up with more good ideas than their industry can realistically commercialize.

## 11.7 THE NEW PRODUCT DEVELOPMENT PROCESS

Some of the most pragmatic and operationally useful research on the new product development process has been carried out by Booz, Allen and Hamilton. Success, they suggest, is most likely to occur when organizations adopt a conscious step-by-step approach that begins with a search for possible new product ideas and then moves progressively through a series of evaluative stages culminating in the launch of the new product. All too often, they argue, organizations for one reason or another rush through the NPD process paying too little attention to the need for detailed evaluation and are then surprised by the product's subsequent poor performance.

The step-by-step approach that Booz, Allen and Hamilton advocate consists of eight stages: idea generation; initial screening; concept development and testing; the development of marketing strategy; business analysis; product development; market testing; and commercialization. These are illustrated in Figure 11.5, which begins with a statement of the new product development strategy.

**FIGURE 11.5**
*The new product development process*

Statement of the new product development strategy

↓

Idea generation

↓

Initial screening

↓

Concept development and testing

↓

Development of the marketing strategy

↓

Business analysis

↓

Product development

↓

Market testing

↓

Commercialization

This process is designed to act as a series of filters with a large number of ideas being poured in at the beginning in the hope and expectation that one or more commercially sound products will emerge at the end. From their initial research in the 1970s, Booz, Allen and Hamilton found that an average of 58 initial ideas were needed in order to generate one worthwhile product. In their latest research, however, this has been reduced to just seven. There are, they suggest, several explanations for this, the most encouraging of which is that many organizations appear to have come to terms with the structure and complexity of new product development and are now far less likely to waste resources by using the shotgun approach that dominated during the 1970s.

**Idea Generation**

The first stage in the new product development process is a search for ideas. Although these ideas can come from a variety of sources (see Illustration 11.3), the search process typically benefits by being structured and by being set against the background of a tight statement of the product and market sectors that are seen by senior management to be of strategic importance.

In addition, the objectives of new product development need to be clearly stated. Are they, for example, related to market share increases or to short-term cash flow? Are they designed to achieve technological leadership or to reduce risk? How much effort should be devoted to developing totally new products and how much to copying competitors and to modifying existing products?

**Idea Screening**

Having generated a series of ideas, the strategist needs then to move on to the first and broadest stage of the evaluative process. In doing this, the purpose is to begin eliminating those ideas which are either weak in absolute terms or which, while possibly attractive to other firms, are of little immediate interest to the

# Illustration 11.3: Sources of Ideas

Ideas for new products can come from a wide variety of sources. The task faced by the strategist is to ensure that these ideas are collected in a systematic fashion, channelled to those who are best able to assess their initial feasibility, and then either discarded, shelved, sold on to another organization, or passed into the next stage of the NPD process. The first step therefore involves setting up a system for collecting ideas. In doing this, attention needs to be paid to customers, competitors, distributors, sales staff, R & D staff, employees in general, the media, and research organizations.

The starting point involves studying *customers' needs and wants*. The richness of this source has been pointed to by a number of writers with the techniques including surveys, group discussions, suggestions, customer complaints and projective techniques.

The second major source consists of the firm's direct and indirect competitors. This can include imitating or improving competitors' products, with particular attention being paid to competitive weaknesses.

*Distributors* are often a valuable source of ideas, since in many markets it is the distributors or dealers who have the closest and most frequent contact with customers.

The company's *sales staff* are again often close to customers and this contact, together with the insights they have to the distribution network and competitors' products, should provide a breadth and depth of perspective. All too often, however, the views of sales staff are either not canvassed sufficiently regularly or are dismissed as being unimportant.

*R & D staff* are particularly valuable in the high-technology industries and here their ideas should be examined within the more general framework of ideas emerging from other scientists, research bodies, inventors, patent lawyers, university and polytechnic laboratories, consultants, advertising agencies and market researchers.

*Employees*, even if they are not in R & D, sales or marketing, should be encouraged, either by the general culture of the organization or by a system of rewards, to search for ideas and put them forward for consideration. Although the number of ideas that have emerged from employees has not been shown to be high and the ideas have generally been biased towards processes rather than products (i.e. improving the organization's manufacturing process in some way), this represents a low-cost source which on occasions proves useful.

The *media* including not only the specialist and technical press, but also newspapers since they can provide general insights to market opportunities and competitors' moves, should be watched closely.

organization. In screening ideas, two types of error can be made: drop errors which occur when an idea with potential is dismissed, and go errors when a product that subsequently proves to be of little value is allowed to move on to the next stage and thereby incur extra costs.

A variety of criteria can be used to screen products at this stage and in order to ensure that the process is both consistent and systematic, the majority of organizations make use of standardized forms. An example of this sort of form appears in Figure 11.6.

**FIGURE 11.6**
*A new product development checklist*

PART A

NEW PRODUCT JUSTIFICATION REPORT NO...

| PRODUCT |
|---|

I.   Discounted cash flow rate... % Payback...years

| | Stage Reached | | | |
|---|---|---|---|---|
| Business Analysis | Development | Testing | Commercial-ization | Follow-up |
| | | | | |

| Year 1 | Year 2 | Year 3 | Year 4 | Year 5 |
|---|---|---|---|---|

II.  Product Contribution
     Sales      A
     Contribution to overheads    B
     Return on sales ($B/A \times 100$)   C

| % | % | % | % | % |
|---|---|---|---|---|

III. Return on investment (cumulative)
     Total investment in new product
       Fixed
       Working capital
       Introduction expenses

                                         Total   D

     Return on investment ($B/D \times 100$)
       (before tax)
     Basic Data
       Volume
       Selling price per unit
       Contribution per unit

| % | % | % | % | % |
|---|---|---|---|---|

PART B

NEW PRODUCT JUSTIFICATION
(Supplementary Schedule)

| PRODUCT |
|---|

REPORT NO.

| Year 1 | Year 2 | Year 3 | Year 4 | Year 5 |
|---|---|---|---|---|

II.  Product Contribution
     Unit: volume per annum    A
     Selling price per unit     B
     Sales ($A \cdot B$)      C
     Variable cost per unit
       Raw materials
       Labour
       Overheads
       Distribution
                                         Total   D
     Variable Cost ($A \cdot D$)    E
     Contribution to product fixed expenses
       ($C - E$)      F
     Product fixed expenses (1)
       Depreciation
       Factory Overheads
       Selling
       Advertising (2)
       Market Research (2)
       R. & D. (2)
                                         Total   G
     Loss of contribution by other products (3)   H
     Contribution to overheads and profits
       ($F - G - H$)      I

Notes:   1. Additional fixed costs arising solely due to introduction of new product. No allocation of existing fixed costs.
         2. Excluding special introduction expenses treated as part of initial investment.
         3. Calculated identically to the contribution by this product.

PART C

NEW PRODUCT JUSTIFICATION
(Supplementary Schedule)

| PRODUCT |
|---|

REPORT NO.

| Year 1 | Year 2 | Year 3 | Year 4 | Year 5 |
|---|---|---|---|---|

III. Total Investment
     *Fixed Assets*
       Land and buildings
       Plant and machinery
       Patents, etc.
       Future obligations (5th year)
       *Less* recovery of existing plant no longer
       required      Total

     *Working Capital*
       Stocks
       Debtors
       *Less* creditors
       *Less* working capital released on any
         product discontinued or reduced
                                         Total

     Introduction Expenses
       Development expenditure
       Special launching expenses (advertising)
       Marketing research prior to commencement
       Losses in early years
       Other (specified)
                                         Total

     Total Investment in New Product

SOURCE: Wilson, R. M. S. (1979), Management Controls and Marketing Planning, Heinemann: London, pp. 184–6

**Concept Development and Testing**

Once the idea has passed through the initial screening process it moves into concept development and testing. Until this point, ideas are, for the most part, only broadly formed. Here, however, the idea is refined into a distinct concept which can be expressed in terms that buyers will understand and which also allows the strategist to begin developing a product and brand positioning map so that the nature of the probable competition can be clearly identified.

The process itself involves testing the concept either physically or symbolically with a group of target buyers. Kotler (1988, p. 420) recommends at this point a series of questions about the concept:

1 *Are the benefits clear to you and believable?*
This measures the concept's communicability and believability. If the scores are low, the concept must be refined or revised.

2 *Do you see this product as solving a problem or filling a need for you?*
This measures the need level. The stronger the need, the higher the expected consumer interest.

3 *Do other products currently meet this need and satisfy you?*
This measures the gap level between the new product and existing products. The greater the gap, the higher the expected consumer interest. The need level can be multiplied by the gap level to produce a need-gap score. The higher the need-gap score, the higher the expected interest. A high need-gap score means that the consumer sees the product as filling a strong need and is not satisfied with available alternatives.

4 *Is the price reasonable in relation to the value?*
This measures perceived value. The higher the perceived value, the higher the expected consumer interest.

5 *Would you (definitely, probably, probably not, definitely not) buy the product?*
This measures purchase intent. We would expect it to be high for consumers who answered the previous three questions positively.

6 *Who would use this product and how often would it be used?*
This provides a measure of user targets and purchase frequency.

In the light of the results that emerge from this, the strategist should then be able to gauge the degree of buyer appeal, the nature and intensity of the probable competition, the broad price bands that are appropriate, and so on.

**The Development of Marketing Strategy**

Having formalized the product concept and gained an understanding of probable buyer reactions, the strategist should be able to begin drafting the preliminary statement of marketing strategy covering, first, the short- and long-term sales, profit and market share objectives, and second, the structure of the marketing mix.

**Business Analysis**

Having developed both the product concept and an initial marketing strategy, the strategist is in a far firmer position to determine the product's attractiveness, and in particular whether sales, costs and profit projections are satisfactory. The problem most commonly encountered is that of predicting the likely level and pattern of sales with any real degree of accuracy. Where the product represents only a small change to what has been offered before, these problems are of course reduced. Where, however, there is any degree of product novelty or when the company is entering a new market segment, the problems of forecasting sales and market share increase significantly. In these circumstances the strategist can take one of several approaches, including comparing the product with similarly radical new products that the organization has launched in the past. There is no easy solution to the task, particularly when it is recognized that sales will depend not just on the product and its qualities, but also on the nature of the marketing mix used to support it, and any competitive action the product's launch might stimulate. However, in order to provide some sort of structure to the forecasting process, the strategist needs to focus on three dimensions:

1 the level and speed of first-time sales;
2 the level of replacement sales;
3 the likelihood and possible level of repeat sales.

Each of these dimensions needs to be calculated for each market segment in which the organization intends to operate, and the results then combined. In this way, the speed of market adoption (see Illustration 11.4), and the probable shape of the product life cycle can be determined.

By contrast, forecasting cost levels is often a relatively straightforward process and the net contribution is calculated with relative ease. This can then be compared with target ROCEs and a decision made on whether the product should move to the next stage or be dropped or shelved.

# Illustration 11.4: The Diffusion of Innovation

Within any given market, potential buyers differ greatly in their speed and willingness to accept new ideas. Recognition of this has led many organizations to move away from mass-market launches of new products to those that are targeted far more precisely on *heavy users* and *early adopters*. Although numerous theories of product adoption have been proposed, the conclusions are all broadly the same:

- adopters of new products move successively through the stages of awareness, interest, evaluation, trial and adoption;
- individuals differ greatly in their willingness to try new products;
- personal influence exerts a significant influence on whether individuals are willing to adopt a new product and, if so, the speed of adoption;
- the nature of the innovation and in particular its novelty and its perceived relative advantages affect the speed of adoption.

These ideas have to a large extent been brought together by Rogers (1962) (see Figure 11.7) who suggested that the five adopter groups that can be identified differ greatly in their value orientations and demographic characteristics. Thus:

- *Innovators* are adventurous and willing to accept risk. They tend to be young, and have higher than average incomes and expectations.
- *Early adopters* are often opinion leaders and, whilst willing to accept a degree of risk, often behave with a degree of caution. Again, they tend to be young, come from higher social groups, and have a high discretionary income. Their sources of information tend to be more numerous, impersonal and cosmopolitan than later adopters. They also typically exhibit a high degree of psychological independence.
- *The early majority* are only rarely leaders and are willing to experiment with new ideas when the risk factor appears not to be unduly high.
- *The late majority* tend to be sceptical and willing to accept new ideas only after their reliability has been thoroughly demonstrated. They tend to place emphasis upon word of mouth and often seek the security conferred by large institutions such as the major retailers.
- *Laggards* are traditionalists, suspicious of change and only accept an idea once it has been available for a considerable period and when in one sense it has become part of a tradition. In demographic terms they tend to be older and from lower social groupings.

**FIGURE 11.7**
*A categorization of adopters based on the speed of innovation*

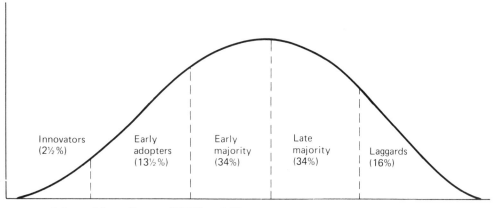

Innovators (2½%)   Early adopters (13½%)   Early majority (34%)   Late majority (34%)   Laggards (16%)

SOURCE: Adapted from Rogers (1962), p. 162

## Product Development

For those product ideas that satisfy the business analysis criteria the next stage involves the physical development of the product in the form of a prototype and, in most cases, a substantial increase in commitment and investment. Once this has been done, the product can then again be tested, although here the tests take on a physical nature. They can, for example, be tested for their functionality to make sure that they perform safely and effectively, and that they achieve the performance levels expected. In the case of foodstuffs, they can be tested for taste and for shelf life. Pharmaceuticals can be tested both for their clinical effectiveness and for any side effects.

## Market Testing

The final stage of the evaluative process is designed to provide a far more formal and realistic setting for the product. The most commonly used technique is that of test marketing where the product is launched into one or more relatively small geographical areas that are seen to be representative of the market as a whole. In doing this, the primary objectives are, first, to arrive at a more reliable forecast of sales, and second to pretest marketing plans. Where, for example, more than one geographical area is being used, it is often possible to compare the sales and profit implications of different marketing mix combinations such as high price/heavy advertising as opposed to low-price/redeemable coupons.

Other possible benefits of test marketing are that weaknesses in the product that have not previously been identified may come to light, insights may be gained into distribution problems, and the behaviour of customers can be seen in greater detail. There are, however, many critics of test marketing who argue that, at best, the results are of only marginal value. In particular, they point to:

- the difficulties of finding areas that are representative of a market as a whole;
- the dangers of competitors either becoming aware of the organization's plans and responding by copying, or of them altering their current sales strategies in order to invalidate the results;
- the difficulties of translating national media plans into local equivalents.

Where, however, a firm does opt for a test market, it has to make a series of decisions:

1 How many test areas should be used?
2 Which test areas should be used?
3 How long should the test last in order to gain a sufficiently valid insight into purchase and repeat purchase patterns?
4 What information should be collected?
5 How should the information collected be used?

Largely because of the difficulties and costs of test marketing, a number of alternatives have been proposed over the past few years. These include *store tests* in which, in return for a fee, a small number of stores carry the product, and *simulated store techniques*.

In the case of a store test, a variety of factors can be tested including shelf location, facings, price levels, and point-of-sale promotions. In a simulated store technique, groups of consumers are invited to view a number of television commercials both for existing and new products, including the one under test. They are then given a sum of money and taken into a store where they can either keep the money or spend it on any item. Researchers then take note of how many opt to buy the product being tested and how many opt for a competitive brand. The group is then asked for its reasons for purchase or non-purchase. Those who did buy are subsequently followed up by telephone to determine usage patterns and satisfaction levels. The results are then put into a mathematical model designed to forecast national sales.

Few of the techniques described so far can be used in industrial markets and here a different approach altogether is often needed. These include: *product-use tests*, where a selection of customers use the product for a short period and report both on their experiences and their likelihood of purchase; *trade shows* where potential buyers can see the product and express interest; and *dealers' display rooms* where the product stands next to existing and possibly competitive products.

Regardless of which approach to testing is used, be it in a consumer or an industrial market, the results from market testing need to be treated with a degree of caution. It is unrealistic to expect to be able to take the results and simply gross them up in order to arrive at a precise measure of sales when the product's full launch takes place. Instead, the strategist should see market testing as an opportunity to gain a greater insight into buyers' reaction patterns and to identify possible faults and problems.

## Commercialization

Because of the sorts of problem that are typically experienced in market testing, many organizations go straight from product development into a full-scale product launch. Regardless of the approach used, the issues in commercialization are the same:

1  *When* should the product be launched? Should it, for example, be launched so that the company is first into the market, or should the launch be delayed until after a competitor has spent money developing the market? Doing this also allows the strategist to learn from the competitor's experiences.
2  *Where* should it be launched? Should the product be launched regionally, nationally or internationally in one go, or should there be a more gradual roll-out in order to learn from localized experiences and reduce the initial expenditure?
3  *Which groups* should be targeted? Should the organization, for example, concentrate on existing customers or new sectors of the market? The answer to this will in practice depend upon both the nature of the product and perceptions of the target market and how it is likely to respond.
4  *How* should it be launched?

## A New Product Development Checklist

Against the background of our discussion so far it is possible to identify a series of questions that need periodically to be posed within the NPD process:

- Does the development strategy reflect the best long-term interests of the organization?
- Are sufficient resources being allocated to the up-front phases?
- Are we targeting the right market sectors?
- Are R & D and marketing working together *effectively*?

- Are we fully utilizing the organization's creative skills?
- Does the product have a core benefit proposition?
- Does the product fulfil the core benefit proposition?
- When we test market, do we make full and effective use of the information generated?
- Do we have a control system to follow the launch?
- Are we maximizing the potential of our mature products?
- Do we have the best people working on and managing our new product development process?

Taken together, these questions lead to a further but very fundamental question:

- *Do we really have a well-formulated new product strategy or do we approach new product development in a haphazard fashion that lacks any real strategic rationale and structure?*

**The Role of Licensing and Technology Transfer**

As an alternative to developing new products in-house, an ever greater number of organizations have over the past decade opted for licensing. The thinking behind this move is straightforward and based on the idea that rather than re-inventing the wheel, substantial savings in time and money, as well as a significant reduction in risk, can be made by making use of the technology developed by others. As an example of this, although there are no properly researched figures available, general agreement exists among those who have made use of technology transfer that time savings of between 50 and 80 per cent can be achieved. These sorts of saving are particularly important given the general trend towards shorter product life cycles and the consequently greater pressures on organizations to achieve a return on investment at the earliest opportunity.

The potential benefits of technology transfer can be considerable, and can be summarized in terms of:

- *Lower costs* with savings that can go as high as 90–95 per cent of going it alone.
- *Reductions in risks*. Commercializing a technology that has already been proven elsewhere is less likely to result in failure.
- *Shorter time-scales and faster reaction periods* are possible as the initial stages of the traditional R & D phases can be short-circuited; an example of how this was done by ICI's Plant Protection Division in the 1970s is cited by Chisnall (1989, p. 240):

> (The company) searched for a suitable post-emergence herbicide to control grass weeds as part of their consistent research programme during which about 10,000 different chemical compounds active against major crop pests are screened each year. Work was stopped on a compound of its own when ICI's toxicological studies revealed that it might not meet the safety standards in crop protection. After 2½ years of complex negotiations, an agreement was reached with a Japanese chemical company for rights to a suitable compound which had been synthesised by them. This enabled ICI to produce Fusilade, which was first marketed in 1981 in Central America and Romania. Later, clearance was obtained virtually worldwide, and so within seven years of first hearing about a potential active ingredient ICI had been able to launch a major new crop protection product. Success was achieved through the efficient co-operation of many innovative scientists and technologists.

Despite the apparent attractions of technology transfer, there are a number of arguments that have been put forward against its wholesale use. It is suggested, for example, that:

- Technology transfer takes the focus away from internal R & D.
- It can make the firm overly reliant upon external sources which can in certain circumstances put the organization at a disadvantage.

- It can reduce the organization's capacity to innovate.
- Transferring technology to another firm can in the long term lead to the creation of another competitor. Michael Porter (1985) is among those who have highlighted the potentially detrimental long-term effects: 'Firms often hurt rather than help their competitive position by awarding licences . . . Firms often fail to perceive who their potential competitors are, and thus award licenses that come back to haunt them.'

The validity of these criticisms has been questioned by a number of writers, many of whom have pointed to the ways in which the Japanese have over the past 45 years made very real strategic use of technology transfer. The key issue appears therefore to be that of management attitudes to new technology. When used as an adjunct to R & D, technology transfer becomes an additional weapon in the NPD armoury, speeding up in-company development processes.

Among those to have used technology transfer successfully are Mazda, Dolby, and Pilkington. In the case of Mazda, the company licensed the technology for the Wankel rotary engine from NSU Wankel. NSU had experienced several problems with the technology, particularly with engine seals. Mazda took the technology, refined it, solved the technical problems and subsequently achieved considerable success.

Both Dolby and Pilkington are examples of companies that have developed a technology which they have then licensed out. In the case of Dolby, the company recognized that they were too small to take on the hi-fi companies, and therefore licensed out their technology to the principal manufacturers partly as a pre-emptive move and partly to generate royalties that have subsequently been used to develop the system further. A similar strategy was used by Pilkington who, having developed the revolutionary 'float glass' process, licensed the process technology first to plate glass manufacturers and later to sheet glass manufacturers.

From the viewpoint of the organization that develops the technology there are six main reasons for engaging in licensing negotiations with others:

1 an inability on the part of the firm to exploit the technology in-house (e.g. Sinclair, who licensed the ZX81 to Timex in the USA);
2 the opening up of markets which other firms are more capable of exploiting;
3 the achievement of a faster standardization of technology;
4 a fragmented industry structure;
5 the creation of 'good' competitors (the issue of good and bad competitors is discussed in Chapter 4);
6 the development of relationships with firms which can then be capitalized on in other areas.

The significance of buying in ideas has also been highlighted by Langrish, et al. (1972) who in a study of 25 important product and process innovations in DuPont, a company with a strong reputation for its success, found that only 10 came from DuPont's own staff.

## 11.8 REASONS FOR NEW PRODUCT FAILURE

It is often suggested that the majority of new products fail, with perhaps the most frequently quoted figure for failure being 80 per cent. There is a problem in identifying with any degree of precision what is meant by failure, and for this reason it is best to see it in terms of products that fail to meet the expectations of their developers. Recognizing the lack of precision and that the term 'failure' can include total and partial failures, Crawford (1979) published a summary of every new product success or failure study covered in the new product's management literature. A summary of his results appears in Figure 11.8.

**FIGURE 11.8**
*Studies of new product failure*

| Study | Percentage of failure |
|---|---|
| Booz, Allen and Hamilton | 37 (Consumer) 38 (Industrial) |
| Buzzell | 27 (Food) |
| Cochran | 30 (Various) |
| Gallagher | 41 (Various) |
| Graf/Nielsen | 42 (Food) |
| Hopkins and Bailey | 40 (Consumer) 20 (Industrial) |
| Mansfield and Wagner | 27 (Industrial) |

SOURCE: Barclay and Benson (1990)

Regardless of just how accurate these figures are, it is generally acknowledged that failure rates are (too) high, that they seem not to change to any great degree over time, and that many firms see failure as one of the prices to be paid for success.

The costs of new product failure can be examined under three headings:

1 *the financial costs* associated with the development and launch processes;
2 *the marketing costs*, which include any damage to the organization's relations with its distributors and customers, lost opportunities, and any publicity given to the product's failure;
3 *the organizational costs*, including any loss of confidence on the part of those involved with the development and launch of the product, and a reduction of top management commitment to future NPD activity.

Although it is typically the first of these three areas that receives the greatest attention, the marketing and organizational consequences of failure should never be either underestimated or ignored. Where failures do occur there is an understandable tendency on the part of those associated with it to distance themselves from the project as far as possible. Often the causes of failure are identified only in broad terms with the result that organizations do not learn as much from the experiences as they otherwise might. The argument for examining failures in considerable detail are therefore strong with the results then being fed back into future new product approaches and strategies.

The research that has been conducted into the causes of failure has tended to pursue one of two themes, with attention being paid either to the reasons for the failure of a specific product (e.g. the Ford Edsel in the 1950s), or to the more general causes of failure across a spectrum of product or market sectors. The first of these has led to the emergence of case histories which, while interesting, have tended to be of relatively limited general applicability. By contrast, the work of, among others, Davidson (1987) and Cooper (1979), has provided a series of guidelines that are of potential value to the strategist.

Davidson, for example, in a study of the groceries market, found that successful products almost invariably exhibited one or more of three characteristics:

1 a significant price or performance advantage;
2 a significant difference from existing products;
3 they were the first into the market.

Although Davidson recognizes that exceptions to these rules exist, they are, he emphasizes, the exception.

Cooper's work among Canadian firms provides an equally useful insight into the causes of failure. His research led him to conclude that the principal sources of failure among industrial firms tended to be market related rather than technical.

Thus:

- competitors proved to be too firmly entrenched with the result that the necessary levels of sales proved difficult to achieve (43 per cent of cases);
- overestimations were made of the numbers of potential users (36 per cent);
- prices were set at too high a level (35 per cent);
- the marketing effort was misdirected (28 per cent).

In only one-third of the companies he examined were technical difficulties experienced.

This pattern of results led Cooper to examine the root causes of failure and to conclude that the areas with the biggest deficiency ratings were:

1 detailed studies of the market (a 74 per cent deficiency rating);
2 test marketing (a 58 per cent deficiency);
3 product launch activities (a 53 per cent deficiency).

A broadly similar pattern of results emerged from work in the United States by Hlavacek, with the causes being identified as:

- inadequate market size;
- distribution problems;
- internal conflicts;
- impatience and resistance on the part of marketing staff;
- poor marketing research.

These sorts of results have led researchers to develop a series of guidelines. The market researchers A. C. Neilsen, for example, have suggested that:

1 the product should be of demonstrably higher quality than those that it will be competing against;
2 it must compare favourably with the competition in terms of:
  - the new product idea,
  - packaging excellence,
  - price/value for money,
  - advertising support,
  - sales support,
  - benefits for the distribution network;
3 it should be capable of bidding for a strong position in the market if levels of brand loyalty are low;
4 care should be taken to guard against distribution hiccups, particularly in the early stages of the product's life;
5 it should not be too far ahead of its time.

Although the bulk of these findings and comments are straightforward and the guidelines for success that emerge largely self-evident, far too many organizations still appear to lack the objectivity that is needed for new products to succeed. In commenting on this, Davidson (1987, pp. 340–2) suggests that there are six possible explanations:

1 *New product development time schedules are often unrealistic*, particularly when the organization is faced with a competitive move. Crash action timetables are brought into play and a lead time of, for example, 18 months is reduced to four. The product that then emerges from this process is likely to be a copycat and lack the strategic thinking and differentiation needed for success.

2 *New product targets are frequently too ambitious* with those responsible for NPD being expected to develop, say, two new products each year. While this can be done, it can often only be achieved by sacrificing quality and strategic thinking in at least one of the two products.

3 *A lack of courage* in stopping a product idea once it has gone beyond the initial stages of the development process.

4 *Vested interests* on the part of those who develop the idea initially and who subsequently fight against the idea being dropped even in the face of evidence which suggests that success is unlikely.

5 *A degree of arrogance* which stems from the size of the company or the strength of its brands and which leads its staff to believe that all new products are guaranteed to succeed.

6 *An over-absorption in the process* which prevents those involved viewing the product objectively (not being able to see the wood for the trees).

Broadly similar patterns of results have emerged from a variety of other studies, including Project Sappho which focused upon the factors influencing successful industrial innovations. The research findings suggested that two marketing factors directly influenced the likelihood of success, first, a detailed understanding of user needs, and second, the attention paid to marketing. In the relative absence of these, failure rates increased dramatically.

## 11.9 LESSONS FROM NEW PRODUCT SUCCESS

The first major study of the factors which contribute to success was conducted in the UK by Carter and Williams (1956). Although the study was somewhat general, their findings highlighted the importance of management talent and the need for communication, both of which have emerged with a high degree of consistency in a variety of subsequent studies. Langrish (1972), for example, published a list of factors associated with success in the area of technological innovation which again gave emphasis to managerial factors. There is, he sugggested, a need for:

- a top person – the presence of an outstanding person in a position of authority;
- other person – some other type of outstanding individual (the 'mechanical genius');
- a clear identification of market needs;
- a realization of the discovery's potential usefulness;
- high levels of cooperation within the organization;
- the availability of resources;
- help from government sources.

The combination of these first two factors has been found to exist in the vast majority of successful companies, particularly the larger ones.

Rothwell (1972, 1974, 1977) and Project Sappho highlighted broadly similar elements:

- successful companies had a higher than average understanding of user needs;
- greater attention was paid to marketing;
- development work was performed effectively, but not always quickly;
- use was made of outside technology and advice;
- the individuals involved in NPD held senior positions and had significant authority.

For Carson and Rickards (1979), the key elements proved to be:

- the establishment of new product teams;
- the creation of an entrepreneurial spirit and approach;

- the development and use of structures designed for systematic opportunity searches;
- a staged progression from idea generation through to commercialization.

The significance of a systematic approach was again reinforced by Project Industriele Innovatie (1980) – as cited in Barday and Benson (1990) – in the Netherlands:

- a step-by-step approach;
- a strong emphasis on teams;
- a strong external focus;
- extensive use of creativity techniques;
- a process-oriented consulting role.

The majority of these factors were brought together by Peters and Waterman (1982) in *In Search of Excellence* (see p. 279). Their findings on consistently innovative companies led them to suggest that success is the result of blending four dimensions:

1 *People*: Emphasize autonomy and entrepreneurship; encourage innovators and leaders; respect the individual; achieve productivity through people; and encourage a bias for action.
2 *Attitude*: Emphasize hands-on, value-driven management, and give leadership and managerial support.
3 *Organization*: Strive for a simple form and lean staff; encourage simultaneous loose/tight properties.
4 *Market*: Get close to the customer and stay close to the business you know (stick to the knitting).

A detailed review of research into new product success led Barclay and Benson (1990, p. 10) to identify five key attributes associated with success:

1 an open-minded, supportive and professional management;
2 a good market knowledge and strategy;
3 a unique and superior product that clearly meets customers wants and needs;
4 good communications and coordination;
5 proficiency in technological activities.

Together, these five attributes form a complex and interrelated set of variables which, perhaps most significantly, are all within the company's control. Success is not, therefore, something which is either entirely or even largely determined by uncontrollable external factors.

## 11.10 Organizing for New Product Development

We suggested at an earlier stage that two principal factors contribute to new product success: first, the structure and effectiveness of the NPD process, and second, the nature of the organizational structure and culture. The significance of this second dimension was for a long time underestimated, although over the past decade a dramatically increased recognition has emerged. At the heart of this has been the acknowledgement that new product development is a process which, if it is to be effective, needs to be handled in a very different way from the vast bulk of day-to-day activities. The implication is that if the organization simply sees NPD as something that can run alongside normal ongoing activities, failure rates are likely to be high. Recognizing this, Booz, Allen and Hamilton (1982) have suggested that the consistently most successful innovators exhibit three characteristics:

1 a significant and sustained commitment of resources to new product development;
2 a new product strategy that is closely linked to the strategic planning process;
3 formal and sophisticated organizational arrangements.

A variety of approaches to organizing for NPD have been suggested, ranging from the responsibility resting with brand managers through to new product venture teams. The pros and cons of each of these approaches are listed in Figure 11.9.

**FIGURE 11.9**
*Approaches to organizing for new product development*

| | **Advantages** | **Disadvantages** |
|---|---|---|
| Brand managers | Close to the market | The more immediate need to focus upon existing brands and products<br>A short-term and narrow perspective<br>A lack of specialist NPD skills |
| New product managers | Provides a strong focus for NPD<br>Adds professionalism | Often lack real authority<br>A tendency to focus upon 'quick-fixes' in the form of a series of small modifications |
| New product committees | Adds weight to the process because members are often drawn from senior positions | Tend to ignore the small, routine changes needed<br>Bureaucratic<br>Often slow and cumbersome<br>Political conflicts frequently emerge<br>Often ad hoc and focus on specific proposals |
| New product departments | Strong focus<br>Adds weight to the process<br>Suited to large organizations with large portfolios | Need strong strategic guidelines<br>Often suffer from communication problems |
| Venture teams (see below) | Encourages entrepreneurial behaviour<br>Can lead to major developments | Expensive if the results are not significant<br>Staff often experience problems re-entering the main body of the organization |

A *venture team* consists of staff brought together from different departments and given the specific responsibility for developing a new product or business. Members are taken away from their normal duties and often moved into a separate physical location. Emphasis is placed upon informal relations and getting the job done, including launching it on to the market. Among those to have used venture teams with some success are Olivetti, 3M, and Dow.

In so far as it is possible to identify the key determinant of success, it is the development and maintenance of an entrepreneurial climate. Where the organization has a poor track record of NPD, the causes can often be traced back to this, as well as to a lack of teamwork. In commenting on this, Kotler (1988, p. 411) suggests that:

> The traditional model of innovation calls for the R & D department to get a bright idea and research it, then have an engineering team design it and the design turned over to the manufacturing department to produce, and then over to sales to sell. But this 'serial' model of innovation led to many problems. The manufacturing people would often send the design back to the engineers saying they could not produce it at the targeted cost; the engineers would then spend time redesigning the product.

When the sales force later showed the product to customers, they would realise that it could not be sold at the targeted price, since consumer needs and wants were not met. The sales people would be mad at the engineers, the R & D people would call the sales force a bunch of incompetents who could not sell, and mutual blaming would be rife.

The solution is clear. Effective product development requires closer teamwork among design, manufacturing, and marketing from the beginning. The product idea must be researched from a marketing point of view, and a marketing person must follow and advise on the idea through its development. Design engineers and manufacturing people must jointly work on the design so that the prototype passes smoothly into manufacture. Studies of Japanese companies show that their new-product success is due in large part to building in much more teamwork in product development from the beginning.

Although effective teamwork undoubtedly makes an important contribution to new product success, the strategist needs also to recognize the potential significance of the *product champion* who, believing strongly in the product, pushes the product forward, argues for resources, and ensures that it receives serious consideration. The importance of the champion was graphically illustrated by a study within Texas Instruments of 50 or so new product introductions which found that failures were *always* associated with the lack of a *volunteer* champion. This work has in turn led to the identification of three types of champion:

- *the product champion* who believes in the project and who is likely to be egotistical and a loner;
- *the executive champion* who is almost invariably an ex-product champion and who has therefore been through the process of fighting for resources;
- *the godfather* who is likely to be older, a leader, and who provides a model for championing.

## 11.11  THE R & D AND MARKETING INTERFACE

The amounts of money spent on research and development (R & D) vary greatly from one industry to another. In some of the high technology industries, for example, it is often around 10 per cent of sales, while in the food area it rarely reaches 1 per cent. The key to success is not expenditure for its own sake, but rather the way in which the money is spent and how it relates to customer needs. Gluck (1985), for example, in discussing 'big-bang' research for companies such as Apple has suggested:

> The raw materials for the big bang are detailed understanding of customers, competitors, markets, and technologies, and the implications of how they are changing.

A similar line of argument applies to virtually every other market.

The need to integrate R & D and marketing is therefore paramount. There are difficulties in doing this, however, largely because of the often very different outlooks of the two departments. In commenting on this, Davidson (1987, p. 189) suggests that whereas marketers give emphasis to risk/reward ratios, speed and timing, a desire for certainty, the short/medium term, facts, and profit-related issues, R & D staff focus on technical issues, detailed insight even at the expense of time, are willing to accept greater uncertainty, the medium/long term, creativity, and the 'validity' of the project.

In an attempt to overcome the potential for conflict that emerges from this, it is possible to identify a series of guidelines:

1 Give priority to priority setting. Recognizing that only a very small minority of ideas ever become commercially viable propositions, R & D efforts need to be focused and priorities allocated. This can be done by considering three questions:
   - What is the idea's marketplace profit potential?
   - What is the likelihood of technical success?
   - What R & D costs and time are likely to be involved in taking the idea through to completion?
2 Turn uncertainty into measures of risk which can then be assessed and a decision made concerning whether to go further.
3 Recognize the need for continuous product improvement.
4 Concentrate on developing superior product benefits.
5 Recognize that small differences can be of strategic significance.
6 Concentrate on *profit* improvements.

## 11.12 SUMMARY

In this chapter we have focused on the nature and importance of product strategy, its role within the marketing mix, and the strategic significance of new product development.

In developing a product strategy recognition needs to be given to the three interrelated elements of the product:

1 the product's physical attributes including its performance, style, and quality;
2 the benefits or 'bundle of satisfactions' that it delivers to the buyer;
3 the marketing support services such as delivery, installation and after-sales service.

The relative importance of these elements can vary considerably from one product to another with buyers in some instances being concerned almost exclusively with the product's physical or objective elements while in other cases their concern is predominantly with the product's image and subjective elements.

An effective product policy is based on an understanding of two main concepts:

1 the product life cycle;
2 portfolio analysis.

Although both the product life cycle and techniques of portfolio analysis have been subjected to a considerable amount of criticism in recent years, both are capable of providing strategic guidelines for the marketing planner.

In developing a product strategy consideration needs to be given to a variety of elements, including environmental factors, past performance, organizational objectives, resource availability and corporate capability. Taken together these elements provide the framework within which the strategist needs to decide among policies based on:

- market leadership;
- market challenging;
- product following;
- me-too.

Within the general framework of the product strategy consideration also needs to be given to the nature of the brand strategy that is to be pursued. Four principal alternatives are open to the organization:

1 corporate umbrella branding;
2 family umbrella branding;

3 range branding;
4 individual branding.

Regardless of which approach is adopted attention needs also to be paid to the various ways in which the brand can be developed. Included within this is the scope that exists for brand stretching.

Against this background we discussed the role of new product development (NPD) and the various ways in which new product development can be carried out cost effectively. We highlighted the differences between proactive and reactive strategies and the implications of each for the NPD process.

Considerable work has been done in recent years in an attempt to extend our knowledge of the determinants of new product success. The findings of this research have pointed to the significance of procedural and structural issues. The principal implications of this are that there is a need for a sequential evaluative approach, adequate resourcing, and a commitment on the part of top management which creates a positive new product development culture. Without this it is likely that the new product development process will lack true direction and the organization's product mix will rapidly become obsolete.

## 12.1 LEARNING OBJECTIVES

When you have read this chapter you should be able to understand:

(a) the strategic role and significance of price;
(b) the ways in which price can be used tactically;
(c) the factors which need to be taken into account when setting a price;
(d) the nature of pricing objectives;
(e) methods of pricing.

These objectives are contained within Figure 12.1.

## 12.2 INTRODUCTION

For many organizations price is potentially the most controllable and flexible element of the marketing mix. It is also in many cases one of the most important elements and, together with the product, a key component of an organization's marketing strategy. In this chapter we therefore focus on the strategic and the tactical roles that price is capable of playing and how pricing decisions influence and interrelate with the other elements of the marketing mix.

## 12.3 THE ROLE AND SIGNIFICANCE OF PRICE

It is generally acknowledged that pricing decisions are among the potentially most difficult that marketing managers are required to make. There are several reasons for this, the most significant of which is the nature and complexity of the interaction that commonly exists between three groups – consumers, the trade, and competitors – and the need that exists to take this interaction into account when either setting or changing a price. An added complexity is that pricing decisions often have to be made quickly and without testing, but almost invariably have a direct effect upon profit. Largely because of this, many marketing managers work to reduce the relative importance of price by, for example, giving far greater emphasis to the product's distinctive values and to its image. In other cases, the pricing decision is taken out of the hands of the marketing strategist by a combination of market-related factors. Prominent among these is the presence of a large and aggressive competitor who in effect determines prices for the industry as a whole and who, with the exception of just one or two small niche players, all other organizations are obliged to follow. The issue faced then by the strategist revolves not around the question of what price to set, but rather how to ensure that costs are contained in such a way that profits can still be made.

Price is undoubtedly a significant strategic variable and in many markets, despite a growth in the importance of non-price factors, it is still the principal determinant of consumer choice. Its significance is further emphasized by the fact

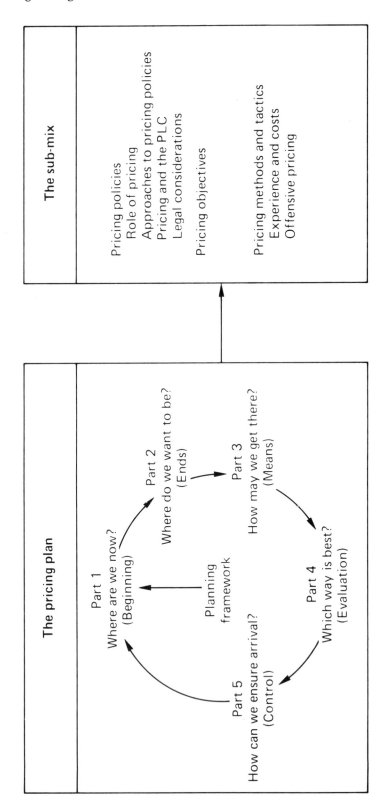

**FIGURE 12.1**
*The pricing plan and its likely submix*

that price is the only element of the mix that generates revenue – the others produce costs. It is perhaps understandable therefore that many marketing strategists treat pricing decisions with an extra degree of caution, which helps to explain why studies on both sides of the Atlantic have suggested that setting prices and dealing effectively with price competition is one of the biggest problems faced by marketing managers. The combination of these factors also goes some way towards explaining why it has often been suggested that relatively few organizations handle pricing well, and why a series of mistakes are commonly made. The most common of these are that:

1  pricing decisions are often too heavily biased towards cost structures and fail to take sufficient account of either competitors' or customers' probable response patterns;
2  prices are often set independently of other mix elements and without sufficiently explicit account being taken of, for example, advertising strategies and market positioning;
3  too little account is taken of the opportunities to capitalize on differentiation;
4  prices often do not vary sufficiently greatly between different segments of the market;
5  prices often reflect a defensive rather than an offensive posture.

Taken together, these points suggest that pricing decisions run the risk of emerging largely as the result either of historical factors or of expediency, rather than of detailed strategic thinking. The likelihood of this risk is further increased by the often haphazard way in which the focus of responsibility for pricing is allocated. In many small firms, for example, pricing decisions are often made not by sales and marketing staff, but by senior management. In larger organizations, although the responsibility for price setting is often devolved downwards, senior management typically retains an overseeing brief.

Perhaps the biggest single source of the problems that are typically associated with pricing stems from the question of whether pricing should be the responsibility of marketing or finance. Although writers on marketing have long argued that price is a marketing variable, a substantial body of evidence exists to suggest that in many organizations price is still seen to be the responsibility of the finance department, and that finance staff guard their possession of this with a degree of jealousy that makes it difficult for marketing to do little more than exert a minimal influence. This is of course a stance to which we do not subscribe.

## 12.4 APPROACHES TO PRICE SETTING

Our earlier comment that in some industries at least organizations have little choice other than to follow the prices set by the market leader, leads to the hypothesis that there are two types of firm:

1  *Price takers* which, by virtue of their size and market position, lack of product differentiation, or passive organizational culture, are either unable or unwilling to adopt a proactive pricing stance. As a result, they follow the lead set by one or more larger and more aggressive organizations within the industry.
2  *Price makers* which, largely as the result of their size and power within the market, are able to determine the levels and patterns of price which others then follow.

It is the price makers with which we are principally concerned here.

In setting a price either for a new or modified product, or for an existing product which is being introduced into a new sector of the market, the strategist needs to give explicit consideration to a variety of factors. These are summarized in Figure 12.2.

**FIGURE 12.2**
*A summary of the influences on pricing strategy*

The firm's corporate and marketing objectives
The firm's product range
The existence or scope for unique selling propositions
The degree of product differentiation
Costs (own and competitors)
Resources
The firm's market position
Previous strategies
The nature of the market
The nature and structure of competition
Opportunities for market growth
Demand elasticities
Consumers' perceptions and expectations
The need for credit
Government influences and constraints upon price
Inflation rates
The costs of raw materials and, when these are brought in from overseas, the effects of currency fluctuations
Interrelationships within the product line

SOURCE: Gilligan and Hird (1986)

Of these, the most significant are:

1 the organization's corporate objectives;
2 the nature and structure of competition;
3 the product life cycle;
4 legal considerations;
5 consumers and their response patterns;
6 costs.

Taken together, these factors allow the strategist to develop the market's price profile (see Figure 12.3) and, subsequently, to gain a greater insight into the market's pricing dynamics.

**FIGURE 12.3**
*The dimensions of a market's price profile*

**Competition**
- Who are our direct and indirect competitors?
- What pricing strategies does each pursue?
- Is price competition an important element of their marketing mix?
- How are they likely to behave when faced with price competition?
- What financial resources do they have available to cope with a price war?
- Are competitors' prices related to particular market segments?

**Legal**
- Are there any constraints upon pricing and re-pricing decisions?
- Are there legal constraints upon margins within the distribution network?
- Is there freedom to engage in price promotions?
- Do prices have to be printed on the product and/or package?
- Does retail price maintenance exist?

**Customers**
- How do consumers perceive these types of product?
- How important is the product's country of origin?
- How is our organization perceived?
- Do any social or cultural factors exist that might influence the prices that consumers are willing to pay?

**Distribution**
- What are the implications of the patterns of distribution for costs and subsequent prices?
- What margins typically exist throughout the channel?
- How are price promotions and special offers likely to be received?

**Other**
- Are there any trade associations that might usefully be consulted before setting prices?
- Is there a consumer group (e.g. The Consumers' Association) which publishes comparative analyses of products which might influence consumers' perceptions of prices?
- Will our price strategy be affected by the behaviour of others in the market in the past?
- How is the market as a whole likely to respond to price changes?

SOURCE: Gilligan and Hird (1986)

## Corporate Objectives

By starting with a statement of the firm's overall objectives and of what it is trying to achieve within each sector of the market, it is possible to identify the broad dimensions of the pricing strategy and the role that price is expected to play. In commenting on this, Majaro (1978, pp. 111–12) suggests that:

> A firm may achieve a volume of profit by catering for a small number of consumers with a high quality product and at a high price. A competitor may opt for a different approach: he may wish to attain a substantial penetration of the market with a lower quality product at a lower price and yet achieve virtually the same amount of profit. The net result of these two extremes may be the same in terms of profit but totally different in terms of turnover, production load, productivity and so on. The underlying considerations in each situation will be different, and it is essential for a person responsible for determining the price of a product to understand these considerations and the goals of the firm that result therefrom. It is the role of the strategic level of the firm to communicate such a fundamental 'input' to the marketing personnel wherever they may be located.

## The Nature and Structure of Competition

Having identified the firm's overall objectives, the focus of attention switches to the nature of competition and to the ways in which the competitive environment is likely to influence the implementation of a pricing strategy. If, for example, the market is dominated by a large and aggressive competitor the firm is likely to be forced into the position of having to follow the market leader with little or no real control over the price charged. This, in turn, may have consequences for prices in other markets either because a policy of price standardization is being pursued, or because it is seen to be necessary to increase prices elsewhere to compensate for these pressures. In other circumstances the firm may find itself in a market in which it has a degree of technological leadership or in which its manufacturing or marketing expertise provides it with a significant competitive advantage and hence a greater degree of pricing flexibility.

The significance of competitive factors in influencing pricing decisions was highlighted by the results of a study conducted by Farris and Reibstein (1979) in which they examined the relationship between relative price, relative quality, and relative advertising. The study, which covered 227 businesses, found that:

1 brands, and particularly those in mature markets, which had an average relative quality but a high relative advertising budget were able to charge higher prices than was possible for less well-known brands;
2 brands with a high relative quality and high relative levels of advertising spend achieved the highest prices;
3 brands with low relative quality and levels of advertising were unable to move away from the lowest prices;
4 the relationship between high prices and high advertising was strongest in the later stages of the product life cycle (PLC).

## The Product Life Cycle

The role of the product life cycle (see pp. 273–8) in marketing strategy was discussed in some detail at an earlier stage in the text and at this point we will do little more than remind the reader that as the firm's products move through their life cycle, so the role of each element of the marketing mix changes. In determining the pricing policy, consideration should therefore be given to three main factors:

1 the probable length of the product's life cycle;
2 the scope that exists for a competitor to introduce a new product or new

technology – possibly from another market – thereby artificially shortening the length of the life cycle;
3 the firm's profit expectations.

The specific implications of the PLC for pricing are spelled out in Figure 12.4.

**FIGURE 12.4**
*The implications of the PLC for pricing decisions*

| Product life-cycle stage | The nature of price decisions |
| --- | --- |
| 1 Pre-launch | Establish price objectives. Analyse the various influences upon price (e.g. forecast levels of demand, costs, competitors, product characteristics, supply factors, legal and other environmental issues). |
| 2 Introduction | Penetration or skimming prices depending on objectives and market characteristics. Determine trade discount structure. Develop special offers to encourage trial. |
| 3 Growth | Use price to combat competition. Make use of economies of scale. Strengthen dealer ties, improve price/value perceptions. |
| 4 Maturity | Price to protect position. Identify incremental opportunities via product differentiation. Increase options. Introduce a low-price fighting brand. Identify alternative distribution channels offering scope for higher prices. |
| 5 Decline | Price to maximize profits, even at the expense of market share. Use price reductions in short-life segments. |

## Legal Considerations

In many markets the pricing policies of large companies and particularly the multinationals are a potentially controversial issue, with some governments, particularly those in the Third World, viewing their strategies as unduly manipulative and against the consumer interest. Because of this a number of countries, including those in the developed world, have at various times experimented with price legislation in one form or another. The nature and significance of this legislation has varied enormously, but most frequently has taken the form of anti-monopoly rules in an attempt to protect small companies, domestic manufacturers and consumers from abuses by large firms.

A second area of concern for governments which has also led to the emergence of legislation is that of *price dumping* whereby an international firm uses its revenues from one market to subsidize abnormally low prices in another. The consequences of dumping have often proved to be disastrous for indigenous manufacturers and at one time or another have affected the steel industry, textile manufacturers, electronics companies, and agricultural machinery manufacturers throughout the world.

At a rather broader level, the influence of the government regulations upon prices has been discussed by Henley (1976, p. 10):

Perhaps the most obvious difference can be found in the realm of legal and philosophical approaches toward competition. Europe, Japan, and the U.S., for example, have far different approaches toward competition policy. In the U.S., antitrust has a long history. Structure and conduct are the principal bases upon which public policy toward competitive activity is formulated. In Europe, antitrust has a history of less than 15 years. Performance is far more important than structure and conduct which would be unheard of in the U.S., provided that performance in terms of public benefits (price, products, service, stable employment, etc.) is acceptable. The Japanese, if the literature is to be believed, coordinate industry, financial institutions, unions, and governments in a manner impossible to duplicate in the other advanced countries. In the developing countries, antitrust is virtually unknown and competition may even be seen as wasteful of fixed plant and equipment.

The final legal issue which needs to be considered here relates to price collusion. In some circumstances, companies may attempt to reduce price competition and establish a greater degree of control over the market by some form of collusion since, by doing this, price is to all intents taken out of the competitive equation. Collusion, however, is seen in many developed countries to be anti-competitive and as such is typically subject to legal sanctions.

### Consumers' Response Patterns and Costs
The last two of the six principal factors which need to be taken into account when setting prices are consumers' response patterns and costs; both elements are discussed in detail at later stages of the chapter.

## 12.5 DECIDING ON THE PRICING OBJECTIVES

Having developed the framework within which pricing decisions are to be made, the marketer needs then to decide upon the specific pricing objectives that are to be pursued. Although the nature of these objectives and their implications for the eventual price charged can vary greatly, the most commonly pursued are described below.

### Survival
Survival is arguably the most fundamental pricing objective and comes into play when the conditions facing the organization are proving to be extremely difficult. Thus prices are reduced often to levels far below cost simply to maintain a sufficient flow of cash for working capital.

### Return on Investment
Prices are set partly to satisfy the needs of consumers, but more importantly to achieve a predetermined level of return on the capital investment involved.

### Market Stabilization
Having identified the leader in each market, the firm determines its prices in such a way that the likelihood of the leader retaliating is minimized. In this way, the status quo is maintained and market stability ensured.

### The Maintenance and Improvement of Market Position
Recognizing that price is often an effective way of improving market share, the firm uses price partly as a means of defending its current position, and partly as a basis for gradually increasing its share in those parts of the market where gains are most likely to be made and least likely to result in competitive action. Toys 'R' Us is just one example of a company that has used price in this way with considerable success.

Chevalier and Carty (1974), however, have highlighted the dangers of using price to pursue market share. Among the disadvantages to which they give emphasis are:

1 gaining market share, particularly in mature markets, is often prohibitively expensive and only rarely cost effective;
2 share gaining price strategies tend to be blunt weapons which do not reflect differences between buyers;

3 at particular stages of the life cycle, market share is an inappropriate goal and can lead to the organization ignoring strategically more important areas such as distribution.

## Meeting or Following Competition

Having entered a market in which competitors are firmly entrenched, the firm may decide quite simply to take its lead in pricing from others until it has built up sufficient experience and established a firm reputation on which it can subsequently build.

## Pricing to Reflect Product Differentiation

For a firm with a broad product range, differences between the products can often be made most apparent by means of price variations related to each market segment. The differences in price are not necessarily linked to the costs of product, but are instead designed to create different perceptions of their products' value, and indirectly to increase profits. Among those who do this with a high degree of success and skill are the volume car manufacturers who offer a variety of derivatives from a basic model.

## Market Skimming

With a skimming objective the marketer enters the market with a high price and only gradually lowers it as he seeks a greater number of market segments. In this way, profits are likely to be relatively high and, by minimizing the degree of commitment at any one time, the levels of risk are minimized. However, for this to be a realistic objective, certain conditions must exist, the most important of which is that the firm has a degree of security in the form of patents, a strong selling proposition (i.e. a high degree of differentiation exists), unique new technology or a new product which discourages or prevents others from undercutting the price and upsetting the strategy. Among the products for which this has been used successfully are compact disc players. Development costs were high and manufacturers wanted to recover these as quickly as possible. At the same time, consumers' perceptions of the product's value were high, allowing a premium pricing strategy to be used. Where barriers to entry are low, however, and there are few if any forms of protection, price skimming is almost invariably doomed to failure since it provides a price 'umbrella' allowing competitors to enter with unnecessary ease.

## Market Penetration

As an alternative to the gradual entry strategy of market skimming, the firm may adopt a far more aggressive approach in which prices are set at a deliberately low level to ensure a high level of sales and to keep competitors at a distance. Among those to have done this consistently and successfully, particularly when entering new markets, are the Japanese.

## Early Cash Recovery

Faced with problems of liquidity or a belief that the life of the product or market is likely to be short, the firm may opt for a policy designed to generate a high cashflow and lead to an early recovery of cash. This can be achieved in a variety of ways, including a rigorous credit control policy, and by a series of special offers and discounts designed to increase immediate sales and achieve prompt payment.

## Preventing New Entry

Because of the potentially powerful role that price can play, a low price may have the effect of preventing others from entering the market as they recognize the low returns available and the dangers of becoming involved in a price war. In this way, the firm may be able to minimize the amount of competition, while recognizing that the returns may be relatively unattractive.

**Pricing Objectives and the Time Dimension**

In deciding on the objective(s) to be pursued, the strategist needs to give consideration not just to the organization's general competitive stance, but also to the issue of time. It is of course always possible for short-term objectives to conflict with long-term objectives; perhaps the most obvious example of this is the scope for conflict that exists between high short-term and long-term profits. Only rarely can the strategist pursue the two simultaneously. Because of this and because of the uncertainty regarding the future, many organizations pursue pricing methods which reflect an essentially short- to medium-term orientation, rather than the long term. This has been commented on by Fisher (1966) who has identified what he suggests are the eight most commonly pursued specific short-term pricing objectives:

1 to penetrate the market and preempt competitors by offering a low price;
2 to skim the market and aim for early profits by opting for a high price;
3 to phase out an old product by raising the price and making it unattractive;
4 to discourage competitors from entering the market;
5 to develop the company's image;
6 to be regarded as 'fair' by customers;
7 to encourage market growth by a low price/high volume policy;
8 to avoid unnecessary provocative action.

**Pricing Problems**

Although in an ideal world the strategist would simply determine the pricing objective(s) and then move on to develop the detail of the pricing structure, there are in practice several problems that are commonly encountered and that conspire to prevent the objectives being achieved unless an allowance is made for them. In commenting on these, Oxenfeldt (1973, p. 50) suggests that they include:

1 prices may be too high when compared with those of competitors and lead either to a reassessment of objectives or an acceptance of an erosion of market share;
2 a given price, while acceptable in one sector of the market, may be too high or low elsewhere;
3 the price may be viewed by sections of the market as exploitative and the company consequently seen as untrustworthy;
4 price differentials across the product line may be illogical;
5 the price may destabilize a previously stable market;
6 the price may lead to a degree of confusion in the market;
7 the price may damage or inhibit brand loyalty;
8 the strategy may well lead to an increase in buyers' price sensitivity.

## 12.6 METHODS OF PRICING

Against the background of our discussion so far it should be apparent that there are four principal factors which influence the pricing decision:

1 the company's marketing objectives;
2 the company's pricing objectives;
3 the determinants of demand including costs, competitors and consumers;
4 the product itself and the extent to which it has any distinguishing features.

The relative importance of these varies considerably from one product and market sector to another. All four, however, need to be taken into account in the choice of the pricing method. This is illustrated diagrammatically in Figure 12.5.

In deciding *how* to price, the strategist has a choice between a range of techniques which, for our purposes here, can be seen to be broadly either *cost oriented* or *market oriented*.

**FIGURE 12.5**
*A framework for
systematic pricing
decisions*

## Cost-Oriented Techniques

The three most commonly used cost oriented pricing techniques are mark-up pricing, target return on investment pricing, and early cash-recovery pricing.

### Mark-up Pricing

In many ways the most straightforward technique available, mark-up or cost-plus pricing simply involves adding a standard mark-up to the total fixed and variable costs of the product. In so far as operational difficulties are encountered with the technique, they stem largely from the problems of identifying and allocating the product's full costs.

Although a commonly used method of pricing, the technique has little to commend it other than its simplicity, since it links prices to the known variable of costs rather than to the uncertainties and realities of demand. It therefore lacks any real logic, and, because it fails to take account either of competitors or the nature of demand, is unlikely to lead to an optimal price. A further limitation of the technique is that when costs rise, prices follow almost irrespective of the implications for demand.

### Target Return on Investment Pricing

The second cost-oriented technique is based on the idea that the organization sets prices in order to achieve a particular level of return on investment. Among those to have used this in the past have been the electricity and gas boards and, in the United States, General Electric and General Motors. The calculation is straightforward:

$$\text{Price to achieve the target ROI} =$$

$$\text{Unit cost} + \frac{\text{Target percentage return} \times \text{Capital invested}}{\text{Unit sales}}$$

In so far as problems exist with the application of the technique, they are broadly similar to those that are associated with mark-up pricing: the method is essentially introspective and market opportunities are likely to be missed. There is also a problem if the price that emerges proves to be too high to achieve the level of sales needed to cover costs and the target return.

### Early Cash-Recovery Pricing (ECR)

Pricing in order to achieve a rapid recovery of the investment involved is often needed when forecasts suggest either that the life of the market is likely to be short (e.g. a fashion-related product), or when the organization anticipates that a larger company will shortly enter the market and, by lowering prices, force others out. In these circumstances emphasis needs to be placed upon pricing at a level which will, as far as possible, maximize short-term revenues and reduce the firm's medium-term risk.

## Market-Oriented Techniques

Because of the shortcomings of cost-oriented techniques, many organizations opt instead for methods of pricing that take a far greater and more explicit account of market and market-related factors. Prices in these circumstances are to be determined by a combination of competitive forces and consumers' perceptions of relative value. In using this general approach, the justification for a price increase has to be that it will add to profit or help gain or increase a competitive advantage. The central focus therefore is the question of what will happen in the short, medium and long term to the sales revenue trend. The most common manifestations of a demand-oriented approach are perceived value pricing, and going rate pricing.

### Perceived Value Pricing

This is based on the idea that in setting a price, costs should be of secondary rather than primary importance. The more important factor is the question of how *customers* perceive the value of the product. This perception can be influenced by several factors, the majority of which are under the control of marketing managers. They include the positioning strategy that is used, the image, the level of support services, and how the lifetime operating costs of the product compare with those of a competitor.

### Going Rate Pricing

As with perceived value pricing, going rate pricing is based on the notion that costs are of only limited direct value when setting a price that customers will respond to most meaningfully. Instead, the benchmark is the price set by a major competitor. The firm then sets its price at the same level or, depending upon the existence or absence of any additional distinguishing features, either just above (premium pricing) or just below (discount pricing) this level.

As a method of pricing, going rate pricing has proved popular not just because of its apparent simplicity and that it appears to reflect what is sometimes referred to as the collective wisdom of the industry, but also because it tends to reduce the likelihood of price wars emerging.

Although going rate pricing involves focusing specifically on competitors, the strategist should, when using this and indeed when using any of the other techniques, take account of the probable impact of the price on others in the market-place. This includes the *distribution network* (how will they view the price?), the *sales force* (will they be able to sell the product at this price?), *suppliers* (will they see an opportunity for increasing their prices of raw materials?), and the *government* (will they perhaps see the price as evidence of a monopoly?).

**Consumers and their Response Patterns**

In setting a price the strategist quite obviously needs to understand in as much detail as possible what effect it will have on levels and patterns of demand. To do this involves taking account of competitors and their probable patterns of behaviour, and of consumers' sensitivity to price. The issue of competition is discussed in the section that follows and here we will focus only on how best to take account of price sensitivity.

Although a number of approaches to measuring price sensitivity have been developed, one of the most useful has been proposed by Nagle (1987, Ch. 3) who suggests that there are nine principal influencing factors:

1  the *unique value effect*: the more distinctive a product is, the less price sensitive buyers become;
2  the *substitute awareness effect*: the more aware consumers become of substitutes, the greater their price sensitivity;
3  the *difficult comparison effect*: the more difficult it is to make direct comparisons between products, the less price sensitive they are likely to be;
4  the *total expenditure effect*: the lower the expenditure is as a proportion of their total income, the lower the degree of price sensitivity;
5  the *end benefit effect*: as perceived benefit increases, so price sensitivity reduces;
6  the *sunk investment effect*: when the product is used in association with products bought previously, price sensitivity is reduced;
7  the *shared cost effect*: price sensitivity is reduced when the costs are shared with one or more other parties;
8  the *price-quality effect*: the greater the degree of perceived quality or exclusiveness, the lower the price sensitivity;
9  the *inventory effect*: when the product cannot be stored and consumption takes place immediately, price sensitivity again reduces.

**Taking Account of Competitors**

One of the recurring themes of this book has been the need for competitive analysis and for the information that is generated through this to be taken into account when developing strategy. In the case of pricing decisions the need to understand competitors' cost levels and their likely patterns of price behaviour is particularly important, since in many industries a competitive attack can be launched most readily and effectively through the price mechanism. Recognizing this, the strategist should monitor particularly closely each competitor's prices and price movements for any evidence of a possible price offensive. By doing this it is possible to build a price profile for each competitor which includes a statement of the firm's likelihood and ability to engage in a price war. This involves taking account of nine factors:

1  each firm's general competitive posture – is it, for example, offensive or defensive and, in Porter's terms (see Chapter 4), a 'good' or a 'bad' competitor?
2  their cost levels and hence the scope that exists for price cutting;
3  the level of resources that would be available in the event of a price war breaking out;
4  their relative dependence upon each product and market sector;
5  the potential returns from cutting prices;
6  the relative importance of each market sector to competitors and hence their probable depth of commitment;
7  their past price history (offensive or defensive);
8  the distinctiveness of each competitor's major products and the apparent degree of brand loyalty that exists;
9  the probable response of distributors and any others in the distribution channel.

Although the information needed under most of these headings is often difficult to obtain with any degree of precision (this is particularly so in the case of costs), the strategic and tactical need for this information should never be under-estimated. The strategist should therefore begin by focusing on the two or three most significant competitors and build the price profile for each firm. The framework can then gradually be developed for the next and less direct level of competition.

## 12.7 USING PRICE AS A TACTICAL WEAPON

The bulk of our discussion so far has centred around the strategic role played by price. In many cases, however, price is used very largely as a tactical weapon, a role to which, because of its flexibility, it is well suited. There are several ways in which this tactical role can be performed, including:

- varying prices to reflect geographic differences;
- offering discounts for early payment, off-season buying, and to encourage high volume purchases;
- trade-in allowances to boost sales when the economy generally is sluggish;
- discriminatory pricing in order to capitalize upon the ability or willingness of particular market segments to pay a higher price;
- optional feature pricing which allows the price of the basic product such as a car to be kept low, but for substantial profits then to be made by adding accessories such as a sunroof;
- hitting at competitors who appear particularly vulnerable.

Perhaps the most obvious and most important tactical role that can be played by price stems from the periodic need or opportunity to raise or lower prices in order to gain or retain a competitive advantage.

Price cutting, for example, can be used to put pressure on competitors and reverse a falling market share. Equally, it can be used to solve the problem of short-term excess capacity. Raising prices can often be a means of overcoming the problems of excess demand and generating an increase in profits.

However, before making any changes to prices, the strategist needs to consider the impact on the triumvirate to which we referred at the beginning of the chapter – consumers, the trade, and competitors – and hence their likely reaction. Faced with a price increase, buyers and distributors may, for example, both respond negatively: buyers by turning to another product and distributors by focusing their attention on competitive products. A price increase might also provide competitors with an opportunity which they then become determined to exploit as far as possible.

Price cutting can, in certain circumstances at least, also create difficulties. Buyers may respond by perceiving the quality to have been lowered, while distributors may feel their margin has been eroded. Even where sales increase, this may simply be as the result of the lower price and does not necessarily lead to any degree of brand loyalty. The implication of this is that when either the price rises at a later stage or when a competitor lowers his price, sales drop. However, perhaps the biggest problem with price cutting is the danger of sparking off a price war.

Faced with a price change that is initiated by a competitor, the strategist has a number of choices:

- follow by increasing prices by the same amount;
- keep prices the same in the hope that those who have previously bought from the competitor will be encouraged to shift supplier;
- cut prices to increase the price differential.

There are of course no hard and fast rules that can be applied. Rather it is the case that the strategist should give full consideration both to the short- and to the long-term implications of any move that is made.

## The Price/ Quality Relationship

The price of a product is capable of communicating a great deal to consumers and can play a powerful role both in attracting attention and gaining sales. It is also, together with the product's performance, the main determinant of a brand's value. The question of where to position a product on quality and price is therefore at the heart of marketing strategy. There are in essence nine possible combinations of price and quality, and it is the decision on these that subsequently effects how the other elements of the marketing mix are used; these nine combinations are illustrated in Figure 12.6.

**FIGURE 12.6**
*The nine price/ quality strategies*

Price

|  |  | Low | Medium | High |
|---|---|---|---|---|
| Product quality | Low | 1 Cheap-value strategy | 2 Out-of-step strategy | 3 Exploitative strategy |
|  | Medium | 4 Above average value strategy | 5 Middle-of-the-road strategy | 6 Overcharging strategy |
|  | High | 7 Superb value strategy | 8 High-value strategy | 9 Premium strategy |

The three most offensive price/quality positioning strategies are 4, 7 and 8; it is these which provide the strongest basis for an attack since each one offers the buyer above average value for money. By contrast, strategies 2, 3 and 6 all involve setting the price above its real value and, particularly in the medium and long-term, are unlikely to succeed. (For a further discussion of how price and quality interrelate and influence patterns of product success and failure, the reader should turn back to p. 317 in which we refer to Davidson's work.)

## Pricing Decisions and Portfolio Analysis

In our discussion of portfolio analysis in Chapter 9 we commented that cashflow and profitability are both closely related to sales volume. Recognizing therefore that products typically follow a well-trodden path through the matrix, portfolio analysis is capable of providing a series of general pricing guidelines. *Question marks*, for example, offer scope either for skimming in order to quickly regain investment (this would be appropriate if the strategist sees the market as having only a limited life), or rapid penetration by means of low prices in order to build share and keep competitors at bay.

In the *star* stage, high prices are appropriate when buyer loyalty is high and/or if a high level of development costs still needs to be recovered. In other markets, a low price may be needed in order to retain share. In the *cash cow* stage, prices are likely to drift down partly because of a general increase in competition as late entrants to the market appear, and partly because the significance of differentiation is often reduced.

For a *dog*, the pricing choice is straightforward. Either price aggressively in order to build share, or where this is felt either not to be possible or worthwhile, raise prices in order to maximize very short-term profits as far as possible and then withdraw.

## 12.8 THE BEHAVIOUR OF COSTS OVER TIME

It has long been recognized that size and market share are primary determinants of profitability. The principal reason for this is that large firms usually have a lower unit cost base. These lower costs are due partly to *economies of scale* in manufacturing, distribution, purchasing and administration, and partly to the *experience effect* whereby the costs of most products decline by a fixed percentage each time an organization's experience of producing and selling them doubles.

Of the two, the nature and sources of economies of scale are by far the best known and it is therefore not our intention to do anything more than to draw the reader's attention to its significance and to emphasize that these economies can provide a significant input to the pricing decision.

The less well-known *experience effect*, however, is of equal, and in some instances of even greater, strategic significance. The concept is based on the discovery that costs decline with cumulative production and that this decline is measurable and predictable. The origins of the effect can be traced to the idea of the *learning curve* which recognizes that the time needed to perform a task decreases as workers become more familiar with it. In the 1960s, however, evidence emerged to suggest that phenomenon was limited not just to labour costs, but applied also to all total value-added costs, including administration, sales, marketing, distribution, and so on. A series of studies by the Boston Consulting Group then found evidence of what was subsequently labelled the *experience effect* in a wide variety of industries covering high technology to low technology products, service to manufacturing, consumer to industrial products, new to mature products, and process to assembly plants. The key feature in each case was, as Abell and Hammond (1979, p. 107) have pointed out:

> That each time cumulative volume of a product doubled, total value-added costs . . . fell by a constant and predictable percentage. In addition, the costs of purchased items usually fell as suppliers reduced prices as their costs fell, due also to the experience effect. The relationship between costs and experience was called the experience curve.

**Sources of the Experience Effect**

The experience effect has a variety of sources, the seven most significant of which have been identified as:

1 greater labour efficiency;
2 work specialization and methods improvement;
3 new production processes;
4 obtaining better performance from existing equipment;
5 changes to the resource mix;
6 greater product standardization;
7 product redesigns.

While these are the principal sources of experience, they do not emerge naturally but are instead, as Abell and Hammond (1979, p. 113) point out:

> the results of substantial, concerted effort and pressure to lower costs. In fact, if left unmanaged, costs rise. Thus experience does not *cause* reductions but rather provides an opportunity that alert managements can exploit. Consequently strategies resulting from market planning should explicitly address how cost reductions are to be achieved.

The strategic implications of the experience curve are potentially significant, since by pursuing a strategy to gain experience faster than competitors (this would normally mean high market share), an organization lowers it cost base and

**FIGURE 12.7**
*The implications of experience for pricing and profitability*

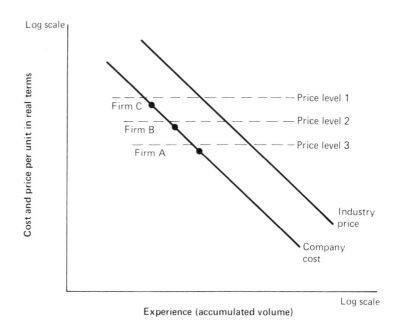

has a greater scope for adopting an aggressive and offensive pricing strategy. This is illustrated in Figure 12.7 in which three organizations are competing.

In this example Firm A has the greatest experience, Firm C has the least. Firm A therefore has a choice of strategies open to it. By setting the price at level 1, all three firms make a profit. However, by forcing the price down initially to level 2 and subsequently to level 3, Firm A puts ever greater pressure on its two competitors and forces firstly Firm C and then Firm B into making a loss. Faced with this, the two firms either make a loss which has to be absorbed or they withdraw from the market.

Although the industry prices are shown in Figure 12.7 to fall steadily, in practice they tend to follow a somewhat different pattern. This is illustrated in Figure 12.8.

In the development phase, prices are below costs.

In the umbrella phase, prices remain relatively stable and profits are readily obtainable. The shake-out occurs either as the result of one company deliberately slashing prices to gain share (this was done with enormous success both in the

**FIGURE 12.8**
*The development of costs over time*

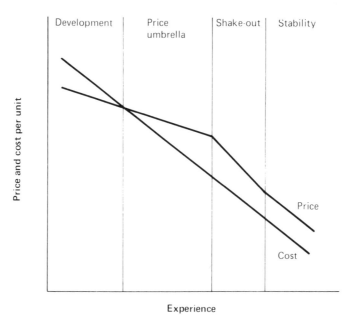

SOURCE: Adapted from Boston Consulting Group (1972), p. 21

hand-held calculator market in the early 1970s and in the personal computer market in the 1980s), or as a defensive move to preempt a competitor's move. At this stage, some companies are likely to withdraw, and the industry then returns to a degree of stability.

Although the experience effect has, as we commented earlier, been found to exist in a wide variety of markets, problems are typically encountered in its use. These include:

- the mistake of plotting cost data against time rather than cumulative experience;
- the difficulties of analysing experience on different cost components;
- the need to take account of inflation;
- the implications of shared experience;
- identifying the correct starting point when measuring experience;
- cost differences between competitors.

Despite these difficulties, the experience effect is of potentially enormous strategic value and has considerable implications for the development of a long-term pricing strategy. A detailed understanding of the experience effect and, more importantly, how it can be used has, for example, provided a strong underpinning for the strategies pursued by the Japanese car industry.

## 12.9 THE PRINCIPLES OF OFFENSIVE PRICING

We commented at an earlier stage that pricing decisions are among the potentially most difficult that marketing managers are required to make. Recognizing this, a number of writers have developed models that are designed to provide the basis for a more highly structured approach to price setting. Among those to have done this is Davidson (1987, Ch. 10) who identifies what he refers to as 'The Eight Principles of Offensive Pricing'. These principles are listed below.

### 1 Know Your Price Dynamics
Pricing decisions must be based on a detailed understanding of the nature and degree of price sensitivity that exists. In some markets, for example, *overall demand* may be generally inelastic whilst the demand for *individual brands* may be highly price responsive. The strategist should therefore consider:

- the frequency of purchase – as a general rule of thumb, levels of price sensitivity increase with the frequency of purchase;
- the degree of necessity – the greater the need, the lower the sensitivity;
- unit price – high prices lead to greater price consciousness;
- the degree of comparability – when this is easy, price awareness increases;
- the degree of fashion or status – as this increases, the direct importance of price reduces.

### 2 Strengthen Your Pricing Muscles
By giving a greater emphasis to non-price features such as higher quality, packaging, advertising and after-sales service, the nature of the selling proposition can be changed in the organization's favour. An example of a company to have done this with considerable success is Marks & Spencer 'which succeeded in widening its price premium by steadily strengthening the appeal of its products over time. Its food products earn a premium because customers perceive them as fresher, of higher quality and more exciting. They also generate (higher) profits' (Davidson, p. 234). Learning from this, other food retailers such as Sainsbury and Tesco have both made significant changes to their product mixes over the past few years.

### 3 Choose Your Price Segments

In choosing segments of the market in which the company is to operate, consideration needs to be given to the implications for pricing and to the organization's ability to operate effectively. In certain market sectors, for example, the prerequisite is not simply that the organization has a low cost base currently, but that it is capable of maintaining this cost base over time. The issues which must therefore be considered include:

- the relative profitability of each segment;
- the degree of organization - segment fit;
- competitors' intentions and capabilities.

### 4 Consider the Alternatives

In what ways might price be integrated most effectively with other elements of the marketing mix and hence the direct significance of price be reduced?

### 5 Manage the Ripples

In most competitive industrial or distributor markets, different buyers pay different prices depending upon their purchase volumes, delivery methods, servicing demands and negotiating skills. Because of the potential sensitivity of this, the strategist needs to give emphasis to:

- a clearly communicated trading strategy;
- understanding the profit implications of altering each of the variables referred to above;
- building long-term relationships so that the implications of problems at a particular level in the organization can be reduced.

### 6 Beware of Profit Cannibalization

This applies where a marketing initiative with one product significantly reduces the profit on another.

### 7 If You Make a Pricing Mistake, Admit it and Remedy it Fast

### 8 Beware of Markets with Falling Prices

This is the case unless you are confident that your organization has a competitive edge which can be maintained and be used to keep competitors on the defence.

## 12.10 HOW DOES BRITISH INDUSTRY PRICE?

The question of how industrial firms approach the pricing task was the subject of a major study, *How British Industry Prices*, published in 1975 but which still provides a clear insight to current practices. The study highlighted a series of points including:

- in most industrial companies, cost-oriented methods predominanted;
- prices were seemingly influenced by marketing policy to only a limited extent;
- little variation in pricing behaviour was found to exist between the three markets covered by the study (capital goods, components and materials);
- the majority of organizations stated that prices were set either by the cost-plus technique or by the target return on investment method;
- less than one-fifth of companies said that prices were primarily affected by factors other than costs;
- the pricing stance was almost invariably defensive;
- prices tended to follow or reflect the patterns set by competitors;

- discounts were only rarely used within the overall framework of marketing objectives, and were instead mechanistically linked to individual or aggregate order size;
- giving discounts appeared to be largely routinized;
- only some 30 per cent of companies conducted any research to determine price acceptability before setting or modifying a price;
- the results of pricing decisions were seldom monitored;
- in general, pricing tended to be handled in an ad hoc rather than a systematic fashion.

## 12.11 SUMMARY

It is generally acknowledged that pricing decisions are among the potentially most difficult decisions that marketing managers are required to make. Within this chapter we explored the complexities of the pricing decision and discussed how the marketing strategist can use price both tactically and strategically.

Organizations can be broadly characterized as being either *price takers* or *price makers*. Our concern within this chapter was with the price makers (those firms which are able to operate with at least a degree of pricing freedom).

Prices are influenced by a series of factors, the most significant of which are:

- corporate objectives;
- the competitive stance;
- the nature and structure of competition;
- the product life cycle;
- legal considerations;
- consumers and their response patterns;
- cost structures.

A detailed understanding of each of these elements *and their interrelationships* is needed whenever setting or modifying a price.

A variety of pricing objectives exist, the most common of which are:

- survival;
- return on investment;
- market stabilization;
- the maintenance or improvement of market position;
- meeting or following competitive moves.

Methods of pricing can be broadly categorized as:

- cost oriented (mark up, target ROI, and early cash recovery);
- market oriented (perceived value and going rate pricing).

Because of its flexibility price can be used in a variety of ways as a tactical weapon, including boosting short-term sales, and reflecting geographical or segmentation differences.

Strategically, price can be a powerful marketing tool although if its full potential is to be used the strategist needs a detailed understanding of competitive objectives and relative cost structures. This was discussed in the context of the experience curve.

We concluded by examining the eight principles of offensive pricing and the various ways in which British industry goes about pricing. The starting point for an offensive approach involves understanding the organization's pricing dynamics and choosing price segments with care, two points which according to the research tend to be understood only by a minority of British organizations.

# 13 | The promotional plan

## 13.1 LEARNING OBJECTIVES

When you have read this chapter you should:

(a) have achieved an understanding of the role of promotion in the marketing mix;
(b) know that promotion is composed of a sub-mix of elements which need to be integrated harmoniously;
(c) be familiar with the promotional planning process and the major decision areas within this element of the marketing mix;
(d) be able to interrelate promotional planning with other aspects of the overall marketing plan.

## 13.2 INTRODUCTION

Promotion here refers to the major forms of marketing communications, namely advertising, personal selling, sales promotion and PR, which we can call the promotional mix.

Some writers (e.g. Kotler, 1986) use the term 'communications mix' rather than promotional mix, in the same context, while others (e.g. Jefkins, 1990) use the term 'communications' to represent company-wide communications rather than just marketing communications.

Just as the elements of the marketing mix need to be integrated and tailored to the needs of particular market segments – see Chapter 8 – so the elements of the promotional mix should be harmonized in order to avoid conflict and confusion in messages being sent to the target audience and to achieve maximum communication effectiveness.

The role of the promotional mix is essentially to make the target audience favourably aware of the availability of products and services in the market-place. Each element of the promotional mix can play a distinctive part in this role.

Attempts to distinguish between advertising as 'above-the-line' and sales promotion as 'below-the-line' are somewhat artificial and arise from the fact that advertising agents receive commission on space bookings from the media. For this reason advertising agencies used to 'draw a line' in their accounts above which were the commissionable items (media advertising) and below which were the non-commissionable items (sales promotion).

Other attempts have been made to distinguish more clearly between elements of the promotional mix. For our purposes we would say that:

● advertising is non-personal persuasive communication in media not owned by the company.
● sales promotion is non-personal persuasive communication in media owned by the company,
● selling is personal persuasive communication by sales people employed by the company.

PR is used by some large companies in a wider context than marketing and has been defined by the Institute of Public Relations as:

> ... the deliberate, planned and sustained effort to establish and maintain mutual understanding between an organisation and its publics.

In this sense we are talking about corporate PR rather than product PR.

In view of the above definition some authors prefer to use the word 'publicity' to mean the subfunction of PR which seeks to gain favourable editorial publicity in the media about company products and services.

As pointed out earlier in this book any writer on marketing planning faces the problem of just what to include under the marketing mix and submix headings so as to represent what he/she feels to be the best interests of the readers. Different product markets involve different emphases. For example, industrial marketers typically have little interest in packaging as a form of promotion, while fast-moving consumer goods manufacturers often see this as a key success factor.

An attempt to depict an acceptable coverage of the promotional submix is made in Figure 13.1.

**FIGURE 13.1**
*The promotional submix expanded*

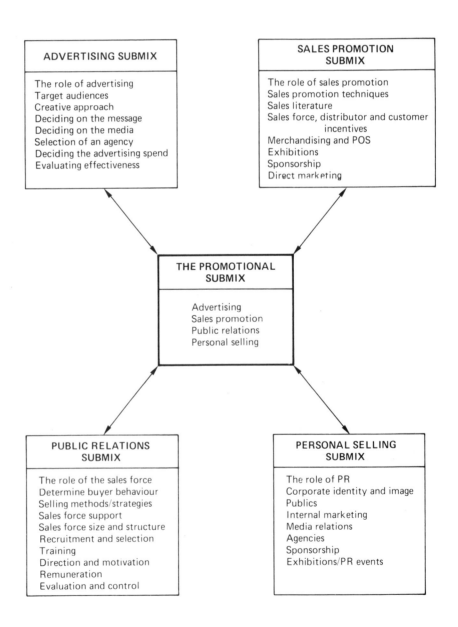

**ADVERTISING SUBMIX**

The role of advertising
Target audiences
Creative approach
Deciding on the message
Deciding on the media
Selection of an agency
Deciding the advertising spend
Evaluating effectiveness

**SALES PROMOTION SUBMIX**

The role of sales promotion
Sales promotion techniques
Sales literature
Sales force, distributor and customer incentives
Merchandising and POS
Exhibitions
Sponsorship
Direct marketing

**THE PROMOTIONAL SUBMIX**

Advertising
Sales promotion
Public relations
Personal selling

**PUBLIC RELATIONS SUBMIX**

The role of the sales force
Determine buyer behaviour
Selling methods/strategies
Sales force support
Sales force size and structure
Recruitment and selection
Training
Direction and motivation
Remuneration
Evaluation and control

**PERSONAL SELLING SUBMIX**

The role of PR
Corporate identity and image
Publics
Internal marketing
Media relations
Agencies
Sponsorship
Exhibitions/PR events

It can be seen that an element in the submix can be included under more than one heading. For example, exhibitions have relevance to both sales promotion and PR. A certain amount of overlapping is therefore desirable when planning submixes, in order to ensure harmony.

We have already distinguished between corporate PR and product PR. There are a number of examples of sponsorships which can be applied to both these areas. For example, Cornhill's sponsorship of test cricket would be classed as corporate PR since it promotes the company name, while Embassy's sponsorship of the world snooker championships is promoting the brand or product. Most product PR could be said to incorporate some element of advertising.

We have observed that the promotional plan consists of a number of sub-elements each of which requires an individual subplan.

While these subplans have of necessity been presented separately in the pages that follow, they do need to integrate harmoniously as a total promotional mix in the same way as the elements of the marketing mix.

**FIGURE 13.2**
*Integrating elements of the promotional mix*

In order to do this there are a number of major steps to be taken:

1 identify the target audiences;
2 determine the promotional objectives;
3 create the messages;
4 select the channels of communication;
5 decide the details of the promotional mix;
6 agree the total promotional budget;
7 measure the results;
8 manage the total promotional plan.

Many companies find they can increase the effectiveness of any single element of the promotional mix by blending it with one or more of the other elements. For example, the sales force communicates more effectively by using presentation materials and samples; advertising recall is enhanced by the placement of point-of-sale display material; consumer incentives and PR benefit from advertising, etc.

There are two basic strategies. The *push* strategy aims at intermediaries in the channel of distribution such as wholesalers and retailers and their industrial equivalents. These are the manufacturer's primary publics or target audiences. The promotional objective is to encourage the stocking and display of products so that ultimate consumers/users receive the maximum exposure to them. In short, goods are *pushed* into the channel and through the middleman in the way depicted in Figure 13.3.

The *pull* strategy is aimed at the ultimate consumer or user (rather than the intermediary) and directly attempts to create demand for the manufacturer's

**FIGURE 13.3**
*Pull and push
promotional
strategies*

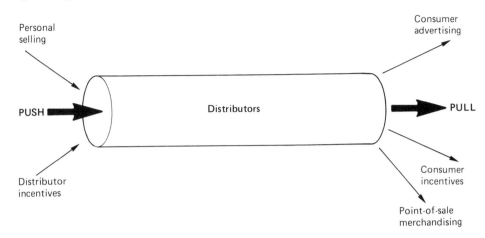

goods so as to persuade distributors to place orders and stock them. The strategy
thus *pulls* goods through the shops from the consumer end of the channel.

In simpler terms it is said that personal selling's role is to *sell in* whereas
advertising's job is to *sell out*.

In practice, however, things are not that simple and a sales person will use the
promise of extensive advertising support to help sell in. Equally, fmcg companies
will often provide teams of sales merchandisers to help the store to sell out. In
short, a mix of strategies is more often the case. Sales people's visits tend to be
more effective when backed up with trade advertising.

As previously illustrated in Chapter 9, promotional strategies for particular
products should be adjusted according to their stage in the product life cycle and
position in the Boston matrix. Heavy advertising to create awareness is necessary
at the introductory stage of a product launch (see p. 276), while promotional
support might be substantially reduced in the cash cow position of the Boston
matrix (see Chapter 11).

The total planning structure advocated in this book at its outset has been
employed for each of the four subplans in the promotional mix which follow so as
to demonstrate the applicability of this overall planning format to particular
elements and indeed sub-elements of the marketing mix.

## 13.3 THE ADVERTISING PLAN

**Introduction**

The planning of advertising can be particularly problematical in that the question
'Does advertising pay?' is often raised, in answer to which Lord Leverhulme's
dilemma is sometimes quoted, namely that half of all advertising is wasted but the
problem lies in knowing which half.

However, it is not always true that we cannot determine the effectiveness of
advertising. In the case of mail order where products are advertised in, say, the
national newspapers (see Figure 13.4) then not only can the sales response to a
given advertisement be accurately measured but its profit contribution as well.
We can compare the costs and profit contribution of different forms of
advertising in the same medium and/or of the same advertisement in one
newspaper with another newspaper. This can be done simply by keying the
address with a particular code or having some other means of identifying the
stimulus of the response, such as a box number.

It can be observed that organizations advertise regularly, presumably in the
belief if not the certain knowledge that it does pay. An organization cannot make
sales without some form of communication, and advertising is one of the major
forms of communication adopted by most concerns. As Jefkins (1990, p. 129)
says 'advertising . . . is both the cheapest way of reaching a large number of

**FIGURE 13.4**
*An example of a
mail-order
advertisement in a
daily newspaper*

strangers who may be potential customers, and the most expensive way of doing so. Costs are relative to results'.

What then are the major decisions that we need to take when planning advertising? Logically these would be:

1  What is the role of advertising within the promotional mix and the marketing mix?
2  With whom do we wish to communicate?
3  What do we want to say?
4  How can we best say it?
5  Where (i.e. in what media) should we say it?
6  How much will it cost?
7  Should we use an advertising agency?
8  How shall we evaluate effectiveness?

These questions form the basis of the advertising submix within advertising planning, as depicted in Figure 13.5.

**Where Are We Now? The Advertising Audit**

The first step when planning advertising is to determine the current situation (where are we now?) in order to decide more clearly where we want to be. This would involve measuring the amount of expenditure (and other resources used) on advertising in the recent past and making comparisons with competitors not only on the amount spent but also on the media used and the types of advertisements placed.

We should also attempt to determine the effectiveness of previous advertising. This can be done in a discrete way as indicated in Figure 13.6.

**FIGURE 13.5**
*The advertising plan*

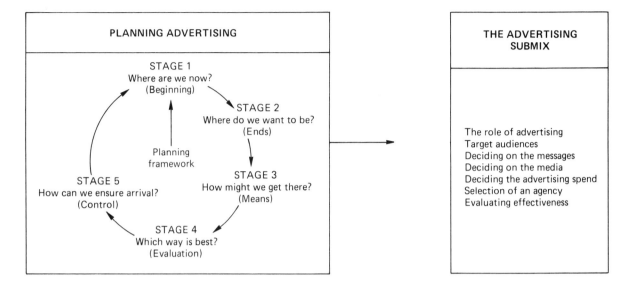

However, a more strategic approach would be to attempt to assess advertising's effect not only in terms of sales response but also on company profit, competitive position and organizational effectiveness (see Chapter 15).

**FIGURE 13.6**
*Some quantitative and qualitative ways of auditing a company's advertising*

| QUANTITATIVE | QUALITATIVE |
| --- | --- |
| Sales response | Awareness |
| Number of enquiries | Unprompted recall |
| Coupon returns | Prompted recall |
| Number of advertisements | Saliency |
| Sizes of audiences reached | Recognition |
| Media spread | Comprehension |
| Costs | Attitude change |
| Competitor spend | Liking |
|  | Likelihood |

**Where Do We Want To Be? The Role of Advertising and Advertising Objectives**

Gilligan and Crowther (1976, p. 27) discuss this issue in the following manner:

Those who contend that the task of advertising should be to achieve a communication goal argue that sales cannot serve as a realistic objective primarily because they are the result not only of advertising but of advertising in conjunction with the other marketing variables. There is the consequent difficulty, therefore, of determining the extent to which advertising has contributed to the achievement of any particular level of sales experienced. By way of contrast, the degree of communication achieved can be measured relatively easily and accurately by the use of research techniques. Advocates of this latter view – known as DAGMAR (Defining Advertising Goals, Measuring Advertising Results) – therefore suggest that the task of advertising is best stated in terms of communication effects.

However, although the adoption of communications objectives overcomes the disadvantages inherent in the use of a sales goal, a significant drawback still exists. With few exceptions, the ultimate purpose of advertising is to create sales and, unless there is clear cut evidence regarding the relationship between communication and subsequent sales, it is not necessarily realistic to assume that a high degree of brand awareness of the existence of a favourable attitude towards a product will lead to an increase in the company's sales performance. The attainment of a communication goal may therefore be misleading in so far as it is not always reflected in the company's performance in the market place.

With these considerations in mind the reader should appreciate that it is not feasible to generalise about the type of objectives which should be pursued by advertising or to state that a sales objective is either any better or any worse than a communication objective. Instead, the choice should be seen to be dependent upon the particular circumstances in which the company is operating. For example, if it is possible to determine that there is a direct functional relationship between communication and subsequent sales, it is safe to use communication objectives. If there are not these obvious relationships then the task of advertising should be expressed in terms of both sales and communication objectives.

With the above discussion in mind we can now categorize advertising objectives as follows:

*Some possible broad objectives:*
1  to enhance organizational effectiveness;
2  to generate greater profits;
3  to improve our competitive position.

*Some possible specific objectives (quantitative):*
4  to increase sales from X to Y;
5  to raise the level of awareness of a given product from P to Q;
6  to generate N enquiries/coupon responses.

*Some possible sub-objectives (qualitative):*
7  to convey information;
8  to create desire;
9  to improve the image of product X or brand Y;
10  to mitigate the effect of a premium price (e.g. Heinz Beans).

## How Might We Get There?– Advertising Strategies

When deciding how best to attain the sort of advertising objectives described above, the advertiser needs a clear idea of the target audience. This audience may be existing and/or potential buyers, deciders or influencers. The audience could be individuals or groups, particular publics or the general public.

The target audience will, to a large extent, influence advertising decisions on what we want to say, how best to say it, where and when it is to be said. For example, the manufacturer of a new toy aimed at 11 to 14-year-old boys might choose to advertise this in appropriately simple language, using line drawings to show a boy using the toy, in a boys' comic or magazine, in the run-up to the Christmas period.

Generally speaking, the bigger the investment in advertising, the greater the number of people that can be made aware of the advertiser's products or services. However, the law of diminishing returns will eventually operate, that is to say the extra cost of the extra people reached will outweigh the extra sales potential (see Chapter 1).

There is also the possibility of greater cost effectiveness in deploying other elements of the promotional mix to achieve the objectives set.

No matter how many people are made aware of a company's products through advertising, the potential sales effectiveness is to a large extent governed by the impact of the advertisements themselves. If these are not believed and/or remembered then it is unlikely that people will be persuaded to buy.

Advertising agencies play a major role in the creative process resulting in an effective advertising campaign. For this reason the selection of the right agency is a key success factor.

We shall now look at these decisions in more detail, starting with the creative strategy since this will affect the expenditure required and possibly the selection of an appropriate advertising agency.

There are three major components in an advertisement, namely, words (copy), pictures (illustration) and their juxtaposition or relationships (layout). These three components are the tangible expression of the creative input.

Before deciding on the creative approach it is necessary to analyse the characteristics of both the market and the product in order to determine the product's required positioning in the target market segment as explained in previous chapters. Having done this there are two main schools of thought concerning the development of creative appeals: one suggests that the potentially most successful advertisements are based on the creation of a distinct brand image, while the other argues that success is more likely if emphasis is placed on developing a unique selling proposition (USP). In addition to these two main theories there are a number of less well-known and less frequently used approaches including the identification of a product's inherent drama.

## Deciding the Advertising Spend

Kotler (1988, pp. 604–6) and other authors offer evidence to show that there are four or five generally used methods of deciding on the advertising spend, namely:

1  what the organization can currently afford;
2  matching competitors' spends or the norm for the industry;
3  a fixed percentage of past sales;
4  a fixed percentage of past profit;
5  the objective and task approach.

We can evaluate these methods as shown below.

### 1 Affordable Approach

In the affordable approach, the advertising appropriation is set simply on the basis of an assessment of what the company can afford to spend in the forthcoming financial year. It is therefore an extremely arbitrary method which, although it has the advantage of being simple to operate and of ensuring that the company does not over-extend itself, suffers from several severe limitations.

The two fundamental weaknesses of the affordable approach are, first, that it does not encourage the development of long-term planning of advertising expenditure (the amount the company can afford to spend may vary greatly from year to year and these variations cannot easily be predicted), and second, that short-term advertising opportunities are likely to be overlooked. Despite these weaknesses many companies use the affordable approach, seemingly without encountering problems. Difficulties are likely to arise, however, if the company's sales revenue begins to decline. Faced with this situation the instinctive reaction is to spend less on 'luxuries' such as advertising. But any decrease in the amount of advertising may well lead to a further decrease in sales. The effects of using the affordable approach in such a situation are therefore likely to be cumulative.

A slight variation of the basic affordable approach has been suggested by Joel Dean (1951, pp. 363–75) who pointed out that the utility to management of any funds left over after allowing for an acceptable return on capital is low compared with the possible return to the organization of diverting all of these excess funds into advertising.

However, the value of Dean's idea notwithstanding, the affordable approach to setting the appropriation has little to commend it and offers little promise to the advertiser who wishes to determine the appropriation in a logical manner by attempting to relate advertising costs and advertising effects.

## 2 Competitive Parity

When applying the principle of competitive parity, the advertiser sets the appropriation at a level to match the advertising outlay of a competitor. This can be done in one of two ways: either by setting the appropriation to match exactly, or nearly exactly, the expenditure of a competitor, or by setting the appropriation on the basis of a ratio of share of market to share of advertising. To apply this second method it is necessary to collect data on total sales and total advertising by all the firms in the market. If, having collected this information, a correlation appears to exist between advertising expenditure and subsequent sales performance it is possible to compute approximately how much money needs to be spent on advertising to achieve any given market share. To illustrate this, assume that the information in Table 13.1 has been collected:

Table 13.1

|  | Percentage of industry sales | Percentage of industry advertising |
| --- | --- | --- |
| Brand A | 30 | 60 |
| Brand B | 15 | 30 |
| Brand C | 3 | 6 |
| Others (including private brands) | 52 | 4 |
|  | 100% | 100% |

On the basis of the figures in Table 13.1 the marketer can conclude that for every 1 per cent share of the market gained by a specific brand, an expenditure of 2 per cent of total industry advertising was required. Therefore, if the manufacturer of Brand B wishes to maintain his 15 per cent share of the market, he must ensure that his advertising appropriation is at least 30 per cent (15 times 2) of the industry's advertising expenditure. Knowledge of the existence of any such relationship is obviously of value although in practice it is likely to occur only in a very stable market in which there is no aggressive action on the part of any one company.

Two justifications are normally advanced for the competitive parity approach. The first is that in some mystical way competitors' expenditure represents what is known as 'the collective wisdom of the industry'. The second is that by maintaining a competitive parity, aggressive action is minimized and advertising wars avoided.

In practice both arguments lack validity. The only true justification for basing the appropriation upon that of a competitor is if both companies are facing exactly the same market conditions, have exactly the same opportunities, are pursuing the same goals, have the same reputations, are intending to allocate advertising funds in the same way to the same media, and are operating the company in the same manner. However, even if we assume that these conditions are satisfied (which in itself is most unlikely), then there still exists the distinct possibility that the competitor from whom the company takes its lead is allocating money unwisely. In addition, there are two practical difficulties in implementing this approach. Companies traditionally handle their financial affairs with some attempt at secrecy and there are likely to be problems encountered in discovering the amount a competitor intends to spend in the forthcoming period. Finally, even assuming that this information is obtained, the imitator may be unable to afford to spend the money necessary to achieve parity.

With regard to the second justification of the approach, little or no evidence exists to suggest that maintaining parity does stabilize industry expenditures.

Thus, although an awareness of a competitor's advertising appropriation is undoubtedly useful, the competitive parity approach is unlikely to lead to an optimal solution to the problem. A worthwhile guideline in this respect was laid down by Burton and Miller (1970, p. 99): 'Watch what your competitor does. Profit from what he does; but set your own course.'

### 3 & 4  Percentage of Sales or Profit

Of the numerous approaches to determining the appropriation, the concept of percentage of sales is the most popular. In its simplest form percentage of sales involves applying a predetermined percentage figure to the value of sales achieved in the previous financial period. This percentage figure remains constant for a number of years. Thus, if the advertiser had sales last year of £1 million and the percentage figure he has used in the past is 5 per cent, the appropriation for the forthcoming year is £50,000 (5 per cent of £1 million). A slight variation which has gained ground in recent years involves the percentage being applied not to the previous year's sales, but to a forecast of sales for the period covered by the appropriation.

The obvious attraction of a percentage of sales or profit is its simplicity. In addition, the amount of funds allocated to advertising will tend to vary with what the company can afford, and, assuming that competing firms tacitly agree to let advertising expenditures follow a percentage of sales, some degree of competitive stability will result.

However, despite these advantages, the method represents a very mechanical approach to decision making, and is hard to support analytically. The weaknesses of the method are, first, that circular reasoning is employed as sales act to determine advertising, rather than the other way round. Second, because the funds made available will vary as sales or profits fluctuate, there is likely to be only limited scope for engaging in long-term planning of advertising programmes. Third, because funds will vary with what the company can afford, there is no facility for engaging in counter-cyclical advertising. Fourth, there is no apparent logical figure which should be employed. In the example given earlier the percentage could equally be 4 per cent or 6 per cent. In addition, implicit in the approach is the fact that once the percentage figure has been chosen it is adhered to rigidly. This inflexibility is obviously undesirable in the face of changing goals and market conditions and is likely to lead to short-term opportunities being overlooked. Finally, having used percentage of sales to determine the appropriation, there is a tendency to allocate the budget in the same way rather than in a more constructive fashion such as on the basis of opportunities.

Thus, despite its popularity, the percentage of sales or profit approach has no apparent logical foundation and, like the affordable and competitive parity methods, is unlikely to lead the advertiser to the profit maximizing outlay.

### 5  Objective and Task

In the objective and task method, the approach used in the previous four methods is reversed. Instead of determining the size of the appropriation and then allocating it by product and sales area, objective and task requires the advertiser to set the appropriation on the basis of the cost of achieving the advertising objectives.

The approach can be illustrated by the following five steps:

(i)   establish the advertising objectives;
(ii)  select the media and determine the number of insertions needed to achieve these objectives;
(iii) calculate the cost of the media programme and add to it the production costs;

(iv) examine the relationship between costs and objectives to determine whether the cost of achieving the objectives is justified and whether the company can 'afford' the costs;

(v) if necessary, revise the goals and methods to a level the company can afford.

Although objective and task is accepted as being logically the most superior of all those in common use, many advertisers avoid using it because of the amount of analysis required initially to operate it properly. In addition, an interesting observation has been made by Frey and Halterman (1970, p. 372) who point out that advertisers:

> who state that they use the method often have trouble in explaining just how they arrived at the amount of advertising necessary to reach the established objectives. They may even find it difficult to explain how they arrived at the objectives. The objectives themselves may be established with too little regard for their implications.

## Selecting the Advertising Agency

Selection of the right media and of the right messages are the means by which advertising objectives are achieved. Both involve the need for expertise, which for many companies is provided by an advertising agency. Generally speaking advertising agencies traditionally booked space in above-the-line media on behalf of advertisers, for which they received commission normally varying from 10 to 15 percent from the media. This activity led naturally to the development of expertise not only in the strengths and weaknesses of an individual medium, in the nature of the audience reached and its cost effectiveness – but also in what has become known as the creative strategy. The real worth of advertising agencies to their clients lies more in their creative abilities which stretch from innovative copy writing to illustration, layout and music, than in their service of booking space.

To help the advertising agency in its creative efforts, the client needs to take the agency into its confidence and provide all the necessary information, including the products benefits and its unique selling proposition (USP) if any.

Today, advertising agencies exist in a wide range of types and provide a variety of services. They range from large international concerns such as Saatchi and Saatchi offering a full service, to very small ones perhaps specializing only in creative work – known as 'à la carte' agencies.

A full service agency, as the name implies, offers not only media planning/research and creative services but will also handle exhibitions, sales literature, PR and other below-the-line aspects, as well as marketing research. Other agencies prefer to specialize – for example those known as 'media independents' limit their services to media planning and media buying. Some agencies may even specialize in particular types of advertisements, e.g. recruitment advertising.

While selection of the right agency will to a large extent depend on the specific nature of the work required there are a number of generally agreed criteria covering this choice.

**FIGURE 13.7**
*Some choice criteria in advertising agency selection*

Size of agency relative to client
Specialisms of agency, e.g. industrial or consumer
The advertising agency's client portfolio (no competitors)
Track record
Creative strategies offered
Compatibility in terms of working relationships
Range of services provided
Standing and reputation

When selecting an advertising agency the question of terms will almost certainly arise. There are a number of different ways in which an agency may be paid for its services but these fall mostly into three basic systems: a flat fee, a retainer or by commission received from the media.

**Evaluation and Control of the Advertising Plan**

Much has been written about the difficulties of evaluating advertising and the small amount spent on research to this end when compared with total advertising expenditure.

There are, however, marketing research agencies (mainly in London) that specialize in the pre-tracking and post-tracking of advertising campaigns. For campaigns aimed at establishing a new or improved corporate image, pre-tracking would establish the bench-marks and post-tracking the extent to which favourable change had occurred.

Continuous tracking, i.e. studies taking place during the campaign, can be helpful in that changes can be made before it is too late to avoid damage.

Post-tracking on the government's campaign against the spreading of AIDS showed that while attitudinal and behavioural changes had been wrought in the population at large, the minority of people most responsible for the spread of AIDS had scarcely been affected. It was alleged therefore that insufficiently accurate targeting had occurred, but the real problem was that of specifically identifying the people most at risk.

Advertisements can be pre-tested using a variety of research techniques. Such techniques would normally be pre-tested for attributes of:

- communications effectiveness (copy-testing);
- sales effectiveness.

*Communications effectiveness research* would test a proposed advertisement for its quality of impact and retention. For example, in the case of a magazine advertisement a dummy magazine can be passed among the readers who are asked to say which advertisements they can remember having seen and what the advertisements said.

*Sales effectiveness research* would test a proposed advertisement for its qualities of liking, conviction and propensity to buy. Taken a stage further, test-marketing could establish the actual number of trials achieved and the proportion of repeat purchases, but it should be noted that these would be affected by other elements in the marketing mix as well as advertising.

The models used for auditing advertising suggested earlier in Figure 13.6 are other specific ways of evaluating the advertising plan, but for a more strategic approach to this readers should turn to Chapter 15.

Readers are also reminded of the potential value of experimentation in aiding decision taking, evaluation and control processes, as discussed in Chapters 1, 3 and 16.

## 13.4 THE SALES PROMOTION PLAN

**Introduction**

Americans use the term 'sales promotion' in the same way that some British authors use the term 'promotion', i.e. to describe all forms of communication including advertising and personal selling. McDonald (1984, p. 110) in bemoaning the state of confusion caused by the various definitions states that, in practice, 'sales promotion is a specific activity, which can be defined as the making of a featured offer to defined customers with a specific time limit'.

The Institute of Sales Promotion defines sales promotion as 'a range of tactical marketing techniques designed within a strategic marketing framework to add value to a product or service in order to achieve specific sales and marketing objectives'.

For the purposes of this discussion, sales promotion can be best defined as any marketing communications other than personal selling, advertising and PR. In this way it includes all the items shown in Figure 13.8.

**FIGURE 13.8**
*The sales promotion plan*

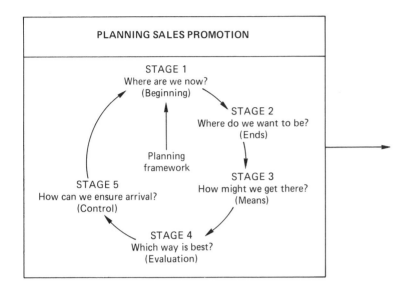

PLANNING SALES PROMOTION

STAGE 1
Where are we now?
(Beginning)

STAGE 2
Where do we want to be?
(Ends)

Planning framework

STAGE 3
How might we get there?
(Means)

STAGE 5
How can we ensure arrival?
(Control)

STAGE 4
Which way is best?
(Evaluation)

SALES PROMOTION SUBMIX

The role of sales promotion
Sales promotion techniques
Sales literature
Salesforce, distributor and
    customer incentives
Merchandising and POS
Exhibitions
Sponsorship
Direct marketing

Public relations (PR) has become important enough (especially in the larger concerns) for it to be treated now in most texts as a separate element of the promotional mix.

Hood (1983, p. 77) draws attention to the risks of sales promotion inherent in its high visibility and considerable effect on the personality of the product: 'Thus it is possible for an advertiser to spend half his promotion fund in the press to emphasize the high quality of his product, and the other half in various promotion devices that cheapen it, debasing the impression of quality.'

This statement re-emphasizes the importance of harmonization of the elements of the promotional mix referred to in the introduction to this chapter.

**Where are We Now? The Sales Promotion Audit**

A. C. Neilson, a company prominent in retailing research, have stated that it is now generally agreed that below-the-line expenditure in the UK currently exceeds that of above-the-line, although precise figures cannot be quoted.

The increase in expenditure on sales promotion relative to advertising can be accounted for partially by its efficacy. Certain forms of sales promotion such as incentive schemes and exhibitions lend themselves to cost-benefit analysis to a greater extent than advertising. For example, the sales effect of a precise markdown and the number of redemptions of prize incentives (i.e. people claiming prizes) can be calculated with a high degree of accuracy, as can the amount of orders taken at a particular exhibition.

Most larger companies in consumer goods and service have sales promotion managers and departments whose activities need to be audited in the same way as other elements of the promotional mix.

The sales promotion audit should cover at least the following items:

1 the effectiveness of sales promotion activites in total;
2 a review of the extent to which various types of sales promotions are used relative to competitors;
3 costs of the various types of sales promotions employed, together with trends;
4 results of individual sales promotions against objectives set;

5 a review of the extent to which sales promotions contribute to and harmonize with other elements of the marketing mix;

6 research to determine the degree to which sales promotion activities are welcomed by distributors, customers and potential customers, and how they influence buying decisions.

## Where Do We Want To Be? Sales Promotion Objectives

Sales promotion helps to maintain a high level of awareness of the supplier and of the brand in several ways:

- through packaging impact at the point of sale;
- through other point-of-sale display materials;
- by obtaining prime positions in retail outlets;
- through the use of in-store merchandising activities such as free sampling;
- by special offers and other incentives, e.g. competitions;
- through exhibitions;
- by the use of sponsorship;
- by the use of sales literature and other selling aids (videos, samples, etc.).

Not only do sales promotions win and help to maintain the patronage of customers but they also build the goodwill of dealers and distributors who enjoy increases in store traffic and rates of stockturn. They also encourage the trial and repeat purchases of services. Direct mail shots can generate enquiries for industrial goods and services leading to increases in order levels.

Other more specific objectives may be set, for example:

- to increase sales from X to Y during the promotional period and to retain 10 per cent of this increase in the post-promotional period;
- to gain a given number of product trials;
- to increase penetration of CTN outlets from X per cent to Y per cent;
- to double the amount of display space allocated to the product and retain X per cent of this following the promotion;
- to gain window displays in N outlets;
- to produce N enquiries from an exhibition;
- to generate N responses from a direct mail campaign.

While sales incentives such as price markdowns are used to boost sales of a product line it should be remembered that the majority of the boost can only be

**FIGURE 13.9**
*Sales promotion series as a means of building market share*

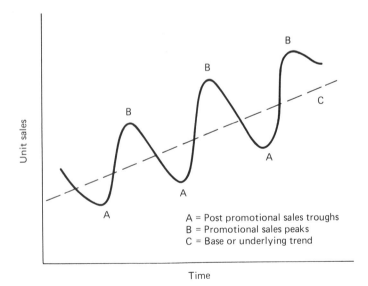

A = Post promotional sales troughs
B = Promotional sales peaks
C = Base or underlying trend

temporary. Buyers may switch loyalties only for the period of the promotional offer and then revert to their normal brand purchase. The real benefit of a good promotion is to convert some of the brand switchers to loyal repeat purchasers of your brand. In this way market share can be increased by a *series* of promotions as illustrated in Figure 13.9.

The positions marked A are the pre- and post-promotion sales troughs, while those marked B represent the promotional peaks. It can be seen that position A settles progressively at a higher sales point due to the retention of a proportion of the previous promotional increase. The dotted line C indicates steadily rising sales stimulated by the series of product-line promotions.

**How Might We Get There? Sales Promotion Strategy**

We have discussed the notions of push and pull promotional strategies in the introduction to this chapter. When we examine the role of sales promotion in relation to these two notions in more detail we can observe that its various techniques can be used in both these contexts, as shown in Figure 13.10.

When deciding whether or not to stock a new product a distributor can often be swayed by the amount and quality of consumer sales promotion support. This is because the distributor's main fear is that of the product not selling, and consumer incentives will help to ensure that products stocked are sold. In this way consumer incentives can help a sales force to sell in to the distribution channel. However, many manufacturers will also offer distributors some special incentives to stock and display a new product or to feature an existing product, such as case bonuses, special trial offers, special display fittings, etc.

**FIGURE 13.10**
*Sales promotion as a push and pull strategy*

In the above ways sales promotion can be seen as an important contributor to the selling in process as well as to that of selling out. More detail on particular techniques follows in the next section.

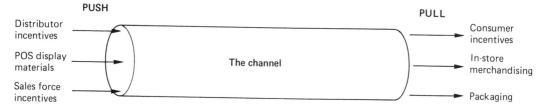

**Sales Promotion Tactics**

A variety of techniques can be employed in a short-term or tactical way to increase sales without committing the promoter to longer-term changes. For example, a consumer markdown may be used to clear out stocks of winter fashions at the end of a season. This does not constitute a permanent reduction in prices.

The wide variety of sales promotion techniques can be categorized as shown below.

### Consumer Incentives
Some of these can be retailer originated as well as supplier originated, and take a wide variety of forms which seem to increase each year as more ideas are created. Some of the more well known of these are:

- *Price markdowns*: which can be on-pack or off-pack, on showcards or in the form of coupons featured in newspapers/magazines or distributed door to door, which customers then offer for redemption.
- *Premium offers*: these can be extra quantities of the same product at the regular price or small free gifts either in the pack or attached to it, e.g. plastic toys or more specifically the inclusion of sachets of Ovaltine in Shredded Wheat packs.

- *Self-liquidating premium offers*: these are where, for example, a cake slicer at a specially reduced price is offered by a cake supplier in return for proof of purchase of N cake cartons. The offer is usually made on-pack. The cake supplier will usually have negotiated a bulk purchase of cake slicers from the slicer manufacturer at a big discount allowing the cake supplier to offer the cake purchaser a slicer at say half its normal price. The cake purchaser thus obtains a premium. The cost of the offer is self-liquidating to the cake supplier on account of the discount negotiated with the slicer manufactuer and the extra cake sales made. That is to say the cost of the promotion is compensated by the profit on the extra sales made and an increment on the price paid for the slicer.
- *Banded packs*: these are usually related items such as a toothbrush banded to toothpaste at a reduced price for the two combined.
- *Stamp collecting schemes*: stamps are given to purchasers in proportion to the spend usually by retail outlets such as the Co-op and petrol stations as a patronage incentive. Other forms include free prize game or 'scratch' cards and coupons which can be collected and exchanged for promotional offers.
- *Free sample or tasting offers*: the giving away, often in-store, of samples, usually by a merchandising person supplied by the promoter. Popular for food and drink items such as cheeses and wines.
- *Prize competitions*: usually on-pack and with questions related to knowledge of the supplier's goods.
- *Personality promotions*: are used to attract greater in-store traffic as well as promote sales of particular items. Thus a well-known footballer may be seen at a bookshop giving autographs or personally signing books on football.
- *In-store demonstrations*: of new gadgets or machines again help to build store traffic and sales.
- *Special displays*: help to attract attention and build sales. These can be assisted by the provision of materials and/or staff by the suppliers – see merchandising/POS.

### Dealer Incentives

- *Cash bonuses*: may be in the form of one extra case for every 10 ordered, cash discounts or straight cash hand-outs to encourage volume sales, period stock-building, display or in support of a cut-price to consumers.
- *Credit terms*: may be extended to support promotions aimed at bulk retail buyers.
- *Staff incentives*: may be payments or prizes provided by suppliers for the attainment of particular promotional targets. Staff training by suppliers could also be considered as falling under this heading.

### Sales Force Incentives

These usually take the form of cash payments or prizes for the achievement of specific promotional objectives. Holmes and Smith (1987, pp. 35–40) give typical objectives for sales force incentives as:

1 to increase sales volume (total);
2 to increase sales of specific products;
3 to increase sales of a high profit product;
4 to reduce high inventory;
5 to introduce new products;
6 to balance seasonal sales variations;
7 to gain new accounts;
8 to reactivate 'old' customers;
9 to decrease credit exposure.

The ultimate objectives, however, may be to increase market share and/or profit.
A higher motivational effect may be gained from a sales force if a competitive

incentive element is introduced (e.g. an exotic holiday for two is offered for the best performance within a group) in addition to individual rewards. Incentives can be applied on a team rather than on an individual basis where appropriate.

Non-financial incentives involving an appeal to pride or status can also prove extremely effective, such as 'best sales person' awards, the use of a special car or the temporary use of the best sales person's special car-parking spot.

For companies that continuously offer sales force incentives, special services have been developed by a number of promotional entrepreneurs. One of these is a system whereby prize points are continuously available and can be exchanged for goods and services featured in a catalogue. The service company will normally handle all the administration of such a scheme on behalf of its clients.

## Merchandising, Window Displays and Point-Of-Sale Display Material

There are a number of books specializing in the detail of these aspects of sales promotion. For example, Cox and Brittain (1988) in chapters 15 and 16 render a succinct description of the contribution these aspects make to the retail marketing mix. Large consumer goods manufacturers such as Mars and Walls employ teams of merchandisers either directly or through agencies such as CPM (Counter Products Marketing) to arrange their product ranges in particular ways so as to generate greater sales turnover. At its simplest this means using whatever space is allocated to the supplier's products to best advantage – usually allocating prime spots and most space to the best selling lines. Experiments have been conducted which demonstrate that the large increase in sales engendered by a professionally merchandised fixture more than offsets the cost of its merchandising. Many of the travel agent multiples also subcontract point-of-sale display to specialists recognizing its prime importance and the particular skills needed for this operation.

Window displays are instrumental in enticing potential customers into shops and stores. Specialist staff can be employed either directly or through agencies. Consumer goods manufacturers will often offer retailers purpose-made display material for the privilege of having their merchandise on view in these prime positions. Such materials can vary from showcards and models to spectacular moving displays with intricate lighting effects.

Point-of-sale display (POS) material is subject to jargon and includes:

- aisle banners (large cards or banners positioned directly over the aisles between fixtures);
- shelf talkers (double-sided strips which stick out of the shelf bases at right angles so as to attract attention from both up and down the aisle);
- window bills (posters for doors and windows);
- spinners (circular free-standing rotatable display units);
- dump bins (temporary containers for specially featured items on promotion and usually sited on gondola ends for short periods only).

POS supplied by manufacturers may need to conform to the house colours and styles of the major multiples in order to gain acceptance. Suppliers' representatives may be given special incentives based upon the amount of POS material they are able to place in-store.

## Exhibitions

Exhibitions are widely used in industrial, commercial and consumer goods and services markets as a means of promoting sales (see p. 372 for their role in PR).

At some exhibitions such as the Boat Show, the Ideal Home Exhibition and the Motor Show, orders may be actually taken on the exhibition stand, thereby enabling their cost effectiveness to be established. By way of illustration an article in *The Times*, (1 March 1990, p. 41) stated that five British show manufacturers who had joined forces to make a strong pitch at the Tokyo Shoe Fair took

£250,000 in firm orders. What we are not told by this article is the cost of getting these orders or the likelihood of repeat business. However, at other exhibitions such as those concerned with engineering it is relatively rare to receive orders and effectiveness is more often measured by the number of enquiries received and/or the visits made by particularly important customers.

Figure 13.11 is a short special report in *The Times* (1 March 1990) on plans for Expo '92, a huge exhibition held in Seville, Spain, for which 102 countries signed up to have pavilions. The article concerns the British pavilion and interestingly reveals an interface between three types of promotion, namely exhibitions, PR

**FIGURE 13.11**

*Advance details on 'Expo 1992' international exhibition advance*

Expo '92, the world fair to be held in Seville in 1992, has been timed to coincide with the 500th anniversary of Christopher Columbus's discovery of the New World (*Peter Strafford writes*). Its organizers have chosen 'The Age of Discovery' as its theme, and that will be interpreted in their various ways by the countries and organizations taking part.

There will be a record number of participants. So far, 103 countries have signed up and will have pavilions of their own. The number is well above the figures for the three previous exhibitions of this kind: Osaka in 1970 (77), Montreal in 1967 (62), and Brussels in 1958 (52).

In addition, 19 international organizations, including the European Community, and about 20 multi-national corporations will take part; and every one of Spain's 17 autonomous regions will have its pavilion.

For the moment, much of the exhibition area looks like little more than a building site. But that is deceptive, because work began in January 1987 and since then progress has been made on the huge task of providing roads, electrical power, plumbing, wiring, landscaping, and all the facilities needed to cater for the exhibition pavilions – and the expected 18 million visitors.

The foundations have been laid for the lake and canal, which will be one of the main features of the exhibition. New groves of transplanted palm trees are already in place, a small proportion of the 15,000 trees that are being brought on to the site to provide shade and colour.

The site is a convenient one, a man-made island within walking distance of the centre of Seville, which had almost no buildings on it until 1987. Known as La Cartuja, it was formed in 1975, when, in order to put an end to the flooding of low-lying Seville by the Guadalquivir River, a new river bed was dug further to the west. La Cartuja lies between the old and the new arms of the river.

But it also has symbolic significance. La Cartuja means Carthusian, and on it there are the surviving buildings of a 15th-century Carthusian monastery, Santa Maria de la Cuevas, where Columbus often stayed, and where he and other members of his family were buried – though Columbus's own remains were later removed.

More recently, in 1839, after the monastery had been abandoned, its buildings were bought by a British industrialist, Charles Pickman, who built a pottery in them. As a result there is a striking contrast between the tall kilns of the pottery and the monastery chapel with its *mudejar*, or Muslim, style.

But Pickman was highly thought of by the Spanish authorities of the day, who created him Marqués de Pickman, and the pottery is seen as symbolic of the industrial revolution. So while the monastery is being extensively restored, and will be used by King Juan Carlos as the site for his own personal pavilion, the kilns will remain in the background.

Expo '92 will be open from April 20 to October 12, 1992. Planning is based on the expectation that many of the visitors will come more than once, making a total of 37 million visits. They will be able to see not just the pavilions put up by the various countries and organizations taking part, but exhibitions on single themes put up by the Spanish organizers, on such topics as navigation, discoveries, and present and future. A cable car will bring visitors across the river to the exhibition and a monorail will take them round it. Fountains and vegetation are being used in an effort to reduce the effect of the heat.

Once the exhibition is over, the site will remain active as a centre for research and development. It will mean that Seville, which until now has tended to expand to the east, away from the Guadalquivir, will spread across the river to the west. Two new bridges have already been built, and seven new ones are planned.

The overall cost, of course, is formidable. But while the public authorities will pay for the main communications projects across Andalusia, the calculation is that Expo '92 will pay for itself.

There will be income from ticket sales, and rent for the buildings after 1992. But about 40 per cent of the cost is expected to be covered by sponsorship and other such arrangements, and the organizers speak confidently of raising a record sum for an occasion of this sort.

and sponsorship. About 40 per cent of the cost of this exhibition is expected to be covered by sponsorship in various forms. The exhibition will run for almost six months (20 April to 12 October 1992).

Companies need to take decisions as to:

- aims to be achieved;
- which exhibitions if any they need to show at;
- the size of stand to hire;
- the location of the stand;
- the layout of the stand and its facilities;
- staffing of the stand.

Choice criteria would include:

- the nature of the exhibition and the types of people likely to attend;
- the numbers of people likely to attend and their geographical locations (e.g. whether groups from overseas countries will be attending);
- costs;
- competitors showing or likely to book stands;
- timing: whether exhibitions might coincide with the launch of a new product;
- assessments of impact on customer relations;
- opportunities for publicity and enhancement of corporate image.

It is of course possible to arrange private exhibitions, a good example of which would be the holding of shows in hotels by fashion houses. The advantage of doing this is that you have the attention of the audience entirely to yourselves, albeit at a higher cost than a public exhibition. Then there is the possibility of a mobile exhibition which can be used to demonstrate equipment to potential buyers at their place of employment, with the benefit of convenience. The travelling exhibition is particularly appropriate where a wide DMU (decision-making unit) is involved, i.e. there are a number of influencers in the buying decision such as the health and safety officer, trade union officials and training personnel, who would not normally all attend a public exhibition.

## Trade Presentations and Talks

Manufacturers and suppliers can make presentations to decision takers, buyers and influencers as a group in hotels or other suitable venues. Despite the probable need to provide expensive hospitality as a means of attracting the audience, such presentations can be more cost effective than the one-to-one personal sell.

A related activity is that of providing speakers for meetings of interested groups, such as the branch members of an institution, so as to promote greater and more favourable awareness. Such activities also incorporate an element of PR.

## Packaging

Davidson (1972, p. 214) claims that 'packaging is one of the lowest cost and highest leverage areas of marketing activity. Changes in design are relatively expensive but can bring quite large business gains ... Packaging unlike advertising, can close a sale once it operates at the point of purchase'.

The word 'leverage' here is taken to mean positional advantage and return on cost. Davidson also provides a useful detailed checklist for packaging development based upon the following four aspects:

- protection of contents;
- consumer convenience;
- trade appeal;
- consumer sales appeal.

The importance of the aspect of trade appeal is echoed by Cox and Brittain (1988, p. 173) in their comment on pack design as follows:

> Because so many products are prepacked and because there is such a fight for shelf space, pack design is important to the retailer who may decide to accept or reject a pack just on the basis of its design rather than its contents, e.g. because of its dimensions or its 'stackability'.

Packaging is the 'silent salesman' in a self-service world, and without packaging noticeability, the product will be unlikely to be selected from the supermarket shelves.

Opportunities exist through the package design for uniqueness and to add value. The shape and attractiveness of a bottle can greatly influence the sale of a liqueur or perfume, while secondary uses (e.g. empty coffee jars for storage) add value to the product.

Other ways in which the packaging can add value have been described above under the heading of consumer incentives and branded packs.

A great deal of thought is put into packaging impact across the range of products being offered by major companies. When Boots last redesigned their packaging for the entire range of own-label medicines great care was taken to ensure *total* harmony and impact in-store. Sales improved dramatically as a result and Boots regained share against competitive proprietary medicines.

### Character Merchandising

The use of characters such as 'Mr Men' can greatly enhance sales of items like mugs and T-shirts to children. Manufacturers pay a royalty and/or a fee for the privilege to the owners of the copyright of the character.

Some companies invest in building up their own characters as promotional devices, such as the famous Spillers flour graders or the Tetley Tea Bag characters.

Coulson-Thomas (1983, pp. 283–4) refers to the practice of associating sportswear and goods with particular sporting personalities under this heading. He also cites the application of the technique to the Pope's visit to Ireland when the Catholic Church entered into a joint venture arrangement with a professional merchandising company in order to profit from the product of an extensive range of 'official' souvenirs.

### Sponsorship

The practice of sponsorship has increased greatly in recent years, and databanks exist which record the companies active in this form of promotion and the types of sponsorship in which they are involved. The association of Cornhill with test cricket is a good example.

Some reference to the PR elements of sponsorship has already been made earlier in this chapter – Jefkins (1990, p. 200) points out that, while sponsorship may be genuinely altruistic, it more usually fulfils a PR, advertising or marketing communications objective of some kind and that many sports sponsorships aim quite blatantly to gain TV coverage.

TI Raleigh, the bicycle manufacturers, sponsored a Tour de France team for several years at a reputed cost of over £500,000 per annum before the team finally succeeded. However, the company found that the benefits simply in terms of the cost of the TV coverage obtained more than compensated for the costs of sponsorship. TI Raleigh's share of the European cycle market increased considerably as a result of their win.

Jefkins (1990, p. 201) cites a list of 16 potential objectives of sponsorship, some of which are concerned with PR, advertising, corporate identity and product positioning rather than sales promotion *per se*. However, some ways in which sponsorship can be seen to contribute to sales promotion objectives are:

- inspiring the sales force, making them proud and providing extra talking points in building better customer relations;
- giving a boost to the trade which is seen to be selling products associated with major events and constantly in the news (e.g. Jaguar dealers following motor-racing success);
- providing a means of offering greater hospitality to very important customers as when sponsoring horse racing and show jumping.

Head (1981, p. 74) quotes the case of Schweppes regarding its sponsorship programme as a vitally important part of its overall marketing strategy, with objectives of 'extra sales, publicity, and enhanced image, increased awareness, a closeness to the community and an opportunity to entertain customers in attractive surroundings'.

## Direct Marketing

Direct marketing is said to be one of the fastest growing elements of the marketing mix. There are a number of interesting developments within this form of sales promotion and distribution which are contributing to its success – including the technology and management of databases and the combination of retailing with selling via catalogues. Formerly direct marketing was largely confined in the UK to business-to-business marketers, the mail-order catalogue companies, and big US-owned publishers such as the *Readers' Digest*.

Today banks and credit card companies regularly enclose leaflets with their statements inviting direct mail orders. We have also become used to receiving offers with our electricity and gas bills for related items and services such as gas boiler maintenance.

Help is available from the British Direct Marketing Association, an increasing number of specialist agencies and a Direct Mail Services Standards Board.

The Post Office is a very keen supporter of direct marketing and offers substantial incentives for first-time users as well as a wide range of helpful booklets on this technique, free of charge. The Post Office has recently introduced Mailsort to replace the old Rebate system which offers substantial discounts providing your bulk mail is at least 75 per cent postcoded. Postcoding services for address lists are available at recognized bureaux. Companies can either develop their own direct marketing databases or purchase lists of addresses from brokers. Mailing houses offer a wide variety of services including the stuffing of envelopes, sealing and postage.

Telemarketing (the direct soliciting of orders by telephone), on the other hand, is taking longer to gain respectability in the UK and does not yet have its own trade body (see pp. 381–2 on telephone selling).

The effectiveness of household door-to-door media distribution has been improved by the selectivity now available through the breakdown of the population into neighbourhood classifications. These classifications group types of neighbourhood together in respect of their buying behaviour patterns and give indices for particular goods and services. Three of the best-known neighbourhood data services are:

- ACORN – offered by CACI;
- MOSAIC – offered by CCN Systems Limited;
- PIN – offered by Pinpoint Systems Limited.

An increasing number of retailers, e.g. W. H. Smith, Allied Carpets and Dixons, are becoming involved in direct response marketing, and a Mintel report (1988) on non-store alternatives states that 'non-store shopping is becoming an alternative part of the increasing segmentation of retailing generally rather than a separate entity'.

Apart from convenience, credit facilities and 'money back if not satisfied' policies, future increases in non-store shopping may be stimulated by factors such as:

- the increasing difficulty of urban driving and parking;
- city centre crime and violence;
- time savings becoming more valuable as more women work.

Argos in the UK is an outstanding example of the combination of catalogue selling and retailing. Shoppers enter retail premises in city centres and select goods from catalogues which are then delivered from the adjacent warehouse to the point of sale.

Laura Ashley's successful entry into the US market in 1974 and the building up of a chain of 63 stores within 10 years was based on the development of a catalogue customer database interface. For example, when considering Denver they found they already had 9000 catalogue customers within a relatively small area of that city. Siting a new store in that vicinity almost guaranteed a good start. Laura Ashley's database logs people who have:

1 ordered a catalogue from a direct response magazine advertisement;
2 ordered a catalogue by mail or telephone;
3 purchased in a store.

The Next Directory, was another example of success resulting from a combination of retailing with catalogue selling. Next made history by charging potential customers £3 towards the £9 cost of the Directory (catalogue) which was launched in a fanfare of publicity in 1988 following Next's acquisition of Grattan's mail-order business in 1986. Next's target of enrolling 500,000 creditworthy respondents in the first season was exceeded by 50 per cent according to an article in the *Marketing Guides*, 1989, No. 4. These respondents were reached via a mix of shop displays, PR, advertising and direct mail.

Although different list systems and legalities are present in Europe, direct mail offers a relatively easy way of communicating with a European market.

## Sales Promotion Budgets, Evaluation and Control

Deciding on the total spend on sales promotion and the allocation of this spend to the various types of sales promotion is as problematical as for other elements of the communications mix. Mention has already been made of the claims that below-the-line expenditure in the UK now exceeds above-the-line expenditure. Consumer goods companies will tend to spend more heavily (in absolute terms) on sales promotion than those operating in industrial markets.

*Marketing Guides*, 1989, No. 12, mentions two surveys which indicate increasing expenditures on sales promotion. One (published in May 1989 by *Marketing*) found that the UK's top 50 sales promotion agencies had experienced a turnover increase from £135m to £185m during 1987–1988, i.e. 37 per cent growth. The other recent survey of 300 companies in the US, Canada and Western Europe gives an indication of the scale of the international development of sales promotion over a 10-year period. It reveals that the proportion rose from 40 per cent to 55 per cent within an expanding total promotional investment.

Setting the budget for sales promotion takes place within the context of the total promotional plan and against a number of criteria:

- What are our communications objectives and what part should sales promotion play in their achievement?
- What are the needs of our sales force for sales promotion support in the attainment of their targets?
- What are our competitors spending on sales promotion and how effective are they in gaining and maintaining market share?

- What case histories do we have or can we acquire with regard to the cost effectiveness of various types of sales promotions within our product-market area?

Kotler (1988, pp. 653–5) offers valuable advice on evaluating and controlling the sales promotion programme. He suggests that some promotions can be tested quickly and inexpensively for visual impact and that some large companies test alternative strategies in selected areas with each of their national promotions.

Sales promotions can be market tested and this is recommended – particularly when damage to the corporate image is at risk (e.g. from over-redemption of prize incentives or premium offers). Packaging can also be pre-tested against a variety of criteria, including impact, using, for example, the tachistoscope research technique. This is where a picture of a completely merchandised fixture is flashed for an instant on to a screen and watchers are asked to say which products (if any) they have noticed. Pupil dilation is also measured to show physical reaction.

Sales promotion effectiveness can be measured by examining sales performance before, during and after a particular campaign. Barclaycard has done this since 1988 with its Profile Points scheme.

Effectiveness of some forms of sales promotion such as sales literature can be established by asking the sales force and/or customers what they think of it in terms of its utility in getting orders, enhancing the company image, etc.

## 13.5 THE PUBLIC RELATIONS PLAN

**Introduction**

Public relations (PR) is at its simplest the way in which an organization manages its relations with its publics. In some companies there appears to be relatively little management or even recognition of this important function.

Marketing is concerned with satisfying the needs of customers. In endeavouring to satisfy customer needs, marketing also has to manage relations with those people who are responsible for producing and distributing goods and services. Thus marketing and PR are very much interlinked and there is a public relations element in every aspect of marketing communications. However, PR extends beyond marketing in that it is concerned with the total communications of the organization, embracing the community as a whole, funding bodies and shareholders, political and legal interfaces, the media, the organization's employees and their trade unions. Thus the Institute of Public Relations defines PR as noted on p. 346.

Within this definition is the word 'planned', which leads us naturally to the planning framework that can be applied to all functions, and the major decision areas appertaining to PR. This is shown in Figure 13.12.

**FIGURE 13.12**
*The PR plan*

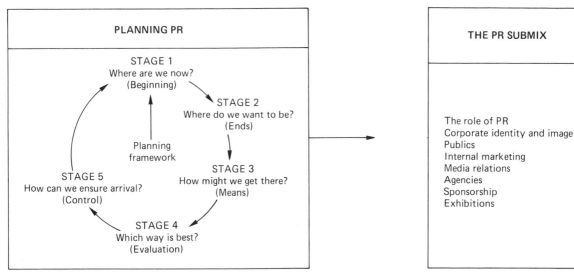

## Corporate Identity and Corporate Image

Olins (1989) distinguishes between corporate personality, corporate identity and corporate image as follows:

*Corporate personality:*

> . . . embraces the subject at its most profound level. It is the soul, the persona, the spirit, the culture of the organisation manifested in some way. A corporate personality is not necessarily something tangible that you can see, feel or touch – although it may be.

*Corporate identity:*

> . . . the tangible manifestation of a corporate personality . . . It is the identity that projects and reflects the reality of the corporate personality.

*Corporate image:*

> . . . is what people actually perceive of a corporate personality or corporate identity.

The components of a corporate identity scheme will therefore be everything that is visible about an organization including premises, literature, staff dress and vehicles. The aspects of branding and packaging have already been discussed and many companies such as ICI, Bass, Boots, etc., use these opportunities to establish a strong corporate identity by the use of common colours, logo and typography.

## The Value of a Clearly Defined Identity

David Bernstein (1984) makes the following claims about a good corporate identity scheme:

> At its basic it minimises the risk of confusion. At its most effective it creates a synergy (2 + 2 = 5) whereby each of the company's diverse communication activities is helping the rest. The corporate identity reinforces the image of the company. The image of the company in turn strengthens the selling 'argument' of the individual company product. A corporate identity represents added value.

This view of corporate identity as an aid to selling is reinforced by Olins (1989) in the following statement:

> If a company's style is clear, consistent and logical and the potential customer happens to like it then that company will win. If a company style is confused, confusing and anonymous it has that much less chance. Corporate identity is for the purpose of selling things . . .

British Telecom spent at least £100 million in 1991–92 on a new corporate identity according to press reports typified by the article in Figure 13.13.

**Where Are We Now? The PR Audit**

This is in effect an audit of all the communications by corporate organizations, including those with its employees. Jefkins (1986, p. 35) suggests eight basic groups or publics with which an organization needs to communicate. These are shown in Figure 13.14.

Some of the above relate to stakeholders (see Chapter 1). However, specific lists need to be drawn up and Jefkins (1986, pp. 36–9) goes on to indicate by examples how these might extend to include visitors, wage tribunals, potential

**FIGURE 13.13**

*Press report on the cost of British Telecom's new corporate identity*

British Telecom is to change its trading name to BT and adopt a new corporate identity in an effort to shake off nationalistic public service perceptions that have dogged the company since flotation.

The BT board meets this month to approve final details. The new look will coincide with completion of organizational restructuring on April 2. Yesterday BT rebuffed as 'a vast exaggeration' suggestions that the cost of the relaunch could reach £200 million.

A new logo, including a Pan-like figure with pipes, and a red and blue colour scheme, will be progressively introduced. The identity will be deployed on the company's 66,000 vehicles, on 86,000 pay phone installations, on 100,000 engineers' uniforms and throughout 90 BT shops.

The new identity is the result of two years' collaboration between BT and Wolff Olins, the design consultancy. BT said the new look was intended to assist in its determination to become 'a major global player' in telecommunications. Faced with restrictions on its UK growth as a result of government determination to open telecommunications to more competition, British Telecom is concentrating on cost-cutting at home and expansion overseas.

Once BT's new structure is in place, the company is seeking to slim its UK workforce by 30,000 to 210,000 by the end of 1993.

Overseas expansion is made difficult by high levels of state control over wired networks worldwide. But BT has already become controlling shareholder in Mitel Corporation, the Canadian equipment maker, McCaw Cellular Communications, America's biggest mobile phone operator, and BT Tymnet, a data network company in America. British Telecom is also in talks with IBM about worldwide cooperation.

A BT spokesman said the company is unable to use its existing 'T' symbol in several overseas countries because of similarities with logos of other groups. Using the trading name BT, rather than British Telecom, may enable it to be more readily accepted by overseas customers. BT stressed that the legal name would remain unchanged.

BT will replace the illuminated sign atop the British Telecom tower in central London. The distinctive yellow livery of its vehicles, which form the largest commercial fleet in Europe, will also be changed.

BT has begun a programme to brief senior staff on the changes. Presentations to the workforce may be delayed until details of the new logo and livery have been unveiled publicly in March.

First reactions in the City, to the style of the new identity and the need for tens of millions of pounds to be spent on it, were largely sceptical.

'Even supposing they spend £100 million, that is an awful lot of money to be spending over two years,' said one analyst who declined to be named. 'The real test of this company is its ability to become more efficient, to devise new services and to become service-oriented.' BT shares eased 4p to 280p.

Ross Tieman
*Industrial Correspondent*

SOURCE: *The Times*, 3 January 1991

**FIGURE 13.14**

*Eight basic publics for PR*

1 **The community at large** – people living near the site and/or affected by it

2 **Employees** – categorized by type, e.g. factory workers, office staff, management and their trade unions

3 **Customers** – past, present and future

4 **Suppliers of materials and services** (other than financial)

5 **The money market** – shareholders, banks, insurance companies, potential investors

6 **Distributors** – agents, wholesalers, retailers, etc.

7 **Potential employees**

8 **Opinion leaders** – all those whose opinions may help or harm the organization, including media editors

residents and so on. We should perhaps also add governments (central and local) to Jefkins's list of basic publics and pressure groups (e.g. Greenpeace, Friends of the Earth) representing 'society'.

In conducting the PR audit of communications with the various publics inside and outside the organization, a number of aspects need to be considered:

1 the extent and frequency of the communications with that public;
2 the degree of importance attached to the communications in terms of their ability to harm or help the organization;
3 the effectivenes of these communications in achieving objectives.

It can be seen that some aspects are quantifiable (e.g. frequency of communications), while other aspects are qualitative or judgemental (e.g. degrees of importance). The extent to which the PR audit needs to be conducted by a specialist agency is perhaps conditioned by these considerations. Some parts (for example, that of customer relationships) might be better conducted by an outside agency on the grounds of objectivity, while other parts (e.g. the number and seriousness of complaints received), are better handled by the organization itself. The extent to which complaints are monitored and acted upon has a direct relationship with the level of customer service.

The amount of publicity gained in the media can be assessed quantitatively (in terms of space) but the extent to which this publicity is favourable or unfavourable requires the exercise of judgement.

## Where Do We Want To Be? PR Objectives

While the PR audit could be said to be concerned with the analysis of communication strengths and weaknesses, PR objectives are more concerned with maximizing communication opportunities and minimizing communication threats.

Most marketing activities have PR consequences and, if mishandled, these can easily harm a corporate reputation. One of the functions of PR is to establish a system for dealing quickly and effectively with crisis occurrences (Coulson-Thomas, 1983, p. 197).

Ray Palin (1985, p. 3) says:

> What we are concerned with in formulating our public relations programme, in a nutshell, is finding out people's attitudes towards a product or company; and then devising a programme of communications which will seek to modify those attitudes in such a way as to create understanding and win preference.

While the above statement presupposes that attitudes will require modification, it does crystallize how PR objectives should harmonize with marketing and corporate planning in attempting to establish a preference for the company's goods and/or services against those of competitors.

Palin goes on to emphasize the importance of defining clear and specific PR objectives but refrains from giving practical examples. Jefkins (1986, pp. 31–4) has no such qualms. After stating that 'Objectives and results are the essentials of tangible cost-effective, accountable PR' he goes on to list no less than 34 possible PR objectives ranging from making known a change of name to organizing the recall of a faulty product.

Kotler (1988, p. 658) distinguishes between corporate PR and marketing PR, seeing marketing PR as a means of achieving marketing objectives. He points out that PR contributes strongly to objectives of:

- building awareness;
- building credibility;
- stimulating sales force and dealer enthusiasm;
- holding down promotion costs.

In stating that *specific* objectives should be set for every PR campaign, Kotler cites the example of a company wishing to convince people that wine drinking is a pleasurable part of good living, with a view to improving the image and market share of particular wines. Specific PR objectives were:

- to develop magazine stories about wine and get them placed in named magazines;
- to develop articles about wine's many health values and direct them to the medical profession;
- to develop specific publicity for the young adult market, college market, governmental bodies and various ethnic communities.

These objectives were then refined into quantified targets so that results could subsequently be evaluated (for example, the number to be featured in particular magazines was specified).

## How Might We Get There? PR Strategies

There are a number of broad ways in which PR objectives can be met. In minimizing the threat of a crisis occurrence a contingency plan can be invoked whereby all communications concerning that crisis are centralized and channelled through experienced executives (or an agency) so as to limit damage to the corporate image and sales. When, for example, an aircraft crashed on the bank of the M1 motorway in January 1989 causing serious loss of life, the managing director of the airline concerned personally handled the media.

In seeking to exploit communication opportunities, good relationships need to be established with the media. This would entail a study of the media and a selection of those considered to be key. Important personnel within these key media can then be targeted for a continuous communications programme. Specific PR events may also be planned in the form of media conferences or receptions. Individual invitations to visit the organization are also a useful way of establishing good relationships. Care needs to be taken not to use minor or flippant events which might be considered a waste of time by the media which, in the final analysis, are looking for proper newsworthy events with which to stimulate and entertain their own target audiences.

In order to ensure that communication opportunities are adequately exploited and communication threats averted, a responsibility for PR needs to be allocated ideally to an experienced professional within the organization or to a PR consultant.

## PR Tactics

A more detailed way in which PR objectives can be achieved might involve regular and programmed communication releases to the various publics. In order to make this effective the personnel responsible for PR need a communications network within the organization. Thus news regarding product developments may be automatically channelled to PR via the R & D department reports, or the PR manager could have regular personal meetings with the head of R & D to find out at first hand what is going on. The latter tactic offers obvious advantages over the method of copy reports which might not get read or might not be understood. Similar meetings with the sales manager might reveal a particularly large order or one from abroad that might have news value.

Reductions in staff have potentially harmful PR effects, while increases present PR opportunities. Every advertisement for new staff offers an opportunity to transmit favourable information about the progressive nature of the recruiting organization under its corporate logo. An example of how to exploit this opportunity is afforded by the Nissan advertisement in Figure 13.15.

A company or corporate logo may be a registered trademark or a symbol which appears on all communications media – buildings, letterheads, visiting cards, company vehicles, advertisements. This device helps to build up instant recognition. Examples include the letters ICI in a circle which appears in television advertisements and on all product packaging, and the British Rail arrows which symbolize quick two-way travel.

An interesting development is the use of hot-air balloons and airships to display corporate logos and company names. These can lend an image of modernity and

**FIGURE 13.15**

*Exploiting corporate image opportunities in recruitment advertising*

Nissan Motor Company plans to establish its own dealer network in the UK, to be operational from early 1992. Nissan is dedicated to providing the highest quality in all its services, from dealer support to customer service.

Here in Europe, Nissan enjoys the outstanding facilities of a leading car manufacturer, offering an exciting range of vehicles and exemplary customer services.

Nissan's comprehensive organisation in Europe encompasses local manufacturing plants at Sunderland in the UK and Barcelona in Spain; design, technology and development centres in the UK, Belgium and Spain; a pan-European parts distribution centre in the Netherlands, and the appropriate in-house financial services.

As well as support such as this to ensure prompt response to their needs, dealers will enjoy selling a superb range of vehicles; the brand new Primera, Sunny and Micra, for example; the stunning 300ZX, Maxima, 200SX, Prairie and Patrol; and the hard-working Pickup, Urvan, Vanette and Cabstar.

Nissan's range is evidence of our dedication to quality; a dedication enshrined in the corporate philosophy you'll see below. We would like to extend a welcome to dealers who share our belief in that philosophy, to join Nissan's team for the 1990's.

For more details, please contact us at the address below. All correspondence will, of course, be treated in the strictest confidence.

Dealer Development Department, Nissan Europe N.V. (London), 5 Arlington Street, London SW1A 1RA. Telephone: 071-409 7988.

*Corporate philosophy*
Our first commitment is to customer satisfaction. Through diligent efforts to develop new customers and expand our customer base we are contributing to the ongoing progress and enrichment of society.

SOURCE: *The Times*, 15 January 1991

adventure to the sponsor as in the case of the Goodyear (Tyres) airships with their flashing night signs.

Even personnel not having direct contact with the customer can adversely affect relationships. For example, a works foreman being obstructive with a member of staff progressing delivery of an important order is indirectly obstructing the customer. Similarly a careless packer or package handler may generate subsequent customer dissatisfaction.

Newsletters, house journals and quality circles (internal discussion groups with the aim of improving quality) are means of establishing good internal relationships. Presentation of awards for long service, news about past employees, social information on current employees and their external activities all help to generate a good, lasting team spirit and maintain a reputation as a good employer.

Exhibitions, while coming under the heading of sales promotion in a previous section, also offer excellent opportunities for PR before, during and after the event. Good PR here can extend the target audience beyond actual visitors to potential buyers unable to visit but nevertheless influenced by what they read in the trade media. Similar remarks apply to conferences, seminars and trade presentations organized by the company.

Sponsorship can be treated as a special form of sales promotion, or as a means of advancing a better corporate identity. Most companies will need to justify sponsorship in both these terms. Jefkins (1990, pp. 200–3) lists 16 hard reasons for investing in sponsorship, including:

- to position a product (e.g. Coca-Cola with youthful sports);
- to enhance the corporate image by showing a company as socially responsible in sponsoring the arts (e.g. Midland Bank);
- to provide hospitality for important customers (e.g. inviting guests to sponsored events such as horse racing).

Head (1981, p. 4) grapples with the distinction between sponsorship and patronage but feels the *Economist* Intelligence Unit probably came closest with its 1977 statement that:

The essential elements of the term sponsorship as it is used in the UK today are: (i) a sponsor makes a contribution in cash or kind – which may or may not include services and expertise – to an activity which is in some measure a leisure pursuit, either sport or within the broad definition of the arts; (ii) the sponsored activity does not form part of the main commercial function of the sponsoring body (otherwise it becomes straightforward promotion, rather than sponsorship); (iii) the sponsor expects a return in terms of publicity.

## The PR Budget

The major components of the PR budget are likely to be the costs of staff and/or external consultants. To these costs must be added expenses which are similar to those of the sales force, with perhaps a greater emphasis on the entertainment aspects.

Specific PR companies will, however, attract their own special costs which might involve the production of videos or indeed extend to expensive television advertisements.

Jefkins (1990, Chapter 6) contains some excellent outlines of specific PR budgets, covering:

1 a press reception;
2 an in-company facility visit;
3 a budget for the production of a film;
4 a budget for producing a house journal;
5 a budget for PR support of an exhibition.

Quotations for current costs can be obtained from PR consultancy firms. Alternatively other companies engaged in PR activities can be asked for an indication of the size of their budgets for given items.

## PR Evaluation and Control

Since PR is about effecting change for the better, a basic evaluation procedure would be to take stock of the current situation prior to conducting a PR campaign and then establish the new situation following the campaign. This procedure is similar to the pre-advertising and post-advertising tracking studies referred to in a previous section.

In this way checks can be made on the improvement of the corporate image, assuming this to be one of the PR objectives. An organization might find that its image scored high rankings on some attributes such as reliability, but a low ranking on modernity (i.e. was considered old fashioned by a majority of potential customers). A campaign to improve the modernity ranking might include the development of articles highlighting R & D activities targeted at particular media with copies direct mailed to particular buyers. This could be coupled with a series of in-company visits to computerized/robotized production plants again targeted at particular buyers. Such a campaign would of course need to be scheduled over a period of time and would incur costs which would need to be budgeted and approved. The extent to which buyers' attitudes had then changed could be established by a post-campaign survey and increases in orders measured against set targets.

A simpler way of evaluating PR activity as a whole is to measure the amount of media coverage in terms of the amount of space gained in newspapers/magazines and/or the amount of viewing/listening time gained on television and radio. Assessing its value would be more problematical but subjective judgements could be made by a panel of company executives.

More specific measures can be made against specific objectives. For example, a PR objective of establishing a better reputation as an employer in the local community might evaluate results by comparing labour turnover rates prior to and following the activities carried out and/or the amount of new recruits from the area involved.

Internal marketing PR could be assessed by means of staff surveys or group discussions. These could focus on particular aspects such as the rating of an in-house journal or the knowledge of and understanding of the company's mission statement.

In summary, we have tried to show that PR (which is thought by many to be the most ephemeral element of the marketing mix) can and indeed should be subject to the planning, evaluation and control process which govern other elements of the promotional mix, whether conducted in-house or through PR consultants. In the latter case, clear briefs covering objectives, budgets, reporting and evaluation procedures will be required in much the same way as when briefing advertising agents.

## 13.6 PLANNING PERSONAL SELLING

**Introduction**

In a sense, the sales plan is of focal importance in that the income generated by it provides most of the means for expenditure not only on marketing research, promotion and distribution but also on the production of goods or the supply of services in the majority of companies. There are of course exceptions! For example, when a company markets its products and/or services by mail-order gaining sales by receiving direct orders against offers advertised in newspapers and magazines and where no personal selling is involved. However, even in this extreme example, receivers of goods may have complaints or queries and contact the company by telephone, asking for the sales department and being put through to a person who could be categorized as dealing with customers and therefore in telephone sales. As for the other elements in the promotional mix, a normal planning framework can be applied to the selling function and then decomposed into a specific submix as indicated in Figure 13.16.

**FIGURE 13.16**
*Components of the sales plan*

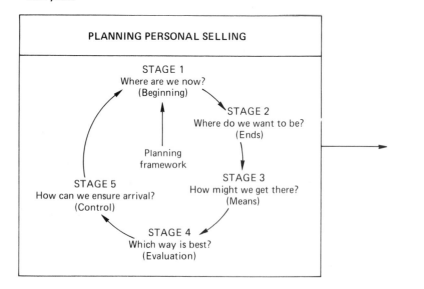

**Where Are We Now? The Sales Audit**

It could be said that the sales function is the most extensively and continuously monitored aspect of the marketing mix, in that sales volumes and values are totalled at least weekly in most organizations and compared against targets or budgets. This recording and checking is usually carried out at the individual sales person's level, as well as at area, regional and national levels.

However, we perhaps need to go beyond these basic measures when auditing the sales function and endeavour to identify the sales force's effectiveness in carrying out sales strategies and as an element of the promotional mix. This may involve, for example, determining the numbers of new customers gained or the proportion of sales achieved for new products. Certainly we also need to measure the selling costs involved in each of these activities in order to determine sales force effectiveness.

The sales audit might seek to establish customer/non-customer attitudes toward the sales force and sales force attitudes towards the company.

The *sales audit* would normally involve comparisons of the sales force with competitors on aspects such as those listed below in an effort to determine its relative effectiveness and form a basis for improvement:

- relative size of the sales force;
- reward systems and levels of earnings;
- rate of sales force turnover;
- sales per sales person;
- sales force support systems;
- relative level of training;
- recruitment system;
- control systems;
- relative images of sales forces.

**Where Do We Want To Be? Sales Objectives**

Sales objectives are perhaps the most quantified and time-scaled of any objectives within the marketing mix, probably because revenue is so important to the company's ability to pay bills, and hence to its survival. They are also the most easily measured and monitored. Quantified objectives would normally be set covering at least items 1, 2 and 3 in Figure 13.17.

**FIGURE 13.17**
*Major quantified sales objectives*

| Overall objectives | Split down by: |
|---|---|
| 1 Total annual volume of products<br>2 Total annual value of products<br>3 Total annual selling costs<br>4 Total annual profit contribution | A Quarter, month and week<br>B Product line<br>C Region and sales area<br>D Type of customer |

As pointed out in Chapter 6, marketing mix objectives are means to ends (strategies) at corporate planning level, and this is known as the cascade effect or hierarchy of objectives as described in McDonald (1984, p. 98). Overall marketing objectives have to be broken down into sub-objectives which, when taken all together, will achieve the overall objectives.

There are therefore a great many other potential quantifiable objectives for the sales force which underpin the above items. Some of these are illustrated in Figure 13.18.

All the above objectives and sub-objectives can be broken down into those for individual members of the sales force, to enable comparisons to be made between sales people, between regions and between periods.

There are also a great many potential qualitative rather than quantitative sales objectives such as those listed in Figure 13.19.

**FIGURE 13.18**
*Some typical quantified sales sub-objectives*

**FIGURE 13.19**
*Some qualitative sales objectives*

1 To provide a high level of customer care
2 To present an image of professionalism
3 To maintain high sales force morale
4 To gain prime in-store positions
5 To establish and maintain point-of-sales displays
6 To maintain a good safety record
7 To provide continuous market/competitor reporting
8 To train customers' sales forces
9 To establish good personal relationships
10 To provide technical advice and/or services
11 To identify new product opportunities

Some of the above (e.g. numbers 1, 2, 9 and 10) are particularly important in the building of longer-term relationships with repeat buying customers so as to gain a competitive advantage (see the section on relationship marketing which follows).

The exact amount and types of sales objectives set will depend on the particular markets in which the company operates, as well as its overall corporate and marketing objectives. For example, a company with European operations would wish to set quantified objectives by country, which might include the desired degrees of penetration of particular groups of outlets within those countries. The exact nature of sales objectives will also depend on the *role of the sales force*. Where the role is seen as being ambassadorial or advisory rather than the strict

**FIGURE 13.20**
*The role of the sales force – some examples*

1 Obtain orders
2 Give advice
3 Staff exhibitions
4 Demonstrate equipment
5 Show samples
6 Undertake merchandising activities
7 Handle complaints
8 Deliver goods
9 Collect payment
10 Establish creditworthiness
11 Entertain customers
12 Maintain stock
13 Maintain equipment
14 Train dealer sales forces
15 Disseminate literature
16 Co-design/create designs
17 Obtain free trials
18 Give talks/presentations

obtaining of orders, then objectives will be likely to be more qualitative than quantitative. Some of the ways in which a sales force can be used are given in Figure 13.20.

Figure 13.20 illustrates the diversity of sales settings. For example, in van sales the salesman will be required to deliver goods and collect payment (as for milk and bread). In furniture marketing, manufacturers' sales forces are usually required to train dealers' showroom sales staff in product knowledge so as to be able to pass this on to potential customers.

## How Might We Get There? Sales Strategies

In a very real sense the sub-objectives and the splits of overall quantified sales objectives contained in the above figures represent some of the sales strategies to be employed.

For example, overall sales revenue objectives might be reached by concentrating on particular areas or on particular types of customers with particular product lines.

The establishment of POS display material and/or the training of customers' sales forces are means of obtaining sales.

Lancaster and Jobber (1985, pp. 50–3) in their discussion of sales strategies confine this to the marketing mix rather than addressing sales strategy *per se* – an approach shared by most authors on selling and sales management. This might be because until recently personal selling has been seen as a rather more tactical element in the marketing mix. However, it is increasingly being recognized that personal interfaces with customers and potential customers present an important opportunity for which a clearly defined strategy is required.

West (1987, p. 215) observes that:

> Surprisingly, there is little discussion of the implications of the interaction between a firm's salesforce and its marketing strategy and tactics . . .
>
> The substantial growth in the service sector has led certain authors to identify further factors; people (the nature of the people employed in the organisation), process (the way in which the service is carried out), and physical (the environment in which the service is performed). The salesforce will have important influences in almost all these areas . . .

Sales strategies – like any other element in the marketing mix – are linked to overall marketing objectives so that a marketing objective of increased market share could be translated into a market penetration strategy, which would then become a sales objective of selling more of Product X to existing customers, as illustrated in Figure 13.21.

How to sell more of Product X to existing customers entails the selection of a sales strategy which might be that of initiating a series of presentations emphasizing the benefits of Product X to groups of store managers in convenient hotels using incentives of refreshments and post-presentation entertainment.

At an individual sales person's level an objective of increased sales from existing customers with existing products will demand an individual strategy or way of getting there. He/she may decide to give more attention to a particular geographic area or select particular customers who are known to possess the most potential for increased business.

There are other ways of viewing sales strategy. For example, we can take an *organizational approach* to selling as a means achieving sales objectives. Some companies organize their sales forces on levels which reflect those of their major customers. In the case of a manufacturer marketing through multiple grocers, van salesmen may call on individual store managers, area sales managers on group store managers (i.e. those over-managers of a small group of stores), regional sales managers on regional store managers, and so on.

Similarly in industrial marketing the sales organization can be tailored to better represent its market segment customers. Thus for the same product – such as

**FIGURE 13.21**
*The relationship of sales strategies to marketing and corporate plans*

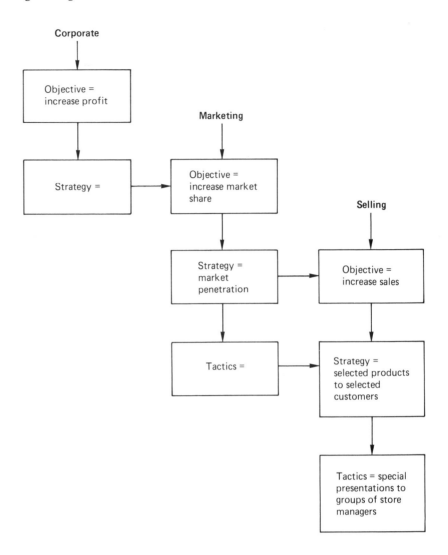

industrial cooling equipment – a company can have a sales engineer calling on mechanical engineering companies, a chemical engineer on companies in the chemical industry, etc. This strategy enables the company to offer specialist advice on different applications for the same types of equipment. It improves communications over the alternative of using sales personnel to cover a wide variety of complex technologies and can lead to increased sales and greater organizational effectiveness.

A further approach to the formulation of sales strategy lies in the choice of broad selling methods and the type of relationship that is desired with the prospective customer. Companies can choose between a hard sell approach and a soft sell approach. Hersey (1989) distinguishes between these two approaches in a manner similar to that shown in Figure 13.22.

**FIGURE 13.22**
*Hard sell versus soft sell strategies*

| Hard sell | Soft sell |
|---|---|
| ● Concern for self | ● Concern for customer |
| ● Canned presentation | ● Questions for discussion |
| ● Talking | ● Listening |
| ● Pushing product | ● Providing buying opportunity |
| ● Presenting features | ● Presenting benefits |
| ● Advocating without acknowledging | ● Acknowledging needs |

## Relationship Marketing and Sales Strategy

Following Peters and Waterman's (1982) analysis of excellent companies, many large organizations have introduced mission statements and customer care programmes, endeavouring to involve all employees in improving customer relations. The concept of total quality has been written about extensively and programmes adopted by companies such as British Telecom, Ilford and Rank Xerox.

The positioning of marketing relative to these issues has until now been somewhat uncertain. However, in 1990 the Chartered Institute of Marketing itself expressed a desire to achieve the British Standard – BS5750 – for the quality of its marketing services. At about the same time Witcher (1990) expressed concern at too narrow a definition of marketing by the marketing profession.

Christopher, Payne and Ballantyne (1991) claim that relationship marketing is emerging as a new focus for integrating the elements of quality and customer concern with marketing.

The emphasis is changing towards *keeping* customers rather than getting them as it is increasingly realized that replacing lost customers becomes more difficult and expensive. A factor influencing the emerging importance of relationship marketing may be that more and more Japanese companies (which have a tradition of preferring longer-term and deeper relationships with suppliers, in their own customer interests) are setting up operations in the UK.

Hakansson (1981) in reporting on research which compared buyer–seller relationships in five European countries concluded that British industrial companies are relatively poor in managing long-term relationships.

All this suggests that some companies need to reappraise their marketing and sales strategies and consider the advantage in moving towards a 'high concern for the customer, high concern for the sale' position as illustrated in Figure 13.23.

While the hard sell approach may be adopted where repeat sales are unlikely (such as in selling encyclopaedias or double glazing door-to-door), this approach is not advocated when a long-term trading relationship needs to be built up.

**FIGURE 13.23**
*Relationship marketing and sales strategy*

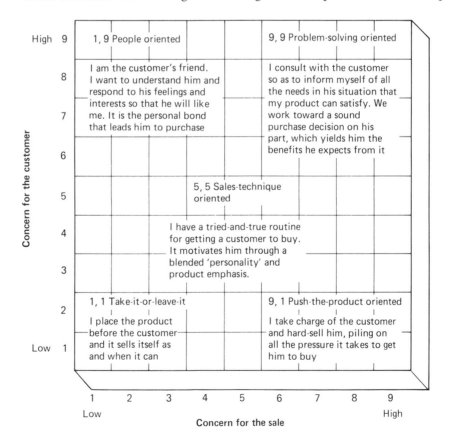

A pure hard sell approach is perhaps also a tempting strategy in situations when time is limited and when the customer appears to want his mind making up for him. It seems to be more frequently used when salespeople are working on commission only.

## Selling Tactics

The detailed selling methods chosen, the size of the sales force, its recruitment, training and motivation are tactical considerations which are determined to a great extent by the type of sales setting in which the company is operating. For example, the methods used in an electricity company showroom setting will be different from those used in an fmcg setting and different again from those used in a highly technological setting. In this sense the word 'setting' is used to encompass the physical situation, the nature of the product and indeed the buying behaviour involved. Buying behaviour patterns may, for example, dictate a team selling approach in a complex technological product setting.

In a computer equipment setting the selling process is likely to involve a series of visits stretching over several months, and talks with a number of influencers in the decision-making unit. In dealing with specifiers the objective is not to sell products *per se* but to get your products specified so as to ensure an eventual order from the contractors. In other settings a great deal of negotiation may take place over terms, after-sales service, etc. Some of the more obvious settings are listed in Figure 13.24.

The number of possible permutations is too large to be covered here in any detail. However, it can be seen, for example, that the number of salespeople, the type of person required, etc., will differ greatly between a setting of fmcg being sold to UK independent retail shop owners and the negotiation of a large civil engineering contract in a Middle East country. In the former setting a large number of relatively homogeneous salespeople requiring little in the way of formal qualifications would be needed. In the latter setting a smaller but varied and highly qualified team would be needed, including experts in legal and financial aspects as well as engineering technology.

## Sales Force Size

The factors determining the number of representatives needed are:

1  the number of customers/potential customers needing visits;
2  the frequency of visits, i.e. call cycle;
3  interview or face-to-face selling time required;
4  travelling time needed;
5  how often the competitors call;
6  identified customer needs.

If there are 800 potential or actual customers wanting visits once every four weeks, then 200 visits per week are needed which could be covered in a perfect situation by eight people each making 25 visits per week. However, allowances have to be made for holidays, illness, staff turnover, meetings, exhibitions, training, etc.

Many companies adopt differential calling frequencies, which means that particularly large or profitable customers get a higher frequency of call, say fortnightly, while small potential customers are visited only once every 12 weeks. This approach can make better use of the high-cost sales force. Other companies make use of intermediate telephone calls in between visits so as to conserve time but preserve contact. While customers can be asked how often they would like to be visited, companies run the risk of calling less often than competitors, with a potential loss of business as a result.

**FIGURE 13.24**
*Some different potential sales settings*

### Telephone Selling

More and more companies are adopting this method of selling. Telephone selling can vary from pure selling (e.g. the selling of advertising space by a large provincial newspaper such as the *Nottingham Evening Post* by a dedicated telephone sales force) to converting enquiries into sales and/or the trading up of telephone orders. Companies dealing in vehicle spare parts and accessories, through motor factors for example, may have a telesales force armed with VDUs and software programs which show on screen at the touch of a button the recent stock and order pattern of the customer ringing in a small order. This enables the telesales person to suggest that the caller is getting low in the stock of a given item and should perhaps add this to the order or indeed suggest that a larger quantity ordered less frequently would save the caller considerable time and inconvenience.

Other companies, such as Weleda (manufacturing pure natural medications marketed partially through healthcare outlets), have initiated telesales operations to supplement rather than support their field sales force. Outlets are telephoned by a given person at a predetermined time each week to check on sales, stock of point-of-sale material such as leaflets, etc. Topping-up orders are then taken and administered by the telesales personnel, leaving the field force free to concentrate on gaining new outlets and initiating promotional support for existing outlets. Other companies may require their telesales personnel to gain new customers as well as develop business from existing customers.

## Sales Force Support

Since selling is generally agreed to be a high-cost operation, it makes sense to support it to the utmost so as to increase efficiency and effectiveness. A telephone sales department is only one way of supporting the field sales force.

All other elements of the communications mix (i.e. advertising, sales promotion and PR) combine to help the field salesperson in engendering favourable awareness of the company's presence in the market-place. Professional selling aids, such as 'sales presenters', help efficiency by cutting down the amount of time needed to make the presentation and encourage effectiveness in getting the message across to the receiver with more impact.

The list shown in Figure 13.25 indicates some of the ways in which companies may support their field sales forces.

**FIGURE 13.25**

*Twenty ways of supporting the sales function*

```
 1 Sales presentation aids – from folders to audio visuals
 2 Sample provision
 3 Demonstrations
 4 Field accompaniments – by manager, technologists, etc.
 5 Telephone sales back-up operations
 6 Advertising
 7 Point-of-sale display material
 8 Dealer promotions
 9 Consumer promotions
10 Sales force incentives
11 Refresher sales training
12 New product introduction seminars
13 PR
14 Mailshots
15 Newsletters and sales bulletins
16 Complaint handling
17 Competitive lead times
18 Exhibitions
19 Merchandising
20 Quality and speed of quotation service
```

In industrial selling for example a salesman may labour hard to persuade a heating and ventilating engineering company to send enquiries for quotations. The speed with which quotations are then furnished by the estimating department can be instrumental in getting orders, in that the enquirer has to meet deadlines specified in the tender of documents to be considered.

## Sales Force Recruitment and Selection

In order to determine who best to recruit we should analyse the nature of the job to be carried out, the conditions under which the tasks will be performed and the responsibilities involved. This job analysis needs to result in a written job description which should also state how the job holder is to be evaluated.

The more thorough the analysis the clearer the picture that will emerge of the ideal person to do the job, or the person profile. However, we may be prepared to accept some deviation from the ideal (in order to be able to recruit under conditions of shortage of applicants or simply because a particular requirement is not stringent).

For example, while the ideal person would be 30 years old we are prepared to accept applicants between 25 and 35, or while the ideal qualification is a higher certificate in electronics we will consider lower certificates and degrees in this

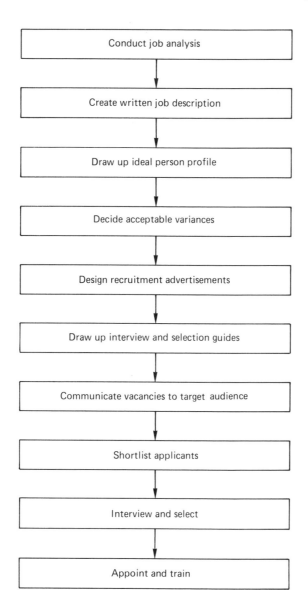

**FIGURE 13.26**
*The sales force recruitment and selection process*

technology. Having decided this issue we would then be in a position to design the recruitment advertising and/or other recruitment communications and continue the process, as indicated in Figure 13.26.

However, the relative importance of any given personal characteristic can vary considerably. For example, appearance and grooming might be extremely important for a beauty consultant but less important for a technical representative.

The amount of effort put into recruitment and selection of the sales force can be seen to occupy a spectrum ranging from companies (often selling door to door) which will recruit with very little discrimination, give no training and pay by results only, to companies like IBM which recognize the focal importance of their field sales force and which make strenuous efforts to recruit only the most suitable people by using sophisticated selection procedures.

### Sales Force Remuneration

There are five basic ways of remunerating the sales force. These are shown in Figure 13.27.

A bonus can be defined as a specific and discretionary payment for a specific purpose or task, as opposed to a commission on sales which is ongoing and previously agreed. Thus a bonus can be used to compensate a salesperson for

1 Salary only
2 Commission only
3 Salary plus commission
4 Salary plus bonus
5 Salary plus commission plus bonus

losses of commission due to staffing exhibitions or training new sales personnel. It can also be used to reward a team of salespeople where no one particular person could be said to have been solely responsible for the gaining of a national contract. Bonuses in the form of a share in profits or the issue of free shares are used by some managements as sales force incentives but are of course conditional on a profit being achieved during the trading period in question.

The choice of remuneration method is to some extent conditioned by custom and practice in the sales setting concerned. Companies can, however, evaluate the options by considering the advantages and disadvantages of each from the respective viewpoints of the company and the salesperson.

Some of the advantages and disadvantages are general. For example, an advantage of commission-only schemes may be that payment is related to results for both the company and the representative. A common disadvantage of commission-only schemes may be the uncertainty involved, which may be more meaningful to representatives worried about paying the mortgage than to the company which may be more concerned with the difficulty of administering the scheme.

However, since all five payment systems are in use (sometimes within a given sales setting), it is clear that different companies see particular advantages in the various methods. This may well be due to considerations of image and product positioning and whether a hard sell or a soft sell approach is being adopted. Hence a long-established company positioning its product well up-market, using exclusive distribution and sustaining a campaign of prestige advertising/PR, may prefer to reward its sales force with a high salary only system so as to discourage hard selling techniques and engender a greater degree of stability in terms of staff turnover.

## Direction and Motivation

Training can of course be used as a means of direction and motivation. It can be the prime reason why the person applied for a selling job with the company in the first place. Equally, poor training can de-motivate. In this context Allen (1989), in writing on the psychological bases of training, points to the individual's reasons for becoming a salesperson, which may be:

- to make more money;
- as a means of self-development;
- out of a liking for travel and meeting people;
- numerous other reasons.

When examining incentives as a means of motivation it can be useful to distinguish between financial incentives (such as salary, commission, bonuses, prizes, car, travelling and out-of-pocket expenses) and non-financial incentives (such as training, level of management support, prestige of company, longevity, opportunities for promotion, etc.).

A mix of financial and non-financial incentives would seem to comprise the best motivation for a sales force in that it is more likely to generate the right degree of enthusiasm combined with a sense of team spirit and pride. Such a working environment can be dynamic without suffering from the high rates of staff turnover experienced by companies relying on financial incentives alone.

In directing the sales force, sales managers need to appreciate the relatively high degree of independence and initiative in the typical sales person's character. Over-direction can cause resentment and be counter-productive, while under-direction can lead to chaos. Certainly the sales manager needs to be a leader and to maintain discipline. Equally, leadership studies suggest that the sales manager will gain the most commitment from a team of salespeople if he or she can be seen to work with them, to listen to them and to champion their causes when appropriate.

West (1987) also points to the interaction which can take place between the firm's sales force and its marketing strategy and tactics. Thus the sales force can influence the setting of prices, the development of products and the nature of sales promotions.

Good communications play a vital role in the directing of a sales force. Two-way verbal communications are the most flexible and effective form, which is why a heavy emphasis tends to be placed on meetings and conferences in the selling function.

The degree of direction the sales manager needs to give is to a large extent governed by the product-market situation. In fmcg, where young sales forces tend to be the mode, the number of visits to be made, their sequence, the amount of time to be given to each call and even the journey plan can be strictly laid down by sales management.

This would contrast with a technical sales engineer who would tend to be older, technically qualified, more experienced and who might be left to his own devices to a much greater extent.

## Evaluation and Control

In evaluating sales force performance comparisons should be made with competitors with regard to what has been achieved both quantitatively in terms of market share and qualitatively in terms of image in the market-place. This will typically entail the use of competitor intelligence and market research.

Some companies use a field sales trainer who will accompany sales representatives intermittently to appraise selling skills and give practical advice. An appraisal form that is used for this purpose and that may also be viewed as an evaluation and control technique is shown in Figure 13.28.

At the individual sales person's level it is not necessarily the person with the highest sales who should receive the most praise. There could be territorial advantages applying. High sales might have been achieved by high-pressure tactics leading to customer alienation. Such a high performer might be forced into obtaining a high proportion of businesses from new customers at the expense of losing existing customers. Similarly, a high total sales performance might not be achieved with the right degree of balance throughout the product range or throughout the year.

Other factors to be taken into account are the amount of competitor intelligence obtained, the quality of reporting, contribution to team events and the level of selling expenses incurred.

Where possible the contribution towards profits generated by a given salesperson's territory should be evaluated, particularly when that person has responsibility for price or discount negotiation. High sales do not necessarily mean high contributions. Quite apart from low prices, too many small orders can decrease the profit contribution considerably.

What we should be most concerned with are productivity and effectiveness (issues which have been discussed earlier in Chapters 1 and 3) and how best to evaluate overall performance, a problem which is addressed more fully in Chapters 15, 16 and 18.

**FIGURE 13.28**
*A selling skills appraisal form*

| Questions | Answers | Reasons why | Score |
|---|---|---|---|
| 1  Was the call well planned?  [Planning] | Yes / No | | |
| 2  Did he gain the prospect's attention with POSITIVE OPENING PHRASES?  [Attention] | Yes / No | | |
| 3  Did he maintain the prospect's interest?  [Interest] | Yes / No | | |
| 4  Did he use his sales aids correctly?  [Sales aids] | Yes / No | | |
| 5  Did he ask sensible questions?  [Questions] | Yes / No | | |
| 6  Did he listen and react correctly?  [Listen] | Yes / No | | |
| 7  Did he explain the benefits of his products?  [Benefits] | Yes / No | | |
| 8  Did he deal with objections satisfactorily?  [Objections] | Yes / No | | |
| 9  Did he communicate enthusiasm?  [Enthusiasm] | Yes / No | | |
| 10  Would you have bought his proposition?  [Order] | Yes / No | | |

## 13.7 SUMMARY

This chapter has endeavoured to show in some detail how the elements of the promotional mix are each composed of a submix to which a formal planning structure can be applied. Since each element of the promotional mix is fundamentally concerned with communications, it is particularly important that these are properly integrated to present a coherent, homogenous and favourable whole.

The role that each element plays in the total promotional mix has been described, and a range of specific objectives suggested. The relationship of promotion to other elements of the marketing mix has also been discussed.

With regard to strategy the question of whether to adopt an overall pull or push approach has been addressed, together with their integration.

A number of specific issues (such as the level of spend and selection of an advertising agency) have been investigated in this chapter on the grounds that these matters worry practitioners. Below-the-line activities are said to be attracting a greater and greater proportion of the total promotional spend and therefore merit a detailed consideration of the tactical decisions involved.

Recent trends towards more direct marketing, greater customer care and longer-term relationship marketing have not been neglected since these present new opportunities for progressive marketers.

In recognition of its importance in industrial marketing, a relatively full treatment of personal selling was included in the final section.

The chapter has been necessarily wide ranging but has endeavoured to show that promotion lends itself to a creative approach to a greater extent than other elements of the marketing mix, offering, for example, the opportunity of gaining a competitive edge in terms of the overall image presented by advertising, packaging, merchandising, PR activities and the sales force.

It is hoped that readers will have been left in no doubt as to the contribution that promotion can make to the achievement of overall marketing objectives.

# 14 | The distribution plan

## 14.1 LEARNING OBJECTIVES

When you have read this chapter you should be able to:

(a) understand the role of distribution as an element of the marketing mix;
(b) understand the range of decisions to be taken with regard to the distribution plan and the major criteria on which to base these decisions;
(c) know the types of distribution strategy in general operation;
(d) appreciate the contribution that distribution makes to overall marketing strategy.

## 14.2 INTRODUCTION

Having discussed in the previous chapter the process by which orders are obtained (i.e. the promotional mix), we now need to turn our attention towards the problem of fulfilling these orders: see Figure 14.1.

**FIGURE 14.1**
*The relationship of order getting to order filling*

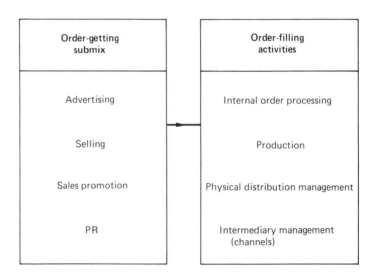

| Order-getting submix | Order-filling activities |
| --- | --- |
| Advertising | Internal order processing |
| Selling | Production |
| Sales promotion | Physical distribution management |
| PR | Intermediary management (channels) |

The success of order-getting activities will determine the volume and hence the scale of the order-fulfilling activities. This influences planning and control in a significant way.

Equally, the level of customer satisfaction engendered by order-fulfilling processes will affect the placing of repeat orders, and so once again the interdependency of the elements of the marketing mix is emphasized – in this case that of promotion with distribution.

There are two major aspects to the problem of order fulfilment. One is whether to use intermediaries in managing the flow of goods from manufacturer or supplier to user or consumer. The other aspect of the problem is that of physical transportation from the point of manufacture to the point of purchase or consumption. Both these aspects are affected by scale and frequency considerations.

**FIGURE 14.2**
*Two major aspects of order fulfilment*

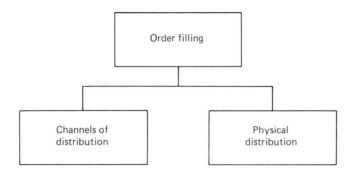

These two aspects can be integrated under the total distribution concept or, as it has come to be known, logistics, defined by Christopher (1986, p. 1) as:

> The process of strategically managing the movement and storage of materials, parts and finished inventory from suppliers, through the firm and on to customers.

In the event, physical distribution operations will be affected in their detail by whether or not a manufacturer or supplier markets direct to users or consumers.

The paramount consideration when deciding distribution strategy is the level of customer service the organization is aiming to provide (see later pages) and its value in the hierarchy of buying and/or patronage motives. A consumer may have been persuaded by advertising to buy Mr Kipling cakes for their quality or taste (buying motives) but prefers to buy them from Sainsbury rather than another supplier on account of the more pleasurable shopping environment (patronage motive).

In supplying Sainsbury with their cakes, Mr Kipling would be concerned to guard against stockouts (the situation when the consumer wants to purchase but the seller cannot fulfil this requirement immediately from stock). In the case of a stockout the consumer may purchase an alternative brand of cakes. The danger here is that the consumer may find this alternative brand preferable so that Mr Kipling loses not only the immediate sale but also future sales of much greater value (by losing the customer). In this example we see how the two aspects of order fulfilment – channels of distribution and physical distribution – can vitally affect sales.

When considering distribution strategy, marketing managers might endeavour to gain competitive advantage by seeking a higher level of customer service. In this context, customer service is defined as: *all parts of the distribution process which add value to the transaction from the customer's viewpoint.* Higher levels of customer service, however, can mean higher costs of distribution and might therefore reduce price competitiveness (see Figure 14.3).

Wilson (1979, pp. 148–9) points out the need to view costs as a whole because a reduction in one area can cause a disproportionate increase in another. For example, it might be cheaper in total terms, and more efficient in speed of delivery, to use an expensive means of transportation (e.g. air freight) than to maintain a number of local warehouses (see pp. 448–9).

**FIGURE 14.3**
*Levels of customer service and their costs*

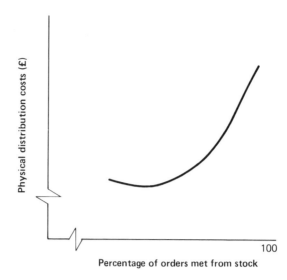

The distribution plan is possibly more difficult to manage than other elements of the marketing mix in that its operational decisions involve other functions to a greater extent. It is perhaps because of this fragmentation of responsibility that the concept of distribution as an integrative activity in business has only relatively recently developed.

It can be seen from Figure 14.4 that the distribution submix will involve the production function with regard to transportation and depots/warehouses, plus the management accounting function with regard to channel costing and perhaps the ordering system. Marketing is more directly concerned with channels of distribution, dealer relationships, the degree of penetration (proportion of available outlets served) and, of course, the level of customer service.

With the formation during the 1970s within the British Institute of Management of a specialist group of people interested in Physical Distribution Management (PDM) a great deal more attention was focused on this area, and activity increased to the stage at which a separate institution became necessary, now known as the Institute of Logistics and Distribution Management.

**FIGURE 14.4**
*The distribution plan and its likely submix*

PDM encompasses all aspects concerned with the physical movement of goods in and out of stock or between manufacturer and customer.

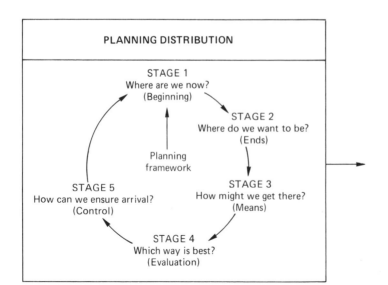

Some companies have adopted the concept of a fully integrated distribution system under the control of a professional distribution manager, and have reaped the reward of considerable gains in effectiveness and competitive advantage. Some years ago Courage Ales made spectacular gains in increasing customer service while reducing unit delivery costs by means of a complete overhaul of their distribution systems, including the installation of new prototype plant.

The Boots Company have also played an innovatory role in computerizing warehouse systems and in originating shared stock centres for geographically proximate groups of stores.

As indicated in the preamble to Stage Three, aspects of the planning structure other than strategy and tactics have been lightly touched on in this chapter so as to illustrate the outline of a total distribution plan. However, Chapter 2 and Chapters 15 onwards provide a much fuller treatments of auditing, evaluation and control.

## 14.3 WHERE ARE WE NOW? THE DISTRIBUTION AUDIT

The need for all marketing mix audits emanates from change, and the distribution element has perhaps been subject to more change than any other element of the mix in the UK in recent years. Particular changes have been seen in:

1 containerization;
2 computerization;
3 distribution channels.

Most consumer goods and some industrial goods are today transported in containers which can be observed daily in their hundreds on the motorways and in the ports by any traveller. Containers are claimed to have reduced lead times as well as reducing damage and pilferage.

Computerization of ordering and stocking systems has progressed with the advent of more higher-quality and lower-cost software, contributing to speedier response in deliveries against orders received.

Changes in distribution channels include the growth of cash and carry outlets as opposed to traditional wholesaling; the trend towards fewer but much larger retail outlets; out-of-town and one-stop shopping centres, e.g. the MetroCentre in Gateshead, Meadowhall in Sheffield, and Brent Cross in London; and last, but by no means least, the growth in channel domination by multiple retailers.

Since competitive advantage gained by other elements of the marketing mix can be lost by poor distribution, the auditing of competitors' distribution systems is particularly important.

The sales force should be directed to ask customers about competitors' distribution efficiencies as part of their regular reporting. Other competitor auditing methods include store checks, test ordering and simple observation.

Store checks are personal visits to retail stores to observe at first hand competitors' displays and sitings. Test ordering entails placing actual orders with competitors to identify their lead times and service levels.

Marketing research may be needed as part of the distribution audit to determine market shares by channel members. The distribution monitors produced quarterly by the government in the UK indicate sales by type of outlet and therefore make a good starting point.

Companies can also subscribe to a retail audit to establish the percentage of total outlets for particular types of retailer as well as percentage of total sales, as illustrated in Figure 14.5.

**FIGURE 14.5**
*Shop numbers and turnover by type of shop and region*

**MULTIPLE, CO-OPERATIVE AND INDEPENDENT GROCERS, SHOP NUMBERS, 1st Jan 1989**

|  | Multiples | Co-op's | Independents | Total |
|---|---|---|---|---|
| **Total GB** | **4,251** | **2,704** | **42,941** | **49,896** |
| **By Nielsen Region** |  |  |  |  |
| London | 897 | 245 | 6,431 | 7,573 |
| Anglia | 192 | 291 | 2,641 | 3,124 |
| Southern | 401 | 177 | 3,038 | 3,616 |
| Wales, West and Westward | 440 | 259 | 5,404 | 6,103 |
| Midlands | 564 | 443 | 7,797 | 8,804 |
| Lancashire | 631 | 357 | 6,144 | 7,132 |
| Yorkshire | 466 | 368 | 5,321 | 6,155 |
| Tyne Tees | 277 | 192 | 2,202 | 2,671 |
| Scotland | 383 | 372 | 3,963 | 4,718 |
| **By Metropolitan Area** |  |  |  |  |
| Greater London | 476 | 102 | 3,816 | 4,394 |
| Greater Manchester | 191 | 116 | 2,139 | 2,446 |
| Merseyside | 131 | 46 | 1,078 | 1,255 |
| South Yorkshire | 102 | 77 | 1,168 | 1,347 |
| Tyne and Wear | 107 | 48 | 961 | 1,116 |
| West Midlands | 173 | 59 | 2,222 | 2,454 |
| West Yorkshire | 129 | 123 | 1,991 | 2,243 |
| Metropolitan Areas Total | 1,309 | 571 | 13,375 | 15,255 |
| Non Metropolitan Areas | 2,942 | 2,133 | 29,566 | 34,641 |
| **By Size** |  |  |  |  |
| Under 10,000 sq. ft. | 2,806 | 2,451 | – | – |
| 10,000–25,000 sq. ft. | 944 | 179 | – | – |
| Over 25,000 sq. ft. (Superstores) | 501 | 74 | – | – |

*Source:* Nielsen Grocery Trade Report

**TURNOVERS AND AVERAGE WEEKLY SALES PER SHOP, 1986–1988**

|  | Turnover £ million | Average Weekly Sales per Shop. £ |
|---|---|---|
| **Total GB** |  |  |
| 1986 | 27,451 | 8,801 |
| 1987 | 29,675 | 9,694 |
| 1988 | 32,667 | 12,590 |
| **1988 by Nielsen Region** |  |  |
| London | 8,058 | 20,462 |
| Anglia | 2,164 | 13,321 |
| Southern | 3,029 | 16,109 |
| Wales, West and Westward | 3,417 | 10,767 |
| Midlands | 4,754 | 10,384 |
| Lancashire | 3,725 | 10,044 |
| Yorkshire | 3,185 | 9,951 |
| Tyne Tees | 1,490 | 10.728 |
| Scotland | 3,845 | 11,596 |
| **1988 by Shop Type** |  |  |
| Multiples | 24,135 | 109,182 |
| Co-operatives | 3,555 | 25,283 |
| Independents | 4,977 | 2,229 |

*Source:* Nielsen Grocery Trade Report

A retail audit will also provide details of sales for your brands and competitor brands by type of shop and by region.

The Centre for Interfirm Comparison in the UK is a useful source of information when conducting the audit, in that it can help in providing figures indicating the percentage of distribution costs to total sales for similar companies. These can act as benchmarks to guide objectives.

## 14.4 WHERE DO WE WANT TO BE? DISTRIBUTION OBJECTIVES

McDonald (1984) makes useful distinctions between sellers' distribution objectives, sellers' requirements of middlemen, and distributors' requirements of sellers, in Figure 14.6.

**FIGURE 14.6**
*Distribution objectives and consumer satisfaction*

**Sellers' distribution channel objectives**

Market/segment share
Profit objective by market segment
Channel member allegiance
Consumer brand loyalty

**Ultimate consumer needs – satisfaction required by ultimate consumers**

Price/value
Convenience
Availability
Choice

**Sellers' channel requirements – support required to achieve distribution channel and marketing objectives**

High penetration factor
High service levels
Wide range       } Inventory
Promotion
Market intelligence
Market development

Consumer satisfaction

**Distributors' requirements – compensation expected by resellers for providing seller support**

Satisfactory rate of stockturn
Gross margin and overhead contribution – ROI on inventory/selling area
Promotional allowance and other below the line benefits
Distribution exclusivity
Continuity of supply
Market development
Credit

Reseller support programmes

SOURCE: McDonald, 1984, p. 151

It can be seen from this figure that manufacturers and middlemen need to cooperate fully together in their common objective of satisfying consumer needs profitably.

However, conflict can occur when a manufacturer or a middleman seeks domination and/or becomes dissatisfied with the relationship. Such conflict can be resolved to some extent by backwards or forwards integration, as when a retailer takes over a manufacturer or a manufacturer obtains its own retail outlets.

Conflict also occurs, of course, between competing retailers in a channel, and can even occur between branches of the same retail chain where, for example, a regional promotion involves some branches but excludes others.

We can set distribution objectives in addition to those concerned with channels and these might cover the logistics aspects. Examples of such objectives might be:

- to reduce unit transportation costs from £5 per case to £4.50;
- to reduce delivery times from seven days to five days;
- to reduce the incidence of stockouts from 10 per cent to 5 per cent.

We now need to examine the strategies and tactics that might be employed to achieve both the channel and logistics objectives.

## 14.5 HOW MIGHT WE GET THERE? DISTRIBUTION STRATEGIES

Assuming that market segments have been identified and product positioning decisions taken, then an overriding consideration might be the level of customer service required. This level might be the distinguishing factor in the company's marketing mix.

Christopher, et al. (1979) define customer service as: 'a system organised to provide a continuing link between the time that the order is placed and the goods are received with the objective of satisfying customer needs on a long-term basis'. While this definition extends that given on p. 389 it still omits pre-sales services. A broader perspective of customer service is afforded by Blenel and Bender (1980) who suggest three missions:

1  the first mission of service is to protect the company's customer base;
2  service's second mission is to enhance the product's saleability;
3  the third mission of service, from the marketing perspective, is to generate income.

La Londe and Zinszer (1976) and other commentators have suggested a number of common elements of customer service from a distribution viewpoint:

- speed of response (time taken to deliver from receipt of order);
- consistency and reliability of delivery;
- stock availability;
- order size constraints;
- convenience of ordering system (customer friendliness);
- flexibility of delivery times;
- invoicing procedures and reliability;
- claims and complaints procedures;
- order status information system;
- condition of goods on delivery.

Research is needed, however, to determine the rank ordering of these elements from customers' viewpoints.

In seeking to improve customer satisfaction at a profit through distribution, the manufacturer needs to decide whether to market direct or, if not, which channels of distribution to select. Questions assisting this decision are:

1  can we effect distribution better than intermediaries at an equivalent cost?
2  can we effect distribution as well as intermediaries at a lower cost?

If the answer to either of these questions is yes, then the manufacturer should consider direct distribution. However, a barrier to direct marketing might exist in the form of entrenched buying behaviour. That is to say people get used to buying certain goods through particular intermediaries and have an in-built inertia to change.

Figures 14.7 and 14.8 illustrate potential savings through the use of intermediaries or middlemen.

It can be seen that the total number of transactions has been reduced from 20 in Figure 14.7 to 12 in Figure 14.8. The customer now has to deal with only one supplier instead of two. Each manufacturer deals with just one middleman instead of 10 customers.

Substantial savings are therefore possible in the ordering system and in transportation costs for the manufacturers concerned. Lead times are potentially reduced by the middleman maintaining stocks. The 'penalty' in using the

**FIGURE 14.7**
*Direct marketing to 10 customers by two manufacturers*

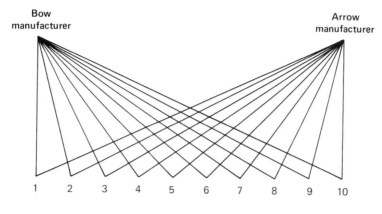

**FIGURE 14.8**
*Marketing to 10 customers by two manufacturers through one middleman*

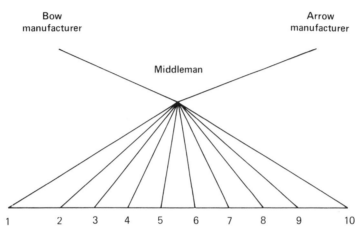

middleman approach is, of course, the mark-up on price exacted for this service. However, middlemen can provide extra benefits by, for example, offering a wider range of particular goods at a convenient location and in congenial surroundings.

## Channels of Distribution

A number of options exist in the choice of distribution channels in the UK, the major ones being illustrated in Figure 14.9.

In Figure 14.9 we can observe that voluntary group retailers (i.e. independent retailers trading under a common group facia or symbol such as Spar and acting as a group for buying purposes) will purchase from wholesalers outside the group as well as from those within the group. Co-operative Society retailers will act in a similar way when expedient.

Co-operative Society wholesalers will buy from other manufacturers as well as from their own manufacturing units in the same way that Boots the Chemists do in order to offer their customers a more attractive choice of goods.

Companies can, of course, use more than one channel of distribution and this is fairly common in the clothing industry in the UK, where a manufacturer may sell direct to the public ex factory, while also supplying garments to mail-order companies, multiple retailers, agents and even market traders.

Not all retailers will want to stock all manufacturers' products. Assuming a manufacturer of matches was able to offer a small independent retailer an equivalent product at a lower price and therefore a higher potential mark-up, it may not be worth the retailer's while to deal with that manufacturer for a single item, especially when the weekly sales value of matches might amount to only a few pounds. The small independent retailer is likely to deal with a local cash and carry wholesaler for a full range of items on the grounds of convenience and economy of effort.

**FIGURE 14.9**
*Principal UK channels of distribution*

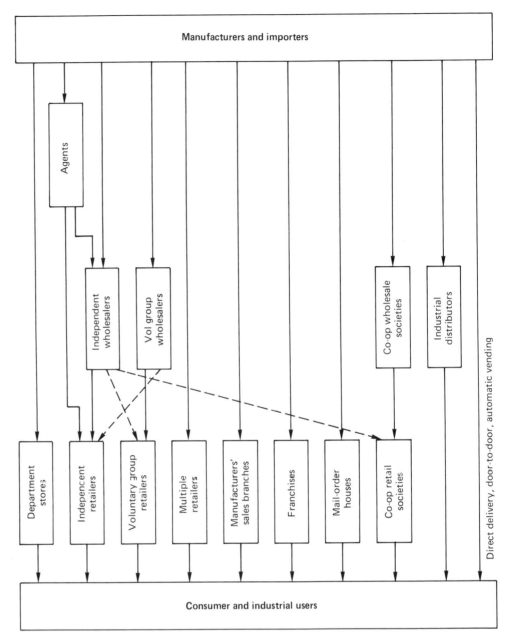

Similarly, large multiple retailers' shelf space is fought over by many suppliers and is unlikely to be easily available to a new manufacturer. However, assuming that a choice among distribution channels or within distribution channels can be made, the manufacturer will apply a number of criteria, which might include the following:

1 number of outlets;
2 sales turnover of outlets;
3 geographical location and accessibility;
4 competitive products stocked;
5 image of outlets;
6 terms of business;
7 stocking policies and conditions of storage;
8 promotional cooperation;
9 pricing policies;
10 level of customer service;
11 profitability;
12 level of sales force.

For example, a manufacturer of fine upholstered furniture wishing to maintain a prestige image might seek a selected number of well-established, good-class outlets in relatively expensive shopping locations which would cooperate in a high-price, high customer service policy. These outlets' salespeople would be of above-average calibre and be trained by the manufacturer in product knowledge.

The choice of potential distribution channels appears to be widening. We have witnessed in recent times, for example, the successful development of hybrids such as the Argos stores which combine the principles of retailing with catalogue selection as used in mail order.

When a manufacturer wishes to market through retail outlets but feels that insufficient exposure would be gained by sharing these with other manufacturers, then the possibility of opening its own dedicated shops might be considered. Should the manufacturer feel that the capital required for its own shops cannot feasibly be raised and/or the risk entailed in going into retailing is too great, then the possibility of operating via franchise should be examined. In this context the relevant form of franchise is where a manufacturer or entrepreneur offers the retailing rights of a unique product, service or trade name under a contractual agreement to franchisees willing to invest their own capital in a retail outlet in return for promotional and other support by the franchisor. The advantage to the franchisor is in rapidly gaining market coverage without high capital costs, while still maintaining market control. The British Franchise Association offers considerable expertise to would-be franchisors as well as attempting to safeguard standards. A number of specialist media (e.g. *Franchise World*) are now available in the UK, through which potential franchisees may be recruited.

Since the risk of business failure has been observed to a be great deal less under a properly established franchise operation than for small businesses generally, the major banks have all now set up franchise departments to facilitate this new form of retailing. They will lend up to 70 per cent of the capital required for an established franchise such as Oliver's Hot Bread Shops, which was one of the National Westminster Bank's bespoke schemes. Figure 14.10 shows a typical assessment for this type of franchise at the time of its growth.

**Distribution Channel Penetration**

A manufacturer choosing the retail channel needs to decide whether to aim to sell products in all the available outlets, in a selection of the available outlets in an area, or even to limit distribution to one outlet per area only.

These three alternatives strategies are known as:

* intensive distribution;
* selective distribution;
* exclusive distribution.

*Intensive distribution* is often sought by manufacturers of high-volume, low-value products in mass demand, for which the typical buying behaviour is one of habit and convenience. A manufacturer of cigarettes, for example, will aim to distribute these intensively in all available outlets from tobacconists to fish-and-chip shops, from theatre foyers to vending machines.

*Selective distribution* is used by manufacturers of consumer durables for which the established buying behaviour is typically one of 'shopping around'. Most consumers will make an effort to compare the offerings of various outlets. For this reason the manufacturer need not have the product in all available outlets. A dishwashing machine might therefore be found in electricity showrooms and in department stores in town centres rather than all available outlets.

Clearly the number of outlets it is necessary to communicate with is a great deal fewer than in intensive distribution, with consequent implications for the promotional plan. Selective distribution also offers opportunities to develop closer relationships with middlemen and enables manufacturers to gain adequate market coverage with less cost and more control than intensive distribution.

**FIGURE 14.10**

*An illustrative assessment for an Oliver's Hot Bread Shop franchise*

Budget trading accounts for a typical sized unit – class A bakery

| What it might cost . . . | £ |
|---|---|
| *Shopfitting* | |
| Joinery/building/ceilings | |
| Electrical | |
| Plumbing | |
| Tiling | |
| Ventilation/airconditioning | |
| Painting/decorating | |
| Prep room | |
| Carpets | |
| Tables & chairs | *90,000 |
| *Major items of capital equipment* | |
| Counters (display, refridgerated, heated) | *14,000 |
| Bakery equipment | 16,800 |
| Catering equipment | 6,100 |
| *Sundry equipment* | 4,600 |
| *Franchise fee* | 10,000 |
| *Legal & stamp duty* | 8,000 |
| *Retained estate agents* | 3,000 |
| *Chartered surveyor* (Structural report where required) | 350 |
| *Architects* | |
| Site visits | |
| Clerk of works | |
| Quantity surveying | |
| Design, drawings, schedules etc | |
| Printing, etc. | |
| Planning applications & fees | |
| Advertising required by planning authorities | 9,00 |
| *Start-up costs* (Transparencies, pictures overalls, stationery) | *2,000 |
| *Pre-trading wages* (For training) | 2,000 |
| | £165,850 |

| . . . and what it might earn | £ |
|---|---|
| *Annual sales 100%* | 350,000 |
| Purchases 35% | 122,500 |
| Wages 20% | 70,000 |
| | 192,500 |
| *Gross profit 45%* | 157,000 |
| Rent, rates & insurance | 50,000 |
| Power, office & sundries | 15,500 |
| Repairs & maintenance | 2,000 |
| Advertising 2% | 7,000 |
| Management fee 6% | 21,000 |
| *Total expenses* | 95,500 |
| Profit before tax, depreciation and finance | 62,000 |

**Notes**

*While gross profit is estimated at 45% after charging material costs, packaging and all direct wage costs, the owner/manager's salary is not included. Time take to achieve the projected gross profit will vary and depends very much on sound management practices

*Varies depending on size and rent of property.

These costs are based on current information at the time of compilation. Obviously inflation, design improvements and modifications may vary above projected costs and it should be noted that 30% of the total cost should come from you own personal resources.

Above costs do not include VAT

Estimated opening costs.

Assume the premises are leased and not purchased.

Source: Oliver's Hot Bread Shop.

SOURCE: Adapted from *Moneycare* magazine, National Westminster Bank PLC

*Exclusive distribution* is where the manufacturer limits the number of intermediaries more strictly to one per geographical area. The dealer receives exclusive rights to distribute the manufacturer's products in that geographical area in return for agreeing not to carry competing products. The manufacturer will therefore receive a greater commitment from the outlet and more control over image and price. Rolls Royce cars are a good example of this type of distribution strategy.

The decision will depend to a large extent on the nature of the product, the target market segment and the product positioning. Lancaster and Massingham (1988) suggest that some of the factors which would persuade a company towards a more exclusive form of distribution would include:

- where the customer needs or expects specialist advice, facilities or service;
- where the manufacturer and/or distributor would gain from the enhanced image associated with selective/exclusive distribution;
- where potential sales volume would not warrant more intensive distribution;
- where the manufacturer wishes to exercise more control over channel members' marketing activities;
- where more intensive distribution might result in conflicts between channel members.

The need for integration between manufacturer and distributors in meeting consumer or user needs cannot be overstressed and covers all aspects of the marketing mix. Room for conflict rather than cooperation occurs not only between manufacturer and distributor but also between different levels in the channel (e.g. wholesaler and retailer) and between one retailer and another.

**Order Processing**

There are a number of aspects which warrant consideration by marketers, including:

- the minimum size of order;
- conditions of sale and purchase;
- the system used to process orders;
- the time taken to process orders.

To some extent these are interdependent since the time taken to process an order depends on the system used, which then determines the cost of processing, which in turn dictates the minimum size of order that can be economically handled.

Mention needs to be made here again of electronic point-of-sales systems (EPOS) which link sales ordering systems with automatic stock control and stock reordering systems through the computer. A further sophistication currently being implemented is EFTPOS (electronic funds transfer at the point of sales) which simultaneously debits the buyer's bank account. Cox and Brittain (1988, p. 267) give the major benefits of EPOS to retailers in both 'hard' and 'soft' varieties as follows:

- *hard benefits*
  - up to 15 per cent increase in checkout productivity,
  - labour savings in not having to price individual items,
  - reduced 'miss-rings' at the checkout,
  - easier price changing;

- *soft benefits*
  - more management information on customer flows, line sales over time periods, merchandising/promotional effectiveness,
  - better stock control.

## 14.6 EVALUATION AND CONTROL – DISTRIBUTION COST ANALYSIS AND CHANNEL PROFITABILITY

Figure 14.11 gives indications of costs by industry sector and by company size for different categories of distribution cost.

While there are some obvious anomalies brought about by the small sample sizes in some categories, it is clear that in general small companies operate at a cost disadvantage compared with their larger competitors. This situation is particularly noticeable among industrial companies and indeed throughout nearly all the manufacturing sectors. The situation is less critical for retailers and wholesalers, as factors such as the product range and the type of outlets will have a significant impact on the results. However, these results are entirely consistent with previous surveys and indicate significant economies of scale for many larger operators.

Wilson (1979, pp. 147–56) provides a great deal more specific help on how to analyse distribution costs in detail with a view to improving the effectiveness of this element of the marketing mix.

## 14.7 SUMMARY

This chapter positions distribution in the role of order-fulfilling activities as opposed to promotion that can be viewed as a series of order-getting activities.

We have seen that there are two major aspects to the process of order fulfilment, namely, the choice of intermediaries between manufacturer and user, *and* the management of physical distribution including stocking and transportation. Both these aspects involve strategic decisions of a crucial nature since they

**FIGURE 14.11**
*Distribution costs as percentages of turnover*

| | | No. of companies | Storage | Inventory | Transport | Admin. | Packaging | Total | Average |
|---|---|---|---|---|---|---|---|---|---|
| Food Drink Tobacco | Manufacturing | | | | | | | | |
| | Small | 31 | 4.4 | 1.5 | 5.1 | 1.0 | 3.3 | 15.3 | |
| | Medium | 26 | 2.4 | 0.8 | 4.1 | 0.8 | 0.1 | 8.2 | |
| | Large | 13 | 1.8 | 0.6 | 3.3 | 1.6 | 0.7 | 8.0 | 8.4 |
| | Retail | | | | | | | | |
| | Small | 31 | – | – | – | – | – | 0.0 | |
| | Medium | 26 | 1.1 | 0.9 | 0.6 | – | 0.0 | 2.6 | |
| | Large | 13 | 1.8 | 0.5 | 1.1 | 0.4 | 0.0 | 4.0 | 3.9 |
| | Wholesale | | | | | | | | |
| | Small | 31 | 2.0 | 2.7 | 2.8 | 0.7 | 0.2 | 8.4 | |
| | Medium | 26 | 1.4 | 0.1 | 0.8 | – | 0.0 | 2.3 | |
| | Large | 13 | – | – | – | – | – | – | 3.6 |
| Consumer goods | Manufacturing | | | | | | | | |
| | Small | 31 | 3.9 | 3.6 | 2.9 | 0.7 | 0.4 | 11.4 | |
| | Medium | 26 | 1.9 | 1.0 | 2.3 | 0.4 | 0.1 | 5.7 | |
| | Large | 13 | 4.1 | 0.1 | 2.6 | 0.2 | 0.0 | 7.0 | 7.5 |
| | Retail | | | | | | | | |
| | Small | 31 | 5.5 | 1.3 | 5.4 | 2.0 | 0.2 | 14.4 | |
| | Medium | 26 | 1.9 | 2.3 | 0.6 | – | 0.1 | 4.9 | |
| | Large | 13 | 3.5 | 1.2 | 4.6 | 0.3 | 0.0 | 9.6 | 9.3 |
| | Wholesale | | | | | | | | |
| | Small | 31 | 20.8 | 5.9 | 5.0 | 15.2 | 1.3 | 48.2 | |
| | Medium | 26 | 1.1 | – | 0.7 | – | 0.2 | 2.0 | |
| | Large | 13 | – | – | – | – | – | 0.0 | 34.0 |
| Industrial | | | | | | | | | |
| | Small | 31 | 4.3 | 3.1 | 3.0 | 1.2 | **0.6** | 12.2 | |
| | Medium | 26 | 2.2 | 1.8 | 2.5 | 2.3 | **1.2** | 10.0 | |
| | Large | 13 | 0.9 | 1.1 | 3.0 | 0.3 | **0.3** | 5.6 | 9.0 |
| Total | | | | | | | | | |
| | Small | 31 | 4.3 | 2.9 | 3.3 | 1.4 | **0.8** | 12.7 | |
| | Medium | 26 | 2.0 | 1.7 | 2.5 | 1.1 | **0.5** | 7.7 | |
| | Large | 13 | 2.2 | 1.1 | 2.9 | **0.5** | **0.2** | 6.9 | 7.4 |

SOURCE: The Institute of Logistics and Distribution Management, Survey, 1989–90 can make or mar long-term customer relationships through the level of customer service that they afford.

Distribution can be seen to present opportunities for gaining distinctive competences relative to competitors. While an enterprise can offer good products at competitive prices, communicated effectively to the right people, all these factors are let down if the products are not available in the right place and at the right time. Distribution can therefore either take away from or add value to other elements in the marketing mix.

In its treatment of the choice of channels of distribution the chapter refers to the possibilities of franchise, since this is a relatively new and growing opportunity for retailers and some manufacturers. Other aspects of channel choice have been covered, including the use of exclusive, selective or intensive modes of distribution.

Some indications have also been made of the levels of distribution costs and (by reference to other chapters) how the analysis and control of these can greatly improve the effectiveness of the distribution element of the marketing mix and thereby the effectiveness of the total offering to the customer.

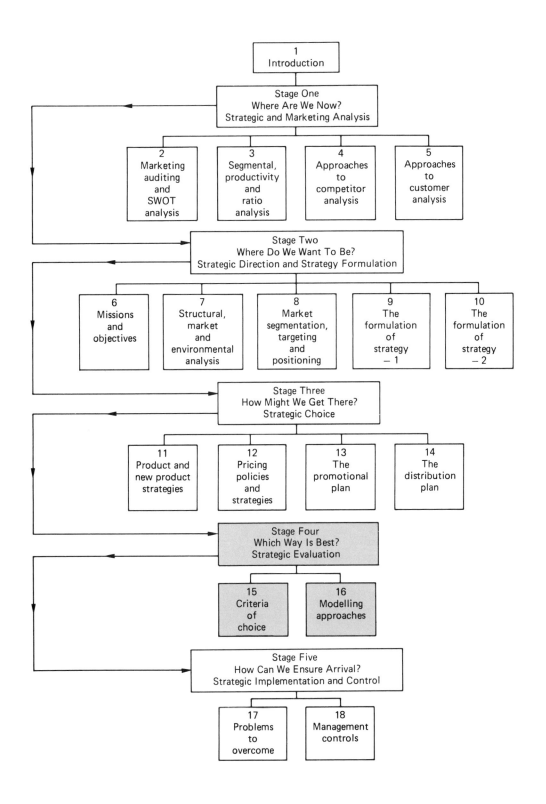

| | 1 |
|---|---|
| | Introduction |

Stage One
Where Are We Now?
Strategic and Marketing Analysis

| 2 | 3 | 4 | 5 |
|---|---|---|---|
| Marketing auditing and SWOT analysis | Segmental, productivity and ratio analysis | Approaches to competitor analysis | Approaches to customer analysis |

Stage Two
Where Do We Want To Be?
Strategic Direction and Strategy Formulation

| 6 | 7 | 8 | 9 | 10 |
|---|---|---|---|---|
| Missions and objectives | Structural, market and environmental analysis | Market segmentation, targeting and positioning | The formulation of strategy − 1 | The formulation of strategy − 2 |

Stage Three
How Might We Get There?
Strategic Choice

| 11 | 12 | 13 | 14 |
|---|---|---|---|
| Product and new product strategies | Pricing policies and strategies | The promotional plan | The distribution plan |

Stage Four
Which Way Is Best?
Strategic Evaluation

| 15 | 16 |
|---|---|
| Criteria of choice | Modelling approaches |

Stage Five
How Can We Ensure Arrival?
Strategic Implementation and Control

| 17 | 18 |
|---|---|
| Problems to overcome | Management controls |

# Stage Four
## Which Way Is Best?
### Strategic Evaluation

## PREAMBLE

The overall concern within this stage is with the choice among alternative marketing strategies that were suggested in Stages Two and Three. This concern reduces to two principal questions:

1 What criteria of choice should be employed? This is dealt with in Chapter 15.
2 How might alternative marketing programmes be evaluated given the criteria articulated in 1? This is addressed in Chapter 16.

Prior to moving on to Chapters 15 and 16 it may be useful to consider some of the evidence that is available on the effectiveness of marketing activities within the UK. This will provide useful background material as we move through Stages Four and Five of the book.

In their study on the effectiveness of British marketing (Lynch, et al., 1988), the Bradford-based research team followed up an earlier study they had undertaken (Hooley, et al., 1984). Their main interest was in identifying the characteristics of the more successful organizations across a sample that was broadly representative of British companies in terms of size, sector and business type.

No magic formula was found that might guarantee the success of marketing activities. However, the better performers showed a firmer grasp of the key marketing concepts and a greater consistency in applying those concepts across their range of operations. There was, in fact, a stronger commitment to marketing principles resulting in a consistent marketing-oriented culture within the more successful enterprises. In summary, the prevalent attitudes among the better performers were found to be:

- a greater emphasis on identifying and meeting customers' needs;
- the chief executive sees marketing as a guiding philosophy for the whole organization;
- more aggressive, expansionist objectives;
- more likely to pursue longer-term marketing goals rather than short-term financial objectives;
- great importance is attached to marketing training.

With regard to marketing practices, the better performing companies exhibited the following characteristics:

- a greater input was made by marketing to overall strategic planning;
- there was more evidence of formal, long-term marketing planning;
- marketing objectives were more aggressively specified;
- prepared to attack the whole market and take on any competition;
- more prepared to take calculated risks;
- adopted superior quality, high-price positioning strategies;
- competitive advantages are built through reputation and quality;
- more active in new product development in order to achieve market leadership.

In overall terms the more successful enterprises showed impressive consistency in implementation derived from a combination of their clearer marketing grasp and their more focused marketing structures and systems.

Other studies that have examined the success of marketing activities include those by Verhage and Waarts (1988) who looked at Dutch and British companies on a comparative basis, and those by Doyle, Saunders and Wright (1988) and Wong, Saunders and Doyle (1988) who looked at the comparative quality of marketing activities in British, Japanese and US companies. Results from the last two studies highlighted significant weaknesses in the marketing effectiveness of British companies which were exacerbated by an excessive emphasis on short-run financial gains. Given that the focus was on comparative performance within UK markets it was found that US firms were less committed to the UK market than were their Japanese rivals. While the Japanese were working to close the technological gap between themselves and their US competitors, the latter were demonstrating a short-term profit focus. This makes it likely that US market positions will deteriorate since the Japanese showed themselves to be unmistakably aggressive, single-minded in their pursuit of market share, and undeniably more market-oriented than their US or British counterparts.

In its 1991 Survey of the UK's 77 top marketing companies (see the reprinted article on pp. 404–12), *Marketing Week* found that Mars was in the lead with British Rail bringing up the rear. The sectors covered by the survey and the criteria used in making the assessments, along with other details, are given below.

**The combination of three phenomenally successful ice-cream bar launches and the long, hot summer gave Mars the edge to push Kellogg from the top slot in the *Marketing Week* 1991 Top Marketing Companies survey. By Jane Sturges**

# Mars in the Ascendant

Mars is rated the best company at marketing in the UK, according to *Marketing Week's* 1991 Top Marketing Companies survey. It knocked last year's winner Kellogg from the top slot, but interestingly with a lower rating – 7.46 points out of ten, compared with 7.59 – than it achieved last year.

Overall this year, companies tended to move nearer to the average: this year's bottom score of 4.29 was recorded by beleaguered British Rail, but was somewhat higher than last year's lowest of 4.05, achieved by the Co-op.

The overall score is the average of the scores companies receive across the nine categories.

This year's result shows the growing marketing strength of retailers. Marks & Spencer moves up to second place, only 0.05 of a point behind Mars. It gains the top rating in six of the nine categories included in the survey: the quality of products or services; the design of products or services; the ability to attract, develop and keep talented people; overall financial performance in its sector; the profitable pricing of products or services; and the successful development of existing products or services where it shared top position with Mars. Last year M&S came top in only two categories, which suggests that it has shown the most dramatic improvement in the top ten this year.

Sainsbury has moved up three places to the number three position and Boots and Tesco have entered the top ten. Boots, in sixth position, has moved up 11 places and improved its overall score from 6.64 to 7.02; Tesco, in joint tenth position, has shot up from 34th place last year.

Outside the top ten, WH Smith, in 13th place, Asda, up 27 places, and House of Fraser have all improved their standing.

## Top marketing companies 1991

| Rank | Name | Score | Rank | Name | Score |
|------|------|-------|------|------|-------|
| 1 | Mars | 7.46 | 40 | British Gas | 5.78 |
| 2 | Marks & Spencer | 7.41 | 41= | Brooke Bond Foods | 5.75 |
| 3 | Sainsbury | 7.23 | 41= | Kraft General Foods | 5.75 |
| 4 | Guinness | 7.08 | 43 | Rothmans | 5.73 |
| 5 | BMW | 7.03 | 44= | Halifax Building Society | 5.71 |
| 6 | Boots | 7.02 | 44= | Argyll Group | 5.71 |
| 7 | Procter & Gamble | 6.99 | 44= | Shell UK | 5.71 |
| 8 | Kellogg | 6.97 | 47 | House of Fraser | 5.70 |
| 9 | Cadbury | 6.96 | 48= | Barclays Bank | 5.68 |
| 10= | Lever Brothers | 6.87 | 48= | Mercury | 5.68 |
| 10= | Tesco | 6.87 | 50 | Whitbread | 5.66 |
| 12 | Mercedes-Benz | 6.81 | 51 | Imperial Tobacco | 5.59 |
| 13 | WH Smith | 6.78 | 52 | Beecham | 5.55 |
| 14 | Heinz | 6.76 | 53= | St Ivel | 5.51 |
| 15 | Vauxhall | 6.72 | 53= | Allied Breweries | 5.51 |
| 16 | VAG | 6.56 | 53= | Nabisco | 5.51 |
| 17= | British Airways | 6.41 | 56 | National Westminster Bank | 5.50 |
| 17= | Grand Metropolitan | 6.41 | 57 | Nissan | 5.48 |
| 19 | Ford | 6.35 | 58= | The Electricity Council | 5.43 |
| 20 | Bass | 6.33 | 58= | Reckitt & Colman | 5.43 |
| 21 | British Telecom | 6.27 | 60= | Lloyds Bank | 5.42 |
| 22 | Nestlé | 6.23 | 60= | Woolworth | 5.42 |
| 23= | United Biscuits | 6.22 | 62= | Lyons Tetley | 5.39 |
| 23= | Peugeot Talbot | 6.22 | 62= | Woolwich Building Society | 5.39 |
| 25 | Rover Group | 6.15 | 64 | Gallaher | 5.38 |
| 26 | Gillette | 6.13 | 65 | Nationwide Anglia Building Society | 5.31 |
| 27 | Toyota | 6.07 | | | |
| 28 | Birds Eye | 6.06 | 66 | Commercial Union | 5.25 |
| 29= | Beecham Toiletries | 6.01 | 67 | Post Office | 5.07 |
| 29= | Scottish & Newcastle | 6.01 | 68 | Midland Bank | 5.05 |
| 31 | Seagram | 5.99 | 69 | Sun Alliance | 5.03 |
| 32 | BP | 5.95 | 70 | Citroën | 5.01 |
| 33 | Courage | 5.94 | 71 | Renault | 4.90 |
| 34= | Dixon Group | 5.91 | 72 | Co-op | 4.87 |
| 34= | Alliance & Leicester | 5.91 | 73= | Mazda | 4.78 |
| 34= | Scott/Andrex | 5.91 | 73= | Leeds Permanent | 4.78 |
| 37 | Asda | 5.89 | 73= | Gateway | 4.78 |
| 38 | Esso UK | 5.88 | 76 | Fiat UK | 4.71 |
| 39 | Abbey National | 5.82 | 77 | British Rail | 4.29 |

# POINTERS TO PERFORMANCE

**This year's result shows the growing strength of retailers, and their progress seems to be at the expense of food companies**

The Top Marketing Companies Survey, carried out for *Marketing Week* by research company ICM, aims to measure the performance of 77 companies over the past year.

Companies in seven sectors were included in the survey:

- Retail and household stores
- Motor manufacturers
- Toiletries and household products
- Drinks and tobacco
- Food
- Finance
- Miscellaneous

Apart from the miscellaneous group, companies were selected according to the ratio of ad spend (figures from MEAL) to annual turnover, and in the case of financial institutions, the ratio of ad spend to assets.

For each sector, 100 interviews were conducted with senior marketing personnel, who were asked to rate companies on a scale of nought to ten. No one was asked to rate their own company.

Each interviewee was asked to give points out of ten for nine criteria: the development of successful new products or services; the successful development of existing products or services; the ability to attract, develop and keep talented people; the creative and effective use of advertising; the quality of products or services; the effective use of marketing in the development of corporate strategy; the design of products or services; the profitable pricing of products or services; and the overall financial performance.

## Using marketing effectively in development of company strategy

**Top 5**

| | | |
|---|---|---|
| 1 | Mars | 7.75 |
| 2 | Procter & Gamble | 7.63 |
| 3 | Kellogg | 7.59 |
| 4 | Lever Brothers | 7.51 |
| 5 | Marks & Spencer | 7.47 |

**Bottom 5**

| | | |
|---|---|---|
| 73 | Post Office | 5.02 |
| 74 | Imperial | 5.00 |
| 75 | Fiat | 4.89 |
| 76 | British Rail | 4.81 |
| 77 | Co-op | 4.20 |

## The quality of products or services

**Top 5**

| | | |
|---|---|---|
| 1 | Marks & Spencer | 8.45 |
| 2 | BMW | 8.28 |
| 3 | Mercedes-Benz | 8.24 |
| 4 | Mars | 7.98 |
| 5= | Cadbury | 7.87 |
| 5= | Kellogg | 7.87 |

**Bottom 5**

| | | |
|---|---|---|
| 73 | Leeds Permanent Building Society | 5.24 |
| 74 | Post Office | 5.07 |
| 75 | Co-op | 4.87 |
| 76 | Fiat | 4.53 |
| 77 | British Rail | 3.86 |

## Design of products or services

**Top 5**

| | | |
|---|---|---|
| 1 | Marks & Spencer | 7.89 |
| 2 | BMW | 7.72 |
| 3 | Cadbury | 7.41 |
| 4 | Guinness | 7.37 |
| 5 | Boots | 7.31 |

**Bottom 5**

| | | |
|---|---|---|
| 73= | Leeds Permanent | 5.34 |
| 73= | Post Office | 5.34 |
| 75 | Fiat | 4.75 |
| 76 | Co-op | 4.43 |
| 77 | British Rail | 4.40 |

As in last year's survey, some of the worst performers are also retailers. Although the Co-op has finally moved up from the bottom position on the table – the first time it has done so in the five years the survey has been run – it still only stands 72nd in the table.

This puts the store marginally ahead of Gateway – last year in 74th place – which shares 73rd position in the 1991 survey, despite the launch of its Somerfield chain.

While many food companies still manage to record scores in the top half of the table, their ratings and positions are generally lower than they were last year.

Three food companies remain in the top ten. While Mars has moved up, Kellogg and Cadbury have slipped back to eighth and ninth positions respectively, compared with their first and third positions last year.

Kellogg, Cadbury, Heinz, United Biscuits, Nestlé, Kraft General Foods, Brooke Bond Foods, Beecham, St Ivel, Lyons Tetley and Nabisco have all slipped back in the ratings on the Top Marketing Companies table, some quite significantly. United Biscuits, for example, has fallen from 14th to 23rd equal place, Nestlé from 12th to 22nd and St Ivel from 24th to 53rd equal. Birds Eye, included for the first time this year, out-performs many of its competitors in 28th place.

But the fact that scores have moved towards the average this year may mean that many food companies' performance is merely static, rather than deteriorating.

This effect also means that Guinness, which in last year's survey took joint seventh position, has moved up to fifth place, despite only increasing its overall score by 0.01 of a point to 7.08.

Grand Metropolitan moves up 15 places to joint 17th position with a rating of 6.41, compared with 6.30 last year. Bass moves up seven places, despite its score slipping from 6.39 to 6.33.

On the other hand both Scottish & Newcastle and Seagram show a genuine improvement. S&N moves up 23 places to 29th position with a score of 6.01, compared with 5.58 last year. Seagram is ten places higher with a score of 5.99 compared with 5.80 last year.

Car manufacturers continue to show a big disparity between those rated highly such as BMW and those still lurking at the bottom of the table. While companies such as Vauxhall and VAG have improved their position, car manufacturers now occupy four of the bottom positions in the table: Citroën is in 70th position, with a score of 5.01, a drop of 22 places; Mazda is down 11 places at 73; Renault down six at 71; and Fiat down one place to 76.

The only car company to show a marked improvement on its previous position is Rover which has leapt a staggering 47 places from 72nd to 25th.

Financial services companies appear to be making little headway with marketing. The only one to show a substantial improvement on last year's poor overall ratings is the Alliance & Leicester Building Society, up 27 places but still only in 34th place.

Midland Bank, beset by difficulties, has fallen 23 places to 68th position; Sun Alliance lies in 69th place; and the Leeds Permanent Building Society, is just off the bottom of the table in joint 73rd position.

Lloyds Bank, the Woolwich Building Society, Nationwide Anglia Building Society and Commercial Union all fall in the bottom 20 companies.

The miscellaneous sector of the survey includes national institutions such as British Telecom, British Rail, the Post Office and British Airways, as well as oil companies BP, Esso and Shell.

Less than half of these make it into the top half of the table, and only one makes it into the top 20, British Airways, which slips back three places to joint 17th position with a rating of 6.41, compared with 6.74 last year.

All three of the oil companies surveyed move down the table and the Post Office marginally improves its score to escape the bottom ten. It will come as no surprise to see British Rail at the bottom of the table with a score of 4.29. It comes out worst in six of the nine categories on which the survey is based: the development of successful new products or services; the successful development of existing products or services; the ability to attract, develop and keep talented people; the design of products or services; the quality of products or services; and the profitable pricing of products or services. Its poor position must have been further compounded by recent safety and weather problems.

# Retail and household stores sector

| 1 | Marks & Spencer | 7.41 |
|---|---|---|
| 2 | Sainsbury | 7.23 |
| 3 | Boots | 7.02 |
| 4 | Tesco | 6.87 |
| 5 | WH Smith | 6.78 |
| 6 | Dixon Group | 5.91 |
| 7 | Asda | 5.89 |
| 8 | Argyll Group | 5.71 |
| 9 | House of Fraser | 5.70 |
| 10 | Woolworth | 5.42 |
| 11 | Co-op | 4.87 |
| 12 | Gateway | 4.78 |

# Toiletries and household products sector

| 1 | Procter & Gamble/ Richardson Vicks | 6.99 |
|---|---|---|
| 2 | Lever Brothers | 6.87 |
| 3 | Gillette | 6.13 |
| 4 | Beecham Toiletries | 6.01 |
| 5 | Scott | 5.91 |
| 6 | Reckitt & Colman | 5.43 |

# Miscellaneous sector

| 1 | British Airways | 6.41 |
|---|---|---|
| 2 | British Telecom | 6.27 |
| 3 | BP | 5.95 |
| 4 | Esso | 5.88 |
| 5 | British Gas | 5.78 |
| 6 | Shell | 5.71 |
| 7 | Mercury | 5.68 |
| 8 | Electricity Council | 5.43 |
| 9 | Post Office | 5.07 |
| 10 | British Rail | 4.29 |

# Drinks and tobacco sector

| 1 | Guinness | 7.08 |
|---|---|---|
| 2 | Grand Metropolitan | 6.41 |
| 3 | Bass | 6.33 |
| 4 | Scottish & Newcastle | 6.01 |
| 5 | Seagram | 5.99 |
| 6 | Courage | 5.94 |
| 7 | Rothmans | 5.73 |
| 8 | Whitbread | 5.66 |
| 9 | Imperial | 5.59 |
| 10 | Allied | 5.51 |
| 11 | Gallaher | 5.38 |

# M&S scores on quality and services

Retailers are at last getting wise to the value of marketing, and this has helped them make a strong showing in the Top Marketing Companies survey. Five firms are in the top 15 compared with just two last year.

Marks & Spencer and Sainsbury have improved last year's placing by three points, taking second and third positions respectively.

Boots has made an 11-place leap into position six, while Tesco has jumped 24 places to take tenth slot. The Dixon Group has gone up 19 places, Asda 27 places, the Argyll Group six and House of Fraser 12.

According to Verdict's Richard Hyman, retailers are only just shaking off the belief that their shops do the marketing for them, whereas food manufacturers have always marketed their products. "Retailers are realising that the greater control they have over their destinies, the more likely they are to achieve success. Therefore it is important for them to market themselves as brands," he says.

M&S scores in the high sevens and eights for most sectors, achieving a respectable 8.45 for quality of products and services. M&S's innovation over the past year, culminating in its Christmas gift range Penny Bazaar, has been impressive.

Meanwhile, Boots commercial director Steve Russell believes the fruition of a four-year plan to emphasise the chemist's traditional values prompted its move up the table. "In the past three to four years we have gone back to Boots' old values on products and services, and this has been more visible over the past year. Perception of what we have been doing is reflected in this [result]." he says.

The company scores highly in areas such as design of products or services and ability to attract and keep talented people. Its development of successful new products, however, falls down with a score of 6.67. Russell is disappointed with that figure. "Eight to ten per cent of our turnover comes from new products," he says. "We've had some notable successes such as our Natural range and Shapers diet range."

Boots spends £20m through Col-

lett, Dickenson Pearce and Publicis. But Russell admits the company's image is rather overshadowed by single product advertising. Commenting on an advertising effectiveness score of 6.35, he says: "Boots' ad recall is not as high as we would like."

Food retailers, with the exception of Gateway and Co-op, have improved their standing in the table. Tesco's highly successful £24m ad campaign using Dudley Moore has improved brand awareness and put it in a strong position to threaten market leader Sainsbury.

Sainsbury marketing director Anthony Rees believes his store has not progressed at the same rate as Tesco because it does not have the same need to update its image. "We have always evolved as a company and our consistent approach is one of our strengths. Tesco has invested heavily in changing perceptions," he says.

Rees compares Tesco's £24m ad spend with Sainsbury's £10m and claims his company's superior position in the table proves it. But Sainsbury is "conscious of a lack of TV presence" and intends to use the medium more through Abbott Mead Vickers.

Asda's leap of 27 places reflects its status as a company that is finally moving with the times. In the eight-

ies, Asda lost ground in a sector where some of the world's best marketers exist. By improving its internal structure and distribution, and investing in advertising to project a brand image, the supermarket chain scored 6.14 for effective marketing in development of corporate strategy. The "It 'asda be Asda" campaign through Publicis represented a 46 per cent increase in ad spend to £14.26m (*MW* Top 100 advertisers, February 22).

Maybe it is Gateway's meagre £2.6m ad spend (Media Register) that accounts for its poor performance in the table – it dropped two points to hover just one place from the bottom.

Its low score of 4.78 for new product development must be a blow considering its recent introduction of new chain Somerfield.

Gateway is desperately trying to alter its position without the need for radical change. Improvements to the Gateway brand are timely but still score a low 4.92 – the chain cannot shake off its image as a company peddling fast but getting nowhere.

Retail marketing is in its infancy, but the table shows that those who have been operating long enough are beating the food manufacturers at their own game.

**Helen Slingsby**

## Development of successful new products or services

| Top 5 | | |
|---|---|---|
| 1 | Mars | **7.60** |
| 2 | Marks & Spencer | **7.51** |
| 3 | Procter & Gamble | **7.31** |
| 4 | Lever Brothers | **7.03** |
| 5 | Sainsbury | **7.01** |

| Bottom 5 | | |
|---|---|---|
| 73 | Renault | **4.95** |
| 74 | Leeds | **4.71** |
| 75 | Fiat | **4.35** |
| 76 | Co-op | **4.19** |
| 77 | British Rail | **3.99** |

# Classy brands help speed Rover's return

Few sectors have been hit by the recession as badly as the car industry, where sales dropped by 14 per cent last year. After four years of growth, purchases began to decline towards the end of 1989, shortly after the last *Marketing Week* top marketing companies survey. The present poll is thus a gauge of motor companies' response to the depressed market.

Marketing honours since October 1989 have been shared between those companies which have responded strongly to the challenge of a squeezed market, such as the Rover Group and VAG, and those which have rested on their marketing laurels such as BMW.

Rover's turnaround has been the most dramatic. In the motor sector, it has risen from twelfth to seventh – the best showing in its sector. Kleinwort Benson motor industry analyst Gavin Launder says: "Rover was lost in the mid-Eighties, but has pulled itself round with the new products, the 200 and 400, and their classier, sportier image. The company is aiming to price its models at the top of every sector in which it is a player."

Improvement has been made by focusing on fewer, stronger brands. Rover chief executive George Simpson says: "Competition is at its most intense for many years. We have created a series of business units with full accountability for themselves, aiming at service, quality and speed of action on product development."

VAG, which markets the Volkswagen and Audi ranges, has also clawed further up the motor manufacturers tables from sixth to fourth. VAG marketing manager John Meszaros identifies deferred purchases by private buyers as the key element in last year's slump.

"VW does well in a tight market when people move away from frivolous ad-ons and closer to the core issues of well-built, long-lasting cars with good residual value," he says.

Meszaros says: "We recognise that the priorities of purchase motivation are changing with ecology and safety becoming more important and many people less excited by 0–60 figures. VW is launching the new Polo, which will be the first small car that you cannot buy without a catalytic converter. You cannot get a dirty Polo."

Since the last survey, VAG has moved ahead of Fiat as Europe's largest car manufacturer, aided by its gaining control of Skoda in December and the opening up of the East German market.

Whereas VAG's marketing has polished its brand associations with German engineering and reliability, Fiat Auto (UK) has failed to earn continental respect for the name.

Fiat remains firmly at the bottom of the car marketing table, coming in the worst five in all but one category.

Launder says: "The Uno and Tipo still suffer in the popular memory from image of rust and breaking down and are on none of the fleet-buying lists which are essential for market share in this country. Fiat has 14 per cent of the European market and two per cent in the UK."

The major French manufacturers, Renault and Citroën, share a low marketing score on new product launches and existing product development. Both are rated in the bottom five companies from the overall list for these two categories.

German quality marques BMW and Mercedes retain their hold on the top two places in the sector. Examining interviewees' responses to each category, it is clear that both thrive on solid German corporate values – quality of products and services, good design and ability to attract talented people.

BMW continues to trade on its successful "driving machine" advertising from the mid-eighties, with increasing emphasis on successful, young people buying their first non-company car. However, the sportier side of this market is under increasing pressure from Japanese firms Honda and Toyota.

Mercedes launched its first new model for 11 years at this year's Geneva motor show, the £80,000 S-Class. The arrival is timely since the brand has slipped from the overall top ten as companies retrench during the recession.

Mercedes passenger car director Walter Greaves says: "To be seen driving a big car at a time when jobs are being cut and wages slipping does not look right even though it may be a sound economic decision.

"By moving on to TV for the first time last year, we have attempted to modernise our advertising approach. Until confidence returns, this will affect the quality sector throughout, although we hope the S-Class will produce a halo effect that filters across the other brands."

For both luxury and budget cars, however, the next five years will witness high-profile advertising challenges from the Japanese. Nissan, the sixth biggest manufacturer in the UK, has long since mastered volume selling, despite the current imbroglio between maker and UK distributor. Toyota's Lexus has shown that luxury is equally within their reach, and is likely to signal a concentrated marketing effort.

**Chris Boulding**

# Mars makes a cool killing with its ices

Mars' accession to the top slot in this year's survey can be summed up in one word – ice-cream. The company's success in creating a new market sector and with it a £60m brand – Mars Bar ice-cream – has rightly impressed the industry and led to a spate of me-too launches.

In toppling Kellogg, the secretive US-owned company reinforces its image as the marketers' marketing company – it often seems as if every senior food marketer in the UK is a graduate of the Mars academy.

Mars also, not surprisingly, tops the table for development of successful new products, and is joint first on successful development of existing products. Further inroads have been made into the ice-cream market with Mars' Snickers, Bounty and Galaxy variants. But within the food industry, Mars is the only company to achieve a better rating this year than last, when food companies dominated the top ten. Observers speculate that in a depressed economic climate, food trades more on its necessity value using less sophisticated, lower-profile marketing.

While this might be a factor, there are more specific reasons for individual companies' declining performance.

Kellogg's fall from the top slot to number eight this year can be attributed to the rather muted success (by Kellogg standards) of its Common Sense products, despite heavy advertising support. The brand generated considerable controversy when it was launched for what were seen as exaggerated health claims, and has never really performed to expectations. Kellogg's market share has slipped in recent years and the company is facing stiff competition from the Nestlé/General Mills joint venture Cereal Partners.

Heinz has lost its top ten ranking with a four-place drop to number 14 after a quiet year which saw little in the way of new products and a lower than usual advertising profile.

Cadbury, which has slipped six places to number nine, and UB, down nine at 23, are widely believed to have been slow off the mark in gearing up for 1992, though UB has made up some ground with a series of acquisitions. Other factors which probably contributed to UB's reduced performance include a number of senior personnel changes, the perceived failure of last year's McVities umbrella ad campaign and the closure of some of the Ross Young's frozen food operation.

Birds Eye/Wall's, new to the sample this year, makes a creditable entry at number 28. Wall's has held onto its market share despite the formidable challenge of Mars, and the Unilever-owned company has benefited from the creation of two separate marketing functions.

If food manufacturers appear to have slipped overall in this year's survey, they still make a good showing in several categories.

Three companies, Mars, Kellogg and Cadbury, appear in the top five for creative and effective use of advertising. All three have continued to spend heavily despite the recession.

There is solace for food companies too in the fact that none appears in the bottom five in any category.

It is likely that an upturn in the general economy would quickly restore many of these companies to their previous rankings in the survey, as marketing directors throw off the caution of the past twelve months or so and put the creativity back into food marketing.

**Lindsay McMurdo**

Reprinted with permission from *Marketing Week*, 22 March 1991, pp. 26–33.

## Food sector

| | | |
|---|---|---|
| 1 | Mars | 7.46 |
| 2 | Kellogg | 6.97 |
| 3 | Cadbury | 6.96 |
| 4 | Heinz | 6.76 |
| 5 | Nestlé | 6.23 |
| 6 | United Biscuits | 6.22 |
| 7 | Birds Eye | 6.06 |
| 8= | General Foods | 5.75 |
| 8= | Brooke Bond Foods | 5.75 |
| 10 | Beecham Foods | 5.55 |

## Profitable pricing of products or services

| | | |
|---|---|---|
| **Top 5** | | |
| 1 | Marks & Spencer | 7.64 |
| 2 | Mars | 7.63 |
| 3 | Cadbury | 7.43 |
| 4 | Procter & Gamble | 7.38 |
| 5 | BMW | 7.37 |
| **Bottom 5** | | |
| 73 | Fiat | 5.25 |
| 74 | Gallaher | 5.09 |
| 75 | Imperial | 4.98 |
| 76 | Midland | 4.86 |
| 77 | British Rail | 4.54 |

## Overall financial performance in own sector

**Top 5**

| | | |
|---|---|---|
| 1 | Marks & Spencer | 8.21 |
| 2 | Sainsbury | 7.89 |
| 3 | Procter & Gamble | 7.82 |
| 4 | Lever Brothers | 7.64 |
| 5 | Mars | 7.62 |

**Bottom 5**

| | | |
|---|---|---|
| 73 | Renault | 4.88 |
| 74 | Co-op | 4.58 |
| 75 | Fiat | 4.48 |
| 76 | British Rail | 4.24 |
| 77 | Midland Bank | 3.72 |

## The creative and effective use of advertising

**Top 5**

| | | |
|---|---|---|
| 1 | Guinness | 7.38 |
| 2 | Mars | 7.32 |
| 3 | Kellogg | 7.29 |
| 4 | Scott | 7.27 |
| 5 | Cadbury | 7.87 |

**Bottom 5**

| | | |
|---|---|---|
| 73 | Gateway | 4.69 |
| 74 | Nissan | 4.55 |
| 75 | Mazda | 4.47 |
| 76 | Fiat | 4.39 |
| 77 | Co-op | 3.88 |

## Financial sector

| | | |
|---|---|---|
| 1 | Alliance & Leicester | 5.91 |
| 2 | Abbey National | 5.82 |
| 3 | Halifax | 5.71 |
| 4 | Barclays | 5.68 |
| 5 | NatWest | 5.50 |
| 6 | Lloyds | 5.42 |
| 7 | Woolwich | 5.39 |
| 8 | Nationwide Anglia | 5.31 |
| 9 | Commercial Union | 5.25 |
| 10 | Midland | 5.05 |
| 11 | Sun Alliance | 5.03 |
| 12 | Leeds Permanent | 4.78 |

## Motor manufacturers sector

| | | |
|---|---|---|
| 1 | BMW | **7.03** |
| 2 | Mercedes-Benz | **6.81** |
| 3 | Vauxhall | **6.72** |
| 4 | VAG | **6.56** |
| 5 | Ford | **6.35** |
| 6 | Peugeot Talbot | **6.22** |
| 7 | Rover | **6.15** |
| 8 | Toyota | **6.07** |
| 9 | Nissan | **5.48** |
| 10 | Citroën | **5.01** |
| 11 | Renault | **4.90** |
| 12 | Mazda | **4.78** |
| 13 | Fiat | **4.71** |

## Successful development of existing products or services

| **Top 5** | | |
|---|---|---|
| 1= | Marks & Spencer | **7.37** |
| 1= | Mars | **7.37** |
| 3 | Procter & Gamble | **7.31** |
| 4 | Lever Brothers | **7.01** |
| 5 | Cadbury | **7.00** |

| **Bottom 5** | | |
|---|---|---|
| 73 | Post Office | **4.91** |
| 74 | Citroën | **4.86** |
| 75 | Renault | **4.72** |
| 76 | Fiat | **4.29** |
| 77 | British Rail | **4.27** |

## Ability to attract, develop and keep talented people

| **Top 5** | | |
|---|---|---|
| 1 | Marks & Spencer | **7.99** |
| 2 | Mars | **7.70** |
| 3 | BMW | **7.41** |
| 4 | Sainsbury | **7.31** |
| 5 | Heinz | **7.28** |

| **Bottom 5** | | |
|---|---|---|
| 73 | Leeds Permanent | **4.76** |
| 74 | Fiat | **4.37** |
| 75 | Midland Bank | **4.36** |
| 76 | Co-op | **4.18** |
| 77 | British Rail | **4.01** |

# 15 | Criteria of choice

## 15.1 LEARNING OBJECTIVES

When you have read this chapter you should be able to:

(a) understand the role of criteria of choice in the decision-making process;
(b) distinguish between financial and non-financial criteria;
(c) recognize the limitations of using single criteria for making strategic choices;
(d) appreciate the relevance of multiple criteria approaches to strategic choice.

## 15.2 INTRODUCTION

In choosing between alternative courses of action or strategies it is, of course, desirable to choose the best; but how is the 'best' to be recognized? The best from the viewpoint of one stakeholder may not be the best from another stakeholder's viewpoint. Similarly, what is best in the short term may not be best in the long term. Specifying the criteria by which choices are to be made among competing alternatives is a crucial step in working towards improved marketing performance.

It has traditionally been the case that financial criteria have dominated choice processes irrespective of the initial emphasis that may have been given to non-financial criteria. Recent changes in strategic thinking (as reported, for example, by Munro and Cooper (1989)) have suggested that the dominance of financial measure may no longer be appropriate. For instance, the emphasis placed by McDonald's on quality, service, cleanliness and value shows that a financial criterion is insufficient, although there will invariably be one or more financial measures within any enterprise's set of *critical success factors* (see pp. 428–33 below).

A selection of the most important financial and non-financial criteria is given in Figure 15.1, many of which will be discussed in this chapter.

**FIGURE 15.1**
*Financial and non-financial criteria*

| Financial | Non-financial |
|---|---|
| Liquidity | Sales volume |
| Cash generation | Market share |
| Value-added | Growth rate |
| Earnings per share | Competitive position |
| Shareholders' value | Consumer franchise |
| Share price | Risk exposure |
| Profit | Reliance on new products |
| Profitability | Customer satisfaction |
| Cost leadership | Sustainable competitive advantage |

Within the marketing literature there is surprisingly little coverage of effectiveness (i.e. doing the right things) as opposed to efficiency (i.e. doing things right). However, it is implicit in the extensive coverage of efficiency that the results of marketing activities are effective: it is not suggested that effectiveness should be traded off for greater efficiency. Nevertheless, the preoccupation that has existed with inputs rather than outputs tends to mean that outputs such as increased sales revenue, greater market share, or higher profits are taken as being self-evident measures of effectiveness.

The various inputs and outputs cited in the literature on marketing efficiency include those shown in Figure 15.2.

**FIGURE 15.2**
*Marketing efficiency criteria*

| Inputs | | Outputs |
|---|---|---|
| Marketing expense | | Profit |
| Investment | | Sales value |
| Number and quality of employees | **Marketing activities** | Sales volume |
| Quality of decisions | | Market share |
| Technology | | Cash flow |
| Administrative support | | Value added |
| | | Consumer franchise |

If we consider market share to be an appropriate output measure we can relate this back to the discussions of the BCG growth-share matrix and the PIMS model (see Chapter 9, pp. 227–31 and Chapter 10, pp. 252–7 below).

The growth-share matrix was developed for use in portfolio planning (i.e. to generate a balanced portfolio of business activities with reference to cash generation and cash use). Relative market share serves as a proxy for cash generation, with market growth acting as a proxy for cash use.

Market share as an output measure also features prominently in the PIMS model (see Abell and Hammond (1979), Buzzell and Gale (1987), Day (1990)). ROI is the dependent variable in the PIMS model (see pp. 252–7 above) with market share playing a key role in the following sequence:

1 superior relative quality is established by a business for its products;
2 this superiority facilitates the building of market share;
3 greater share brings with it cost advantages due to higher volume and experience curve effects;
4 superior quality allows premium prices to be charged which, in association with lower costs, ensures higher profits.

Whatever measures of input and output are used in an attempt to assess efficiency – and Figure 15.2 offers only a limited number of each – the overriding emphasis is typically on readily quantifiable factors. This gives a means of both asking and answering the question as to whether the enterprise is getting as much output per unit of input as it should, or whether the efficiency of marketing activities might be improved. As we have seen, however, this concern with 'doing things right' begs the question of whether the right things are being done, which requires a fuller consideration of marketing effectiveness. This is provided in Chapter 16 when we deal with such approaches as the marketing audit (which was also covered in Chapter 2) and Bonoma's approach to assessing marketing programmes.

We will proceed through this chapter by examining a range of individual criteria from both the financial and non-financial categories, and then look at more broadly-based, multiple-criteria approaches to evaluating alternatives.

## 15.3 FINANCIAL CRITERIA

**Cash Generation**

Poor liquidity is a greater threat to the survival prospects of an enterprise than poor profitability, hence it is vitally important in choosing a marketing strategy to consider carefully the cashflow implications of available alternatives. This can be vividly illustrated via the BCG growth-share matrix (as discussed in Chapter 9) which classifies products into four categories (see Figure 9.2 on p. 227):

- stars;
- question marks (or wildcats);
- dogs;
- cash cows.

Use of the product portfolio as a frame of reference should ensure that all products, business units, or profit centres are not treated alike and that investment decisions are not seen as being independent of continuing business activities. Nevertheless, a strategic success sequence is likely to emerge through following these steps:

1 The cash generated by cash cows (high market share, low market growth) should be invested in building the market share of question marks. If this is done well sustainable advantage will be provided by which question marks will become stars and then cash cows, and will thereby become capable of financing subsequent strategies.
2 To be avoided is the sequence by which question marks are not supported so that they become dogs when the market matures: low relative share in a low growth market is not the place to find oneself.
3 Also to be avoided is the sequence by which stars lose position and become question marks as market growth slows, with the risk of their becoming dogs.

It should be mentioned that, in focusing on the balancing of operating cashflows, the BCG matrix ignores the existence of capital markets which also have a role to play in balancing cashflows. Moreover, the BCG matrix fails to allow for differential risk.

**Cost Leadership**

A particular strategy may be more desirable than others if it is likely to secure cost leadership (which is one of Porter's key generic strategies). This notion can be illustrated through the *experience curve* which was introduced in Chapter 12.

The essence of the experience curve is that the real costs of generating products and services decline by 20–30 per cent whenever cumulative experience doubles.

Several causes of cost reduction act together within the experience curve, such as:

- the learning experience;
- the effect of labour specialization;
- scale effects due to increased volume.

The experience curve is derived not from accounting costs but by dividing the cumulative cash inputs by the cumulative output of end products, and the cost decline is shown by the rate of change in this ratio over time. From this rate of change managers can see how – and why – their competitive costs are shifting. If estimates can be made of competitors' experience curve effects this should reveal which are the low-cost competitors and which are not, hence which are at risk and from whom.

The main strategic message from the experience curve is that if costs per unit in real terms decrease predictably with cumulative output, then the market leader has the potential to achieve the lowest costs and the highest profits. This is illustrated in Figure 12.7 (see p. 340).

Given the empirical existence of the experience curve it is apparent that the use of cash will be less than directly proportional to a product's rate of growth. Similarly, the generation of cash will be a function of the product's market share, which links back to the BCG product portfolio matrix.

**Profitability Analysis**

Profitability can be defined as the rate at which profit is generated. This may be expressed as profit (i.e. an output measure) per unit of input (e.g. investment, or some measure of effort such as sales calls). Apart from limiting our focus to one output measure (profit) to represent effectiveness, this approach also overlooks such issues as the quality of services rendered, hence its partiality needs to be kept in mind.

As a criterion for strategic decision making, profitability has been criticized by Robinson, et al. (1978), as being insufficient in:

- failing to provide a systematic explanation as to why one business sector has more favourable prospects than another and why one enterprise's position in a particular sector is strong or weak;
- not providing enough insight into the underlying dynamics and balance of an enterprise's individual business units and the balance among them.

Other writers (including Chakravarthy (1986) and Day (1990)) have also criticized profitability as a performance criterion due to its remoteness from the actions that actually create value: it represents an outcome rather than a determinant of performance and cannot be managed directly, hence employees are likely to attach limited importance to it on the grounds that their day-to-day actions would appear to have little impact on profitability.

Feder (1965) has defined good marketing performance as existing when investment in each market segment is made to the point where the expenditure of an additional $1 or £1 would produce greater immediate profits if spent elsewhere. This approach reflects the *marginal responsiveness* that is characteristic of marketing experimentation (i.e. where can the greatest response in terms of improved profit be achieved for a marginal increase in effort?). To take an example, if investment of £1 million in advertising within a given market produces sales of £20 million and a gross margin of £10 million, then the *average* response of profit to advertising is 10:1. If an increase in advertising expenditure of £100,000 produced additional sales of £3 million and a gross margin of £1.5 million, then the *marginal* response would be 15:1.

In assessing marketing performance using this approach it would be logical to determine the average response for the existing allocation of marketing effort, segment by segment, which would highlight those areas in which the company has underspent or overspent relative to their profit potential. Improvements can be made by allocating additional effort in accordance with the anticipated marginal response: the greater the anticipated marginal response the more efficient will be the allocation of effort. In considering whether additional effort might be exerted through direct selling, advertising, or improved terms for intermediaries within distribution channels, for example, the need exists to consider the timing factor since different actions bring results over different time scales.

A less dynamic approach emphasizing profit (rather than profitability) has been suggested by a number of writers. Goodman (1970) and Pyne (1984) both offer modified versions of financial operating statements as bases for assessing marketing performance. These are illustrated in Figures 15.3 and 15.4.

In Figure 15.3 Goodman distinguishes carefully between direct and apportioned costs which is a more relevant distinction than, say, that between fixed and variable costs if one is concerned to identify the performance of a marketing segment: relevance is given priority over the question of cost behaviour. In principle it makes sense to separate the profit attributable to manufacturing, distribution, and so forth, on a direct cost basis. The operational difficulty in doing this stems from the problems associated with identifying the direct costs of Product 123 within a product range of 10 000 items.

Apart from the quantity of products as a measure of performance we might also consider the quality of profits. This depends upon the position of a particular

**FIGURE 15.3**
*Marketing-oriented income statement*

|  | £ | £ |
|---|---|---|
| Proceeds from sales |  | 100.0 |
| Variable cost of goods sold: |  |  |
|   Raw materials | 10.0 |  |
|   Packing | 10.0 |  |
|   Direct labour | 5.0 |  |
| *Variable gross profits* (manufacturing contribution margin) |  | 75.0 |
| Other variable expenses: |  |  |
|   Freight | 3.0 |  |
|   Warehousing | 2.0 |  |
|   Spoilage | 1.0 |  |
|   Commissions | 5.0 |  |
|   Discounts | 3.0 |  |
| *Variable profit* (distribution contribution margin) |  | 61.0 |
| Direct product costs: |  |  |
|   Advertising | 9.0 |  |
|   Promotion | 3.0 |  |
| *Direct product profits* |  | 49.0 |
| Direct division costs: |  |  |
|   Sales management | 12.0 |  |
|   Product management | 3.0 |  |
|   Sales force | 2.8 |  |
|   Sales incentives | 1.0 |  |
|   Market research | 0.2 |  |
| *Division profit contribution* (net contribution margin) |  | 30.0 |
| Allocated fixed expense: |  |  |
|   Factory indirect costs | 21.0 |  |
|   Supervision | 4.0 |  |
|   Other indirect costs | 19.0 |  |
|   Corporate administration | 5.0 |  |
| *Net division profit before taxes* |  | (19.0) |

SOURCE: Adapted from Goodman (1970), p. 38

product within its life cycle. It is evident that the profits from products in the growth phase of the cycle are likely to be more valuable than those in the decline phase since the former have a more promising future.

Pyne's approach is similar in some respects to that of Goodman. For instance, both authors emphasize the need for conventional operating statements (i.e. those having a legalistic format) to be modified to reflect marketing's circumstances and, in so doing, to highlight direct costs.

In Figure 15.4 we can see that Pyne's approach differs in some significant ways from that of Goodman:

- revenue is analysed more fully;
- marketing costs are analysed more fully with headings that help in distinguishing operating from policy-related costs;
- the orientation is more radical than that of Goodman in giving a basis for assessing marketing performance in strategic terms.

The amount of profit an enterprise earns is a measure of its effectiveness if that enterprise has a profit objective. (In this sense we can define effectiveness in terms of achieving that which one sought to achieve.) Since profit = revenue (output) − cost (input), it can be seen to be a measure of efficiency also in that it relates outputs to inputs. Thus an organization having revenues of £100 million and costs of £60 million is more efficient than one in the same industry having revenues of £100 million and costs of £70 million since the former uses less input to produce a given output.

Despite its ability to act as a measure both of effectiveness and efficiency, profit is a less than perfect measure because:

**FIGURE 15.4**

*Marketing-oriented profit statement*

| | |
|---|---|
| *Full revenue sales* (at full sale price to end user) | £ |
| *Lost revenue*<br>Distributors' mark-ups and margins<br>Mark-downs, offers, deals and allowances<br>Third-party costs of delivery to end user paid by the purchaser | _____ |
| *Sales proceeds*<br>Sales taxes and customs duties | £<br>_____ |
| *Net sales proceeds* | £ |
| *Direct marketing expense*<br>Direct selling – field sales expenses<br>Sales promotion – merchandising and display<br>              – samples, point of sales aids<br>              – cooperative allowances to distributors<br>Product packaging and branding expense<br>Product service – installation, warranty and returns<br>Warehousing – storage, receiving and marking, shipping<br>Transportation outward – truck, rail, air; cost, insurance,<br>                        freight and delivery | _____ |
| *Direct marketing contribution* | £ |
| *Managed marketing expense*<br>Order processing<br>Sales and distribution management<br>Brand and product management<br>Marketing direction and administration | _____ |
| *Marketing policy costs*<br>Advertising and publicity<br>Market research and customer relations<br>Product planning, design and development<br>Marketing team training and development | £<br>_____ |
| *Committed marketing costs*<br>Inventory carrying – expense and financing<br>Cost of credit – collection and financing<br>Marketing equipment – maintenance, insurance, financing | £<br>_____ |
| *Net marketing contribution* | £<br>_____ |

*Note*: where appropriate, lost revenue may be broken down by the marketing channels in use, e.g. wholesalers, stockists, retail chains, stores, direct vending outlets, etc.

SOURCE: Pyne (1984), p. 90

1 it is a monetary measure, and monetary measures do not measure all aspects of either input or output;
2 the standards against which profits are judged may themselves be less than perfect;
3 at best, profits are a measure of what has happened in the short run, whereas we must also be interested in the long-run consequences of management actions.

Nevertheless, profit measures can still play a distinctly valuable role in the control effort. For example:

1 A profit measure can provide a simple criterion for evaluating alternatives. (Although it will be necessary to take into account many factors other than profit in making a choice among alternative courses of action, on the face of it option A is more attractive than option B if A will produce more profit than B.)
2 A profit measure will permit a quantitative analysis of alternatives to be made in which benefits can be directly compared with costs. (Assuming a market exists for an enterprise's output, these benefits will be measured by the revenue flow from its sale.)

3 A profit measure can provide a single, broad measure of performance in that it is arrived at after all financial costs and revenues have been taken into account, and it thus subsumes many other aspects of performance.

4 Profit measures permit the comparison of performance to be made over time for one organization, or comparisons at a point in time to be made for a group of organizational units (e.g. divisions or competing enterprises within an industry), even if they are performing dissimilar functions. This is not possible with other measures, although it may be necessary to standardize accounting practices in measuring profits for this purpose and to ensure that the valuations of assets are made on the same bases.

This all sounds very promising, but we need to bear in mind the limitations of the profit measure. Among these are:

1 Organizations have multiple objectives and will often forgo profit opportunities in order to avoid conflict over some other objective (or constraint) such as the desired image for the company or some ethical standard.

2 Social costs and benefits are excluded from corporate profit figures. At best profit is a measure of an enterprise's success as an economic entity, but this does not measure that enterprise's net contribution (or cost) to society such as the training programmes it might offer, or the pollution it might cause.

3 As already mentioned, profit measures typically focus on current rather than long-run performance: actions can be taken to improve the former at the expense of the latter (e.g. by cutting advertising, R & D, training and maintenance budgets).

4 Profit is an inadequate basis for comparing organizations' relative performance or for monitoring one organization's performance over time. The real test is actual versus target profit, but we are really unable to specify this latter figure in any sensible way because it should be based on *profit potential* and a company's profit opportunities are not all identified. It follows that an apparently high profit figure, even when this corresponds with the target figure, may in reality be poor when related to missed opportunities.

5 Accounting rules are also inadequate since they often do not permit the recording of economic reality. (Costs should reflect the use of resources, but accounting practice does not allow this to be measured when it values assets on the basis of historical cost rather than their opportunity cost, i.e. current value in an alternative use, which has an impact on the depreciation charge, etc.)

6 Profit measures are not applicable in certain segments of a business, notably those that incur costs but do not generate revenue (unless a transfer pricing system is introduced to impute revenue flows). Examples of these types of segment are R & D, the legal department, the personnel department and the accounting department.

**Creating Shareholder Value**

Perhaps the majority of evaluative criteria advocated in the literature and used in practice focus on the maximization of profit, profitability, or sales rather than on the return to shareholders (see, for example, McGuire et al. (1986); Chakravarthy (1986)). The key idea behind *creating shareholder value* (e.g. Rappaport (1986); Wenner and LeBer (1989); Reimann (1989)) is that investors only willingly invest in an enterprise when they think that the managers of that enterprise will be able to secure a better return on their funds than they could on their own without additional risk. In contrast to ROI and other short-term measures the creation of shareholder value emphasizes the market's assessment of the long-term health and wealth of the enterprise. Evidence exists to indicate that movements in an enterprise's share price are due (at least in part) to the impact of management's decisions on the long-term value of the enterprise. This is covered by the *efficient markets hypothesis* which suggests that financial markets are adept at capturing information and reflecting the significance of that information in changes in share prices. It follows that decision makers in enterprises having listed shares (which only applies to some 2200 of more than one million companies incorporated in the UK) should pay due attention to the impacts of their decisions on share prices.

Day and Fahey (1988) have sought to demonstrate how a value-based approach can be applied to the evaluation of marketing strategies. The starting point is the recognition that value is only created when the financial benefits of a strategic activity exceed its costs. Since strategic activities are carried out over time – often involving several years – it is necessary to apply discounting methods to the relevant cash inflows and outflows. This is equivalent to the long-established practice of applying discounting techniques to new investments in plant and equipment: the extension of the practice to marketing strategies involves dealing with more intangible elements and embracing a series of issues rather than simply the investment in a single item of plant. We will return to this approach in Chapter 16.

## 15.4 NON-FINANCIAL CRITERIA

**Growth**

The importance of growth as a criterion of choice stems from the following:

1 Its relationship to gaining market share. Consider, for example, the sad case of the motorcycle industry in Britain. During the 1960s the level of output of British motorcycles was fairly constant (at 80 000 units per annum) whereas the exports from Japan increased from 60 000 in 1960 to 2.5 million in 1973, with their production volumes tripling over this period. The British manufacturers failed to recognize the strategic importance of market share *on a worldwide basis* for long-term profitability related to the experience curve effect. While UK production during the 1960s ensured that manufacturing facilities were being adequately employed the significant strategic issue was that Japanese manufacturers' costs were falling whereas those of British manufacturers were not, hence the collapse of the UK motorcycle industry in the early 1970s.
2 The opportunities it provides for investment: as funds are generated they can be reinvested to produce a compound return.

Growth has a significant relevance to an enterprise's relative competitive position. This is most readily measured by relative market share which is defined as the enterprise's market share divided by that of its largest competitor. Since the stronger the relative competitive position the higher the margins should be (due to the effect of the experience curve) this measure has a strategic importance.

The need for growth is shown in Figure 15.5 in which a gap can be discerned between the enterprise's present position and its preferred future position. (Figure 15.5 is a variation on Figure 6.5.) By continuing with current activities on the same scale the level of profits will decline (e.g. due to increasing competition, product obsolescence, etc.). By expanding in either existing markets (i.e. larger market share) or by entering new markets with existing products, or by improving existing products, it may be possible to maintain the level of profits into the future. (Note: these alternatives employ known technology and, in two out of three cases, known markets.)

By expanding the scale of activity within existing markets, improving existing products *and* diversifying into new markets with new products, a much higher level of profit may result, thereby meeting the desired profit target. The choice of strategy, therefore, will be that by which the gaps in Figure 15.5 might be closed.

Growth will usually involve a move outside the enterprise's existing range of activities. Alternative paths for expansion are shown in Figure 6.4 (see p. 156).

**FIGURE 15.5**
*Gap analysis*

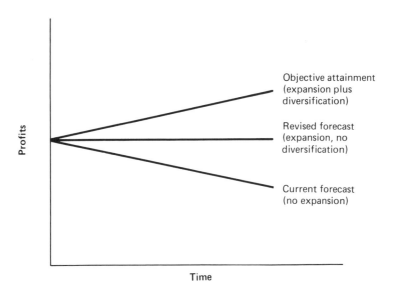

The graph shows Profits (vertical axis) against Time (horizontal axis) with three diverging lines labelled:
- Objective attainment (expansion plus diversification)
- Revised forecast (expansion, no diversification)
- Current forecast (no expansion)

- *Market penetration* entails an increasing share of existing markets with existing products – this would involve more aggressive promotion and distribution;
- *market extension* results from taking existing products into new markets;
- *product development* requires that new products be created to replace existing products in present markets;
- *diversification* involves the development (or acquisition) of new products for new markets.

The risk levels associated with these strategies tend to increase in the sequence in which they are listed above, so a change in product technology is likely to be riskier than a change in target markets, and a change in markets and products will be riskier than a change in only one of these (see Figure 6.7, p. 160).

**Sustainable Competitive Advantage**
(see also Chapter 10, pp. 246–9)

Wensley (1981), Day and Wensley (1988) and Cravens (1988) argue that the most meaningful guidance for strategic decision makers is to be found in returning to basics and focusing on the search for *sustainable competitive advantage*. This focus implies that strategic alternatives should be evaluated in terms of the organization's strengths and weaknesses. Sustainable competitive advantage will be found when opportunities are taken to build on an enterprise's unique capabilities. These capabilities reflect the adequacy of the match between the current core activities of an enterprise and the strategic alternatives under consideration. Thus, for example, if we consider Ansoff's growth matrix (see Figure 6.4) an enterprise's greatest competitive advantage is likely to be found in product-market situations that are similar to those of its core activities (i.e. in Cell 1).

A clear example is that of Gillette. Razors for men were followed by shaving cream for men and razors for women. Razors – whether for men or women – can be manufactured using the same facilities and the marketing has similarities whether it is razors or shaving cream one is considering. A common brand name helps develop a consumer franchise. The distribution system in use for razors can also be used for shaving cream – the products are bought in the same outlets.

At first sight it may appear odd that Gillette ventured into disposable lighters since they do not fit synergistically with the marketing of razors, etc. However, Gillette's special capabilities include:

- mass production of low cost products;
- utilization of precision plastic moulded parts;
- use of mass distribution;
- marketing of low cost, disposable consumer products under the Gillette brand name.

The manufacturing and marketing capabilities ensured Gillette secured competitive advantage in disposable lighters even if the brand name itself was not particularly useful.

## Competitive Position

In considering financial criteria it is usually found that a rather introspective approach is adopted (i.e. *this* enterprise's profit, or *this* enterprise's cashflow). There is a need to adopt a more strategic perspective in dealing with an enterprise's competitive position.

The strategic dimension emerges when the performance of the business in question is compared with that of its competitors. Viewing the business within its competitive context is possible within the framework suggested by Figure 15.6.

**FIGURE 15.6**
*Strategic comparisons*

| | Economic performance of competitive units | | | | |
|---|---|---|---|---|---|
| | Market leader | Dominant challenger | Own business unit | Closest competitor | |
| | | | | A | B |
| **Revenues** **Resource costs** | | | | | |

SOURCE: Adapted from Pyne (1984), p. 90

The details from Figure 15.4 would be entered in the rows of Figure 15.6 under the given headings.

A variation on this theme, focusing on the notion of competitive position, has been developed by Simmonds (1986). This is covered in some detail in the following discussion.

The key notion here is that of an enterprise's position *relative to* competitors' positions. In so far as strategy is concerned with competitive position it has been largely ignored by management accountants, but in a number of papers Simmonds (1981, 1982, 1985, 1986) has proposed how this failing might be overcome.

A basic plank in his argument is the preoccupation that accountants have with the recording, analysing and presentation of cost data relating to existing activities. This 'data orientation' begs some fundamental questions, such as why the data is being collected in the first place. An alternative and preferable approach is one of 'information orientation' which starts with the diagnosis of problems, leading to the structuring of decisions, and thence to the specification of information that will help in making appropriate decisions. The focus shifts from the analysis of costs *per se* to the value of information.

The manager wishing to make decisions that will safeguard his organization's strategic position must know by whom, by how much, and why he is gaining or being beaten. In other words, strategic indicators of performance are required. Conventional measures, such as profit, will not suffice.

Let us take comparative costs as a starting point. It is intuitively the case that organizations having a cost advantage (i.e. lower unit cost for a product of comparable specification) are strong and those having a cost disadvantage are weak. If we relate this to the idea of the experience curve (which was introduced on p. 339 above) it will be appreciated that, if costs can be made to decline predictably with cumulative output, then the enterprise that has produced most should have the lowest unit cost and therefore the highest profits.

Apart from cost, an enterprise may seek to gain strategic advantage via its pricing policy. In this setting the management accountant can attempt to assess each major competitor's cost structure and relate this to their prices, taking care to eliminate the effects of inflation from the figures being used. Applying cost–volume–profit analysis to one's competitors is likely to be more fruitful than simply applying it internally. As Simmonds (1982, p. 207) states:

> Clearly, competitor reactions can substantially influence the outcome of a price move. Moreover, likely reactions may not be self-evident when each competitor faces a different cost-volume-profit situation. Competitors may not follow a price lead nor even march in perfect step as they each act to defend or build their own positions. For an adequate assessment of the likelihood of competitor price reactions, then, some calculation is needed of the impact of possible price moves on the performance of individual competitors. Such an assessment in turn requires an accounting approach that can depict both competitor cost-volume-profit situations and their financial resources.

After dealing with costs and prices the next important (and related) variable to consider is volume – especially market share. By monitoring movements in market share an enterprise can see whether it is gaining or losing position, and an examination of relative market shares will indicate the strength of different competitors.

Reporting market share details along with financial details can help in making managerial accounting reports more strategically relevant.

The significance of competitive position has been highlighted by Simmonds (1986) as being the basic determinant of future profits and of the business' value. Moreover, since competitive position can change over time, so can profits and value, but it should not be assumed that an improvement in competitive position will be associated with an improvement in short-run profits. In fact, the opposite is likely to be the case due to the need to incur costs in building up a competitive position which has the effect of depressing current profits in favour of future profits. This raises the question as to whether competitive position can be measured in accounting terms – not just for a given business, but also for its main competitors; and not just at a point in time, but also over time. Simmonds has attempted to do this by applying strategic management accounting. He makes it clear, however, that it is not possible to express competitive position as a single figure. Instead it is possible to offer an array of indicators relating to the competitive situation. From these indicators managers can gain insights into the competitive position of a business which will help them in judging whether or not things are moving in their favour.

Simmonds recommends that competitive data be built up for the market leader, close competitors, and laggards rather than for all competitors. The following data* might most usefully be developed:

## 1  Sales and Market Share
Sales revenue of each firm relative to the total market is a cornerstone, and changes in market share should be closely monitored. A decrease in market share suggests a loss of competitive position, with unfortunate implications for future profits. Conversely, an increase in market share suggests an improved competitive position with the prospect of improved future profits. By adding market share details to management accounting reports managers are able to make much more sense of what is happening.

*The example that follows is derived from that given in Simmonds (1986) and is used with permission.

Figure 15.7 gives sales and market share data for Firm A and the total market for Product X.

**FIGURE 15.7**
*Sales and market share data, Product X*

| | Firm A | Total market |
|---|---|---|
| Sales (£'000) | | |
| Last year | 1,000 | 5,200 |
| This year | 1,200 | 7,500 |
| % change | +20 | +44 |
| Market share (%) | | |
| Last year | 19 | 100 |
| This year | 16 | 100 |

We can see from Figure 15.7 that, despite an increase in sales revenue of 20 per cent for Firm A, the market share has slipped from 19 per cent to 16 per cent. This is explained by the growth in the total market of 44 per cent. It seems probable that the firm's failure to keep pace with the overall market growth will be reflected in a poorer competitive position: not only might competitors have gained market share at the firm's expense, but this is likely to be accompanied by cost advantages – hence improved profits. Some details are given in Figure 15.8.

**FIGURE 15.8**
*Relative market shares*

| | Sales (£'000s) | Market share (%) | Relative market share |
|---|---|---|---|
| **Total market:** | | | |
| Last year | 5,200 | | |
| This year | 7,500 | | |
| **Firm A:** | | | |
| Last year | 1,000 | 19 | |
| This year | 1,200 | 16 | |
| **Leading competitor:** | | | |
| Last year | 2,200 | 42 | 2.20 |
| This year | 3,600 | 48 | 3.00 |
| **Close competitor:** | | | |
| Last year | 1,200 | 23 | 1.20 |
| This year | 2,200 | 27 | 1.67 |

Relative market share is calculated by dividing each competitor's market share by that of one's own firm, and it indicates any gains or losses. As Figure 15.8 makes clear, Firm A has slipped relative to both the market leader and its closest competitor. The leader's market share has increased to three times that of Firm A, and it will almost certainly have lowered its unit costs.

## 2 Profits and Return on Sales

If a competitor has a high return on sales than Firm A it may well reduce price, or improve quality, or increase its marketing efforts in order to improve its competitive position further.

The data in Figure 15.9 shows sales, market share, relative market share and profit (before tax but after interest) over the last three years for all firms supplying Product X. Over that period the market leader's profit has grown by 400 per cent, the closest competitor's by over 200 per cent, and Firm A's by only 190 per cent. In absolute terms the market leader's profit in Year 3 is almost five times that of Firm A, giving a huge source of funds for expansion, R & D, etc., while in relative terms the leader's return on sales of 22.2 per cent in Year 3 is well ahead of any other competitor.

**FIGURE 15.9**
*Sales, market shares, and profits for all suppliers of Product X*

| | Sales (£'000s) | Market share (%) | Relative market share | Profit (£'000s) | (%) |
|---|---|---|---|---|---|
| **Firm A:** | | | | | |
| Year 1 | 700 | 17.5 | | 90 | 12.8 |
| Year 2 | 1,000 | 19.2 | | 130 | 13.0 |
| Year 3 | 1,200 | 16.0 | | 170 | 14.2 |
| **Leading competitor:** | | | | | |
| Year 1 | 1,400 | 35.0 | 2.0 | 200 | 14.3 |
| Year 2 | 2,200 | 42.3 | 2.2 | 400 | 18.2 |
| Year 3 | 3,600 | 48.0 | 3.0 | 800 | 22.2 |
| **Close competitor:** | | | | | |
| Year 1 | 1,000 | 25.0 | 1.4 | 120 | 12.0 |
| Year 2 | 1,200 | 23.1 | 1.2 | 170 | 14.2 |
| Year 3 | 2,000 | 26.6 | 1.7 | 260 | 13.0 |
| **Laggard 1:** | | | | | |
| Year 1 | 500 | 12.5 | 0.71 | 55 | 11.0 |
| Year 2 | 500 | 9.6 | 0.50 | 60 | 12.0 |
| Year 3 | 500 | 6.7 | 0.42 | 50 | 10.0 |
| **Laggard 2:** | | | | | |
| Year 1 | 400 | 10.0 | 0.57 | 40 | 10.0 |
| Year 2 | 300 | 5.8 | 0.30 | 20 | 6.7 |
| Year 3 | 200 | 2.7 | 0.17 | 5 | 2.5 |
| **Total market:** | | | | | |
| Year 1 | 4,000 | 100.0 | | 505 | 12.6 |
| Year 2 | 5,200 | 100.0 | | 780 | 15.0 |
| Year 3 | 7,500 | 100.0 | | 1,285 | 17.1 |

Firm A's task seems to be to reinforce its competitive position relative to both laggard firms on the one hand, and to develop a defence against the strong competitors on the other.

### 3  Volume and Unit Cost

Details of volume and costs are given in Figure 15.10. Changes in unit costs reveal each firm's relative efficiency: the further a competitor's relative cost falls below unity the more of a threat this becomes, and vice versa. (Costs are calculated by subtracting profit from sales revenue, and unit costs are obtained by dividing the costs by volume, year by year.)

The market leader has a cost advantage in Year 3 of 69p per unit relative to Firm A, whereas Laggard 2 has a cost disadvantage relative to Firm A of 73p per unit. Perhaps more significant than these figures are those that compare volume and cost changes. Thus, for example, Firm A's two main competitors both increased volume between Years 2 and 3 by more than 70 per cent, yet the close competitor's cost per unit only fell by 3 per cent or so while the market leader's cost per unit fell by more than 9 per cent. Is the explanation to be found in the close competitor's investment in competitive position – such as in R & D, marketing programmes, or new plant?

### 4  Unit Prices

In Figure 15.11 are shown the unit prices charged for Product X by each competitor over the last three years, along with costs and the profits and market shares that have resulted. (Unit prices are simply calculated by dividing sales revenue by units sold.)

The pattern of price changes reflects the use of price as a competitive variable, and this can be related to cost and market share data to see how competitive positions are changing. For example, the market leader has reduced the price by more than any other firm, but its price reductions have not been as great as its

**FIGURE 15.10**
*Volume, costs and unit costs*

| | Volume in units (000s) | Increase (%) | Cost (£'000s) | Cost per unit (£) | Relative cost per unit |
|---|---|---|---|---|---|
| **Firm A:** | | | | | |
| Year 1 | 100 | | 610 | 6.10 | |
| Year 2 | 156 | 56 | 870 | 5.58 | |
| Year 3 | 192 | 23 | 1,030 | 5.36 | |
| **Leading competitor:** | | | | | |
| Year 1 | 200 | | 1,200 | 6.00 | 0.98 |
| Year 2 | 350 | 75 | 1,800 | 5.14 | 0.92 |
| Year 3 | 600 | 71 | 2,800 | 4.67 | 0.87 |
| **Close competitor:** | | | | | |
| Year 1 | 140 | | 880 | 6.29 | 1.03 |
| Year 2 | 190 | 36 | 1,030 | 5.42 | 0.97 |
| Year 3 | 330 | 74 | 1,740 | 5.27 | 0.98 |
| **Laggard 1:** | | | | | |
| Year 1 | 70 | | 445 | 6.36 | 1.04 |
| Year 2 | 75 | 7 | 440 | 5.86 | 1.05 |
| Year 3 | 80 | 7 | 450 | 5.62 | 1.05 |
| **Laggard 2:** | | | | | |
| Year 1 | 56 | | 360 | 6.42 | 1.05 |
| Year 2 | 45 | (20) | 280 | 6.22 | 1.16 |
| Year 3 | 32 | (29) | 195 | 6.09 | 1.14 |
| **Total:** | | | | | |
| Year 1 | 566 | | | | |
| Year 2 | 816 | 44 | | | |
| Year 3 | 1,234 | 51 | | | |

cost reductions, hence profit per unit has increased each year – as has the number of units. This places that firm in a very strong competitive position.

Patterns of price, cost, profit and volume change for Firm A and its closest competitor are less clear, but for the laggards the picture of a downward spiral is clear enough.

**FIGURE 15.11**
*Unit prices, profits and market shares*

| | Average price per unit (£) | Average cost per unit (£) | Profit per unit (£) | Market share (%) |
|---|---|---|---|---|
| **Firm A:** | | | | |
| Year 1 | 7.00 | 6.10 | 0.90 | 17.5 |
| Year 2 | 6.41 | 5.58 | 0.83 | 19.2 |
| Year 3 | 6.25 | 5.36 | 0.89 | 16.0 |
| **Leading competitor:** | | | | |
| Year 1 | 7.00 | 6.00 | 1.00 | 35.0 |
| Year 2 | 6.29 | 5.14 | 1.15 | 42.3 |
| Year 3 | 6.00 | 4.67 | 1.33 | 48.0 |
| **Close competitor:** | | | | |
| Year 1 | 7.14 | 6.29 | 0.85 | 25.0 |
| Year 2 | 6.31 | 5.42 | 0.89 | 23.1 |
| Year 3 | 6.06 | 5.27 | 0.79 | 26.6 |
| **Laggard 1:** | | | | |
| Year 1 | 7.14 | 6.36 | 0.78 | 12.5 |
| Year 2 | 6.66 | 5.86 | 0.80 | 9.6 |
| Year 3 | 6.25 | 5.62 | 0.63 | 6.7 |
| **Laggard 2:** | | | | |
| Year 1 | 7.14 | 6.42 | 0.72 | 10.0 |
| Year 2 | 6.66 | 6.22 | 0.44 | 5.8 |
| Year 3 | 6.25 | 6.09 | 0.16 | 2.7 |

### 5 Cashflow, Liquidity and Resource Availability

Competitive gains and losses will arise over longer periods than the financial year, and the capacity of a competitor to continue in the fray is a function of more than simply profit or market share at a particular point in time. A firm's ability to continue to compete will also depend on its liquidity position and the availability of other resources over time. For example, a firm with poor cashflow, a high level of debt, and out-of-date production facilities is not likely to be able to compete for long.

### 6 The Future

Having analysed the relative positions of each firm supplying Product X over the past three years the real crunch comes in attempting to make the next move.

The management of Firm A will be able to see that the market leader is controlling the competitive situation with the highest volume and profits, plus the lowest unit costs and price. If that firm reduced its price by, say, 10 per cent, it would force the laggards out of the market and limit the close competitor's profit (assuming it followed suit and reduced its own price). Firm A needs to reduce its costs and strengthen its position against its two main competitors while there is scope for growth in the overall market for Product X.

Using Figures 15.8 to 15.11 as a basis, various possibilities can be projected for the future, each building on explicit assumptions regarding:

- future market demand;
- likely competitive actions;
- likely competitive reactions;
- competitors' liquidity and solvency.

This takes us a long way from conventional single entity, single-period management accounting, yet the adaptations that need to be made are not so difficult to comprehend – but the benefits from gaining a clearer picture of one's competitive position and how this is changing should be enormous. Strategic management accounting can help realize these benefits.

After seeing the appeal of the approaches suggested by Pyne and Simmonds one might wonder how the necessary competitive information might be gathered. Brock (1984), Pyne (1985), Beerel (1986), Jones (1988), Robert (1990) and others offer a variety of ways forward. We will return to this theme in Chapter 18.

**Consumer Franchise**

It has been argued by Mehotra (1984) that market share and profit measures are unsatisfactory for gauging efficiency since they ignore the purpose of marketing which he sees as being the identification of, and meeting, the needs and wants of end users. His proposed measure is *consumer franchise* which he has developed from an approach within General Electric. The basis of this approach is to be found in a continuum with consumers being arrayed along it in accordance with the probability of their buying a particular brand. An enterprise's core consumer franchise for its brand is represented by consumers having a consistently high probability of buying that brand. Those consumers with a low probability of buying that brand are likely to be either committed to another brand or uncommitted to any brand. It is apparent, therefore, that a brand's sales can be represented by the following equation:

$$\text{Sales} = (P_1 \times N_1) + (P_2 \times N_2)$$

Where: $P_1$ is probability of buying if committed
$N_1$ is number of committed buyers
$P_2$ is probability of buying if uncommitted
$N_2$ is number of uncommitted buyers

The level of sales can be increased by increasing the probability of purchasing by a given consumer or by increasing the proportion of high probability buyers, i.e. the consumer franchise. To achieve the former it is likely that sales promotion methods will be used, whereas advertising and product improvements are more likely for the latter. It can be argued that the use of sales promotions (as inputs) is likely to influence market share but this may only be temporary. On the other hand improvements in the consumer franchise are more likely to be lasting, hence a more desirable output. There is always a risk that some approaches to increasing market share (or sales or profit) may only achieve this in the short term and thereafter actually erode the consumer franchise – this would be reflected in a temporary improvement in efficiency but a reduction in effectiveness. In contrast a brand's consumer franchise might be enhanced by a more substantive and coordinated improvement in the market offering.

## 15.5 MULTIPLE CRITERIA

Let us broaden our perspective and consider criteria that go beyond the single criteria we have been focusing on so far in this chapter. The use of a single criterion is inadequate because:

1 organizations behave ineffectively from some points of view if a single criterion is used;
2 organizations fulfil multiple functions and have multiple goals, some of which may be in conflict. It would be inappropriate to assess strategies purely on the basis of any one criterion.

The difficulty, as will be apparent, lies in identifying those multiple criteria that are necessary and sufficient to ensure corporate well-being and survival. One way is via the application of *Pareto's Law*.

Pareto's Law (or the 80/20 rule) is widely thought to apply to a range of situations in which most of the behaviour or value of one factor is deemed to depend on only a little of another factor. For example, it is often asserted that 80 per cent of inventory movements within an organization are attributable to 20 per cent of items stocked, 80 per cent of sales volume comes from 20 per cent of customers, or 80 per cent of profits are derived from 20 per cent of product lines. The main point here, of course, is that one can effectively control an inventory if one can focus attention on the critical 20 per cent of active items, or one can control the level of sales if the key customers are properly serviced. This can be greatly beneficial both in terms of cost savings (through eliminating unnecessary control effort on the 'insignificant' 80 per cent of items that only make up 20 per cent of stock issues) and in terms of improved organizational effectiveness (due to better control of the key elements).

The application of Pareto's Law is known by a number of different names. Perhaps the most frequently encountered are: key variables, critical success factors (CSF), and key result areas.

To illustrate the idea further we can consider a generalized example, and then a number of specific industry examples (see Rockart (1979)). Figure 15.12 identifies for each main sphere of activity the factors that are likely to be of some major significance to corporate performance. Each factor has financial implications, and if they can be controlled it is probable that the overall company can be controlled.

Within specific industries there is likely to be considerable variation in key variables, as Figure 15.13 illustrates. Johnson (1967), for example, looks in more detail at this key question.

**FIGURE 15.12**
*A general example of key variables*

| Sphere of activity | Critical factors |
|---|---|
| Environment | Economic – interest rates<br>inflation rates<br>concentration<br>Political stability |
| Marketing | Sales volume<br>Market share<br>Gross margins |
| Production | Capacity utilization<br>Quality standards |
| Logistics | Capacity utilization<br>Level of service |
| Asset management | Return on investment<br>Accounts receivable balance |

**FIGURE 15.13**
*Specific industry examples of key variables*

*Food processing:*
- new product development
- good distribution
- effective advertising

*Motor vehicles:*
- styling
- efficient dealer networks
- tight control over manufacturing costs

*Life assurance:*
- development of agency managerial personnel
- effective control of clerical staff
- innovation in creating new types of policies

*Oil:*
- decentralization
- liquidity
- government business relationships
- societal image
- new ventures (to broaden its base)

SOURCE: Adapted from Rockart (1979)

The variables that are critical are those that are causally related to desired outcomes. In seeking to measure the values of variables great care must be taken to avoid the trap of giving attention to variables that are amenable to measurement and overlooking more important variables that are not amenable to measurement (e.g. quantities are more readily measured than qualities, but it does not follow that the latter are less important than the former). Similarly, variables that reflect a short-run focus, such as reported profit or EPS (earnings per share), should not be allowed to dominate the measurement process when variables with a longer-run focus, such as competitive position, are being ignored in that process.

In a study of more than 250 US organizations Steiner (1969) sought to determine the factors most likely to influence future success. He did this by asking the senior managers in the chosen companies to rank 85 factors. The top 10 are shown below:

1 attract and maintain high quality top management;
2 develop future managers for domestic operations;
3 motivate sufficient managerial drive for profits;
4 assure better judgement, creativity, and imagination in decision making at top management levels;
5 perceive new needs and opportunities for products;
6 develop a better long-range planning programme;

7  improve service to customers;
8  provide a competitive return to shareholders;
9  maximize the value of shareholders' investment;
10 develop a better willingness to take risks with commensurate returns in what appear to be excellent new business opportunities in order to achieve growth objectives.

A variety of alternative approaches have been put forward for identifying key variables or critical success factors (see, for example, Leidecker and Bruno (1984); Jenster (1987); Freund (1988); Dace (1990); De Vasconcellos and Hambrick (1989); Hitt and Ireland (1985)). Such approaches usually rely on the views of managers and other experts within the particular industries. It is inherent in these approaches that their validity is questionable and that they do not constitute a clear basis for action. Is it helpful in the food processing industry, from the viewpoint of formulating action plans, to know that NPD, good distribution, and effective advertising are the prescribed critical success factors (as in Figure 15.13)? However plausible the CSFs might be it is difficult to know how they will impact on an enterprise's competitive position.

An alternative approach that Day and Wensley (1988) argue gives more defensible insights is one that relates current *sources* of advantage to the achievement of advantageous competitive *positions* hence superior *performance*. By relating causes (i.e. sources) to effects (i.e. performance) this approach emphasizes linkages in a more explicit way. It is illustrated in Figure 15.14.

An example of operational linkages between CSFs and actions (in the form of specified strategies) is given by Freund (1988) for a life insurance company. These emerged from a process in which:

1  top management identified what it considered were the company's CSFs;
2  departmental managers then identified financial strategies that would allow the CSFs to be achieved.

While CSFs can serve as criteria for choosing among competing strategies they are not equivalent to performance indicators. Figure 15.15 shows CSFs, a selection of strategies, and some performance indicators. The performance indicators are designed to show when – and by how much – strategies are not being achieved once they have been implemented.

In a study of US companies D'Aveni and MacMillan (1990) found that, under normal circumstances, managers in successful enterprises pay equal attention to their internal and external environments but pay more attention to their output environment than to their input environment. When crises relating to demand decline arise they focus their attention on the critical aspects of their external environments.

In contrast, the managers of enterprises that subsequently fail tend to ignore output factors during crises and to pay more attention to their input and internal environments.

These results accord with the view that successful enterprises attend to critical success factors that relate to their output environments (e.g. customers' needs and demand growth).

Relationships between CSFs (described as *corporate distinctive competencies*) and overall performance were examined by Hitt and Ireland (1985) in 185 US industrial enterprises. Their results suggest that distinctive competencies associated with performance vary according to the 'grand strategy' used on the one hand, and on the industry in which the enterprise is based on the other. A grand strategy refers to a predominant strategy covering the whole enterprise, and the view put forward by Hitt and Ireland for testing was that an enterprise should develop distinctive competencies in activities that are important from the point of view of implementing the grand strategy. They distinguish four industry types:

**FIGURE 15.14**
*Comparing competitors*

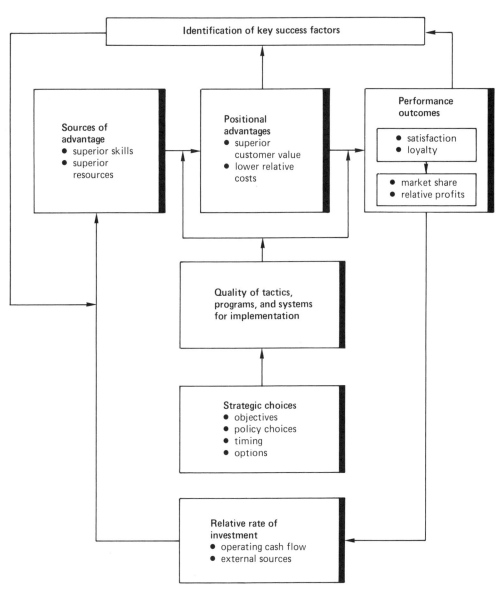

Identification of key success factors

Sources of advantage
● superior skills
● superior resources

Positional advantages
● superior customer value
● lower relative costs

Performance outcomes
● satisfaction
● loyalty
● market share
● relative profits

Quality of tactics, programs, and systems for implementation

Strategic choices
● objectives
● policy choices
● timing
● options

Relative rate of investment
● operating cash flow
● external sources

SOURCE: Day and Wensley (1988), p. 13

**FIGURE 15.15**
*Critical success factors in action*

| Critical success factor | Strategies | Performance indicators |
|---|---|---|
| Ability to achieve critical mass volumes through existing brokers and agents | ● Develop closer ties with agents<br>● Telemarket to brokers<br>● Realign agents' compensation | ● Policies in force<br>● New business written<br>● Percent of business with existing brokers |
| Be able to introduce new products within six months of industry leaders | ● Underwrite strategic joint ventures<br>● Copy leader's products<br>● Improve underwriting skills | ● Elapsed time to introduce<br>● Percent of products introduced within six months<br>● Percent underwriters having additional certification |
| Be able to manage product and product line profitability | ● Segment investment portfolio<br>● Improve cost accounting<br>● Closely manage loss ratio | ● Return on portfolio segments<br>● Actual product cost/revenue versus plan<br>● Loss ratio relative to competitors |

SOURCE: Adapted from Freund (1988), pp. 22–3

- consumer durables;
- consumer non-durables;
- capital goods;
- producer goods (e.g. raw materials).

The message that emerges from this work is that managers should be concerned to develop distinctive competencies that are appropriate for implementing their grand strategies within the context of their particular industries. It is important to match these matters in a balanced way.

It will be apparent that the choice of critical variables is neither neutral nor objective: in choosing what to measure the manager is indicating his/her personal view regarding factors that are considered important in the control process. This can be illustrated via the well-documented (e.g. Lewis (1955), Greenwood (1979)) case of the American company, General Electric (GE).

GE set up a major measurement project which had three principal component parts dealing with:

1 measures designed to assess the overall performance of a department or division as an economic entity;
2 measures designed to assess the performance of the functional activities within the organization (such as engineering, production, marketing, finance, employee relations, and community relations);
3 measures designed to assess the performance of departmental or divisional managers.

The overall measurement project was based on the following principles:

- measures should be designed to provide factual inputs to support judgements in appraising the performance of departments or divisions;
- measures should be designed so as to provide performance indicators relating both to short-run and long-run goals;
- a minimum number of measures should be used at each level within an organization.

In order to determine whether or not a variable qualified as a key success factor (which would require it to be measured) the following question was asked: 'Will continued failure in this area prevent the attainment of management's responsibility for advancing General Electric as a leader in a strong, competitive economy, even though results in all other key result areas are good?'

A range of eight key success factors emerged from this project – see Figure 15.16.

**FIGURE 15.16**
*General Electric's key results areas*

1 Profitability
2 Market position
3 Productivity
4 Product leadership
5 Personnel development
6 Employee attitudes
7 Public responsibility
8 Balance between short-run and long-run goals.

While these eight factors might seem to be generally applicable, it is their precise definition within the context of a particular company's activities that determines how critical they are. This highlights a fundamental aspect of designing any control system: it must be highly 'situational' if it is to be effective. In other words, it must be tailored to the specific characteristics of the situation, which means *this* company's objectives, *this* company's operations, *this* company's managers, and *this* company's environment.

The General Electric approach seeks to balance two conflicting tendencies: on the one hand, the diffusion of effort over multiple goals and the failure to perform as well as might be expected in any one area; and on the other hand, the tendency to emphasize one particular goal with the result that other goals are not attained.

The most common tendency in commercial enterprises is to focus on the short-run maximization of net profit (or sales) without considering the damage that this might do to the long-run position (e.g. by postponing repairs or maintenance work; by cutting back on advertising or on research, training or quality control expenditure; by deferring capital investment outlays; or through exhortations to employees to increase productivity). Short-term 'gains' achieved in this way tend to be illusory because the subsequent need to make up lost ground (e.g. via heavier advertising or training in later periods) more than outweighs short-term gains.

To the extent that effectiveness is a multiple criterion we must avoid the trap of focusing too sharply on one contributing factor. It would be a mistake to assume that effectiveness would be assured simply through selecting and training the right people. Given our definition of effectiveness in Chapter 1, effectiveness may be assessed in terms of a system's capacity:

1 to survive, adapt, maintain itself, and grow – regardless of the functions it fulfils;
2 to achieve 1 through its bargaining position with its environment in relation to the acquisition of resources.

Against this background of criteria for effectiveness at an enterprise level it can be argued that any attempt to deal with the effectiveness of individual elements of marketing, such as advertising or personal selling, is problematic for two major reasons:

1 It is not possible to separate the impact of, say, advertising on the attainment of goals from the impacts of other elements of the marketing mix. The interdependence of the elements of the mix ensures that the selling task is influenced by advertising and by the nature of the product, the price and the channel decisions, all on a *mutatis mutandis* basis. It would not be sensible, therefore, to attempt to consider marketing effectiveness at any level below that of the marketing programme (i.e. the integrated set of marketing activities embracing the entire mix formulated to pursue a given strategy directed at a particular segment).
2 Most criterion measures relating to individual elements of marketing are measures of efficiency rather than effectiveness, focusing on the maximization of output for a given input or the minimization of input to achieve a given level of output. One exception to this is the use of sales quotas which represent output measures and performance is assessed by reviewing how close each sales person came to achieving his/her quota. We can see that this is a measure of effectiveness, albeit on a small scale relative to the overall scheme of things. We will return to this later in the book (see Chapter 18, pp. 585–93).

With these caveats in mind it is possible to identify criteria that are regularly applied in choosing among alternative plans for specific elements of the mix (see, for example, McNamee (1988), pp. 131 and 143; Guiltinan and Paul (1988), pp. 396–8). Examples are given in Figure 15.17.

**FIGURE 15.17**
*Criteria for
functional activities*

| Activity | Criteria |
|---|---|
| • New product programmes | Trial rate<br>Repurchase rate |
| • Product programmes | Contribution margin<br>Controllable margin as percentage of sales |
| • Sales programmes | Contribution by region, salesman<br>Controllable margin as percentage of sales<br>Number of new accounts<br>Travel costs |
| • Advertising programmes | Awareness levels<br>Attribute ratings<br>Cost levels |
| • Promotion programmes | Redemption rates<br>Displacement rates<br>Stock-up rates |
| • Pricing programmes | Price relative to industry average<br>Price elasticity of demand |
| • Distribution programmes | Number of distributors carrying the product |

## 15.6 SUMMARY

In this chapter we have looked at a range of possible criteria for assessing marketing strategies as a basis for making choices. Distinctions have been made among:

- short-term versus long-term criteria;
- financial versus non-financial criteria;
- single versus multiple criteria;
- criteria focusing on overall strategies versus criteria focusing on specific activities;
- criteria focusing on efficiency versus criteria focusing on effectiveness.

Apart from the variety of input and output measures that have been discussed there are additional approaches that deal with factors ranging from the degree of realism in the assumptions underlying the strategy to the capacity of the enterprise to implement successfully the chosen strategy. To take specific examples, Tilles (1963) and Day (1990) both outline sets of criteria that might be applied in assessing strategies. These include:

1 Is there an effective matching of the enterprise's competences with the threats and opportunities from the environment? (If not then there is unlikely to be a basis for achieving sustainable competitive advantage.)

2 Will the strategy place the enterprise in a position to counter known threats, exploit opportunities, enhance current advantages, or provide new sources of advantage?

3 Is the strategy robust enough to adapt to a broad range of anticipated environmental events or is it only likely to work under very specific conditions?

4 Will it be difficult for competitors to deal with the expected advantages to be gained from the strategy?

5 Are the assumptions underlying the formulation of competing strategies realistic? (Such assumptions might relate to price levels, relative market share, market growth, cost levels, timing aspects, competitive reactions, and so on.)

6 What are the potential risks to which the strategy (hence the enterprise) may be vulnerable? (These may be internal – in the form of resource availability or implementation factors – as well as external.)

7 Is the strategy feasible from the viewpoint of the enterprise having the necessary skills and resources? (These would include access to technology, markets, and servicing facilities as well as adequate managerial capabilities.)

8 Is the strategy capable of being effectively communicated so that those who will be responsible for its implementation can understand what is required of them?

9 Will the strategy challenge and motivate key personnel? (This implies that strategies must be accepted by those who are charged with their implementation.)

10 Are the elements within the strategy internally consistent so that it hangs together in a coherent way?

11 Will the expected results from the strategy be acceptable relative to the anticipated risks? (This will require evidence of a clear competitive advantage from which enhanced value to shareholders and other stakeholders' gains will flow.)

12 Does the strategy have an appropriate time frame? (Strategies cannot be achieved overnight, so sufficient time must be allowed for their effective implementation.)

# 16 | Modelling approaches

## 16.1 LEARNING OBJECTIVES

When you have read this chapter you should be able to:

(a) understand more fully the role of modelling approaches;
(b) apply financial models to the short-run and long-run evaluation of marketing plans;
(c) appreciate the contribution that non-financial modelling approaches – such as matrix models and Bonoma's MPA model – can make to evaluating marketing plans;
(d) recognize and handle the problems of allowing for risk and uncertainty in carrying out evaluations.

## 16.2 INTRODUCTION

In broad terms a model is anything that is used to represent something else, and models may be classified as descriptive – those that aim to describe real-world processes; predictive – describing both objectives and events as well as attempting to predict future events; and control models – describing current events, predicting future events, and providing a basis for choice among alternative courses of action.

Management science models are typically mathematical in nature, being sets of equations or other expressions that state the significant variables in a particular situation and indicate the relationship between them. A variable can be defined as any factor that can take on different values under different circumstances, such as:

$$y = a + bx$$

Where: y represents sales (the effect);
x represents consumer income (the cause);
a and b are constants (or parameters), one of which may, for instance, be a time lag.

This shows that mathematical models are symbolic and are based on the axioms of mathematics. The axioms of probability theory, for example, as one branch of mathematics, will be briefly stated (see p. 467 below). Furthermore, most mathematical models are based on a small number of highly aggregated factors that are of overriding importance in explaining the way a system works and determining the outcome of different actions.

Models are useful in that they facilitate conceptions of reality that allow the effects of alternative courses of action to be more readily anticipated and measured. Such conceptions, however, are necessarily simplifications of the real situation because this is usually so complex that it could not possibly be explained by a model. The danger is always present that models may be *over*-simplifications of reality, and this renders them useless. Over-simplification is often a trait of corporate model-building.

The balance sheet is a form of simplified corporate model governed by the principles of financial accounting, but the annual budget is a better operational example of a corporate model. Such models can be used to examine how the workings of a system affect the flow of inputs and outputs and are being used with increasing frequency.

Budgeting, as a means of modelling, is limited in its traditional application by:

1 the inclusion of too few alternative possibilities from which the most satisfactory is to be selected;
2 the difficulty of adjusting traditional operating budgets to rapidly changing conditions – they are at best 'flexible' with respect to changing sales or production levels (see Chapter 8).

It follows that a model permitting the calculation of a larger number of alternatives (based on a larger range of flexible variables and changing parameters) should yield a closer approximation to the ideal solution.

This can be achieved via simulation models, the idea of which is to handle relationships that are too complex to be reduced to simple conclusions by means of mathematical or statistical analysis. These models can then be used to generate predictions about the future course of events.

Two types of simulation are readily identifiable:

1 analogue simulation which tends to be a physical representation – such as the use of a model aircraft to predict the behaviour of a full-scale version;
2 symbolic simulation via mathematical modelling, in which the manipulation of the variables within the model simulates the interaction process and is thereby able to predict the outcomes of particular courses of action.

*Sensitivity analyses* (see pp. 472 and 474 below) can be performed in the symbolic simulation model by varying the inputs to the system (e.g. time, quantities, funds, etc.) and observing the outputs from each alternative combination of inputs. In this way a pattern of responses can be built up to permit predictions to be made of likely future outcomes.

Probability theory is important in any form of simulation since, for instance, the application of probabilities allows the manipulator to estimate the risk of predictions proving to be wrong. This and related techniques show that the value of simulation to management is in its providing the equivalent of a laboratory in which past or proposed operations can be examined and experimental evidence produced concerning the probable future outcomes of present decisions.

The building of any model should be carried out by following a *systematic method* such as the following:

1 specify the objectives to be achieved;
2 formulate the problem to be solved;
3 determine the relationships and major variables in the decision situation, including constraints;
4 construct a model to represent the system under review in such a way that it expresses the effectiveness of the system as a function of the variables isolated in step 3, with at least one of these variables being subject to control;
5 derive a solution from the model;
6 test both the solution and the model to ensure that the effect of changes in the system are accurately predicted in the system's overall effectiveness;
7 establish controls over the solution to allow for variations in the relationships among the variables, otherwise the solution may become invalid;
8 implement the tested solution by translating it into a set of operating

procedures capable of being understood and applied by the personnel who will be responsible for this use;
9 appraise the results.

Within marketing several models have been developed that have general application in such areas as brand share and loyalty determination, media selection, measurement of message effectiveness, competitive strategies, transpor-tation and warehouse location, pricing and the determination of competitive bids. However, these models are usually more complex and less precise than those developed for production and administration purposes. This is due to two major factors:

1 The ease of model construction will generally depend on the number of costs involved and the accuracy with which they are measured. The general absence of well-developed costing systems for marketing means that marketing models must handle less precise data than is desirable.
2 The sheer number of variables in the typical marketing decision is huge, many of which are beyond the decision-maker's control. This results in complex models as well as the need to make a large number of simplifying assumptions.

In many marketing decisions it is behavioural relationships that are of the essence rather than more easily measured physical or economic factors, and, along with other environmental variables, behaviour is difficult to measure in order to accommodate it into a mathematical model. The nature of a behavioural model is shown in Figure 16.1 for predicting sales in the convenience food industry.

**FIGURE 16.1**
*Buyer behaviour model*

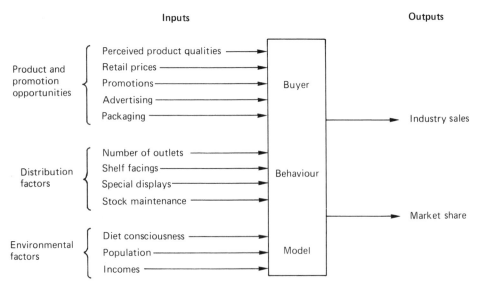

This is a *black-box* model that aims to show which given inputs result in a particular output rather than attempting to explain exactly how this occurs.

Decision models (as illustrated in Figure 16.2) permit a higher degree of explanation than is possible with *black-box* models because the variables contained within them are more readily quantified, and the interrelationships contained within these models are less tenuous than in behavioural models.

Analytical decision models (based on the programming techniques discussed later in this chapter) can result in the selection of the best marketing mix to adopt for both the trade and the consumer. Simulation models, on the other hand, can start from a different point and attempt to evaluate the effect of alternative marketing mix combinations on the company's sales and profits as shown in Figure 16.3.

**FIGURE 16.2**
*Decision model*

**FIGURE 16.3**
*Company sales and profit model*

*Company profit equation:*
Z  =  (P − c) Q − F − A − D

*Company sales equation:*
Q  =  sQi

*Industry sales equation:*
Qi  =  mKN

*Market share equation:*
s   =  R(aA + dD)/Σ [R(aA + dD)]

Where: Z  =  Company profit in Year T
       P  =  Average price of the company's product in Year T
       c  =  Average variable manufacturing cost of the company's product in Year T
       Q  =  Number of units of product sold by the company in Year T
       F  =  Fixed costs of company in Year T
       A  =  Advertising and promotion costs of the company in Year T
       D  =  Distribution and sales force costs of the company in year T
       s  =  Average market share of company in Year T
       Qi =  Industry sales in Year T
       m  =  Convenience food share of total food market
       K  =  Consumption of food per head in Year T
       N  =  Population of market in Year T
       R  =  Preference rating for company's product in Year T
       a  =  Advertising effectiveness index
       d  =  Distribution effectiveness index

There can be little doubt that models can assist considerably in marketing planning and control, but this will only happen if models are developed and used properly.

Models must be designed on a planned basis to ensure that they are geared to the decision maker's objectives and requirements. In addition, models must function as part of the management process, which means that they should not be developed in isolation of an appreciation of the changes in the balance of power that they can produce: political implications are a significant feature of management science applications.

Once developed, the risk exists that models will be incorrectly used. This does not mean that the decision maker must become a specialist in the development of models, but he should understand the essential features of model building and how to apply a model that has been built.

## 16.3 COST–VOLUME–PROFIT ANALYSIS

In deciding on future courses of action management pays a great deal of attention to the alternatives that are available. However, in the case of alternatives that involve changes in the level of business activity with no changes in scale itself it is generally found that profit does not vary in direct proportion to changes in the level of activity. This is due to the interactions of costs, volume, and profits.

Costs can be classified as fixed, variable, and mixed. In a marketing context the costs which are typically fixed in relation to the level of activity (within a specified time-span) are:

- salaries;
- sales administration costs;
- advertising appropriations;
- market research allocations;
- establishment costs of premises.

Many costs depend very much on the volume of business and are often computed on a per unit basis. Such variable costs include:

- commissions;
- delivery costs;
- after-sales service costs;
- cost of credit;
- order processing/invoicing costs.

Mixed costs are those that are neither constant over a period nor directly variable on a per unit basis. An example could be the cost of additional sales staff: a particular level of business may require 30 sales staff to service the relevant outlets, but a rise in business of, say, 10 per cent that involves new outlets will probably require additional sales staff.

The patterns that emerge are shown in Figure 16.4.

**FIGURE 16.4**
*Cost behaviour patterns*

(a) Fixed costs    (b) Variable costs    (c) Mixed costs

Sales revenue is an increasing function of the level of activity and therefore has the behavioural characteristics of the variable cost curve (see Figure 16.4(b)). Profit is a residual that depends on the interaction of sales volume, selling prices and costs. The non-uniform response of certain costs to changes in the level of activity can have a serious impact on profit in companies having a high proportion of fixed costs with the result that a seemingly insignificant decline in sales volume from the expected level may be accompanied by a major drop in expected profit. (This is particularly prevalent in capital-intensive companies producing expensive but specialized industrial equipment.)

On account of the difficulties involved in many industries in accurately predicting the volume of business that may be expected during a forthcoming planning period it is a wise policy to consider the cost–volume–profit picture for each likely level of activity. This can be done by means of a profitgraph (or break-even chart) that illustrates the profit emerging from different cost/revenue combinations.

**FIGURE 16.5**
*Profitgraph*

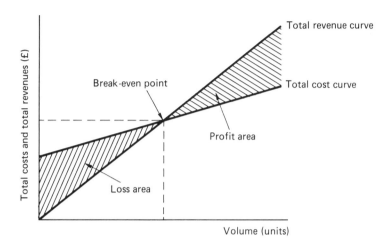

The simple profitgraph in Figure 16.5 is compiled by combining the cost and revenue curves. The total revenue curve is simply the expected unit sales multiplied by price for each level of activity, whereas the total cost curve is made up by splitting mixed costs into their fixed and variable costs elements, and superimposing the total fixed cost curve on to the variable cost curve as shown in Figure 16.6.

**FIGURE 16.6**
*Total cost curve*

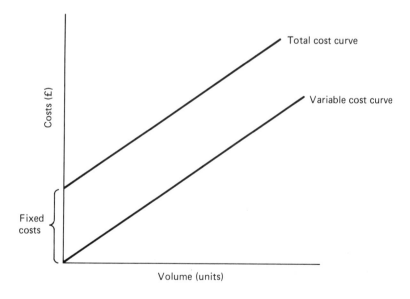

It is characteristic of this modelling technique that significant simplifying assumptions underlie its application. For example:

1 it is assumed that fixed costs are constant and that variable costs vary at a constant rate;
2 it is assumed that all costs can be broken into either fixed or variable categories;
3 it is assumed that only one selling price applies.

**FIGURE 16.7**
*CVP analysis with a market demand schedule*

| Unit price (£) | Market demand (units) | Total revenue (£) | Total costs (£) | Break-even point (units) | Profit (£) |
|---|---|---|---|---|---|
| 5 | 65 000 | 325 000 (a¹) | 362 500 | 80 000 (a) | (37 500) |
| 10 | 55 000 | 550 000 (b¹) | 337 500 | 26 667 (b) | 212 500 |
| 15 | 45 000 | 675 000 (c¹) | 312 500 | 16 000 (c) | 362 500 |
| 20 | 30 000 | 600 000 (d¹) | 275 000 | 11 429 (d) | 325 000 |

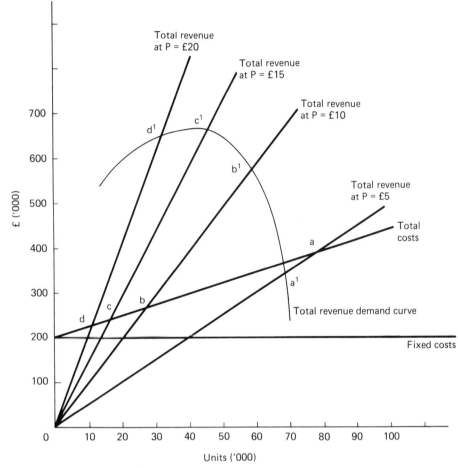

SOURCE: Adapted from Cravens and Lamb (1986)

Any of these (and other) assumptions underlying cost–volume–profit analysis can be modified in order to produce a more realistic model that is better suited to specific circumstances. This can be demonstrated by reference to Figure 16.7 in which assumption 3 above is relaxed (modified from Cravens and Lamb (1986), p. 31). Fixed costs are given at £200,000, the unit variable cost is £2.50, and demand forecasts are shown for a number of different prices: £5, £10, £15 and £20. The greatest profit is generated by the £15 price and can be confirmed by the following calculation:

| | |
|---|---|
| Sales revenue (45 000 units at £15.00) | £675,000 |
| Variable costs (45 000 units at £2.50) | £112,500 |
| | |
| Contribution | £562,500 |
| Fixed costs | £200,000 |
| | |
| Profit | £362,500 |

The break-even volume is derived from the formula:

$$\frac{\text{Fixed costs}}{\text{Unit contribution}}$$

$$= \frac{£200,000}{£15.00 - £2.50} = 16,000 \text{ units}$$

At £15.00 per unit the break-even point expressed in terms of revenue is:

$$16,000 \times £15 = £240,000$$

This gives a margin of safety of

$$\frac{£675,000 - £240,000}{£675,000} \times 100 = 64\%$$

In Figure 16.7 the line connecting the points $a^1$, $b^1$, $c^1$ and $d^1$ constitutes the market demand curve for the product in question.

An alternative form of presentation to the profitgraph is the profit–volume chart. This shows the same relationships but simplifies the picture by netting costs and revenues to show the profit for each level of activity. Figure 16.8 shows such a chart.

**FIGURE 16.8**
*Profit-volume chart.*

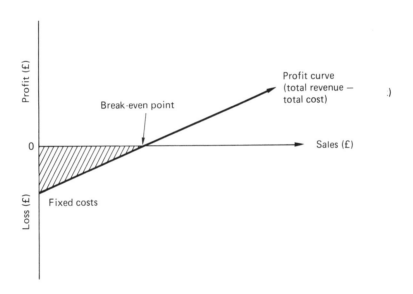

The reason why the total cost curve of Figures 16.5 and 16.6 does not pass through the origin is the same as the reason why the profit curve of Figure 16.8 cuts the vertical axis below the point of zero profit: even when there are no sales the fixed costs must still be paid, and consequently the area below the break-even sales volume represents one of loss, being at its greatest at zero sales.

When constructed, the profitgraph represents in essence a wide range of profit statements for various levels of activity. As such, it can be used as a bench-mark for judging the adequacy of actual performance, or it can be used in the planning phase to portray alternative courses of action. The graphical analysis described above is a simple means of illustrating cost–volume–profit interrelationships, but the managerial applications are better facilitated by algebraic analysis.

The basic equation is simple once mixed costs have been split into their fixed and variable elements and shown as such:

Sales revenue = variable costs + fixed costs + profit.

The break-even (BE) equation is even simpler since at the break-even point there is no profit:

BE sales revenue = variable costs + fixed costs.

In physical volume terms the break-even point can be calculated as follows:

$$\text{BE volume} = \frac{\text{Fixed costs}}{(\text{Sales revenue} - \text{variable costs})/(\text{units sold})}$$

Thus if a firm has fixed costs of £10,000, variable costs of £15,000, and sells 5000 units for £30,000, the break-even volume is:

$$\frac{10\,000}{(30\,000 - 15\,000)/5000} = 3333 \text{ units}$$

In monetary terms the break-even volume can be derived by applying the formula:

$$\frac{\text{Fixed costs}}{1 - (\text{Variable costs/sales revenue})} = \frac{\text{Fixed costs}}{\text{Contribution margin ratio}}$$

Using the data referred to above the break-even volume is equal to:

$$\frac{10\,000}{1 - (15\,000/30\,000)} = \frac{10\,000}{0.5} = £20,000$$

The proof is simple: unit price is £6.00 (i.e. £30,000/5000) and the unit variable cost is £3.00 (i.e. £15,000/5000). The unit contribution towards fixed costs and profit is therefore £6.00 − £3.00 = £3.00 and sufficient units must be sold to cover the fixed costs of £10,000. The solution is thus 3333 units, and at a unit price of £6.00 the break-even revenue is £20,000.

Reference was made in the above example to the contribution margin ratio. This is an important concept that expresses the percentage of a volume change that is composed of variable costs. In the example the revenue from an additional sale is £6.00 and the additional variable cost is £3.00. The contribution margin ratio is therefore 1 − 3/6 = 0.5 or 50 per cent. In other words, half the revenue from a change in volume is sufficient to cover the variable costs and the other half contributes to fixed costs and profits. (The slope of the curve in Figure 16.8 is given by the contribution margin ratio.)

The application of this ratio is based on the assumption that other factors remain constant and it should be evident that this is a somewhat unrealistic assumption. Nevertheless, to continue the above example, if a change in sales of £10,000 takes place the change in profits will be as shown in Figure 16.9.

**FIGURE 16.9**
*Profit-volume variations*

| | Original volume | Increase in volume | Decrease in volume |
|---|---|---|---|
| | (£) | (£) | (£) |
| Sales | 30,000 | +10,000 | −10,000 |
| Variable costs | 15,000 | +5,000 | −5,000 |
| Fixed costs | 10,000 | Unchanged | Unchanged |
| Total costs | 25,000 | +5,000 | −5,000 |
| Profits | 5,000 | +5,000 | −5,000 |

Figure 16.9 shows that with a contribution margin (or profit–volume) ratio of 50 per cent the profit variation for an upward move is the same as that for a downward move, with the former being positive and the latter negative, and with both being equal to one half of the change in sales revenue.

A further equation can be devised to measure the excess of actual (or budgeted) sales over the break-even volume. This is known as the *margin of safety* and is given by the equation:

(Actual sales – sales at break-even point)/actual sales

Again taking data from the earlier example, in monetary terms the margin of safety is:

(£30,000 – £20,000)/£30,000 = ⅓ or 33⅓%

In physical terms it is:

(5,000 – 3,333)/5,000 = ⅓ or 33⅓%

This ratio means that sales can fall by one-third before operations cease being profitable – assuming that the other relationships are accurately measured and remain constant.

The combination of cost–volume–profit analysis with budgeting enables alternative budget figures to serve as the basis for profitgraphs. If a particular budget is shown to be unsatisfactory then the parameters can be recast until a more suitable budget results. It is not surprising that cost–volume–profit analysis has been compared to flexible budgeting in being able to show what the cost and profit picture should be at different levels of sales, but flexible budgets are essentially concerned with cost control whereas cost–volume–profit analysis is more concerned with the predictions of profit.

As with other techniques, cost–volume–profit analysis has its strengths and weaknesses. In its favour is its value as a background information device for important decisions – such as selecting distribution channels, make or buy, and pricing decisions. In this role it offers an overall view of costs and sales in relation to profit requirements.

If simplicity is a virtue, then cost–volume–profit analysis has this virtue since it is easily understood. However, this very simplicity points the way to the weaknesses and limitations of cost–volume–profit analysis. As suggested earlier in this section, the major weakness is in the underlying assumptions: profit varies not only in relation to changes in volume, but also with changes in production methods, marketing techniques, and other factors. Cost–volume–profit analysis is unable to allow for these possibilities, and at best indicates the profit that may be expected under a single set of assumed conditions regarding external factors as well as managerial policies. Thus it is a static representation of the situation it purports to illustrate: a different set of circumstances would obviously result in a different series of cost–volume–profit relationships.

Furthermore, cost–volume–profit analysis can only accommodate objectives that relate to profits, costs and sales levels/revenues, and it tends to treat costs, volume, and profit as if they were independent of each other.

These limitations do not outweigh the value of cost–volume–profit analysis provided that the user is aware of the assumptions and limitations. It is necessary, of course, to supplement the assistance given by any technique with managerial judgement, and cost–volume–profit analysis is no exception to this principle.

The roles of budgeting and cost–volume–profit analysis are illustrated below in another example.

**Examples**

1  ABC Ltd

This is a single-product company with a profit objective that is expressed as 10 per cent of net sales revenue.

**FIGURE 16.10**
*Manufacturing costs and revenues.*

| Forecast percentage share of market | 10% | 12% | 14% | 16% |
|---|---|---|---|---|
| Unit sales | 50 | 60 | 70 | 80 |
| Average net price per unit | £1,500 | £1,500 | £1,450 | £1,400 |
| Forecast net sales revenue | £75,000 | £90,000 | £101,500 | £112,000 |
| Variable manufacturing costs at £300 per unit | £15,000 | £18,000 | £21,000 | £24,000 |
| Contribution | £60,000 | £72,000 | £80,500 | £88,000 |
| Fixed manufacturing costs | £20,000 | £20,000 | £20,000 | £20,000 |
| Gross profit | £40,000 | £52,000 | £60,500 | £68,000 |

For the next planning period the total market potential is estimated to be 500 units. Figure 16.10 indicates the cost and profit outlook at each level of sales that ABC Ltd can expect to achieve.

The behaviour of marketing costs is shown in Figures 16.11 and 16.12 for fixed/mixed and variable costs respectively.

**FIGURE 16.11**
*Fixed and mixed costs*

| Fixed and mixed costs | 10% | 12% | 14% | 16% |
|---|---|---|---|---|
| Sales force (excluding commission) | £6,000 | £6,000 | £9,000 | £9,000 |
| Sales administration | £10,000 | £10,000 | £12,000 | £12,000 |
| Advertising appropriation | £5,000 | £5,500 | £8,000 | £12,000 |
| Establishment costs | £10,000 | £10,000 | £12,000 | £12,000 |
| Marketing research costs | £2,000 | £2,000 | £2,000 | £2,000 |
| Office services | £3,000 | £3,100 | £3,200 | £3,300 |
| Totals | £36,000 | £36,600 | £46,200 | £50,300 |

**FIGURE 16.12**
*Variable cost per unit*

| | |
|---|---|
| Delivery | £10 |
| Order processing/invoicing | £2 |
| Commission | £10 |
| Average cost of credit | £30 |
| After-sales service | £48 |
| | £100 |

The unit costs from Figure 16.12 can be extended to show the variable marketing costs of each anticipated sales level:

| Market share | 10% | 12% | 14% | 16% |
|---|---|---|---|---|
| Variable marketing cost | £5,000 | £6,000 | £7,000 | £8,000 |

The combination of Figures 16.10, 16.11 and 16.12 gives the total cost–volume–profit situation shown in Figure 16.13.

The profit objective of 10 per cent of net sales revenue is only achieved if ABC Ltd secures a 12 per cent market share, but control effort must be rigorously applied because the margin for error is very small.

**FIGURE 16.13**
*Net profits*

| Net profit statement | 10% | 12% | 14% | 16% |
|---|---|---|---|---|
| Gross margin (Figure 16.10) | £40,000 | £52,000 | £60,500 | £68,000 |
| Marketing costs (Figures 16.11 and 16.12) | £41,000 | £42,600 | £53,200 | £58,300 |
| Net profit (loss) | £(1,000) | £9,400 | £7,300 | £9,700 |
| Net profit as percentage sales revenue | −1.33% | 10.44% | 7.19% | 8.66% |

**FIGURE 16.14**
*Cost–volume–profit relationships*

This gives the basic budget for the forthcoming period, and this can be illustrated in a profitgraph as in Figure 16.14.

For the selected course of action (i.e. that aiming for a 12 per cent market share) the total cost make-up is:

| | | |
|---|---|---|
| Variable manufacturing costs | £18,000 | |
| Variable marketing costs | £ 6,000 | |
| | | £24,000 |
| Fixed manufacturing costs | £20,000 | |
| Fixed/mixed marketing costs | £36,600 | |
| | | £56,600 |
| | | £80,600 |

The break-even point is computed by applying the formula given earlier in this section:

$$\frac{£56,000}{(£90,000 - £24,000)/60} = 51 \text{ units}$$

This gives a margin of safety of only 15 per cent calculated thus:

$$(60 - 51)/60 = 15\%$$

A clear and concise summary is given in this way of one particular course of action that provides a standard for management purposes. Separate charts and analyses can easily be drawn up for other alternative courses of action prior to making a choice.

## 2 XYZ Ltd

This example deals with the design of a distribution system.

Whatever the system adopted, it must facilitate the delivery of goods to the company's customers in usable and saleable condition. This requires that they be undamaged, arrive at the specified time and place, and in the right quantities. These requirements are not so simple to meet as they may appear: inadequate packaging, incorrect loading procedures, rough handling in transit and similar matters all hinder their attainment.

The system that is eventually specified will consist of a unique physical distribution network based on decisions on transport, warehousing, inventory management, administration, and the level of service to be provided. The total system's cost is given by the simple equation:

$$D = T + FW + VW + S$$

Where:  D = total distribution cost
        T = total transportation cost
        FW = fixed warehousing cost
        VW = variable warehousing cost (including inventory costs)
        S = cost of lost sales due to average delivery delay.

Each alternative system should be costed and evaluated by using this equation before the best one can be selected. This example should help to clarify the approach that should be adopted.

XYZ Ltd has a national distribution system via six warehouses selling to whole-sale customers. Ninety-five per cent of orders are delivered within 24 hours of receipt. Some figures from the last financial year are:

| | |
|---|---|
| Sales | £5 million |
| Net profit (after tax) | £250,000 |
| Finished goods inventory (average) at factory | £750,000 |
| Finished goods inventory (average) at warehouses | £1 million |

There is only one factory and this works on the basis of maximum–minimum levels of finished goods inventory to maintain the 95 per cent level of service. Each warehouse orders weekly from the factory, with special interim orders being placed for urgent requirements. Warehouse inventory levels are based on lead times of 2 to 12 days from the factory.

The marketing director is interested in the effect on costs of eliminating the warehouses and using outside carriers to make direct deliveries to customers. The estimated effects for the next year are given in Figure 16.15.

On the basis of these figures it appears that the present system is least expensive. But all the relevant costs have not been considered.

It is assumed that both alternatives are based on a 95 per cent level of service, so the cost of lost sales will be the same in each and can thus be ignored for comparative purposes. However, to maintain this level of service under the

**FIGURE 16.15**
*Cost consequences*

|  |  | Shipments to warehouses | Shipments to customers |
|---|---|---|---|
| **Transport:** | To warehouses | 150,000 |  |
|  | Local | 37,500 |  |
|  | Direct |  | 330,000 |
| **Warehousing:** | Rent | 52,500 | 2,500 |
|  | Salaries | 65,000 | 20,000 |
|  | Insurance | 17,500 | 10,000 |
|  | Rates | 7,500 | 5,000 |
|  | Other | 15,000 | 5,000 |
|  | Communications | 22,500 | 30,000 |
| Total distribution costs |  | £367,500 | £402,400 |

existing system involves an investment of £1 million in warehouse stocks. The cost of carrying this stock is:

| Cost of capital | 15% |
|---|---|
| Excess handling | 2% |
| Obsolescence | 8% |
| Deterioration | 2% |
| Administration | 1% |
|  | 28% |

(This figure of 28 per cent excludes an allowance for the risks of price changes, variable markets, etc., which would make it even higher.)

Thus 28 per cent of £1 million is £280,000 which is the amount saved by adopting the proposed alternative of direct delivery, and shows that this is, in fact, the better choice. Further savings could also be made in manufacturing costs as a result of producing for one central inventory rather than for a central inventory plus six warehouses.

The above example shows the need to consider the *total* situation, not merely segments of it. A variation would have been to consider the financial alternatives of owning or leasing the warehouses. The leasing alternative provides greater flexibility and less risk unless volume is large and demand stable. This is so because the cost of storage should be related to the average area (i.e. the number of square metres) in use per period, and leasing charges will be proportional to this area whereas ownership costs remain the same regardless of usage.

Cost–volume analysis can be used to aid the decision maker faced with such choices as:

1 leasing or buying premises;
2 leasing or owning vehicles;
3 using agents or setting up branch offices.

In the case of warehousing Figure 16.16 summarizes the situation, showing the storage space at which ownership costs are identical with leasing charges (B). At greater volume requirements ownership is cheaper, and at lesser volumes leasing is to be preferred.

## 3 Product Line

The product mix is a major part of the overall marketing plan, and the relationship between the mix and the level of profit can be seen to be one of the basic areas against which alternatives can be reviewed in developing the

**FIGURE 16.16**
*Break-even chart for warehousing*

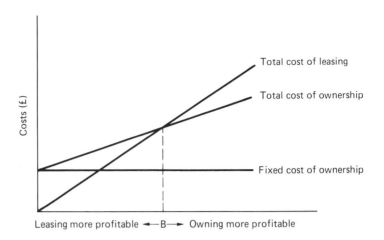

marketing plan. Not only does it involve the consideration of the roles of single products and product groups but it also involves considerations of the related effects of decisions bearing on, for example, the choice and emphasis of alternative sales areas.

However, very few companies appear to be aware of the actual gross profit contributions of either individual products or product groups. Furthermore, large variations would probably be found in gross contributions in most cases, and this could suggest different courses of marketing action if only the gross margins were properly computed. Figure 16.17 gives the example of a six-product mix analysed

**FIGURE 16.17**
*Product mix analysis*

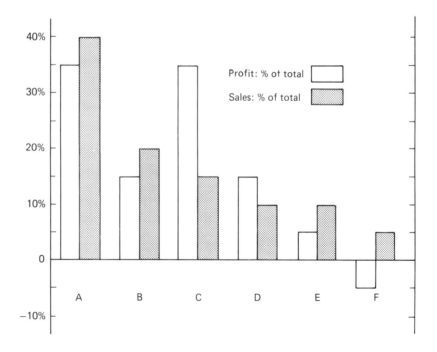

to show how each product contributes to sales and to profit. Product F has a negative contribution of 5 per cent of profit and would thus appear to be a candidate for deletion, while Product C especially, and to a lesser extent Product D, appear to deserve special marketing emphasis because they both have a proportionately greater profitability than their relative volume.

When management adopts direct product costing and distribution cost analysis it can compute the gross contribution of each item in the product range so that the tactical significance of the mix in relation to profit objectives becomes apparent. This can reveal cases of under-recovery of direct costs (as in Product F in Figure

**FIGURE 16.18**

*Product costs and contributions*

| Product | Selling price (SP) | Variable cost (VC) | % contribution (SP-VC)/SP × 100 | % of total sales | Contribution as % of total sales |
|---------|-----|-----|-----|-----|-----|
| A | £5 | £4 | 20% | 10% | 2.0% |
| B | £6 | £5 | 16.6% | 20% | 3.3% |
| C | £8 | £6 | 25% | 30% | 7.5% |
| D | £10 | £7 | 30% | 40% | 12.0% |
| | | | | 100% | 24.8% |

16.17) that could possibly be corrected by modifications in price or cost reduction if it is decided that the product should be retained to fill out the product line.

Direct costing requires the separation of fixed and variable costs, with the latter being treated as 'period costs' (i.e. they are charged to the profit and loss account on a periodic basis rather than being apportioned to units of output and thereby included either in inventory or in the cost of sales). An example should make the picture clear. LMN Ltd markets four products, the most recent financial data for which are shown in Figure 16.18. For each £1 of sales of the existing product mix, therefore, 24.8p is profit contribution. If the fixed costs of LMN Ltd amount to £50,000 and total sales are £250,000, then profit (P) is equal to:

$$(\text{Sales} \times 24.8/100) - \text{fixed costs}$$
$$\therefore\ P = £62,000 - £50,000 = £12,000$$

If it is decided to vary this mix it will be necessary to forecast the costs and sales for the modified mix. For instance, Product E may be launched to replace Product B, having the following characteristics:

| | |
|---|---|
| Selling price per unit | £7 |
| Variable cost per unit | £5.6 |
| Percentage contribution | 20% |
| Increase in fixed costs | £1,000 |

The effects on the product mix are, for a new total sales level of £275,000:

| Product | Former % of sales | Forecast % of sales |
|---------|-----|-----|
| A | 10% | 25% |
| C | 30% | 30% |
| D | 40% | 30% |
| E | – | 15% |
| | | 100% |

The total contribution picture then becomes:

A: 20 × 25/100 = 5%
C: 25 × 30/100 = 7.5%
D: 30 × 30/100 = 9%
E: 20 × 15/100 = 3%
                24.5%

$$\therefore\ P = (275,000 \times 24.5/100) - (50,000 + 1,000)$$
$$P = £67,375 - £51,000 = £16,375$$

The profit improvement is thus £4,357 (i.e. £16,375 − £12,000) on additional sales of £25,000 and this is 17.6 per cent.

This example emphasizes the fact that products must be controlled on the basis of their contribution to fixed costs and profit, and on the basis of their percentage share of total sales.

Future planning and control are both aided by studying the progress of each product over its life cycle since no product can hold its market position indefinitely in the face of changing conditions. The typical curves of Figure 16.19 show the lagged profit curve and the sales revenue curve for a product over the phases of its life. (See also the discussion in Chapter 10 above.) Rates of

**FIGURE 16.19**
*The product life cycle*

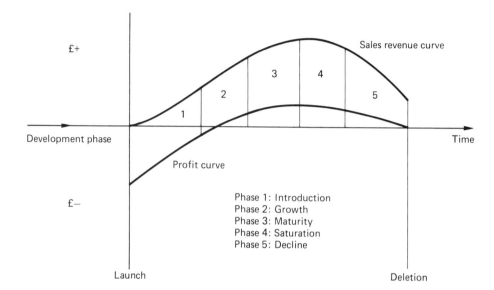

technological change, market acceptance, and ease of competitive entry will collectively determine the lifespan of the product. However, it may be possible to extend the lifespan by either modifying the product, changing its image to appeal to new market segments, or finding new uses for it. Generally it will be necessary to adapt the marketing effort in each phase, and the ideal situation is one in which new products are introduced at such a rate that optimum profits can be maintained by some products reaching maturity at the time that others are beginning to decline, and so on.

In Figure 16.19 the product in question is deleted at the time when it ceases to be profitable, even though it is still selling. But any deletion decision should be preceded by serious consideration of the areas in which it may be possible to improve the product's performance. In particular, areas to consider are selling methods, channels, the advertising message, promotions, the brand image, the pack, the quality and design of the product, and the adequacy of the service offered.

Under no circumstances should a declining product be allowed to continue in decline without evaluation because it may be consuming resources that could more fruitfully be employed elsewhere. A declining product will tend to take up a disproportionate amount of management time; may require frequent price adjustments; will involve short – hence expensive – production runs; and may damage the company's image. Pareto's law will often apply in that 80 per cent of sales will come from 20 per cent of products and the weakest 20 per cent of products may absorb 80 per cent of management's attention.

Reviewing the product line should not be a rare action but should rather be undertaken in a regular and planned manner. For example, all products could be reviewed every three months and any that are less profitable than, say, the average for the range should be the subject of revised plans to improve their performance.

## 4  SRD Example

Heskett (1976, pp. 410–18) gives the example of a marketing proposal from the Safety Razor Division of the Gillette Company for a line of blank audio cassettes. The market penetration of the SRD's razors and blades was such that no further increase was likely, thus growth would have to come via diversification. Estimates of the size and rate of growth of the market for blank audio cassettes made it particularly attractive.

In the USA the most popular tape was the 60-minute one, available as follows:

| *Type* | *Price* |
|---|---|
| Budget quality | $1.00 |
| Standard quality | $1.75–$2.00 |
| Professional quality | $2.98 |

Competition was fierce and price-oriented: some 50 per cent (by value) of tape sales were of budget quality, typically unbranded, with well-known companies supplying standard and professional quality tapes under such brand names as Sony, 3M, Memorex.

If SRD used 10 per cent of its existing sales force's effort to sell cassettes via existing outlets with the 50 per cent discount off retail price that was customary for cassettes, and if an advertising budget for Year 1 was set at $2 million (and $1.2 million per annum thereafter), and if unit costs were as follows:

| | |
|---|---|
| Cassette case (bought out) | $0.159 |
| Standard quality tape (60 minutes) | $0.214 |
| Professional quality tape (60 minutes) | $0.322 |
| Assembly labour | $0.200 |

and if the fixed annual costs of an assembly plant with capacity to handle 1 million cassettes per month were $500,000, there is the basis for an economic appraisal of alternative marketing programmes.

**FIGURE 16.20**
*Economic appraisal of marketing strategy-standard quality at budget prices*

| Item | Computation | |
|---|---|---|
| Price to final consumer | $1.30 per tape | |
| Price to retailer or wholesaler (50 per cent of list price) | $0.650 | |
| Variable costs per tape: | | |
| cassette case | $0.159 | |
| standard quality tape | $0.214 | |
| assembly labour | $0.200 | |
| Total | | $0.573 |
| Contribution | | $0.077 |
| Fixed costs per annum: | | |
| assembly plant | $500,000 | |
| sales force costs (10%) | $550,000 | |
| advertising | $2,000,000 | |
| Total | | $3,050,000 |
| Break-even sales volume: | | $3,050,000 |
| | $0.077 | |
| | = 39,600,000 tapes | |
| 39,600,000 × $1.30 | = $51.5 million retail value | |

SOURCE: Adapted from Heskett (1976)

Figure 16.20 shows an outline programme offering standard quality cassettes at a price that is a little higher than that applicable to budget cassettes. The break-even volume is almost 40 million units per annum, which is greatly in excess of the capacity of the assembly plant. It also represents 85 per cent of the total retail market of budget-priced cassettes (totalling $65 million). On grounds of feasibility this does not appear to be a viable proposition.

Alternative marketing programmes to allow SRD to enter the cassette market might entail:

- raising list price (with or without an increase in quality);
- reducing trade margins;
- using a small sales team and only selling via wholesalers;
- reducing the proposed advertising budget;
- investing in manufacturing facilities (rather than just assembly).

These alternatives might be considered individually (on a *ceteris paribus* basis) or interactively (on a *mutatis mutandis* basis) and there would be knock-on effects for other elements of the marketing mix also.

Significant effort would need to be applied (via market research) to define the market, its segments, growth rates, etc., in order to determine the viability of alternative marketing programmes. Relevant factors would include:

- the quality of forecasts;
- the rate at which market conditions favourable to entry might change;
- alternatives to blank cassette tapes as vehicles for SRD's growth;
- assumed buyer behaviour patterns within the cassette market;
- assumptions about other elements of the marketing mix.

Three alternative marketing programmes have been developed by SRD. The steps through which they were developed are shown in Figure 16.21 and the evaluated alternatives are shown in Figure 16.22. These alternatives are the marketing of budget cassettes, the marketing of standard cassettes at a low price, and the marketing of professional cassettes. Only the last two would use the Gillette brand name, although all three would have to generate an equivalent profit to Gillette's overall level (at 20 per cent of sales revenue). It is clear from Figure 16.22 that alternative 3 is non-viable and that alternative 1, while viable, is more challenging than alternative 2.

## 16.4  INVESTMENT APPRAISAL

Any investment involves the outlay of resources at one point in time in anticipation of receiving a larger return at some time in the future. This return must repay the original outlay as well as providing a minimum annual rate of return (or interest) on that outlay. If an individual invests £100 in a building society he will expect to receive that £100 back at some future time along with compound interest. This is a typical investment situation.

The aim will usually be to secure the maximum net cash flow (after tax) from the investment, and this will be achieved only from investments having the highest rate of return of those available. (This rate will be that on the *outstanding* as opposed to the initial balance over the life of the investment – as determined by the discounting methods of appraisal outlined later in this section.)

Characteristically, an investment decision involves a largely irreversible commitment of resources that is generally subject to a significant degree of risk. Such decisions have far-reaching effects on an enterprise's profitability and flexibility over the long term, thus requiring that they be part of a carefully developed strategy that is based on reliable forecasting procedures.

**FIGURE 16.21**
*A conceptual scheme for the economic appraisal of a marketing programme*

SOURCE: Heskett (1976), p. 415

Typical examples of investment projects are:

1 expansion projects;
2 replacement projects;
3 buy or lease decisions.

Projects for analysis and appraisal do not just appear – a continuing stream of good investment opportunities results from hard thinking, careful planning, and often from large outlays on R & D. Replacement decisions are ordinarily the simplest to make as the enterprise will have a very good idea of the cost savings to be obtained by replacing an old asset along with the consequences of non-replacement. (A central problem is that of accurately predicting the revenues and costs associated with particular projects for many years into the future.)

Over-investment in capital assets will result in heavy fixed costs, whereas under-investment may mean:

1 an enterprise's assets are not sufficiently modern to enable it to operate competitively; or
2 it has inadequate capacity to maintain its share of a growing market.

Investment is one of the main sources of economic growth since it is required not only to increase the total capital stock but also to employ labour in increasingly productive jobs as old plant is replaced by new. The application of reliable means of appraising investment proposals brings out more systematically and reliably the advantages of investing where it will increase efficiency and thus help to secure faster growth.

Various criticisms have been put forward in relation to the methods of appraisal that many companies employ. Among the most important are:

1 although most companies only make investment decisions after careful consideration of the likely costs and benefits as they see them, these decisions

**FIGURE 16.22**
*An economic
analysis of three
alternative
strategies for
designing and
marketing SRD
cassettes*

| | Alternative 1 | Alternative 2 | Alternative 3 |
|---|---|---|---|
| Determination of Product characteristics | Budget cassette, sold under a name other than Gillette | Standard cassette, sold under Gillette name | Professional cassette, sold under Gillette name |
| Elements of marketing program | | | |
| Price (list) to ultimate buyer | $1.20/cassette | $1.50/cassette | $2.50/cassette |
| Channels | Current Gillette retail outlets, wholesalers; total margin = 25% | Current Gillette retail outlets, wholesalers; total margin = 30% | Audio shops, wholesalers; total margin = 60% |
| Promotion | Advertising = $2.0 million per year; personal selling = $.5 million per year | Advertising = $2.0 million per year; personal selling = $.5 million per year | Advertising = $1.0 million per year; personal selling =$.2 million per year |
| Relevant target market | Teenagers for pop music; 50% of total dollar value | Young adults, business people for dictation, letter writing; 40% of total dollar value | Serious audiophiles for convenient high-fidelity recording of music; 10% of total dollar value |
| Calculation of | | | |
| Price to ultimate buyer | $1.20/cassette | $1.50/cassette | $2.50/cassette |
| Price to SRD | $ .90 | $1.05 | $1.00 |
| Variable costs and profit per tape | | | |
| Unloaded cassette | $ .159 | $ .159 | $ .159 |
| Tape of each quality | .214 | .214 | .322 |
| Assembly | .200 | .200 | .200 |
| Profit (20% of sales) | .180 | .210 | .200 |
| Total | $ .753 | $ .783 | $ .881 |
| Contribution to fixed costs | $ .147/cassette | $ .267/cassette | $ .119/cassette |
| Fixed costs for | | | |
| Assembly plant (per year) | $  500,000 | $  500,000 | $  500,000 |
| Sales force salaries | 500,000 | 500,000 | 200,000 |
| Advertising | 2,000,000 | 2,000,000 | 1,000,000 |
| Total | $3,000,000 | $3,000,000 | $1,700,000 |
| Target sales level(units) | $3,000,000/.147 = 20,408,163 | $3,000,000/.267 = 11,235,955 | $1,700,000/.119 = 14,300,000 |
| Value to ultimate customers of target sales level | $24,489,795 | $16,853,932 | $35,800,000 |
| Estimated 1970 target market size ($ and % of $130 million) | $38,000,000 (50%) | $32,000,000 (40%) | $13,000,000 (10%) |
| Appraisal of | | | |
| Likelihood of success (share of target market), including potential for competitive response, channel, and market acceptance of strategy | 38% share of target market required to break even | 32% share of target market required to break even | 275% share of target market required to break even |
| Potential risk | High fixed investment | High fixed investment | Moderate fixed investment |
| Potential return on investment of capacity operations | Would require expanded investment in manufacturing facilities | Would require expanded investment in manufacturing facilities | Would require expanded investment in manufacturing facilities |

No go

SOURCE: Adapted from Heskett (1976), pp. 416–17

are often reached in ways that are unlikely to produce the pattern or level of investment that is most favourable to economic growth – or even most profitable to the company;

2  many companies apply criteria for assessing investment projects that have little relevance to the measurement of the expected *rate of return on investment* (ROI) by which subsequent performance will be gauged;

3  even when a calculation of the anticipated ROI of each project is made, the methods used vary widely and are sometimes so arbitrary as to give almost meaningless results – for instance, a failure to assess returns *after* tax is a frequent weakness of many widely used methods since alternative opportunities can only be effectively compared and appraised on an after-tax basis.

This faulty use of (or use of faulty) means of investment appraisal may result in over-cautious investment decisions in which too high a rate of return is demanded before a proposal is accepted. This will cause delay in economic growth. Alternatively, faulty methods may mean that investment decisions are made that result in the selection of projects that yield an unduly low return. This causes a waste of scarce capital resources which is also unfavourable to economic growth.

From an information flow point of view the use of inadequate means of investment appraisal results in a damaging restriction in the flow of information to top management since these methods are incapable of fully exploiting relevant data. Because a company's future is inextricably linked to its investments, poor methods that give poor information that leads to poor decisions are likely to result in many mistakes.

Realistic investment appraisal requires the financial evaluation of many factors, such as the choice of size, type, location, and timing of investments, giving due consideration to the effects of taxation and alternative forms of financing the outlays. This shows that project decisions are difficult on account of their complexity and their strategic significance.

No matter which technique is adopted for investment appraisal the same steps will need to be followed. These steps are:

1  determine the profitability of each proposal;
2  rank the proposals in accordance with their profitability;
3  determine the cut-off rate (e.g. minimum acceptable rate of return);
4  determine which projects are acceptable and which unacceptable in relation to the cut-off rate; and
5  select the most profitable proposals in accordance with the constraints of the company's available funds.

## Cash flows

In considering investment decisions it does not matter whether outlays are termed 'capital' or 'operating', nor whether inflows are termed 'revenue', 'tax allowance', or whatever. All outlays and inflows must be taken into account in cash flow terms.

*Cash flow* in this context is not the same as the cash flow through a bank account nor is it identical to accounting profit since changes in the latter can occur without any change taking place in the cash flow.

For purposes of investment appraisal the cash flow is the incremental cash receipts less the incremental cash expenditures solely attributable to the investment in question.

The future costs and revenues associated with each investment alternative are:

1  *Capital costs.* These cover the long-term capital outlays necessary to finance a project, and working capital. (Since residual working capital is recoverable at the termination of a project's life, this leads to the investment having a terminal value that should be taken into account.) Typically, additional working capital will be required to cover a higher inventory, or a larger number of debtors, and

to be worthwhile the project must earn a return on this capital as well as on the long-term capital.

2 *Operating costs.*

3 *Revenue.*

4 *Depreciation.* In the case of the discounting methods of appraisal (discussed below) the recovery of capital (i.e. depreciation) is automatically allowed for from the net cash flow so depreciation need not be included as an accounting provision. This has the important advantage that the discounted profitability assessment is not affected by the pattern of accounting depreciation chosen.

5 *Residual value.* As with working capital, the residual assets of the project may have a value (as either scrap or in an alternative use or location). This residual value (net of handling costs and tax allowances or charges) should be included within the net cash flow.

An investment decision implies the choice of an objective, a technique of appraisal, and a length of service – the project's life. The objective and technique must be related to a definite period of time. In a static world that period would quite naturally be taken as being equal to the commercial life of the plan that is the purpose of the investment, which may be known with a good deal of certainty on the basis of past experience. However, in a dynamic world the life of the project may be determined by:

1 technological obsolescence; or
2 physical deterioration; or
3 a decline in demand for the output of the project – such as a change in taste away from the market offering.

No matter how good a company's maintenance policy, its technological forecasting ability, or its demand forecasting ability, uncertainty will always be present because of the difficulty of predicting the length of a project's life.

## Time Value of Money

To permit realistic appraisal the value of a cash payment or receipt must be related to the time when the transfer takes place. In particular it must be recognized that £1 received today is worth more than £1 receivable at some future date because £1 received today could be earning interest in the intervening period. This is the concept of the *time value of money.*

To illustrate this, if £100 was invested today at 5 per cent per annum compound interest it would accumulate to £105 at the end of one year (i.e. £100 × 1.05), to £110.25 at the end of two years (i.e. £100 × 1.05 × 1.05, or £105 × 1.05), and so on. In other words, £110.25 receivable in two years' time is only worth £100 today if 5 per cent per annum can be earned in the meantime (i.e. £110.25/(1.05 × 1.05) = £100).

The process of converting future sums into their present equivalents is known as *discounting*, which is simply the opposite of *compounding* (see Figure 16.23). Compounding is used to determine the *future value of present* cash flows.

**FIGURE 16.23**
*Discounting and compounding*

Another example will clarify this further. An investor who can normally obtain 8 per cent on his investments is considering whether or not to invest in a project that gives rise to £388 at the end of each of the next three years. The present value of these sums is:

$$\frac{£388}{1.08} + \frac{£388}{1.08 \times 1.08} + \frac{£388}{1.08 \times 1.08 \times 1.08} = £1,000$$

If the investment's capital cost is less than the present value of its returns (say £800) then it should be accepted since the present value of the return on this outlay is a larger amount (i.e. £1,000 − £800 = £200 gain from the investment). The gain is the *net present value* of the investment.

The interest rate does not always relate to an outlay of cash as the concept of interest applies equally to the use of internal funds. The reason why interest must be considered on *all* funds in use, regardless of their source, is that the selection of one alternative necessarily commits funds that could otherwise be invested in some other alternative. The measure of interest in such cases is the return foregone by rejecting the alternative use (i.e. the opportunity cost).

## Financial Evaluation

The techniques of evaluation fall into two categories, as shown below.

### Traditional Methods of Evaluation

*The payback period* is the most widely used technique and can be defined as the number of years required to recover the initial investment. By definition, the payback period ignores income beyond this period and it can thus be seen to be more a measure of liquidity than of profitability. In addition, it fails to take account of the time value of money, and these limitations make it seriously defective in the aim of reflecting the relative financial attractiveness of projects.

Projects with long payback periods are characteristically those involved in strategic planning and which determine an enterprise's future. However, they may not yield their highest returns for a number of years and the result is that the payback method is biased against the very investments that are most important to long-term success.

*The accounting rate of return* is defined as the average profit from the project (after allowing for accounting depreciation but before tax) as a percentage of the average required investment.

This method is superior to the payback period but is fundamentally unsound. While it does take account of the earnings over the entire economic life of a project, it fails to take account of the time value of money. This weakness is made worse by the failure to specify adequately the relative attractiveness of alternative proposals. It is biased against short-term projects in the same way that payback is biased against longer-term ones.

These traditional methods of investment appraisal are misleading to a dangerous extent. A means of measuring *cash* against *cash* that allows for the importance of time is needed. This is provided by the discounting methods of appraisal, of which there are basically two, both of which meet the objections to the payback period and accounting rate of return methods.

### Discounting Methods of Evaluation

Both discounting methods relate the estimates of the initial cash outlays on the investment to the annual net after-tax cash flows generated by the investment. As a general rule, the net after-tax cash flows will be composed of profit less taxes (when paid), plus depreciation. Since discounting techniques automatically allow for the recoupment of the capital outlay (i.e. depreciation) in computing time-adjusted rates of return it follows that depreciation implicitly forms part of the discounting computation and so must be added back to profit.

The *internal rate of return* (IRR) (or discounted cash flow) method consists of finding that rate of discount that reduces the cash flows (both inflows and outflows) attributable to an investment project to zero – this being, in principle, the true rate of return. (In other words, this 'true' rate is that which exactly equalizes the discounted net cash proceeds over a project's life with the initial investment outlay.)

If the IRR exceeds the minimum required rate (or *cost of capital*) then the project is *prima facie* acceptable.

Instead of being computed on the basis of the average investment the IRR is based on the funds in use from period to period.

The actual calculation of the rate is a hit-and-miss exercise because the rate is unknown at the outset, but tables of present values are available to aid the analyst. These tables show the present value of future sums at various rates of discount, and are prepared for both single sums and recurring annual payments.

The *net present value* (NPV) method discounts the net cash flows from the investment by the minimum required rate of return, and deducts the initial investment to give the yield from the funds invested. If this yield is positive then the project is *prima facie* worthwhile, but if it is negative the project is unable to pay for itself and is thus unacceptable. An index can be developed for comparative purposes by relating the yield to the investment to give the yield per £1 invested. This is the *present value index* and facilitates the ranking of competing proposals in order of acceptability. (It is not important in their evaluation in terms of profitability that competing proposals require widely different outlays since the index reduces alternatives to a common base.)

## Comparison of Discounting Methods

In ordinary circumstances the two discounting approaches will result in identical investment decisions. However, there are differences between them that can result in conflicting answers in terms of ranking projects according to their profitability.

In formal accept/reject decisions both methods lead to the same decision since all projects having a yield in excess of the minimum required rate will also have a positive net present value. Figure 16.24 shows that this is so.

*Example*: Projects A and B both require an outlay of £1,000 now to obtain a return of £1,150 at the end of Year 1 in the case of A, and £1,405 at the end of Year 3 in the case of B. The minimum required rate of return is 8 per cent.

**FIGURE 16.24**
*Ranking comparisons, 1*

| | | |
|---|---|---|
| Internal rate of return: | A | = 15% |
| | B | = 12% |
| Net present value | A | = (1,150 × 0.926) − 1,000 = £65 |
| | B | = (1,405 × 0.794) − 1,000 = £115 |

Note: 0.926 is the factor that reduces a sum receivable one year hence, at a discount rate of 8 per cent, to its present value; and 0.794 is the discount factor that reduces a sum due three years hence to its present value. These discount factors are derived easily from published tables.

Both projects have rates of return in excess of 8 per cent *and* positive net present values; but on the basis of the IRR method Project A is superior, while on the basis of the NPV method Project B is superior.

Confusion arises because the projects have different lengths of life and if only one of the projects is to be undertaken (i.e. they are mutually exclusive) the IRR can be seen to be unable to discriminate satisfactorily between them. As with any rate of return there is no indication of either the *amount* of capital involved or the *duration* of the investment. The choice must be made either on the basis of net present values or on the return on the *incremental investment* between projects. (In the above example, of course, the same amount of investment is required for each, thus Project B is to be preferred on the strength of its higher net present value.)

The two methods make different implicit assumptions about the reinvesting of funds received from projects – particularly during the 'gaps' between the end of one and the end of another.

Considering the example further, if it is explicitly assumed that the funds

**FIGURE 16.25**
*Ranking comparisons, 2*

| | | | |
|---|---|---|---|
| IRR | A | = (15 + 10 + 10) ÷ 3 | = 11.667% |
| | B | (as Fig. 16.24) | = 12% |
| NPV | A | = [(150 × 0.926) + (115 × 0.857) + (1126 × 0.794)] − 1,000 = | £32 |
| | B | (as Fig. 16.24) | = £115 |
| Terminal value: | A | = (1,150 × 110% × 110%) | = £1,391 |
| | B | (as given) | = £1,405 |

received from Project A can be reinvested at 10 per cent per annum between the end of Years 1 and 3, the situation will be as shown in Figure 16.25.

All three formulations clearly show Project B to be superior, illustrating the importance of project characteristics when only one can be undertaken.

The NPV approach assumes that cash receipts can be reinvested at the company's minimum acceptable rate of return, thereby giving a bias in favour of long-lived projects.

In contrast, the IRR approach assumes that cash receipts are reinvested at the same rate (i.e. a constant renewal of the project), giving a bias in favour of short-lived projects.

It follows that the comparison of alternatives by either method must be made over a common time-period with explicit assumptions being made about what happens to funds between their receipt and the common terminal date.

## Aspects of Application

### Alternative Proposals

The selection of a particular proposal should follow a careful appraisal of both alternative uses for funds and alternative means of performing a particular project. For instance, a company may wish to double the capacity of its production line and determine three means of accomplishing this, namely:

- introduce double-shift working;
- install a second production line;
- scrap the existing production line and build a new line with double the initial capacity.

The choice of a particular alternative will depend on how it accords with the enterprise's established investment objectives, and the choice of projects will depend on both corporate objectives and the availability of funds. But the fact remains that if the most advantageous alternative has been overlooked no amount of technical evaluation and appraisal can overcome this basic omission.

### Capital Rationing

In terms of financing investment projects three essential questions must be asked:

- What funds are needed for capital expenditure in the forthcoming planning period?
- What funds are available for investment?
- How are funds to be assigned when the acceptable proposals require more than are available?

The first and third questions are resolved by reference to the discounted return on the various proposals since it will be known which are acceptable and in which order of preference.

The second question is answered by a reference to the *capital budget*. The level of this budget will tend to depend on the quality of the investment proposals submitted to top management. In addition, it will also tend to depend on:

- top management's philosophy towards capital spending (e.g. is it growth-minded or cautious?);
- the outlook for future investment opportunities that may be unavailable if extensive current commitments are undertaken;
- the funds provided by current operations;
- the feasibility of acquiring additional capital through borrowing or share issues.

It is not always necessary, of course, to limit the spending on projects to internally-generated funds. Theoretically, projects should be undertaken to the point where the return is just equal to the cost of financing these projects.

If safety and the maintaining of, say, family control are considered to be more important than additional profits, there may be a marked unwillingness to engage in external financing, and hence a limit will be placed on the amounts available for investment.

Even though the enterprise may wish to raise external finance for its investment programme there are many reasons why it may be unable to do this, for example:

- the enterprise's past record and its present capital structure may make it impossible, or extremely costly, to raise additional debt capital;
- its record may make it impossible to raise new equity capital because of low yields – or even no yield;
- covenants in existing loan agreements may restrict future borrowing.

Furthermore, in the typical company, one would expect capital rationing to be largely self-imposed.

### Post-audit

Each major project should be followed up to ensure that it conforms to the conditions on which it was accepted, as well as being subject to cost control procedures.

## An Example

The following example illustrates the importance of accurate forecasts of cash flows (representing sales value, cost of sales, operating costs, and initial

**FIGURE 16.26**
*Cash flow projections*

| Proposal | Add a new line of toys. |
|---|---|
| Cash investment (£'000s) | |
| Production equipment | 1,000 |
| Recruiting and training salesmen | 100 |
| Promotional material | 10 |
| Inventory and debtors | 190 |
| | 1,300 |
| Projected sales volume (£'000s) | |
| Year 1 | 600 |
| Year 2 | 1,000 |
| Year 3 | 1,200 |
| Year 4 | 1,000 |
| Year 5 (final year) | 800 |
| Cost of sales | 30% of sales value |
| Direct operating costs | £100,000 per annum |
| Depreciation of equipment | £200,000 per annum. No salvage value. |

SOURCE: Adapted from Winer (1966)

investment). Taxation is deliberately ignored. (The example is adapted from Winer (1966).)

A proposal has been put forward in the form of a marketing plan to launch a new line of toys. Cash flow forecasts are shown in Figure 16.26. Note that depreciation is not, in fact, a cash cost. It is shown here simply as a footnote to indicate that there will be no cash inflow at the end of Year 5 from the sale of the equipment since that equipment is not expected to have any residual value at that point in time.

**FIGURE 16.27**
*Cash flow analysis
and evaluation*

| (£'000s) | Year | | | | | |
|---|---|---|---|---|---|---|
| | 0 | 1 | 2 | 3 | 4 | 5 |
| 1 Cash investment | (1,300) | | | | | |
| 2 Sales revenue | | 600 | 1,000 | 1,200 | 1,000 | 800 |
| 3 Cost of sales | | (180) | (300) | (360) | (300) | (240) |
| 4 Operating costs | | (100) | (100) | (100) | (100) | (100) |
| 5 Recovery of investment in inventory and debtors | | | | | | 190 |
| 6 Cash flows | (1,300) | 320 | 600 | 740 | 600 | 650 |
| 7 Discount factor at 18% | 1.00 | 0.847 | 0.718 | 0.609 | 0.516 | 0.437 |
| 8 Discounted cash flow | (1,300) | 271 | 431 | 451 | 310 | 284 |
| 9 NPV | 447 | | | | | |

SOURCE: Adapted from Winer (1966)

The evaluation of the plan is shown in Figure 16.27 which is largely self-explanatory. Cost of capital is shown as being 18 per cent. This can be taken to be the minimum required rate of return from the plan (thus reflecting equivalent returns from alternative plans of comparable risk). The plan's net present value is £447,000 which results when the discounted inflows and outflows are summed and the initial investment deducted from the total:

| | |
|---|---|
| Total discounted value of inflows and outflows from Year 1 to Year 5 | £1,747,000 |
| Initial investment | £1,300,000 |
| Net present value | £ 447,000 |

From these figures it is also possible to calculate the PV index:

$$\frac{£1,747,000}{£1,300,000} = 1.34$$

In other words, the plan promises to generate £1.34 for every £1.00 invested in it, expressed in terms of current £s. Since the PV index exceeds unity, hence the NPV is positive, the plan appears to be economically viable. However, various additional questions need to be raised, such as:

- Is there sufficient funding available to meet the initial investment requirements of £1,300,000?
- Can the plan be modified to earn even more than £1.34 per £1.00 of investment?
- Are there alternatives available that may be more attractive?
- How sensitive is the plan's NPV to changes in flow estimates, including their timing?

From the data given in Figure 16.27 it is possible to calculate the payback period of the plan and the accounting rate of return, as follows:

Payback period is the length of time it takes to recover the initial investment.

|  |  | £'000s |
|---|---|---|
|  | Year 1 | 320 |
|  | Year 2 | 600 |
| 380/740 | Year 3 | 380 |
|  |  | 1,300 |

It will be 2 years and 187 days (assuming an even pattern of inflows). The investment is exposed, therefore, over half of the anticipated life of the plan.

The accounting rate of return is an accounting (rather than cash flow) measure of the average profitability of the plan.

- Average profits will be (in £'000s):

$$\frac{£(320 + 600 + 740 + 600 + 460)}{5} - £200$$

$$\frac{£2,720}{5} - £200 = £344$$

It is necessary to deduct depreciation as an expense in calculating the average accounting profit.

- Average investment will be (in £'000s)

$$\frac{£1,300 - £190}{2} = £555$$

- The ARR will be:

$$\frac{£344}{£555} \times 100 = 62\%$$

## Valuing Market Strategies

Mention was made in Chapter 15 of the criterion of enhanced shareholder value. This has been adopted by Day & Fahey (1988) in their approach to strategy evaluation. Since the basic premise of this approach is that shareholders' interests should be maximized it will be apparent that it is a partial approach that ignores other stakeholders' interests. Moreover, since maximizing the current market value of shareholders' interests presumes that the shares themselves are listed, this restricts Day & Fahey's approach to a little over 2200 of the total of more than one million limited companies incorporated within the UK.

Value is created whenever the financial gains from a strategy exceed its costs. The use of discounting methods allows for both the timing of cash flows and the inherent riskiness of marketing strategies in measuring the value of the latter. A potential shareholder will only invest in an enterprise if it is his expectation that the management of that enterprise will generate a better return than he could obtain himself, at a given level of risk. The minimum expected return is the cost of capital (i.e that rate used in discounting), hence shareholder value is only created when activities are undertaken that generate a return in excess of the cost of capital.

The usual approach adopted in assessing the shareholder value of an enterprise is to discount the anticipated cash flows by the risk-adjusted cost of capital. If a new strategy is in prospect then the shareholder value will be the sum of the value to be derived from the new strategy plus the 'baseline' value reflecting the value that is expected to result from continuing the existing strategy. This gives a basis for comparing strategic alternatives in a way that highlights their respective contributions to value. Thus:

| Estimated shareholder value if strategy X is selected | = | Estimated value contributed by strategy X | + | Baseline shareholder value |
|---|---|---|---|---|
| ∴ Estimated value of strategy X | = | Estimated shareholder value if strategy X is selected | − | Baseline shareholder value |

When several competing strategies are being evaluated in a situation where there are insufficient resources to undertake all available strategies that meet the specified economic criterion (e.g. offer a positive net present value when discounted at the risk-adjusted cost of capital), the recommended basis for ranking acceptable strategies is by use of the PV index. This shows how much value is created per £1 of investment.

$$\text{PV index} = \frac{\text{Present value of strategy}}{\text{Investment required}}$$

In using this approach to evaluating strategies there needs to be available:

1 cash inflow and outflow forecasts relating to each alternative strategy:
2 cash flow forecasts relating to the baseline strategy;
3 a suitable discount factor (i.e. the risk-adjusted cost of capital);
4 alternative scenarios to allow the sensitivity of the outcomes to changes in the inputs to be tested.

Even if all these information requirements can be met there is inevitably a large element of subjectivity involved: in part this will be included within the estimates of cash flows, etc., and in part it will reflect both the specification of the strategy and the interpretation of results from the analysis. It is suggested that all assumptions involving judgments be specified explicitly in order that their appropriateness can be gauged by others.

The steps to follow in carrying out a strategic evaluation to enhance shareholder value are:

1 derive cash flow forecasts from the managerial judgments relating to competitive and market responses to each strategic alternative;
2 adjust the forecasts from 1 for risk and timing prior to calculating the NPV of each strategy and relating these NPVs to baseline expectations in order to gauge the increase in shareholder value from each alternative;
3 select the strategy that offers the greatest increase in shareholder value and implement it.

It is implicit in this sequence of steps that:

• the value creation potential of each strategic alternative relative to the baseline strategy can be accurately predicted;

- the shareholder value criterion is applicable to all strategic alternatives having cash flow implications;
- the stock market will recognize and reward strategies that enhance shareholder value.

Each of these matters raises fundamental questions. For example, our ability to predict accurately is limited for reasons of uncertainty as well as personal bias, and the stock market is not a perfect market (and so does not have perfect information on which to base its reactions). Nevertheless, by focusing on cash flows rather than accounting data, and by taking a long-term perspective rather than a short-term one, the approach advocated by Day & Fahey has distinct benefits as well as limitations.

Support for variations on this 'economic value' approach has come from a range of sources. Buzzell and Chussil (1985), for example, have argued that it is rare for managers to evaluate strategies in terms of their effects on future value. This suggests that many enterprises are failing to achieve their full potential by using inappropriate methods for strategic evaluation, and by emphasizing short-run financial results at the expense of long-term competitive strength.

## 16.5 ALLOWING FOR RISK AND UNCERTAINTY

In dealing with risk and uncertainty we will draw heavily from management science. Management science is a method or approach to management problem solving rather than a discipline within its own right. The various techniques of management science offer managers an analytical, objective, and (usually) quantitative basis for making better decisions.

Opinions differ as to whether operations research (OR) is synonymous with management science or merely a part of it. For our present purposes the two can be considered to be synonymous. The Council of the Operations Research Society have defined OR (or management science) as 'the attack of modern science on complex problems arising in the direction and management of large systems of men, machines, materials and money in industry, business, government and defence'.

The problems with which management science is concerned are those that involve the effectiveness of the organization as a whole and the conflict of functional interests within the organization. Their satisfactory solution demands a highly refined balance of departmental and overall objectives, and can only be achieved through the application of scientific methodology. The relevant methodology is the systems approach emphasizing the fact that the effectiveness of each department depends on how it fits into the whole and the effectiveness of the whole depends on the way in which each department functions within it.

The basic requirement in decision making is information and a major branch of management science is concerned with the provision of information under conditions of risk and uncertainty. This is the role of *decision theory*.

Information should preferably be in quantitative form, and this presupposes some means of measurement. Furthermore, the information presented should relate to the objective of the decision – it is easier to make the correct decision when one keeps in mind what one is trying to achieve. If there exists more than one objective the decision maker must balance one against the other by making a *trade-off*. For example, the decision maker may trade speed for quality in deciding on a particular means of production if this appears to reflect accurately the relative importance of multiple objectives.

Decisions are made in relation to objectives and they are well made if the objectives are achieved. However, doubts about the future mean that a choice can be wrong, and it also means that a single choice has several possible outcomes. The sales of a new product, for instance, may be at any one of several levels estimated at the time of its launch. The systematic approach of decision theory allows good decisions to be made even in the presence of severe doubts about what the future may hold in store.

Views of the future are of four types:

1 *ignorance* – where the future is seen as a blank;
2 *assumed certainty* – which is a pretence, for all practical purposes, that the future is known exactly and estimates become deterministic;
3 *risk* – where it is not known exactly what will happen in the future but the various possibilities are weighed by their assumed probability of occurrence;
4 *uncertainty* – where a variety of outcomes is possible but probabilities cannot be assigned.

There is little that can be done in cases of ignorance, other than following a systematic approach and attempting to delay making the decision until further information has been gathered. In cases of certainty, of course, there is no such need for delay. This covers situations in which the decision maker has full knowledge.

In relation to decision making under conditions of risk and uncertainty the purpose of expressing an opinion about the likelihood of an event occurring is to facilitate the development of decision-making procedures that are explicit and consistent with the decision maker's beliefs.

## Allowing for Risk

Risk describes a situation in which there are a number of actions or strategies that may be taken, a number of conditions or events that may be experienced (known as *states of nature* because they are beyond the decision maker's control), and consequently a number of possible outcomes each of which will depend on a particular combination of strategy and state of nature.

In the risk situation *probability theory* is central in rational decision making. The probability of a particular outcome of an event is simply the proportion of times this outcome would occur if the event were repeated a great number of times. Thus the probability of the outcome 'heads' in tossing a coin is 0.5 since a large number of tosses would result in 50 per cent heads and 50 per cent tails.

By convention, probabilities follow certain rules, such as:

- the probability assigned to each possible future event must be a positive number between zero and unity, where zero represents an impossible event and unity represents a certain one;
- if a set of events is mutually exclusive (i.e. only one will come about) and exhaustive (i.e. covers all possible outcomes), then the total of the probabilities of the events must add to one.

The probability of an outcome is a measure of the certainty of that outcome. If, for instance, a sales manager is fairly confident that his division will be able to sell 10 000 units in the forthcoming period, he may accord a probability of 0.8 to this outcome (i.e. he is 80 per cent certain that 10 000 units will be sold). By simple deduction, there is a 20 per cent probability that the outcome will be something other than 10 000 units (i.e. 100 − 80 = 20 per cent).

A development of this approach gives rise to the concept of *expected value*. This results from the multiplying of each possible outcome of an event by the probability of that outcome occurring, and this gives a measure of the *pay-off* of each alternative. An example should make this clear: Company XYZ has two new marketable products but only sufficient resources to manufacture and market one of these. The relevant estimates of sales, costs, and profits are shown in Figure 16.28 for the various anticipated levels of sales activity.

**FIGURE 16.28**
*Decision
information*

| | Sales £ | Costs £ | Profit £ | Probability | Expected value £ |
|---|---|---|---|---|---|
| Product A | 1,000 | 500 | 500 | 0.1 | 50 |
| | 1,250 | 600 | 650 | 0.4 | 260 |
| | 1,500 | 700 | 800 | 0.3 | 240 |
| | 1,750 | 800 | 950 | 0.2 | 190 |
| | | | | 1.0 | £740 |
| Product B | 2,000 | 800 | 1,200 | 0.2 | 240 |
| | 2,300 | 950 | 1,350 | 0.4 | 540 |
| | 2,500 | 1,050 | 1,450 | 0.2 | 290 |
| | 2,700 | 1,150 | 1,550 | 0.1 | 155 |
| | 3,000 | 1,300 | 1,700 | 0.1 | 170 |
| | | | | 1.0 | £1,395 |

The calculations are very simple. If sales of product A amount to £1,000, the associated costs – as shown above – are £500, and thus the profit is also £500. But there is only a probability of 0.1 that this outcome will eventuate, giving an *expected value* of £50 (i.e. £500 × 0.1).

This procedure is followed for the other possible outcomes of Product A sales, costs, and profits, and the expected values of each outcome summated to give an expected pay-off of £740. (This is nothing more than a weighted arithmetic average of the data given in Figure 16.28.)

In contrast, Product B has an expected pay-off of £1,395 and this choice is, therefore, the better one of the two, provided that profit is the desired objective, as measured by the pay-off computation.

Apart from the externally given economic and physical conditions surrounding a decision (i.e. the 'states of nature'), the decision maker's own attitudes towards the alternatives must also be taken into account. His scale of values will determine the *desirability* of each possible course of action, whereas the conventional prediction systems merely assign probabilities. Desirability has connotations of 'best' that are unrelated to profit and may be measured in terms of utility, thus:

Expected utility  =  (Probability of success × value of success) –
(Probability of failure × value of failure)

As a result of his sense of values the decision maker will have a general attitude towards risk that may cause him to act as either a *risk acceptor* or a *risk averter*. In the latter case the decision maker will tend to request more and more information before he attempts to make a decision, and this will often mean that decisions are made too late to be optimal, whereas the risk acceptor makes rapid decisions that may not be the correct ones.

Risk attitudes are one of four essential elements to be ascertained in any decision, these being:

1 What are the available courses of action?
2 What are the relevant states of nature?
3 What are the possible outcomes?
4 What is important to the decision maker?

**Applying Risk Analysis**

The application of simple risk analysis is best illustrated by means of an example. Let it be assumed that RST Ltd has two new products, A and B, but only has the resources to launch one of these. The relevant states of nature relate to competitive activity: no matter which product is launched, it may be assumed that the competition will:

1 do nothing; or
2 introduce a comparable product; or
3 introduce a superior product.

On the basis of past experience and current knowledge the management of RST Ltd attach probabilities of 0.25, 0.5 and 0.25 respectively to these states of nature. In the light of these alternative conditions the profit of each strategy can be shown in a *pay-off matrix* (Figure 16.29).

**FIGURE 16.29**
*Pay-off matrix*

| | State of nature | | |
| Strategy | Do nothing | Introduce comparable product | Introduce superior product |
| --- | --- | --- | --- |
| Launch A | £40,000 | £30,000 | £20,000 |
| Launch B | £70,000 | £20,000 | £0 |

This matrix shows that if Product B is launched and a comparable competitive product is introduced a profit of £20,000 will be made, and so forth for the other five possible outcomes. The best decision would *appear* to be to introduce Product B and *hope* that competitive action does not change. But is this so?

By using the concept of expected value it is possible to calculate the expected profit (or pay-off) from each strategy by multiplying the probability of each outcome by the profit from that outcome. Thus, for strategy A (the introduction of Product A), the expected pay-off is given by:

$$(40,000 \times 0.25) + (30,000 \times 0.5) + (20,000 \times 0.25)$$

and is equal to £30,000.

Similarly, for strategy B the expected pay-off is:

$$(70,000 \times 0.25) + (20,000 \times 0.5) + (0 \times 0.25)$$

which equals £27,500.

This analysis clearly shows that strategy A is to be preferred as it has a larger expected profit or pay-off. It is vital, however, that the distinction between the *expected* pay-off and the *most probable* pay-off is understood and attention focused on the former rather than the latter. The most probable pay-off for strategy A is that with the competitive introduction of a comparable product, which has a probability of 0.5 and a profit estimated at £30,000. The most probable pay-off for strategy B has the same state of nature, and a profit estimate of £20,000. But the most probable outcome cannot be used as the basis for decision making because it ignores the other possible outcomes. It is thought to be 50 per cent certain that a comparable competitive product will be launched which means that it is also 50 per cent *uncertain* that this will occur and allowance for this eventuality should accordingly be made. The use of expected pay-off allows for this.

From the information contained in the above example a *decision tree* can be constructed as in Figure 16.30.

Strategies and states of nature are represented by the branches of the decision tree, and at each fork there are as many branches as there are identified possibilities. Only if all of the possible courses of action have been observed and included will the tree be complete. For each alternative combination of strategy

**FIGURE 16.30**
*Decision tree*

and state of nature the outcome can be computed, and the expected pay-off for each strategy derived.

A decision tree is a diagrammatic representation of the relationships between decisions, states of nature, and pay-offs (or outcomes) that helps in structuring problems in a way that allows risk to be assessed at each stage. Further examples will show how a decision tree can be used. Imagine a research project that is in progress with a view to developing a new product for commercial launch. There are several aspects to this issue.

1 the project may be aborted or it may be allowed to continue;
2 if it is continued it may or may not result in a potentially marketable new product;
3 if it does result in a marketable product the organization may choose to launch it immediately or to postpone the launch;
4 competitors may or may not be able to match the organization's endeavours.

Figure 16.31 spells out these aspects and specifies the two major decisions that need to be made. (The squares represent points at which decisions need to be

**FIGURE 16.31**
*A basic decision tree*

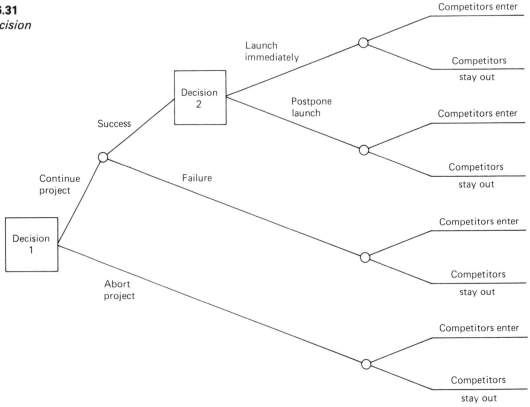

made, while the circles represent subsequent events.) It can be seen that each decision, combined with the states of nature that are assumed to prevail, produces distinct outcomes.

The next step is to introduce quantitative data, so let us assume the following:

1  it will cost an estimated £50,000 to continue the project (which is itself probabilistic);
2  if the company decides to postpone the launch of the product (assuming the project is successful) and competitors enter the market there will be a loss of current business amounting to £125,000;
3  if the project is successful and an immediate launch is undertaken, the company will generate incremental cash flows of £450,000 if competitors stay out of the market but only £250,000 if competitors enter the market.

These figures are shown at the end of each branch of the decision tree in Figure 16.32. We now need to incorporate the probabilities of the events leading to the various possible outcomes, and these are also shown in Figure 16.32. By working back from the right-hand side of the decision tree it is a simple matter to compute expected values. Taking the branch dealing with the immediate launch of a successful project as an example, the expected value is derived as follows:

$$£250,000 \times 0.7 = £175,000$$
$$£450,000 \times 0.3 = £135,000$$

Expected value     £310,000

The figures show that an immediate launch is the better alternative if the project is successful than is postponing it (which has an expected value of −£112,500). But this only gives part of the picture, so the expected values need to be worked through to the next event in the tree (moving across from right to left). The logic

**FIGURE 16.32**
*Decision tree with quantified outcomes*

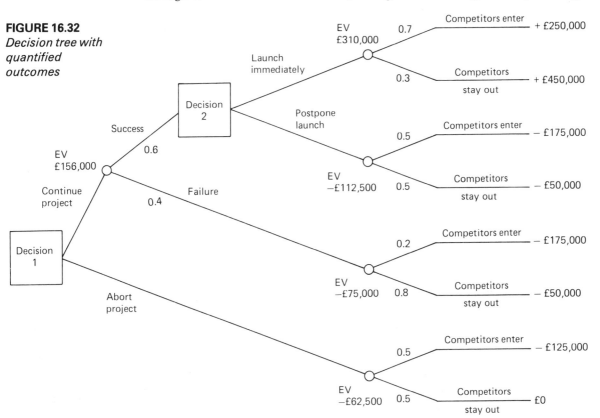

in doing this is straightforward: if the project is successful and the launch is immediate there will be a larger pay-off than if the launch is postponed, so the latter branch can now be ignored. This gives an expected value for continuing the project of £156,000 calculated thus:

£310,000 × 0.6 = £186,000
−£75,000 × 0.4 = −£30,000

Expected value    £156,000

A comparison of this pay-off with the expected value of aborting the project (−£62,500) shows the desirability of continuing with the project.

Risk analysis is applicable to most pricing decisions, such as the situation in which a company can adopt one of three pricing policies for a new product:

1 skimming pricing − $P_1$;
2 intermediate pricing − $P_2$;
3 penetration pricing − $P_3$;

and in which three estimates of demand are available:

1 optimistic forecast − $Q_1$;
2 most probable demand − $Q_2$;
3 pessimistic forecast − $Q_3$;

and in which two sizes of plant are available:

1 small plant − $F_1$;
2 large plant − $F_2$.

The various interrelationships of price, demand and capacity are illustrated in a decision tree format in Figure 16.33.

The pay-off is computed by taking the probability of each level of demand and multiplying it by the forecast level of demand, and then multiplying this by the price. Thus for a penetration pricing policy ($P_3$) with a small factory ($F_1$) and a pessimistic sales forecast ($Q_3$), the pay-off is given by multiplying the $P_3F_1$ price of £4 by 0.2, which is the probability of $Q_3$ occurring, and expressing this in terms of $Q_3$. If values of 50 000, 40 000 and 30 000 are ascribed to $Q_1$, $Q_2$, and $Q_3$, the pay-off column in Figure 16.33 becomes Figure 16.34.

Clearly strategy $P_1F_2$ has the highest expected pay-off because it has the highest price, but each expected pay-off must be related to objectives in order to select the most appropriate in a given situation.

There are several alternatives to the basic decision tree approach to allowing for risk which can be employed. It is not possible within the limits of this volume to cover them, but there is space to refer to *sensitivity analysis*. In its applied organizational setting this has been broadly defined by Rappaport (1967, p. 441) as:

> ... a study to determine the responsiveness of the conclusions of an analysis to changes or errors in parameter values used in the analysis.

Sensitivity analysis seeks to test the responsiveness of outcomes from decision models to different input values and constraints as a basis for appraising the relative risk of alternative courses of action. It is also possible to use sensitivity analysis for helping determine the value of information in addition to its role in strategic decision making.

In effect what sensitivity analysis allows management to do is to experiment in the abstract without the time, cost or risk associated with experimenting with the organization itself. This can be seen symbolically in the following expression:

**FIGURE 16.33**
*Pricing decision tree*

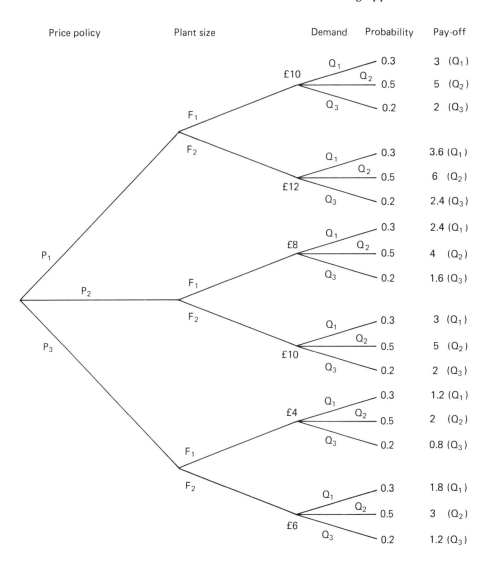

**FIGURE 16.34**
*Expected pay-offs*

| | | | | | |
|---|---|---|---|---|---|
| 3.0 × 50,000 | = | 150,000 | 3.0 × 50,000 | = | 150,000 |
| 5.0 × 40,000 | = | 200,000 | 5.0 × 40,000 | = | 200,000 |
| 2.0 × 30,000 | = | 60,000 | 2.0 × 30,000 | = | 60,000 |
| Expected pay-off $P_1F_1$ | | £410,000 | Expected pay-off $P_2F_2$ | | £410,000 |
| | | | | | |
| 3.6 × 50,000 | = | 180,000 | 1.2 × 50,000 | = | 60,000 |
| 6.0 × 40,000 | = | 240,000 | 2.0 × 40,000 | = | 80,000 |
| 2.4 × 30,000 | = | 72,000 | 0.8 × 30,000 | = | 24,000 |
| Expected pay-off $P_1F_2$ | | £492,000 | Expected pay-off $P_3F_1$ | | £164,000 |
| | | | | | |
| 2.4 × 50,000 | = | 120,000 | 1.8 × 50,000 | = | 90,000 |
| 4.0 × 40,000 | = | 160,000 | 3.0 × 40,000 | = | 120,000 |
| 1.6 × 30,000 | = | 48,000 | 1.2 × 30,000 | = | 36,000 |
| Expected pay-off $P_2F_1$ | | £328,000 | Expected pay-off $P_3F_2$ | | £246,000 |

$$V = f(X,Y)$$

where:

V = a measure of the value of the decision that is to be made;
X = the set of variables that can be directly regulated by the decision-maker (i.e. the decision variables);
Y = the set of factors (variable or constant) that affects outcomes but which is not subject to direct regulation by the decision maker (i.e. the states of nature);
f = the functional relationship amongst V, X and Y.

One can manipulate any element within X or Y and see the consequent impact on V.

Reference has been made in earlier chapters of this book to balancing the cost and value of information. The broad picture is given in Figure 16.35 from which

**FIGURE 16.35**
*Cost and value of information*

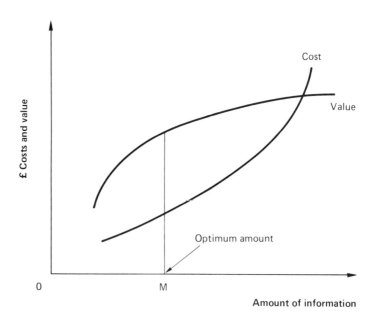

it will be seen that the optimum amount of information in a given situation (OM) is to be found when the difference between the value and cost curves is greatest. For a number of reasons (including overload) the value of information starts to decline as more is made available whereas the cost of providing information increases at an accelerating rate as more is made available (due to increasing accuracy, faster transmission, etc.).

In operational terms how can we assess the value of information? We can readily grasp the principle that by evaluating the consequences of a particular decision based on a given amount of information on the one hand, and then evaluating the consequences of the same decision made with additional information on the other, the difference (in consequences) reflects the value of the extra information. This value gives the maximum sum that should be spent on generating the extra information. To apply this principle requires that we:

1 enumerate the possible outcomes of future information collection efforts;
2 compute the probabilities of these outcomes;
3 indicate how the information will change the decision maker's view of this choice.

These are demanding requirements!

**Allowing for Uncertainty**

Uncertainty arises from a lack of previous experience and knowledge. This results in the decision maker's inability to assign probabilities to the elements within alternative strategies.

Inevitably decision making under conditions of uncertainty is more complicated than is the case under risk conditions. In fact, there is no single *best* criterion (such as expected pay-off) that should be used in selecting a strategy. Of the various available techniques company policy or the decision maker's attitude will determine that which is selected. Four possible criteria are given below.

### 1 Maximin – Criterion of Pessimism

The assumption underlying this technique is that the worst outcome will always come about and the decision maker should therefore select the largest minimum pay-off. Referring back to Figure 16.29, this would mean that strategy A should be adopted; the worst outcome for A is £20,000 and the worst for strategy B is £0 which means that strategy A maximizes the minimum – hence maximin. The philosophy is that the actual outcome can only be an improvement in the majority of instances – the probabilities accorded to strategy A suggest that there is a 75 per cent chance that a better result than £20,000 will be obtained and a 25 per cent chance of its being £20,000.

### 2 Maximax – Criterion of Optimism

This is the opposite of maximin and is based on the assumption that the best pay-off will result from the selected strategy. Referring again to Figure 16.29, the highest pay-offs are £40,000 and £70,000 for A and B respectively. Strategy B has the highest maximum pay-off and will be selected under the maximax criterion.

### 3 Criterion of Regret

This criterion is based on the fact that, having selected a strategy that does not turn out to be the best one, the decision maker will regret not having chosen another strategy when he had the opportunity.

Thus, if strategy B had been adopted (see Figure 16.36) on the maximax assumption that competition would do nothing, and competition actually did

**FIGURE 16.36**
*Regret matrix*

| Strategy | State of nature | | |
| --- | --- | --- | --- |
| | Do nothing | Introduce comparable product | Introduce superior product |
| Launch A | £30,000 | £0 | £0 |
| Launch B | £0 | £10,000 | £20,000 |

nothing, there would be no regret; but if strategy A had been selected the company would have lost £70,000 − £40,000 = £30,000. This measures the *regret* and the aim of the regret criterion is to minimize the maximum possible regret. A regret matrix (Figure 16.36) can be constructed on the above basis.

The maximum regret is, for strategy A, £30,000, and for strategy B £20,000. The choice is therefore B if the maximum regret is to be minimized.

### 4 Criterion of Rationality – Laplace Criterion

The assumption behind this criterion is that, since the probabilities of the various states of nature are not known, each state of nature is equally likely. The expected pay-off from each strategy is then calculated and the one with the largest expected pay-off selected.

For strategy A the expected pay-off under this criterion is:

$$(40,000 \times 0.33) + (30,000 \times 0.33) + (20,000 \times 0.33)$$

which equals £30,000; and for strategy B it is:

$$(70,000 \times 0.33) + (20,000 \times 0.33) + (0 \times 0.33)$$

which is also equal to £30,000.

By chance neither strategy in this example is preferable under this criterion, with the result that the choice must be made on another basis (e.g. in terms of desirability) or under another criterion (e.g. minimax).

Under conditions of risk or uncertainty the decision may appear to be to select one of the available courses of action or to accept none of them. However, another alternative is to postpone the decision and gather more information to aid in the selection process.

Perfect information is rarely available, so the decision maker must be satisfied with imperfect data which will reduce even if it does not eliminate his uncertainty. But there comes a point when it is unnecessary or pointless collecting further information, and at this point a decision must be made. An increasingly popular approach to determining this point is given by the Bayesian approach to statistical decision theory.

The theory of Bayesian inference is one that provides the basic rules whereby one set of probabilities can be mathematically (i.e. logically) determined from another. For example, the probability of heads in tossing a coin is 0.5, and Bayesian inference puts the probability of there being 10 heads in a row as $0.5^{10}$ (about 0.001). Bayesian inference is not restricted to accepting the input of observed data only: it will also accept the decision maker's subjective probabilities.

The most common form of Bayesian inference is prior-posterior analysis which involves the derivation of probabilities posterior to evidence by reweighing prior probabilities according to likelihoods indicated by this evidence. This procedure is an important one. However, since it is beyond the scope of this book to present a detailed exposition of Bayes' theorem the interested reader is referred to Day (1964).

In general the benefits of decision theory are that it requires the decision-making manager to make his uncertainties and other judgments explicit in such a way that they can be incorporated into a formal analysis that will lead to the best decisions being made. This process need not be time consuming, but it does prevent the hurried selection of the most obvious course of action and encourages creative thinking in seeking new solutions to problems.

This is the best way to determine the value of information prior to carrying out research. It differs from traditional statistical techniques by allowing the assignment of numerical probabilities to *unique* rather than to repetitive events, with probabilities being subjectively determined by the decision maker. For example, in relation to a new product launch, Bayesian analysis argues that the manager has some idea of how well it will do based on his experience with other products, and that these expectations can be translated into quantitative terms by assigning probabilities to the various sales levels that may be achieved. The key concept is the 'opportunity loss' which represents either:

1  the actual financial loss due to the new product failing to reach its break-even sales volume; or
2  the potential loss of profit from failing to introduce the product when sales would have been profitable.

In Figure 16.37 the probabilities of the expected sales levels are shown in columns (1) and (2), and the profit/loss consequences are shown in column (3) with the break-even point being 1 400 000. At a sales level of 1 800 000 a profit of £450,000 is expected, and the opportunity *loss of not* introducing the product (if

**FIGURE 16.37**
*Bayesian analysis for product launch*

| Unit sales (1) | Estimated probability (2) | Profit/ loss (3) | Opportunity loss Introduced (4) | Opportunity loss Not introduced (5) | Expected opportunity loss Introduced (6) | Expected opportunity loss Not introduced (7) |
|---|---|---|---|---|---|---|
| 1,800,000 | 0.10 | 450,000 | 0 | 450,000 | 0 | 45,000 |
| 1,600,000 | 0.25 | 200,000 | 0 | 200,000 | 0 | 50,000 |
| 1,400,000 | 0.35 | 0 | 0 | 0 | 0 | 0 |
| 1,200,000 | 0.15 | −150,000 | 150,000 | 0 | 22,500 | 0 |
| 1,000,000 | 0.10 | −250,000 | 250,000 | 0 | 25,000 | 0 |
| 800,000 | 0.05 | −400,000 | 400,000 | 0 | 20,000 | 0 |
| Totals | 1.00 | | | | £67,500 | £95,000 |

this level of sales could be achieved) is £450,000 (i.e. the profit of launching the product is foregone by not launching it). The *expected* opportunity loss is given by the product of the estimated probability and the opportunity loss. For a sales level of 1 800 000 the expected loss is (0.10 × £450,000) = £45,000. The same analysis can be applied to all the other possible sales levels as shown in columns (4) to (7). The sums of columns (6) and (7) show the overall expected opportunity loss of each course of action – introduce the product on the one hand, or do not introduce it on the other. Since the 'introduce' choice has the lowest expected opportunity loss it should be the chosen course of action, and £67,500 is the maximum value of research expenditure.

Although analytical methods can be applied to the evaluation of risk and uncertainty, management may prefer to take other courses of action to reduce risk and uncertainty. Perhaps the best method is to increase the information available to the decision maker prior to his making a decision. For instance, marketing research can supply further information prior to new product launches via product testing or test marketing.

Alternatively, the scale of operations may be increased, or product diversification pursued. Figure 16.38 illustrates the case of two products, with Product A having a seasonal demand pattern that is the opposite of the pattern of Product B. But in combination Figure 16.39 shows that the overall result is one of continuous profitability, whereas either product in isolation would result in a loss during part of its demand cycle.

**FIGURE 16.38**
*Diversified products*

**FIGURE 16.39**
*Combined
profitability*

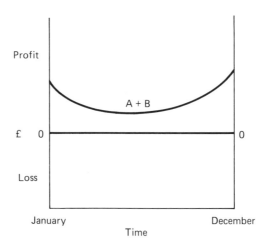

## 16.6 MATRIX MODELS

A number of analytical matrix models were discussed in Chapters 9 and 10 above. In this section we will focus on three available models: the directional policy matrix, the multifactor portfolio matrix, and the product positioning matrix.

**Directional
Policy Matrix**

This was developed to help in identifying:

1 the principal criteria by which a business unit's prospects may be assessed:
2 the criteria by which an enterprise's position in a particular market may be evaluated.

The criteria that emerge are useful in defining *business sector prospects* on the one hand, and the *enterprise's competitive capabilities* on the other. These can be used to label the axes of the matrix itself, as shown in Figure 9.7 (see p. 234).

There are nine cells in this matrix. On the x axis business sector prospects increase in attractiveness as one moves from left to right. The strength of the enterprise's competitive capabilities increases as one moves down the scale on the y axis. Locating an enterprise in any cell of the matrix implies different strategic actions, although the boundaries between cells are less precise than this might suggest: it is more helpful to consider zones rather than cells – even though the zones may be of irregular shapes. Strategies appropriate to the zones shown in Figure 9.7 are (after Cohen (1988), pp. 36–7):

- leader – allocate major resources to the product group;
- try harder – acceptable in the short run but may be vulnerable over the longer run;
- double or quit – major future sources of competitive advantage and profitability should be developed from this zone;
- growth – sufficient resources should be allocated to match market growth;
- custodial – maximize cash generation without any further commitment of resources;
- cash generator – a cash generator with little further need for finance or expansion;

- phased withdrawal – resources can be reallocated to better uses by withdrawing gradually;
- divest – withdraw immediately and redeploy resources elsewhere.

Among the criteria by which business sector prospects might be assessed are:

- market growth rate
  - market growth is needed if profits are to grow;
- market quality, reflected in such factors as
  - whether profitability is high and stable,
  - whether or not margins can be maintained when demand falls below the level of normal capacity,
  - whether the market is supplied by a few or by many enterprises,
  - whether a small group of powerful consumers dominates the market,
  - whether the market offering is free from risks of substitution;
- environmental aspects (e.g. regulations applying to distribution, marketing, or manufacturing).

The criteria for assessing an enterprise's competitive capabilities include:

- its market position (usually specified in terms of market share);
- production capability (including location, number of plants, capacity, access to supplies, technological state of facilities);
- product R & D (as a complete technological package to cover product range, quality, developments in applications, competence of technical service).

It is probably most beneficial if the enterprise in question reviews its competitive capabilities relative to those of significant competitors. Ratings are best determined by a team of relevant personnel attempting to reach a consensus. Alternatively, a more complex set of weights (see multifactor portfolio matrix below) may need to be devised when some criteria (or critical success factors) are deemed to be more important than others.

**Multifactor Portfolio Matrix**

This was developed jointly by General Electric and the consulting firm of McKinsey & Co in order to overcome the limitations of the BCG's growth-share matrix. Like the directional policy matrix it had nine cells with the axes relating to similar notions: industry attractiveness (rather than business sector prospects) and business strengths (rather than the enterprise's competitive capabilities). Figure 9.6 (see p. 232) illustrates the multifactor portfolio matrix. There are three zones dealing with strategies relating to:

- invest;
- manage selectively for earnings;
- harvest or divest;

and these are more clearly defined than are the zones within the directional policy matrix.

Criteria that might be used in establishing industry attractiveness include:

- market size;
- size of key segments;
- market growth rate;
- diversity of market;
- demand seasonality;
- demand cyclicity;
- sensitivity of market to price;

- opportunities;
- competitive structure;
- entry and exit barriers;
- extent of integration;
- degree of concentration;
- bargaining power of suppliers;
- bargaining power of distributors;
- capital intensity;
- capacity utilization;
- raw material availability;
- inflation vulnerability;
- environmental aspects;
- profitability;
- value added.

Measures that reflect business strength include:

- market share;
- enterprise (or SBU) growth rate;
- breadth of product line;
- distributive effectiveness;
- sales effectiveness;
- price competitiveness;
- promotional effectiveness;
- facilities (location, age, capacity, etc.);
- experience curve effects;
- investment utilization;
- raw material cost;
- relative product quality;
- R & D capabilities;
- personnel skills;
- relative market position;
- relative profitability;
- value added.

An enterprise can select whichever measures of industry attractiveness or business strength best suit its circumstances when evaluating plans. The relative importance weightings of the selected measures will need to be determined in order to locate a plan within the matrix. This can be carried out in the following way (after Cohen (1988), pp. 32–5).

1 Identify the major measures of industry attractiveness that are applicable. Let us suppose these are:
   - size of market;
   - growth of market;
   - ease of entry;
   - favourable position in PLC.
2 Weights must be assigned to the chosen measures to indicate their relative importance. If the weightings are 0.30, 0.30 ,0.25 and 0.15 respectively for the criteria shown in 1 above we can see the overall picture in Figure 16.40.
3 Figure 16.40 also shows the points that might be awarded to any given marketing plan in relation to the extent to which the selected criteria are seen to be met by that plan. Points might be awarded on the following basis:
   - very attractive     9
   - attractive          7
   - fair                4.5
   - unattractive        3
   - very unattractive   0

**FIGURE 16.40**
*Weighted score for industry attractiveness*

| Industry attractiveness criteria | Relative importance weightings | Point ratings | Weighted scores |
|---|---|---|---|
| Size of market | 0.30 | 9 | 2.70 |
| Growth of market | 0.30 | 4.5 | 1.35 |
| Ease of entry | 0.25 | 9 | 2.25 |
| Favourable PLC position | 0.15 | 0 | 0 |
| Total weighted score | | | 6.30 |

4  A weighted score relating to industry attractiveness can be calculated for each alternative marketing plan: this is equal to 6.30 for the plan covered by Figure 16.40.
5  Steps 1–4 need to be repeated for business strength in relation to each marketing plan. Let us assume that the applicable criteria are image, productivity, product synergy, and price competitiveness, with weights of 0.40, 0.30, 0.15 and 0.15 respectively. The assessment of points to indicate the extent to which any given plan meets the applicable criteria would be carried out as outlined in 3 above, with the results being shown in Figure 16.41.

**FIGURE 16.41**
*Weighted score for business strength*

| Business strength criteria | Relative importance weightings | Point ratings | Weighted scores |
|---|---|---|---|
| Image | 0.40 | 9 | 3.60 |
| Productivity | 0.30 | 7 | 2.10 |
| Product synergy | 0.15 | 3 | 0.45 |
| Price competitiveness | 0.15 | 4.5 | 0.675 |
| Total weighted score | | | 6.825 |

6  Having calculated weighted scores of 6.30 for industry attractiveness and 6.825 for business strength it is now possible to locate these scores within the matrix. Using the scales shown in Figure 9.6 it is apparent that the coordinates interesect in the top left-hand cell within the *invest* zone of the matrix.
7  Similar plots can be made for alternative marketing plans and an appropriate choice made in accordance with strategic priorities.

It will be evident that the weightings and scoring within this procedure involves considerable subjective judgement. This makes it important that all underlying assumptions should be made explicit to facilitate peer review.

**Product Positioning Matrix**

Among the many other available matrix approaches that can be used for evaluating marketing programmes is that of Wind and Claycamp (1976). This focuses on product line strategy and is comprehensive in that it deals with all the major measures (sales, market share, profitability) that are essential in positioning products by segment.

The first step involves defining:

1  the product (including its subcategories at both the enterprise and industry levels);
2  the strategic market for the product and the key segments within it;
3  the appropriate forms of measurement (e.g. sales in value or volume terms, sales per capita, quarterly time periods).

Following the establishing of suitable definitions the analysis can be undertaken. This will involve the generation of:

- Sales position for the given product within the strategic market, showing enterprise and industry sales along with an indication of when the product is expected to reach each stage within the product life cycle. For this purpose the PLC can be characterized as having three stages:
  - growth (when sales are expected to increase by more than 10 per cent year on year);
  - maturity (where sales are expected to increase in the range of 0–10 per cent year on year);
  - decline (when sales growth is expected to be negative).
- Market share position which can also be characterized by means of a set of decision rules such as:
  - marginal (if market share is likely to be less than 10 per cent).
  - average (if market share is likely to be within the range 10–24 per cent).
  - leading (if market share is expected to be over 25 per cent).
- Profit position, which can be characterized by distinguishing among:
  - above par (where profit from a given segment is expected to be greater than from the rest of the enterprise's business when expressed as a rate of return);
  - par (where the profitability expected from the segment is comparable to that from other segments);
  - below par (where the profitability of the segment is expected to fall below that of other segments).

The expectations relating to product sales, industry sales, market share, and profitability can then be plotted on to the comprehensive product evaluation matrix as shown in Figure 16.42.

It is possible to plot the anticipated positions of the product in question under different assumptions regarding sales, market share and profitability. A time dimension can be built in as suggested in Figure 16.42.

**FIGURE 16.42**
*Product positioning matrix.*

| Industry sales / Market share | Profitability | Decline — Below par | Decline — Par | Decline — Above par | Maturity — Below par | Maturity — Par | Maturity — Above par | Growth — Below par | Growth — Par | Growth — Above par |
|---|---|---|---|---|---|---|---|---|---|---|
| Growth | Leading | | | | | | | | | |
| Growth | Average | | | | | | | | | |
| Growth | Marginal | | | | | | | | | |
| Maturity | Leading | | | | | | | $B_{19X2}$ | | |
| Maturity | Average | | | | | $B^1_{19X2}$ ← $B_{19X1}$ → $B^2_{19X2}$ | | | | |
| Maturity | Marginal | | | | | | | | | |
| Decline | Leading | | | | | | | | | |
| Decline | Average | $A_{19X1}$ | | | | $A^1_{19X2}$ | | | | |
| Decline | Marginal | $A_{19X2}$ | | $A^2_{19X2}$ | | | | | | |

SOURCE: Adapted from Wind and Claycamp (1976)

This figure shows for two products – A and B – the current position (i.e. A as at 19X1 and B as at 19X1) along with projections into the future. Such projections are built up from estimates of each constituent element (sales, market share, profit outcome) for each alternative marketing programme. We can see, for example, that Product A is a poor performer as at 19X1: it is in a declining industry with declining sales, has only an average market share and is achieving a profit performance that is below par. If no change occurs it is anticipated that Product A's position will get worse. In an attempt to improve the position of Product A two alternative marketing plans are proposed: plan $A^1$ is predicted to reposition Product A in an improved situation in 19X2 by moving it from its 19X1 position to a position offering stable sales and profits at par, although it is not expected that the decline in industry sales can be changed.

An alternative to plan $A^1$ is given by plan $A^2$ which anticipates an improvement in the profit performance but a continuing decline in sales and also in market share between 19X1 and 19X2.

Product B is in a much stronger position in 19X1. It is increasing its sales level within a mature market, thereby increasing its market share but showing poor profit performance. If no changes occur in the marketing plan for B the expectation is that, by 19X2, it will have achieved a leading market position with profit performance continuing to be below par. Two alternative marketing plans are proposed for Product B. The first, $B^1$, will lead to a stable level of sales and an improvement in profit performance from below par to above par. Plan $B^2$ is expected to produce continuing growth and a better profit position.

For Product A management must consider the trade-off between a modest improvement in profit with an increase in sales, and a large improvement in profit with a decrease in sales. In the case of Product B the choice is between taking profits in the near future (plan $B^2$) or investing for the longer term in increased market share.

## 16.7 THE MARKETING PERFORMANCE ASSESSMENT MODEL

Bonoma and Clark (1988) set out to develop a means of assessing the performance of marketing programmes in a way that avoids the limitations of measures that focus narrowly on either economic issues or efficiency. They do this by relating programme results to management's expectations, thereby focusing on effectiveness via a measure of satisfaction. Efficiency is assessed by means of the effort that needs to be expended to achieve a given level of satisfaction. The effort comprises the skills that must be exercised by a marketing programme's managers and the support structures that are provided for the programme.

Finally, Bonoma and Clark allow for those factors that are beyond the enterprise's control but that affect the performance of the marketing programme – such as competitors' actions, changes within distribution channels or in legal, economic, or demographic variables. It is possible to determine programmes that succeed (or fail) on the basis of luck rather than effort by utilizing these factors.

In summary, they seek to offer an approach to marketing performance assessment that measures:

1 the degree to which a marketing programme satisfies strategic requirements;
2 the effort that is necessary to produce the satisfaction in 1, above;
3 the effect of uncontrollable variables on the programme.

The approach is operationalized via a testable model of *marketing performance assessment* (MPA) which is defined as the adjudged quality of marketing programmes, directed by strategy, as these programmes are executed in the market-place. The model seeks to combine elements of efficiency and effectiveness in assessing marketing performance. In addition it incorporates managers' judgements in an explicit way.

The motivation behind this work was a concern to identify whether a set of principles exists that explains 'quality marketing practice' (i.e. the *doing* of marketing in an effective and efficient way rather than just the *planning* of marketing). In part this motivation stemmed from the following dissatisfactions that Bonoma felt with the literature on marketing practice:

1 there is a widespread tendency to ignore the role of managers, hence their values, etc., which implies that all managers act in similar ways – something we know is not the case;
2 it is implicit in the advice offered to guide marketing practice that the causal link is strategy–causes–practice whereas there is good reason to believe that the reverse causal link exists (i.e. practice–causes–strategy) in some circumstances, which is akin to ex post-rationalization.

Bonoma conceives of marketing practice as an attempt by managers with particular skills (relating to organizing, allocating, interacting and monitoring), values and expectations to achieve specified results. The managers in question operate within an organizational context characterized by particular ways of doing things – whether through particular programmes, systems or policies – which collectively represent a structure for guiding marketing actions. In turn the organization is located within its environment, with its array of threats, opportunities and constraints, and the link between the organization and its environment is found via the marketing strategy of the organization.

These relationships are portrayed in Figure 16.43 which represents a rudimentary model of marketing implementation.

It is suggested by Figure 16.43 that:

Quality marketing practice  =  f (market results)
and
Market results  =  f (environment, strategy, structure, skills).

The combination of structure (in the form of programmes, systems and policies) and skills on the part of individual managers allows strategies to be implemented – within the organization's environment – and results achieved. The extent to which the results represent an effective level of marketing performance will depend on managerial expectations, but Bonoma's contribution is significant in that he builds into his model the idea of effort expended in achieving results as well as the level of satisfaction that managers derive from the results of their efforts plus an explicit recognition that results are influenced by events outside the enterprise over which managers have no direct control. These elements are brought together in the following expression:

$$MP = \frac{SAT}{EFF} \times EXT$$

Where   MP  =  marketing performance
        SAT  =  managers' satisfaction with the results of effort expended in marketing programmes
        EFF  =  effort expended to achieve the results
        EXT  =  the impact of external events on marketing effort.

A variety of implications concerning the relationship between satisfaction and effort stem from the discussion above. These are summarized in Figure 16.44 and indicate how the MPA model predicts optimal marketing performance when a low level of effort is associated with a high level of satisfaction.

**FIGURE 16.43**
*A rudimentary model of marketing implementation*

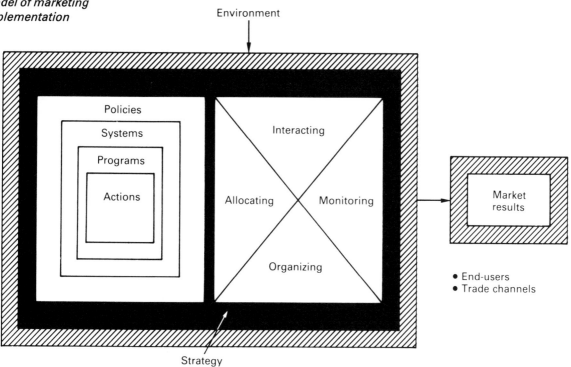

Quality practice = f (Marketplace results) = f (Environment, Strategy, Structure, and Skills)

SOURCE: **Bonoma and Clark (1988), p. 59**

*Notes to Figure 16.43*

**Structural variables**

*Actions* relate to low-level execution issues (e.g. selling, NPD, distributor management, etc.).

*Programs* deal with integrated sets of actions (e.g. a specific marketing mix tailored to a particular segment).

*Systems* focus on formal controls and decision aids (e.g. decision-support systems, order processing systems, etc.).

*Policies* are broad rules of conduct promulgated by top management to guide marketing operations (e.g. segments to develop, technology to use in NPD).

**Skills**

*Interaction skills* focus on how managers deal with each other and with staff, customers, etc., in order to influence events.

*Allocation skills* relate to an ability to assign resources to tasks in an effective and efficient way.

*Monitoring skills* concern the design and use of feedback mechanisms to measure and control marketing activities.

*Organizing skills* deal with 'networking' behaviour by which a manager copes when the formal organization is not relevant.

Adapted from Bonoma and Crittenden (1988)

The determinants of satisfaction are seen as being expectations and results: if expectations are not met the consequences can be high satisfaction (when expectations are exceeded) or high dissatisfaction (when expectations are not realized). Figure 16.45 shows how the lowest level of satisfaction occurs when poor results and high expectations interact, and the highest level of satisfaction arises when low expectations interact with good results.

**FIGURE 16.44**
*Marketing performance: satisfaction and effort*

| | Management's perceived effort is | |
|---|---|---|
| **Management's perceived satisfaction with results is** | **Low** | **High** |
| **High** | Maximum performance | Adequate performance |
| | Achieving the most results with the least effort, in complete contravention of the Protestant ethic. By definition, low effort is more easily achieved through systematized or routinized procedures than through 'exception management'. | High satisfaction is the 'due consequence' of high effort. Effort, however, is costly, resulting in only adequate performance because much was expended to produce the results. Usually, effort is high when routinized systems and procedures cannot be delegated to do the job 'automatically'. |
| **Low** | Adequate performance | Low performance |
| | There is little to be satisfied with, but little effort was expended in achieving the low performance. The lack of effort is seen as justifying or explaining the lack of performance. | Much effort was expended to little avail in terms of results. This is the worst possible state. |

SOURCE: Bonoma and Clark (1988), p. 65

**FIGURE 16.45**
*The determinants of satisfaction: results and expectations*

| | Results from marketing efforts are | |
|---|---|---|
| **Management's expectations for results are** | **Poor** | **Good** |
| **High** | High dissatisfaction | Moderate satisfaction |
| | Results achieved do not live up to expectations. Management is unhappy with performance given prior expectations and promise. | Results match goals – which, after all, is only what should have happened. There are no surprises, either pleasant or unpleasant. |
| **Low** | Moderate dissatisfaction | High satisfaction |
| | Poor results match the low expectations held for the program. The poor results are only moderately unsettling because of the low expectations. | Good results far exceed what was hoped or planned. Top management loves these kinds of surprises, despite its suspicion about being sandbagged. |

SOURCE: Bonoma and Clark (1988), p. 66

Within any organization the quality of marketing skills will depend on the availability of suitably trained and motivated staff. The application of marketing skills through the organization's marketing structure (i.e. programmes, systems, policies) will determine the effort that is to be expended in order to achieve results. Skills might be strong or weak, and structures might be flexible or rigid. As shown in Figure 16.46, there are various combinations of skills and structure that determine the effort available, and the way in which that effort might be applied.

**FIGURE 16.46**
*The determinants of effort: management skills and marketing structures*

|  | Marketing structures are | |
|---|---|---|
|  | Flexible | Rigid |
| Management's marketing skills are | Maximum effort | Moderate effort |
| Strong | Weak structures cannot help routinize repetitive decisions; all problems receive 'custom' solutions from strongly skilled managers. While all get solved, the fixes are expensive and people-dependent. | Strong structures help routinize decisions, but strongly skilled managers come into conflict with structural constraints. Decisions with which the system cannot cope are handled on an exception basis by management. This is expensive but highly effective as long as systems and managers do not conflict destructively. |
|  | Low effort | Minimal effort |
| Weak | Weak structures do not routinize well. Poorly skilled management does not or cannot exert itself to bridge the shortcomings between structural shortfalls and marketing requirements. | Strong structures routinize marketing decisions. Weakly skilled managers let the structure do the job, and are not compelled to intervene in its operation. This works superbly efficiently, and is effective as long as the environment remains stable. |

SOURCE: Bonoma and Clark (1988), p. 70

## 16.8 SOME OTHER APPROACHES TO MODELLING

In this section we will reinforce earlier coverage of marketing experimentation as a modelling approach by which marketing plans might be assessed. In addition we will look at programming and networking as further approaches to modelling by which alternative plans can be evaluated.

**Marketing Experimentation**

In an experiment attempts are made to identify all the factors that affect a particular independent variable, and these factors are then manipulated systematically (in so far as it is within the firm's power to do so) in order to isolate and measure their effects on the performance of the dependent variable (see pp. 13–15 above).

It is not possible to plan or control all the conditions in which an experiment is conducted; for example, the timing, location, and duration of an experiment can be predetermined, but it is necessary to measure such conditions as the weather and eliminate their effects from the results.

The independent variable that is the subject of marketing experimentation may be the demand for one of the company's various products, or one of the environmental factors it faces, and the dependent variable may be one of the company's objectives. Profit is a dependent variable of both the particular marketing strategy adopted and of the external conditions prevailing at the time that strategy is executed.

Because experiments are concerned with the deliberate manipulation of controllable variables (i.e. such variables as prices and advertising effort), a good deal more confidence can be placed in conclusions about the effects of such manipulation than if the effects of these changes are based purely on historical associations or vague projections rather than on the basis of experimentation.

Ideas for experiments can result from marketing cost studies. The following questions are fairly representative of those that can be answered as a result of experimentation (as we saw in Chapter 3, pp. 63–4, above):

1  By how much (if any) would the net profit contribution of the most profitable products be increased if there were an increase in specific marketing outlays, and how would such a change affect the strategy of competitors in terms of the stability of, say, market shares?
2  By how much (if any) would the net losses of unprofitable products be reduced if there were some decrease in specific marketing outlays?
3  By how much (if any) would the profit contribution of profitable products be affected by a change in the marketing effort applied to the unprofitable products, and vice versa, and what would be the effect on the total marketing system?
4  By how much (if any) would the total profit contribution be improved if some marketing effort were diverted to profitable territories or customer groups from unprofitable territorial and customer segments?
5  By how much (if any) would the net profit contribution be increased if there were a change in the method of distribution to small unprofitable accounts or if these accounts were eliminated?

Only by actually carrying out properly designed marketing experiments can management realistically predict with an acceptable degree of certainty the effects of changes in marketing expenditure on the level of sales and profit of each differentiated product, territory or customer segment in the multi-product company.

Experiments must be conducted under conditions that resemble the real-life conditions of the market-place insofar as this is possible. It is pointless, for example, carrying out an experiment to prove that the sale of £1's worth of Product X in Southampton through medium-sized retailers contributes more to profit than does the sale of £1's worth of Product Y through small retailers in Leeds, if the market for Product X is saturated and no reallocation of marketing resources can change the situation. This points to the danger of confusing what is happening now with what may happen in the future – ascertaining that Product X is more profitable than Product Y may be the right answer to the wrong question.

The style of question should be 'What will happen to the dependent variable in the future if the independent variables are manipulated now?' If the concern is with the allocation of sales effort, the aim of an experiment may be to show how changes in the total costs of each sales team can be related to changes in the level of sales. In such a simple case where only one type of marketing effort is being considered this effort should be reallocated to those sales segments where an additional unit of effort will yield the highest contribution to profits.

The experiment can be designed to show which sales segment produces the highest value when the following equation is applied to each:

(Additional sales − additional variable costs)/additional expenditure

If an additional budget allocation of £1,000 to the London sales force results in extra sales of £5,000 with additional variable costs amounting to £2,000, then the index of performance is $(5,000 − 2,000)/1,000 = 3$. It may happen that the same index computed for the Midlands sales force has a value of 4, in which case selling effort should be reallocated to the Midlands *provided* due consideration has been given to the expected level of future demand.

As a result of the high costs involved, experiments must usually be conducted with small samples of the relevant elements. This is generally valid so long as the samples are properly determined and representative. However, it is believed by some that marketing experimentation is not a feasible means by which information can be obtained as a basis for making important decisions.

There are certainly a lot of difficulties to be overcome in planning and executing experiments, and the need to keep special records and make repeated measurements is both expensive and time consuming. The risk is always present that the results of an experiment will not be of any value because they may not be statistically significant. A further risk is that even temporary and limited experimental variations in the marketing mix may damage sales and customer relationships both during and after the experiment.

Other problems that are involved in marketing experimentation include:

1 the measuring of short-term response when long-term response may be of greater relevance;
2 accurate measurements are difficult to obtain – apart from the high expense involved;
3 it is almost impossible to prevent some contamination of control units by test units since it is difficult to direct variations in the marketing mix solely to individual segments;
4 making experiments sufficiently realistic to be useful is hindered by such difficulties as the national media being less flexible than may be desired, and the fact that competitors may not react to local experimental action in the same way as they would to a national change in policy.

These problems and difficulties, while discouraging, are insufficient to discount completely the use of experimentation as a valuable means of obtaining information to increase the efficiency of marketing operations. Indeed, it is likely that the use of experimental techniques will become increasingly widespread, as has been the case with test marketing which is the best known form of experimentation in marketing.

## Programming

Programming is a form of analytical modelling that is useful in allocation problems. The most widely-used technique is *linear programming* which aims to determine the optimum allocation of effort in a situation involving many interacting variables: in other words, it produces that solution which maximizes or minimizes a particular outcome in accordance with given constraints (e.g. how should sales effort be allocated among regions to maximize the level of sales subject to a maximum availability of 10 000 units of product per period, or what product mix should be sold – subject to demand – in order to give the maximum profit?). Other forms of programming include integer programming which is concerned with optimizing subject to the constraint that the solution must be in the form of whole numbers, and dynamic programming which is applicable to problems involving a series of interdependent decisions.

In all cases the marketing manager will be interested in making the best use of his limited resources and the constraints that exist will set the upper limit to the level of performance that is possible. The company cannot spend more on advertisng each product than it has in its advertising appropriation, thus:

$$a_1(W) + a_2(X) + a_3(Y) + a_4(Z) \leqslant A$$

Where: $\leqslant$ means 'equal to or less than'
      A is the total advertising appropriation
      $a_1(W)$ is the amount spent on advertising Product W
      $a_2(X)$ is the amount spent on advertising Product X
      $a_3(Y)$ is the amount spent on advertising Product Y
      $a_4(Z)$ is the amount spent on advertising Product Z

Similarly, a constraint exists in relation to every fixed budget or limited resource such as sales force time and warehouse space:

$$b_1(W) + b_2(X) + b_3(Y) + b_4(Z) \leqslant B$$

Where: B is the total available sales force time
$b_1(W)$ is the time devoted to selling Product W, etc.

And:

$$c_1(W) + c_2(X) + c_3(Y) + c_4(Z) \leqslant C$$

Where: C equals the available warehouse space
$c_1(W)$ is the space occupied by the inventory of Product W, etc.

The basis on which resources are allocated is the *marginal response*. If the expenditure on advertising of £100,000 produces sales amounting to £500,000 then the *average response* is 5/1; and if an increase in advertising expenditure of £1,000 produces additional sales totalling £10,000 this gives the measure of marginal response, which is equal to 10/1. Marginal response can thus be seen to be a measure of the value of opportunities presented.

If a company's advertising budget is set at £100,000 for a period, the optimal allocation to each of the company's products (A, B, and C) is given by equating the marginal responses because this gives the situation where it will not be beneficial to reallocate funds from one product to another. The requirement is to find the best solution to the equation:

$$a_1(A) + a_2(B) + a_3(C) = £100,000$$

where $a_1(A)$ is the advertising budget for product A, $a_2(B)$ for product B, and $a_2(C)$ for product C. This is given when:

$$d\ YA/d\ XA = d\ YB/d\ XB = d\ YC/d\ XC$$

where $d\ YA/d\ XA$ is the marginal response for product A measured as change in sales/change in advertising outlay, and so on for products B and C.

Linear programming must be applied in the absence of uncertainty, which means that uncertainty must be eliminated before variables are incorporated into a linear programme. Moreover, all the relationships of problems put into a linear programming format are assumed to be linear, and this may not apply under all possible conditions. For example, costs rarely rise in direct proportion to increases in sales. But even with this discrepancy linear programming is able to indicate the best direction for allocating resources to segments. This technique can be used to determine the best (i.e. optimal) solution to allocation decisions in the following circumstances:

1 where there is a clear, stated objective;
2 where feasible alternative courses of action are available;
3 where some inputs are limited (i.e. where constraints exist);
4 where 1 and 2 can be expressed as a series of linear equations or inequalities.

Let us consider the application of linear programming to a short-run product selection problem in which the decision maker's objective is to maximize profits. (This illustration is adapted from Dev (1980).) The products in question both offer positive contributions, and market demand is buoyant and likely to be sustained, but there are insufficient resources in prospect to allow for unlimited output. The problem is, therefore, to choose that allocation of available resources which leads to maximized profits.

Boam Brothers produce two products, M and S, and the following data reflects estimated prices, variable manufacturing costs, and contributions for each product for the following financial year:

|  | | *Product M* | *Product S* |
|---|---|---|---|
| Selling price per unit | | £22.20 | £14.00 |

*Less* avoidable costs:

| | | | | | |
|---|---|---|---|---|---|
| Material A @ £1.00 per kilo | | | | | |
| | 12 kilos | 12.00 | | 4 kilos | 4.00 |
| Labour @ £3.00 per hour | | | | | |
| | 1 hour | 3.00 | | 2 hours | 6.00 |
| | | | 15.00 | | 10.00 |
| Contribution per unit | | | £7.20 | | £4.00 |

It is assumed that the material and labour input requirements per unit and the contribution per unit are constant no matter what the level of output. This emphasizes the 'linear' aspect of linear programming.

Available inputs for next year are expected to be subject to possible constraints as suggested below:

| | |
|---|---|
| Material A | 1,200,000 kilos |
| Labour | 400,000 hours |

Fixed costs have been budgeted at £560,000. Assume that there are no opening or closing inventories of M, S or A, and that the selling price will stay constant irrespective of the level of sales.

Three possible situations can be envisaged:

1 *No resource constraints*, in which case Boam Brothers would produce as much of M and S as they are able (since both make a positive contribution).
2 *One resource constraint*, which we might take as material A being limited to 1,200,000 kilos. The solution is derived via the limiting factor: priority will be given to the product generating the highest contribution per unit of the limiting factor. We can see that this is product S from the following computation:

| | *Product M* | *Product S* |
|---|---|---|
| Contribution per unit | £7.20 | £4.00 |
| Kilos of A per unit | 12 | 4 |
| Contribution per kilo of A | £0.60 | £1.00 |

With the available amount of A the maximum output would be:

$$\frac{1,200,000}{12} = 100,000 \text{ units M}; \quad \frac{1,200,000}{4} = 300,000 \text{ units S},$$

and the maximum contribution would be:
M: 100,000 × £7.20 = £720,000  S: 300,000 × £4.00 = £1,200,000
(or 1,200,000 × £0.60 = £720,000 for M, and 1,200,000 × £1.00 = £1,200,000 for S).

The optimal choice is to produce 300,000 units of S and to give up producing M.

If, on the other hand, the scarce resource was labour hours the analysis would show the following:

|  | Product M | Product S |
|---|---|---|
| Contribution per unit | £7.20 | £4.00 |
| Labour hours per unit | 1 | 2 |
| Contribution per labour hour | £7.20 | £2.00 |

The maximum output with 400,000 labour hours available would be:

$$\frac{400,000}{1} = 400,000 \text{ units M}; \quad \frac{400,000}{2} = 200,000 \text{ units S},$$

and their respective contributions would be:

M: 400,000 × £7.20 = £2,880,000   S: 200,000 × £4.00 = £800,000.

The optimal output is to produce 400,000 units of M and no units of S.

3 *Two resource constraints.* This is a more difficult situation than 2 above since the material constraint favours production of S and the labour constraint favours the production of M. Four logical alternatives present themselves:

- produce M but no S;
- produce S but no M;
- produce some combination of M and S;
- produce neither M nor S.

The last alternative can be discarded because the contributions of both products are positive. A choice from the remaining alternatives can be made by formulating the problem as follows:

Maximize C = 7.20 $Q_m$ + 4.00 $Q_s$

Subject to 12$Q_m$ + 4 $Q_s$ ≤ 1,200,000
$Q_m$ + 2 $Q_s$ ≤   400,000
$Q_m$ ⩾ 0; $Q_s$ ⩾ 0

Where:  C   = total contribution
$Q_m$  = units of product M to be produced
$Q_s$  = units or product S to be produced

The resource constraints are expressed as inequalities (i.e. 'less than or equal to') because it may not be necessary to use all 1,200,000 kilos of A or all 400,000 labour hours. In addition, a non-negativity constraint is included in the problem formulation to show that negative quantities of either M or S are not desired.

A solution can be derived either by algebraic or graphic methods (and can easily be handled by standard computer programs). Figure 16.47 shows a graphic approach to the solution. Units of M and S are shown on the x and y axes respectively, with line AB showing the maximum output of each under the labour constraint and line CD showing the maximum output of each under the material constraint. AB connects all the possible combinations of M and S within the labour constraint while CD connects all the combinations that are feasible within the material constraint. However, when we take both constraints into account the combinations of M and S within the triangles ACE and DBE are not feasible because they require more labour and material respectively than is available. This leaves OAED as a *feasible region* within which all the combinations of M and S can be achieved. But which is the best combination (in terms of maximizing profit)?

**FIGURE 16.47**
*Graphical presentation of solution*

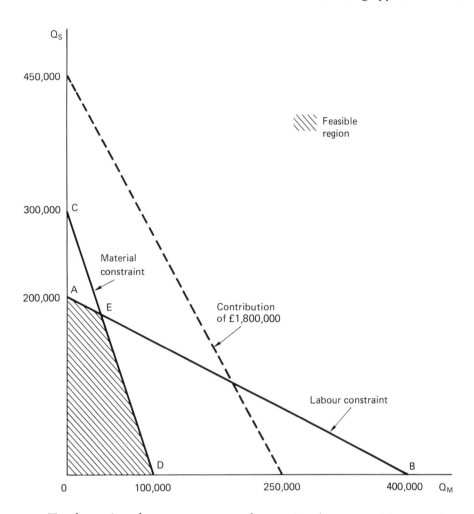

To determine the answer we need to move from quantities to relative contributions. Let us take a contribution figure of, say, £1,800,000. This can be generated by

$$\frac{1,800,000}{7.20} = 250,000 \text{ units M or } \frac{1,800,000}{4.00} = 450,000 \text{ units S.}$$

A curve showing these limits is superimposed on the graph in Figure 16.47 but none of the possibilities suggested by this line is within the feasible region. By moving back towards the origin with parallel contribution lines we arrive at point E which is within the feasible region, and this gives us the optimal combination of M and S. (The lines will be parallel because the contribution per unit of M and S will be the same regardless of the level of output.) It should be apparent that the closer the contribution line is to the origin the lower will be the total contribution (since the smaller will be the output), so the best point is at a tangent to the feasible region: point E.

The output levels at this point (from the graph) are 40 000 units of M and 180 000 units of S, with the following financial outcome:

Contribution:
| | | |
|---|---|---|
| M | 40,000 × £7.20 | 288,000 |
| S | 180,000 × £4.00 | 720,000 |

| | |
|---|---|
| Total contribution | 1,008,000 |
| Fixed costs | 560,000 |
| Net profit | £448,000 |

You may care to manipulate the combination of M and S represented in this solution to see if any marginal change could improve the profit outcome. (For example, if five units less M were produced this would free 60 kilos of A and five hours of labour which could be used to produce two more units of S – with one hour of labour and 52 kilos of A left over. However, the contribution gained from S would only be £8.00, whereas the contribution lost by M would be £36.00, so it would be a suboptimal change.)

## Networks

Network analysis is a method of problem solving that is based on analysing systematically and logically the relationships and time factors involved in carrying out a particular project. An appropriate project is any activity that can be considered as having a definable beginning and end, and this includes:

1 developing and launching a new product, which involves coordinating many complex and interrelated factors along with the need to be able to assess quickly the effects of changes in order to show where corrective action can best be taken;
2 product modification;
3 large-scale promotional campaigns;
4 many smaller activities that would benefit from a more rigorous approach, such as catalogue preparation; planning exhibitions, sales conferences, and training courses; carrying out market research studies; and the building of models.

Network analysis is made possible by two techniques developed during the late 1950s: critical path analysis (CPA) and programme evaluation and review technique (PERT). Networks developed by these techniques show the relationships among all the activities that must be performed in terms of time in completing the project in question. Three estimates of time are characteristically used for each activity – an optimistic, a pessimistic and a 'most likely'. The expected time for each activity can then be calculated on a probability basis, and since some activities must be completed before others can be commenced, the various activities can be laid out along a diagrammatic time-scale.

Figure 16.48 relates to the launching of a new washing-up liquid and shows that a network diagram is a graphical representation of a project, indicating how the activities are linked. It is drawn by using three basic symbols:

1 a solid line represents an *activity*;
2 a circle represents an *event* or intersection between activities;
3 a dotted linee represents a *dummy* activity which is a means of showing logical relationships that are not physical activities – they may be thought of as transfers of information between events.

When the network is first drawn it is usual to omit duration times for reasons of simplicity in ascertaining the correct sequences and dependencies. After times have been incorporated it is possible to find the overall project time that is determined by those activities in sequence – the critical path. A certain amount of time ('float') will usually be available on those activities that are not on the critical path to permit flexibility in executing the project.

Basic networks only cover the time dimension, so further analysis requires the introduction of a cost dimension. This is the role of the PERT/cost technique. Both PERT and PERT/cost are designed for use in single large-scale projects, and resource allocation and multiproject scheduling (conveniently abbreviated to RAMPS) has been developed to deal with the problem of allocating resources to several projects when a number of projects are being undertaken simultaneously but there is a restriction in the availability of resources.

Although drawing up a valid network for a project is difficult, the procedure

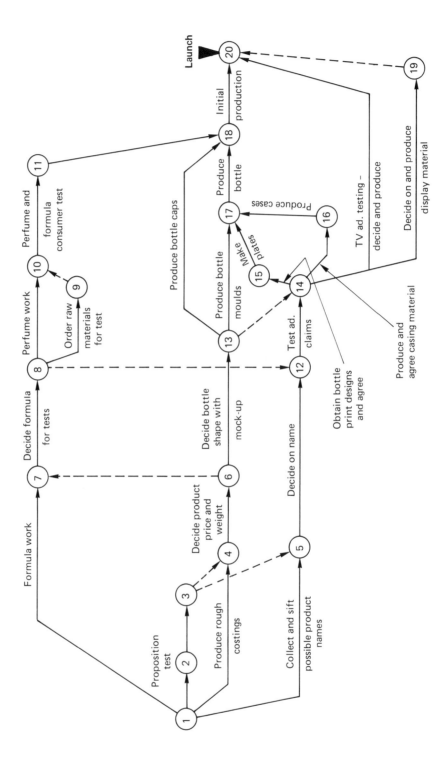

**FIGURE 16.48**
*Network for launching a new product*

demands thorough and systematic analysis, and this discipline means that relationships that might otherwise have been overlooked are included. Furthermore, it specifies the decisions that must be made and thus provides a framework for control as well as permitting planning and scheduling.

Network analysis can fail in practice for such reasons as lack of top management support, the use of excessive detail, bad presentation, a failure to update, and the absence of feedback.

A different type of network is shown in Figure 16.49. This relates to the development of new products which was discussed in Chapter 11.

**FIGURE 16.49**
*New product development network*

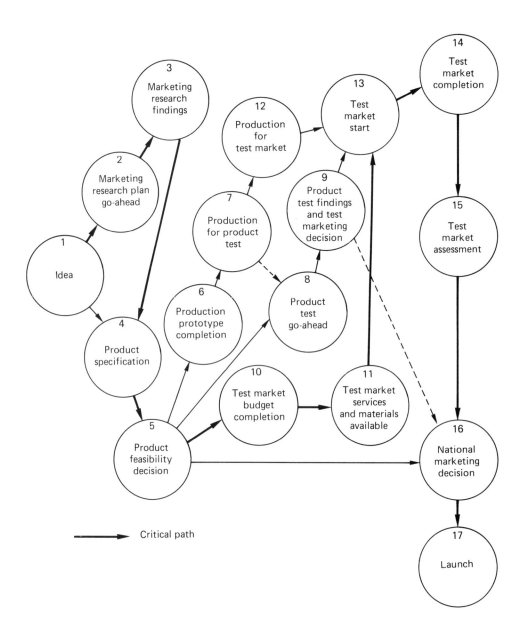

## 16.9 SUMMARY

Given the specification of marketing programmes in Chapters 11 to 14, and the specification of choice criteria in Chapter 15, this chapter has sought to show some of the ways in which marketing programmes might be evaluated by using modelling approaches embodying the appropriate criteria.

The principles of modelling were reviewed and developed via a consideration of short-run financial modelling (using cost–volume–profit analysis) and long-run financial modelling (using investment analysis).

Risk and uncertainty are inevitably present whenever choices need to be made among alternative claims on scarce resources. A variety of ways of accommodating risk and uncertainty were discussed and illustrated, including probability analysis, sensitivity analysis, decision trees and, briefly, Bayesian analysis.

Some alternative matrix models were covered – the directional policy matrix, the multifactor portfolio matrix, and the product positioning matrix – and their application to evaluating marketing plans illustrated.

Bonoma's MPA (marketing performance assessment) model warranted special attention as the most ambitious of the approaches considered. It is still in its development phase but holds great promise for the future.

Finally, brief coverage was given to some further modelling approaches which can be used to test the robustness, feasibility and desirability of marketing plans: marketing experimentation, networking and programming.

# Stage Five
## How Can We Ensure Arrival?
### Strategic Implementation and Control

## PREAMBLE

This stage of the book focuses on implementation and control. In this endeavour there are lots of problems to be overcome (e.g. relating to organizational as well as to environmental matters) which are discussed in Chapter 17.

Management controls to help in ensuring arrival are dealt with in Chapter 18. Some of these are social/behavioural in character while others are analytical.

The successful implementation of strategy is neither easy nor widely discussed in the marketing literature. If implementation is left to compete with the internal pressures of coping with crises, reacting to competitors' actions, company politics, personal career needs, and so forth, it is likely to be swamped or disrupted.

The implementation of plans poses a fundamental dilemma since to be effective it requires the reconciliation of two opposing forces: forces leading to organizational integration must be reconciled with forces leading to organizational segmentation (see Lawrence and Lorsch (1967)). In seeking to achieve this balance it is helpful if:

1 the messages contained in the plan are communicated so that there is clear recognition of what the plan says;
2 the plan must be understood so that all who need to play a role in its implementation are aware of what their roles are;
3 there is consensus about the wisdom of pursuing the plan in order to secure commitment to its accomplishment.

A flowchart showing how a strategic marketing plan might be implemented is shown in Figure 6. This suggests that a number of key elements within the organization need to be matched with the plan. These elements are:

- leadership;
- organizational culture;
- organizational structure;
- functional policies;
- resources;
- evaluation and control procedures.

There is a logical sequencing of the key elements, although some may occur simultaneously or in a different order in practice. Feedback loops are shown linking the elements in an iterative process (see McNamee (1988), pp. 323–35).

No matter how brilliant the analysis behind the formulation of plans and strategies it is only possible to out-perform one's competitors if those plans and strategies are executed brilliantly.

This requires, inter alia, an overriding concern for quality. Japanese success in the post-war period is a clear testimony to the pursuit of quality, as reflected in the pioneering work of W. Edwards Deming. (See, for example, Mann (1989).) This success is built upon

**FIGURE 6**
*A flowchart showing schematically how
a strategy may be implemented*

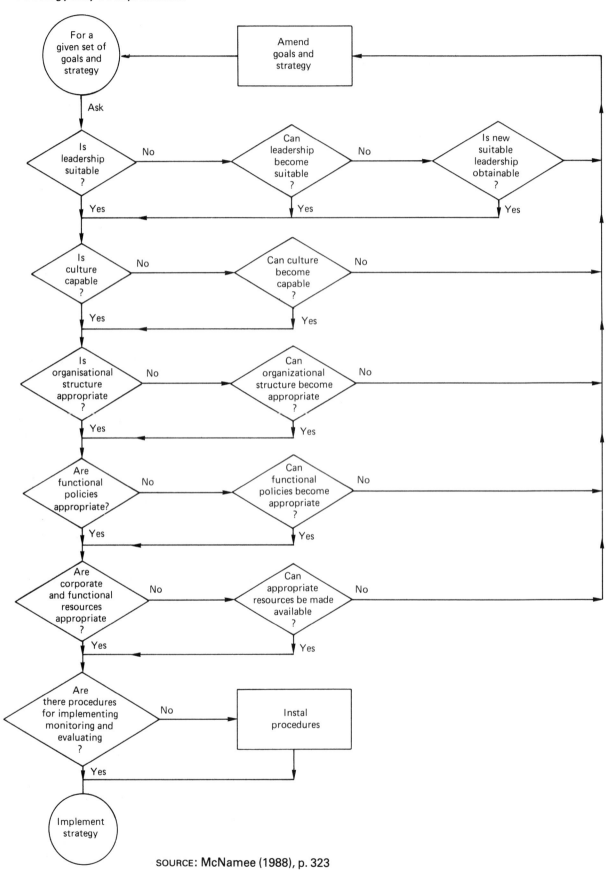

SOURCE: McNamee (1988), p. 323

# Marketing needs new sales pitch

British companies need to wake up to what the customer wants. Staying ahead when hundreds of others are going under means taking a new look at quality and service, says Ian Griffith.

AT A TIME when the newspapers are full of stories about companies closing, there are two developments that encourage optimism.

First, there is a call from a number of chief executives for better performance in the market-place. This is a clear sign that the improvement of marketing and sales is accepted as a priority for business.

Second, quality is shaping up as one of the most important ways of staying ahead of competitors in the 1990s. Many leading companies are already on the road to total quality, where the need to identify and satisfy customer needs is given the highest priority.

The customer has not always been paramount in British business. Products have failed, not necessarily because they were poorly made but because they were not what people wanted.

The Japanese, on the other hand, have understood only too well for the past 20 years that the customer comes first. Before entering a market, they take pains to make sure they have a full understanding of customer needs and expectations. They also weigh up the competition. The Americans and the Germans have not ignored the Japanese lesson; they too are customer-conscious. If Britain is to maintain healthy businesses after 1992, it will also have to become much more market and customer focused.

The only way that this can be achieved is for companies to concentrate on improving marketing and sales effectiveness. Responsibility for this should lie with marketing departments, which not only have to represent the needs of the customer but also ensure that the company has the capability and commitment to satisfy demand with quality goods and services.

How well prepared are marketing and sales people to meet this challenge? In my experience, they are often not. Marketing is still treated by too many companies as a tactical discipline that is involved with publicity and promotion as opposed to a business philosophy

that is concerned with how the whole company deals with its customers.

When competition is intensifying, this is a serious issue. Marketing must represent the customers' viewpoint as well as interests in the company boardroom.

However, reforming attitudes, ideas and quality within companies raises the questions of how people achieve such goals, how they measure that achievement and how they can maintain those standards.

The British Standard BS5750 set out the principles for product quality a decade ago, but it did not lay down how companies should identify and meet customer needs and expectations. Could those standards, which have attracted about 12,000 registrations from British companies, be applied to marketing? It was with all this in mind that the concept of Marketing Quality Assurance (MQA) was developed.

MQA, launched last October, is a third-party certification body that assesses the quality of marketing, sales and customer service in companies. It awards a certificate of excellence, and the right to use the MQA mark, if companies achieve the required standard. This is a way of signalling that the certified company is one that has independent recognition, and is a sign of marketing excellence to customers, competitors, employees and potential employees.

The specification, which is an international first and based on good practice, took five years to research and develop. An important consideration in drafting the 58 requirements in the specification was to ensure that companies were aware of the need for high-quality marketing and sales people and also understood their aspirations.

Findings showed that the most successful people are those who are able to provide a disciplined and well-planned approach based on a real understanding of the market-place and competition. They are good communicators who are able to co-ordinate the work of all parts

of the organisation concerned with meeting and satisfying customer needs.

Perhaps most important, they are people who can provide a creative and innovative approach, which has become vital in differentiating one organisation from another.

MQA has captured all of these needs through its specification which covers: business plans; review of market needs; marketing and sales planning; marketing and sales operations; customer assurance; purchasing of marketing and sales services; resources, personnel, training and organisation structure; quality policy, systems, control and procedures, records and audit.

MQA's specification is an associated document to the International Quality Standard ISO 9000 and therefore – as a third-party certification organisation – can grant registration to ISO 9001, EN 290012 and BS 5750 Part 1 for a company's marketing, sales and customer-assurance activities.

So the stage is set for another big step forward as the marketing enlightenment of the 1980s becomes the quality assured marketing of the 1990s.

Early indications would suggest that many chief executives acknowledge the considerable extent to which MQA registration moves their companies towards the ultimate goal of total quality, as well as providing improved marketing effectiveness.

More than 25 companies have applied for registration, with organisations such as Kodak, Sorbus, Newcastle Breweries and Southern Electric already well down the track.

There are those, however, who imagine that a formal set of standards would bring too much bureaucracy to the essentially creative business of marketing. This is not so, for marketing is more than coming up with bright ideas; it is putting those ideas into practice and making sure they work.

● *Ian Griffith is the managing director of Marketing Quality Assurance, Park House, Wick Road, Egham, Surrey TW20 0HW. Telephone: 0784 430953*

**FIGURE 7**
*Marketing quality assurance*

SOURCE: *The Sunday Times*, 7 July 1991, p. 4.13

the notion of being 'right first time' which is much more than a catchy slogan: it implies providing exactly what is required by those using an organization's outputs. The *total quality management* (TQM) approach is built around this ideal.

Oakland (1989, pp. 14–15) defines TQM as '... an approach to improving the effectiveness and flexibility of businesses as a whole. It is essentially a way of organizing and involving the whole organization; every department, every activity, every single person at every level. For an organization to be truly effective, each part of it must work properly together, recognizing that every person and every activity affects, and in turn is affected by, others'.

A slightly different emphasis is offered in the definition put forward by Atkinson and Naden (1989, p. 6). They see TQM as being '... a strategy which is concerned with changing the fundamental beliefs, values and culture of an organization, harnessing the enthusiasm and participation of everyone ... towards an overall ideal of "right first time"'.

As the exhibit in Figure 7 shows, a variation on TQM can be used in a marketing context to attain BS 5750: Marketing Quality Assurance (or MQA).

In the task of implementing plans it is helpful to consider the core skills that are needed if sustainable competitive advantage is to be achieved. These core skills are the critical capabilities that the organization must possess as distinct from the skills of individuals within the organization. This is not a trivial distinction since individuals may come and go but the organization needs to have core skills (such as effective training programmes, clear performance guidelines, well-designed information systems, and incentive schemes that generate high levels of motivation) to link planning and the successful implementation of plans.

A vivid example is that of Marriott Hotels. As with many hotel chains the basic strategy is to go after business travellers with a level of service that is consistently excellent. However, the success of Marriott (as reflected in an occupancy rate that is some 10 points above the industry average) is to be found in its ability to implement the strategy in a superior way. This is achieved by institutionalizing among its 200 000 employees a fanatical eye for detail (e.g. maids follow a 66-point guide in making up bedrooms). The outcome is that Marriott Hotels is invariably at the top in customer surveys: the core organizational skill of excellent service gives a sustainable competitive advantage.

Another example can be taken from the fast food sector. In 1968 both Burger King and McDonald's had less than 1000 outlets. By 1990, despite backing from its parent company, Burger King had increased its outlets to a total of only 5500 or so, while McDonald's had emerged as the clear industry leader with over 10 000 outlets and with sales growing at 13 per cent per year. The explanation is to be found in the core skills – see Figure 3 (Irvin and Michaels, 1989, p. 7). McDonald's has the competitive edge on all counts.

**FIGURE 8**
*Contrasting execution of core skills*

| Core skills | McDonald's | Burger King |
|---|---|---|
| Site selection | 'Penchant for finding the *plum*'. | 'Generally good locations'. |
| High-quality service | '*Unparalleled* consistency'. | 'Suffers from operational sloppiness'. |
| Product innovation | 'A *knack* for product development'. | 'Spotty record with new products'. |
| Communications | 'Surrogate man'. | 'Comes off as aggressive, masculine and distant'. |

SOURCE: Irvin and Michaels (1989), p. 7

There are good examples to be found in the manufacturing sector as well as in the service sector, such as the VF Corporation (which makes Lee and Wrangler jeans, Jantzen swimsuits and Vanity Fair lingerie). The strong position of this company over the last 10 years is largely due to:

- high quality at competitive prices, thus offering superior value to consumers;
- accurate forecasting which means lower inventories, fewer stockouts, and less plants than most competitors;
- managing the risk that is inherent in the clothing industry by means of a focused and disciplined approach to the development of new lines.

It is important to recognize that identifying and creating core skills is far from easy. Both organizations and individuals develop particular ways of doing things and managing the process of change may require that the behaviour of thousands of people be changed in dozens of different locations. If success depends on it, then this nettle must be grasped. The approach adopted in grasping it will influence how effective the outcome is likely to be. For example, employees are more likely to show a willingness to accept change if they have a clear understanding of what is required of them, coupled with the assurance that there is some latitude for them to exercise judgement. This can be built in to the following steps *en route* to developing core skills:

1 establish a clear link between the chosen strategy and the required core skills, such as quick delivery requiring excellent distribution facilities;
2 be specific as well as selective in defining core skills so that employees will know what to do and how to do it, but in a focused way (e.g. covering no more than five core skills);
3 clarify the implications for pivotal jobs (hence recruitment and training requirements, support systems, reward schemes, etc.);
4 provide leadership from the top since the single most powerful discriminating factor between success and failure in developing core skills is the degree of top management involvement;
5 empower the organization to learn, which requires that individuals within the organization have scope for learning by doing – thereby seeing what works and what fails to work in building core skills through which strategies can be successfully implemented.

While a number of authors have written on the implementation of strategy (e.g. Lorange (1982); Bourgeois and Brodwin (1984); Nutt (1987, 1989); Reed and Buckley (1988); Reid (1989)), or more specifically on the implementation of marketing strategy (e.g. Spekman and Grønhaug (1983); McTavish (1989); Piercy and Morgan (1989a, 1989b, 1990)) as pointed out earlier there is relatively little guidance available on this important theme. Outstanding strategies are worthless if they cannot be put into effect, as Piercy and Morgan (1990), p.20 state:

> In short, the . . . reality the marketing executive faces is that implementing plans and strategies successfully is often dependent on managers and employees who are far removed from the excitement of creating new marketing strategies – people like service engineers, customer service units . . . field sales personnel, and so on.

The same authors (1989a) give examples of a museum failing to deliver a theme park strategy because employees cannot change from being 'policemen' to 'entertainers'; marketing strategies that rely on customer service failing because of employees' negative attitudes at the point of sale; and strategies based on integration and divisional cross-selling foundering because nobody recognized the human costs of change. It is not enough to develop marketing plans by focusing exclusively on customers, competitors and distributors (all *outside* the company) and ignoring those *within* the company. Almost all plans involve substantial human and organizational change: this requires 'internal marketing' which has goals such as to:

1 gain the support of key decision makers and facilitators;
2 change attitudes among those employees who deal with customers;
3 obtain employees' commitment to making the marketing plan work by involving them in the 'ownership' of the plan and by rewarding them on the plan's attainment;
4 train staff to allow them to develop new skills that will contribute to the effective implementation of plans.

Training (or management development) has been enthusiastically promoted (e.g. Hussey (1985), Brache (1986)) as a means of implementing plans. It was suggested by Hussey (1985, p. 32) that training can contribute to some of the problems of strategy implementation identified by Alexander (1985). Of the 10 most frequently encountered strategy implementation problems in US organizations, training can probably help with the top six (Figure 9).

**FIGURE 9**

*Implementation
problems*

| Problem | Percentage of enterprises reporting problem |
|---|---|
| 1 Implementation took more time than originally allocated. | 76 |
| 2 Major problems surfaced during implementation that had not been identified beforehand. | 74 |
| 3 Coordination of implementation activities was not effective enough. | 66 |
| 4 Competing activities and crises distracted management from implementing decisions. | 64 |
| 5 Capabilities of employees involved were insufficient for the task. | 63 |
| 6 Training and instructions given to lower level employees were inadequate. | 62 |

SOURCE: Adapted from Alexander (1985)

Bonoma and Crittenden (1988) have put forward a well-considered case showing that the successful implementation of marketing plans results from the interaction of structure and skills. In this context *structure* is seen to consist of:

- actions,
- programmes,
- systems,
- policies,

as portrayed in Figure 16.43 (see p. 485). Managerial *skills* embrace:

- interacting;
- allocating;
- monitoring;
- organizing.

Through a series of discussions with managers involved in implementing marketing plans Bonoma and Crittenden derived an interesting set of propositions concerning the relationship between structure and skills. These propositions are as follows:

1 There is normally a tension rather than a synergy between the enterprise's marketing structures and the skills of its managers. Whether this tension is productive or harmful depends on environmental factors.
2 The interaction between marketing structures and management skills is partially predictable using the rate of market change.
3 In low-change markets, structures and their associated systems dominate skills. Quality marketing practices result more often, and more cheaply, when strong systems and weak management skills are combined.
4 In high-change markets the reverse is true. Enterprises with weak structures and highly skilled managers get more desirable market-place results, more cheaply, than do enterprises having strong structures.
5 The complexity of tasks that marketing faces suggests whether structure or skills should dominate.
6 Routine, repetitive tasks (i.e. low complexity) are done more efficiently under strong structures with less strong execution skills.
7 Highly complex tasks require stronger execution skills and a weaker structure.

Propositions 1 to 7 can be portrayed diagrammatically (see Figure 10). If strong structures exist in circumstances characterized by rapidly changing markets and complex tasks it is likely that the enterprise's ability to adapt quickly to market needs will be constrained by rules and procedures. Conversely, if skills are dominant in a situation

**FIGURE 10**
*Structure/skills dynamics*

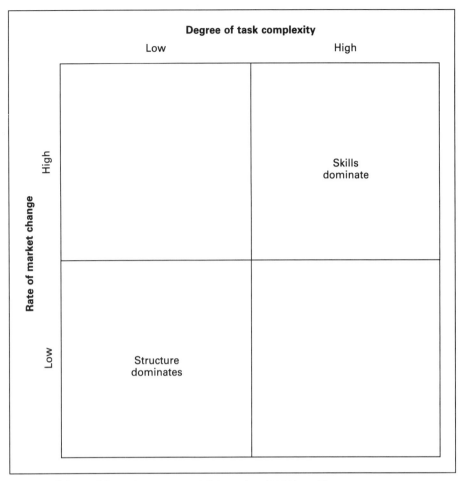

SOURCE: Adapted from Bonoma and Crittenden (1988), p. 12

involving low market change and low task complexity, the enterprise will be unable to increase its efficiency by relying on standard operating procedures.

Propositions 2 to 4 can be linked to phases of the PLC via a further proposition:

8  In the turbulent periods of the PLC (e.g. introduction, rapid growth, and, subsequently, maturity/decline) management skills will dominate execution structures in those enterprises performing better than average. In the more stable phases of the PLC structures will dominate skills.

The idea of balancing 'external' and 'internal' marketing in the implementation of marketing plans is portrayed in Figure 11.

This shows the distinction between strategy and tactics (developed with an external focus) and their implementation (via operations). However, part of the strategic thinking must be to ensure that those who will be responsible for carrying out operations are properly equipped for their tasks. If this is not the case then implementation will be poor, and failure is likely to result. Figure 12 offers the logical possibilities. Failure will follow whenever either the strategy/tactics are inappropriate or the implementation is poor.

**FIGURE 11**
*Strategy/tactics and operations*

| **External marketing –**<br>**strategy and tactics** | **Internal marketing –**<br>**operations** |
|---|---|
| External focus: setting direction | Internal focus: attaining direction |
| Effectiveness: doing the right thing | Efficiency: doing things right |
| Designing the plan | Executing the plan |
| Commits resources | Uses resources |

SOURCE: Adapted from Kotler, et al. (1985), p. 245

**FIGURE 12**
*Consequences of
strategic and
tactical
implementation*

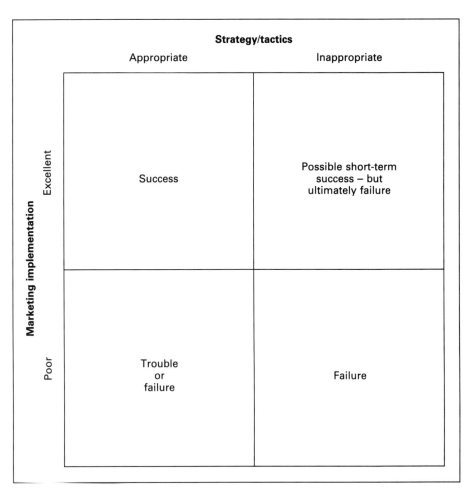

SOURCE: Adapted from Bonoma (1984), p. 72

# 17 | Problems to overcome

## 17.1 LEARNING OBJECTIVES

When you have read this chapter you should be able to:

1 understand the importance of implementation as part of the overall process of marketing planning and control;
2 recognize the problems that need to be addressed in implementing marketing plans and controlling marketing activities;
3 appreciate the need for marketing orientation and a positive approach to planning if marketing objectives are to be achieved;
4 identify the organizational design issues that are relevant to marketing planning, implementation, and control.

## 17.2 INTRODUCTION

Of the two major operating functions, production and marketing, the former has lent itself to rigorous analysis over many years with the result that it has been studied in great detail. Marketing, however, has not lent itself so much to critical examination until relatively recently, and for this reason it has received an unjustifiably low proportion of analytical attention. The marketing function is the most difficult area to plan and control since it is the source of sales forecasts and revenue estimates that can rarely be predicted accurately, and there is the further need to plan and control expenditure in addition to dealing with the human dimensions.

The scale of operations is determined by the sales forecast, but it may be found that the level of projected sales exceeds the short-term productive capacity of the enterprise. In such an event it may be necessary to:

1 expand the productive facilities;
2 raise prices in an attempt to ration the available output;
3 subcontract production to outside suppliers;
4 rely on inventories.

On the other hand, it may be that the projected level of sales is insufficient to produce the desired return on investment (i.e. profit objective). Apart from increasing the overall level of sales activity it may be appropriate to reconsider the means of distribution to ensure that it is the most cost-effective, or the existing sales effort may not be properly allocated (e.g. consider exporting – see Pilcher (1989)) or individual product profit margins may be subject to adjustment by product modifications, or an analysis of credit losses may cause credit extension policies to be amended to improve profitability (see, for example, Allenza (1989)).

The study, and to a lesser extent the practice, of financial management has been reduced almost to a science in parallel with the study of production. The importance of human rather than technical factors in the marketing subsystem, coupled with the complexity of the marketing interfaces with internal and external subsystems, have been the causes of the delays in rigorous marketing analysis. This chapter considers some of the problems that must be overcome in controlling marketing activities along the lines suggested in Chapter 18. Problem areas that are discussed include business pressures, problems in the marketing subsystem, problems of marketing feedback and information adequacy, cost problems, problems relating to marketing orientation and problems relating to planning. Consideration is also given to the organizational problems associated with the implementation and control of marketing plans.

## 17.3 PRESSURES

King (1991, p. 3) has pointed out that the pressures on marketing organizations during the 1980s were formidable and it is likely that these pressures will intensify as we move through the 1990s. Similar views are offered by Buckley (1991) and Hussey (1989).

**FIGURE 17.1**

*The influence of external factors*

SOURCE: Wilson (1983), p. 209

The range of external factors impacting on organizations is shown in Figure 17.1 (Wilson, 1983, p. 209), although this is not intended to be an exhaustive portrayal. Many of these factors were discussed in Chapter 7. Pressures that are expected to have an increasing significance as we head towards the year 2000 include:

1 More confident customers due to increasing consumer awareness via consumerism, a greater willingness to experiment, more readiness to trust their own judgement, less tolerance of products that fail to contribute to their own values, higher levels of disposable income, and increased individualism.
2 New concepts of quality that reflect *real* values rather than superficial styling, plus personal added values, and a requirement for increased customer care.
3 Changing demographic and social patterns, such as fewer school leavers and a higher proportion of retired people, a shortage of skills relative to 2 above, demands for improved social conditions, and the continuing importance of 'green' issues.
4 An intensification of competition via increased global marketing, the fragmentation of markets, and the risk of excess capacity in many markets.

5 The formation of joint ventures and strategic alliances when outright acquisition is neither feasible nor desirable, or when organic expansion is not possible (see, for example, Clarke and Brennan (1988) and Devlin and Biggs (1989)) and the growing use of shared services.

6 Political changes, including deregulation, political, economic and financial integration, and change in trade policies (see, for example, Quelch, Buzzell and Salama (1990)).

7 Technological imperatives in product and process innovations, the acceleration of technological change with an emphasis on new product development, hence shorter PLCs, and changes in the provision of service (e.g. via EFTS) – especially in retailing.

8 The harnessing of information technology in ways that build competitive advantage, which places a greater responsibility on managers both to understand the meaning of the results from the use of analytical techniques and to ensure that the quality of information in use is high.

9 Restructuring of the world economy and restructuring at a micro-economic level due to mergers, management buy-outs, leveraged buy-outs, building, unbundling, etc.

10 More market-focused organizations (i.e. increasing marketing orientation – see pp. 527–30 below), and an acceleration in the shift from a manufacturing to a service economy.

11 Short termism. On the question of short termism Heller (1990) observed that it has been argued that the spectre of the City of London has cast a shadow over British managers which makes them so uneasy that they tend to concentrate on short-term financial goals to the detriment of long-term results. However, the core of Heller's argument is that the short-term demons are, in fact, lurking within the managers themselves rather than within the City institutions (which are rarely inclined to act on a short-term basis). Managers who attach more importance to this year's results than to the organization's likely situation in the twenty-first century, or whose rewards are wholly-related to current performance, are not acting in the best interests of the organization as a whole.

The CBI set up a task force to report on the phenomenon of short termism: the resulting report (entitled *Investing for Britain's Future*) also showed short termism to be a myth insofar as it is attributable to City institutions. To the extent that it does exist it is attributable to poor management on the one hand and to underlying economic and political factors (such as high interest rates) on the other. Ferguson (1989, p. 68) has observed that share prices typically react well to announcements of strategic commitments but that 'British companies have a curious reticence about heralding their grand schemes'. The fact that there is good empirical support underlying the efficient markets hypothesis was pointed out in Chapter 15 (p. 419) (see also Puxty and Dodds (1991), pp. 69–86).

If only a few of these pressures were to occur there would be significant implications for marketing planning and control. Since most (if not all) of them are already occurring it is evident that managers must develop understanding, commitment and skills to deal proactively with new situations.

Lewis (1989) has grouped the pressures for change into four main areas, as in Figure 17.2.

The axes range from task-focused to people-focused pressures on the horizontal plane and from external to internal pressures on the vertical plane. Within the resulting cells we have:

1 market pressures, with keywords being change, variety and complexity;
2 external – people pressures involving increasing liaison with customers and developments such as the Green movement;

**FIGURE 17.2**
*Pressures for*
*change*

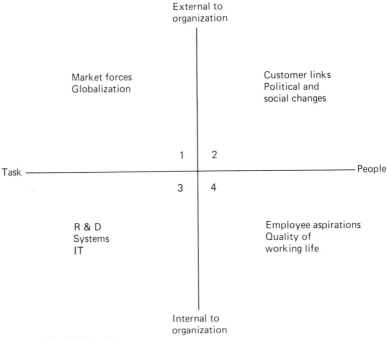

SOURCE: Lewis (1989)

3  internal – task pressures for cost reduction and systems development as well as
   R & D activities;
4  internal – people pressures, including increased autonomy among employees
   and demands for more flexibility in the way in which staff are treated in the
   face of reduced job security.

There are no blanket formulae for structuring organizations or motivating staff
in order to cope with the problems of constant change. It is evident, however, that
not all managers or their subordinates are equally amenable to change. Figure
17.3 gives one approach to assessing resistance to change (adapted from Witte
(1990), p. 30).

An organization that is highly resistant to change will exhibit characteristics
such as the following:

- large;
- established;
- centralized;
- hierarchic management structures;
- predictable tasks;
- manufacturing base;
- paternal orientation;
- vertical information systems;
- autocratic management style;
- unskilled workforce;
- non-professional;
- undifferentiated product lines;
- immobile workforce.

In contrast, an organization that has a low resistance to change will have
characteristics as follows:

- small;
- new;
- decentralized;
- flat management structures;

**FIGURE 17.3**
*Change resistance grid*

SOURCE: Adapted from Witte (1990)

- unpredictable tasks;
- service base;
- fraternal orientation;
- horizontal information systems;
- participative management style;
- skilled workforce;
- professional;
- differentiated product lines;
- mobile workforce.

The ideal environment in which to initiate change is one in which employees trust the organization but feel dissatisfied with the status quo. A classic example of this is to be found in the Virgin Group: it is a relatively young, decentralized, fast-growing service organization with diverse and innovative product lines. The workforce is skilled and mobile, the management structures are flat, and the management style is both participative and fraternal with an ethos that is virtually synonymous with change.

Innovation is clearly more likely in low-resistance organizations provided that they do not attempt too much too quickly or fail to carry through the changes that are initiated.

It has been contended (see Ulrich and Lake (1991)) that the 'traditional' means of securing competitive advantage (i.e. via financial, strategic and technological capabilities) cover only part of what managers will need to do to build sustainable competitive advantage in the 1990s. Existing capabilities must be supplemented by *organizational capability* – which can be defined as the enterprise's ability to manage people to gain competitive advantage by establishing internal structures and processes that influence its members to create organization-specific competences. This entails more than simply recruiting good people; it requires the deliberate development of competences by which employees will act to ensure the enterprise stays ahead of its competitors. Two outstanding examples of where this is being done are the Marriott Corporation (covering hotels and food) to which reference was made on p. 501, and Borg-Warner (which deals with chemicals, automotive components and financial services).

## 17.4 PROBLEMS IN THE MARKETING SUB-SYSTEM

Several facets of the marketing sub-system that give rise to problems of control have been highlighted by Kotler (1972). These include the following:

1  the outputs of the marketing function have repercussions on the outputs of other corporate functions, such as credit collection having a significant bearing on the controller's cash flow situation;
2  these outputs of other functional sub-systems in turn affect subsequent outputs of the marketing sub-system, so that a poor cash flow may lead to a need to cease extending credit and hence to a lower level of sales and profit;
3  the interface of the marketing sub-system with the sub-systems formed by external agents is fraught with difficulty since the marketing manager must attempt to exercise some degree of control over advertising agents, PR consultants, wholesalers, and shipping companies;
4  the human factor that is at the heart of marketing creates problems of control because of the difficulties involved in co-ordinating the activities of sales-people, product managers, advertising agents, and marketing researchers, all of whom are essentially creative and individualistic;
5  the usual problems associated with any corporate project, such as launching a new product, entering a new territory, or executing a major promotional campaign are especially noticeable in marketing as a result of the human element and the external interfaces.

To these we can add the problem of assessing performance.

Defining marketing performance has proved to be a difficult task due to a number of problems, including (as suggested by Bonoma and Clark (1988)):

* the nature of marketing as a complex discipline having many dimensions and interfaces (e.g. internally with functions such as production, and externally with intermediaries, agencies, etc.), each of which has an impact on performance;
* the need for marketing to behave in an adaptive way in the light of environmental changes (such as competitive activities or shifts in the pattern of consumer demand) which renders performance bench-marks perishable;
* the tendency to focus on inputs rather than outputs with the presumption being that the desired outputs (such as increased market share) are 'obvious' thereby playing down the importance of both marketing performance and the implementation of marketing plans.

The marketing manager must find means of securing better co-ordination among the various functional sub-systems that are not directly under his control, including production, purchasing, and materials control. This may be achieved by improving communications and inter-organizational understandings about what is in the interest of the enterprise as a whole.

In addition, the marketing manager must strive to influence external agents as well as to motivate his internal staff to carry out their respective duties in the enterprise's best interests. This requires both flexibility in terms of tactics and adequate feedback from operations.

A co-ordinated approach requires that marketing plans are developed alongside production plans, staffing plans, financial plans, and so forth. The need for this close co-ordination is due to elements of one plan being the starting point for others: thus a sales forecast (as an element of the marketing plan) is the cornerstone of the production plan (see Chapter 15 of Fisk (1967) and Chapter 9 of Schaffir and Trentin (1973)).

Systems theory provides a framework within which management can effectively integrate the various activities of the organization, including the marketing function. The major benefit of the systems approach lies in the facility it gives to management in recognizing the proper place and function of sub-systems within the whole, thereby focusing attention on broader issues than those contained in a single department. With particular reference to marketing, the application of systems thinking (Lazer (1962b); Wilson (1970b)) should result in at least three developments of significance to improved management:

- a more concerted emphasis on marketing planning and control;
- better systems of marketing intelligence to provide management with a clearer perspective for its marketing actions:
- following from both of the above items, a better understanding of marketing as an adjustment mechanism that is able to employ corporate resources to meet changing market conditions successfully.

With particular regard to functional co-ordination, the common flows through all departments are information, physical resources, and funds, so one or more of these can be a vehicle for integration. Let us consider some examples.

## Production–Marketing Interface
A failure to control this interface effectively can lead to such problems as the sales force promising early delivery to secure an order that then causes difficulties in both production programming and delivery scheduling. Such behaviour could easily jeopardize future orders. Plant capacity and flexibility, standardization, and quality requirements must all be taken into account by planners attempting to integrate production and marketing operations.

## Purchasing–Marketing Interface
Effective co-operation here should prevent material shortages from appearing and should also help to avoid the holding of excessive raw material/component stocks due to marketing management's failing to inform the purchasing department of reduced requirements. Such failure causes funds to be tied up unnecessarily in an unprofitable use, which is very inefficient.

## Personnel–Marketing Interface
Although selection procedures are imperfect this in itself is an insufficient cause to ignore the methods that are available and to rely on personal judgement. Those who are to be responsible for recruiting, training, and inducting marketing personnel must have a sound knowledge of the work done in, and skill requirements of, the marketing area.

## Finance–Marketing Interface
The question of co-ordination and communication between marketing and the financial control function is of fundamental importance (e.g. Ratnatunga (1983, 1988); Ward (1989); Wilson (1970, 1975, 1981)). Our present interest is not with the keeping of books of accounts and the subsequent reporting to outside parties (e.g. via the statutory annual balance sheet and profit and loss account). This is but one decreasingly important function of the financial controller generally referred to as the *stewardship function*. (It is so called because the

controller acts as the shareholders' steward in keeping records, paying bills, collecting debts, and safeguarding the assets of the business.)

In contrast with stewardship is the controller's *service function* through which he aims to develop information flows and reporting systems to facilitate improved planning, decision making and control.

Marketing controllership is concerned with the controller's service to marketing management, and this will become increasingly important as the marketing concept is more widely adopted and as marketing becomes more dominant within the typical company.

To offer the best service to marketing involves the controller studying the company's marketing organization and its problems. One approach to this is shown in Figure 17.4 (Bancroft & Wilson (1979), p. 29).

**FIGURE 17.4**
*A framework for improved management accounting – marketing interaction*

SOURCE: Bancroft and Wilson (1979), p. 29

A greater mutual understanding between marketing managers and management accountants, coupled with the greater involvement of members from both groups in the decision process, should lead to more effective outcomes. The most effective communication, and the best information flows, tend to occur where members of the controller's staff are located within the marketing function with line responsibility to the controller but with a close working relationship with the marketing staff. In their US study Schiff and Melman (1962) found this arrangement in very few companies, and in their UK study Wilson and Bancroft (1983) found a similar situation, but a deeper interest in analysing the costs of marketing seems to have developed since then, along with the spread of the marketing concept. Nevertheless, comparatively little attention has been given to marketing costs as opposed to the extensive attention given to production costs despite the very substantial scale of the former.

## 17.5 PROBLEMS OF MARKETING FEEDBACK

The importance of feedback is paramount since unbalanced and unstable conditions, along with an inability to exercise effective control, can develop within the marketing area if prompt, adequate, and undistorted feedback is not present.

However, the marketing manager can rarely benefit from the advantages of statistical feedback to provide an automatic corrective control over marketing activities in the same way that the production manager can use such control over much of his plant. It is necessary for the marketing manager frequently to base his decision on experience alone, and control by relying on his ability to motivate his staff and external agents after he has personally received the feedback.

The two major reasons for the rare use of pure automatic feedback in marketing are simple to discern.

1 The fact that performance deviations can arise from a multitude of different causes. For example, a drop in sales may be caused by a price increase with elastic demand, as a result of competitive products or promotions, or as a result of a decline in the level of business activity over the trade cycle, and so forth.
2 The plans and standards used in the control process may be as much at fault as the apparent performance. The inability, say, of a salesman to achieve his quota may be due to poor quota setting or unrealistic sales forecasting as well as poor performance. An investigation into such matters may result in a revision of standards or plans, but a feedback mechanism can hardly be expected to deal with mistakes in the basis of performance measurement.

All these problem areas demand that flexibility be maintained in relation to both planning and controlling marketing operations. Accordingly, the marketing manager must be able to redeploy his salesmen, adapt the advertising campaign, or change the various aspects of his market offer (price, packaging, product features, etc.) to meet changing conditions. This means that he is charged with the almost impossible tasks of knowing the changes to make and being able to make them.

Of the greatest importance in this setting is the suitability of the information system in enabling the marketing manager to be flexible in devising alternative plans as a matter of contingency rather than necessity. As in all such matters, the costs and benefits should be balanced in the securing of fuller control.

In considering feedback it is inevitable that delays of one kind or another will be experienced. To a large extent delay is inevitable since feedback is, by definition, *ex post*, thus only arising after the event. However, we can break delays down into their constituent categories as shown in Figure 17.5.

**FIGURE 17.5**
*Major delays in a feedback system*

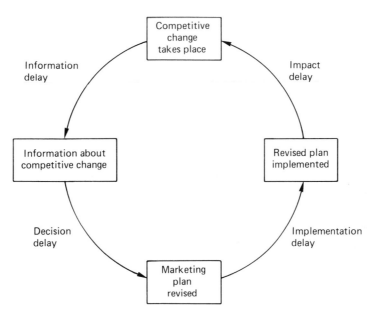

SOURCE: Adapted from Kotler (1972), p. 770

If a competitor introduces a significant change in his market offering there is a delay until this information is relayed to the marketing team. It takes time to devise a suitable response, involving revisions to marketing plans. Once the revisions are decided upon there will be a lag until they are implemented. Finally, at least for this iteration, there will be a delay following implementation before it becomes apparent what the impact of the revised course of action is on the competitive change. By the time these delays have been incurred it is quite possible that the competitor may have established a clear competitive advantage, hence feedback delays must be minimized in responding to competitive threats – or to any other relevant change. This latter situation is illustrated in Figure 17.6 (derived from Forrester (1965), pp. 357, 358 and 361) which shows positive and negative feedback loops relating to the sales growth pattern of a newly launched product.

**FIGURE 17.6**
*Feedback effects on
sales growth*

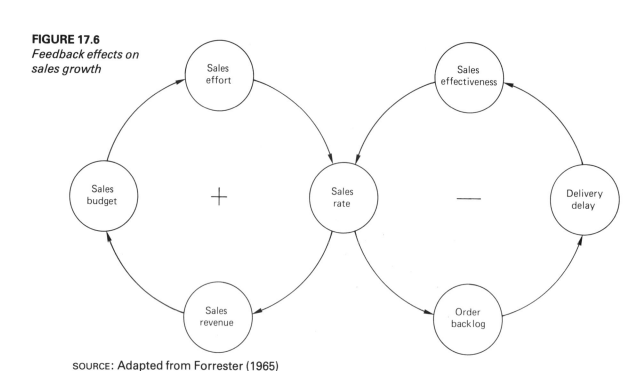

SOURCE: Adapted from Forrester (1965)

The rates of sales of the new product (i.e. the point of intersection of the positive and negative feedback loops in Figure 17.6) is a function of sales effort on the one hand and sales effectiveness on the other. If the sales rate generates a profitable level of sales revenue this is likely to lead to an increase in the sales budget, hence to further increases in the amount of sales effort. These linkages are shown in the left-hand (positive feedback) loop, and it would appear that continuous sales growth is in prospect. However, if there is insufficient productive capacity to meet the increased sales rate an order backlog will build up, along with delays in delivery. This will almost certainly cause a decrease in sales effectiveness which, in turn, will dampen the sales rate as shown in the right-hand (negative feedback) loop.

As the two loops interact it becomes clear that sales will grow when there is available productive capacity to ensure that order backlogs are avoided. Whenever the sales rate exceeds full capacity the result is that sales will then decrease due to the order backlogs, etc. This rather simplified example highlights not only the lack of synchronizing in terms of timing but also the importance of functional coordination.

## 17.6 INFORMATION ADEQUACY

How effective a manager is in his job will depend on how much, how relevant, and how good his information is, and how well he interprets and acts upon it.

Nevertheless, one hears frequent complaints from management that information is too late, of the wrong type, unverified, or even suppressed. It is evident, therefore, that if information is to be of value it must be clear, detailed, timely, accurate, and complete – and must not consist of vague figures thrown out by an unplanned system.

It is not enough, for example, to observe that the purpose of a particular set of procedures is to provide the information required for planning and controlling the company's marketing operation. The information requirements must be made more explicit, and the aim of a marketing analysis system defined. The aim may be to produce the internal data needed for effective planning and control of marketing activities and the requirements specified as follows:

*Marketing planning*
● establishing sales quotas by territory, product, industry and channel;
● developing the advertising budget, and planning the allocation of funds amongst specified media;
● evaluating the character and size of the product line;
● developing additional outlets and new channels of distribution;
● determining the need for, and location of, additional warehouses.

*Measurement and control of results by:*
● salesman;
● geographic area;
● distribution channel;
● customer group;
● product.

Management must decide what needs to be done, who is to do it, ensure that it is done, and evaluate the success with which it was done. None of these functions can be performed without the necessary information. But *all* the available information may not be helpful, so the marketing manager must pay great attention to the quality, quantity, and relevance of the information that he seeks.

It is characteristic of decision making that in selecting one particular course of action the manager thereby prevents himself from moving in another direction. This constitutes a major difficulty in making decisions, and it follows that the manager's ability to make better decisions involves relying upon information that:

1 reduces the uncertainty associated with following one particular course of action;
2 improves his power to act in the right direction.

The sources of such improvement lie in the methodical selection, collection, processing, analysis, and communication of relevant information, along with the ability to formulate sound assumptions as a basis for making more accurate forecasts and decisions on the basis of that information.

However, while to manage a business is to manage information, it may be that either too much or too little information is presented. The economic wastage that results from an excess of information is *not* the incremental clerical cost of producing it, but rather the loss of executive effectiveness that it causes. This comes about in two major ways:

1 the manager may ignore the great volume of information that is presented to him, thus missing the vital as well as the irrelevant;
2 the manager may become overburdened, or even enslaved, by the excess.

On the other hand, should there be insufficient information presented for optimal decision making, it may be wise to postpone the decision until more information is available. A similar situation involving delay is that in which sufficient information is presented but its accuracy is in doubt and extra time must be spent if this accuracy is to be improved. In either situation the loss of control that results from delay must be weighed against the value of improved information in reducing the uncertainties implicit in the making of most decisions.

Only a limited amount of the information that flows through the typical organization is of real management significance. That which is of value, therefore, must be identified and developed in line with organizational requirements – observing the important information qualities of impartiality, validity, reliability, and internal consistency.

The organizational structure of an enterprise and its information requirements are inextricably linked. In order to translate a statement of his duties into action the manager must receive and use information. This involves using all the relevant data and intelligence – financial and non-financial – that is available, instead of merely relying on an existing system and the reports it produces.

As frequently happens the manager may not know precisely what information he requires or, alternatively, what information is available. Consultants can help by observing the types of decisions made, testing the adequacy of existing information, suggesting alternative information flows, and indicating the means (and costs) of collection.

The aim, then, is to provide the right information to the right people in the right quantity at the right time, and at minimum cost. The purpose of collecting, analysing, and using information is essentially the same in any size of business, whether for routine purposes or for special projects. The difference is in the relative employment of manual as opposed to computer-based systems. The increasing adoption of electronic data processing should ensure that fewer managers have cause to complain about insufficient, inaccurate or delayed information. This depends, of course, not only upon accurate information flows but also upon systematic storage in order to facilitate rapid retrieval. The need to react quickly to a changing environment demands fast and accurate retrieval as facts that take too long to find and compile are often useless when time is of the essence.

Discussions about information systems can usefully be considered against the background of the *theory of communication*. Relative to the broad subject of communication there are three major problems:

1  the accuracy with which the symbols of communication can be transmitted – the technical problem;
2  the precision with which the transmitted symbols convey the desired meaning – the semantic problem;
3  the effectiveness with which the received meaning affects behaviour in the desired manner – the effectiveness problem.

Figure 17.7 illustrates how these problems can arise in the process of selecting a message and transmitting it (i.e. in the usual decision-making process of using an information system).

In the process of being transmitted it is unfortunately characteristic that certain things are added to (or omitted from) the signal that were not intended by the information source. Such errors, distortions, and changes are collectively termed 'noise'.

The transmitter could take a written message and use some code to encipher it into, say, a sequence of numbers (as on punched cards or tape), which could then be sent over the channel as the signal. The general purpose of the transmitter thus becomes one of encoding, and the purpose of the receiver one of decoding.

**FIGURE 17.7**
*The
communication
system*

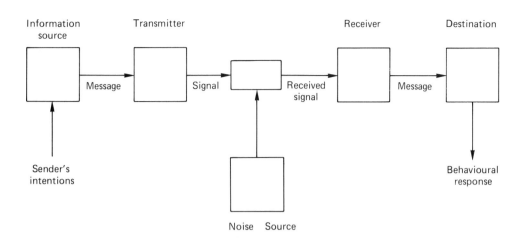

However, as one makes the coding more and more nearly ideal one is forced into longer and longer delays in the process of coding, and this requires the establishing of balance. But no matter how careful one is in the coding process it will always be found that, after the signal has been received, there remains some undesirable uncertainty (noise) about the precise nature of the message.

It is emphasized throughout this book that the manager needs information to assist him in decision making, to indicate performance, and to help him in making plans, setting standards and controlling outcomes. In this light the key to developing a dynamic and usable management information system is to move beyond the limits of conventional reporting and to conceive of information as it relates to the two vital elements of the management process – planning and control.

A great deal of information, while useful for planning and control, is primarily raised for some other purpose that is only tangentially related to planning and control. This covers much of the output of the accounting routine in many companies. Such information is derived from:

1 payroll procedures;
2 the order-processing cycle, beginning with the receipt of an order and ending with the collection of accounts receivable;
3 the procurement and accounts payable cycle.

The adequacy of these information flows as a basis for decision systems is highlighted by the omission of:

1 information about the future;
2 data expressed in non-financial terms, such as market share, productivity, quality levels, adequacy of customer service, etc.
3 information dealing with external conditions as they might bear on a particular enterprise's operations.

Effective business planning requires three types of information – environmental, competitive and operating. Accounting alone, therefore, is insufficient; but if the controllership function exists within a company it should ensure that economic and marketing research and forecasting are closely integrated with the systems function.

Information is the medium of control, but the flows required for planning are not necessarily the same as those required for control. Figure 17.8 outlines the general nature of information flows for planning and control. Their uses in control revolve around communication, motivation, and performance, whereas forecasting, establishing objectives, and deciding among alternatives are more important in planning.

**FIGURE 17.8**
*The anatomy of
management
information*

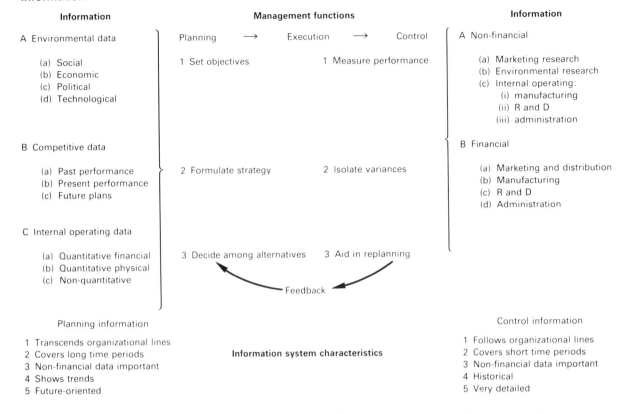

| Information | Management functions | Information |
|---|---|---|

**Planning information**
1 Transcends organizational lines
2 Covers long time periods
3 Non-financial data important
4 Shows trends
5 Future-oriented

**Information system characteristics**

**Control information**
1 Follows organizational lines
2 Covers short time periods
3 Non-financial data important
4 Historical
5 Very detailed

In summary, a management information system is the means of bringing to each level of management the necessary and complete information that is accurate, timely and sufficient (but not in excessive detail), so that each manager can fulfil his responsibilities to the organization. The central purpose, then, is to aid decision making, and the system should be based on sound data, be sufficiently flexible to allow new techniques to be used, and be operated at minimum cost commensurate with the overall system results.

The three basic information flows in marketing are:

1 the inflow of environmental data;
2 internal operating data;
3 communication (usually of a persuasive nature) directed to external audiences.

The effectiveness of each flow should be continually tested by the posing of questions such as:

1 Does the procedure for developing delivery quotations to customers produce the information required to ensure that delivery promises are realistic?
2 Does the procedure for handling customers' enquiries regarding the status of their orders provide for rendering a superior form of customer service?
3 Do the sales statistical procedures produce the best internal data required to plan sales strategy, to control selling effort, and to spotlight opportunities for major improvements in the distribution programme?
4 Do the clerical support activities provided for the sales force help to increase each sales person's productivity by maximizing the amount of time spent in direct selling work?

These representative questions point to the main uses of a marketing information system in the control effort and these fall into the following groups:

1 to spot things that are going wrong and to take corrective action before serious loss results, which constitutes the most fruitful and constructive use of control information;
2 to highlight things that have actually gone wrong and guide marketing management in either cutting the losses of failure or turning apparent failure to future advantage;
3 to determine exactly how and why failures or deviations from plan have arisen and to suggest steps that should be taken to prevent their recurrence, which is another highly constructive application since mistakes need not be repeated even if they cannot be avoided.
4 to find out who is to blame for failure which, if not done in the proper way and followed up by corrective action, is the least constructive of uses.

Careful consideration must always be applied to deciding which elements of information to include in a marketing information system if cost is not to be a prohibitive factor. The types of decisions that must be made will obviously determine the types of information that the system should provide. A few examples are given below.

## Pricing (See also Chapter 12)
Before any decision on price can be made information should be available on:

1 competitive pricing policies and product prices;
2 consumer attitudes to price;
3 the relative profitability of the company's products at various prices;
4 distribution and production costs as a basis for 3, above;
5 volume factors (covering both market share and potential along with capacity details).

## Product Management (See also Chapter 11)
This function depends completely on adequate flows of information from a variety of sources if it is to be successfully carried out. Information should be related to the PLC since this indicates when to launch new products, when to phase out declining products, and when to revitalize the marketing effort behind other products. The life cycle must be viewed in terms of total sales and market penetration on the one hand, and costs and profitability on the other. Forecasts of costs and revenues will follow from forecasts of total market size and the share that is to be achieved.

## Sales Operations
Up-to-date details of each live account should be an essential part of a marketing information system because this facilitates analyses that are invaluable to sales planning and control. In addition, accurate customer records mean that new salesmen can be assigned to territories or customer groups and learn a good deal about the accounts before visiting them: this prevents the situation when a poor salesman is kept on because he is the only person knowing about his accounts in the absence of proper records, and the total sales job can be smoothly transferred to the case of promotion, transfer, or departure only if such records exist.

Analyses from sales records will give essential information to marketing management on product profitability, customer-group profitability, and regional profitability, and actual performance can be compared to the requirements of the profit plan. The extent to which variances arise from volume changes, variations in price, or adjustments in the mix of products sold can be analysed, and the usual budgetary procedures will provide information on selling expenses.

The role of the sales person as an information intermediary between the enterprise and its outlets and customers must not be overlooked since a sales person who appreciates the importance of rapid information dissemination and feedback can help his or her organization to promote new products as well as adapting quickly to environmental change.

## 17.7  COST PROBLEMS

The essence of control in marketing, as in any other activity, is measurement. In relation to marketing costs, however, this measurement is not as straightforward as it may seem.

Figure 17.9 illustrates the basic elements of financial marketing performance that need to be controlled. The importance of marketing as the 'revenue generator' is made clear, but the other aspect of the financial sphere – cost incurrence – requires further consideration (see the discussion of definitions in Chapter 3, Section 3.3).

**FIGURE 17.9**
*Key financial
factors in marketing
performance*

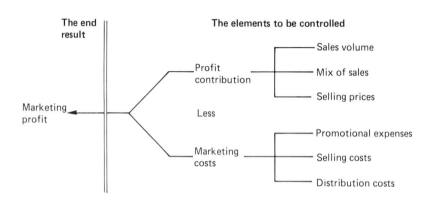

It is invariably found that the costs stemming from marketing activities are difficult to plan and control. The lowest costs are not necessarily to be preferred since these may not result in the effective attainment of the desired sales volume and profit. Most order-getting costs are programmed rather than variable and tend to influence the volume of sales rather than being influenced by it.

The characteristics of marketing costs lead to problems in analysis. Such characteristics include (after Wilson (1979, 1988) but see also Kjaer-Hansen (1965) and Wilson (1992)):

1  Long-run effects (e.g. the effect of an advertising campaign lasts longer than the campaign, and is usually lagged).
2  The difficulty in measuring productivity since standards are not easily determined. (Standards can be set for sales activities, e.g. cost to create £1 of sales, average costs of each unit sold, cost to generate £1 of profit, cost per transaction, cost per customer serviced. However, in product decisions, levels of performance may be expressed in terms of the minimum required level of sales per product or the minimum profit contribution required.)
3  The non-symmetrical nature of costs. (For example, costs increase more in changing from regional to national distribution than would be saved by changing from national to regional distribution.)
4  Costs are frequently indivisible or joint costs, often intended to support a product group.
5  Some costs have discontinuities, or a stepped character shape. The special structure of marketing costs raises problems. The cost structure of every activity is related to the interaction of fixed costs (that do not vary with the level of sales activity) and variable costs (such as shipping costs that do vary with the level of activity), and is reflected in the cost per unit produced or sold at different rates of activity. However, a large number of marketing costs are semi-fixed, including, for example, sales force costs: when a sales person is appointed his or her salary is a fixed cost, but the number of sales people and the level of commission and expenses are variable, thus giving rise to a

semi-fixed expenses category. In the case of marketing, which accounts for a considerable proportion of total expenditure, these stepped costs of a semi-fixed nature determine the behaviour of many other costs.

Planning in the light of these characteristics must be based to a significant extent on past experience, knowledge of competitive activities, test marketing exercises, and the estimated expenditure that desired profits at various levels of activity will permit.

Accounting data in the more conventional form provides a point of departure for marketing cost analyses, but these data must be reworked on the basis of units that are subject to management control. (The relevant control unit will depend on the purpose of the analysis, but may be a product, product line, sales territory, marketing division, customer group, etc.).

6 The costs of performing the two main tasks of marketing – order getting and order filling – have different effects and must be treated differently. The minimization principle should be applied to distribution activities whereby a given quantitative target is aimed for at the lowest possible cost. But this principle cannot be applied to promotion since the relationship between promotion and sales means that a variation in promotional expenditure will affect turnover so minimal promotion may mean minimal sales. Consequently an optimization principle must be applied and a balance struck between the desired level of sales and the level of promotional expenditure necessary to achieve that level of sales.

7 The allocation of indirect marketing costs raises questions that require solutions. Along with a general increase in the proportion of fixed costs that exists in modern businesses there has been an increasing adoption of direct costing systems (i.e. in which indirect costs are not allocated to products) which often result in indirect costs being ignored. The significance of marketing costs is so great that they must necessarily be subjected to detailed control via responsibility centre accounting (see Chapter 18, pp. 554–64) rather than be left uncontrolled as inevitable indirect outlays.

8 Further cost problems relate to the greater number of essentially different marketing conditions that have to be controlled continually and rationally. Financial control in marketing is complicated because a number of factors are influenced by the costs incurred – the product, the territory, the customer group, and the salesman's profitability, in contrast to the product alone that is the centre of attention in production accounting. The addition of varying conditions to a series of control bases makes it difficult to know which costs are to be controlled and in relation to which base.

9 Special cost control problems arise in attempting to evaluate the results of each element of the marketing mix. It is almost impossible to isolate the role played by, say, direct selling in the marketing operation from the roles played by promotion, price, and product features. Measures of individual parameter effectiveness must be related to detailed market analyses on a before and after basis, but this requires a more comprehensive system of marketing intelligence and information than is found in the typical company.

10 The enormous range of strategic possibilities makes it impossible to include all of them in a formal analysis. Any particular marketing strategy will involve a particular combination of the elements of the marketing mix, with particular assumed environmental conditions. The number of different possible combinations is vast. This does not mean that quantitative techniques are useless, but it does mean that measurement problems arise to complicate the issue.

11 The ever-changing environment – including the impacts of competitive activities, developments in technology, changes in consumer tastes, government action, and the other factors depicted in Figure 17.1 – makes planning difficult. As a result control is made more difficult since it is no longer clear which variances were avoidable and which unavoidable.

12 In considering the range of possible strategies the uncertainty that any one constituent factor may change at almost any time makes the question of choice even more difficult.

13 The effectiveness of costs (i.e. productivity or efficiency) is not easy to measure. The interdependent variety of elements involved and their varying long- and short-run effects are the cause of this difficulty.

14 The tendency towards 'conglomeration', with its attendant diversification of activities and sheer size, results in an increasing complexity that challenges the best efforts in securing control.

In addition there is the problem relating to the setting up and operating of decision models which strictly require a knowledge of the substitution or supplementation of the elements of the marketing mix. As with the major problem areas discussed above the latter one (i.e. understanding substitution and supplementation) is concerned with evaluating the efficiency of the marketing effort and rationalizing the pattern of expenditure. In every case it is helpful to relate marketing costs to a profitability base since this is both a measure of efficiency and of goal attainment.

Essentially, costs are incurred in marketing to obtain a sufficient level of sales to give the desired profit. The necessary sales volume can be expressed as either a particular market share, or a desired depth of market penetration, in which event the interrelationships are illustrated in Figure 17.10.

**FIGURE 17.10**
*Marketing costs, profits and penetration*

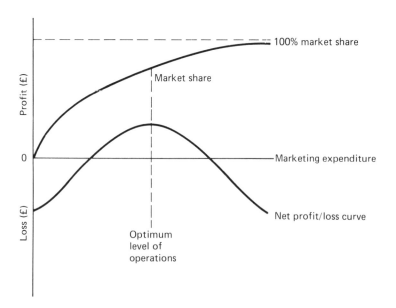

The important point made by Figure 17.10 is that increasing profitability is not necessarily a function of increasing market share, nor necessarily of increasing marketing expenditure. A frequently met obsession with sales managers is that of maximizing *sales volume* whereas the action that they should be recommending is the optimizing of profits. The relationship between sales and profitability should follow one of the following patterns:

1 an increase in sales with a proportionately lower increase in costs should lead to improved profitability;
2 an increase in sales with constant costs should improve profitability;
3 an increase in sales with a decrease in costs should improve profitability;
4 the maintaining of sales at a constant level with a decrease in costs should improve profitability.

The outcome of these various matters in operational terms is that, in order to improve the effectiveness of control in marketing, the following requirements must be met:

- a frequent and accurate monitoring of the three main constituents discussed – costs, sales volume, and profit;
- a regular monitoring of the total market environment in order to detect movements and aid in evaluating the effectiveness of marketing expenditures;
- a detailed breakdown of marketing effort (expressed in financial terms) into functional/managerial responsibility centres.

In many manufacturing enterprises the costs of marketing greatly exceed the costs of production yet very little attention has been given to the analysis of marketing costs compared to the extensive attention given to production costs.

It is instructive to consider some of the reasons for this state of affairs, and these include the following:

1 While the costs of productive labour and materials can be associated with specific machines, processes, and products, the costs of the elements of the marketing mix cannot be associated so readily with outputs (such as sales and profit levels).
2 Marketing activities tend to be less routine and repetitive than is the case with many standardized production activities.
3 The dependency of marketing activities on outside agencies distinguishes them further from the more internally-regulated and predictable manufacturing activities.
4 Marketing activities tend to be performed in many locations, often distant from each other, rather than on one site.
5 Within manufacturing there is the relatively simple choice to be made between using the product or the process as the cost object. In contrast, within marketing there are many more possible cost objects – such as the product line, product range, customer, customer/industry group, salesman sales territory, size of order, channel of distribution, etc.
6 The cost behaviour patterns of many marketing activities are the reverse of those for manufacturing activities in the sense that marketing costs tend to determine sales volume (hence manufacturing costs). Marketing costs are committed in anticipation of sales. Whereas manufacturing costs *necessarily* increase as sales volume rises, marketing costs must be *permitted* to increase. Thus, for a given level of activity, the lower the manufacturing costs the better, while the right level (and mix) of marketing costs is a matter of judgement. It can be argued that the 'best' approach is to focus on *technical efficiency* in relation to marketing outlays (i.e. to maximize the outputs for a given level of input) and on *economic efficiency* in relation to manufacturing outlays (whereby one aims to minimize the inputs for a given level of output). This indicates the analytical complexity inherent in accounting for marketing costs.
7 Since marketing costs are rarely included in inventory valuations (being treated instead as period costs) financial accounting principles, etc., provide little incentive for detailed analysis.
8 Manufacturing activities typically have a short-run focus whereas marketing operations must pay attention to long-run considerations. This also produces a conflict over financial accounting practice in that promotional outlays in a particular period are invariably matched with the sales achieved during that period notwithstanding the fact that much promotional expenditure (and other order-getting outlays) are in the nature of capital investment intended to stimulate sales over several time periods.

9 Personnel in manufacturing roles often have a greater cost consciousness and discipline than their marketing colleagues.
10 The risk of suboptimization (whereby one particular aspect is maximized to the possible detriment of the whole) is much greater in a complex marketing context than it is in manufacturing.
11 Many marketing activities have an intangible quality that distinguishes them from the tangible characteristics of production activities. Among the intangible factors is the psychological dimension of purchase predisposition.

Although these problems are many they do not mean that no attempts should be made to plan and control marketing activities successfully. However, there is evidence to show that most accountants are not yet in tune with marketing thinking. First, accountants lack the knowledge and understanding of the information requirements necessary for the marketing function. Second, accountants in general do not accept marketing as a distinct and separate managerial function. This seemingly blind attitude was found in a survey (reported by Williamson (1979)) to be well ingrained and is an appalling indication of the failure of accountants to see the real essence of business activity (i.e. product-market interactions) and of a misplaced arrogance in looking down on a group whose purpose and function they so clearly misunderstand. Lastly, organizational design may impede adequate communications between functions. This could (and does) happen to such an extent that the accounting and marketing departments may be geographically diverse from one another, although marketing *activities* are geographically diverse in any event.

A long-established organizational design could also hinder a new pattern of resource allocation. It may be such that available resources are channelled towards the order-filling production and distribution functions rather than to the order-getting processes such as advertising, sales promotion and selling. Allocating to the former in preference to the latter is tantamount to saying that a firm can sell what it can make – the old sales concept – rather than the marketing concept of making what the consumers want.

The practical consequences of these inhibitions manifest themselves in the ways described below.

Schiff and Mellman (1962), in an almost isolated empirical study, noted deficiencies of the accounting function in supplying marketing with sufficient information in certain areas, such as:

- lack of effective financial analyses of customers, channels of distribution and salespeople;
- an over-emphasis on net-profit based reporting (or the full cost allocation approach);
- inadequacies in marketing cost classification (e.g. little distinction was made betwen fixed and variable costs or between controllable and non-controllable costs);
- return on investment was rarely used;
- there was a general lack of integration between the accounting and marketing functions.

Goodman (1970) in a later study found that accounting did not appear to have made much progress in satisfying the needs of marketing planning. These areas of failure he saw as being:

- non-use of sufficient return-on-investment criteria;
- insistence on using the traditional full-costing for decision analyses;
- inability to separate the reporting obligation of accounting from the service function;

- imperfect understanding of the marketing concept;
- lack of minimum acceptable goal criteria;
- disregard for the implications of working capital.

As various authorities have observed, there are fundamental differences between accounting and marketing. For example, accounting builds from an analysis of internal financial data, whereas marketing builds from the diagnosis of external market situations. The respective perspectives are literally poles apart (see Simmonds' Foreword in Wilson (1981)). Thus the marketing view that profit stems from an enterprise's position relative to its competitors (i.e. reflecting its differential advantage) and is not a function of arbitrary financial periods is not likely to meet with full-blooded approval – or even understanding – on the part of the average accountant who invariably fails to link his own profit measures either to market share or to changes in market size.

## 17.8 MARKETING ORIENTATION

In the absence of marketing orientation it will be difficult to implement and control marketing activities effectively since there will be no marketing plan. (The following discussion draws heavily from Wilson and Fook (1990).)

The well-documented and long-run decline in Britain's industrial competitiveness has often been attributed to a lack of adequate marketing orientation on the part of UK firms. It is widely felt that the more successful firms demonstrate a higher level of marketing orientation than their less successful rivals, although hard evidence to support this is rather rare. Nevertheless, despite a minority view that a preoccupation with marketing orientation is a cause of competitive decline when the former is focused on the short-run requirements of customers, there is a strong case for arguing that marketing orientation leads to improved marketing effectiveness which, in turn, leads to improved corporate effectiveness: see Figure 17.11.

**FIGURE 17.11**
*The role of marketing orientation*

SOURCE: Wilson and Fook (1990), p. 22

If a business is to seek to improve its effectiveness in this way it needs to ask the following questions:

- What is marketing orientation?
- How can marketing orientation be recognized?
- How can marketing orientation be developed?

In this section we will address these three questions and suggest how an enterprise might develop its marketing orientation in order to improve its effectiveness.

**What is Marketing Orientation?**

A business can exhibit any one of a number of different orientations such as:

- production orientation;
- cost orientation;
- engineering orientation;
- sales orientation;
- marketing orientation.

The last of these is the broadest and highlights the concern the enterprise has with satisfying its customers via the adoption of the marketing concept.

Marketing orientation is concerned with implementing the marketing concept and, as such, is action oriented. However, rather than seeing it as a set of activities it is more helpful to think of marketing orientation as a process by which an enterprise seeks to maintain a continuous match betwen its products/services and its customers' needs. With a little elaboration we can build this into a formal definition:

> Marketing orientation is the process by which an enterprise's target customers' needs and wants are effectively and efficiently satisfied within the resource limitations and long-term survival requirements of that enterprise.

Doubt has been expressed by many marketing authorities on the extent to which the philosophy underlying the marketing concept has been adequately implemented – hence upon the extent to which marketing orientation really exists. Given that the practical manifestations of marketing orientation are not well known prompts our next question.

## How can Marketing Orientation be Recognized?

While it should not be assumed that the following items are in order of priority, it is intended that they should be seen as constituting a comprehensive listing of the requirements that must be met if marketing orientation is to be effective.

1  Is there a good understanding within the enterprise of the needs, wants and behaviour patterns of targeted customers?
2  Is the enterprise profit-directed rather than volume-driven?
3  Does the chief executive see himself as the enterprise's senior marketing strategist or 'marketing champion'?
4  Does the enterprise have a market-driven mission (for example, a cosmetics company should see itself as being in the beauty business and the Post Office should see its market as users of communications)?
5  Do the enterprise's strategies reflect the realities of the market-place (including the competitive situation)?
6  Is marketing seen as being more important by managers within the enterprise than other functions and orientations?
7  Is the enterprise organized in such a way that it can be more responsive to marketing opportunities and threats than its less successful competitors?
8  Does the enterprise have a well-designed marketing information system?
9  Do managers within the enterprise make full use of marketing research inputs in their decision making?
10  Are marketing costs and revenues systematically analysed in relation to marketing activities to ensure that the latter are being carried out effectively?
11  Is there a strong link between the marketing function and the development of new products/services?
12  Does the enterprise employ staff in the marketing area who are marketing professionals (rather than, say, sales oriented in their approach)?
13  Is it understood that marketing is the responsibility of the entire organization if it is to be effective?
14  Are decisions with marketing implications made in a well-co-ordinated way and executed in an integrated manner?

These points can be linked to McKinsey & Co's 'Seven S' framework to show what is required in an effective, marketing-oriented enterprise (see Figure 17.12).

If an enterprise's responses to the points listed above contain a lot of negative answers the next question becomes important if matters are to be improved.

**FIGURE 17.12**
*Requirements of marketing orientation*

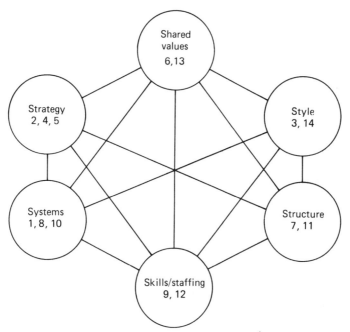

SOURCE: Adapted from Wilson and Fook (1990)

## How can Marketing Orientation be Developed?

Developing marketing orientation is a long-term process and needs to be thought of as a form of investment. To a large extent this investment is in changing the organization's culture so that common values relating to the need to highlight service to customers, a concern for quality in all activities, and so forth are shared throughout the organization. This is not an appropriate target for the 'quick fix'.

Steps to be taken in order to enhance an enterprise's degree of marketing orientation are:

1 Secure top management support since a bottom-up approach would be doomed from the outset given the company-wide implications of marketing orientation.
2 Specify a mission relating to the development of marketing orientation. This should have a plan associated with it, and the necessary allocation of resources to enable it to be executed.
3 A task force should be set up as part of the plan to bring together managers from across the company (and consultants who can help considerably) to carry out tasks such as:
   • identifying the current orientation of the company;
   • carrying out a training needs analysis as a basis for a management development programme to change the company's culture in a desired way;
   • advising on structural changes within the company to support marketing activities;
   • ensuring commitment to change via the system of rewards (such as bonuses and promotion) that will apply to facilitate change.
4 Maintain the momentum of change by means of continuous monitoring of marketing performance to ensure that inertia does not set in. Progress towards improved marketing orientation can be measured by regularly asking questions of the following type:
   • Are we easy to do business with?
   • Do we keep our promises?
   • Do we meet the standards we set?
   • Are we responsive?
   • Do we work together?

**FIGURE 17.13**
*Steps in developing marketing orientation*

SOURCE: Wilson and Fook (1990), p. 23

These elements of a process for developing marketing orientation are shown in Figure 17.13.

Developing marketing orientation requires a focus on customers, competitors, the changing environment, and company culture. Achieving it is an expensive and time-consuming endeavour. However, those companies that really make the effort are likely to have a higher level of marketing effectiveness and greater organizational effectiveness than their competitors.

## 17.9 PLANNING ORIENTATION

What benefits does planning offer? Among the most important are the following:

1 Planning requires effective communication which improves the functional co-ordination of efforts throughout the organization (see pp. 532–46 below). In part this will be due to the clearer definition of objectives and policies that planning presupposes (see Porter and Roberts (1977)).

2 Planning motivates by showing what is expected of each member of the organization, and if plans have been agreed between superiors and subordinates in an appropriate way there should be a high degree of commitment to their attainment.

3 Planning should lead to the making of better decisions by requiring an explicit statement of assumptions underlying choices as well as the enumerating of alternative courses of action and relevant states of nature. In other words, systematic thought needs to be given to the future, thereby ensuring that effort is not wholly absorbed in the present.

4 Planning encourages a favourable attitude towards change, which is due in part to a better state of preparation for sudden variations (anticipated and otherwise) so that they can be turned to the organization's advantage, but which is also due to constantly striving to create a desired future. As pointed out by Charles St Thomas (1965, p. 9):

> ... the manager who successfully undertakes his planning work must begin by recognising that the primary key to his effectiveness lies in his capability to adapt.

5 Planning enables standards of performance to be established, and these in turn allow the control process to be effective.

Despite the obvious appeal of planning there are those who believe that any attempt to lay out specific and rational plans is either foolish, dangerous, or downright evil. Churchman (1968, p. 14 and pp. 215–26) refers to these individuals as anti-planners:

> ... there are all kinds of anti-planners, but the most numerous are those who believe that experience and cleverness are the hallmarks of good management.

It is easy to see what a contrast there is between the 'practical' approach based on intuition and experience and the more analytical approach being recommended in this book. Particular arguments against the adoption of planning in any given organization might include the fear that it will take power away from the chief executive, or make excessive demands on line managers, or consume time and other resources for results that cannot be guaranteed, or be a waste of effort because market forecasts are never wholly correct, and so on (see Hussey (1971), pp. 9–10).

Failings in strategic marketing planning may arise as a result of:

1 A chief executive who is not committed to planning, or who makes every decision of significance alone.
2 A planner who is too narrow in his view, or too restricted in his ability, to consider all the essential aspects of marketing planning and their impacts throughout the organization.
3 Small-scale operations which are unable adequately to support a planning function.
4 A state of corporate decline that is progressing too rapidly for planning to arrest it (see Stonich (1975)).
5 Too much emphasis being placed on *where* to compete and not enough on *how* to compete given that the latter rather than the former secures sustainable competitive advantage (see Simmonds (1985)).
6 Too little focus on uniqueness and adaptability with a tendency in many industries (e.g. security dealing, semi-conductors, biotechnology, retailing) towards a herd instinct that encourages sameness on the one hand and a limited adaptive capability on the other.
7 Inadequate emphasis on *when* to compete – such as being first into new markets or first with new products as opposed to being fast followers.
8 Too much attention being paid to competing organizations rather than focusing on individuals as competitors (e.g. chief executives' pronouncements in annual reports, etc., effectively lock their organizations into specified courses of action which highlight opportunities for others).
9 Using the wrong measures of success – especially when these favour short-term results to the detriment of long-term performance.

   Assessing marketing performance is difficult due to problems of both definition and measurement. The traditional approach has been to attempt to measure outputs relative to inputs (e.g. marketing productivity analysis – see Chapter 3). While this is feasible in broad terms, e.g. for an entire organization, it becomes more problematic as one looks in more detail at specific activities or marketing programmes. Much in marketing is unquantifiable and it follows that inputs and outputs cannot be adequately measured and manipulated if some are qualitative. Moreover, the typical result of relating inputs and outputs is the assessment of efficiency whereas effectiveness is of much greater significance. (See Bleeke (1988) for a fuller discussion of 5–9.)
10 Planning becoming a mindless ritual rather than an opportunity for sound strategic thinking.
11 Senior staff get involved in 'us versus them' battles with lower level colleagues.

12 Information that is held in one part of the organization is withheld, or only begrudgingly provided, to those who need it elsewhere in the organization.

13 Key information on which plans are based (such as sales estimates) are biased to justify a particular position rather than providing a sound basis for comparing alternatives (see Lowe and Shaw (1968)).

14 The results of the planning process are ignored when actual decisions with strategic consequences for marketing are made (such as acquisitions).

(Further coverage of points 10–14 will be found in Chapter 9 of Abell and Hammond (1979).)

## 17.10 ORGANIZATIONAL ISSUES

**Introduction**

Suggestions have been made, for example by Hayhurst and Wills (1972), that changing organizational needs may lead to the disintegration of a corporate marketing organization. This could be achieved by the separation of operational activities on the one hand and planning activities on the other. Selling and distribution might fall into the former category.

It is clear (e.g. Hooley, et al. (1984)) that the increasingly competitive environment in which marketing is undertaken has created a recognition that organizational flexibility is a necessary element of marketing orientation.

To a large extent the successful implementation of marketing strategies relies upon an appropriate structure. As Hughes (1980) has pointed out:

> Many marketing plans fail because the planner did not consider the fact that the organization was not capable of implementing the plan. Short-range plans will require adaptation to the existing organization, whereas long-range plans may require redesigning the organization.

There is thus an interdependence between strategy and structure, and this warrants our considering the issue of organizational structures in marketing. For example, organizing marketing around products or markets – rather than around functional tasks – can give an important source of competitive advantage (see Levitt (1980)). Moreover, many writers have argued that organizational structure is a key determinant of marketing effectiveness, marketing failures, and the successful implementation of the marketing concept. (See, for example, Tookey (1974), Hakansson, et al. (1979), Cascino (1967).)

The study of organizations has developed in an interdisciplinary way:

* The *classical approach* emphasized the division of labour within a pyramid of centralized control. Highlights of this approach are:
  – specialization,
  – functional specification,
  – unity of command,
  – separation of line and staff,
  – equality of authority and responsibility,
  – span of control.
  (See Sofer (1972).)
* The *contingency approach* emphasizes the need to structure an organization according to certain key variables – such as:
  – size,
  – technology,
  – environment.
  (See Ruekert et al. (1985).)

Lawrence and Lorsch (1967) distinguished betwen the need for organizational units (or divisions) to be differentiated in order that they might deal with their particular environments, and the need for integration among divisions in order that the organization as a whole might act in a co-ordinated way with full recognition of the interdependence among the differentiated units.

Evidence suggests that the greater the differentiation among divisions the greater are the problems of integration (such as conflicts of interest and functional differences). The demise of the conglomerates built up in the 1960s illustrates this well: there was no underlying industrial, technological or marketing logic to their emergence – they were based wholly on a fragile financial logic which gives no grounds for satisfactory integration. In contrast, high-performing organizations are those having an underlying logic that allows for differentiation while facilitating integration.

The work of Burns and Stalker (1961) has been influential in the emergence of contingency theory. They distinguished between mechanistic and organic organizational structures which were at different ends of a notional continuum. At the mechanistic end was a rigid differentiation of tasks; a precise definition of roles and responsibilities; various ways of reinforcing the formal hierarchy; an emphasis on formal superior–subordinate communications; and a stable environment. At the organic end, in the setting of an unstable environment, was a higher level of unpredictable change. This was associated with less rigid departmental differentiation; higher levels of individual contributions to common tasks; a less formal hierarchy for responsibility and communication; a higher level of commitment; and a flow of advice and information down the organization (rather than just instructions and decisions).

## Organizational Design

Apart from serving as a means of linking the organization to its environment, thereby ensuring that the outputs and activities are compatible with the external milieu in which the organization is operating, planning also serves as a means of integrating the goal-striving activities of the organization into a coordinated whole. This latter role is facilitated by effective organizational design, as Nathanson, et al. (1982, p. 93) point out:

> Organization design is conceived to be a decision process to bring about a coherence between the goals or purposes for which the organization exists, the pattern of division of labor and interunit coordination and the people who will do the work.

Organization design has similarly been defined by Pfeffer (1978) as:

> . . . the process of grouping activities, roles or positions in the organization to co-ordinate effectively the interdependencies that exist . . . the implicit goal of the structuring process is achieving a more rationalized and co-ordinated system of activity.

In considering a framework for organizational design (OD) we can be guided by Child's 1977 classification of the major issues within the domain of OD:

- allocating task responsibilities to individuals;
- designating formal relationships leading to hierarchical levels and spans of control;
- grouping individuals into departments, departments into divisions, etc;
- designing systems for integration and communication;
- delegating authority and evaluation;
- providing systems for appraisal and reward.

Galbraith has developed a conceptual framework (Figure 17.14) in which a number of organizational variables over which choices must be made by

**FIGURE 17.14**
*Organizational
variables*

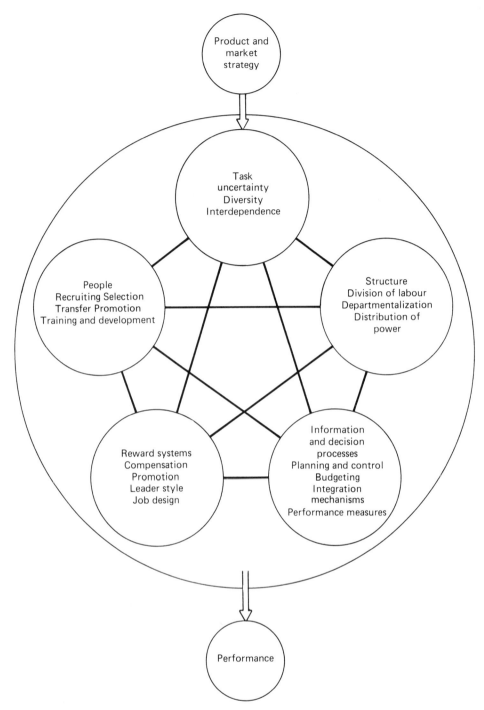

SOURCE: Nathanson et al. (1982)

managers in creating an organization design are identified. These are task,
structure, information and decision processes, reward systems and people. In
choosing how to balance these elements top management has considerable scope
for varying and influencing all five. However, the organization design that
emerges should be one that fits the product-market strategy of the enterprise. If a
consciously developed strategy is to be effectively implemented this needs to be
done via a properly designed organization: the process of organization design is
the link between strategy formulation and implementation.

As Figure 17.14 indicates, all the variables are interrelated but the starting
point is the specification of tasks, their diversity and associated levels of
uncertainty which all stem from the product-market strategy. Staff must be

recruited and located within a suitable structure which is determined by the amount of role differentiation, the number of hierarchic levels, the arrangement of departments, and the distribution of power. Resource allocation and coordination processes are superimposed on the structure by means of planning and control systems. Finally, the task structure must be matched by a reward system that deals with such matters as compensation and promotion policies.

If any one of these variables is changed it will be necessary for all the others (on a *mutatis mutandis* basis) to vary in order that a revised design might result. It follows also that any modification in the strategy itself will lead to a series of revisions among the organizational variables (which collectively constitute the structure).

It is clear that choices exist in designing appropriate organizational structures. An appropriate structure in this context is one that facilitates the implementation of the marketing concept, the attainment of sustainable competitive advantage, and improvements in organizational performance. We must recognize, however, that there are many factors contributing to performance: it is not simply a function of organizational structure. Nevertheless, there are some clear examples of structural deficiences that can lead to poor performance. As Child (1984) has pointed out (see Figure 17.15), there are symptoms and causes of these deficiencies.

**FIGURE 17.15**
*Symptoms of structural deficiencies*

| Symptoms | Possible causes |
|---|---|
| Low motivation and morale | Decisions seem inconsistent/arbitrary, with no standardized rules.<br>People see insufficient delegation.<br>Ambiguous requirements on individuals.<br>People are subject to conflicting pressures.<br>People are overloaded because of inadequate support systems. |
| Slow or low-quality decision making | Information is communicated too late.<br>Decision making is decentralized and not coordinated.<br>Decision makers are overloaded because of insufficient delegation.<br>Lack of procedures to evaluate similar decisions made before. |
| Conflict and lack of coordination | Conflicting goals with no established priorities.<br>No mechanisms operate to achieve integration.<br>Operations and planning are isolated from each other. |
| Lack of innovation | No specialized attention to environmental scanning.<br>No focus on programming and resourcing change.<br>Lack of coordination of market information and R & D. |
| Escalation in administrative costs | Too many supervisors/administrators.<br>Too much effort on procedures and paperwork.<br>Some or all of the other organizational problems exist. |

SOURCE: Adapted by Piercy (1985) from Child (1984)

The organizational design choices in marketing can be summarized, as in Figure 17.16.

In generating answers to these OD questions some regard must be had to the particular circumstances of a given enterprise. This is necessary since the environmental characteristics, technological considerations, and corporate content of each individual enterprise will vary from those influencing other enterprises. Organizational design choices, therefore, will be contingent upon the circumstances facing each individual enterprise. Piercy (1985, p. 202) has produced a checklist of contingencies for OD in marketing: see Figure 17.17.

**FIGURE 17.16**
*A checklist of
organizational
design choices*

**Specification of jobs**
What specializations can be identified as necessary and desirable?
What degree and type of control should be maintained?
What will be the scope/responsibility of jobs?
What type of reward system is most appropriate?

**Span of organization**
Should the structure be 'tall' or 'flat' in the number of levels of management and the spans of control created for individual managers?
What are the implications of these alternatives for communications, motivation, and costs?

**Grouping activities**
What activities should be grouped together?
What should be the logic for grouping and separating activities – function, product, etc.?
Can the advantages of different logics be combined at different levels in an overlay or matrix arrangement?

**Integration**
Do the different groups created require intensive integration – what type of interdependency exists?
What types of integration mechanism could be used?

**Control**
What degree and type of management control is appropriate?
Which decisions should be centralized and which delegated?
How formal should standardized procedures and controls be – how should they be used?

**Change**
What are the changing structural needs implied by the strategic development plans of the organization?
What are the implications of new information technology for the design of structure and the new choices made available?
What are the stimuli or pressures for organizational change – how will they be recognized?
What are the situational problems and costs of reorganization?

SOURCE: Adapted by Piercy (1985) from Child (1984)

**FIGURE 17.17**
*A checklist of
contingencies in
organizational
design for
marketing*

**Environmental contingencies**
What areas of the environment are producing the greatest workload – how is this expected to change?
Which are the first order elements of the environment to study, which the second, and so on – how is this expected to change?
Which are the areas of greatest uncertainty – complexity, interconnectedness, unpredictability – how is this expected to change?
What is the present environmental information-processing burden – in quality and quantity – how is this expected to change?
How do these present and forecast burdens compare with the information-processing capacity of our marketing structures?
Are there signs of coping problems in the structure – can such problems be expected?

**Technological contingencies**
What is the information-processing burden created by integration and control compared with the structures operated?
What are the present and likely future implications of new information technology for the marketing organization?

**Corporate contingencies**
What is the implication of corporate and marketing strategic plans for structural needs?
What are the implications of new technology for marketing strategy and structure?
What are the constraints imposed by problems of reorganization?
What are the preferred organizational outcomes or different interests?
Who is likely to attempt to influence marketing organizational designs – and how?
What are the implications for the distribution of power and the emergence of political behaviour of the organizational changes that can be identified?

SOURCE: Piercy (1985), p. 202

Nathanson, et al. (1982, p. 110) have proposed a series of 'fit' relationships which indicate the best 'fit' between particular strategies and structures. The main choices consist of:

1 single business with a functional structure;
2 a business having related products (which implies common technology and possibly common manufacturing facilities) with a multidivisional structure;
3 a business having unrelated products (hence no technological commonalities) with a holding company structure.

An enterprise's chosen strategy is a key determinant of its relationship with the environment, which in turn places particular information-processing requirements on the management of the enterprise. Different strategies help in defining different environmental settings, thus giving rise to different information processing requirements. (As an example consider the different circumstances of an enterprise choosing a strategy taking it into a high-technology sector and another enterprise adopting a strategy that focuses on a traditional, labour-intensive sector.) A good fit is found when the structure – which includes information processing among its elements – matches the strategy and produces the desired outcomes.

Figure 17.18 illustrates the best combinations of strategy and structure. ('Product relatedness' refers to common technology and 'market relatedness' refers to common customers.)

**FIGURE 17.18**
*Fit relationships*

| Strategic situation Product-market strategy | Operating organization Structure | Planning process |
|---|---|---|
| 1. High product relatedness with high market relatedness | Functional structure: necessary because of product market and geographic relatedness. No need to divisionalize. | Business-level planning focus on: competition, competitive advantage, distinctive competences, product-market segmentation, stage of product-market evolution. Synergy-integration of different functional areas. Market share, production efficiencies, technological innovation. |
| 2. High product relatedness with low market relatedness | Functional structure: necessary because of product relatedness. | SBUs to deal with the market or geographic diversity, to focus attention on each market and allocate the functional resources to markets in most efficient manner, and to keep abreast of each market's opportunities and threats. |
| 3. Low product relatedness with high market relatedness | Divisionalized structure: necessary because of different technologies and manufacturing processes inherent in the product. | SBUs to provide strategic approach to the market and eliminate counterproductive competition within the market-place. |
| 4. Low product relatedness with low market relatedness | Multidivisional or holding company structure: the high degree of diversity calls for much decentralization. | SBUs, because of the large size of most of the firms in this category, the focus is primarily on goal formulation and setting on a financial basis, to place emphasis on the 'stars' that are small and might otherwise be overlooked, to serve as a span of control reducer, and to overlap any interdependencies (relatedness) that might exist. |

SOURCE: Nathanson, et al. (1982)

**An Information- Processing Approach**

Tushman and Nadler (1978) argued that information processing provides a key integrating mechanism in the context of organizational design. The assumptions underlying this view are that organizations should be seen as:

1 open social systems that must deal with work-related uncertainty;
2 information-processing systems where a basic function of structure is to create work units that facilitate information processing;
3 sets of subunits that are interdependent and share scarce resources.

These assumptions are reflected in the model (Figure 17.19), as are a number of propositions, including:

- the tasks of organizational subunits vary in their degree of uncertainty (which is related to the characteristics of the subunit, its environment, and its interdependence);
- as work-related uncertainty increases so does the need for increased amounts of information, hence the need for increased information-processing capacity;
- different organizational structures have different capacities for effective information processing – more specifically, the information processing capacity of a subunit is affected by:
  - the organismic-mechanistic nature of the subunit's structure,
  - the nature of the co-ordination and control mechanisms which seek to tie interdependent units together.

**FIGURE 17.19**
*An information-processing model of organization design*

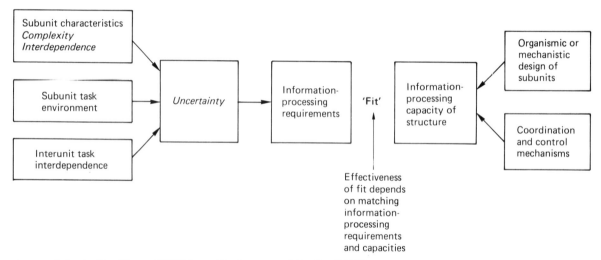

SOURCE: Adapted by Piercy (1985) from Tushman and Nadler (1978)

Piercy (1985) has put forward a very powerful case for viewing the marketing organization as an information-processing structure. His basic model is shown in Figure 17.20.

In developing this model Piercy reviewed major approaches to organization theory. His most significant point of departure from the traditional approach lies in his examination of information-processing models of structure and the implications of such models for organizational power and political behaviour.

Such an approach focuses on the processes required to cope with task and environmental uncertainty:

> ... in the sense both that uncertainty imposes an information-processing burden that a given structure may or may not be able to cope with, and that coping with these uncertainties critical to the organisation provides a source of power and political strength to certain sub-units or individuals.
>
> (Piercy (1985), p. 38)

**FIGURE 17.20**
*The organizational dimensions of marketing*

SOURCE: Piercy (1985), p. 17

The link between marketing structures and the environment, and hence to marketing decision making, is provided by the idea of information processing. The question follows as to which organizational structure is best suited to processing the information required by marketing tasks, but this question has been largely ignored by marketing experts.

One approach to dealing with some aspects of the question is provided by Weitz and Anderson (1981). They suggest that the environment may be analysed in terms of:

- *complexity* – which refers to the number of elements relevant to the organization (such as the number of product markets served);
- *interconnectedness* – which is concerned with the interdependence of key elements within the environment;
- *predictability* – which relates to the degree to which the environment is stable or unstable, hence to the degree of uncertainty.

See Figure 17.21 which relates these aspects of the environment to marketing organizations.

The tendency towards increasingly unpredictable and discontinuous change implies that organizational forms need to be considered as being short term and subject to adjustment in response to frequent changes in the contingencies that underpin them. Doyle (1979) points to such factors as an increased focus on integration, a change from volume to productivity orientation, and a move towards portfolio management as indicating that a traditional functional structure is becoming less and less appropriate. A more complex and ambiguous set of alternatives is to be found in divisional and matrix forms of organization, but these too may be transitory.

An extreme view has been put forward by Haller (1980a, 1980b) and Wills (1980a, 1980b) to suggest that marketing – as a unified function – will disappear either as a result of its being subsumed within strategic management (see Figure 17.22), or as a result of marketing planning being taken under the wing of a corporate planning department and a sales director on the one hand and a distribution director on the other emerging to take over the operational activities, with no marketing director.

**FIGURE 17.21**
*Environmental
dimensions and
marketing
organization*

Environmental unpredictability and interconnectedness

| | Low | High |
|---|---|---|
| **High** (Environmental complexity) | 1   Decentralized organization<br>e.g. product divisions<br>High differentiation<br>i.e. marketing is organized around<br>different products<br>Conventional integration methods<br>e.g. hierarchical reporting,<br>planning systems | 2   Matrix organization<br>e.g. organized into product<br>groups drawing on functional<br>resources<br>High differentiation<br>i.e. marketing is organized<br>around different projects<br>Unconventional integration methods<br>e.g. programming managers |
| **Low** | 3   Functional organization<br>e.g. sales, advertising,<br>marketing research, etc.<br>Low differentiation<br>i.e. marketing is general for<br>all products and markets<br>Conventional integration methods<br>e.g. hierarchical reporting,<br>planning systems | 4   Brand management<br>e.g. product managers plus<br>functional specialists<br>Low differentiation<br>i.e. marketing is general for<br>all brands<br>Unconventional integration methods<br>e.g. brand and market managers |

SOURCE: Adapted from Weitz and Anderson (1981)

**FIGURE 17.22**
*A strategic
management
organizational
structure*

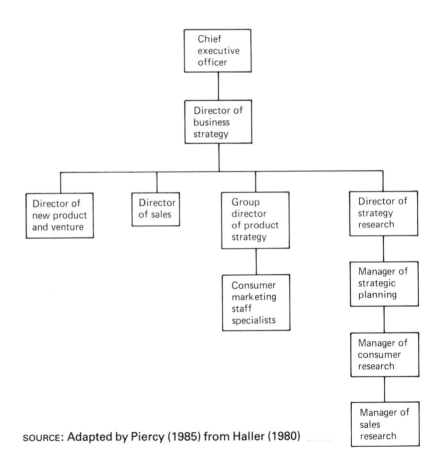

SOURCE: Adapted by Piercy (1985) from Haller (1980)

Such views contrast sharply with the traditional approach to marketing structures where the primary concern has been with differentiation within the marketing department. The basis of this differentiation may be products, functions, markets, geographical regions or customer groups, each of which allows some degree of specialization via the division of labour. See Figures 17.23 and 17.24.

It has been argued that the functional structure is likely to be abandoned in favour of a product-based structure as the number of products in the range

**FIGURE 17.23**
*Marketing
structures – bases
of differentiation*

(a) Functional marketing structure

(b) Product marketing structure – product management

(c) Product marketing structure – product groups

(d) Market-based marketing structure

(e) Product/market overlay

SOURCE: Piercy (1985)

**FIGURE 17.24**

*Comparison of marketing structures*

| Form | Advantages | Disadvantages | Situational indicators |
|---|---|---|---|
| Functional | Specialization in task activities to develop skills. Marketing tasks and responsibilities clearly defined. | Excess levels of hierarchy may reduce unity of control. Direct lines of communication may be ignored. Conflicts may emerge. Integration problem for CME*. | Simple marketing operations. Single primary product/market. |
| Product/brand | Specialization in products/brands. More management attention to marketing requirements of different products/brands. Fast reaction to product-related change. | Dual reporting. Too much product emphasis. More management levels and cost. Conflict. | Wide product lines sold to homogeneous groups of customers, but sharing production/marketing systems, i.e. proliferation of brands and diversified products requiring different skills/activities. |
| Market/customer/geographical | Specialization in a market entity – focus on customer needs. Fast reaction to market-related changes. | Duplication of functions. Coordination problems. More management levels. | Limited, standardized homogeneous product line sold to customers in different industries, i.e. proliferation of markets each meriting separate efforts. |
| Product/market overlay | Advantages of functional product and market specialization and integration. | Allocation of responsibilities is difficult. Duplication inefficiencies. | Multiple products and multiple markets. |

\* Chief Marketing Executive
SOURCE: Piercy (1985)

increases (Hughes, 1980), or in favour of a market-based structure as the number of markets served increases (Ames, 1971). A further variation is to adopt a hybrid approach in which product and market structures are combined in a form of matrix organization.

Much has been written on the product management approach to marketing organization. In principle it appears to be an ideal means for implementing the marketing concept in an integrated way in multiproduct enterprises. The evidence, in contrast, includes lots of instances of the failure of product management, although it is still widespread. See Figure 17.25 for a summary of advantages and disadvantages.

An alternative approach to that of PM is the matrix structure which can be thought of as a vehicle for increasing the information-processing capacity of an organization. However, this type of structure can give rise to major problems of a political nature.

In essence a matrix organization is one that seeks to coordinate functions and programmes, with resources being provided by the functions and each programme being a plan for serving a particular market segment. Among the distinguishing characteristics of a matrix organization are that:

- its members are allocated to two groups (i.e. one function and one programme) and so have two superiors;
- the groupings are work-related (albeit on two different bases);
- the groups are formal rather than informal;
- the groups are continuing rather than ad hoc.

**FIGURE 17.25**
*Advantages and disadvantages of product management*

---

**Advantages**

* *Meeting complex needs:* with increased diversity and complexity and the proliferation of brands, PM provides a way of coping with marketing problems.
* *Flexibility:* The basic PM concept can be adapted and shaped to the needs of a specific situation.
* *Integration:* PM provides a focus of attention on a product or brand and mechanism for integrating/coordinating efforts at this point.
* *Training:* PM provides a training role for future marketing managers.

**Disadvantages**

* *Responsibility and authority:* product responsibility greater than authority is an organizational anomaly, as is the existence of more than one superior in the hierarchy, leading potentially to conflict and political behaviour.
* *Level of responsibility/role ambiguity:* product managers may assume too much responsibility. The product manager may be subject to role conflict and ambiguity.
* *Too many interfaces:* the diversity of interfaces may be too great for the product manager to cope with the informational burden they represent, leading to delays, etc.
* *Isolation:* with growth, the product manager may become isolated from both top managers (by the intervening levels of hierarchy) and the market-place (by the sales force).
* *No specialist expertise:* the PM system may lead to the abandonment/lack of development of advertising management, marketing research and other areas of specialism.
* *Trivialization:* the PM role may degenerate into handling only trivial tasks.
* *Personnel implications:* PM may be staffed with inexperienced, junior executives, and be associated with high turnover as they progress to other posts. There are training problems in PM and for this and other reasons possibly low job satisfaction.

---

SOURCE: Piercy (1985)

The advantages and disadvantages of the matrix structure have been summarized by Piercy (1985, pp. 160–1) in the following terms:

Advantages
● Programme focus is achieved without the loss of functional specialization.
● Information-processing capability is increased to allow simultaneous response to a range of environmental stimuli.
● Decision making can be decentralized in the knowledge that information-processing ability exists.
● Accountability exists in two directions: functionally relating to resources, and for the achievement of programme goals.
● A means of co-ordination is provided in situations of high reciprocal and complex interdependence.
● The adaptability of an organic structure is provided via the matrix, with scope for increased participation and commitment.

Disadvantages
● Conflict is inevitable between the functional and programme managers.
● Ambiguity is inevitable in both individual roles and reporting relationships.
● The increased demands for information will generate higher costs.
● Changes in attitude are needed to balance power within a matrix organization, but such changes are difficult to bring about. See Figure 17.26.

A suggested development from the matrix organization is the network model (Daniell (1990)). This closely resembles the physical configuration of a modern integrated information systems network. Interdependence among the activities and units within the network is emphasized, with any one activity or unit drawing on the capabilities of the entire network to strengthen its performance, thereby improving the overall collective performance of the network.

**FIGURE 17.26**
*Mission-based
matrix in marketing*

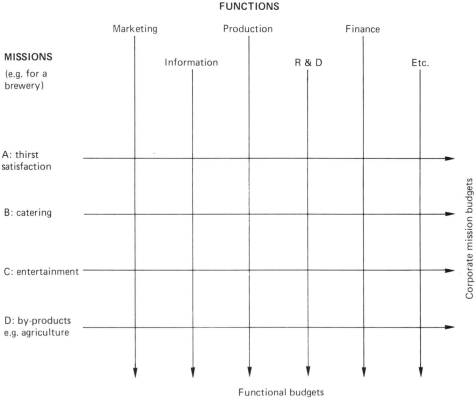

SOURCE: Adapted from Wills, et al. (1972)

## Centralization Versus Decentralization

We need to recognize that in the context of large, complex organizations it is not simply the creation of a single marketing department (along with its status and integrative characteristics) that is of concern but rather the allocation of marketing responsibilities and activities among different levels in the organizational structure.

In the study that was cited in the Preamble to Stage Four (see p. 403), Lynch, et al. (1988) found that the better performing British companies exhibited the following organizational characteristics:

- more likely to have a marketing department;
- more likely to have marketing represented directly at board level;
- more likely to adopt a market-based organizational structure;
- work more closely with other functional areas.

The study of large organizations has consistently emphasized the process of divisionalization beyond the point at which a traditional organizational structure (i.e. of a functional form) becomes incapable of effectively coping with such issues as geographic expansion, volume growth, vertical integration and product diversification (e.g. Chandler, 1962).

Buell (1966) suggested a fourfold categorization of divisionalized marketing organization:

- *Divisionalized companies with self-sufficient divisions.* At the corporate level of marketing (if it exists) policy guidelines and advice are provided, and the marketing performance of divisions is evaluated, but no marketing services are provided.
- *Divisionalized companies with corporate marketing services.* Divisions are responsible for production and selling but central marketing services deal with advertising, marketing research, etc.

- *Geographically divisionalized companies.* Divisions provide some marketing activities for their areas but central marketing services are also provided, along with national/international coordination.
- *Centralized manufacturing/decentralized marketing.* All manufacturing is centralized and marketing is undertaken through divisions.

There are benefits from both centralization and decentralization. For example, Heskett (1976) has identified the following.

### Centralized control
- Facilitates the coordination of marketing.
- Makes up for low management expertise in some areas.
- Can lead to better control.
- Ensures the transfer of ideas among marketing groups.
- Avoids duplication of effort.

### Decentralization
- Encourages more effective local performance.
- Improves management development opportunities.
- Favours the development of marketing programmes that are more sensitive to local needs.

Deciding whether centralization is to be preferred to decentralization will depend on the specific circumstances of a given enterprise. For example, an enterprise having a complex and dynamic environment on the one hand and a variety of product groups on the other might be better suited to a decentralized structure. As Nonaka and Nicosia (1979) put it:

> A simple centralized organization of a marketing department is sufficient to process environmental information that is homogeneous and certain. But a complex, decentralized organization for a marketing department is required to process environmental information that is heterogeneous and uncertain . . . only organisms with high internal variety can cope with and survive high variety in the environment.

See Figure 17.27.

**FIGURE 17.27**
*Environmental variety and marketing centralization*

SOURCE: Adapted from Nonaka and Nicosia (1979)

Whether or not the marketing organization should be centralized is likely to be a function of uncertainty which, in turn, reflects environmental turbulence. A centralized structure is able to cope with a relatively stable – hence predictable –

environment whereas a decentralized structure is more appropriate when the environment is unstable – hence more uncertain.

## 17.11 SUMMARY

In this chapter we have reviewed an array of problems that need to be addressed if marketing plans are to be properly developed, adequately implemented, and the outcomes effectively controlled. The origins of problems include:

- pressures from a variety of sources (embracing consumer behaviour, economic conditions, technology, societal expectations, politics) all of which are associated with change and the imperative for enterprises to adapt to change if they are to be successful;
- the marketing subsystem with its interdependencies;
- the nature of marketing feedback;
- the adequacy of information;
- cost issues and the analysis of marketing costs as a means of establishing the effectiveness – in financial terms – and efficiency of marketing activities;
- the degree of marketing orientation that exists within the enterprise;
- the resistance to planning that is still to be found.

Successful implementation and control will be facilitated by:

- a balance between short-run programme-related measures and longer-term performance criteria;
- the attainment of synergy among the various elements of the marketing mix;
- the use of appropriate criteria for assessing performance within segments;
- the use of appropriate criteria for allocating resources to segments, coupled with flexibility in adaptive reallocations;
- executing product-market decisions in the broader context of business-level considerations relating to strategic marketing.

The need to balance strategy with a suitable structure was discussed in some detail. An emphasis was given to the principles of organizational design and the view (put forward most strongly by Piercy) of the marketing organization as an information-processing structure within an uncertain environment.

The control structure of an organization embraces the organization structure, responsibility centres, performance measures and the system of rewards. This structure needs to be properly designed if resources are to be allocated effectively in decentralized decision making.

There is a clear need for the control structure to be co-ordinated with the organization's planning system if desired behaviour is to be achieved. In assessing the adequacy of results it would be too limiting to rely solely on traditional measures such as costs, profits and profitability (e.g. return on investment) since these are partial on the one hand and on the other emphasize a relatively short-term orientation. It is better to relate short-term measures to strategic performance measures, including changes in market share, changes in growth and changes in competitive position.

# 18 | Management controls

## 18.1 LEARNING OBJECTIVES

When you have read this chapter you should be able to:

(a) understand the nature of the control process;
(b) appreciate some different approaches to control;
(c) see the importance of the behavioural aspects of control;
(d) carry out variance analyses in a marketing context;
(e) recognize how to use competitive and environmental intelligence in devising corrective responses.

## 18.2 INTRODUCTION TO CONTROL

Since control is a process whereby management ensures that the organization is achieving desired ends, it can be defined as a set of organized (adaptive) actions directed towards achieving a specified goal in the face of constraints.

To bring about particular future events it is necessary to influence the factors that lie behind those events. It is the ability to bring about a desired future outcome at will that is the essence of control. In this sense it can be seen that control itself is a *process* and not an event. Moreover, the idea of control can be seen to be synonymous with such notions as adaptation, influence, manipulation and regulation. But control is *not* synonymous with coercion in the sense in which the term is used in this book. Nor does it have as its central feature (as so often seems to be thought) the detailed study of past mistakes, but rather the focusing of attention on current and, more particularly, on future activities to ensure that they are carried through in a way that leads to desired ends.

The existence of a control process enables management to know from time to time where the organization stands in relation to a predetermined future position. This requires that progress can be observed, measured, and redirected if there are discrepancies between the actual and the desired positions.

Control and planning are complementary, so each should logically presuppose the existence of the other. Planning presupposes objectives (ends), and objectives are of very limited value in the absence of a facilitating plan (means) for their attainment. In the planning process management must determine the organization's future course of action by reconciling corporate resources with specified corporate objectives in the face of actual, and anticipated, environmental conditions. This will usually involve a consideration of various alternative courses of action and the selection of the one that is seen to be the best in the light of the objectives.

In seeking to exercise control it is important to recognize that the process is inevitably value laden: the preferred future state that one is seeking to realize is unlikely to be the same for individual A as for individual B, and that which applies to individuals also, within limits, applies to organizations.

In seeking to exercise control the major hindrances are uncertainty (since the relevant time horizon for control is the future, which cannot be totally known in advance) and the inherent complexity of socio-economic and socio-technical systems (such as business organizations). If one had an adequate understanding of the ways in which complex organizations function, and if this facilitated reliable predictions, then the information stemming from this predictive understanding would enable one to control the organization's behaviour. In this sense it can be seen that information and control have an equivalence.

Behind the presumption, therefore, that we can control anything there is an implied assertion that we know enough about the situation in question (e.g. what is being sought, how well things are going, what is going wrong, how matters might be put right, etc.).

## 18.3 CONTROL DEFINED

There are as many different definitions of control, and of management control, as there are authors.

Maciariello (1984, p. 5), for example, offers the following definitions of management control (MC) and management control system (MCS):

> Management control is the process of ensuring that the human, physical, and technological resources are allocated so as to achieve the overall purposes of an organization. An MCS attempts to bring unity of purpose to the diverse efforts of a multitude of organizational subunits so as to steer the overall organization and its managers toward its objectives and goals. An MCS consists of a structure and a process.

A control system's structure has relative permanence and focuses on what the system is (i.e. the designated responsibility centres, delegated authority, performance measures, etc.). Its process focuses on the way in which decisions are made to establish goals, allocate resources, evaluate performance, revise strategies, etc., in a purposive manner.

Itami (1977) emphasized the fact that management control is control within an organizational context, which implies that it is of a multi-person nature. This is also evident in Tannenbaum's (1964, p. 299) definition of control as being:

> . . . any process in which a person (or a group of persons or organization of persons) determines or intentionally affects what another person or group or organization will do.

However, the idea of interpersonal influence was broadened by Hofstede (1968, p. 11) to embrace impersonal control also:

> Control within an organizational system is the process by which one element (person, group, machine, institution or norm) intentionally affects the action of another element.

The interpersonal nature of control within organizations needs to be recognized in order to relate to motivation, goal congruence and the reward system. Within Figure 18.1 there is no explicit recognition of this requirement, whereas Figure 18.2 allows for it via 'nesting'.

Within the nested model the superior exercises control by influencing the subordinate's behaviour – largely through the assessing of the subordinate's performance against agreed plans.

The behavioural aspect is highlighted by Merchant (1985, p. 4) who also refers to the strategic aspects of control:

> *Control* is seen as having one basic function: to help ensure the proper behavior of the people in the organization. These behaviors should be consistent with the organization's strategy . . .

**FIGURE 18.1**
*The control process*

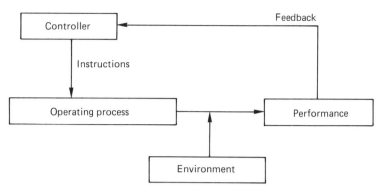

**FIGURE 18.2**
*A nested model of
control systems*

The need for control arises because individuals within the organization are not always willing to act in the organization's best interests.

Whilst strategy may be seen as being related to control it is usually separable. Thus it is possible for an enterprise having good strategies to fail because it has a poor control system, and vice versa. In general, however, the better the formulation of a strategy the greater will be the number of feasible control alternatives and the easier their implementation is likely to be.

Anthony (1988, pp. 7 and 10) also refers both to the links between control and strategic implementation on the one hand, and the interaction among individuals on the other:

> *Control* is used in the sense of assuring implementation of strategies. The management control function includes making the plans that are necessary to assure that strategies are implemented.
>
> Management control is the process by which managers influence other members of the organization to implement the organization's strategies.

Merchant (1985, p. 1) has pointed out a number of problems that have inhibited a greater understanding of control:

1 the lack of a comprehensive and generally-accepted control framework with supporting terminology;
2 control problems and solutions are discussed at different levels of analysis;
3 the solutions that are proposed also differ in accordance with the orientation of their proposers:
4 some authors argue that control should deal with (historical) facts whereas others argue that control should be future-oriented.

## 18.4 BASIC CONTROL CONCEPTS

In this section, which draws on Wilson and Chua (1992), we will distinguish between:

- open-loop control; and
- closed-loop control.

We shall also distinguish between two main forms of closed-loop control:

- feedforward control; and
- feedback control.

**Open-loop Control**

This form of control exists when an attempt is made by a system (for example, an organization) to achieve some desired goal, but when no adjustments are made to its actions once the sequence of intended acts is under way. A very simple example is that of a golfer hitting a golf ball: his aim is to get the ball into the hole, and with this in mind he will take into account the distance, the hazards, and so forth, prior to hitting the ball. Once the ball is in the air there is nothing that the golfer can do but hope that he did things right.

Two possible refinements to the basic open-loop model are:

1 To introduce a monitoring device for the continual scanning of both the environment and the transformation process of the system (that is, the process by which the organization converts inputs into outputs). This will provide a basis for modifying either initial plans or the transformation process itself if it appears that circumstances are likely to change before the plan has run its course and the goal realized. This is *feedforward control* and is illustrated in Figure 18.3.

**FIGURE 18.3**
*A feedforward control system*

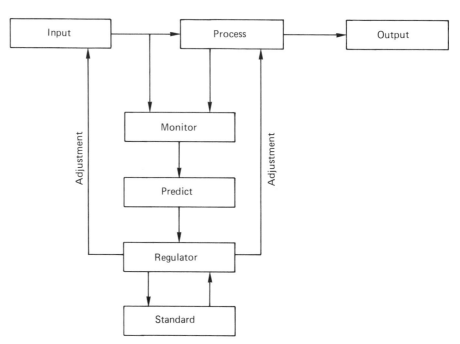

2 To monitor the outputs achieved against desired outputs from time to time, and take whatever corrective action is necessary if a deviation exists. This is *feedback control* and is illustrated in Figure 18.4.

Both feedback and feedforward control entail linking outputs with other elements within the system, and this explains why they are termed *closed-loop* control systems.

**FIGURE 18.4**
*A feedback control system*

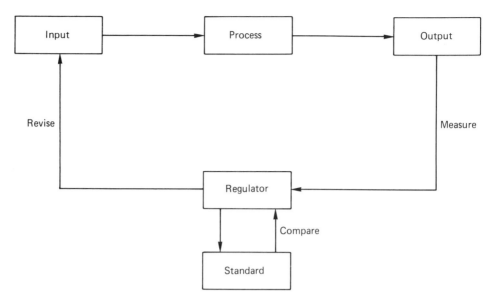

## Closed-loop Control

In an open-loop system errors cannot be corrected as it goes along, whereas likely errors can be anticipated and steps taken to avoid them in a feedforward control system, and actual errors along the way can be identified and subsequent behaviour modified to achieve desired ends in a feedback control system.

The inadequacy of open-loop systems as a basis for organizational control (and hence for the design of MCS) largely stems from our limited knowledge of how organizational systems operate, which in turn reflects the complexity of organizations and their environments, plus the uncertainty that clouds the likely outcome of future events. If we possessed a full understanding of organizational processes and had a perfect ability to predict the future then we would be able to rely on open-loop systems to achieve the ends we desire since we would be able to plan with the secure knowledge that our plans would be attained due to our perfect awareness of what was going to happen, and how, and when (i.e. control action would be independent of the system's output).

In our current state of awareness we must rely on closed-loop systems, whether feedforward or feedback, in which control action is dependent upon the actual or anticipated state of the system.

It is helpful to think of four types of outcome in connection with the application of closed-loop systems to the problem of organizational control. These are:

$S_0$ = Initial *ex ante* performance (e.g. a budget based on a set of expectations which might include: inflation at 5 per cent per annum; market growth of 10 per cent per annum; no labour disputes).

$S_1$ = Revised *ex ante* performance (e.g. an updated budget that has taken into account the experience of operating the system to date).

$S_2$ = *Ex post* performance (e.g. a revised budget based on what should have been achieved in the circumstances that prevailed during the period in question, say: inflation at 7 per cent per annum; market growth of 12 per cent per annum, and a strike lasting three weeks).

$A_0$ = Observed performance (i.e. that which actually occurred).

An organization's forecasting ability is shown by $A_0 - S_0$ (under feedback control) and, more precisely, by $A_0 - S_1$ (under feedforward control). The extent to which the organization is not using its resources to maximum advantage (its opportunity cost of operating) is given by $A_0 - S_2$.

A feedforward control system will function in a way that keeps revising $S_0$ as events are proceedings with a view to producing an eventual outcome in which

$A_0 = S_1$. On the other hand, a feedback control system will, from time to time, compare $A_0 - S_0$ and $S_0$ will only be revised if a discrepancy has been experienced.

It is apparent that feedforward control tends to be:

- ex ante,
- proactive,
- continuous;

and seeks to predict the outcomes of proposed courses of action, while feedback control tends to be:

- ex post,
- reactive,
- episodic.

Let us look at each a litle more closely.

## Feedforward Control

A feedforward system can be defined as:

> A measurement and prediction system which assesses the system and predicts the output of the system at some future date.
>
> (Bhaskar and Housden (1985), p. 199)

This differs from a feedback system in that it seeks to anticipate, and thereby to avoid, deviations between actual and desired outcomes. According to Cushing (1982, p. 83), its components are:

1 an operating process (which converts inputs into outputs);
2 a characteristic of the process (which is the subject of control);
3 a measurement system (which assesses the state of the process and its inputs, and attempts to predict its outputs);
4 a set of standards or criteria (by which the predicted state of the process can be evaluated);
5 a regulator (which compares the predictions of process outputs to the standards, and which takes corrective action where there is likely to be a deviation).

For a feedforward control system to be effective it must be based on a reasonably predictable relationship between inputs and outputs (i.e. there must be an adequate degree of understanding of the way in which the organization functions).

Guidelines for developing feedforward control systems are as follows:

1 thorough planning and analysis are required (reflecting as much understanding as possible about the links amongst inputs, process, and outputs);
2 careful discrimination must be applied in selecting those variables that are deemed to have a significant impact on output;
3 the feedforward system must be kept dynamic to allow for the inclusion of new influences on outputs;
4 a model of the system to be controlled should be developed and the most significant variables (along with their effects on process and outputs) defined within it;
5 data on significant variables must be regularly gathered and evaluated in order to assess their likely influence on future outcomes;
6 feedforward control requires action focused on the future (rather than on the correction of past errors).

**Feedback Control**

Feedback control should ensure self-regulation in the face of changing circumstances once the control system has been designed and installed. The essence of feedback control is to be found in the idea of *homeostasis* which defines the process whereby key variables are maintained in a state of equilibrium even when there are environmental disturbances.

As a hypothetical illustration let us consider a company planning to sell 100 000 cassette players during the next 12 months. By the end of the third month it finds that the pattern of demand has fallen to an estimated 80 000 units due to the launch by another company of a competing product. After a further three months the competitor puts up the price of its product while the original company holds its own price steady, and this suggests that the level of demand may increase to 150 000 units. Feedback signals would ensure that the company is made aware, e.g. by monthly reports, of the actual versus planned outcomes (in terms of sales levels). The launch of the competitive cassette player would be identified as the reason why sales levels were below expectations in the early months, and the competitor's price increase would be identified as the reason why sales levels subsequently increased. In response to deviations between actual and desired results (i.e. feedback) an explanation needs to be found and actions taken to correct matters. Amending production plans to manufacture fewer (or more) cassette players, allowing inventory levels to fall (or rise) to meet the new pattern of demand, modifying promotional plans to counter competitive activities and so forth, could all stem from a feedback control system.

If deviations (or *variances* to give them their usual accounting name) are minor it is probable that the process could absorb them without any modifications, and inventory control systems, for example, are normally designed to accommodate minor variations between expected and actual levels of demand with buffer stocks being held for this purpose. But in the case of extreme variations – such as the pattern of demand shifting from 100 000 units to 80 000 and then to 150 000 – it will be necessary to amend the inputs in a very deliberate way once the causes of the variations have been established. Inevitably there are costs associated with variances, and these will tend to be proportional to the length of time it takes to identify and correct them.

Some principles for the proper functioning of a feedback control system can be suggested (e.g. Cushing (1982), p. 80), and might include:

1 The benefits from the system should be at least as great as the costs of developing, installing, and operating it. This is the problem of 'the cost of control'. It is often difficult to specify precisely either the benefits (other than in broad terms – e.g. 'better customer service', 'increased efficiency') or the costs relating to different system designs, but it should be possible to make approximate assessments of both.
2 Variances, once measured, should be reported quickly to facilitate prompt control action. (This is analogous to the feedback – known as *knowledge of results* – in psychological learning theory: if one has been tested on what one has learnt it is important to be told quickly whether one is right – to reinforce the learning – or wrong – to facilitate remedial learning.)
3 Feedback reports should be simple, easy to understand, and highlight the significant factors requiring managerial attention.
4 Feedback control systems should be integrated with the organizational structure of which they are a part. The boundaries of each process subject to control should be within a given manager's span of control.

**Feedforward Versus Feedback Control**

The most significant features of feedforward and feedback control are shown in Figure 18.5.

Feedback systems are typically cheaper and easier to implement than are feedforward systems, and they are more effective in restoring a system that has gone out of control. Their main disadvantage, however, is that they can allow

**FIGURE 18.5**
*Relative strengths*

| Characteristic | Feedforward | Feedback |
|---|---|---|
| Low cost<br>Ease of implementation<br>Effectiveness<br>Minimal time delays<br>Self-regulation | √ | √<br>√<br>√<br><br>√ |

variations to persist for as long as it takes to detect and correct them. Feedforward control systems, as we have seen, depend critically for their effectiveness on the forecasting ability of those who must predict future process outputs. Both feedforward and feedback systems lend themselves to self-regulation.

The most effective approach to control comes from using the two approaches as complements since few (if any) processes could be expected to operate effectively and efficiently for any length of time if only one type of control was in use. (For example, in controlling inventory, feedback data can be used in connection with stock outs, rates of usage, etc., while feedforward data needs to be generated in gauging the raw material requirements for predicted levels of demand and the ability of suppliers to deliver on time.)

Both types of control are fundamentally intertwined with the design of MCS. In a feedback control system the functions that the system will carry out are:

- standard setting;
- performance measurement;
- reporting of results.

Within a feedforward control system the role of the MCS will encompass:

- standard setting;
- monitoring process inputs;
- monitoring operations;
- predicting process outputs.

The degree of overlap is modest relative to the degree of complementarity.

## 18.5 RESPONSIBILITY ACCOUNTING

In analysing organizations with a view to securing control over them there are five key variables to which one must pay attention. A change in any one of these will have consequences for one or more of the others (on a *mutatis mutandis* basis rather than a *ceteris paribus* basis). These variables are:

1 the task of the organization (i.e. the purpose to be served by the outputs from the organization);
2 the technology of the organization (i.e. the means whereby the inputs are converted into outputs);
3 the structure of the organization (i.e. the roles, rules, etc.);
4 the people of the organization (including their expectations, career development, etc.);
5 the environment of the organization (i.e. those factors beyond the organization's boundary).

In this section we will be concerned with aspects of 3 – the structure, as reflected through individuals' assigned responsibilities.

If a company is organized in such a way that lines of authority are clearly defined, with the result that each manager knows exactly what his or her responsibilities are and precisely what is expected of him or her, then it is possible to plan and control costs, revenues, profits, etc., in order that the performance of each individual may be evaluated and, one hopes, improved. In addition, a meaningful basis can be given to the design of the reporting system if it is geared to areas of responsibility.

That is the essence of responsibility accounting which is a system of accounting that is tailored to an organization so that costs, revenues, profits, etc., can be planned, accumulated, reported, and controlled by levels of responsibility within that organization. Responsibility accounting requires that costs be classified by:

- responsibility centre;
- their degree of controllability within their responsibility centre (on the premise that each responsible individual in an organization should only be charged with those costs for which he or she is responsible and over which he or she has control);
- their nature.

This approach to classification will facilitate:

- self-appraisal by lower and middle management;
- subordinate appraisal by top management;
- activity appraisal (by which top management might evaluate the performance of the overall range of corporate activities).

**FIGURE 18.6**
*Appraisal of performance*

See Figure 18.6.

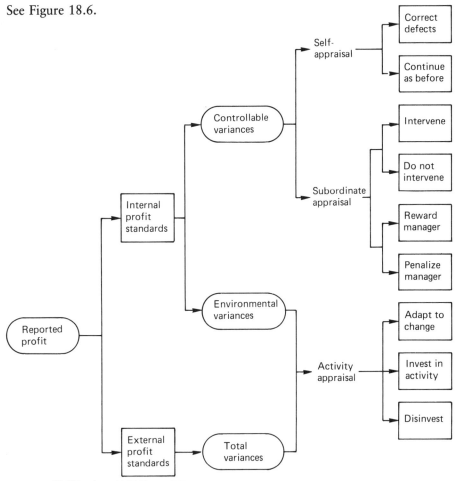

SOURCE: Shillinglaw (1964), p. 158

However, it is essential to the success of any control system that an individual is only held responsible for results when the following conditions prevail:

1 that he knows what he is expected to achieve;
2 that he knows what he is actually achieving;
3 that it is within his power to influence what is happening (i.e. that he can bring 1 and 2 together).

When all these conditions do not occur simultaneously it may be unjust and ineffective to hold an individual responsible, and it will be impossible to achieve the desired level of organizational performance.

From the above comments it will be apparent that targets or results should be compiled in a way that reflects one individual's 'uncontaminated' performance. Thus Manager A's budget should contain a clear set of items which are deemed to be controllable at his level of authority and a further set of items that are either fixed by company policy or are otherwise beyond Manager A's influence. These latter items are uncontrollable from A's viewpoint, and his performance should not be assessed in relation to costs, etc., over which he has no control.

Costs (as well as revenues, profits, and so forth) can only be controlled if they are related to the organizational framework: in other words, costs should be controlled in accordance with the concept of responsibility – a cost should be controlled at whatever level it is originated and initially approved by the individual who did the initiating and approving. In this way it will be clear that certain costs are the responsibility of, and can only be controlled by, the chief executive of a company (such as corporate public relations expenditure) whereas others are controllable by responsible individuals at lower levels of the organizational hierarchy (e.g. a departmental manager will be responsible for the salary expense of those who work within his department). It is important to distinguish between costs that are controllable at a given level of managerial authority within a given period of time and those that are not. This distinction is not the same as the one between variable costs and fixed costs. For example, rates are a fixed cost that are uncontrollable, for a given time period, by any managerial level, whereas the annual road licence fee for a particular vehicle is a fixed cost that is controllable by the fleet manager who has the power to dispense with the vehicle. In the same way the insurance premium payable on inventories is a variable cost (fluctuating with the value of the inventory from month to month) that is not controllable at the storekeeper level, but it is controllable at the level of the executive who determines inventory policy (subject, of course, to the environmental vagaries of such factors as consumer demand which can never be removed).

Controllability is affected by both managerial authority and the element of time – a short-run fixed cost will be a long-run variable cost. (Thus the managing director's salary is fixed for 12 months but variable thereafter.) All costs are controllable to some extent over the longer term even if this involves a change in the scale of operations or a relocation of the company.

The problem of distinguishing between controllable and uncontrollable costs is more difficult in relation to indirect as opposed to direct costs. It is vitally important that costs be regulated at source, and this means that for many indirect items the beneficiary of cost incurrence is very often not the person to be charged with the cost. Obvious examples are central services – maintenance, the personnel department, post room/switchboard facilities – from which all members of the company derive benefits but for which cost responsibility is accorded to the respective supervisors and managers of these service functions.

To sum up so far, the approach to control that is based on the concept of responsibility accounting involves designing the control system to match the organizational structure in order that it reflects realistically the responsibilities of departmental managers, supervisors, etc. (This method of tackling control permits the collecting and reporting of data in such a way that the performance of organizational sub-units can be evaluated.) In devising a control system for securing control that accords with the organizational structure it will usually be found necessary to define more closely the duties of responsible individuals, and various responsibilities will have to be reassigned in order to give a logical structure to an organization that may have grown in a haphazard manner. All subsequent organizational changes that lead to changes in individual responsibilities should be accompanied by suitable modifications to the control system.

Organizational charts are useful if properly detailed. Apart from showing the chain of command (i.e. who reports to whom) such a chart should also include a schedule defining the duties of those individuals and any limitations to their authority. In this way responsibilities can be unambiguously assigned, and this knowledge clearly communicated to all concerned. Figure 18.7 represents a possible marketing organization structure, giving details of duties within each functional area.

**FIGURE 18.7**
*Marketing organization structure*

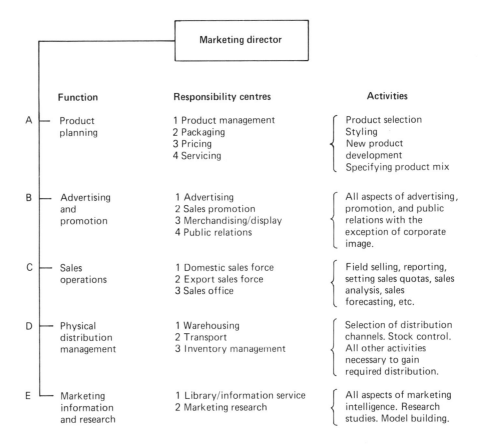

The implications of fixing responsibility and of implementing control via responsibility centres are:

- the organizational structure must be clearly defined and responsibility delegated so that each person knows his or her role;
- the extent and limits of functional control must be determined;
- the responsible individuals should be fully involved in preparing plans if they are to be held responsible for results;
- responsible individuals must be serviced with regular performance reports;
- means must be established to enable plans to be revised in line with actual performance in such a way that responsible individuals are involved;
- every item should be the responsibility of some individual within the organization.

The ability to delegate is one sign of a good manager and responsibility accounting facilitates this. The act of passing responsibility down the line to the lowest levels of supervision gives these advantages:

- it helps to create an atmosphere of cost consciousness throughout the organization;
- it tends to get control action quickly without delays resulting from the need for a senior executive to receive a monthly report before decisions can be made;
- it helps to give all levels of management a sense of team spirit with a common purpose.

A central notion in considering control is the evaluation of performance – whether *ex ante* (as in feedforward control) or *ex post* (as in feedback control). This can be undertaken at several levels: at the societal level, at the level of the enterprise as a whole, at the level of a division or other segment – such as activities, or at the levels of the group or individual. In essence what is required is a comparison of desired outcomes with expected or actual outcomes, an assessment of any divergences, and proposals for future courses of action. Putting this another way, three questions need to be posed:

1 What has happened?
2 Why has it happened?
3 What is to be done about it?

The need to view performance evaluation within a control context is highlighted by our posing all three questions, rather than just the first two.

The concept of performance measurement is a simple one to comprehend but it can only be put into practice if plans are carefully prepared before decisions are made. In the absence of a plan (expressed in terms of standards and budgeted levels of performance) there is no bench-mark for evaluating the performance of segments of an enterprise, individuals in responsible positions, or the organization as a whole, and attempting to improve them. The existence of standards of performance eliminates many of the opportunities and excuses for poor performance, and provides a reference point for improvements.

Measuring the performance of the various types of responsibility centre (i.e. cost, profit and investment) will usually focus on financial aspects of an organization's activity. This will not always be appropriate, although it tends to be the general case that managers are held accountable in terms of quantifiable performance rather than performance that is qualitative (such as employee morale or public relations). It is necessary to know from time to time how actual performance compares with desired performance, and this chapter focuses on this issue.

This comparison answers the question about *what* is happening, and responsibility accounting ensures that managers know *who* is to be accountable. Establishing *why* divergences occur is problematic, as is the question of deciding *how* to apply corrective action in order that control may be effective.

Individuals learn through assessing their experience and organizations learn through their members. However, the extent to which individuals – and thus organizations – can learn is constrained by the rules of the organization (governing decision making, delegation, membership and other restrictions). Dery (1982) has pursued this question by focusing on the links between erring (e.g. when variances arise) and learning. His argument is as follows:

1 the recognition of errors is a function of interpretation rather than simply an observation of events – it requires that desired and actual outcome be compared and interpreted before one can assert that an error exists;

2 the interpretation of events is influenced by organizational rules, etc., which also serve to constrain the extent to which learning can take place;
3 it is insufficient to assume that better learning at the organizational level can stem from the learning ability of individual members since the latter is constrained by the rules of the former, hence an additional factor is required that will change the organization's rules.

The level of performance of a responsibility centre from a control viewpoint can be evaluated by obtaining answers to three pairs of questions;

*Quantity*
● How much was accomplished?
● How much should have been accomplished?

*Quality*
● How good was that which was accomplished?
● How good should it have been?

*Cost*
● How much did the accomplishment cost?
● How much should it have cost?

Performance measurement presupposes a standard of comparison. An obvious example comes from the comparison of actual results with budgeted results – the latter being the predetermined standard of performance. Standards can be compiled for almost every business activity, such as:

● number of customer complaints;
● production costs;
● unit costs of handling and transporting products;
● market share;
● employee turnover;
● downtime;
● unfilled orders;
● return on investment;
● percentage of late deliveries of orders;
● a variety of cost/revenue ratios.

Any standard can only be an effective aid to control if it is seen to be equitable: those who are being judged (i.e. the responsible individuals whose performance is being measured) must be consulted in the setting of standards otherwise no attempt may be made to reach them if they are considered to be either too high or too low. This ruins any attempt to control.

Luck and Ferrell (1979) have portrayed the links among marketing strategy, plans and standards as shown in Figure 18.8.

Control reports should be suited to the various areas of individual responsibility and as one moves further up the managerial hierarchy more items will be contained, albeit in summary form, in reports prepared for each level since more items are controllable as the scope of managerial responsibility enlarges. Top management will therefore receive a summary of all items of income and expenditure.

Such summary reports can do little to rectify past mistakes but by indicating exceptions to plans they can ensure that causes are investigated and appropriate corrective actions are taken to help in preventing future mistakes. The appropriate orientation should clearly be to the future rather than to the past.

A *responsibility centre* is made up of the various cost and revenue items for

**FIGURE 18.8**
*Standards in the
marketing control
process*

SOURCE: Adapted from Luck and Ferrell (1979), p. 421

which a given individual is responsible. It is consequently a personalized concept that may be made up of one or more of the following.

- a cost centre;
- a profit centre; or
- an investment centre.

Let us look at each of these in turn.

### A Cost (or Expense) Centre

This is the smallest segment of activity, or area of responsibility, for which costs are accumulated. In some cases the cost centre may correspond with a department, but in others a department may contain several cost centres.

A cost centre may be created for cost control purposes whenever management feels that the usefuless of accumulating costs for the activity in question justifies the necessary effort.

Only input costs are measured for this organizational unit: even though there is some output this is not measured in revenue terms. Thus a production unit will produce X units at a given total (or unit) cost, with the output being expressed either as a quantity or in terms of input costs.

### A Profit Centre

This is a segment, department or division of an enterprise that is responsible for both revenue and expenditure. This is the major organizational device employed to facilitate decentralization (the essence of which is the freedom to make decisions). See Illustration 18.1.

Among the arguments favouring decentralized profit responsibility are:

1 a divisional manager is only in a position to make satisfactory trade-offs between revenues and costs when he has responsibility for the profit outcome of his decisions (failing which it is necessary for many day-to-day decisions to be centrally regulated);

# Illustration 18.1: BR to Split National Network into Local Areas

British Rail is to embark on one of the most far-reaching changes in the organisation of the rail network since nationalisation in 1948, John Welsby, British Rail's chief executive, said yesterday.

From the end of April, the five regions, inherited from the days of private ownership, London Midland, Eastern, Western, Southern, and Scottish, will be progressively abolished and replaced by about 20 smaller units, or profit centres.

The Railways Board will retain responsibility for strategic matters, such as investment programmes, financial targets and railway safety, but most aspects of the day-to-day running of the railway will be devolved to the profit centres.

British Rail's three passenger sectors, InterCity, Network SouthEast, and Regional Railways, will be sub-divided into several profit centres, run by a director, who will effectively own all the rolling stock, track and signalling equipment needed.

Malcolm Rifkind, the transport secretary, has pledged to introduce a bill to privatise British Rail after the next general election. Transport officials are still examining the options, which include privatisation of BR as a single unit, the creation of a track authority and its break-up into regional companies.

Under the reorganization, Network SouthEast, which provides rail services in London and the South East region, will be divided into nine semi-autonomous divisions. Some of these divisions will be substantial businesses. South West, for example, which embraces all services from Waterloo, has an income of £252 million a year, employs about 8,000 staff and covers 500 route-miles. Others, such as the London, Tilbury and Southend division, with an income of £65 million, employs about 1,500 and covers 70 route-miles, will be considerably smaller.

InterCity will be divided into five route divisions. Regional Railways, which provides commuter, passenger and cross-country services, will also be split into five sub-divisions.

In an effort to make each profit centre more cost conscious, charges will be levied on trains from one profit centre using the tracks of another. Directors will know exactly what they are responsible for and accountability for shortcomings will be instant. "There will be no more alibis," Mr Welsby said.

The division of the national rail network into what is effectively 20 semi-autonomous railways, is the final phase of the radical reorganisation of the rail network introduced in the early 1980s by Sir Robert Reid, the former British Rail chairman.

By reorganising British Rail's passenger sectors around the markets rather than the regions they serve, Mr Welsby is determined to bring about a substantial improvement in the quality of services. "I'm not changing the organisation for the fun of it," he said. "The changes are vital to improve the quality of service to passengers."

The move is being watched closely by continental rail organisations, particularly those in France and Germany, which are already following the example set by British Rail with the introduction of the five sectors in the 1980s.

The reorganisation is expected to take about a year to complete, and is likely to cost in the region of £50 million. Mr Welsby said that British Rail was not trying to facilitate or impede government plans to privatise the railways.

*Source:* The Times, 11 April, 1991, p. 24

2 a manager's performance can be evaluated more precisely if he has complete operating reseponsibility;

3 managers' motivation will be higher if they have greater autonomy;

4 the contribution of each division to corporate profit can be seen via divisional profit reports.

The advantages of profit centres are that they resemble miniature businesses and are a good training ground for potential general managers.

When it comes to defining profit measures several alternatives are available. An example built up from the data in Figure 18.9 will help to illustrate some of them.

**FIGURE 18.9**
*Division A's operating data for July*

| | |
|---|---|
| Sales revenue generated by Division A | £100,000 |
| Direct costs of Division A: | |
| Variable operating costs | £45,000 |
| Fixed operating costs under control of manager of Division A | £25,000 |
| Fixed costs not under the control of manager of Division A | £10,000 |
| Indirect costs of Division A: | |
| Apportioned central costs | £15,000 |

This data can be analysed in ways such as those suggested in Figure 18.10. One can identify strengths and weaknesses relating to each alternative measure of profit. The *contribution margin* is useful for short-run decision making since it is not clouded by the inclusion of costs that do not respond to short-run volume changes. From a performance evaluation point of view, however, it is unsatisfactory in that it excludes all non-variable costs.

*Controllable profit* is a much better measure of the divisional manager's performance because it includes all the costs – whether fixed or variable – that are

**FIGURE 18.10**
*Analysis of Division A's operating data*

| | Division A contribution margin £ | Division A controllable profit £ | Division A direct profit £ | Division A net profit £ |
|---|---|---|---|---|
| Sales revenue | 100,000 | 100,000 | 100,000 | 100,000 |
| Direct costs: | | | | |
| Variable | 45,000 | 45,000 | 45,000 | 45,000 |
| **Contribution margin** | £55,000 | | | |
| Fixed controllable | | 25,000 | 25,000 | 25,000 |
| **Controllable profit** | | £30,000 | | |
| Fixed non-controllable | | | 10,000 | 10,000 |
| **Direct profit** | | | £20,000 | |
| Indirect costs | | | | 15,000 |
| **Net profit** | | | | £5,000 |

within his control. When non-controllable fixed costs are taken into account we have the *direct profit* of the division. This is more a measure of the division's performance than it is of the divisional manager's performance, so one needs to consider what it is that one is seeking to assess before one chooses a measure.

Finally, *net profit* (as pointed out in Chapter 3) helps us in assessing a division's performance in full cost terms, but this is not a relevant means of gauging the divisional manager's performance on account of the categories of cost that he is unable to influence either directly or indirectly. It could be argued that divisional managers benefit from seeing the full cost of their division's operations, but if the controllable elements are dwarfed by the uncontrollable (at the divisional level) it may not be highly motivational!

From the above we can reasonably conclude that controllable profit is the best of the specified measures for assessing a divisional manager's performance – at least in principle. In practice it may be found that the manager of a division acts in ways that improve his short-run profit position at the expense of both the division's long-run profit potential and the best interests of the organization as a whole. Examples might include:

1 eliminating training and management development activities;
2 cutting back on advertising, routine maintenance or R & D.

Countering these ways of 'playing the system' must be devised by top management in the form of policy guidelines, etc. But any measure of profit is inevitably sub-optimal as an index of divisional performance for at least one of the following reasons:

1 it typically includes items (such as interest and taxation) that are not under the control of divisional managers;
2 it only tells part of the story – something needs to be said about the investment that is needed to generate profit. The next sub-section picks up this point.

### An Investment Centre

This is a segment, department or division of an enterprise that is not only responsible for profit (i.e. for revenue and expenditure) but that also has its success measured by the relationship of its profit to the capital invested within it (i.e. profitability). This is most commonly measured by means of the rate of return on investment (ROI).

The logic behind this concept is that assets are used to generate profits, and the decentralizing of profit responsibility usually requires the decentralization of control over many of a company's assets. The ultimate test, therefore, is the relationship of profit to invested capital within a division. Much of its appeal lies in the apparent ease with which one can compare a division's ROI with earnings opportunities elsewhere – inside or outside the company. However, ROI is an imperfect measure and needs to be used with some scepticism and in conjunction with other performance measurements.

The value of the controllable/uncontrollable cost split is primarily found in fixing responsibility and measuring efficiency. Time is an important ingredient in this context since all costs are controllable at some organizational level if a sufficiently long time-span is taken. Controllable costs are those that can be directly regulated by a given individual within a given time period.

The division of costs into controllable and uncontrollable categories is important in order that performance levels may be evaluated and also for securing the cooperation of managers at all levels. The manager who is involved in planning his performance level in the knowledge that those controllable costs for which he is responsible will be monitored, accumulated, and reported, is likely to be motivated towards attaining his predetermined level of performance. In this way it can be seen that the collecting of controllable costs by responsibility centres serves as a motivating force as well as an appraisal mechanism.

While the ideal procedure is for each responsibility centre to be assigned those costs over which its manager has sole control and for which he or she is therefore responsible, in practical terms this cannot usually be achieved. It is rare for an individual to have complete control over *all* the factors that influence a given cost element.

Apart from those costs over which a responsible individual actually has control, his responsibility centre may be charged with costs that are beyond his direct control and influence but about which management wishes him to be concerned. A good example is the cost of a company's personnel department: an operating manager may be charged with a proportion of the personnel department's costs on the grounds that either:

- he will be careful about making unnecessary requests for the services of the personnel department if he is made to feel somewhat responsible for its level of costs; or
- he may try to influence the personnel manager to exercise firm control over his department's costs.

Allocating general overheads to responsibility centres is done by many companies that practise responsibility accounting (and that therefore recognize that such costs are beyond the control of those to whom they are allocated) on the grounds that each responsible individual will be able to see the magnitude of the indirect costs incurred to support this unit. There is a major disadvantage that should be seriously considered: the manager of a small responsibility centre incurring directly controllable costs at his level in a given time period of, say, £10,000 may be allocated £45,000 of general overhead costs. In relation to the overall level of overhead costs the manager may feel that those costs for which he is responsible are so insignificant that he may give up trying to control them. The point to note is that each cost must be made the responsibility of whoever can best influence its behaviour, and allocating costs beyond this achieves at best very little from a control viewpoint and may be distinctly harmful to the cost control effort. (Since a specific example of uncontrollable costs has not been given so far the general overheads of £45,000 referred to above can be used as a suitable example. For control purposes the costs that are being considered are the costs that can be directly influenced at a given level for a specified time-span.)

While the head of a responsibility centre may not have sole responsibility for a particular cost item this item may reasonably be considered to be controllable at his level if he has a significant influence on the amount of cost incurred, and in this case his responsibility centre can properly be charged with the cost. This is one aspect of the wider problem that arises because few (if any) cost items are the sole responsibility of just one person. Guidelines that have been established for deciding which costs can appropriately be charged to a responsibility centre are, in summary:

- If an individual has authority over both the acquisition and the use of a cost incurring activity, then his responsibility centre should bear the cost of that activity.
- If an individual does not have sole responsibility for a given cost item but is able to influence to a significant extent the amount of cost incurred through his own actions, then he may reasonably be charged with the cost.
- Even if an individual cannot significantly influence the amount of cost through his own direct action, he may be charged with a portion of those elements of cost with which management wishes him to be concerned in order that he may help influence those who are more directly responsible.

That which applies to costs also, in essence, applies to revenues and assets.

## 18.6 APPROACHES TO CONTROL

**Anthony's Approach to Control**

The views of Robert Anthony of Harvard on management control have been very influential. They are stated in Anthony 1965 and 1988.

When Anthony published his 1965 *Framework*, the management control function was not generally recognized as a discrete activity. This has changed.

Management control is one of three types of planning and control activities that occur within organizations; the other categories are strategic planning and task control. Anthony's definition of management control, given earlier (see p. 549) presumes that goals and strategies exist, but that these do not arise automatically, hence (1988, p. 10):

> Strategic planning is the process of deciding on the goals of the organization and the strategies for attaining these goals.

Authors often distinguish between

- planning (i.e. deciding what to do); and
- control (i.e. ensuring that desired results are obtained).

Anthony argues that both planning and control are undertaken at different organizational levels, hence it is more helpful to look at the mix, as shown in Figure 18.11:

**FIGURE 18.11**
*The planning and control mix*

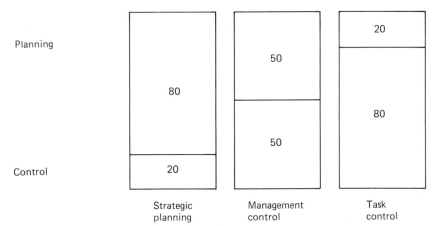

SOURCE: Adapted from Anthony (1988)

> Strategies are the courses of action that an organization has adopted as a means of attaining its goals. They include the assignment of overall responsibility for implementation . . .
>
> Strategies are big plans, important plans. They state in a general way the *direction* in which the organization is supposed to be headed. They do not have a time dimension: that is, they exist until they are changed.
>
> (1988, p. 31)

> The purpose of the MC process is to carry out the strategies arrived at in the SP process and thereby to attain the organization's goals.
>
> (1988, p. 34)

The 1988 approach links MC to the implementation of strategies in a direct way rather than to the attainment of objectives which is an indirect purpose of MC.

The key difference between MC and SP is that the latter is unsystematic: the need for strategic decisions can arise at any time – whether in response to a threat or an opportunity.

Another difference is that SP is undertaken by top management and it involves a great deal of judgement. In contrast, MC is systematic, done at all levels, and involves considerable personal interaction but less judgement than SP. SP sets the boundaries within which MC takes place.

The third element in Anthony's approach is task control:

> Task control is the process of ensuring that specific tasks are carried out effectively and efficiently.

> (1988, p. 12)

Anthony's framework is shown in Figure 18.12 (1988, p. 19). While dealing with SP and TC, Anthony's 1988 book focuses primarily on MC which can be described in terms of a process and the environment within which it takes place. The environment is partly external and partly internal, with the latter comprising:

- the organization's structure;
- a set of rules, procedures, etc.;
- a culture.

**FIGURE 18.12**
*Anthony's framework*

SOURCE: Anthony (1988), p. 19

The external environment contains influences that affect the level of uncertainty faced by the organization. At a highly uncertain extreme are:

- newly developed products;
- differentiated products;
- aggressive competition;
- uncertain sources of inputs;
- uncertain political circumstances.

At a less uncertain extreme are:

- mature products;
- commodity products;
- price competition;
- secure sourcing of inputs;
- political stability.

Within a highly uncertain setting an organization is likely to pay great attention to programming; to make broad budget estimates; to revise budgets frequently; to set limits to discretionary costs; to permit a good deal of management latitude; to insist on a rapid flow of information; to evaluate performance subjectively in terms of results rather than process; and to have a high proportion of bonus within the reward package.

The opposite characteristics are likely to apply in a relatively certain environment.

**Merchant's Approach to Control**

An organization's control system is comprised of a variety of mechanisms, including:

- personal supervision;
- job descriptions;
- rules;
- standard operating procedures;
- performance appraisal;
- budgets;
- standard costing;
- incentive compensation schemes.

However, it would be wrong to think of 'controls' – such as the above – as being the plural of 'control', and it would also be wrong to assume that more 'controls' would automatically give us more 'control' since this would assume that they meant the same thing, which they do not.

'Controls' has the same meaning as measurement, or information, whereas 'control' is more akin to direction. 'Controls' is concerned with means while 'control' is concerned with ends, and they deal respectively with facts (i.e. events of the past) and expectations (i.e. desires about the future). From this it will be appreciated that 'controls' tend to be analytical and operational (concerning what was and is) and 'control' tends to be normative (concerning what ought to be). A summary of key differences is shown in Figure 18.13.

The increasing ability to develop 'controls' has not necessarily increased our ability to 'control' organizations. If controls are to lead to control they must encourage human actors to behave in a way that facilitates adaptive behaviour on the part of the organization as a whole.

The complexity and uncertainty of the control problem are apparent when, for example, controls reveal that 'profits are falling'. But this does not indicate how one might (or should) respond – indeed, it would not be possible even to identify the whole array of potential responses. What is needed, therefore, if control is to

**FIGURE 18.13**
*The different focus of control and controls*

$\Sigma$ CONTROLS $\neq$ CONTROL
$\Delta$ CONTROLS $\neq$ $\Delta$ CONTROL

**Controls**

*Parts
 ($\therefore$ simple)
*Measurement

**Control**

*Wholes
 ($\therefore$ complex)
*Direction

Information

*Measurable symptoms
*Means
*Present/past orientation
 ($\therefore$ facts)
*Positive
 (what was/is)
*Efficiency
*Hardware
 (machines, physical
 processes)

*Unmeasurable causes
*Ends
*Future orientation
 ($\therefore$ expectations)
*Normative
 (what ought to be)
*Effectiveness
*Software
 (through human
 actors)

SOURCE: Wilson (1983), p. 57

be effective, is a basis for forming expectations about the future as well as understanding about the past that will enable us to combine these in order that we might behave in an adaptive way by either anticipating external changes and preparing to meet them, or by creating changes.

From this arises the basic question – how do we control? In large part this is resolved by the answer to another question – what do we measure in order to control? Care must be taken in measuring the key elements in any situation rather than those elements that lend themselves to easy measurement. ('Controls' are only helpful in 'control' if they are designed in the context of the overall control problem.)

Merchant (1985) offers some valuable advice on a range of controls but with a control perspective. He classifies these controls under the headings given below:

### Results Controls

Reward systems – in which an individual's pay, promotion prospects, etc., depend on his performance – are a good example of results control. It is not unusual for desired results to be expressed in quantitative terms – whether financial (e.g. ROI, EPS) or not (e.g. growth rate, market share) – which gives a bench-mark for exercising results control. At senior management levels this form of control predominates since it is compatible with decentralized organizational structures. At middle-management levels, where financial goals may be less dominant, results control can be exercised through MbO (management by objectives) systems.

The effectiveness of results controls derives from the ability of this approach to address some key control problems. In particular motivational problems are eased since individuals are influenced to produce the results which will enhance both the organization's performance and their own rewards. By focusing on future expectations the results approach to control can be useful in informing managers as to what is expected of them. This emphasizes a feedforward orientation.

Three conditions need to be fulfilled before results control can be employed:

1 it is known what results are desirable;
2 the desired results can be controlled to some extent by those whose actions are being influenced;
3 the controllable results can be measured.

## Action Controls
Action controls are used:

> ... to ensure that individuals perform (or do not perform) certain actions that are known to be beneficial (or harmful) to the organization.
>
> (Merchant (1985), p. 29)

Categories of action controls are:

- behavioural constraints (whether physical or administrative);
- preaction reviews;
- action accountability;
- redundancy (in which more resources are allocated to a task than is strictly necessary which increases the likelihood of its accomplishment).

Two conditions need to be fulfilled if action controls are to be effective:

1 knowledge must exist as to which actions are desirable (or undesirable);
2 the ability must be present to ensure that the desirable actions occur (or that the undesirable ones do not).

## Personnel Controls
There are two categories of personnel control that can be usefully harnessed as part of the management control endeavour:

1 individual self-control which, as a naturally present force, motivates most people to want to do a good job;
2 social control which is exerted by other members of a group on those individuals who deviate from group norms and values.

If these two categories are insufficient they can be augmented by:

- selection and placement;
- training;
- cultural control.

There are several advantages that personnel controls have over results controls and action controls:

- feasibility is not a serious constraint;
- there are fewer harmful side-effects;
- their cost is typically lower.

## Financial Controls
Financial controls are a form of results control which constitute the single most important type of control used in organizations of any size. The reasons favouring financial controls are fairly obvious:

- financial objectives are very important in commercial life;
- financial performance indicators are easy to derive;
- since financial results can be achieved via various routes, the use of financial controls allows for some managerial discretion;
- using financial measures is relatively inexpensive since accounting systems exist within all enterprises.

Inevitably there are negative effects which can outweigh the advantages of using financial controls. The most serious are:

- behavioural displacement – especially when the control system encourages managers to be overly concerned with short-term profits rather than longer-term strategic ends, or when it causes excessive risk aversion;
- gamesmanship.

It has been argued that there is a tendency for financial measures to drive out non-financial measures (see, for example, Munro & Cooper, 1989) within MCS design which, given the partiality of financial measures (i.e. they measure those things that can be measured in financial terms), is unfortunate.

## The Approach of Johnson and Scholes

Strategic marketing involves strategic change. Johnson and Scholes (1988) have argued that there are two ways in which an organization can cope with strategic change:

1 make use of control and regulatory systems to ensure that the tasks of implementation are clear, that their execution is monitored, that individuals and groups have the capabilities to implement change, and that they are rewarded for so doing;
2 ensure that those charged with implementing change understand and work within the social, political and cultural systems that regulate organizational behaviour, and which can give rise to a resistance to strategic change.

**FIGURE 18.14**
*The influence of organization systems on strategy implementation*

SOURCE: Adapted from Johnson and Scholes (1988), p. 292

Their approach to dealing with these issues is reflected in Figure 18.14. If we take the information and control systems first, it is widely recognized that quantitative measures are needed to see if desired results are being achieved. Such measures will typically include:

- financial analysis;
- market analysis;
- sales and distribution analysis;
- physical resource analysis;
- human resource analysis.

A set of guidelines for ensuring the effective design and operation of control systems would deal with such aspects as:

1 distinguishing between various levels of control (as proposed by Anthony (1965 and 1988)), since different levels will require different information;
2 creating responsibility centres as a means of delegation and motivation, ensuring information is provided in a suitable form for each responsible manager;

3 identifying the critical success factors and supplying information relating to these in a way that highlights their interrelationships;
4 avoiding misleading measurements by accepting that quantitative indicators of performance are not available for every activity and it is not helpful to use a measurable index as a surrogate for an unmeasurable characteristic;
5 being wary of negative monitoring in which only poor performance is reported since this can lead to risk adverse behaviour or a tendency to 'pass the buck'.

The next means for ensuring the implementation of strategic change is via regulatory systems. These might range from training to the management style of an organization:

- training and development to ensure staff are capable of implementing change, which involves both new skills and attitudes;
- incentive and reward systems to encourage compliance with required change, whether in the form of pay increases or non-monetary rewards (such as promotion);
- organizational routines by which tasks are carried out may exhibit inertia so deliberate steps need to be taken to redesign them in order to facilitate change;
- management style, which embodies the organization's culture, its circumstances, and the characteristics of its managers, needs to be appropriate to the task of strategic implementation.

Moving on from regulatory systems brings us to culture change. At its most basic this focuses on the need for change to be recognized within the organization in a way that ensures those responsible for bringing change about believe in what they are doing. This can be achieved in two stages, both of which are concerned with cognitive change:

1 the beliefs and assumptions underlying the way in which the organization's members make sense of their organizational world need breaking down;
2 a reformulated set of beliefs needs to be put in their place to reorientate the culture from the past to the future. For cultural change to be meaningful it must impact upon the day-to-day experiences of individuals within the organization.

Finally there is the political system to consider. The overlaps among control systems, regulatory systems, culture and political systems is largely self-apparent, but it is important to emphasize that planning and control are inherently political rather than neutral. This will be illustrated later when we discuss the notion of entrapment.

## The Approach of Luck and Ferrell

Once the plan/strategy has been determined and steps taken (e.g. via a suitable organization) to put this into effect, the control process exists to ensure that the plan will be achieved (in so far as this is feasible).

Control can operate at different levels. For example, Figure 18.15 shows *tactical* control which focuses on the implementation of plans on the right, and *strategic* control which focuses on the possible revision of strategy on the left. This is developed further in Figure 18.16.

Tactical control typically relates to adjustments in the execution of an established marketing plan – such as fine tuning on pricing or advertising schedules.

Strategic control deals with the reformulation of the plans themselves. For example, actual buyer behaviour patterns may indicate that a plan has been based

**FIGURE 18.15**
*A basic control model for marketing*

SOURCE: Adapted from Luck and Ferrell (1979), p. 15

on false premises. Strategic rethinking will thus be necessary in developing a new marketing plan (as shown in the lower half of Figure 18.16).

The role of the information system needed to facilitate tactical and strategic control is indicated in Figure 18.17.

**FIGURE 18.16**
*Strategic and tactical marketing control*

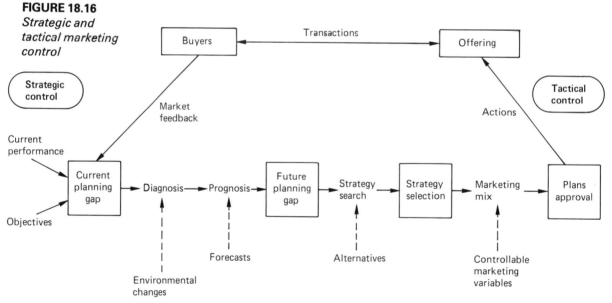

SOURCE: Adapted from Luck and Ferrell (1979), p. 416

## 18.7 CONTROLS

**Forms of Control**

In large organizations there are a number of insidious and unobtrusive controls to be found. These are all the more dangerous and powerful because they are so deceptive. Their deceptiveness is shown in their *not* causing participants to feel their presence – there is no feeling of being oppressed by a despot. Instead there is perhaps just the experience of conforming to the logic of a situation, or of performing in accordance with some internalized standard.

**FIGURE 18.17**
*The role of
information in
marketing control*

SOURCE: Luck and Ferrell (1979), p. 418

Beyond this source of 'control' there are other sources. To the extent that the behaviour of members of organizations is controlled (i.e. appears to be regular and predictable) such regularity may derive from the norms and definitions of subcultural groups within the organization rather than from official rules and prescriptions. The idea that organizational rules constitute the blueprint for all behaviour within organizations is not a tenable one.

Nevertheless, the most significant form of power within organizations is the power to limit, guide and restrict the decision making of organizational personnel such that even when they are allowed (or obliged) to use their own judgement they do not deviate from official expectations. In part this is due to the organization's structure, which can be seen as a series of limitations and controls over members' decision making, and which results from powerful, senior organizational personnel choosing what the structure should be (and hence determining who is allowed to do what).

It is something of a paradox that the modern individual is freer from coercion through the power of command of superiors than most people have ever been, yet individuals in positions of power today probably exercise more control than any tyrant ever did. This is largely due to contemporary forms of power exercised within organizations and by organizations in society. There is a distinct trend that places less reliance on control through a fixed chain of command while placing more reliance on indirect forms of control. Let us pursue this in greater detail.

Forms of control have changed with the passage of time, and these forms have had impacts not only within organizations but also through them, on contemporary society.

Organizations have taken advantage of a variety of control mechanisms from time to time, ranging from ones that are obviously bureaucratic in nature (e.g. command authority and discipline) to ones that are quite unbureaucratic (such as the controlling power that is rooted in expert knowledge).

We can consider the following range of control mechanisms:

1 The prototype (bureaucratic control) is the authority exercised through a *chain of command* in which superiors give subordinates instructions which must be obeyed. This coercive form of control has strong military overtones, and an essential element is rigorous discipline that must be enforced through coercive sanctions. Such discipline is not usually a characteristic of contemporary industrial life.

2 The establishing of explicit regulations and procedures to govern decisions and operations gives a programmed form of control. Discipline is involved in this mechanism also, and close links can be seen between the idea of a set of rules that must be followed and the idea of following orders via a chain of command. However, explicit rules do restrict the arbitrary exercise of power by superiors because they apply to rulers as well as to the ruled.

In specifying rules on how to behave in particular circumstances it is unlikely that all possible situations will be catered for. It follows that rules should ideally be related to the principles underlying decisions rather than to particular decisions – thus specifying *criteria* for decision making will be less restrictive than the stipulating of *how* specific decisions should be made.

3 Incentive systems constitute a further control mechanism. Salaries and career advancement clearly make individuals dependent to a large extent on the organization that employs them, thereby constraining them to submit to the authority exercised within that organization.

Incentives are often tied directly to performance, piece-work rates and sales commissions being the most obvious examples. However, performance measures can be developed for most organizational roles, and adjustments in salary levels and promotion decisions will depend at least to some extent on measured achievements.

4 Technology provides a control mechanism in two forms:
   • production technology constrains employees' performance, thereby enabling managers to control operations (e.g. the speed of an assembly line can be used to regulate productivity);
   • the technical knowledge possessed by an organization's 'technocrats' gives them the ability to understand and perform complex tasks and thereby maintain control of a situation. Management is thus able to control operations, albeit indirectly, by hiring staff with appropriate professional/technical skills to carry out the required responsibilities.

   This reduces the need to use alternative mechanisms, such as detailed rules or close supervision through a chain of command.

5 Expert knowledge is a vital requirement in managing organizations. (It could even be argued that successful management comes about through the exercising of control over the basic knowledge.) It follows that recruiting suitable technocrats is a key mechanism for controlling the organization. If technically-qualified individuals are selectively recruited and if they have the professional ability to perform assigned tasks on their own, then if the organization gives such individuals the appropriate discretion to do what needs to be done within the broad framework of basic policies and administrative guidelines, it should be possible for control to be effective.

6 The allocation of resources (including personnel) is the ultimate mechanism of organizational control since this facilitates certain actions and inhibits others.

Within most organizations one will find several of these mechanisms of control in operation, yet there seems to be a trend towards a decreasing reliance on control through a chain of command and an increasing reliance on indirect forms of control, e.g. via recruitment policies. Incentive systems and machine technologies are perhaps the most prevalent mechanisms of contemporary organizational control: control via recruitment and resource allocation is indicative of the likely future pattern.

Controls may be informal as well as formal. The former are unwritten mechanisms that can influence either individual or group behaviour patterns within organizations in profound ways. A distinction can be made among different types of informal control by means of the level of aggregation (i.e. from individual through small groups to large groups) chosen (see, for example, Jaworski (1988)). Three categories are:

1 Self-control in which individuals establish their own personal objectives and attempt to achieve those objectives by monitoring their own performance and adapting their behaviour whenever this is necessary. This can lead to high levels of job satisfaction but it may fail to achieve the outcomes sought by top management (i.e. those relating to the organization rather than specific individuals). In order to motivate individuals to act in accordance with top management's wishes a system of incentives will be needed.

2 Social control is applied within small group settings by members of the group. It is typically found that groups (e.g. marketing teams) set their own informal standards of behaviour and performance with which group members are expected to conform. These standards represent values and mutual commitments towards some common goal. Whenever a member of the group behaves in a deviant way by violating a group norm the other members of the group will attempt to use subtle pressures – such as humour or hints – to correct the deviance. If this fails and violations are repeated the group's reaction is likely to be to ostracize the deviant individual. In a marketing context there may be group norms for, say, expenses and sales volumes within a sales team.

3 Cultural control applies at a corporate (or divisional) level and stems from the accumulation of rituals, legends and norms of social interaction within the organization. Once an individual has internalized the cultural norms he/she can be expected to behave in accordance with those norms. This gives reason to see cultural control as being the dominant control mechanism for senior management positions involving non-routine decision making: the judgemental factor will reflect the manager's cultural conditioning.

In contrast to informal controls there are formal controls – written management-initiated mechanisms that influence the probability that individuals, or groups, will act in a manner that is supportive of marketing objectives. Three categories of formal controls can be identified, with timing being the distinguishing factor (i.e. these controls echo the sequence of managerial processes):

1 Input controls consist of measurable actions that are taken prior to the implementation of plans, such as specifying selection criteria for recruiting staff, establishing recruitment and training programmes, and various forms of resource allocation. The mix of these inputs can be manipulated in an attempt to secure control.

2 Process control relates to management's attempts to influence the means of achieving desired ends, with the emphasis being on behaviour and/or activities rather than on the end results – such as requiring individuals to follow establishing procedures. There is no clear agreement in the literature as to whether the organization's structure represents a control mechanism or not. Since it can be seen to influence and shape individual and group behaviour it is not unreasonable to think of structure as being part of process control.

3 Output controls apply when results are compared with performance standards, as in feedback control.

In considering control in marketing one might emphasize the control of marketing activities in a relatively detached and impersonal way, as is done by strategy formulation (feedforward control) and variance analysis (feedback control). Alternatively, one might emphasize the control of marketing personnel which involves finding ways to influence the behaviour of those engaging in marketing activities in order that desired ends might be achieved. Since it seems likely that marketing activities can only be controlled through marketing personnel the best way forward would seem to be a balanced combination of both approaches: in other words, feedforward and feedback need to be combined with marketing activities by those who devise and execute marketing activities.

The ultimate test of any control system is the extent to which it brings about organizational effectiveness and it is fair to say that there is little rigorously formulated evidence to demonstrate clear linkages between any approach to control and organizational effectiveness.

## Audits

One approach towards assessing marketing effectiveness is the marketing audit (dealt with in detail in Chapter 2 above).

The marketing audit exists to help correct difficulties and to improve conditions that may already be good. While these aims may be achieved by a piecemeal examination of individual activities it is better achieved by a total programme of evaluation studies. The former approach is termed a 'vertical audit' as it is only concerned with one element of the marketing mix at any one time. In contrast, the latter approach, the 'horizontal audit', is concerned with optimizing the use of resources, thereby maximizing the total effectiveness of marketing efforts and outlays. As such, it is by far the more difficult of the two, and hence rarely attempted.

No matter which form of marketing audit is selected, top management (via its audit staff) should ensure that no area of marketing activity goes unevaluated and that every aspect is evaluated in accordance with standards that are compatible with the total success of the marketing organization and of the firm as a whole. This, of course, requires that all activities be related to the established hierarchy of objectives.

### The Distribution Audit

In the planning and control of costs and effectiveness in distribution activities the management audit can be of considerable value. Not surprisingly, however, it entails a complex set of procedures right across the function if it is to be carried out thoroughly. The major components are the channel audit, the PDM audit, the competitive audit, and the customer service audit. Each of these will be considered briefly in turn.

1 *The channel audit*

Channels are made up of the intermediaries (such as wholesalers, factors, retailers) through which goods pass on their route from manufacture to consumption. The key channel decisions include:
   - choosing intermediaries;
   - determining the implications (from a PD point of view) of alternative channel structures;
   - assessing the available margins.

It follows from the nature of these decisions that the main focus of a channel audit will be on structural factors on the one hand and on cost/margin factors on the other.

2 *The PDM audit*

There are three primary elements within this audit: that of company profile (which includes the handling cost characteristics of the product range and the service level that is needed in the light of market conditions); PDM developments (both of a technological and contextual nature); and the current system's capability.

Cost aspects exist in each of these elements, but operating costs loom largest in the last since it is predominantly concerned with costs and capacity. For example, some of the items that will be subjected to audit will include those shown in Figure 18.18.

3 *The competitive audit*

Through this phase it should be possible to ascertain the quality of competitors' distribution policies, etc., and especially the level of service that competitors are able to offer (and maintain). Within the competitive audit regard should also be had to channel structures, pricing and discount policies and market shares.

4 *The customer service audit*

Given that the level of service is at the centre of physical distribution management it is essential to monitor regularly its cost and quality characteristics.

A very thorough approach to the distribution audit is that developed at the Cranfield School of Management by Christopher and his colleagues (see Christopher, et al. (1977)).

Kotler (1984) has offered the view that auditing is the ultimate control measure, although it can be seen as a means of linking the notions of efficiency and effectiveness. It achieves this latter purpose by not only evaluating performance in terms of inputs used and outputs generated but also by evaluating the assumptions underlying marketing strategies. The fact that audits are expensive and time consuming – especially when undertaken in a comprehensive, horizontal manner – may appear to contradict the striving for efficiency. However, by focusing on doing the right thing they should help in ensuring effectiveness which is of greater importance.

Selecting the right person to carry out the audit has been addressed by Kling (1985). He observed that a balance of experience and objectivity is needed which tends to favour outside auditors who have a broader range of experience than insiders and who can stand back in a reasonably impartial way from policies and procedures that they were not involved in either formulating or implementing. The range of possible auditors includes:

1 self-audit;
2 audit from across (i.e. by a colleague in another function but at the same level as the manager whose activities are being audited);
3 audit from above (i.e. by the manager's superior);
4 company auditing office;
5 company task-force audit (i.e. a team set up specifically to conduct the audit);
6 outside auditors.

It may be better to have a combination of 6 with one of 2–5, thereby bringing together an external view with the perspective of insiders in a joint endeavour. There is little evidence of support for 1, although it exists as a possibility in the absence of any alternative.

In carrying out a marketing audit it will be evident that the enterprise needs to exhibit adaptive behaviour if it is to remain goal striving in a dynamic environment. Effectiveness is concerned with this ability to achieve goals in an ever-changing context.

**Budgeting**

Budgeting (or profit planning) is perhaps the widest-ranging control technique in that it covers the entire organization rather than merely sections of it.

A budget is a quantitative plan of action that aids in the co-ordination and control of the acquisition, allocation and utilization of resources over a given

**FIGURE 18.18**

*System capability factors*

| Capacity utilization | • Warehouse<br>• Transportation<br>• Flexibility and expansion scope |
|---|---|
| Warehouse facilities | • Total costs<br>• Age and maintenance costs<br>• Flexibility throughput/period<br>• Total throughput/period<br>• Returns handled – number<br>                 – recovery time<br>• Picking accuracy<br>• Service levels/back orders<br>• Cube utilization<br>• Cost of cube bought out |
| Inventory | • Total inventory holding costs<br>• Product group costs<br>• Service levels – total<br>                 – plant<br>                 – field<br>• Field inventory holding costs<br>• Transfers – number<br>              – volume<br>• Stock out effects – loss of business<br>              – rectification costs |
| Transportation | • Total costs<br>• Production to field units<br>• Field units to customers<br>• Vehicle utilization<br>• Vehicle cube utilization<br>• Total volumes shipped<br>• Cost per mile – volumes shipped<br>            – cases/pallets shipped<br>• Costs of service bought out<br>• Costs by mode/comparisons |
| Communications | • Total costs<br>• Order communication times – method<br>             – cost<br>• Time and costs per line item per order method for:<br>  – order processing and registration<br>  – credit investigation<br>  – invoice and delivery note preparation<br>  – statement preparation<br>• Number and cost of customer queries<br>• Salesmen's – calls/day<br>          – calls/territory/day<br>          – calls/product group/day<br>          – calls/customer group/day<br>• Salesmen's use of time – selling<br>            – inventory checking<br>            – merchandising<br>            – order processing |
| Unitization | • Total costs<br>• Volumes shipped<br>• Unitization method/proportions of<br>  – pallets<br>  – roll pallets<br>  – containers<br>• Costs of assembly and handling by load type |
| Service achieved<br>(by market segment) | • Total costs<br>• Service levels operated/costs<br>• Delivery times<br>• Delivery reliability<br>• Order processing and progressing<br>• Order picking efficiency<br>• Claims procedure/time/cost |
| Volume throughput | • Total throughput – volume<br>             – weight<br>             – units<br>• Total costs<br>• Throughput/field locations – volume<br>                – weight<br>                – units<br>• Throughput fluctuations<br>• Flexibility (capacity availability/time) |

period of time. The building of the budget may be looked upon as the integration of the varied interests that constitute the organization into a programme that all have agreed is workable in attempting to attain objectives.

Budgetary planning and control work through the formal organization viewing it as a series of responsibility centres and attempting to isolate the performance measurement of one module from the effects of the performance of others.

Budgeting involves more than just forecasting since it involves the planned manipulation of all the variables that determine the company's performance in an effort to arrive at some preferred position in the future. The agreed plan must be developed in a co-ordinated manner if the requirements of each sub-system are to be balanced in line with company objectives. Each manager must consider the relationship of his responsibility centre (or department, or sub-system) to all others and to the company as a whole in the budgetary planning phase. This tends to reduce departmental bias and empire building, as well as isolating weaknesses in the organizational structure and highlighting problems of communication. Furthermore, it encourages the delegation of authority by a reliance on the principle of management by exception.

Having determined the plan, this provides the frame of reference for judging subsequent performance. There can be no doubt that *budgeted* performance is a better bench-mark than past performance on account of the inefficiencies that are usually hidden in the latter and the effect of constantly changing conditions.

There are essentially two types of budget – the long-term and the short-term. Time obviously distinguishes one from the other, and this raises the point that users of budgets should not be unduly influenced by conventional accounting periods: the budget period that is most meaningful to the company should be adopted. For example, the life cycle of a product from its development right through to its deletion is in many ways a more natural budgetary period than calendar units because it links marketing, production, and financial planning on a unified basis. The actual choice of a budget period will tend to depend very much on the company's ability to forecast accurately.

Typically, however, budgets tend to be compiled on an annual basis, with this time-span being broken down into lesser time intervals for reporting, scheduling and control reasons (i.e. half years, quarters, months, and even weeks in the case of production and sales activities).

Within this framework of one year the *operating budget* is prepared. This is composed of two parts, with each part looking at the same things in a slightly different way, but both arriving at the same net profit and return on investment. These two parts are:

1 The programme (or activity) budget that specifies the operations that will be performed during the forthcoming period. The most logical way to present this budget is to show, for each product, the expected revenues and their associated costs. The result is an impersonal portrayal of the expected future that is useful in ensuring that a balance exists amongst the various activities, profit margins, and volumes – in other words, this is the plan.
2 The responsibility budget that specifies the annual plan in terms of individual responsibilities. This is primarily a control device that indicates the target level of performance, but the personalized costs and revenues in this budget must be controllable at the level at which they are planned and reported.

The significance of these two ways of dealing with the operating budgets is of importance as the programme budget is the outcome of the planning phase whereas the responsibility budget is the starting point for the control phase. The former need not correspond to the organizational structure but the latter must. Consequently, the plan must be translated into the control prior to the time of execution and communicated to those involved in order that no one will be in any doubt as to precisely what is expected of him (or her).

Given these two complementary aspects of the operating budget there are two basic ways in which the budget may be prepared:

1 Periodic budgeting in which a plan is prepared for the next financial year with a minimum of revision as the year goes by. Generally the total expected annual expenditure will be spread over the year on a monthly basis on the strength of the behaviour of the elemental costs. Thus 'salaries' will be spread over the months simply as one-twelfth of the expected annual cost per month, but seasonal variations in sales will require a little more attention to be paid to marketing and production costs and their behaviour over time.
2 Continuous (or rolling) budgeting in which a tentative annual plan is prepared with, say, the first quarter by month in great detail, the second and third quarters in lesser detail, and the fourth quarter in outline only. Every month (or perhaps every quarter) the budget can then be revised by adding the required detail to the next month (or quarter), filling in some of the vagueness in the other remaining months (or quarters), and adding on a new month (or quarter) in such a way that the plan still extends one year ahead. Such a budgeting procedure attempts to accommodate changing conditions and uncertainty, and is highly desirable in that it forces management constantly to think in concrete terms about the forthcoming *year* regardless of where one happens to be in the present *financial* year.

Periodic budgeting will often be satisfactory for companies in stable industries that are able to make relatively accurate forecasts covering the planning period. Conversely, rolling budgeting is of greater value in the more usual cases of somewhat irregular cyclical activity amid the uncertainties of consumer demand.

Whether the concern is with long-term or short-term budgeting, or with continuous or period budgeting, there are certain fundamental requirements that must be met if budgeting is to be of maximum value. Briefly, these requirements are:

1 established objectives;
2 top management sponsorship and support;
3 a knowledge of cost behaviour;
4 flexibility;
5 a specified time period;
6 adequate systems support;
7 an effective organizational structure;
8 a sufficient level of education in budgetary practice.

If these prerequisites exist, then budgeting should enable the company to improve its effectiveness by planning for the future and controlling the execution of the plan by comparing actual results with the desired level of performance.

Deviations between actual and budgeted results will be of managerial concern for such reasons as the following:

1 to highlight errors in budgeting procedures;
2 to indicate the need for budget revision;
3 to pinpoint those activities requiring remedial attention.

The principles of management by exception should be applied to this process of comparison with the focusing of attention on *significant* variations. However, if the budgeted level of activity differs from the actual level of activity it will be apparent that variances of an artificial nature arise – such variances are based purely on volume rather than efficiency. This emphasizes the need for flexibility within the budgeting system: it should be able to allow for varying circumstances by recognizing and adapting to significant changes in the fundamental operating conditions of the firm. Such adaptability can be achieved by a *flexible budget*.

In a flexible budgeting system the budgeted cost is adjusted in accordance with the level of activity experienced in the budget period. For example, a budget that is based on sales of 10 000 units during a particular period is of little value for control purposes if 12 000 units (or 8000 units) are actually sold. The sales manager will be necessarily held responsible for the volume variance, but the level of commission, order processing/invoicing, freight, and similar cost-incurring activities will tend to depend on the actual level of activity which requires that the budget be adjusted in order to show the efficient budgeted level of expenditure for the achieved level of activity.

A simple way of building a flexible budget is to start with a budget for the most likely level of activity and then to derive budgets for 5 per cent, 10 per cent, 15 per cent above and below this level.

The major advantage of the flexible budget is its ability to specify the budgeted level of costs, revenues and profits *without revision* when sales and production programmes are changed. It achieves this by distinguishing between those costs that vary with changes in the level of activity and those that do not. In other words, it is based on a thorough knowledge of cost behaviour patterns.

A static budget (i.e. a fixed budget that relates to a single level of activity) can result in misleading actions. An example should make this clear. Figure 18.19

**FIGURE 18.19**
*Fixed budget analysis*

|  | Budget | Actual | Variance |
|---|---|---|---|
| Sales (units) | 10,000 | 11,000 | +1,000 |
| Sales revenue | £15,000 | £16,500 | +£1,500 |
| Expenditure: Direct | 10,000 | 11,000 | +1,000 |
| Indirect | 4,000 | 4,200 | +200 |
| Profit | £1,000 | £1,300 | +£300 |

shows the comparison of a budgeted level of 10 000 units with an actual sales level of 11 000 units. It appears that profit has improved by £300 *but* not all costs vary in the same way, so a flexible budget analysis is called for. This is shown in Figure 18.20 and indicates clearly that the comparison should be between the actual level of activity and the budgeted costs, revenue, and profit for that level. While profit was higher than the budgeted figure, the difference was only £20 rather than £300.

The need to distinguish fixed costs (which remain constant in total during a period) from variable costs (which remain constant per unit of output) is of paramount importance, and any costs that are neither one nor the other (i.e. semi-fixed or semi-variable expenses) can usefully be classified as mixed costs.

**FIGURE 18.20**
*Flexible budget analysis*

|  | Fixed budget | Flexible Actual | Actual | Variance |
|---|---|---|---|---|
| Sales (units) | 10,000 | 11,000 | 11,000 | – |
| Sales revenue | £15,000 | 16,500 | 16,500 | – |
| Expenditure: Direct | 10,000 | 11,000 | 11,000 | – |
| Fixed indirect | 1,500 | 1,500 | 1,450 | −50 |
| Variable indirect | 2,000 | 2,200 | 2,240 | +40 |
| Mixed indirect | 500 | 520 | 510 | −10 |
| Profit | £1,000 | £1,280 | £1,300 | +20 |

Apart from showing the cost breakdown in some detail, Figure 18.20 shows the target level of activity (i.e. the fixed budget) as well as the efficiency with which the actual level of activity was attained. This information is vital to effective control.

It is important to appreciate that budgeting cannot take the place of management but rather forms a vital aid to management. Indeed, budgets are based on estimates, and judgement must be applied to determine how valid the estimates are and, consequently, how significant deviations are from those estimates. The adequacy of planning and controlling operations hinges critically upon the adequacy of managerial judgement.

In the light of the need for judgement it is clear that budgeting should not introduce unnecessary rigidity into the management process. A budget should be a flexible framework that is capable of accommodating changing circumstances, but care must be exercised lest the budgetary targets come to supersede the objectives of the company. The budget is a means to an end, not an end in itself.

In its traditional application budgeting has a major weakness in planning and another in control: in the planning phase there is usually consideration of too few alternative courses of action from which the best is to be selected, and in the control phase it is difficult to adjust operating budgets to reflect rapidly changing conditions – they are at best flexible with respect to changing sales or production levels.

Nevertheless, these weaknesses should not outweigh the general role of budgeting in drawing attention to problem areas, encouraging forward thinking, and developing company-wide cooperation.

## Other Approaches to Budgeting: ZBB and PPBS

In order to accommodate the particular needs of non-profit organizations (such as government agencies) as well as providing a focus for more rigorous thinking in relation to *programmed* or *discretionary costs* (i.e. those which are determined purely by managerial discretion – such as R & D, training, and many marketing outlays), a number of recent developments in budgeting techniques are worthy of mention. In particular, zero-base budgeting (ZBB) and output budgeting (which is also known as a planning-programming-budgeting system, hence the initials PPBS) have generated considerable interest, so we will take note of them at this point.

- *Zero-base budgeting*
  Among other failings it is generally agreed that traditional budgeting (or *incremental budgeting* as it is often known due to the tendency to add on a bit more – an increment – to last year's budget level in order to arrive at a figure for next year) is number-oriented, fails to identify priorities, and starts with the existing level of activity or expenditure as an established base, whereas it might be more useful to managers to have a technique that was decision-oriented, helped in determining priorities, and sought to reassess the current level of expenditure.

  It will be appreciated from this last point that in taking as given the current level of expenditure, and the activities that this represents, the traditional approach to budgeting, by looking only at desired increases or, occasionally, decreases, is ignoring the majority of the organization's expenditure. This is rather myopic.

  The zero-base budgeting alternative is to evaluate *simultaneously* existing and new ways of achieving specified ends in order to establish priorities among them which could mean that there are trade-offs between existing and new activities. For example, a new Project A that is considered to be more desirable than an existing Project B may be resourced by terminating Project B. In essence the approach is carried out in two stages:
  (a) Decision packages are identified within each decision unit. These decision units are essentially discrete activities that can be described in a way that

separates them from other activities of the organization. The decision packages cover both existing and projected incremental activities, and the organizational units responsible for carrying them out are much akin to the responsibility centres that were discussed earlier in the chapter. The object is to define for each decision unit the basic requirements that are needed if it is to perform the function for which it was established. Any costs in excess of this basic level are deemed increment. (It will be seen, therefore, that the title 'zero base' is something of a misnomer since the base is certainly greater than zero!) In considering what is needed in order to fulfil a particular purpose, over and above the base level, it is probable that alternative ways of achieving the same end will be identified, and these should be described and evaluated as they arise: these are the decision packages.

(b) Once the manager of a decision unit has submitted his statement of evaluated decision packages to his superior it is the latter's job to assign priorities to the various submissions from all his subordinates, and to select the highest-ranking decision packages that come within his available budget limit. There are a number of ways in which priorities can be determined, all of which presuppose some explicit criterion of effectiveness in order that competing packages may be ranked.

This approach is logical and has much to commend it in relation to discretionary outlays.

- *Output budgeting*

In the traditional approach to budgeting there tends to be an overall emphasis on the functional areas of an organization. Thus one has the budget for the marketing function, and that for the data processing department. However, no organization was ever established in order that it might have these functions as a definition of what it exists to achieve, so it is helpful to look at the situation from another angle.

In a typical business organization there will be functions such as those shown in Figure 18.21, but the organization really exists in order to achieve

**FIGURE 18.21**
*Functional activities*

**FIGURE 18.22**
*Missions*

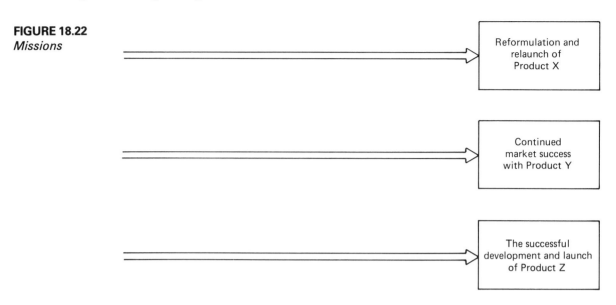

various purposes which have been simplified in the 'missions' of Figure 18.22. In developing a business plan the major concern is with the 'missions', subject to the resource limitations within the functions, etc., whereas the development of controls will usually be via the responsibility centres that are contained within the functions.

If we now superimpose the (horizontal) missions over the (vertical) functions we have the crux of the output budgeting approach. What this does is to focus attention on the purposes to be served by the organization, as shown by the missions, and the contribution that each function must make to each mission if the missions are to be successful. Figure 18.23 suggests this in the most simplified manner.

**FIGURE 18.23**
*A simplified output budgeting format*

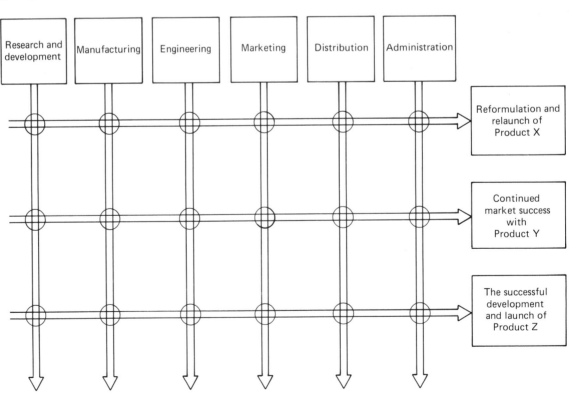

**Variance Analysis**

When actual selling prices differ from standard selling prices a *sales price variance* can be computed. Standard selling prices will be used in compiling budgets, but it may be necessary to adapt to changing market conditions by raising or lowering prices, so it becomes desirable to segregate variances due to price changes from variances due to changes in quantity and product mix.

Quantity and mix are the two components of *sales volume variances*, and variations in profit can be explained to some extent by analysing sales quantity and sales mix.

The formulae for computing sales variances are:

- sales price variance = actual units sold × (actual price − standard price);
- sales volume variance = sales quantity variance + sales mix variance;
- sales quantity variance = budgeted profit on budgeted sales − expected profit on actual sales;
- sales mix variance = expected profit on actual sales − standard profit on actual sales.

'Expected profit on actual sales' is calculated as though profit increases or decreases proportionately with changes in the level of sales. 'Standard profit on actual sales' is the sum of the standard profit for all units sold. (For a single product enterprise, or in one where the profit per unit of sales is constant over the product range, the standard profit on actual sales is equal to the expected profit on actual sales, and the sales mix variance will necessarily be nil.)

Let us clarify the methodology with an example. Assume budgeted sales of a company's two products for a forthcoming period were as follows:

Product A  500 units at £2.00 per unit
Product B  700 units at £1.50 per unit

and their costs were:

Product A  £1.75 per unit
Product B  £1.30 per unit

Actual sales for the period were:

Product A  560 units at £1.95 per unit
Product B  710 units at £1.40 per unit

| | | | |
|---|---|---|---|
| Budgeted sales revenue | = £[(500 × 2.00) + (700 × 1.50)] = £2,050 | | |
| Actual sales revenue | = £[(560 × 1.95) + (710 × 1.40)] = £2,086 | | |
| Budgeted profit | = £[(500 × 0.25) + (700 × 0.20)] = | £265 | |
| Actual profit | = £[(560 × 0.20) + (710 × 0.10)] = | £183 | |
| Total sales variance | | | −£82 |

| | | | |
|---|---|---|---|
| Sales price variance | = £[560 × (1.95 − 2.00)] + [710 × (1.40 − 1.50)] = | | −£99 |
| Sales volume variance: | | | |
| Quantity variance | = £265 − [2,086/2,050 × 265] = | +£4 | |
| Mix variance | = £269 − [(560 × 0.25) + (710 × 0.20)] = | +£13 | |
| Sales volume variance | | | +£17 |
| Total sales variance | | | −£82 |

Standards can be developed for repetitive activites, and it is possible to determine standards in a marketing context for the following illustrative activities:

1 cost per unit of sales;
2 cost per sales transaction;
3 cost per order received;
4 cost per customer account;
5 cost per mile travelled;
6 cost per sales call made.

The degree of detail can be varied to suit the particular requirements. Thus 'cost per unit of sales' may be 'advertising cost per £ of sales revenue for product X' and so on.

It is clearly more difficult to establish precise standards for most marketing activities than is the case in the manufacturing or distribution functions. Physical and mechanical factors are less influential; psychological factors are more prominent; objective measurement is less conspicuous; tolerance limits must be broader; and the range of segments for which marketing standards can be developed is much greater. But the discipline of seeking to establish standards can generate insights into relationships between effort and results that are likely to outweigh any lack of precision.

It is possible for an organization to develop marketing standards by participating in an interfirm comparison scheme (such as the one run by the Centre for Interfirm Comparison). As Westwick (1987) has shown, integrated sets of ratios and standards can be devised to allow for detailed monitoring of performance.

When budget levels and standards are being developed it is vitally important to note the assumptions on which they have been based since it is inevitable that circumstances will change and a variety of unanticipated events will occur once the budget is implemented. Bearing this in mind let us work through an example. Figure 18.24 illustrates an extract from a marketing plan for Product X (column 2), with actual results (column 3) and variances (column 4) being shown for a particular operating period.

**FIGURE 18.24**
*Operating results for Product X*

| Item (1) | Plan (2) | Actual (3) | Variance (4) |
|---|---|---|---|
| Revenues: | | | |
| Sales (units) | 10,000,000 | 11,000,000 | 1,000,000 |
| Price per unit (£) | 1.00 | 0.95 | 0.05 |
| Total revenue (£) | 10,000,000 | 10,450,000 | 450,000 |
| Market: | | | |
| Total market size (units) | 25,000,000 | 30,000,000 | 5,000,000 |
| Share of market (%) | 40.0 | 36.7 | (3.3) |
| Costs: | | | |
| Variable cost per unit (£) | 0.60 | 0.60 | – |
| Contribution: | | | |
| Per unit (£) | 0.40 | 0.35 | 0.05 |
| Total contribution (£) | 4,000,000 | 3,850,000 | (150,000) |

The unfavourable contribution variance of £150,000 shown at the foot of column 4 is due to two principal causes:

1 a variance relating to contribution per unit; and
2 a variance relating to sales volume.

In turn, a variance relating to sales volume can be attributed to differences between:

3 actual and anticipated total market size; and
4 actual and anticipated market share.

Therefore a variation between planned and actual contribution may be due to variations in price per unit, variable cost per unit, total market size and market penetration.

In the case of Product X we have:

1 Profit variance:
$$(C_a - C_p) \times Q_a = £(0.35 - 0.40) \times 11{,}000{,}000$$
$$= (£550{,}000)$$

2 Volume variance:
$$(Q_a - Q_p) \times C_p = (11{,}000{,}000 - 10{,}000{,}000) \times £0.40$$
$$= £400{,}000$$

3 Net variance:                 £

| | £ |
|---|---|
| Profit variance | (550,000) |
| Volume variance | 400,000 |
| | £(150,000) |

where:   $C_a$ = actual contribution per unit;
        $C_p$ = planned contribution per unit;
        $Q_a$ = actual quantity sold in units;
        $Q_p$ = planned quantity of sales in units.

Figure 18.25 illustrates the relations.

**FIGURE 18.25**
*Marketing variances, 1*

However, 2 can be analysed further to take into account the impact of market size and penetration variations.

4 Market size variance:
$$(M_a - M_p) \times S_p \times C_p = (30{,}000{,}000 - 25{,}000{,}000) \times 0.4 \times 0.4$$
$$= £800{,}000$$

5 Market share variance:
$$(S_a - S_p) \times M_a \times C_p = (0.367 - 0.40) \times 30{,}000{,}000 \times 0.4$$
$$= £(400{,}000)$$

6  Volume variance:

| | £ |
|---|---|
| Market size variance | 800,000 |
| Market share variance | (400,000) |
| | £400,000 |

where:  $M_a$  =  actual total market in units;
$M_p$  =  planned total market in units;
$S_a$  =  actual market share;
$S_p$  =  planned market share.

See Figure 18.26 which illustrates these relationships.

**FIGURE 18.26**
*Marketing variances, 2*

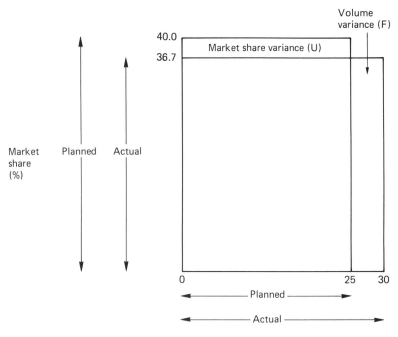

In summary, the position now appears thus:

| | £ | £ |
|---|---|---|
| Planned profit contribution | | 4,000,000 |
| Volume variance: | | |
|   Market size variance | 800,000 | |
|   Market share variance | (400,000) | 400,000 |
| Profit variance | | (550,000) |
| Actual profit contribution | | £3,850,000 |

But this is not the end of the analysis! Variances arise because of unsatisfactory performance and unsatisfactory plans. It is desirable, therefore, to distinguish variances due to the poor *execution* of plans from those due to the poor *establishing* of plans. In the latter category are likely to be found forecasting errors reflecting faulty assumptions, and the estimates of total market size may constitute poor bench-marks for gauging subsequent managerial performance.

It is difficult to determine categorically whether market share variances are primarily the responsibility of forecasters or of those who execute the plans based on forecasts. On the face of it the primary responsibility is likely to be attached to the latter group.

In interpreting the variances for Product X it can be seen that the favourable volume variance of £400,000 resulted from two variances relating to market size and market share. Both of these are undesirable since they led to a lower contribution than intended. Had the forecasting group correctly anticipated the larger total market it should have been possible to devise a better plan to achieve the desired share and profit contribution. The actual outcome suggests that competitive position has been lost due to a loss of market share in a rapidly growing market. This is a serious pointer.

Lower prices resulted in a lower level of contribution per unit, and hence a lower overall profit contribution. The reasons for this need to be established and future plans modified as necessary.

As an approach to improved learning about the links between effort and results – especially in the face of active competitive behaviour – it is helpful to take the above analysis further and to evaluate performance by considering what *should have happened* in the circumstances (which is akin to flexible budgeting in a manufacturing setting).

At the end of the operating period to which Figure 18.24 refers it may become known that a large company with substantial resources made an aggressive entry into the market-place using lots of promotions and low prices. Furthermore, an unforeseen export demand for Product X may have arisen due to a prolonged strike in the USA's main manufacturer. On the basis of these details it becomes possible to carry out an *ex-post* performance analysis in which the original plans are revised to take account of what has since become known.

A clearer distinction can be made via *ex-post* performance analysis along these lines since a distinction can be made between:

1 planning variances due to environmental events that were:
  - foreseeable,
  - unforeseeable;
2 performance variances that are due to problems in executing the plans.

The situation is summarized in Figure 18.27.

**FIGURE 18.27**
*Ex-post performance analysis*

Legend

| Subscripts | Variables |
|---|---|
| a = actual | Q = Quantity |
| p = planned | C = Contribution margin |
| r = revised | S = Share |
| | M = Market |

SOURCE: Adapted from Hulbert and Toy (1977)

This example has focused on a single product line (Product X), but multiproduct companies will typically have product lines with differing cost structures, prices and hence profit characteristics. It will be apparent, therefore, that the *mix* of products sold will have an impact on the overall profit outcome. For example, an enterprise may offer three product lines with budgeted characteristics relating to the next operating period as given in Figure 18.28.

**FIGURE 18.28**
*Budgeted operating results by product line*

|  | Product A | Product B | Product C | Total |
|---|---|---|---|---|
| Budget sales (units) | 100,000 | 200,000 | 50,000 |  |
| Budgeted unit selling price | £12.00 | £10.00 | £20.00 |  |
| Budgeted unit variable cost | £6.00 | £4.50 | £8.00 |  |
| Budgeted unit contribution | £6.00 | £5.50 | £12.00 |  |
| Budgeted contribution | 50% | 55% | 60% |  |
| Budgeted contribution | £600,000 | £1,100,000 | £600,000 | £2,300,000 |

Each product line has a different contribution per unit, so the total contribution from all lines is dependent upon the particular mix of sales across all product lines. If the actual outcomes for the period in question were as shown in Figure 18.29 we can explain the total variance of £275,000 U (i.e. actual profit contribution £2,025,000 minus budgeted profit contribution £2,300,000) as in Figure 18.30.

**FIGURE 18.29**
*Actual operating results by product line*

|  | Product A | Product B | Product C | Total |
|---|---|---|---|---|
| Actual sales (units) | 90,000 | 220,000 | 45,000 |  |
| Actual unit selling price | £12.00 | £9.00 | £20.00 |  |
| Actual unit variable cost | £6.00 | £4.50 | £9.00 |  |
| Actual unit contribution | £6.00 | £4.50 | £11.00 |  |
| Actual contribution | 50% | 50% | 55% |  |
| Actual contribution | £540,000 | £990,000 | £495,000 | £2,050,000 |

In summary we have:

|  | £ |
|---|---|
| Volume variance | 32,863 F |
| Mix variance | 42,863 U |
| Profit variance | 265,000 U |
| Total variance | £275,000 U |

In other words the total variance was partly due to overall volume being higher than budgeted (355 000 units rather than 350 000, as budgeted), which gives a favourable variance of £32,863 made up of favourable volume variances for each individual product line; the actual mix of sales differed from budget in a way that produced an unfavourable variance of £42,863 made up of unfavourable variances for Products A and C which were partly offset by a favourable variance for product line B; and the actual margins were less than budgeted for product lines B and C, giving an unfavourable profit variance of £265,000.

The volume variance can be analysed further along the lines suggested in the previous example, but the main point to note from this example is the impact that variations in the mix of products sold can have on the profit outcome. If all

**FIGURE 18.30**
*Marketing variances, 3*

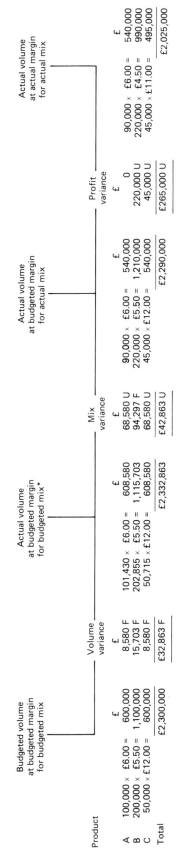

| Product | Budgeted volume at budgeted margin for budgeted mix | | Volume variance | Actual volume at budgeted margin for budgeted mix* | | Mix variance | Actual volume at budgeted margin for actual mix | | Profit variance | Actual volume at actual margin for actual mix | |
|---|---|---|---|---|---|---|---|---|---|---|---|
| | | £ | £ | | £ | £ | | £ | £ | | £ |
| A | 100,000 × £6.00 = | 600,000 | 8,580 F | 101,430 × £6.00 = | 608,580 | 68,580 U | 90,000 × £6.00 = | 540,000 | 0 | 90,000 × £6.00 = | 540,000 |
| B | 200,000 × £5.50 = | 1,100,000 | 15,703 F | 202,855 × £5.50 = | 1,115,703 | 94,297 F | 220,000 × £5.50 = | 1,210,000 | 220,000 U | 220,000 × £4.50 = | 990,000 |
| C | 50,000 × £12.00 = | 600,000 | 8,580 F | 50,715 × £12.00 = | 608,580 | 68,580 U | 45,000 × £12.00 = | 540,000 | 45,000 U | 45,000 × £11.00 = | 495,000 |
| Total | | £2,300,000 | £32,863 F | | £2,332,863 | £42,863 U | | £2,290,000 | £265,000 U | | £2,025,000 |

*The budgeted mix was 100,000/(100,000 + 200,000 + 50,000) = 100,000/350,000 = 28.57% for product A, and so on.
Applying this proportion to actual sales units gives 0.2857 (90,000 + 220,000 + 45,000) = 101,430 for product A, and so on for B and C.

product lines had the same percentage margin there would be no mix variance, but this situation is not normal, so we need to be aware of the impact of mix changes.

### Variance Analysis for Distribution Cost Control

As with production costing the analysis of cost variances in distribution costing is the first step towards the goal of identifying the factors that caused the difference between the standard and actual costs so that any inefficiencies can be eliminated. To do this each enterprise will have to decide what specific variance analyses it may want to use. Often companies only compute a net variance for their distribution costs and do not attempt to break the variance down into causal factors. This practice is not to be encouraged, however, since it tends to hide inefficiencies. If the analysis is to be meaningful the variance must be further explained in terms of price and efficiency components. Such price and quantity or efficiency variances can be computed for distribution activities. The price variance is given by:

(standard price − actual price) × actual work units;

and the quantity (or efficiency) variance is given by:

(budgeted work units − actual work units) × standard price.

### A Variance Reporting Example

The distribution costs of the Hill Company are analysed by territories: data for the southern territory is shown in Figure 18.31. The warehousing and handling function's standards are:

| | *Total standard for direct and indirect costs (£)* |
|---|---|
| *Variable costs:* | |
| Receiving | 21 per shipment |
| Pricing, tagging and marking | 6 per unit handled |
| Sorting | 5 per order |
| Handling returns | 10 per return |
| Taking physical inventory | 0.50 per unit warehouse unit |
| Clerical handling of shipping orders | 2 per item |
| | |
| *Fixed costs:* | |
| Rent | 600 per month per territory |
| Depreciation | 450 per month per territory |

The following units of variability were budgeted and recorded for the month of January, 1992:

| | Budgeted | Actual |
|---|---|---|
| Shipments | 400 | 420 |
| Units handled | 200 | 223 |
| Orders | 110 | 108 |
| Returns | 70 | 71 |
| Warehouse unit | 1,600 | 1,630 |
| Item | 750 | 780 |

Southern territory's actual direct costs for the month of January, 1992, were as follows:

| | |
|---|---|
| Receiving | £6,400 |
| Pricing, tagging and marking | 1,115 |
| Sorting | 565 |
| Handling returns | 680 |
| Taking physical inventory | 880 |
| Clerical handling of shipping orders | 500 |
| Rent | 650 |
| Depreciation | 445 |

The company allocates the following actual indirect costs to its southern and northern territories:

| | |
|---|---|
| Receiving (allocated on actual shipments: southern 420, northern 80) | £2,500 |
| Clerical handling of shipping orders (allocated on actual items: southern 780, northern 120) | 1,223 |

- *Efficiency variance*
  Shipments received is the unit of variability chosen for the receiving function. There were a total of 420 shipments made, while only 400 shipments were budgeted. This results in an unfavourable efficiency variance because actual shipments exceeded those budgeted. (It should be noted here that care must be used in analysing distribution cost variances because it is easy to misinterpret the results associated with such costs. Each cost variance is considered favourable or unfavourable as far as that individual detailed function is concerned, not for its effect on the overall company.) The efficiency variance in this case is unfavourable because 20 more shipments were made than planned. Hence, orders of larger quantities should be encouraged to save costs in receiving.

- *Price variance*
  The actual cost of £20.238 (i.e. £8,500 total actual cost of receiving as shown in Figure 18.31 ÷ 420 actual units) for each shipment received is less than the standard price of £21.00 which results in a favourable price variance. This difference in price is multiplied by the actual shipments to give a total favourable price variance of £320. It is not necessary to compute the actual cost per unit using the format illustrated in Figure 18.31 since the price variance can be determined by comparing total actual cost to the actual units at standard price shown in Column 2.

Efficiency and price variance are computed for variable costs only. Only a net variance is computed for the two fixed expenses shown in Figure 18.31. This measures the difference between budgeted costs (budgeted units at standard price) and actual costs (actual units at actual price).

## Other Models

A useful model for assessing product line performance has been proposed (and tested) by Diamantopoulos and Mathews (1990). The model is based on the need to evaluate product performance in a multiproduct setting using readily-available product information and widely-used performance indicators in a systematic way. Not least of all it was deemed essential that the model be clearly understood by its intended users (product managers) otherwise, from an implementation point of view, it would not have been worthwhile. Figure 18.32 shows the model.

**FIGURE 18.31**
*Distribution cost variances*

**HILL COMPANY – SOUTHERN TERRITORY**
**Expense variance report – warehousing and handling**
**January 1992**

| Detailed function: | Units of variability | (1) Actual cost (actual @ actual price) | (2) Actual units @ standard price | (3) Budgeted costs (budgeted units @ standard price) | (2 – 1) Price variance | (3 – 2) Efficiency variance | (3 – 1) Net variance |
|---|---|---|---|---|---|---|---|
| Receiving: | | | | | | | |
| direct costs | Shipment | £ 6,400 | | | | | |
| indirect costs | $(420/500 \times £2,500)$ | 2,100 | | | | | |
| Total | | £ 8,500 | £8,820 (420 × £21) | £ 8,400 (400 × £21) | £320 F | £420 U | £100 U |
| Pricing, tagging and marking: | | | | | | | |
| direct costs | Unit handled | 1,115 | 1,338 (223 × £6) | 1,200 (200 × £6) | 223 F | 138 U | 85 F |
| Sorting: direct costs | Order | 565 | 540 (108 × £5) | 550 (110 × £5) | 25 U | 10 F | 15 U |
| Handling returns: | | | | | | | |
| direct costs | Return | 680 | 710 (71 × £10) | 700 (70 × £10) | 30 F | 10 U | 20 F |
| Taking physical inventory | Warehouse unit | 880 | 815 (1,630 × £0.50) | 800 (1,600 × £0.50) | 65 U | 15 U | 80 U |
| Clerical handling of shipping orders: | | | | | | | |
| direct costs | Item | £ 500 | | | | | |
| indirect costs | $(780/900 \times £1,223)$ | 1,060 | | | | | |
| Total | | £ 1,560 | 1,560 (780 × £2) | 1,500 (750 × £2) | 0 | 60 U | 60 U |
| Total variable expense | | £13,300 | | £13,150 | £483 F | £633 U | £150 U |
| Fixed expense: | | | | | | | |
| rent | | 650 | | 600 | | | 50 U |
| depreciation | | 445 | | 450 | | | 5 F |
| Total warehousing and handling | | £14,395 | | £14,200 | | | £195 U |

F = favourable;   U = unfavourable

594   *Strategic Marketing Management*

**FIGURE 18.32**
*A model for
product
performance
analysis*

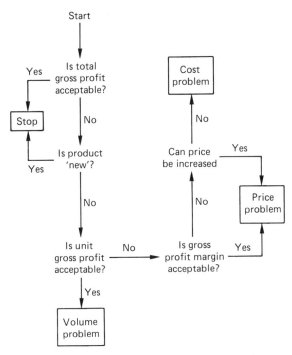

SOURCE: Diamantopoulos and Mathew (1990), p. 9

Gross profit is used as the primary performance indicator since this measure is easily provided without additional analysis. If the gross profit being generated is below par this may be due to:

- insufficient sales volume;
- high unit cost;
- prices that are too low.

Investigation should reveal which of these possible causes applies. If the *unit* gross profit is satisfactory, for example, but the product line's *overall* gross profit is unsatisfactory, the remedy may be to increase volume by revising the marketing mix in a suitable way. There may be products having unsatisfactory gross margins that are not amenable to corrective action. In this case their continued role in the range needs to be questioned.

Areas in which the model is particularly useful are:

1 pricing (especially the effectiveness of existing pricing policies in terms of profit and volume results);
2 new product introductions (by using previous introductions to set realistic bench-mark expectations for new products);
3 product deletions (using warning signals as the stimulus to further investigations).

Despite the need to specify target values for each element of the model (i.e. total gross profit, unit gross profit, newness of product, gross profit margin, and price) this does not take away the importance of managerial judgement in arriving at an overall assessment of each product's performance. Indeed, judgement is needed in specifying the quantified target values themselves as well as in interpreting any given product's standing relative to those targets. When a particular product's performance is considered satisfactory it is not self-evident that it should be ignored: in order to ensure *sustained* satisfactory performance it may be necessary to take action in anticipation of future environmental changes (i.e. feedforward control).

**FIGURE 18.33**
*Analysing sales deviations*

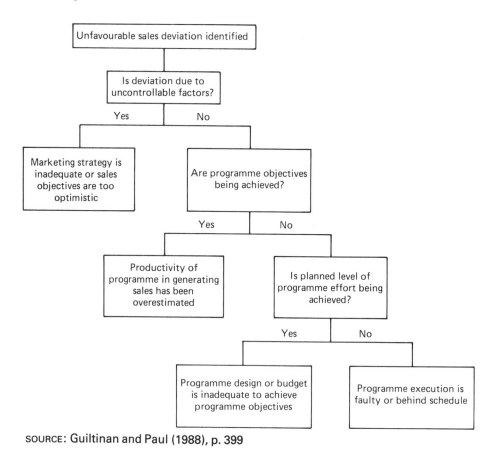

SOURCE: Guiltinan and Paul (1988), p. 399

A variation on the product line model that deals with sales deviations from plan is shown in Figure 18.33.

This protocol follows a series of logical steps. Having identified a variance that is deemed to be significant (i.e. is unlikely to have arisen by chance) the question is raised as to whether this may be due to controllable or uncontrollable factors. ('Uncontrollable' is used here in the sense of being beyond the influence of managers in the given enterprise, or beyond the forecasting ability of relevant personnel, which might cover changing market conditions leading to a decline in industry sales, or unanticipated competitive actions.)

If the explanation for the variance is not found at this first stage the next stage raises the question of the performance of marketing programmes. This can be addressed at two levels:

1  the degree to which programme objectives are being achieved;
2  the degree to which planned programme effort is being achieved.

If the degree of effort (as represented by actual sales levels, or advertising coverage) is not as planned it is unlikely that either programme objectives or sales objectives are being achieved. On the other hand, if the planned input of effort is being achieved but programme objectives (such as brand awareness levels or the number of new accounts) are not, it is probable that either the budget is inadequate or the design of the programme (e.g. sales appeal, pricing level, advertising copy) is ineffective.

It may be found that the sales variance is not attributable to faulty programmes or lack of effort but is due to the sales productivity of the programme being overstimulated, or the implementation of the programme being behind schedule.

Insofar as sales variances reflect revenue generation there is a corresponding need to examine the variances among the costs incurred and budget figures to secure control over the profit consequences of sales activities.

## The Variance Investigation Decision

A major inhibiting factor in seeking to control via feedforward systems is our limited ability to make reliable estimates of the outcomes of future events. (This reflects our modest understanding of causal relationships both within the sub-systems of the enterprise and between the enterprise and its environment.) All planning is based on estimates (e.g. of prices, costs, volumes) and actual outcomes will rarely be precisely in line with these estimates: some variation is inevitable. Should we expect a manager to investigate every variance that might be reported when we know that some deviation between actual outcomes and budgeted outcomes is bound to occur? On the other hand, if no variances are investigated the control potential of this form of managerial control system is being ignored. An appropriate course of action lies somewhere between these two extremes.

Causes of variances (or 'deviations') can be categorized in the following broad way (after Demski (1980)) with particular variances often being due to one or more deviations:

1 Implementation deviation results from a human or mechanical failure to achieve an attainable outcome, e.g. if the mileage rate payable to employees using their own vehicles for business trips is 35p per mile, but due to clerical error this is being paid at only 25p per mile, the required corrective action is easy to specify. The cost of correction will be exceeded by the benefits.

2 Prediction deviation results from errors in specifying the parameter values in a decision model, e.g. in determining overhead absorption rates *ex-ante* predictions must be made of, *inter alia*, the future level of activity. If the predictions are wrong then the overhead absorption rate will be wrong and variances will result.

3 Measurement deviation arises as a result of error in measuring the actual outcome – such as incorrectly adding up the number of calls made in Region X, or the number of units sold of Product P.

4 Model deviation arises as a result of an erroneous formulation in a decision model. For example, in formulating a linear programme the constraints relating to the availability of input factors may be incorrectly specified.

5 Random deviations due to chance fluctuations of a parameter for which no cause can be assigned. These deviations do not call for corrective action, but in order to identify the causes of variances it is helpful to separate random deviations from deviations 1–4 above, in order that the significance of the latter might be established.

While these five categories of deviation appear to be mutually exclusive their interdependencies should not be underestimated. The traditional view is to assume that variances are due to implementation deviations but this is patently simplistic. It is also potentially inequitable since it may deem individual managers to be responsible for variances that arise from reasons beyond their control (such as 3 and 5 above).

In setting up bench-marks (e.g. budget targets or standard costs) it is important to recognize that a range of possible outcomes in the vicinity of the bench-mark will usually be acceptable. In other words, random variations around the bench-mark are to be expected, and searching for causes of variances within the acceptable range of outcomes will incur costs without generating benefits. Only when variances fall outside the acceptable range will further investigation be desirable.

This prompts the operational question of how one actually determines whether a variance should be investigated. As Figure 18.34 suggests, if it was known in advance that a variance arose on a random basis it would not be necessary to investigate it since there will be no assignable cause. On the other hand, if a variance is of a non-random nature it would not pay to ignore it if it was significant.

**FIGURE 18.34**
*The variance
investigation
decision*

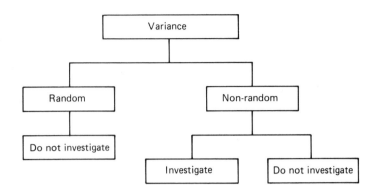

How can significance be determined? This boils down to a statistical question, and the technique that is of proven help is that developed for use in quality control situations to which we will turn very shortly.

A more conventional approach to evaluating the significance of variances is either to:

1 look at the absolute size of the variance (i.e. actual − standard) such that all variances greater than, say, £1,000 are investigated; or
2 compute the proportionate size of the variance (i.e. variance/standard) and investigate all those exceeding, say, 10 per cent.

Both 1 and 2 must depend upon the manager's intuition or some arbitrary decision rule when it comes to deciding whether or not to investigate a given variance.

The advantages of 1 and 2 are their simplicity and ease of implementation, but both fail to deal adequately with the issues of significance (in statistical terms) and balancing the costs and benefits of investigation. We can resolve these issues with the help of the approach adopted in *statistical quality control*.

Statistical quality control (SQC) is based upon the established fact that the observed quality of an item is always subject to chance variability. Some variability in the observed quality of an item will be due to assignable causes which exist beyond the boundaries due to chance cause. (Assignable causes are, by definition, identifiable and steps can be taken to remove them.) The major task of SQC is to distinguish between assignable and chance causes of error in order that the assignable causes may be identified, their causes discovered and eliminated, and acceptable quality standards maintained.

These basic principles of SQC can be applied in areas other than production. An example is given of a control chart for monitoring advertising expenditure as a percentage of sales in Figure 18.35.

**FIGURE 18.35**
*Advertising control
chart*

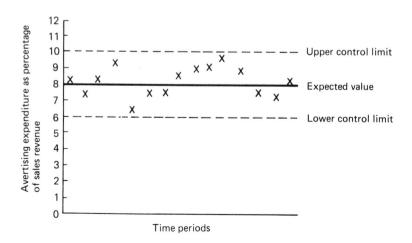

The standard of performance that is expected is that advertising expense will be 8 per cent of sales revenue, but random causes (i.e. chance) can make this figure vary from 6 per cent to 10 per cent of sales revenue. If the range of 6–10 per cent represents three standard deviations on either side of a mean of 8 per cent (i.e. $\bar{x} = 8$ with confidence limits of $\pm 3\,\theta$), then observations would be expected to fall within this range in 998 out of 1000 cases.

However, when an observation falls outside these limits two opposing hypotheses can be put forward to explain the situation:

1 The observation is the freak one out of 1000 that exceeds the control limits by pure chance, and the company still has the situation under control.
2 The company has lost control over the situation due to some assignable cause such as a new competitor entering the market.

If hypothesis 1 is accepted it is unnecessary to investigate – with the risk that something has actually happened to cause the situation to fall out of control. On the other hand, if hypothesis 2 is accepted and investigations are begun into assignable causes there is always the risk – albeit very small – of the first hypothesis being correct and hence investigation being unecessary.

Investigations to identify the causes of variances – even when the latter are deemed to be significant – involve costs, so we must again reflect on the cost-benefit issue: if the likely penalty from *not* identifying and correcting the cause of the variance is less than the likely cost of the investigation it hardly seems worth the trouble.

Consider a hypothetical case in which the cost of investigating a reported variance is estimated at £200 while the penalty for not identifying a correctable cause is likely to be £600 (which could be the value of cost savings – or extra profit – that will arise once the cause of the variance is removed). If an investigation is undertaken and no cause is discovered, the enterprise will be £200 worse off, whereas it will be £400 better off (i.e. £600 − £200) if a cause is ascertained and corrected.

## 18.8 SOME BEHAVIOURAL FACTORS

Management control (MC) is based on interactions between an organization's members, hence the control process must reflect how individuals behave, as well as their knowledge, skills and personality traits.

In participating in organizations, individuals are seeking to satisfy various needs, some of which are extrinsic (i.e. satisfied by the actions of others) while others are intrinsic (i.e. satisfied by the feelings individuals have about themselves and their achievements).

The extent to which a given individual might be motivated to engage in organizational activities has been argued to be a function of:

1 beliefs regarding the outcomes that are likely to result from this individual's actions;
2 how attractive these outcomes are in relation to satisfying the individual's needs.

In designing and operating control systems, therefore, it is necessary to consider:

1 the actions that individuals are motivated to take in their perceived self-interest;

2 the best interests of the organization.

> MC is a blend of rational and behavioural considerations, and neglecting either type leads to erroneous generalizations.
>
> (Anthony (1988), p. 22)

It can also lead to harmful side effects.

Some side effects stemming from the design and implementation of control systems are inevitable and an inherent characteristic of certain types of control. On the other hand, some harmful side effects are avoidable – such as those stemming from poor design, the implementation of the wrong type of control system for a given situation, or both.

The major side effects of a negative nature are as follows.

## 1 Behavioural Displacement

This arises when the behaviours encouraged by the control system are inconsistent with the strategy the organization seeks to pursue. In the case of results controls, displacement can occur when there is a poor understanding of desired results or an excessive reliance on easily quantified results. In the case of action controls there is the risk of displacement due to means–ends inversion when individuals are (wrongly) encouraged by the control system to pay more attention to what they are doing (the means) rather than to what they should be accomplishing (the ends). Displacement in the context of action controls can also arise when rules and standard operating procedures are followed in a rigid, non-adaptive manner.

There is also the risk of behavioural displacement when social controls (such as group norms) induce a degree of routinized conformity that stifles any form of creative adaptation.

## 2 Gamesmanship

This refers to the tendency among managers to 'play the system' by means of actions intended to improve their measures of performance without producing any positive economic effects. It is particularly prevalent when either results or action controls are in use. In both, it is possible for data to be manipulated, thus rendering the control system ineffective.

## 3 Negative Atittudes

Such negative effects as job tension, frustration, conflict and resistance can arise even when control systems are well designed. This is most likely to be the case with poor performers since their limitations become more apparent the better the control system. However, negative attitudes can also arise in the case of potentially good performers if the control system is poorly designed.

Potential consequences of negative attitudes include gamesmanship, sabotage, or turnover, all of which can impede the achievement of strategic ends.

## 4 Short-termism

> ... if long term growth of profits is the aim then rewards based on short term achievement of sales targets are not likely to be helpful.
>
> (Johnson and Scholes (1988), p. 298)

An organization's reward system is supposed to encourage goal congruence. However, control systems tend to focus on short-term results even though managers are expected to achieve both short- and long-run objectives. The reason for this is simple: the control system tends to report what has happened (e.g. over the past month) and is less capable of specifying what might happen in the long-term future.

> Our lack of knowledge about how best to measure a manager's performance is probably the most serious weakness in MCS.
>
> (Anthony (1988), p. 74)

For example, performance in a given period may not reflect the manager's real performance. Reasons for this may be that:

- outcomes (hence performance) in that period will be influenced by the actions taken in earlier periods as well as by actions of managers in other responsibility centres;
- current actions will have a lagged impact on future outcomes and it is virtually impossible to eliminate these effects from the measurement of current performance.

Dent (1990, p. 3) has commented on the way in which accounting practices have been drawn into the argument over short-termism:

> The extensive use of short-run financial calculations to appraise managerial performance is deemed to have diverted managerial attention away from fundamental value-creating activities, motivating instead opportunistic behaviours with less permanent benefits . . .

## 5 Entrapment and Escalation

Anthony's framework (see Figure 18.12, p. 566 above) distinguishes between MC of operating activities and MC of projects. Our focus so far has been on the former, but there are some aspects of the latter which warrant our attention.

A project can be defined as a set of activities intended to accomplish a specified end result of sufficient importance to be of interest to management.

> In a project, the focus of control is on the project itself, rather than on activities in a given time period in individual responsibility centers, as is the case with the management control of ongoing operations.
>
> (Anthony (1988), p. 16)

There are three aspects of particular interest within a project:

- its scope (i.e. the specifications for the end product);
- its schedule (i.e. the time required);
- its cost.

Trade-offs among scope, schedule and cost are usually possible in projects. For example, costs might be reduced by decreasing the project's scope, or the schedule might be reduced by increasing the cost. This is not always easy to plan since performance standards are likely to be less reliable for a one-off project than for on-going activities. Moreover, projects tend to be influenced to a greater extent by the external environment than is the case with continuing operations.

The prospect of being assessed as part of the control endeavour – whether in relation to projects or ongoing activities – typically affects the behaviour of individuals, often with dysfunctional consequences. Control activities are far from neutral in their impact, as can be shown by means of a phenomenon of recent interest: entrapment. This occurs when a responsible individual increases his commitment to an ineffective course of action in order to justify the previous allocation of resources to that task. Entrapment is seen as being one example of a broader psychological process that focuses on commitment. The commitment of an individual to a particular course of action is likely to depend on, *inter alia* (see Brockner et al. (1986), p. 110):

1 responsibility for the action;
2 responsibility for the consequences of the action;
3 the salience of the action;
4 the consequences of the action.

While entrapment is not easily explained in terms of economic rationality, there are various plausible explanations reflecting psychological rationality. For example:

- there is a need for the decision maker to assert himself and reaffirm the wisdom of his initial decision;
- the initial commitment was made as a result of the decision maker's belief in the goodness of the course of action, hence self-justification, justification to others, and the norms of consistency are served by continuing;
- continuing avoids the waste of the investment already made (which is known as the sunk-cost fallacy);
- further investment gives further opportunities for the project to come good;
- negative feedback is treated as a learning experience (i.e. a cue to revise the inputs rather than cancel the project);
- negative feedback, alternatively, may be seen as a chance variation;
- a state of inertia has been created by which a project's financial past cannot be divorced from its future – prior investment then motivates the decision to continue;
- decisions are not made in a social vacuum, hence social costs and benefits must be considered relating to self-image, organizational image, reputation and face saving – continue so long as the social and psychological benefits are greater than the economic costs;
- information processing has behavioural underpinnings, such as selective perception in which we see what we want to see;
- an organization's reward system may work to encourage the decision maker to overlook short-term setbacks and continue with the original project through bad times.

Prospect theory (Kahneman and Tversky, 1984) has been used to explain the phenomenon of entrapment, and Figure 18.36 illustrates this. A value function (i.e. the curve in Figure 18.36) shows the relationship between objectively defined gains and losses and the subjective value placed on these by the decision maker.

**FIGURE 18.36**
*The value function*

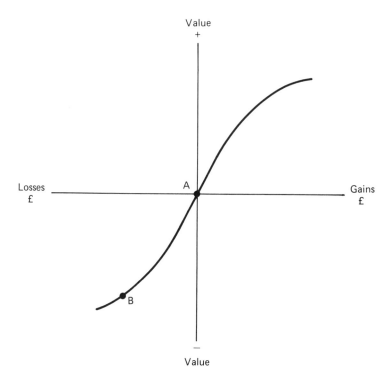

At the outset the decision maker is at point A, but if the decision is unsuccessful he will find himself at point B where further losses do not result in large decreases in value. On the other hand, any gains will result in large increases in value, thus, at point B, the decision maker will risk further losses in the hope of making gains. Despite the sunk costs, risky behaviour is much more likely at point B than it was at point A.

A variation on the theme of entrapment is that of escalation (e.g. see Staw and Ross, 1987a, 1987b). These two phenomena are often related but are analytically separable: entrapment may exist in the absence of escalation. Vivid examples of escalation have been experienced in many major projects when the cost out-turns prove to be much greater than anticipated: the Sydney Opera House, Chicago's sewage system, Concorde, the Channel Tunnel.

## 18.9 TAKING CORRECTIVE ACTION

Having implemented plans, monitored performance, and analysed significant variances, the next step is to decide on the corrective action that is needed. In this section we will concentrate on responding to environmental changes – especially those of a competitive nature.

How should an enterprise respond to environmental changes? There are many ways, and Barrett (1986) has pointed out two opposing possibilities. On the one hand there is the *deterministic approach* in which it is felt that the enterprise's environment determines its actions, hence strategies and even its structure. This takes the idea of adaptation to environmental change to an extreme: changes in the environment – whether in the form of opportunities or threats – will result in changes in competitive strategy and the implementation of these changes may well bring about changes in organizational structure.

In contrast there is the *strategic approach* in which the environment is seen as constraining the enterprise's freedom of action rather than determining it. This concentrates more on the enterprise's strengths (and weaknesses) and its ability to influence its environment rather than simply being influenced by it. One example is the strategy of raising barriers to entry which modifies the environment against the interests of potential competitors.

Marketing intelligence has a role to play in both these approaches by identifying environmental change as a basis for reactive or proactive responses. The response process is reflected in the model portrayed in Figure 18.37.

Various response stages are highlighted, with any given one being triggered when the intelligence signals pass thresholds. Thus, for example, a strong signal indicating a significant change in the environment will cross a number of thresholds and activate an appropriate high-level response. Weaker signals will cross fewer thresholds and hence prompt lower-level responses. Barrett sets his model within a framework of power relationships – especially those involved in the allocation of resources via the budgeting process. This leads to the building in of 'slack' (i.e. a greater amount of resource than is strictly needed to carry out a given task) in certain parts of the enterprise in accordance with the distribution of power. Figure 18.38 indicates in some detail the links between stages in the response process and thresholds. The sequence of stages presumes that each subsequent stage consumes more slack resources than prior stages, thereby reducing the power given from the existence of slack resources.

How should an enterprise respond to environmental changes that manifest themselves either through the gathering of environmental data (e.g. by means of a competitor intelligence system – see Cvitkovic (1989), or environmental scanning – see Sanderson and Luffman (1988)) or via variance analysis? Help is available from the technique of *competitor profiling*. The steps in this technique, developed by SRI International, are:

**FIGURE 18.37**
*Response model*

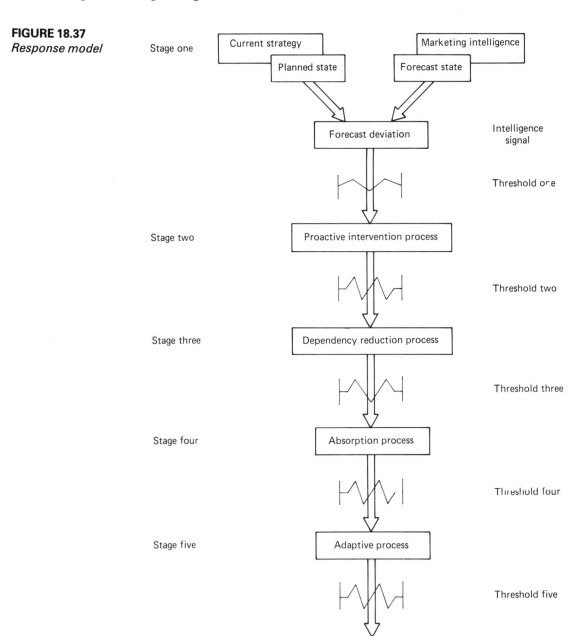

SOURCE: Barrett (1986), p. 37

**FIGURE 18.38**
*Signal thresholds and response stages*

**Stage one**
The first stage of the model suggests that the organizational plan, or budget, is based on a forecasted state of the market environment. Market intelligence provides a constantly updated forecast of the environment in which the organization operates. Differences between the original planned state of the environment on which the organization is acting, and the revised forecasted state provided by the intelligence function, gives a 'forecast deviation'.

**Threshold one**
In setting market budgets, marketing executives may build in slack, most of which will usually be cut back in the budget setting process. It is possible that not all the slack will be removed and the marketing revenue budget will be artificially high. Unless market intelligence indicates that this budget allowance is likely to be exceeded no action will be taken on the basis of the market intelligence report. The market signal will not then cross the first threshold.

### Stage two: the proactive intervention process

If the market intelligence report indicates that the budget allowance will be exceeded, the second stage of the model is entered. In this stage the market executives may be motivated to act to prevent the forecast deviation. This proactive intervention is an attempt to engineer the market into an acceptable state. In its simplest form it may merely necessitate a minor market push. This proactive intervention in the market will, however, consume at least some of the slack resources available to the marketing executive. Successful proactive intervention may, however, require resources in excess of the slack available. In this case the intelligence report will be used to support a plea for additional marketing resources, e.g. to undertake an unabridged campaign to protect a product's position against the anticipated attack of a competitor.

### Stage three: the dependency reduction process

This process is an attempt by the organization to reduce its dependency on the market in question and so reduces the significance to the organization of the perceived market adversity. This decoupling may be achieved in a number of ways – diversification, the switching of resources, adapting plant previously devoted to the market to service other markets, and so on. Dependency reduction may, however, require a long lead time and for this reason organizations are likely to engage in diversification as a policy rather than awaiting detailed intelligence reports. However, market signals which cross threshold two are likely to spur this activity. The dependency reduction process, e.g. diversification, requires the use of slack resources.

### Stage four: the absorption process

This process is an attempt by the organization to sit out the market change, or at least that proportion of the change which has not been dampened by proactive intervention or dependency reduction processes. Such an absorption process consumes the stock of slack resources available to the organization. 'Belt tightening' and 'shedding' indicate the extent of the rundown of slack. All members of the organizational coalition are likely to be affected if the absorption process continues for any extended period.

### Stage five: the adaptive process

In the adaptive process the organization seeks to realign its strategy and/or structure to the perceived changed environment in which it operates. It engages the organization in a 'change mode' and requires the ability by the organizational executives to adapt or react to the forecast market change. Their ability to do so is dependent on the slack resources available and the ease with which such resources can be marshalled to implement strategy/structure changes.

### Stage six: the crisis process

In this, the final process, the organization is dependent on a market which is changing. It has insufficient slack to absorb the change, and both proactive intervention and adaptive response are perceived to be ineffective. Such organizations now face the possibility of being 'selected out' by the market change. The perception that such is the case is likely to induce organizational crisis leading to trauma and the termination of the organization at least in the form in which it existed prior to the onset of the market change.

### Threshold two

Should the power elite within the organization be unwilling or unable to make available sufficient resources to allow successfully proactive intervention, the second threshold is crossed and the third stage of the model is entered.

### Threshold three

If the organization cannot, or chooses not to, utilize its slack resources in proactive market intervention, or in dependency reduction, the market signal indicating market change will pass over the third information threshold and the fourth stage of the model is entered.

### Threshold four

For organizations which do not have sufficient slack to endure the forecast market change, the intelligence signal traverses the fourth threshold and stage five of the model is entered.

### Threshold five

Should the organization be unable or unwilling to adapt to the change signalled by the market intelligence report and if the lower order processes cannot effectively be engaged, the intelligence signal will cross the fifth threshold and the sixth stage is entered.

SOURCE: Barrett (1986), p. 38

1  Identify the industry's four key competitive strengths. Figure 18.39 shows one set of possibilities applicable to a manufacturing situation. It is implicitly assumed that both current and future success in the industry is a function of a competitor's ability to:
   - meet customers' needs and communicate products' attributes;
   - understand and control relevant technology;
   - make superior products in a cost effective way;
   - manage the co-ordination of human, financial, and technological resources.

**FIGURE 18.39**
*Key competitive strengths*

SOURCE: Cvitkovic (1989), p. 28

2  Select a single specific measure of success for each of the four key competitive strengths identified in step 1 above. See Figure 18.40 for some proposals: sales level, investment in R & D, capacity utilization, and ROI are suggested for marketing, technology, manufacturing and management respectively.

**FIGURE 18.40**
*Measures of success*

SOURCE: Adapted from Cvitkovic (1989), p. 28

3  Define linkages between adjacent pairs of competitive strengths to demonstrate their interdependence. In Figure 18.41 price has been used to link marketing and technology; quality to link technology and manufacturing; integration to link manufacturing and management; and growth to link management and marketing.

**FIGURE 18.41**
*Linkages between competitive strengths*

SOURCE: Adapted from Cvitkovic (1989), p. 29

**FIGURE 18.42**
*Average competitor*

Conventions:
outside the circle = better than average
inside the circle = below average

SOURCE: Adapted from Cvitkovic (1989), p. 29

4 Determine average performance scores for the measures specified in step 2 and the linkages defined in step 3. This has the effect of setting up an 'average competitor' to use as a yardstick in assessing competitors' relative positions. In Figure 18.42 average performance for the industry is shown as a circle. Above-average performance for any competitor would be plotted outside the circle and below average performance on any aspect would be plotted inside the circle. Scoring can be done by using a scale of 1 (= excellent) to 5 (= inadequate) to assess a competitor's standing on each dimension shown in Figure 18.41 and then plotting these scores and joining them up (as shown in Figure 18.43).

**FIGURE 18.43**
*Competitive profiles*

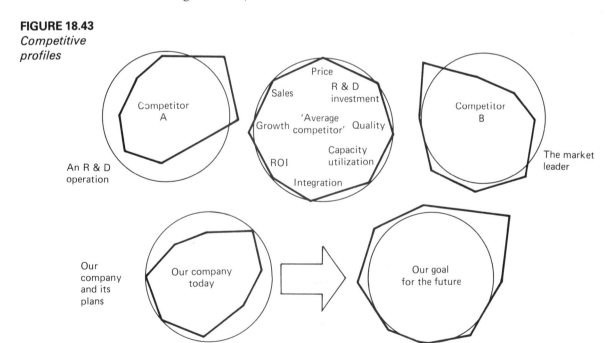

SOURCE: Adapted from Cvitkovic (1989), p. 30

5 Generate competitors' profiles in order to identify relative strengths and weaknesses as a basis for taking action. The strengths and weaknesses are shown (as in Figure 18.43) relative to the 'average competitor'.

In monitoring competitors' activities the categories of activity most relevant in relation to the strategic needs of the user must be determined. Once the categories are established, frequency of monitoring must be set. Prescott and Smith (1989) reported on a study they undertook in the USA to identify categories and frequencies. Details are given in Figure 18.44.

**FIGURE 18.44**
*Competitive information categories and their frequency of monitoring*

| Continuous | Periodic | Ad hoc |
|---|---|---|
| * General industry trends | * Organizational goals and assumptions | * Public and international affairs |
| * Marketing and sales | * Customers<br>* Acquisition/divestment programmes | * Human resources<br>* General administrative structure |
| * Financial | * Services provided | |
| * Technological development | * Operations<br>* Channels of distribution | * Supplier and procurement practices |

SOURCE: Adapted from Prescott and Smith (1989), p. 10

A further aspect of the study was the extent to which different categories of information were subjected to analysis (see Figure 18.45). Three levels of analysis were used in the questionnaire sent out by Prescott and Smith – extensive, basic, and little/no analysis – with the extent to which implications were drawn from the analysis being limited to the first two levels.

**FIGURE 18.45**
*Extent of analysis of categories of information*

| Extensive analysis undertaken and implications derived | Basic analysis with some implications | Little or no analysis and no implications |
|---|---|---|
| • General industry trends | • Technological developments | • Distribution channels |
| • Potential competitors | • Acquisition/divestment programmes | • Human resources |
| • Marketing and sales | • Customers | • General administrative structure |
| • Financial | • Services provided | • Public and international affairs |
| • Organizational goals and assumptions | | • Supplier practices |

SOURCE: Adapted from Prescott and Smith (1989), p. 11

Competitor cost analysis methods have been proposed by a number of authors (e.g. Beerel (1986), Brock (1984), Jones (1988), Pyne (1985) and most notably Porter (1980, 1985)). Brock (1984, p. 226) has related his discussion to the *strategic triangle* (Ohmae (1983)), see Figure 18.46.

The focal points of the triangle were initially customers, competitors, and the company in question, but Brock has emphasized the cost differences between one's own company and competitors as a potential source of competitive advantage. Cost differentials stem from the asset bases of competing companies coupled with the way in which assets are utilized. The importance of being cost effective is evident when one considers the need to deliver value to customers at prices that are competitive while generating an adequate rate of reward to

**FIGURE 18.46**
*The strategic triangle*

SOURCE: Brock (1984), p. 226

shareholders. As an example let us take a comparison between an integrated steelmaker (Maxi) and a small competitor (Mini) with the latter using scrap steel and electric furnace technology. A detailed examination of annual reports, public statements of Mini's chief executive (who was a promoter of the mini-mill industry), and general trade literature gave sufficient information to allow the comparative profile shown in Figure 18.47 to be compiled.

**FIGURE 18.47**
*Cost advantages and disadvantages*

SOURCE: Adapted from Brock (1984), p. 228

It is evident that Mini's manufacturing costs are only 59 per cent of those relating to Maxi per ton of hot rolled steel ready for finishing. With a price set at £425 (as opposed to Maxi's £500) Mini not only has a clear price advantage of £75 per ton but also a gross margin advantage of £175 versus £70 which will allow for even more aggressive pricing. Maxi can see from this type of analysis that its position is being eroded, and appropriate decisions need to be made to avoid a forced decline.

Without this type of information Maxi would not be able to see how the strong strategic position it has held hitherto is being undermined by Mini. Detailed guidance on carrying out this type of cost analysis can be found in Jones (1988).

## Bench-marking

This is an analytical process through which an enterprise's performance can be compared with that of its competitors. It is used by organizations such as Xerox and Ford in order to:

- identify key performance measures for each business function;
- measure one's own performance as well as that of competitors;
- identify areas of competitive advantage (and disadvantage) by comparing performance levels;
- design and implement plans to improve one's own performance on key issues relative to competitors.

Furey (1987) offers a number of US case studies showing bench-marking in use. One of these concerns a company (Company Y) that is a major vendor of telecommunications equipment in which the senior management was curious about the cost and productivity of its sales force. The comparisons shown in Figure 18.48 were developed through a bench-marking exercise using the largest direct competitor and the best-in-class vendor of data processing equipment.

**FIGURE 18.48**
*Sales force bench-marking*

| | Company Y | Direct competitor | Best-in-class competitor |
|---|---|---|---|
| **Cost bench-marks** | | | |
| Average total sales rep. compensation | $38,000 | $44,000 | $55,000 |
| % compensation earned from commission | 10% | 15% | 30% |
| Revenue per sales rep. | $835,000 | $900,000 | $1,200,000 |
| Compensation as % of revenue | 4.6% | 4.9% | 4.6% |
| **Performance bench-marks** | | | |
| Average number of calls per week per rep. | 16–18 | 13–16 | 20+ |
| Revenue quotas | Yes | Yes | No |
| New account quotas | Informal | No | Yes |

SOURCE: Adapted from Furey (1987)

The cost of sales representatives (as a percentage of revenues) was found to be very competitive in Company Y (at 4.6 per cent), but the low commission paid by the company relative to that paid by its main competitors was matched by low productivity (in terms of revenue generated). Moreover, the direct competitor's sales force was generating more revenue with fewer calls in the absence of new account quotas than was the case in Company Y. The best-in-class competitor was paying a high rate of commission to its sales force and aggressively pursuing new customers via numerous sales calls and quotas for new accounts.

Company Y's response to this situation was to restructure the sales team's compensation and split the team into two. By raising the rate of commission substantially, and by having one part of the sales force dealing with existing accounts and the other part dealing with new accounts, Company Y's relative market share improved within six months.

Bench-marking is applicable in other functional areas and has the potential, when properly communicated throughout the enterprise, to help change the corporate culture. In the case of bench-marking products or services offered by customers but not by itself, an enterprise's senior managers can gain insights to guide its decisions: by keeping abreast of new developments in this way it will be easier to assess how to respond (see, for example, Schmid (1987) and Fifer (1989)).

In considering how to take corrective action it is important to make some assessment of the probable response of competitors to any action that might be taken. This is a vital aspect of strategic behaviour. It is assumed that the identities of the enterprise's competitors – both actual and potential – are known, although this should not be taken for granted. Once the competitors' identities are known they can be profiled (see Chapter 4) and possible responses can be explored, taking into account conjectures regarding the beliefs that competitors have of one's own enterprise (including its resources, capabilities, and strategies).

Let us look further at this, drawing on the approach of Amit, et al. (1988). In a simple situation involving an Enterprise X and its sole competitor, Y, there are four possible price policies available. In Figure 18.49 these possibilities for X are shown as the headings for the rows; the column headings show competitor Y's likely reactions. The figures in the cells represent the changes in X's profits that are expected to result from the various interactive outcomes contained in the

**FIGURE 18.49**
*Reaction function*

| Enterprise X's price policy (% change in price) | Competitor Y's reaction (% change in price) | | | |
|---|---|---|---|---|
| | 0% | −5% | −10% | −20% |
| 0% | 0 | −10 | −15 | −20 |
| −5% | +7 | −5 | −12 | −22 |
| −10% | +30 | +15 | −8 | −25 |
| −20% | +12 | +8 | +5 | −30 |

SOURCE: Adapted from Amit, et al. (1988), p. 432

matrix. Thus if X reduces its price by 10 per cent and Y responds by reducing its price by 20 per cent, then X's profits will fall by 25 per cent. If the data in the figure is valid, the optimal course of action for X will depend on the likelihood of Y responding in a particular way. For example, if it is felt to be most likely that Y will react to a price reduction on the part of X by reducing price by half as much as X, then the optimal choice for X is to reduce its price by 10 per cent, giving an increase in profits of 15 per cent. It will be apparent that additional information is needed on Y's likely reaction. This can be provided via *conjectural variations*, which are beliefs about competitors' views of one's own enterprise and of their likely reactions to actions taken by one's own enterprise.

In order to gauge a competitor's likely reactions it is necessary to have information on:

- the structural characteristics of the industry and the technical ability plus desire of competitors to respond;
- competitors' conjecture about one's own behaviour.

Figure 18.50 illustrates a hypothetical situation involving different conjectural possibilities relating to a price reduction of 10 per cent. The derivation of conjectural variations is explored in detail elsewhere (see Amit, et al. (1988)) but we need to note here that it ranges from zero (when the competitor believes that the enterprise in question will not respond to changes in the competitor's strategy) to unity (when the competitor expects the enterprise in question to match any changes in strategy on the part of the competitor).

**FIGURE 18.50**
*Conjectures and a price reduction policy*

SOURCE: Amit, et al. (1988), p. 433

From Figure 18.50 it can be seen that when the competitor's conjectural variation is near to unity it believes the enterprise in question will respond aggressively to a shift in pricing policy. The obvious consequence of this will be a price war if the competitor were to match a reduction in price. As a result of this belief the competitor is unlikely to match the price reduction for fear of the consequences. The opposing situation (i.e. when the conjectural variation is near zero) is likely to have the opposite result.

## 18.10 MANAGEMENT REPORTS

An effective management reporting system is one that uses the available information flows to control the company's activities in accordance with objectives and plans. The process of controlling business operations depends in no small part on the devising, compiling and constant revising of an adequate and up-to-date system of reports. This should result in better decision making, faster action, greater management flexibility, and vastly improved co-ordination.

The controller must be aware of the types of decisions made at each managerial level, and the related information needs, if the best reports are to be compiled at the appropriate frequencies. In developing reports the controller must assess their ultimate utility to their recipients, which requires that they be designed specifically for the individuals who are to receive them, with due consideration being given to the conditions that govern the business and the way in which it is managed. Reports should supply information that is considered important, and this should be arranged and analysed in such a way that it is most convenient and immediately useful to those who must make decisions on the basis of it. To achieve the aim of successfully communicating the essential facts about the business to those who manage it, the controller must have a clear idea of the purposes, possibilities and limitations of the many different types of statement and report. He must, therefore, understand the problems and viewpoints of those who receive his reports and ensure that these people understand the true meaning and limitations of the information contained in those reports.

Reports should be designed to emphasize those factors that are especially important in determining success: the critical success factors.

Such factors have the following characteristics:

1 they are important in explaining success or failure;
2 they are volatile (i.e. they can change quickly);
3 prompt action is needed when a significant change occurs;
4 change is not easy to predict;
5 they can be measured.

In specifying what is to be reported at each level of management, especially at lower levels, the controller must pose two questions:

1 What are the necessary and controllable factors relevant to the level of authority in question?
2 In what form are these factors best presented to aid in decision making at this level?

The level of management in question will determine whether reports are to relate results to long-range objectives expressed in aggregate terms, or whether they should relate results to standard costs in great detail. The principles of control are the same for these extremes of top management and supervisory management, but the form of report is different.

The adoption of a structured approach to reporting, with results being reported by areas of responsibility, will enable top management to view the results and efficiencies of individual departments in the light of their contribution to overall performance and objectives. It may be, however, that the need for control action on the part of top management indicates a failure to achieve control at a more appropriate but lower level.

Similarly, a long delay between actual events and the reporting of these events via the top management control system may create the need for corrective action that is more drastic, more complex, and involves more people than if such action had been initiated at a lower level of control more closely associated with the actual events.

Within the control framework the characteristics of good reports are that they should:

1 be oriented towards the user, taking into account both his level and his function;
2 give as much information as possible in quantitative terms, and flow both ways in the organization (i.e. up and down);
3 be based on a flexible system that allows quick changes to meet new conditions;
4 be oriented towards action rather than towards curiosity.

On a tangible plane succinctness is a great virtue in reporting, while on an intangible plane a major contribution made by an adequate reporting system is that the recipient of a report is made to pause and think over the contents of that report and its implications for the enterprise.

## 18.11 SUMMARY

Many commentators (e.g. Lamb and Shrivastava (1986)) have observed that the study of strategy implementation and control has received far less attention than its importance warrants. No matter how brilliant the formulation of strategy, it is quite useless if it cannot be effectively implemented and the subsequent performance of the organization controlled.

An array of approaches to control that focus in part on social/behavioural issues and in part on analytical techniques have been considered. Feedforward and feedback control, formal and informal controls and the approaches of authorities such as Anthony, Merchant and others were discussed. Budgeting and variance analysis were dealt with in some detail, as was the use of competitive intelligence in devising adaptive responses. Some relevant techniques, including ratio analysis, marketing audits, and networking, have been dealt with in earlier chapters. The importance of social and behavioural issues is that analytical control techniques function only in an organizational context: social and analytical controls are complements rather than substitutes.

It can be argued (e.g. Maciariello (1984), p. 54) that the hierarchical structure of an organization is a response to the limited information-processing ability of decision makers. At each level within the hierarchy it is desirable from the viewpoint of co-ordination and control to identify the responsibilities that need to be undertaken if successful outcomes are to be achieved. One approach to this task is to define the *key success factors* over which each organizational unit has control and to assign responsibilities in accordance with these factors. The basic idea behind this approach is a simple one: if a manager's cognitive limitations constrain the amount of information that can be processed at any time it makes sense to be deliberately selective by focusing on the information that is most important in terms of fulfilling the manager's designated responsibilities.

Selecting key success factors that adequately reflect these responsibilities gives a basis for:

- establishing appropriate performance measures;
- determining resource allocation procedures;
- specifying reward systems.

The identification of key success factors gives focus to the control process. In essence the following question is being posed: to which factors are desired outcomes most sensitive? The greater the degree of sensitivity (or responsiveness) between a factor and an outcome, the more critical is that factor in controlling the organizational unit in order to bring about the desired outcome.

It is inevitable that some critical factors (such as macroeconomic variables, government actions, competitive behaviour, and suppliers' behaviour) cannot easily be influenced by a given organization, while other critical factors (which might include product design, quality, price, and level of customer service) are more readily influenced by the organization's managers. However, in control terms the point to note is that the outcome that is desired (e.g. sustained competitive advantage) can be achieved if the manager understands how the key variables behave (i.e. how they change over time and why those changes occur), since this gives the manager the ability to make future predictions. Through the ability to make accurate predictions of each key variable's future value, the manager is in a position to control the outcome of events. In part this will require the manipulation of those variables that can be directly influenced, and in part it will require an awareness of the anticipated future values of variables that the manager is unable directly to influence. Control is achieved when desired outcomes are realized, hence it is possible to be in control even though one is unable to manipulate the values of all variables. It is worth repeating the major elements underlying the above discussion:

- an understanding of the behaviour of key variables gives a basis for making predictions about their likely future values;

- on the basis of good predictions it is possible to bring about desired outcomes by manipulating the variables over which one has influence in the knowledge of the expected behaviour of those variables over which one has no direct influence.

In seeking to control marketing activities the requirements of effective control systems are:

- they must provide timely information;
- they must measure the essential nature of the activity being assessed;
- they should provide information on trends;
- they must facilitate action;
- they must be economical;
- they must be meaningful.

One developing field that is likely to increase in importance is that of expert systems (see McDonald and Wilson (1990)).

# Bibliography

Aaker, D. A. and Day, G. S. (1972), 'Corporate Response to Consumerism Pressures', *Harvard Business Review*, Vol. 50, No. 6, November–December, pp. 114–24.

Aaker, D. A. and Day, G. S. (eds) (1974), *Consumerism*, New York: Free Press, 2nd ed.

Abbott, L. (1955), *Quality and Competition*, New York: Columbia University Press.

Abell, D. F. (1980), *Defining the Business: The Starting Point of Strategic Planning*, Englewood Cliffs, NJ: Prentice-Hall.

Abell, D. F. and Hammond, J. S. (1979), *Strategic Market Planning: Problems and Analytical Approaches*, Englewood Cliffs, NJ: Prentice-Hall.

Abratt, R. (1986), 'Industrial Buying in High-Tech Markets', *Industrial Marketing Management*, Vol. 15, pp. 293–8.

Ackoff, R. L. (1970), *A Concept of Corporate Planning*, New York: Wiley.

Adler, L. (1960), 'Phasing Research into the Marketing Plan', *Harvard Business Review*, Vol. 38, No. 3, May–June, pp. 118–21.

Adler, L. (1967), 'Systems Approach to Marketing', *Harvard Business Review*, Vol. 45, No. 3, May–June, pp. 105–18.

Aguilar, F. (1967), *Scanning the Business Environment*, New York: Macmillan.

Albrecht, K. (1979), *Stress and the Manager*, Englewood Cliffs, NJ: Prentice-Hall.

Alexander, L. (1985), 'Successfully Implementing Strategic Decisions', *Long Range Planning*, Vol. 18, No. 3, pp. 91–7.

Alexander, R. S., Cross, J. S. and Cunningham, R. M. (1961), *Industrial Marketing*, Homewood, Illinois: Irwin.

Allen, P. (1989), *Selling: Management and Practice*, London: M & E Handbooks.

Allenza, N. (1989), 'Cash in on Bad Debts', *AA*, May, pp. 51, 53–5

American Accounting Association (1972), 'Report of Committee on Cost and Profitability Analyses for Marketing', Supplement to *The Accounting Review*, Vol. 47, pp. 575–615.

American Management Association (1959), 'The Marketing Audit: Its Nature, Purposes and Problems', in *Analyzing and Improving Marketing Performance*, AMA Management Report No. 32.

American Marketing Association (1957), 'The Values and Uses of Distribution Cost Analysis', *Journal of Marketing*, Vol. 21, No. 2, April, pp. 395–400.

Ames, B. C. (1968), 'Marketing Planning for Industrial Products', *Harvard Business Review*, Vol. 46, No. 5, September–October, pp. 100–11.

Ames, B. C. (1971), 'Dilemma of Product/Market Management', *Harvard Business Review*, Vol. 49, No. 2, March–April, pp. 66–74

Ames, B. C. (1989) 'How to Devise a Winning Business Plan', *Journal of Business Strategy*, Vol. 10, No. 3, May–June, pp. 26–30.

Amit, R. (1986), 'Cost Leadership Strategy and Experience Curves', *Strategic Management Journal*, Vol. 7, No. 3, May–June, pp. 281–92.

Amit, R., Domowitz, I. and Fershtman, C. (1988), 'Thinking One Step Ahead: The Use of Conjectures in Competitor Analysis', *Strategic Management Journal*, Vol. 9, pp. 431–42.

Anandarajan, A. and Christopher, M. G. (1987), 'A Mission Approach to Customer Profitability Analysis', *International Journal of Physical Distribution and Materials Management*, Vol. 17, No. 7, pp. 55–68.

Andreason, A. R. and Belk, R. W. (1980), 'Predictors of Attendance at the Performance Arts', *Journal of Consumer Research*, Vol. 7, No. 2, September, pp. 112–20.

Ansoff, H. I. (1957), 'Strategies for Diversification', *Harvard Business Review*, Vol. 25, No. 5, September–October, pp. 113–24.

Ansoff, H. I. (1968), *Corporate Strategy*, Harmondsworth: Penguin Books.

Ansoff, H. I. (1984) *Implementing Strategic Management*, Englewood Cliffs, NJ: Prentice-Hall.

Anthony, R. N. (1965), *Planning and Control Systems: A Framework for Analysis*, Cambridge, Mass: Harvard University Press.

Anthony, R. N. (1988) *The Management Control Function*, Boston, Mass: Harvard Business School Press.

Armitage, H. M. (1987), 'The Use of Management Accounting Techniques to Improve Productivity Analysis in Distribution Operations', *International Journal of Physical Distribution and Materials Management*, Vol. 17, No. 2, pp. 40–50.

Armstrong, J. S. (1982), 'The Value of Formal Planning for Strategic Decisions: Review of Empirical Research', *Strategic Management Journal*, Vol. 3, pp. 197–211.

Ashton, D. J., Hopper, T. M. and Scapens, R. W. (eds) (1991) *Issues in Management Accounting*, London: Prentice-Hall.

Aspinal, L. (1962), 'The Characteristics of Goods Theory' in *Managerial Marketing*, edited by Lazer, W. and Kelley, E., Homewood, Illinois: Irwin.

Assael, H. (1987), *Consumer Behavior and Marketing Action*, Boston, Mass.: Kent Publishing.

Atkin, B. and Skinner, R. N. (1975), *How British Industry Prices*, London: Industrial Market Research Association.

Atkinson, P. E. and Naden, J. (1989), 'Total Quality Management: Eight Lessons to Learn from Japan', *Management Services*, Vol. 33, No. 3, pp. 6–10.

Baker, K. (1982), quoted in Clark, E., 'Acorn Finds New Friends', *Marketing*, 16 December, p. 13.

Baker, M. J. (1985), *Marketing Strategy and Management*, London: Macmillan.

Bancroft, A. L. and Wilson, R. M. S. (1979), 'Management Accounting in Marketing', *Management Accounting*, (CIMA), Vol. 57, No. 11, December, pp. 25–30.

Banks, S. (1964), *Experimentation in Marketing*, New York: McGraw-Hill.

Barclay, I. and Benson, M. (1990), 'Success in New Product Development: Lessons from the Past', *Leadership and Organisation Development Journal*, Vol. 11, No. 6, pp. 4–12.

Barksdale, H. C. and Harris, C. E. (1982), 'Portfolio analysis and the PLC' *Long Range Planning*, Vol. 15, No. 6, pp. 74–83.

Barnard, C. I. (1956), *The Functions of the Executive*, Cambridge, Mass: Harvard University Press.

Barrett, T. F. (1980), 'Modular Data Base System', *International Journal of Physical Distribution and Materials Management*, Vol. 10, No. 4, pp. 135–46.

Barrett, T. F. (1986), 'When the Market Says "Beware!" ...' *Management Decision*, Vol. 24, No. 6, pp. 36–40.

Barrett, T. F. (1987), 'A Surrogate Case Flow Model of Marketing Strategy', *Irish Marketing Review*, Vol. 2, pp. 117–25.

Bartels, R. (ed.) (1963), *Ethics in Business*, Columbia, Ohio: Bureau of Business Research, Ohio State University.

Bastable, C. W. and Bao, D. H. (1988), 'The Fiction of Sales-Mix and Sales-Quantity Variances', *Accounting Horizons*, Vol. 2, No. 2, June, pp. 10–17.

Baumol, W. J. and Sevin, C. H. (1957), 'Marketing Costs and Mathematical Programming', *Harvard Business Review*, Vol. 35, No. 5, September–October, pp. 52–60.

Beer, S. (1967), *Decision and Control*, New York: Wiley.

Beerel, A. (1986), 'Strategic Financial Control Can Provide Light and Guidance', *Accountancy*, Vol. 97, No. 1114, June, pp. 70–4.

Beishon, J. and Peters, G. (eds) (1972), *Systems Behaviour*, London: Harper & Row.

Bellis-Jones, R. (1989), 'Customer Profitability Analysis', *Management Accounting*, (CIMA) Vol. 57, No. 2, pp. 26–8.

Bennett, R. C. and Cooper, R. G. (1982), 'The Misuse of Marketing: an American Tragedy', *McKinsey Quarterly*, Autumn, pp. 52–69.

Bernstein, D. (1984), *Company Image and Reality*, Eastbourne: Holt, Rinehart & Winston.

Bhaskar, K. N. and Housden, R. J. W. (1985), *Accounting Information Systems and Data Processing*, Oxford: Heinemann.

Biggadike, R. (1977), *Entering New Markets: Strategies and Performance*, Cambridge, Mass: Marketing Science Institute.

Bleeke, J. A. (1988), 'Peak Strategies', *Across the Board*, Vol. 25, No. 2, February, pp. 45–50.

Blenel, W. H. and Bender, H. E. (1980), *Product Service Planning*, New York: Amacom.

Bliss, M. (1980), *Market Segmentation and Environmental Analysis*, unpublished MSc thesis, University of Strathclyde.

Boag, D. A. (1987), 'Marketing Control and Performance in Early-Growth Companies', *Journal of Business Venturing*, Vol. 2, No. 4, pp. 365–9.

Bonini, C. P., Jaedicke, R. K. and Wagner, H. M. (eds) (1964), *Management Controls: New Directions in Basic Research*, New York: McGraw-Hill.

Bonoma, T. V. (1984), 'Making Your Marketing Strategy Work', *Harvard Business Review*, Vol. 62, No. 2, March–April, pp. 68–76.

Bonoma, T. V. and Clarke, B. H. (1988), *Marketing Performance Assessment*, Boston, Mass: Harvard Business School Press.

Bonoma, T. V. and Crittenden, V.L. (1988), 'Managing Marketing Implementation', *Sloan Management Review*, Vol. 29, No. 2, Winter, pp. 7–14.

Bonoma, T. V. and Shapiro, B. P. (1983), *Segmenting the Industrial Market*, Lexington, Mass: Lexington Books.

Bonoma, T. V. and Shapiro, B. P. (1984), 'Evaluating Market Segmentation Approaches', *Industrial Marketing Management*, Vol. 13, pp. 257–68.

Booth, J. (1986), 'If You're Not Sure Then Ask', *Accountancy*, Vol. 98, No. 1119, November, pp. 94–5.

Booz, Allen and Hamilton, (1982), *New Product Management for the 1980s*, New York: Booz, Allen & Hamilton.

Boston, Consulting Group (1971), *Perspectives on Experience*, Boston, Mass: Boston Consulting Group.

Boston Consulting Group (1982), Annual Report.

Bourantas, D. and Mandes, Y. (1987), 'Does Market Share Lead to Profitability?', *Long Range Planning*, Vol. 20, No. 5, pp. 102–8.

Bourgeois, L. J. and Brodwin, D. A. (1984), 'Strategic Implementation: Five Approaches to an Elusive Phenomenon', *Strategic Management Journal*, Vol. 5, No. 3, pp. 241–64.

Boyd, S. H. and Britt, J. S. (1965), 'Making Marketing Research More Effective by Using the Administrative Process', *Journal of Marketing Research*, Vol. 2, No. 1, February, pp. 13–19.

Brache, A. (1986), 'Strategy and the Middle Manager', *Training*, Vol. 23, No. 4, April, pp. 30–4.

Brighton, M. (1977), 'Pinning Down the Angels', *Market Research Society Newsletter*, No. 133, April, pp. 8–10.

Brion, J. (1967), *Corporate Marketing Planning*, New York: Wiley.

Broadbent, S. (1979), *Spending Advertising Money*, London: Business Books, 3rd edition.

Brock, J. J. (1984), 'Competitor Analysis: Some Practical Approaches', *Industrial Marketing Management*, Vol. 13, pp. 225–31.

Brockner, J., et al. (1986), 'Escalation of Commitment to an Ineffective Course of Action', *Administrative Science Quarterly*, Vol. 31, No. 1, March, pp. 109–26.

Brownlie, D. T. (1983), 'Analytical Frameworks for Strategic Market Planning', in Baker, M. J. (ed.) (1983), *Marketing: Theory and Practice*, London: Macmillan.

Brownlie, D. T. (1987), 'Environmental Analysis', in Baker, M. J. (ed.) (1987), *The Marketing Book*, London: Heinemann.

Brownlie, D. T. and Saren, M. A. (1983), 'A Review of Technological Forecasting Techniques and Their Application', *Management Bibliographies and Reviews*, Vol. 9, No. 4.

Buckley, P. J. (1991), 'Developments in International Business Theory in the 1990s', *Journal of Marketing Management*, Vol. 7, No. 1, January, pp. 15–24.

Bucklin, L. P. (1978), *Productivity in Marketing*, Chicago: American Marketing Association.

Buckner, H. (1967), *How British Industry Buys*, London: Hutchinson.

Buell, V. P. (1966), *Marketing Management in Action*, New York: McGraw-Hill.

Bureau, J. R. (1981), *Brand Management*, London: Macmillan.

Burnett, L. (1961), *Communications of an Advertising Man*, New York: Leo Burnett.

Burns, T. and Stalker, G. M. (1961), *The Management of Innovation*, London: Tavistock.

Burton, P. W. and Miller, J. R. (1990), *Advertising Fundamentals*, Scranton, Pa: International Textbook Company.

Business Week (1977), 'The Market Mishandles a Blue Chip', *Business Week*, 20 June, p. 17

Buzzell, R. D. and Chussil, M. J. (1985), 'Managing for Tomorrow', *Sloan Management Review*, Vol. 26, No. 4, Summer, pp. 3–13.

Buzzell, R. D., Cox, D. F. and Brown, R. V. (1969), *Marketing Research and Information Systems*, New York: McGraw-Hill.

Buzzell, R. D. and Gale, B. T. (1987), *The PIMS Principles: Linking Strategy to Performance*, New York: Free Press.

Buzzell, R. D., Gale, B. T. and Sullivan, R. G. M. (1975), 'Market Share: a Key to Profitability', *Harvard Business Review*, Vol. 53, No. 1, January–February, pp. 97–106.

Buzzell, R. D. and Nourse, R. M. (1967), *Product Innovation in Food Processing*, Boston, Mass: Division of Research, Harvard Business School.

Buzzell, R. D. and Wiersema, F. D. (1981), 'Successful Share Building Strategies', *Harvard Business Review*, Vol. 59, No. 1, January–February, pp. 135–44.

Byars, L. L. (1984), *Strategic Management*, New York: Harper & Row.

Calingo, L. M. R. (1989), 'Achieving Excellence in Strategic Planning Systems', *SAM Advanced Management Journal*, Vol. 54, No. 2, Spring, pp. 21–3.

Cannon, J. T. (1968), *Business Strategy and Policy*, New York: Harcourt, Brace & World.

Cardozo, R. N. (1980), 'Situational Segmentation of Industrial Markets', *European Journal of Marketing*, Vol. 14, No. 5/6, pp. 264–76.

Cardozo, R. N. and Smith, D. K. (1983), 'Applying Financial Portfolio Theory to Product Portfolio Decisions: An Empirical Study', *Journal of Marketing*, Vol. 47, Spring, pp. 110–19.

Carson, and Rickards (1979), 'Structured Creativity and Integrated Modelling for Industry, Technology and Research (SCIMITAR)', cited in Barclay, I. and Benson, M. (1990).

Carson, R. (1963), *Silent Spring*, Boston, Mass: Houghton Mifflin.

Carter, C. F. and Williams, B. R. (1958), *Investment in Innovation*, London: OUP.

Cascino, A. E. (1967), 'Organizational Implications of the Marketing Concept' in Kelley, E. J. and Lazer, W. (eds) (1967), *Managerial Marketing: Perspectives and Viewpoints*, Homewood, Illinois: Irwin.

Chakravarthy, B. S. (1986), 'Measuring Strategic Performance', *Strategic Management Journal*, Vol. 7, pp. 437–58.

Chandler, A. D. (1962), *Strategy and Structure*, Cambridge, Mass: MIT Press.

Channon, D. (1987), 'Through the Eyes of Customers', *Banking World*, November, pp. 26–9.

Chevalier, M. and Charty, B. (1974), 'Don't Misuse Your Market Share Goal', *European Business*, Spring, pp. 43–51.

Child, J. (1977), *Organization*, London: Harper & Row. 1st edition.

Child, J. (1984), *Organization*, London: Harper & Row. 2nd edition.

Chisnall, P. M. (1989), *Strategic Industrial Marketing*, London Prentice-Hall, 2nd edition.

Christopher, M. G. (1986), *The Strategy of Distribution Management*, London: Heinemann.

Christopher, M. G. and Walters, D. W., with Gattorna, J. L. (1977), *Distribution Planning and Control*, Farnborough: Gower.

Christopher, M. G., Majaro, S. and McDonald, M. H. B. (1987), *Strategy Search*, Aldershot: Gower.

Christopher, M. G., Jeffries, J., Kirkland, J. and Wilson, R. M. S. (1968), 'Status Report on Marketing Theory', *British Journal of Marketing*, Vol. 2, No. 3, Autumn, pp. 230–42.

Christopher, M. G., Payne, A. and Ballantyne, D. (1991), *Relationship Marketing*, Oxford: Heinemann.

Christopher, M. G., Schary, P. and Skjott-Larsen, T. (1979), *Customer Service and Distribution Strategy*, London: Associated Business Press.

Christopher, W. F. (1977), 'Marketing Achievement Reporting: A Profitability Approach', *Industrial Marketing Management*, Vol. 6, pp. 149–62.

Chua, W. F., Lowe, E. A. and Puxty, A. G. (eds) (1989), *Critical Perspectives in Management Control*, Basingstoke: Macmillan.

Churchman, C. W. (1968), *The Systems Approach*, New York: Delacorte Press.

Clarke, C. and Brennan, K. (1988), 'Allied Forces', *Management Today*, November, pp. 128–31.

Clarke, C. and Pratt, S. (1985), 'Leadership's Four Part Progress', *Management Today*, March, pp. 84–6.

Clifford, D. K. and Cavanagh, R. E. (1985), *The Winning Performance: How America's High and Mid-Size Growth Companies Succeed*, New York: Bantam Books.

Coates, D., Finlay, P. and Wilson, J. (1991), 'Validation in Marketing Models', *Journal of the Market Research Society*, Vol. 33, No. 2, April, pp. 83–90.

Cochran, E. and Thompson, G. (1964), 'What New Products Fail', *The National Industrial Conference Board Review*, October, pp. 11–18.

Cohen, W. A. (1988), *The Practice of Marketing Management: Analysis Planning and Implementation*, New York: Macmillan.

Cohn, C. (1990), 'Agents of Argent', *Management Today*, March, pp. 97–8, 101.

Coleman, R. P. (1961), 'The Significance of Social Stratification in Selling', in Bell, M. (ed.) (1961) *Marketing*, New York: American Marketing Association.

Cook, V. J. Jr. (1985), 'The Net Present Value of Market Share', *Journal of Marketing*, Vol. 49, Summer, pp. 49–63.

Cooper, R. G. (1979), 'The Dimensions of New Product Success and Failure', *Journal of Marketing*, Vol. 43, No. 2, Summer, pp. 93–104.

Cooper, R. G. (1980), 'Factors in New Product Success', *European Journal of Marketing*, Vol. 14, Nos. 5/6, pp. 277–92.

Coulson-Thomas, C. J. (1983), *Marketing Communications*, London: Heinemann.

Cowley, P. R. (1985), 'The Experience Curve and History of the Cellophane Business', *Long Range Planning*, Vol. 18, No. 6, pp. 84–90.

Cox, K. K. and Enis, B. M. (1969), *Experimentation for Marketing Decisions*, Scranton, Pa: Intertext.

Cox, R., Alderson, W. and Shapiro, S. J. (eds) (1964), *Theory in Marketing*, Homewood, Illinois: Irwin.

Cox, R. and Brittain, P. (1988), *Retail Management*, London: M & E Handbooks.

Cox, W. E. (1967), 'Product Life Cycles as Marketing Models', *Journal of Business*, Vol. 40, No. 4, October, pp. 375–84.

Crainer, S. (1990), 'A Niche for High Performance', *Marketing Business*, Issue 13, October, pp. 14–15.

Cravens, D. W. (1981), 'How to Match Marketing Strategies with Overall Corporate Planning', *Management Review*, Vol. 70, No. 12, December, pp. 12–19.

Cravens, D. W. (1986), 'Strategic Forces Affecting Marketing Strategy', *Business Horizons*, Vol. 29, No. 5, September–October.

Cravens, D. W. (1988), 'Gaining Strategic Marketing Advantage', *Business Horizons*, Vol. 31, No. 5, pp. 44–54.

Cravens, D. W. (1990), *Strategic Marketing*, Homewood, Illinois: Irwin. 3rd edition.

Cravens, D. W. and Lamb, C. W. (1986), *Strategic Marketing Cases and Applications*, Homewood, Illinois: Irwin. 2nd edition.

Crawford, C. M. (1979). 'New Product Failure Rates – Facts and Fallacies', *Research Management*, September, pp. 9–13.

Crissy, W. J. E., Fischer, P. M. and Mossman, F. H. (1973), 'Segmental Analysis: Key to Marketing Profitability', *MSU Business Topics*, Vol. 21, No. 2, Spring, pp. 42–9.

Crissy, W. J. E. and Kaplan, R. M. (1963), 'Matrix Models for Marketing Planning', *MSU Business Topics*, Vol. 11, No. 3, Summer, pp. 48–66.

Cross, R. H. (1987), 'Strategic Planning: What it Can and Can't Do', *SAM Advanced Management Journal*, Vol. 52, No. 1, Winter, pp. 13–16.

Culliton, J. W. (1948), *The Management of Marketing Costs*, Boston, Mass: Division of Research Harvard Business School.

Cunningham, M. I. and Roberts, D. A. (1974), 'The Role of Customer Service in Industrial Marketing', *European Journal of Marketing*, Vol. 8, No. 1, Spring, pp. 15–19.

Cushing, B. E. (1982), *Accounting Information Systems and Business Organizations*, Reading, Mass: Addison-Wesley.

Cyert, R. M. and March, J. G. (1963), *A Behavioral Theory of the Firm*, Englewood Cliffs, NJ: Prentice-Hall.

Cvitkovic, E. (1989), 'Profiling Your Competitors', *Planning Review*, Vol. 17, No. 3, May–June, pp. 28–30.

Dace, R. W. (1990), 'Exporting to Japan – Key Factors for Success', *Quarterly Review of Marketing*, Vol. 16, No. 1, October, pp. 1–7.

Dale, E. and Michelon, L. C. (1969), *Modern Management Methods*, Harmondsworth: Penguin.

Daniell, M. (1990) 'Webs We Weave', *Management Today*, February, pp. 81–4.

D'Aveni, R. A. and MacMillan, I. C. (1991), 'Crisis and the Content of Managerial Communications: a Study of the Focus of Attention of Top Managers in Surviving and Failing Firms', *Administrative Science Quarterly*, Vol. 35, No. 4, December, pp. 634–57.

Davidson, J. H. (1987a), *Offensive Marketing or How to Make Your Competitors Followers*, Harmondsworth: Penguin. 2nd edition.

Davidson, J. H. (1987b), 'Going on the Offensive', *Marketing*, 16 April, pp. 24–9.

Davies, G. (1988), Marks & Spencer UK Case Study. Manchester Polytechnic.

Davies, H. L. (1970), 'Dimensions of Marital Roles in Consumer Decision Making', *Journal of Marketing Research*, Vol. 7, No. 2, May, pp. 168–77.

Davis, J. (1970), *Experimental Marketing*, London: Nelson.

Day, G. S. (1983) 'Gaining Insights through Strategy Analysis', *Journal of Business Strategy*, Vol. 4, No. 1, pp. 51–8.

Day, G. S. (1984), *Strategic Market Planning: the Pursuit of Competitive Advantage*, St Paul, Minnesota: West Publishing.

Day, G. S. (1986), *Analysis for Strategic Marketing Decisions*, St Paul, Minnesota: West Publishing.

Day, G. S. (1990), *Market Driven Strategy*, New York: Free Press.

Day, G. S. and Fahey, L. (1988), 'Valuing Market Strategies', *Journal of Marketing*, Vol. 52, No. 3, July, pp. 45–57.

Day, G. S., Weitz, B. and Wensley, J. R. C. (eds) (1990), *The Interface of Marketing and Strategy*, Greenwich, Conn: JAI Press.

Day, G. S. and Wensley, J. R. C. (1988), 'Assessing Advantage: A Framework for Diagnosing Competitive Superiority', *Journal of Marketing*, Vol. 52, No. 2, April, pp. 1–20.

Dean, J. (1951), *Managerial Economics*, Englewood Cliffs, NJ: Prentice-Hall.

De Jouvenal, B. (1967), *The Art of Conjecture*, New York: Basic Books.

De Kluyver, C. A. and Pessemier, E. A. (1986), 'Benefits of a Marketing Budgeting Model: Two Case Studies', *Sloan Management Review*, Vol. 28, No. 1, Fall, pp. 27–38.

Dempsey, W. A. (1978), 'Vendor Selection and the Buying Process', *Industrial Marketing Management*, Vol. 7, pp. 257–67.

Demski, J. S. (1980), *Information Analysis*, Reading, Mass.: Addison-Wesley, 2nd edition.

Dent, J. F. (1990), 'Strategy, Organization and Control: Some Possibilities for Accounting Research', *Accounting, Organizations and Society*, Vol. 15, No. 1/2, pp. 3–26.

Deran, E. (1987), *Low-Cost Marketing Strategies*, New York: Praeger.

Dery, D. (1982), 'Erring and Learning: An Organizational Analysis', *Accounting, Organizations and Society*, Vol. 7, No. 3, pp. 217–23.

Dev, S. F. D. (1980), 'Linear Programming and Production Planning', Chapter 7 (pp. 121–47) in Arnold, J. A., Carsberg, B. V. and Scapens, R. W. (eds) (1980), *Topics in Management Accounting*, Deddington: Philip Allen.

De Vasconcellos, J. A. S. and Hambrick, D. C. (1989), 'Key Success Factors: Test of a General Theory in the Mature Industrial-Product Sector', *Strategic Management Journal*, Vol. 10, No. 4, pp. 367–82.

Devlin, G. and Biggs, I. (1989), 'Partners in the Strategic Quickstep', *Accountancy*, Vol. 104, No. 1155, November, pp. 144–6.

Dhalla, N. K. and Yuspeh, S. (1976), 'Forget the Product Life Cycle Concept', *Harvard Business Review*, Vol. 54, No. 1, January–February, pp. 102–12.

Diamantopoulos, A. and Mathews, B. P. (1990), 'A Model for Analysing Product Performance', *Quarterly Review of Marketing*, Vol. 15, No. 3, April, pp. 7–13.

Dickinson, R. A. (1967), *Buyer Decision Making*, Berkeley, California: Institute of Business and Economic Research.

Diffenbach, J. (1983), 'Corporate Environmental Analysis in Large US Corporations', *Long Range Planning*, Vol. 16, No. 3, pp. 107–16.

Dolan, R. J. (1981), 'Models of Competition: a Review of Theory and Empirical Evidence', in Enis, B. M. and Roering, K. J. (eds), *Review of Marketing*, Chicago: American Marketing Association.

Dominguez, L. V. and Page, A. (1984), 'Formulating a Strategic Portfolio of Profitable Retail Segments for Commercial Banks', *Journal of Economics and Business*, Vol. 36, No. 3, pp. 43–57.

Doyle, D. (1985), 'Marketing and ZBB', *Management*, (Eire), December, pp. 33–4.

Doyle, P. (1979), 'Management Structures and Marketing Strategies in UK Industry', *European Journal of Marketing*, Vol. 13, No. 5, pp. 319–31.

Doyle, P. (1987), 'Marketing and the British Chief Executive', *Journal of Marketing Management*, Vol. 3, No. 2, Winter, pp. 121–32.

Doyle, P. and Newbould, G. D. (1974), 'Advertising Management for Building Societies', *Advertising Quarterly*, No. 42, Winter, pp. 19–23.

Doyle, P. and Saunders, J. (1986), 'Measuring the True Profitability of Sales Promotions', *Journal of the Operational Research Society*, Vol. 37, No. 10, October, pp. 955–66.

Doyle, P., Saunders, J. and Wong, V. (1986), 'Japanese Marketing Strategies in the UK: A Comparative Study', *Journal of International Business Studies*, Vol. 17, No. 1, pp. 27–46.

Doyle, P., Saunders, J. and Wright, L. (1988), 'A Comparative Study of British, US, and Japanese Marketing Strategies in the British Market', *International Journal of Research in Marketing*, Vol. 5, No. 3, pp. 171–84.

Driver, J. C. (1990), 'Marketing Planning in Style', *Quarterly Review of Marketing*, Vol. 15, No. 4, July, pp. 16–21.

Drucker, P. F. (1955), *The Practice of Management*, London: Heinemann.

Drucker, P. F. (1959), 'Long Range Planning: Challenge to Management Science', *Management Science*, Vol. 5, No. 3, April, pp. 238–49.

Drucker, P. F. (1963), 'Managing for Business Effectiveness', *Harvard Business Review*, Vol. 41, No. 3, May–June, pp. 53–60.

Drucker, P. F. (1969), *The Age of Discontinuity*, New York: Harper & Row.

Drucker, P. F. (1973), *Management: Tasks, Responsibilities and Practices*, New York: Harper & Row.

Duffy, M. F. (1989), 'ZBB, MBO, PPB, and Their Effectiveness within the Planning/Marketing Process', *Strategic Management Journal*, Vol. 10, No. 2, pp. 163–73.

Düro, R. (1989), *Winning the Marketing War*, New York: Wiley.

Dutton, J. E. and Duncan, R. B. (1987), 'The Influence of the Strategic Planning Process on Strategic Change', *Strategic Management Journal*, Vol. 8, pp. 103–16.

Eells, R. and Nehemkis, P. (1984), *Corporate Intelligence and Espionage: A Blueprint for Executive Decision-Making*, New York: Macmillan.

Ehrenberg, A. S. C. (1965), 'News and Notes: American Marketing Association – 50th Anniversary Speech', *Operational Research Quarterly*, Vol. 16, No. 3, September, pp. 406–12.

Emery, F. (ed.) (1981), *Systems Thinking*, Harmondsworth: Penguin. Two vols.

Engel, J. F., Kollat, D. T. and Blackwell, R. D. (1968), *Consumer Behavior*, New York: Holt, Rinehart and Winston.

Evans, F. B. (1959), 'Psychological and Objective Factors in the Prediction of Brand Choice: Ford versus Chevrolet', *Journal of Business*, Vol. 32, No. 4, October, pp. 340–69.

Fahey, L., King, W. R. and Narayanan, V. K. (1981), 'Environmental Scanning and Forecasting in Strategic Planning – the State of the Art', *Long Range Planning*, Vol. 14, No. 1, February, pp. 32–9.

Farris, P. W. and Reibstein, D. J. (1979), 'How Prices, Expenditure and Profit are Linked', *Harvard Business Review*, Vol. 57, No. 6, November–December, pp. 173–84.

Feder, R. A. (1965), 'How to Measure Marketing Performance', *Harvard Business Review*, Vol. 43, No. 3, May–June, pp. 132–42.

Feldman, W. and Cardozo, R. N. (1968), 'The Industrial Revolution and Models of Buyer Behavior', *Journal of Purchasing*, Vol. 4, November.

Feldwick, P. (ed.) (1990), *Advertising Works - 5*, London: Cassell.

Ferguson, A. (1989), 'Hostage to the Short Term', *Management Today*, March, pp. 68, 70–72.

Fern, R. H. and Tipgos, M. A. (1988), 'Controllers as Business Strategists: A Progress Report', *Management Accounting*, (NAA), Vol. 69, No. 9, March, pp. 25–9.

Festinger, L. (1957), *A Theory of Cognitive Dissonance*, Stanford, California: Stanford University Press.

Fifer, R. M. (1989), 'Cost Benchmarking Functions in the Value Chain', *Planning Review*, Vol. 17, No. 3, May–June, pp. 18–23, 26–7.

Filiatrault, P. and Chebat, J–C. (1987), 'Marketing Budgeting Practices: An Empirical Study', *Developments in Marketing Science*, Vol. 10, pp. 278–82.

Filiatrault, P. and Chebat, J–C. (1990), 'How Service Firms Set their Marketing Budgets', *Industrial Marketing Management*, Vol. 19, pp. 63–7.

Fisher, L. (1966), *Industrial Marketing*, London: Business Books.

Fisk, G. (1967), *Marketing Systems*, New York: Harper & Row.

Fisk, G. and Dixon, D. F. (eds) (1967), *Theories for Marketing Systems Analysis*, New York: Harper & Row.

Flamholtz, E. G. and Das, T. K. (1985), 'Toward an Integrative Framework of Organizational Control', *Accounting, Organizations and Society*, Vol. 10, No. 1, pp. 35–50.

Forrester, J. W. (1961), *Industrial Dynamics*, New York: Wiley.

Forrester, J. W. (1965), 'Modeling of Market and Company Interactions', pp. 353–64, in Bennett, P. D. (ed.) (1965), *Marketing and Economic Development*, Chicago: American Marketing Association.

Fox, H. W. (1986), 'Financial ABCs of Test Marketing', *Business Horizons*, Vol. 29, No. 5, September–October, pp. 63–70.

Foxall, G. (1987), 'Consumer Behaviour' in Baker, M. J. (ed.) (1987), *The Marketing Book*, London: Heinemann.

Freeman, C. (1965), 'Research and Development in Electronic Capital Goods', *National Institute Economic Review*, No. 34, November, pp. 40–91.

Freund, Y. P. (1988), 'Critical Success Factors', *Planning Review*, Vol. 16, No. 4, July–August, pp. 20–3.

Frey, A. W. and Halterman, J. C. (1970), *Advertising*, New York: The Ronald Press. 4th edition.

Frey, J. B. (1982), 'Pricing Over the Competitive Life Cycle', speech presented at the 1982 Marketing Conference, New York.

Frey, J. B. (1987), *Pricing Over the Competitive Life Cycle*, The Conference Board, New York.

Fruhan, W. E. (1972), 'Pyrrhic Victories in Fights for Market Share', *Harvard Business Review*, Vol. 50, No. 5, September–October, pp. 100–7.

Fuld, L. M. (1985), *Competitor Intelligence*, New York: Wiley.

Fuld, L. M. (1988): *Monitoring the Competition: Finding Out What's Really Going on Over There*, New York: Wiley.

Furey, T. R. (1987), 'Benchmarking: The Key to Developing Competitive Advantage in Mature Markets', *Planning Review*, Vol. 15, No. 5, September–October, pp. 30–2.

Gabb, A. (1991), 'How the Discovery Took Off', *Management Today*, October, pp. 64–8.

Gaedeke, R. M. and Etcheson, W. W. (1972), *Consumerism*, New York: Harper & Row.

Galbraith, J. K. (1958), *The Affluent Society*, Harmondsworth: Penguin Books.

Galbraith, J. K. (1977), *The Age of Uncertainty*, London: BBC/André Deutsch.

Gale, B. T. and Swire, D. J. (1988), 'Business Strategies that Create Wealth', *Planning Review*, Vol. 16, No. 2, March–April, pp. 6–13, 47.

Gallagher Report (1973), Supplement to Vol. 21, No. 13, 26 March, p. 1.

Garsombke, D. J. (1989), 'International Competitor Analysis', *Planning Review*, Vol. 17, No. 3, May–June, pp. 42–7.

Ghemewat, P. (1986), 'Sustainable Advantage', *Harvard Business Review*, Vol. 64, No. 5, September–October, pp. 53–8.

Gilligan, C. T. and Crowther, G. (1976), *Advertising Management*, Deddington: Philip Allen.

Gilligan, C. T. and Hird, M. (1986), *International Marketing: Strategy and Management*, London: Routledge.

Gluck, F. (1985), 'Big Bang Management', *Journal of Business Strategy*, Vol. 6, No. 1, Summer, pp. 59–64.

Gofton, K. (1984) 'The Fed Loses its Reserve', *Marketing*, 2 August, p. 15.

Goldsmith, W. and Clutterbuck, D. (1988), *The Winning Streak*, London, Weidenfeld & Nicholson.

Goodman, S. R. (1970), *Techniques of Profitability Analysis*, New York: Wiley.

Goold, M. C. and Campbell, A. E. C. (1987a), *Strategies and Styles*, Oxford: Basil Blackwell.

Goold, M. C. and Campbell, A. E. C. (1987b), 'Many Best Ways to Make Strategy', *Harvard Business Review*, Vol. 65, No. 6, November–December, pp. 70–6.

Goold, M. C. and Quinn, J. J. (1990), *Strategic Control: Milestones for Long-term Performance*, London: Hutchinson.

Govindarajan, V. and Shank, J. K. (1989), 'Profit Variance Analysis: A Strategic Focus', *Issues in Accounting Education*, Vol. 4, No. 2, Fall, pp. 396–410.

Graf, F. (1967), A speech by the A. C. Nielsen Vice-President to a grocery manufacturers' executive conference, cited by G. T. Gerlach and C. A. Wainwright (1968), *Successful Management of New Products*, New York: Hastings House, pp. 125–6.

Grashof, J. F. (1975), 'Conducting and Using a Marketing Audit' in McCarthy, E. J., Grashof, J. F. and Brogowicz, A. A. (eds) (1975), *Readings in Basic Marketing*, Homewood, Illinois: Irwin.

Green, P., Faris, P. and Wind, Y. (1968), 'The Determinants of Vendor Selection: the Evaluation Function Approach', *Journal of Purchasing*, Vol. 4, August.

Greenley, G. E. (1986a), *The Strategic and Operational Planning of Marketing*, London: McGraw-Hill.

Greenley, G. E. (1986b), 'The Interface of Strategic and Marketing Plans', *Journal of General Management*, Vol. 12, No. 1, pp. 54–62.

Greenwood, R. G. (1974), *Managerial Decentralization: A Study of the General Electric Philosophy*, Lexington, Mass: D.C. Heath.

Griffith, I. (1986) 'Cost-Cutting Doesn't Move Merchandise', *Financial Decisions*, October, pp. 77, 78, 80, 82.

Griffith, I. (1991), 'Marketing Needs New Sales Pitch', *The Sunday Times*, 7 July, p. 4.13.

Grönroos, C. (1983), *Strategic Management and Marketing in the Service Sector*, Bromley: Chartwell-Bratt.

Grundy, A. (1986), 'Why Accountants and Marketing Men Should Be Friends', *Certified Accountant*, November, pp. 12–15.

Guiltinan, J. P. and Paul G. W. (1988), *Marketing Management: Strategies and Programs*, New York: McGraw-Hill. 3rd edition.

Hakansson, H. (ed.) (1981), *International Marketing and Purchasing of Industrial Goods: an Interaction Approach*, Chichester: John Wiley.

Hakansson, H., et al. (1979), 'Industrial Marketing as an Organizational Problem', *European Journal of Marketing*, Vol. 13, No. 3, pp. 81–93.

Haley, R. J. (1963), 'Benefit Segmentation: a Decision Orientated Research Tool', *Journal of Marketing*, Vol. 27, No. 3, July.

Haller, T. (1980a), 'An Organization Structure to Help You in the 1980s', *Advertising Age*, Vol. 51, No. 36, pp. 45–6.

Haller, T. (1980b), Strategic Planning: Key to Corporate Power for Marketers', *Marketing Times*, Vol. 27, No. 3, pp. 18–24.

Hambrick, D. G. and Cannella, A. A. (1989), 'Strategy Implementation as Substance and Selling', *The Academy of Management Executive*, Vol. 3, No. 4, November, pp. 278–85.

Hamermesh, R. G., Anderson, M. J. and Harris, J. E. (1978), 'Strategies for Low Market Share Businesses', *Harvard Business Review*, Vol. 65, No. 3, May–June, pp. 95–102.

Harding, M. (1966), 'Who Really Makes the Purchasing Decision?', *Industrial Marketing*, September, p. 76.

Harris, D. (1990) 'British Shoe Exports Shine', *The Times*, 5 March, 1990, p. 41.

Hart, N. A. (1978), *Industrial Advertising and Publicity*, London: Associated Business Programmes. 2nd edition.

Hartman, B. P. (1983), 'The Management Accountant's Role in Deleting a Product Line', *Management Accounting*, (NAA), Vol. 65, No. 2, August, pp. 63–6.

Harvey-Jones, Sir J. (1988), *Making it Happen*, London: Collins.

Haspelagh, P. (1982), 'Portfolio Planning: Its Uses and Limits', *Harvard Business Review*, Vol. 60, No. 1, January–February, pp. 58–73.

Hay Management Consultants (1989), *Headlines 2 000: The World as We See It*, London: Hay.

Hayhurst, R. and Wills, G. S. C. (1972), *Organizational Design for Marketing Futures*, London: Allen & Unwin,

Head, V. (1981), *Sponsorship: The Newest Marketing Skill*, Woodhead-Faulkner in association with the Institute of Marketing.

Hedley, B. (1977), 'Strategy and the Business Portfolio', *Long Range Planning*, Vol. 10, No. 1, pp. 9–15.

Heller, R. (1990), 'Pinstripe Devils', *Management Today*, September, p. 36.

Henderson, B. D. (1981), 'Understanding the Forces of Strategic and Natural Competition', *Journal of Business Strategy*, Vol. 2, Winter, pp. 11–15.

Henderson, B. D. (1982), *Henderson on Corporate Strategy*, New York: Mentor.

Henderson, B. D. (1984), *The Logic of Business Strategy*, Cambridge, Mass.: Ballinger.

Hendon, D. W. (1979), 'A New Empirical Look at the Influences of Reference Groups on Generic Product Strategy and Brand Choice: Evidence from Two Nations', in Proceedings of the Academy of International Business, *Asia Pacific Dimensions of International Business*, Honolulu: College of Business, University of Hawaii, December, pp. 752–61.

Henley, D. S. (1976), 'Evaluating Product Line Performance: A Conceptual Approach', pp. II–10 and II–11 in *Multinational Product Management*, Cambridge, Mass: Marketing Science Institute.

Hersey, P. (1988), *Selling: A Behavioral Science Approach*, Englewood Cliffs, NJ: Prentice-Hall.

Hershey, R. (1980), 'Commercial Intelligence on a Shoe-String', *Harvard Business Review*, Vol. 58, No. 5, September–October, pp. 22–4, 28, 30.

Herzberg, F. (1966), *Work and the Nature of Man*, London: Collins.

Heskett, J. L. (1976), *Marketing*, New York: Macmillan.

Hill, R. W. (1972), 'The Nature of Industrial Buying Decisions', *Industrial Marketing Management*, Vol. 2, October, pp. 45–55.

Hirsch, R. (1990), 'Getting the Ratios Right', *Management Today*, April, pp. 107–8, 110.

Hise, R. T. and Strawser, R. H. (1970), 'Application of Capital Budgeting Techniques to Marketing Operations', *MSU Business Topics*, Vol. 18, No. 3, Summer, pp. 69–75.

Hitt, M. A. and Ireland, R. D. (1985), 'Corporate Distinctive Competence, Strategy, Industry and Performance', *Strategic Management Journal*, Vol. 6, pp. 273–93.

Hlavacek, J. D. (1974), 'Towards More Successful Venture Management', *Journal of Marketing*, Vol. 38, No. 4, pp. 56–60.

Hofer, C. W. and Schendel, D. E. (1978), *Strategy Formulation: Analytical Concepts*, New York: West.

Hofstede, G. H. (1968), *The Game of Budget Control*, London: Tavistock.

Holmes, G. and Smith, N. (1987), *Salesforce Incentives*, London: Heinemann.

Hood, P. (1983), 'Sales Promotion and Merchandising' in Hart, N. A. and O'Connor, J. (eds) (1983), *The Practice of Advertising*, London: Heinemann, 2nd edition.

Hooley, G. J., West, C. J. and Lynch, J. E. (1983), *Marketing Management Today*, Cookham, Berks: Chartered Institute of Marketing.

Hooley, G. J., West, C. J. and Lynch, J. E. (1984), *Marketing In the UK – A Survey of Current Practice and Performance*, Cookham, Berks: Chartered Institute of Marketing.

Hopkins, D. S. and Bailey, E. L. (1971), 'New Product Pressures', *The Conference Board Record*, June, pp. 16–24.

Howard, J. (1983), 'Marketing Theory of the Firm', *Journal of Marketing*, Vol. 47, No. 4, Fall. pp. 90–100.

Howard, K. (1972), 'Network Analysis and Marketing Decisions', *European Journal of Marketing*, Vol. 6, No. 4, Winter, pp. 270–80.

Huegy, H. W. (ed.) (1963), *The Conceptual Framework for a Science of Marketing*, Urbana, Illinois: University of Illinois.

Hughes, G. D. (1980), *Marketing Management: A Planning Approach*, Reading, Mass: Addison-Wesley.

Hulbert, J. M. and Toy, N. E. (1977), 'A Strategic Framework for Marketing Control', *Journal of Marketing*, Vol. 41, No. 2, April, pp. 12–20.

Hurst, E. G. Jr. (1982), 'Controlling Strategic Plans', Ch. 7, pp. 114–23, in Lorange (ed.) (1982).

Hussey, D. E. (1971), *Introducing Corporate Planning*, Oxford, Pergamon.

Hussey, D. E. (1985), 'Implementing Corporate Strategy: Using Management Education and Training', *Long Range Planning*, Vol. 18, No. 5, pp. 28–37.

Hussey, D. E. (1989), 'Management in the 1990s', *Management Training Update*, September.

Irvin, R. A. and Michaels, E. G. (1989), 'Core Skills: Doing the Right Thing Right', *The McKinsey Quarterly*, Summer, pp. 4–19.

Itami, H. (1977), *Adaptive Behavior: Management Control and Information Analysis*, Sarasota, Florida: American Accounting Association (Studies in Accounting Research, No. 15).

Jackson, K. F. (1975), *The Art of Solving Problems*, London: Heinemann.

Jacobson, R. and Aaker, D. A. (1985), 'Is Market Share All That It is Cracked Up To Be?', *Journal of Marketing*, Vol. 49, No. 4, Fall, pp. 11–22.

Jain, S. C. (1985), *Marketing Planning and Strategy*, Cincinnati, Ohio: South-Western Publishing Company. 2nd edition.

James, B. G. (1966), 'Emotional Buying in Industrial Markets', *Scientific Business*, Vol. 3, No. 12, Spring, pp. 326–30.

James, B. G. (1985), *Business Wargames*, Harmondsworth: Penguin.

Jaworski, B. J. (1988), 'Toward a Theory of Marketing Control: Environmental Context, Control Types, and Consequences', *Journal of Marketing*, Vol. 52, No. 3, July, pp. 23–39.

Jaworski, B. J. and MacInnis, D. J. (1989), 'Marketing Jobs and Management Controls: Toward a Framework', *Journal of Marketing Research*, Vol. 26, No. 4, pp. 406–19.

Jefkins, F. (1986), *Planned Press and Public Relations*, Glasgow: Blackie, 2nd edition.

Jefkins, F. (1990), *Modern Marketing Communications*, Glasgow: Blackie.

Jenster, P. V. (1987), 'Using Critical Success Factors in Planning', *Long Range Planning*, Vol. 20, No. 4, pp. 102–9.

Johnson, G. and Scholes, K. (1988), *Exploring Corporate Strategy*, London: Prentice-Hall. 2nd edition.

Johnson, H. G. (1967), 'Key Item Control', *Management Services*, Vol. 4, No. 1, January–February, pp. 21–6.

Johnson, H. G. and Flodhammer, A. (1980), 'Industrial Customer Segmentation', *Industrial Marketing Management*, Vol. 9, July, pp. 201–5.

Johnson, R. A., Kast, F. E. and Rosenzweig, J. E. (1973), *The Theory and Management of Systems*, New York: McGraw-Hill. 3rd edition.

Jones, C. M. (1986), 'GTE's Strategic Tracking System', *Planning Review*, Vol. 14, No. 5, September–October, pp. 27–30.

Jones, G. R. and Butler, J. E. (1988), 'Costs, Revenue and Business-Level Strategy', *Academy of Management Review*, Vol. 13, No. 2, April, pp. 202–13.

Jones, L. (1988), 'Competitor Cost Analysis at Caterpillar', *Management Accounting*, (NAA), Vol. 70, No. 4, October, pp. 32–8.

Joseph, L. and Yorke, D. (1989), 'Know Your Game Plan', *Quarterly Review of Marketing*, Vol. 15, No. 1, Autumn, pp. 8–13.

Kahneman, D. and Tversky, A. (1984), 'Choices, Values and Frames', *American Psychologist*, Vol. 39, pp. 341–50.

Keiser, B. E. (1987), 'Practical Competitor Intelligence', *Planning Review*, Vol. 15, No. 5, September–October, pp. 14–18.

Kelley, W. J. (1972), *Marketing Planning and Competitive Strategy*, Englewood Cliffs, NJ: Prentice-Hall.

Kerin, R. A., Mahajan, V. and Varadarajan, P. R. (1990), *Contemporary Perspectives on Strategic Market Planning*, Englewood Cliffs. N.J: Prentice-Hall.

Kettlewood, K. (1973), 'Source Loyalty in the Freight Transport Market', Unpublished MSc Dissertation, UMIST.

Kight, L. K. (1989), 'The Search for Intelligence on Divisions and Subsidiaries', *Planning Review*, Vol. 17, No. 3, May–June, pp. 40–1.

King, S. (1991), 'Brand-building in the 1990s', *Journal of Marketing Management*, Vol. 7, No. 1, January, pp. 3–13.

King, W. (1968), 'A Conceptual Framework For Advertising Agency Compensation', *Journal of Marketing Research*, Vol. 5, No. 2, May, pp. 177–80.

Kjaer-Hanson, M. (ed.) (1965), *Cost Problems in Modern Marketing*, Amsterdam: North-Holland.

Klein, H. E. and Linneman, R. E. (1984), 'Environmental Assessment: An International Study of Corporate Practice', *Journal of Business Strategy*, Vol. 5, Summer, pp. 66–75.

Kling, N. D. (1985), 'The Marketing Audit: An Extension of the Marketing Control Process', *Managerial Finance*, Vol. 11, No. 1, pp. 23–6.

Klir, G. J. and Valach, M. (1967), *Cybernetic Modelling*, London: Iliffe.

Kortge, G. D. (1984), 'Inverted Break-even Analysis for Profitable Marketing Decisions', *Industrial Marketing Management*, Vol. 13, pp. 219–24.

Kotler, P. (1971), *Marketing Decision-Making: A Model-Building Approach*, New York: Holt, Rinehart & Winston.

Kotler, P. (1972), *Marketing Management: Analysis, Planning and Control*, Engelwood Cliffs, NJ: Prentice-Hall, 2nd edition.

Kotler, P. (1972), 'What Consumerism Means for Marketers', *Harvard Business Review*, Vol. 50, No. 3, May–June, pp. 48–57.

Kotler, P. (1977), 'From Sales Obsession to Marketing Effectiveness', *Harvard Business Reveiw*, Vol. 55, No. 6, November–December, pp. 67–75.

Kotler, P. (1980), *Marketing Management: Analysis, Planning and Control*, Engelwood Cliffs, NJ: Prentice-Hall, 4th edition.

Kotler, P. (ed.) (1984), *Marketing Management and Strategy: A Reader*, Engelwood Cliffs, NJ: Prentice-Hall, 5th edition.

Kotler, P. (1987), *Marketing: An Introduction*, Englewood Cliffs, NJ: Prentice-Hall.

Kotler, P. (1988), *Marketing Management: Analysis, Planning, Implementation and Control*, Engelwood Cliffs, NJ: Prentice-Hall, 6th edition.

Kotler, P., Fahey, L. and Jatusripitak, S. (1985), *The New Competition*, Engelwood Cliffs, NJ: Prentice-Hall.

Kotler, P., Gregor, W. T. and Rodgers, W. H. (1977), 'The Marketing Audit Comes of Age', *Sloan Management Review*, Vol. 18, No. 2, Winter, pp. 25–43.

Kotler, P., Gregor, W. T. and Rodgers, W. H. (1989), 'The Marketing Audit Comes of Age', *Sloan Management Review*, Vol. 30, No. 2, Winter, pp. 49–62.

Kuehn, A. A. (1961), 'A Model For Budgeting Advertising', in Bass, F. M., et al. (eds) (1961), *Models and Methods in Marketing*, Homewood, Illinois: Irwin.

Lalonde, B. J. and Zinszer, P. H. (1976), *Customer Service: Meaning and Measurement*, Chicago: NCPDM.

Lamb, R. and Shrivastava, P. (eds) (1986), *Advances in Strategic Management*, Greenwich, Conn: JAI Press. Volume 4.

Lambert, D. M. and Sterling, J. U. (1987), 'What Types of Profitability Reports Do Marketing Managers Receive?', *Industrial Marketing Management*, Vol. 16, pp. 295–303.

Lancaster, G. and Jobber, M. D. (1985) *Sales: Technique and Management*, London: MacDonald & Evans.

Lancaster, G. and Massingham, L. (1988), *Essential of Marketing: Text and Cases*, London: McGraw-Hill.

Langrish, J., Gibbons, M., Evans, W. G. and Jevon, F. R. (1972), *Wealth from Knowledge – Studies of Innovation in Industry*, London: Macmillan.

Lawrence, P. R. and Lorsch, J. (1967), *Organization and Environment*, Boston, Mass: Harvard University Press.

Lazer, W. (1962a), 'The Role of Models in Marketing', *Journal of Marketing*, Vol. 26, No. 2, April, pp. 9–14.

Lazer, W. (1962b), 'The Systems Concept in the Evolution of Marketing Management Thought' in *Marketing Precision and Executive Action* – Proceedings of 49th Annual Conference of the American Marketing Association.

Lehmann, D. R. and O'Shaughnessy, J. (1974), 'Differences in Attribute Importance for Different Industrial Products', *Journal of Marketing*, Vol. 38, No. 2, April, pp. 36–42.

Lehmann, D. R. and Winer, R. S. (1990), *Analysis for Marketing Planning*. Homewood Illinois: Irwin, 2nd edition.

Leidecker, J. K. and Bruno, A. V. (1984), 'Identifying and Using Critical Success Factors', *Long Range Planning*, Vol. 17, February, pp. 23–32.

Leppard, J. and McDonald, M. H. B. (1987), 'A Re-Appraisal of the Role of Marketing Planning', *Journal of Marketing Management*, Vol. 3, No. 2, pp. 159–71.

Levitt, T. (1960), 'Marketing Myopia', *Harvard Business Review*, Vol. 38, No. 4, July–August, pp. 45–56.

Levitt, T. (1966), 'Innovative Imitation', *Harvard Business Review*, Vol. 44, No. 5, September–October, p. 63.

Levitt, T. (1976), 'The Augmented Product Concept' in Ruthberg, R. R. (ed.) (1976), *Corporate Strategy and Product Innovation*, New York: Free Press.

Levitt, T. (1980), 'Marketing Success Through Differentiation – of Anything', *Harvard Business Review*, Vol. 58, No. 1, January–February, pp. 83–91.

Lewis, R. (1989), 'The Shape of Organisations to Come', *Management Training Update*, December.

Lewis, R. W. (1955), 'Measuring, Reporting and Appraising Results of Operations with Reference to Goals, Plans and Budgets' in *Planning, Managing and Measuring: A Case Study of Management Planning and Control at General Electric Company*, New York: The Controllership Foundation.

Lieberman, M. B. (1987), 'The Learning Curve, Diffusion, and Competitive Strategy', *Strategic Management Journal*, Vol. 8, pp. 441–52.

Little, Arthur D. (1974), see Patel, P. and Younger, M. (1978), 'A Frame of Reference for Strategy Development', *Long Range Planning*, Vol. 11, No. 2, April, pp. 6–12.

Little, J. D. C. (1966), 'A Model of Adaptive Control of Promotional Spending', *Operations Research*, Vol. 14, No. 6, pp. 1075–97.

Lorange, P. (ed.) (1982), *Implementation of Strategic Planning*, Englewood Cliffs, NJ: Prentice-Hall.

Lowe, E. A. (1971), 'On the Definition of "Systems" in Systems Engineering', *Journal of Systems Engineering*, Vol. 2, No. 1, Summer, pp. 95–8.

Lowe, E. A. and Machin, J. L. J. (eds) (1983), *New Perspectives in Mangement Control*, London: Macmillan.

Lowe, E. A. and Shaw, R. W. (1968), 'An Analysis of Managerial Biasing: Evidence from a Company's Budgeting Process', *Journal of Management Studies*, Vol. 5, No. 3, October, pp. 304–15.

Luck, D. J. and Ferrell, O. C. (1979), *Marketing Strategy and Plans*, Englewood Cliffs, NJ: Prentice-Hall.

Luck, D. J., Ferrell, O. C. and Lucas, G. S. (1989), *Marketing Strategy and Plans*, Englewood Cliffs, NJ: Prentice-Hall. 3rd edition.

Lyles, M. A. (1987), 'Defining Strategic Problems: Subjective Criteria of Excellence', *Organization Studies*, Vol. 8, No. 3, pp. 263–80.

Lynch, J. E., Hooley, G. J. and Shepherd, J. (1988), *The Effectiveness of British Marketing*, University of Bradford Management Centre.

McCarry, C. (1972), *Citizen Nader*, London: Jonathan Cape.

McClelland, D. C. (1961), *The Achieving Society*, New York: Free Press.

McColl-Kennedy, J. R., Yau, O. H. and Kiel, G. C. (1990), 'Marketing Planning Practices in Australia: A Comparision Across Company Types', *Marketing Intelligence and Planning*, Vol. 8, No. 4, pp. 21–9.

McDonald, M. H. B. (1984), *Marketing Plans: How to Prepare Them, How to Use Them*, London: Heinemann.

McDonald, M. H. B. and Wilson, H. N. (1990), 'State-of-the-Art Developments in Expert Systems and Strategic Marketing Planning', *British Journal of Management*, Vol. 1, No. 3, September, pp. 159–70.

McGraw-Hill (1963), *Special Report on the Buying and Selling Techniques in the British Engineering Industry*, London: McGraw-Hill.

McGraw-Hill (1963), *How Advertising Affects the Cost of Selling*, London: McGraw-Hill.

McGuire, J., Schneeweis, T. and Hill, J. (1986), 'An Analysis of Alternative Measures of Strategic Performance', pp. 127–54 in Lamb and Shrivastava (eds) (1986).

McKay, E. S. (1972), *The Marketing Mystique*, New York: American Management Association.

MacLuhan, M. (1964), *Understanding Media: the Extension of Man*, London: Routledge.

MacLuhan, M. (1968), *The Medium is the Message*, New York: Random House.

McNamee, P. (1988), *Management Accounting: Strategic Planning and Marketing*, Oxford: Heinemann.

McTavish, R. (1989), 'Implementing Marketing Strategy', *Management Decision*, Vol. 26, No. 5, pp. 9–12.

Machin, J. L. J. (1983), 'Management Control Systems: Whence & Whither?' Ch. 2, pp. 22–42, in Lowe and Machin (eds) (1983).

Maciariello, J. A. (1984), *Management Control Systems*, Englewood Cliffs, NJ: Prentice-Hall.

Magrath, A. J. (1988) 'People Productivity: Marketing's Most Valuable Asset', *Journal of Business Strategy*, Vol. 9, No. 4, pp. 12–14.

Magrath, A. J. and Hardy, K. G. (1986), 'Cost Containment in Marketing', *Journal of Business Strategy*, Vol. 7, No. 2, pp. 14–21.

Majaro, S. (1972), 'A Market Strategy for Europe', in Blake, J. E. (ed.) (1972), *Design For European Markets: A Management Guide*, London: Design Council.

Majaro, S. (1978), *International Marketing*, London: George Allen and Unwin.

Makens, J. C. (1989), *The 12-Day Marketing Plan*, Wellingborough: Thorsons.

Mann, N. R. (1989), *The Keys to Excellence: The Deming Philosophy*, London: Mercury.

Mansfield, E. and Wagner, S. (1975) 'Organizational and Strategic Factors Associated with Possibilities of Success in Industrial R&D', *Journal of Business,* April, pp. 179–98.

March, J. G. and Simon, H. A. (1958), *Organizations*, New York: Wiley.

Market Research Society (1990), *Occupational Groupings: A Job Dictionary*, London: MRS.

Markovitz, Z. N. (1987), 'Hidden Sector Competitor Analysis', *Planning Review*, Vol. 15, No. 5, pp. 20–4, 46.

Martilla, J. C. (1971), '"Word of Mouth" Communication in the Industrial Adoption Process', *Journal of Marketing Research*, Vol. 3, No. 2, pp. 173–8.

Maslow, A. E. (1954), *Motivation and Personality*, New York: Harper & Row.

Mathur, S. S. (1986), 'Strategy: Framing Business Intentions', *Journal of General Management*, Vol. 12, No. 1, pp. 77–97.

Mehotra, S. (1984), 'How to Measure Marketing Productivity', *Journal of Advertising Research*, Vol. 24, No. 3, pp. 9–15.

Meldrum, M. J., Ward, K. and Srikanthan, S. (1987), 'Needs, Issues and Directions in the Marketing Accountancy Divide', *Quarterly Review of Marketing*, Vol. 12, Nos. 3–4, pp. 5–12.

Meldrum, M. J., Ward, K. and Srikanthan, S. (1986), 'Can You Really Account for Marketing?', *Marketing Intelligence & Planning*, Vol. 4, No. 4, pp. 39–45.

Merchant, K. A. (1985), *Control in Business*, Boston: Pitman.

Merchant, K. A. (1988), 'Progressing Toward a Theory of Marketing Control: A Comment', *Journal of Marketing*, Vol. 52, No. 3, pp. 40–4.

Miles, R. E. (1980), *Macro Organisational Behavior*, Glenview, Illinois: Scott, Foresman.

Miles, R. E. and Snow, C. C. (1978), *Organizational Strategy, Structure & Process*, New York: McGraw-Hill.

Milton, F. and Reiss, T. (1985), 'Competitive Strategy', *Accountancy Ireland*, Vol. 17, No. 5, pp. 13–17.

Milton, F. and Reiss, T. (1985), 'Developing a Competitive Strategy', *Accountancy Ireland*, Vol. 17, No. 5, pp. 19–23, 28.

Mintel Report (1988), 'Retailing: The Non-Store Alternatives – 1987', London: Mintel.

Mintzberg, H. (1987), 'Crafting Strategy', *Harvard Business Review*, Vol. 65, No. 4, pp. 66–75.

Montgomery, D. B. and Urban, G. L. (1969), *Management Science in Marketing*, Englewood Cliffs, NJ: Prentice-Hall.

Montgomery, D. B. and Urban, G. L. (eds) (1969), *Applications of Management Science in Marketing*, Englewood Cliffs, NJ: Prentice-Hall.

Morrison, A. and Wensley, J. R. C. (1991), 'Boxing Up or Boxed In?: A Short History of the Boston Consulting Group Share/Growth Matrix', *Journal of Marketing Management*, Vol. 7, No. 2, pp. 105–29.

Mossman, F. H., Fischer, P. M. and Crissy, W. J. E. (1974), 'New Approaches to Analyzing Marketing Profitability', *Journal of Marketing*, Vol. 38, No. 2, pp. 43–8.

Mossman, F. H. and Worrell, M. L. (1966), 'Analytical Methods of Measuring Marketing Profitability: A Matrix Approach', *MSU Business Topics*, Vol. 14, No. 4, pp. 35–45.

Mulvaney, J. (1969), *The Use of Network Analysis in Marketing*, Cookham: Chartered Institute of Marketing.

Munro, R. J. B. and Cooper, P. (1989), 'The Impact of Changes in Strategic Thinking on Management Control Systems: the Selection of Non-Financial Measure in a Functional Structure'. Paper given at the Annual Conference of the British Accounting Association, University of Bath, March.

Myers, J. H. and Samli, A. C. (1969), 'Management Control of Marketing Research', *Journal of Marketing Research*, Vol. 6, No. 3, pp. 267–77.

Myers, S. and Marquis, D. G. (1969), *Successful Industrial Innovations: a Study of Factors Underlying Innovations in Selected Firms*, New York: National Science Foundation.

Nagle, T. T. (1987), *The Strategies and Tactics of Pricing*, Englewood Cliffs, NJ: Prentice-Hall.

Naisbitt, J. and Aburdene, P. (1982), *Megatrends: Ten New Directions Transforming Our Lives*, New York: Warner Books.

Naisbitt, J. and Aburdene, P. (1990), *Megatrends 2000*, London: Sidgwick & Jackson.

Narver, J. C. and Savit, R. (1971), *The Marketing Economy*, New York: Holt, Rinehart & Winston.

Nathanson, D. A., Kazanjian, R. K. and Galbraith, J. R. (1982), 'Effective Strategic Planning and the Role of Organization Design', Chapter 6 (pp. 91–113) in Lorange, P. (ed.).

Nicosia, F. M. (1966), *Consumer Decision Processes*, Englewood Cliffs, NJ: Prentice-Hall.

Nonaka, I. and Nicosia, F. M. (1979), 'Marketing Management, its Environment and Information Processing: A Problem of Organization Design', *Journal of Business Research*, Vol. 7, No. 4, pp. 277–301.

Nutt, P. C. (1987), 'Identifying and Appraising How Managers Install Strategy', *Strategic Management Journal*, Vol. 8, pp. 1–14.

Nutt, P. C. (1989), 'Selecting Tactics to Implement Strategic Plans', *Strategic Management Journal*, Vol. 10, pp. 145–61.

Oakland, J. S. (1989), *Total Quality Management*, Oxford: Butterworth-Heinemann.

O'Brien, S. and Ford, R. (1988), 'Can We at Last Say Goodbye to Social Class?', *Journal of the Market Research Society*, Vol. 30, No. 3, pp. 289–332.

Ogilvy, D. (1964), *Confessions of an Advertising Man*, London: Longmans Green.

Ohmae, K. (1983), *The Mind of the Strategist*, London: Penguin.

Olins, W. (1989), *Corporate Personality – an Enquiry into the Nature of Corporate Identity*, London: Wolff Olins.

Olins, W. (1989), *Corporate Identity*, London: Thames & Hudson.

Openshaw, S. (1989), 'Making Geodemographics More Sophisticated' *Journal of the Market Research Society*, Vol. 31, No. 1, pp. 111–31.

Otley, D. T. and Berry, A. J. (1980), 'Control, Organization and Accounting', *Accounting, Organizations and Society*, Vol. 5, No. 2, pp. 231–46.

Ouchi, W. (1983), *Theory Z*, Reading, Mass: Addison-Wesley.

Oxenfeldt, A. R. (1973), 'A Decision Making Structure for Price Decisions', *Journal of Marketing*, Vol. 37, No. 1, January, pp. 48–54.


Packard, V. (1957), *The Hidden Persuaders*, Harmondsworth: Penguin Books.

Palin, R. (1985), 'Operational PR' in Howards, W. (ed.) (1985), *The Practice of Public Relations*, London: Heinemann.

Pearson, G. J. (1979), 'Setting Corporate Objectives as a Basis for Action', *Long Range Planning*, Vol. 12, August, pp. 13–19.

Peattie, K. J. and Notley, D. S. (1989), 'The Marketing and Strategic Planning Interface', *Journal of Marketing Management*, Vol. 4, No. 3, pp. 330–49.

Peters, T. J. and Waterman, R. H. (1982), *In Search of Excellence: Lessons from America's Best Run Companies*, New York: Harper & Row.

Pettigrew, A. M. (1975), 'The Industrial Purchasing Decision as a Political Process', *European Journal of Marketing*, Vol. 9, No. 1, pp. 4–19.

Pfeffer, J. (1978), *Organizational Design*, Arlington Heights, Illinois: AHM.

Piercy, N. F. (1985), *Marketing Organisation: An Analysis of Information Processing, Power and Politics*, London: Allen & Unwin.

Piercy, N. F. (1986), *Marketing Budgeting*, London: Croom Helm.

Piercy, N. F. (1987), 'Servicing the Needs of Marketing Management', *Management Accounting*, (CIMA), Vol. 65, No. 3, March, pp. 42–3.

Piercy, N. F. (1987), 'The Marketing Budgeting Process: Marketing Management Implications', *Journal of Marketing*, Vol. 51, No. 4, October, pp. 45–9.

Piercy, N. F. (1991), *Market-led Strategic Change*, Wellingborough: Thorsons.

Piercy, N. F. and Morgan, N. (1989a), 'Good Plans Need Internal Marketing', *The Sunday Times*, 10 September, p. E1.

Piercy, N. F. and Morgan, N. (198b), 'Learning to Love the Marketing Task', *The Sunday Times*, 12 November, p. E14.

Piercy, N. F. and Morgan, N. (1990), 'Making Marketing Strategies Happen in the Real World', *Marketing Business*, Issue 9, February, pp. 20–1.

Pilcher, R. (1989), 'Managing Exports Effectively', *Accountancy*, Vol. 103, No. 1148, April, pp. 75–8.

Pilditch, J. (1987), 'Winning Companies Concentrate on Their People and Products', *The Times*, 25 June, p. 29.

*Planning Review*: Competitve Intelligence Issues: Vol. 15, No. 5, September–October 1987; Vol. 17, No. 3, May–June 1989.

Platchta, J. (1990), 'Does Sweet Talk Pay?', *Management Today*, March, pp. 91–2, 94.

Ploos Van Austel, M. J. (1987), 'Physical Distribution Cost Control', *International Journal of Physical Distribution and Materials Management*, Vol. 17, No. 2, pp. 67–78.

Poczter, A. and Siegel, J. G. (1986), 'How to Finance Your Marketing Strategy', *FE*, Vol. 2, No. 2, February, pp. 41–4.

Polli, R. and Cook, V. (1969), 'The Validity of the Product Life Cycle', *Journal of Business*, Vol. 42, No. 4, October, pp. 385–400.

Porter, L. M. and Roberts, K. H. (eds) (1977), *Communication in Organizations*, Harmondsworth: Penguin.

Porter, M. E. (1979), 'How Competitive Forces Shape Strategy', *Harvard Business Review*, Vol. 57, No. 2, March–April, pp. 137–45.

Porter, M. E. (1980), *Competitive Strategy*, New York: Free Press.

Porter, M. E. (1985), 'How to Attack the Industry Leader', *Fortune*, Vol. 111, 29 April, pp. 97–9, 102, 104.

Porter, M. E. (1985), *Competitive Advantage: Creating and Sustaining Superior Performance*, New York: Free Press.

Porter, M. E. (1990), *The Competitive Advantage of Nations*, New York: Free Press.

Posner, M. (1986), 'Sales and Finance Staff Should Harmonise', *Accountancy*, Vol. 98, No. 1116, August, pp. 113–14.

Powers, T. L. (1987), 'Breakeven Analysis with Semifixed Costs', *Industrial Marketing Management*, Vol. 16, No. 1, February, pp. 35–42.

Prescott, J. E. (ed.) (1989), *Advances in Competitor Intelligence*, Vienna, Virginia: Society of Competitor Intelligence Professionals.

Prescott, J. E., Kohli, A. K. and Venkatraman, N. (1986), 'The Market Share – Profitability Relationship: An Empirical Assessment of Major Assertions and Contradictions', *Strategic Management Journal*, Vol. 7, No. 4, July–August, pp. 377–94.

Prescott, J. E. and Smith, D. C. (1989), 'The Largest Survey of 'Leading Edge' Competitor Intelligence Managers', *Planning Review*, Vol. 17, No. 3, May–June, pp. 6–13.

Project SAPPHO (n.d.) *A Study of Success and Failure in Innovation*, Science Policy Research Unit, University of Sussex.

Puxty, A. G. and Dodds, J. C. (1991), *Financial Management: Method and Meaning*, London: Chapman & Hall. 2nd edition.

Pyne, F. G. (1984), 'Better, Operating Statements for the Marketing Director', *Accountancy*, Vol. 95, No. 1086, February, pp. 87–90.

Pyne, F. G. (1985), 'Accountancy that Helps to Meet and Beat Competition', *Accountancy*, Vol. 96, No. 1104, August, pp. 104–7.


Quelch, J. A., Buzzell, R. D. and Salama, E. R. (1990), *The Marketing Challenge of 1992*, Reading, Mass: Addison-Wesley.


Rabino, S. and Wright, A. (1984), 'Applying Financial Portfolio and Multiple Criteria Approaches to Product Line Decisions', *Industrial Marketing Management*, Vol. 13, pp. 233–40.

Rapp, S. and Collins, T. (1987), *Maxi Marketing*, New York: McGraw-Hill.

Rappaport, A. (1967), 'Sensitivity Analysis in Decision-Making', *The Accounting Review*, Vol. 42, No. 3, July, pp. 441–56.

Rappaport, A. (1986), *Creating Shareholder Value: The New Standard for Business Performance*, New York: Free Press.

Ratnatunga, J. T. D. (1983), *Financial Controls in Marketing: The Accounting-Marketing Interface*, Canberra: Canberra College of Advanced Education.

Ratnatunga, J. T. D. (1988), *Accounting for Competitive Marketing*, London: CIMA (Occasional Paper Series).

Reading, B. (1988), 'Why it's Time for Us to Save', *The Sunday Times*, 11 December.

Reed, R. and Buckley, M. R. (1988), 'Strategy in Action – Techniques for Implementing Strategy', *Long Range Planning*, Vol. 21, No. 3, pp. 67–74.

Reeves, R. (1961), *Reality in Advertising*, New York: Knopf.

Reid, D. M. (1989), 'Operationalizing Strategic Planning', *Strategic Management Journal*, Vol. 10, pp. 553–67.

Reid, D. M. and Hinckley, L. C. (1989), 'Strategic Planning: The Cultural Impact', *Marketing Intelligence and Planning*, Vol. 7, No. 11/12, pp. 4–11.

Reimann, B. C. (1989), *Managing for Value*, Oxford: Basil Blackwell.

Resnik, A. J., Turney, P. B. B. and Mason, J. B. (1979), 'Marketers Turn to Countersegmentation', *Harvard Business Review*, Vol. 57, No. 5, September–October, pp. 100–6.

Rhyne, L. C. (1986), 'The Relationship of Strategic Planning to Financial Performance', *Strategic Management Journal*, Vol. 7, pp. 423–36.

Richards, M. (1978), *Organizational Goal Structures*, St Paul, Minnesota: West Publishing Company.

Richardson, P. R. (1988), *Cost Containment: The Ultimate Advantage*, New York: Free Press.

Richardson, W. and Richardson, R. (1989), *Business Planning: a Strategic Approach to World Markets*, London: Pitman.

Ries, A. and Trout, J. (1982), *Positioning: the Battle for Your Mind*, New York: Warner Books.

Riesman, D., Glazer, N. and Dinny, R. (1950), *The Lonely Crowd*, Newhaven, Conn: Yale University Press.

Roach, J. D. C. (1981), 'From Strategic Planning to Strategic Performance: Closing the Achievement Gap', *Outloook*, Spring, New York: Booz Allen & Hamilton.

Robert, M. M. (1990), 'Managing Your Competitor's Strategy', *Journal of Business Strategy*, Vol. 11, No. 2, pp. 24–8.

Robertson, R. S. (1967), 'The Process of Innovation and the Diffusion of Innovation', *Journal of Marketing*, Vol. 3, No. 1, January, pp. 14–19.

Robinson, P. J., Faris, C. W. and Wind, Y. (1967), *Industrial Buying and Creative Marketing*, Boston, Mass: Allyn & Bacon.

Robinson, S. J. Q., Hichens, R. E. and Wade, D. P. (1978), 'The Directional Policy Matrix – Tool for Strategic Planning', *Long Range Planning*, Vol. 11, No. 3, June, pp. 8–15.

Robinson, W. T. and Fornell, C. (1985), 'Market Pioneering and Sustainable Market Share Advantages', *PIMSletter*, 39, Cambridge, Mass: Strategic Planning Institute.

Robinson, W. T. and Fornell, C. (1985), 'Sources of Market Pioneer Advantages in Consumer Goods Industries', *Journal of Marketing Research*, Vol. 22, No. 3, August, pp. 305–17.

Rockart, J. F. (1979), 'Chief Executives Define Their Own Data Needs', *Harvard Business Review*, Vol. 57, No. 2, March–April, pp. 81–93.

Rodger, L. W. (1965), *Marketing in a Competitive Economy*, London: Hutchinson.

Rogers, E. M. (1962), *Diffusion of Innovations*, New York: Free Press.

Rothman, L. J. (1989), 'Different Measures of Social Grade', *Journal of The Market Research Society*, Vol. 31, No. 1, pp. 139–40.

Rothschild, W. E. (1984), *How to Gain (and Maintain) the Competitive Advantage*, New York: McGraw-Hill.

Rothwell, R. (1972), Project SAPPHO: An Interim Report, Working Paper, Science Policy Unit, University of Sussex.

Rothwell, R. (1974), SAPPHO Updated – Project SAPPHO Phase II, *Research Policy*, Vol. 3, pp. 258–91.

Rothwell, R. (1977), 'The Characteristics of Successful Innovators and Technically Progressive Firms', *R & D Management*, Vol. 7, No. 3, pp. 191–206.

Ruekert, R. W., Walker, O. C. and Roering, K. J. (1985), 'The Organization of Marketing Activities: A Contingency Theory of Structure and Performance', *Journal of Marketing*, Vol. 49, pp. 13–25.


St. Thomas, C. E. (1965), *Practical Business Planning*, New York: AMA.

Salancik, G. R. and Upah, G. D. (1978), Directions for Interorganisational Marketing, Unpublished paper, University of Illinois, August.

Sanderson, S. M. and Luffman, G. A. (1988), 'Strategic Planning and Environmental Analysis', *European Journal of Marketing*, Vol. 22, No. 2, pp. 14–27.

Saunders, J. (1987), 'Marketing and Competitive Success' in Baker, M. J. (ed.) (1987), *The Marketing Book*, London: Macmillan.

Schaffir, K. H. and Trentin, H. G. (1973), *Marketing Information Systems*, New York: Amacom.

Scherer, F. M. (1980), *Industrial Market Structure and Economic Performance*, Chicago: Rand McNally. 2nd edition.

Schiff, M. and Mellman, M. (1962), *The Financial Management of the Marketing Function*, New York: FERF.

Schiffman, L. G. and Kanuk, L. L. (1983), *Consumer Behavior*, Englewood Cliffs, NJ: Prentice-Hall. 2nd edition.

Schmid, R. D. (1987), 'Reverse Engineering a Service Product', *Planning Review*, Vol. 15, No. 5, September–October, pp. 33–5.

Schoderbeck, P. P. (ed.) (1971), *Management Systems: A Book of Readings*, New York: Wiley. 2nd edition.

Schoderbek, P. P., Kefalas, A. G. and Schoderbek, C. G. (1975), *Management Systems: Conceptual Considerations*, Dallas: Business Publications.

Schoeffler, S. (1977), 'Market Position: Build, Hold or Harvest?', *The PIMSletter on Business Strategy*, No. 3, Cambridge, Mass: Strategic Planning Institute.

Schwartz, D. (1973), *Marketing Today*, New York: Harcourt, Brace, Jovanovich.

Schwartz, G. (ed.) (1965), *Science in Marketing*, New York: Wiley.

Sevin, C. H. (1965), *Marketing Productivity Analysis*, New York: McGraw-Hill.

Shapiro, B. P., et al. (1987), 'Manage Customers for Profits (Not Just Sales)', *Harvard Business Review*, Vol. 65, No. 5, September–October, pp. 101–8.

Shapiro, S. J. and Kirpalani, V. H. (eds) (1984), *Marketing Effectiveness*, Boston: Allyn & Bacon.

Shell Chemical Company (1975), *The Directional Policy Matrix: a New Aid to Corporate Planning*, London: Shell.

Sheth, J. N. (1969), *The Theory of Buyer Behavior*, New York: Wiley.

Sheth, J. N. (1973), 'Industrial Buyer Behavior', *Journal of Marketing*, Vol. 37, No. 4, October, pp. 50–6.

Shillinglaw, G. (1964), 'Divisional Performance Review: An Extension of Budgetary Control', in Bonini, C. P., Jaedicke, R. K. and Wagner, H. M. (eds) (1964).

Shuchman, A. (1950), 'The Marketing Audit: its Nature, Purposes and Problems', in Oxenfeldt, A. R., & Crisp, R. D. (eds) *Analysing and Improving Marketing Performance*, New York: American Management Association Report No. 32.

Simmonds, K. (1980), 'Strategic Mangement Accounting', Paper presented to ICMA Technical Symposium, Oxford.

Simmonds, K. (1981), 'Strategic Management Accounting', *Management Accounting*, Vol. 59, No. 4, April, pp. 26–9. Reprinted in Cowe, R. (ed.) (1988), *Handbook of Management Accounting*, Aldershot: Gower (2nd edition) pp. 14–36.

Simmonds, K. (1982), 'Strategic Management Accounting for Pricing: A Case Example', *Accounting and Business Research*, Vol. 12, No. 47, Summer, pp. 206–14.

Simmonds, K. (1985), 'How to Compete', *Management Today*, August, pp. 39–43, 84.

Simmonds, K. (1986), 'The Accounting Assessment of Competitive Position', *European Journal of Marketing*, Vol. 20, No. 1, pp. 16–31.

Simmonds, K. (1989), 'Strategic Management Accounting: The Emerging Paradigm', Plenary lecture given at 12th Annual Conference of the European Accounting Association, University of Stuttgart, April.

Simmons, W. W. (1972), 'Practical Planning', *Long Range Planning*, Vol. 5, No. 2, June pp. 32–9.

Simon, H. A. (1960), *The New Science of Management Decision*, New York: Harper & Row.

Simons, R. (1987), 'Accounting Control Systems and Business Strategy: An Empirical Analysis', *Accounting, Organizations and Society*, Vol. 12, No. 4, pp. 357–74.

Simons, R. (1990), 'The Role of Management Control Systems in Creating Competitive Advantage: New Perspectives', *Accounting, Organizations and Society*, Vol. 15, Nos. 1/2, pp. 127–43.

Slevin, D. P. and Pinto, J. K. (1987), 'Balancing Strategy and Tactics in Project Implementation', *Sloan Management Review*, Vol. 29, No. 1, Fall, pp. 33–41.

Smith, D. C. and Prescott, J. E. (1987), 'Demystifying Competitive Analysis', *Planning Review*, Vol. 15, No. 5, September–October, pp. 8–13.

Sofer, C. (1972), *Organizations in Theory and Practice*, London: Heinemann.

Spekman, R. E. and Grønhaug, K. (1983), 'Insights on Implementation: A Conceptual Framework for Better Understanding the Strategic Marketing Planning Process', AMA Conference Proceedings, 1983, Chicago: American Marketing Association.

Srikanthan, S., Ward, K. and Meldrum, M. J. (1986), 'Reducing the Costs of the Marketing Game', *Management Accounting*, (CIMA), Vol. 64, No. 10, November, pp. 48–51.

Srikanthan, S., Ward, K. and Meldrum, M. J. (1987), 'Segment Profitability: A Positive Contribution', *Management Accounting*, (CIMA) Vol. 65, No. 4, April, pp. 27–30.

Srikanthan, S., Ward, K. and Meldrum, M. J. (1987), 'Marketing: The Unrecognised Asset', *Management Accounting*, (CIMA), Vol. 65, No. 5, May, pp. 38–42.

Stapleton, C. (1991), 'Strategic Alliances', *Management Consultancy*, April, pp. 40, 43.

Starr, M. K. (1971), *Management: A Modern Approach*, New York: Harcourt, Brace, Jovanovich.

Stasch, S. F. (1972), *Systems Analysis for Marketing Planning and Control*, Glenview, Ill: Scott, Foresman.

Staw, B. M. and Ross, J. (1987a), 'Knowing When to Pull the Plug', *Harvard Business Review*, Vol. 65, No. 2, March–April, pp. 68–74.

Staw, B. M. and Ross, J. (1987b), 'Behavior in Escalation Situations: Antecedents, Prototypes and Solutions', *Research in Organizational Behavior*, Vol. 9, pp. 39–78.

Steiner, G. (1969), *Strategic Factors in Business Success*, New York: FERF.

Stern, M. E. (1966), *Marketing Planning: A Systems Approach*, New York: McGraw-Hill.

Stonich, P. L. (1975), 'Formal Planning Pitfalls and How to Avoid Them', *Management Review*, No. 64, July.

Strauss, G. (1962), 'Tactics of Lateral Relationships: The Purchasing Agent', *Administrative Science Quarterly*, Vol. 7, No. 3, September, pp. 161–86.

Sturges, J. (1991), 'Top Marketers', *Marketing Week*, 22 March, pp. 26–33.

Sutton, H. (1988), *Competitive Intelligence* (Research Report No. 913), New York: The Conference Board.

Swan, J. E. and Rink, D. R. (1982), 'Variations on the Product Life Cycle', *Business Horizons*, Vol. 25, No. 1, January–February, pp. 72–6.


Tannenbaum, A. S. (1964), 'Control in Organizations: Individual Adjustment and Organizational Performance', in Bonini, Jaedicke and Wagner (eds) (1964).

Test, D. L., Hawley, J. D. and Cortright, M. F. (1987), 'Determining Strategic Value', *Management Accounting*, (CIMA), Vol. 68, No. 12, June, pp. 39–42.

Thomas, M. J. (1984), 'The Meaning of Marketing Productivity Analysis', *Marketing Intelligence and Planning*, Vol. 2, No. 2, pp. 13–28.

Thomas, M. J. (1986), 'Marketing Productivity Analysis: A Research Report', *Marketing Intelligence and Planning*, Vol. 4, No. 2,

Thomas, M. J. (1987a), 'Does Your Marketing Pay?', *Management Decision*, Vol. 25, No. 4, pp. 41–5.

Thomas, M. J. (1987b), in Baker, M. J. (ed.) (1987), *The Marketing Book*, London: Heinemann.

Thomas, P. S. (1980), 'Environmental Scanning – the State of the Art', *Long Range Planning*, Vol. 13, No. 1, pp. 20–8.

Tilles, S. (1963), 'How To Evaluate Corporate Strategy', *Harvard Business Review*, Vol. 41, No. 4, July–August, pp. 111–21.

Tocher, K. (1970), 'Control', *Operational Research Quarterly*, Vol. 21, No. 2, June, pp. 159–80.

Tocher, K. (1976), 'Notes for Discussion on "Control"', *Operational Research Quarterly*, Vol. 27, No. 2, June, pp. 231–39.

Toffler, A. (1970), *Future Shock*, New York: Bantam Books.

Toffler, A. (1980), *The Third Wave*, New York: Bantam Books.

Tookey, D. A. (1974), 'The Marketing Function in its Organisational Context', in *Marketing as a Non-American Activity*, Proceedings, MEG Conference, July.

Turnbull, P. (1987), 'Organisational Buying Behaviour', in Baker, M. J. (ed.) (1987), *The Marketing Book*, London: Heinemann.

Turnbull, P. W. and Cunningham, M. T. (1981), *International Marketing and Purchasing*, London: Macmillan.

Tushman, M. L. and Nadler, P. A. (1978), 'Information Processing as an Integrating Concept in Organizational Design', *Academy of Management Review*, Vol. 3, No. 3, pp. 613–24.

Udell, J. G. (1964), 'How Important is Pricing in Competitive Strategy?', *Journal of Marketing*, Vol. 28, No. 1, pp. 44–8.

Ule, M. (1957), 'A Media Plan for Sputnik Cigarettes', *How to Plan Media Strategy*, American Association of Advertising Agencies.

Ulrich, D. and Lake, D. (1991), 'Organizational Capability: Creating Competitive Advantage', *The Executive*, Vol. 5, No. 1, February, pp. 77–92.

Vangermeersch, R. and Brosnan, W. T. (1985), 'Enhancing Revenues Via Distribution Cost Control', *Management Accounting*) (NAA), Vol. 67, No. 2, August, 56–60.

Veblen, T. (1899), *The Theory of the Leisure Class*, London: Macmillan.

Vella, C. M. and McGonagle, J. J. (1987), 'Shadowing Markets: A New Competitive Intelligence Technique', *Planning Review*, Vol. 15, No. 5, September–October, pp. 36–8.

Venkatesan, M. and Holloway, R. J. (1971), *An Introduction to Marketing Experimentation: Methods, Applications and Problems*, New York: Free Press.

Verhage, B. J. and Waarts, E. (1988), 'Marketing Planning for Improved Performance: A Comparative Analysis', *International Marketing Review*, Vol. 8, No. 5, Summer, pp. 20–30.

Vickers, Sir G. (1965), *The Art of Judgement*, London: Chapman & Hall.

Vickers, Sir G. (1968), *Value Systems and Social Process*, London: Tavistock.

Vickers, Sir G. (1972), *Freedom in a Rocking Boat: Changing Values in an Unstable Society*, London: Penguin.

Vidale, M. L. and Wolfe, H. B. (1957), 'An Operations Research Study of Sales Responses to Advertising', *Operations Research*, Vol. 5, No. 3, June, pp. 370–81.

Walker, O. C. and Ruekert, R. W. (1987), 'Marketing's Role in the Implementation of Business Strategies: A Critical Review and Conceptual Framework', *Journal of Marketing*, Vol. 51, No. 3, July, pp. 15–33.

Wall, S. L. (1974), 'What the Competition is Doing: You Need to Know', *Harvard Business Review*, Vol. 52, No. 6, November–December, pp. 22–4, 28, 30, 32, 34, 36, 38, 162–6, 168, 170.

Walleck, A. S., O'Halloran, J. D. and Leader, C. A. (1991), 'Benchmarking World Class Performance', *The McKinsey Quarterly*, No. 1, pp. 3–24.

Walters, C. G. and Paul, G. W. (1970), *Consumer Behavior: An Integrated Framework*, Homewood, Illinois: Irwin.

Ward, A. J. (1968), *Measuring, Directing and Controlling New Product Development*, London: In Com Tec.

Ward, K. (1989), *Financial Aspects of Marketing*, Oxford: Heinemann.

Webster, F. E. (1970), 'Informal Communications in Industrial Markets', *Journal of Marketing Research*, Vol. 7, No. 2, May, pp. 186–9

Webster, F. E. and Wind, Y. (1972), *Organisational Buying Behavior*, Englewood Cliffs, NJ: Prentice-Hall.

Weigand, R. (1966), 'Identifying Industrial Buying Responsibilities', *Journal of Marketing Research*, Vol. 3, No. 1, February, pp. 81–4.

Weigand, R. (1968), 'Why Studying the Purchasing Agent is Not Enough', *Journal of Marketing*, Vol. 32, No. 1, January, pp. 41–5.

Weinberg, R. (1969), Paper presented at a seminar on Developing Marketing Strategies for Short-Term Profits and Long-Term Growth, sponsored by Advanced Management Research, Inc. Regency Hotel, New York, 29 September.

Weinshall, T. D. (ed.) (1977), *Culture and Management*, Harmondsworth: Penguin.

Weitz, B. A. and Anderson, L. (1981), 'Organizing the Marketing Function', in *AMA Review of Marketing 1981*, Chicago: American Marketing Association.

Wells, W. D. and Gubar, G. (1966), 'Life Cycle Concepts in Marketing Research', *Journal of Marketing Research*, Vol. 3, No. 4, November, pp. 355–63.

Wenner, D. L. and LeBer, R. W. (1989), 'Managing Shareholder Value – From Top to Bottom', *Harvard Business Review*, Vol. 67, No. 6, November–December, pp. 1–8.

Wensley, J. R. C. (1981), 'Strategic Marketing: Betas, Boxes or Basics', *Journal of Marketing*, Vol. 45, No. 3, Summer, pp. 173–83.

Wensley, J. R. C. (1987), 'Marketing Strategy', in Baker, M. J. (ed.) (1987), *The Marketing Book*, London: Heinemann.

Wernerfelt, B. (1986), 'The Relation Between Market Share and Profitability', *Journal of Business Strategy*, Vol. 6, No. 4, Spring, pp. 67–74.

West, A. (1967), *Modern Sales Management*, London: Macmillan Education.

Westfall, R. (1962), 'Psychological Factors in Predicting Product Choice', *Journal of Marketing*, Vol. 36, April, pp. 34–40.

Westwick, C. A. (1987), *How to Use Management Ratios*, Aldershot: Gower, 2nd edition.

White, J. (1969), Some Aspects of The Marketing of Machine Tools in Great Britain, unpublished PhD thesis, UMIST.

Williamson, R. J. (1979), *Marketing for Accountants and Managers*, London: Heinemann.

Wills, G. S. C. (1980a), 'Sweeping Marketing Overboard', *European Journal of Marketing*, Vol. 14, No. 4, p. 1.

Wills, G. S. C. (1980b), 'Commercial Phoenix', *European Journal of Marketing*, Vol. 14, No. 6, p. 1.

Wills, G. S. C., Christopher, M. G. and Walters, D. W. (1972), *Output Budgeting in Marketing*, Bradford: MCB.

Wills, G. S. C., Wilson, R. M. S., Hildebrandt, R. and Manning, N. (1972), *Technological Forecasting*, London: Penguin Books.

Wilson, A. (1982), *Marketing Audit Check Lists*, London: McGraw-Hill.

Wilson, R. M. S. (1970), 'Accounting Approaches to Marketing Control', *Management Accounting*, (CIMA), Vol. 48, No. 2, February, pp. 51–8.

Wilson, R. M. S. (1970), 'The Development and Application of a Systems Approach', *Marketing Forum*, July–August, pp. 5–28.

Wilson, R. M. S. (1971), 'The Role of the Accountant in Marketing', *Marketing Forum*, May–June, pp. 21–33.

Wilson, R. M. S. (1971), 'Implications of Technological Forecasting for Industrial Marketing', Ch. 21 (pp. 326–46) in Wills, G. S. C. (ed.) *Exploration in Marketing Thought*, London: Crosby Lockwood/Bradford University Press.

Wilson, R. M. S. (1971), 'The Role of Marketing in Conglomerates', *European Journal of Marketing*, Vol. 5, No. 3, Autumn, pp. 116–22.

Wilson, R. M. S. (1972), 'Financial Control of Physical Distribution Management: Some Basic Considerations', *International Journal of Physical Distribution*, Vol. 3, No. 1, Autumn, pp. 7–20.

Wilson, R. M. S. (1973), *Management Controls in Marketing*, London: Heinemann.

Wilson, R. M. S. (1974), *Financial Control: A Systems Approach*, London: McGraw-Hill.

Wilson, R. M. S. (1975), 'Marketing Control: A Financial Perspective', *The Business Graduate*, Vol. 5, No. 2, Summer, pp. 15–20.

Wilson, R. M. S. (1979), *Management Controls and Marketing Planning*, London: Heinemann.

Wilson, R. M. S. (ed.) (1980), *The Marketing of Financial Services*, Bradford: MCB.

Wilson, R. M. S. (compiler) (1981), *Financial Dimensions of Marketing*. London: Macmillan. Two volumes.

Wilson, R. M. S. (1983), *Cost Control Handbook*, Aldershot: Gower. 2nd edition.

Wilson, R. M. S. (1984), 'Financial Control of the Marketing Function', Ch. 12 (pp. 130–53) in Hart, N. A. (ed.), *The Marketing of Industrial Products*, London: McGraw-Hill. 2nd edition.

Wilson, R. M. S. (1986), 'Accounting for Marketing Assets', *European Journal of Marketing*, Vol. 20, No. 1, pp. 51–74.

Wilson, R. M. S. (1988), 'Cost Analysis', Ch. 11 (pp. 150–88) in Lock, D. and Farrow, N. A. E. (eds), *The Gower Handbook of Management*, Aldershot: Gower. 2nd edition.

Wilson, R. M. S. (1988), 'Marketing and the Management Accountant', Ch. 13 (pp. 255–95) in Cowe, R. (ed.) (1988), *Handbook of Management Accounting*, Aldershot: Gower. 2nd edition.

Wilson, R. M. S. (1990), 'Strategic Cost Analysis', *Management Accounting*, Vol. 68, No. 9, October, pp. 42–3.

Wilson, R. M. S. (1991), 'Strategic Management Accounting', Ch. 5 (pp. 82–105) in Ashton, D. J., Hopper, T. M. and Scapens, R. W. (eds) *Issues in Management Accounting*, London: Prentice-Hall.

Wilson, R. M. S. (1991), 'Corporate Strategy and Management Control', Ch. 4, (pp. 115–65) in Hussey, D. E. (ed.), *International Review of Strategic Management*, Chichester: Wiley.

Wilson, R. M. S. (1992), *Accounting for Marketing*, London: Academic Press.

Wilson, R. M. S. and Bancroft, A. L. (1983), 'Management Accounting for Marketing – Some Industry Practices', *Management Accounting*, (CIMA), Vol. 61, No. 2, February, pp. 26–8.

Wilson, R. M. S. and Bancroft, A. L. (1983), *The Application of Management Accounting Techniques to the Planning and Control of Marketing*, London: CIMA.

Wilson, R. M. S. and Bennett, M. D. (1992), *How To Control Costs*, Aldershot: Gower.

Wilson, R. M. S. and Chua, W. F. (1992), *Managerial Accounting: Method and Meaning*, London: Chapman & Hall. 2nd edition (1st edition, 1988).

Wilson, R. M. S. and Fook, N. Y. M. (1990), 'Improving Marketing Orientation', *Marketing Business*, Issue 11, June, pp. 22–3.

Wilson, R. M. S. and McHugh, G. J. P. (1987), *Financial Analysis*, London: Cassell.

Wind, Y. (1978), 'Issues and Advances in Segmentation Research', *Journal of Marketing Research*, Vol. 15, No. 3, August, pp. 317–37.

Wind, Y. and Claycamp, H. J. (1976), 'Planning Product Line Strategy: A Matrix Approach', *Journal of Marketing*, Vol. 40, No. 1, January, pp. 2–9.

Winer, L. (1966), 'A Profit-Oriented Decision System', *Journal of Marketing*, Vol. 30, No. 2, April, pp. 38–44.

Witcher, B. J. (1990), 'Total Marketing: Total Quality and the Marketing Concept', *The Quarterly Review of Marketing*, Vol. 15, No. 2, Winter, pp. 1–6.

Witte, M. (1990), 'Organising to Make the Most of Change', *Management Consultancy*, March, pp. 29–30, 32–3.

Wong, V., Saunders, J. and Doyle, P. (1988), 'The Quality of British Marketing: A Comparison with US and Japanese Multinationals in the UK Market', *Journal of Marketing Management*, Vol. 4, No. 2, pp. 107–30.

Woo, C. Y. and Cooper, A. C. (1982), 'The Surprising Case for Low Market Share', *Harvard Business Review*, Vol. 60, No. 6, November–December, pp. 106–13.

Wright, R. V. L. (1974), *A System for Managing Diversity*, Cambridge, Mass: Arthur D. Little.

Yale, J. P. (1964), *Modern Textiles Magazine*, February, p. 33.
Yankelovich, D. (1964), 'New Criteria for Market Segmentation', *Harvard Business Review*, Vol. 42, No. 2, March–April, pp. 83–90.
Young, S. (1972), 'The Dynamics of Measuring Unchange', in Haley, R. I. (ed.) (1972), *Attitudes Research in Transition*, Chicago: American Marketing Association.

Zabriskie, N. B. and Huellmantel, A. R. (1985), 'The New Marketing-Finance Interface in Corporate Portfolio Management', *Managerial Planning*, Vol. 33, No. 5, March–April, pp. 27–30.
Zakon, A. (1971), *Growth and Financial Strategies*, Boston, Mass: Boston Consulting Group.
Zaltman, C., Pinson, C. R. A. and Angelmar, R. (1973), *Metatheory and Consumer Research*, New York: Holt, Rinehart & Winston.

# Index

## AUTHOR INDEX

# SUBJECT INDEX